Intimate Relationships

EIGHTH EDITION

Rowland S. Miller
Sam Houston State University

Mc
Graw
Hill
Education

INTIMATE RELATIONSHIPS, EIGHTH EDITION

Published by McGraw-Hill Education, 2 Penn Plaza, New York, NY 10121. Copyright © 2018 by McGraw-Hill Education. All rights reserved. Printed in the United States of America. Previous editions © 2015, 2012, and 2009. No part of this publication may be reproduced or distributed in any form or by any means, or stored in a database or retrieval system, without the prior written consent of McGraw-Hill Education, including, but not limited to, in any network or other electronic storage or transmission, or broadcast for distance learning.

Some ancillaries, including electronic and print components, may not be available to customers outside the United States.

This book is printed on acid-free paper.

3 4 5 6 7 8 9 LCR 21 20 19

ISBN 978-1-259-87051-4
MHID 1-259-87051-0

Portfolio Manager: *Jamie Laferrera*
Product Developer: *Francesca King*
Senior Marketing Manager: *Ann Helgerson*
Lead Content Project Managers: *Sandy Wille,*
Jodi Banowetz
Senior Buyer: *Sandy Ludovissy*

Content Licensing Specialist: *Melisa Seegmiller*
Cover Image: *©Art Collection 2/Alamy Stock Photo*
ISE Cover Image: *Digital image courtesy of the*
Getty's Open Content Program.
Compositor: *Aptara®, Inc.*

All credits appearing on page or at the end of the book are considered to be an extension of the copyright page.

Library of Congress Cataloging-in-Publication Data
Names: Miller, Rowland S., author.
Title: Intimate relationships/Rowland S. Miller, Sam Houston State
    University.
Description: Eighth Edition. | Dubuque : McGraw-Hill Education, [2018] |
    Revised edition of the author's Intimate relationships, [2015] | Includes
    bibliographic references and indexes.
Identifiers: LCCN 2017029323 | ISBN 9781259870514 (alk. paper) |
    ISBN 1259870510 (alk. paper)
Subjects: LCSH: Family life education. | Interpersonal relations.
Classification: LCC HQ10 .B735 2017 | DDC 302—dc23 LC record available at
https://lccn.loc.gov/2017029323

The Internet addresses listed in the text were accurate at the time of publication. The inclusion of a website does not indicate an endorsement by the authors or McGraw-Hill Education, and McGraw-Hill Education does not guarantee the accuracy of the information presented at these sites.

mheducation.com/highered

Contents

PREFACE   *vii*

ABOUT THE AUTHOR   *ix*

1.   The Building Blocks of Relationships   1

     THE NATURE AND IMPORTANCE OF INTIMACY   2

     THE INFLUENCE OF CULTURE   7

     THE INFLUENCE OF EXPERIENCE   14

     THE INFLUENCE OF INDIVIDUAL DIFFERENCES   20

     THE INFLUENCE OF HUMAN NATURE   33

     THE INFLUENCE OF INTERACTION   37

     THE DARK SIDE OF RELATIONSHIPS   38

     FOR YOUR CONSIDERATION   38

     CHAPTER SUMMARY   39

2.   Research Methods   41

     THE SHORT HISTORY OF RELATIONSHIP SCIENCE   42

     DEVELOPING A QUESTION   46

     OBTAINING PARTICIPANTS   47

     CHOOSING A DESIGN   50

     THE NATURE OF OUR DATA   53

     THE ETHICS OF SUCH ENDEAVORS   59

     INTERPRETING AND INTEGRATING RESULTS   61

     A FINAL NOTE   62

     FOR YOUR CONSIDERATION   63

     CHAPTER SUMMARY   63

3.   Attraction   65
    THE FUNDAMENTAL BASIS OF ATTRACTION   65
    PROXIMITY: LIKING THOSE NEAR US   66
    PHYSICAL ATTRACTIVENESS:
        LIKING THOSE WHO ARE LOVELY   72
    RECIPROCITY: LIKING THOSE WHO LIKE US   85
    SIMILARITY: LIKING THOSE WHO ARE LIKE US   87
    SO, WHAT DO MEN AND WOMEN WANT?   96
    FOR YOUR CONSIDERATION   98
    CHAPTER SUMMARY   98

4.   Social Cognition   100
    FIRST IMPRESSIONS (AND BEYOND)   101
    THE POWER OF PERCEPTIONS   107
    IMPRESSION MANAGEMENT   123
    SO, JUST HOW WELL DO WE KNOW OUR PARTNERS?   128
    FOR YOUR CONSIDERATION   133
    CHAPTER SUMMARY   133

5.   Communication   136
    NONVERBAL COMMUNICATION   138
    VERBAL COMMUNICATION   151
    DYSFUNCTIONAL COMMUNICATION
        AND WHAT TO DO ABOUT IT   161
    FOR YOUR CONSIDERATION   168
    CHAPTER SUMMARY   168

6.   Interdependency   171
    SOCIAL EXCHANGE   171
    THE ECONOMIES OF RELATIONSHIPS   180
    ARE WE REALLY THIS GREEDY?   192
    THE NATURE OF COMMITMENT   199
    FOR YOUR CONSIDERATION   204
    CHAPTER SUMMARY   204

7. Friendship   207
    THE NATURE OF FRIENDSHIP   208
    FRIENDSHIP ACROSS THE LIFE CYCLE   216
    DIFFERENCES IN FRIENDSHIP   221
    FRIENDSHIP DIFFICULTIES   226
    FOR YOUR CONSIDERATION   237
    CHAPTER SUMMARY   237

8. Love   240
    A BRIEF HISTORY OF LOVE   241
    TYPES OF LOVE   242
    INDIVIDUAL AND CULTURAL DIFFERENCES IN LOVE   260
    DOES LOVE LAST?   264
    FOR YOUR CONSIDERATION   268
    CHAPTER SUMMARY   268

9. Sexuality   270
    SEXUAL ATTITUDES   270
    SEXUAL BEHAVIOR   275
    SEXUAL SATISFACTION   292
    SEXUAL COERCION   299
    FOR YOUR CONSIDERATION   301
    CHAPTER SUMMARY   301

10. Stresses and Strains   303
    PERCEIVED RELATIONAL VALUE   303
    HURT FEELINGS   305
    OSTRACISM   308
    JEALOUSY   310
    DECEPTION AND LYING   322
    BETRAYAL   326
    FORGIVENESS   330
    FOR YOUR CONSIDERATION   332
    CHAPTER SUMMARY   332

11. Conflict 335
    THE NATURE OF CONFLICT 335
    THE COURSE OF CONFLICT 339
    THE OUTCOMES OF CONFLICT 353
    FOR YOUR CONSIDERATION 358
    CHAPTER SUMMARY 359

12. Power and Violence 360
    POWER AND INTERDEPENDENCE 360
    VIOLENCE IN RELATIONSHIPS 374
    FOR YOUR CONSIDERATION 385
    CHAPTER SUMMARY 385

13. The Dissolution and Loss of Relationships 388
    THE CHANGING RATE OF DIVORCE 388
    THE PREDICTORS OF DIVORCE 394
    BREAKING UP 403
    THE AFTERMATH OF BREAKUPS 408
    FOR YOUR CONSIDERATION 418
    CHAPTER SUMMARY 418

14. Maintaining and Repairing Relationships 420
    MAINTAINING AND ENHANCING RELATIONSHIPS 422
    REPAIRING RELATIONSHIPS 430
    IN CONCLUSION 439
    FOR YOUR CONSIDERATION 440
    CHAPTER SUMMARY 440

REFERENCES   R
NAME INDEX   I
SUBJECT INDEX   I-16

Preface to the Eighth Edition

Welcome to *Intimate Relationships!* I'm very pleased that you're here. I've been deeply honored by the high regard this book has enjoyed, and I'm privileged to offer you another very thorough update on the remarkable work being done in relationship science. The field is busier and broader than ever, so this edition contains *hundreds* and *hundreds* of citations of brand-new work published in the last 3 years. You'll find no other survey of relationship science that is as current, comprehensive, and complete.

Readers report that you won't find another textbook that's as much fun to read, either. I'm more delighted by that than I can easily express. This is a scholarly work primarily intended to provide college audiences with broad coverage of an entire field of inquiry, but it's written in a friendly, accessible style that gets students to read chapters they haven't been assigned—and that's a real mark of success! But really, that's also not surprising because so much of relationship science is so *fascinating*. No other science strikes closer to home. For that reason, and given its welcoming, reader-friendly style, this book has proven to be of interest to the general public, too. (As my father said, "Everybody should read this book.")

So, here's a new edition. It contains whole chapters on key topics that other books barely mention and cites hundreds more studies than other books do. It draws on social psychology, communication studies, family studies, sociology, clinical psychology, neuroscience, demography, and more. It's much more current and comprehensive and more fun to read than any other overview of the modern science of close relationships. Welcome!

What's New in This Edition

This edition contains 686 (!) new references that support new or substantially expanded discussion of topics including

Porn	Technoference
Rituals	Dark Triad traits
Oxytocin	Frequency of sex
Infidelity	Marital paradigms
Phubbing	Sexual satisfaction
Dating apps	Relational cleansing
Dealbreakers	Mismatches in looks
Cohabitation	Sexual growth beliefs
Pupil dilation	The effects of familiarity
Virtual reality	Instrumentality in attraction

What Hasn't Changed

If you're familiar with the seventh edition of this book, you'll find things in the same places. Vital influences on intimate relationships are introduced in chapter 1, and when they are mentioned in later chapters, footnotes remind readers where to find definitions that will refresh their memories.

Thought-provoking **Points to Ponder** appear in each chapter, too. They invite readers to think more deeply about intriguing phenomena, and they can serve equally well as touchstones for class discussion, topics for individual essays, and personal reflections regarding one's own behavior in close relationships.

The book's singular style also remains intact. There's someone here behind these pages. I occasionally break the third wall, speaking directly to the reader, both to be friendly and to make some key points (and because I can't help myself). I relish the opportunity to introduce this dynamic, exciting science to a newcomer— what a remarkable privilege!—and readers report that it shows.

Finally, this new edition is again available as a digital SmartBook that offers a personalized and adaptive reading experience. Students do better when their text *tells* them which concepts are giving them trouble, so if you haven't examined the SmartBook for *Intimate Relationships*, I encourage you to do so.

Kudos and thanks go to Sharon Brehm, the original creator of this book, and to Dan Perlman, the co-author who enticed me into doing it in the first place. I've also been grateful for the wonderful support and assistance of editorial and production professionals, Jamie Laferrera, Francesca King, Sandy Wille, Erin Guendelsberger, Reshmi Rajeesh, Melisa Seegmiller, David Tietz, Dheeraj Kumar, and Ryan Warczynski. Thanks, y'all.

I'm glad you're here, and I hope you enjoy the book.

About the Author

Rowland S. Miller is a University Distinguished Professor of Psychology at Sam Houston State University in Huntsville, Texas. He has been teaching a course in Close Relationships for over 30 years, and he won the 2008 Teaching Award from the International Association for Relationship Research (primarily as a result of this book). He's also been recognized as one of the most outstanding college teachers in Texas by the Minnie Stevens Piper Foundation, which named him a Piper Professor of 2016. He is a Fellow of the Association for Psychological Science, and a winner of the Edwin Newman Award for Excellence in Research from Psi Chi and the American Psychological Association. His parents were happily married for 73 years, and he'd like to have as long with his wonderful wife, Carolyn. He's pictured here with another of his favorite companions, Foster Bear (who isn't his best friend but who, on a good day, comes close).

Courtesy of Rowland S. Miller

The 8th edition of Intimate Relationships *is now available online with Connect, McGraw-Hill Education's integrated assignment and assessment platform. Connect also offers SmartBook for the new edition, which is the first adaptive reading experience proven to improve grades and help students study more effectively. All of the title's website and ancillary content is also available through Connect, including:*

- *A full Test Bank of multiple choice questions that test students on central concepts and ideas in each chapter.*
- *An Instructor's Manual for each chapter with full chapter outlines, sample test questions, and discussion topics.*
- *Lecture Slides for instructor use in class.*

 **connect®**

McGraw-Hill Connect® is a highly reliable, easy-to-use homework and learning management solution that utilizes learning science and award-winning adaptive tools to improve student results.

Homework and Adaptive Learning

- Connect's assignments help students contextualize what they've learned through application, so they can better understand the material and think critically.
- Connect will create a personalized study path customized to individual student needs through SmartBook®.
- SmartBook helps students study more efficiently by delivering an interactive reading experience through adaptive highlighting and review.

Connect's Impact on Retention Rates, Pass Rates, and Average Exam Scores

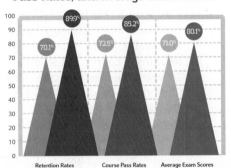

Retention Rates	Course Pass Rates	Average Exam Scores

■ without Connect   ■ with Connect

Over **7 billion questions** have been answered, making McGraw-Hill Education products more intelligent, reliable, and precise.

Using **Connect** improves retention rates by **19.8%**, passing rates by **12.7%, and** exam scores by **9.1%**.

73% of instructors who use **Connect** require it; instructor satisfaction **increases** by 28% when **Connect** is required.

Quality Content and Learning Resources

- Connect content is authored by the world's best subject matter experts, and is available to your class through a simple and intuitive interface.
- The Connect eBook makes it easy for students to access their reading material on smartphones and tablets. They can study on the go and don't need internet access to use the eBook as a reference, with full functionality.
- Multimedia content such as videos, simulations, and games drive student engagement and critical thinking skills.

Robust Analytics and Reporting

- Connect Insight® generates easy-to-read reports on individual students, the class as a whole, and on specific assignments.
- The Connect Insight dashboard delivers data on performance, study behavior, and effort. Instructors can quickly identify students who struggle and focus on material that the class has yet to master.
- Connect automatically grades assignments and quizzes, providing easy-to-read reports on individual and class performance.

©Hero Images/Getty Images

Impact on Final Course Grade Distribution

without Connect		with Connect
22.9%	A	31.0%
27.4%	B	34.3%
22.9%	C	18.7%
11.5%	D	6.1%
15.4%	F	9.9%

More students earn **As** and **Bs** when they use **Connect**.

Trusted Service and Support

- Connect integrates with your LMS to provide single sign-on and automatic syncing of grades. Integration with Blackboard®, D2L®, and Canvas also provides automatic syncing of the course calendar and assignment-level linking.
- Connect offers comprehensive service, support, and training throughout every phase of your implementation.
- If you're looking for some guidance on how to use Connect, or want to learn tips and tricks from super users, you can find tutorials as you work. Our Digital Faculty Consultants and Student Ambassadors offer insight into how to achieve the results you want with Connect.

CHAPTER 1

The Building Blocks of Relationships

THE NATURE AND IMPORTANCE OF INTIMACY ◆ THE INFLUENCE OF CULTURE ◆ THE INFLUENCE OF EXPERIENCE ◆ THE INFLUENCE OF INDIVIDUAL DIFFERENCES ◆ THE INFLUENCE OF HUMAN NATURE ◆ THE INFLUENCE OF INTERACTION ◆ THE DARK SIDE OF RELATIONSHIPS ◆ FOR YOUR CONSIDERATION ◆ CHAPTER SUMMARY

How's this for a vacation? Imagine yourself in a nicely appointed suite with a pastoral view. You've got high-speed access to Netflix and Hulu, video games, plenty of books and magazines, and all the supplies for your favorite hobby. Delightful food and drink are provided, and you have your favorite entertainments at hand. But there's a catch: No one else is around, and you have no phone and no access to the Web. You're completely alone. You have almost everything you want except for other people. Texts, tweets, Instagram, and Facebook are unavailable. No one else is even in sight, and you cannot interact with anyone else in any way.

How's that for a vacation? A few of us would enjoy the solitude for a while, but most of us would quickly find it surprisingly stressful to be completely detached from other people (Schachter, 1959). Most of us need others even more than we realize. Day by day, we tend to prefer the time we spend with others to the time we spend alone (Kahneman et al., 2004), and there's a reason prisons sometimes use *solitary confinement* as a form of punishment: Human beings are a very social species. People suffer when they are deprived of close contact with others, and at the core of our social nature is our need for intimate relationships.

Our relationships with others are central aspects of our lives. They can bring us great joy when they go well, but cause great sorrow when they go poorly. Our relationships are indispensable and vital, so it's useful to understand how they start, how they operate, how they thrive, and how, sometimes, they end in a haze of anger and pain.

This book will promote your own understanding of close relationships. It draws on psychology, sociology, communication studies, family studies, and neuroscience, and it reports what behavioral scientists have learned about relationships through careful research. It offers a different, more scientific view of relationships than you'll find in magazines or the movies; it's more reasoned, more cautious, and often less romantic. You'll also find that this is not a how-to manual. There are many insights awaiting you in the pages ahead, and there'll be plenty of news you can use, but you'll need to bring your own values and personal experiences to bear on the information presented here. Our intent is to survey the scientific study of close relationships and to introduce you to the diverse foci of relationship science.

To set the stage for the discoveries to come, we'll first define our subject matter. What are intimate relationships? Why do they matter so much? Then, we'll consider the fundamental building blocks of close relationships: the cultures we inhabit, the experiences we encounter, the personalities we possess, the human origins we all share, and the interactions we conduct. In order to understand relationships, we must first consider who we are, *where* we are, and how we got there.

THE NATURE AND IMPORTANCE OF INTIMACY

Relationships come in all shapes and sizes. We can have consequential contact with almost anyone—cashiers, classmates, colleagues, and kin—but we'll focus here on our relationships with friends and lovers because they exemplify *intimate* relationships. Our primary focus is on intimate relationships between adults.

The Nature of Intimacy

What, then, is intimacy? That's actually a complex question because intimacy is a multifaceted concept with several different components (Prager et al., 2013). It's generally held (Ben-Ari & Lavee, 2007) that intimate relationships differ from more casual associations in at least seven specific ways: **knowledge, interdependence, caring, trust, responsiveness, mutuality,** and **commitment.**

First, intimate partners have extensive personal, often confidential, *knowledge* about each other. They share information about their histories, preferences, feelings, and desires that they do not reveal to most of the other people they know.

The lives of intimate partners are also intertwined: What each partner does affects what the other partner wants to do and can do (Fitzsimons et al., 2015). *Interdependence* between intimates—the extent to which they need and influence each other—is frequent (they often affect each other), strong (they have meaningful impact on each other), diverse (they influence each other in many different ways), and enduring (they influence each other over long periods of time). When relationships are interdependent, one's behavior affects one's partner as well as oneself (Berscheid et al., 2004).

The qualities that make these close ties tolerable are caring, trust, and responsiveness. Intimate partners *care* about each other; they feel more affection for one another than they do for most others. They also *trust* one another, expecting to be treated fairly and honorably (Thielmann & Hilbig, 2015). People expect that no undue harm will result from their intimate relationships, and if it does, they often become wary and reduce the openness and interdependence that characterize closeness (Jones et al., 1997). In contrast, intimacy increases when people believe that their partners understand, respect, and appreciate them, being attentively and effectively *responsive* to their needs and concerned for their welfare (Winczewski et al., 2016). Responsiveness is powerfully rewarding, and the perception that our partners recognize, understand, and support our needs and wishes is a core ingredient of our very best relationships (Reis, 2013).

As a result of these close ties, people who are intimate also consider themselves to be a couple instead of two entirely separate individuals. They exhibit a high degree of *mutuality,* which means that they recognize their close connection and think of themselves as "us" instead of "me" and "him" (or "her") (Soulsby & Bennett, 2017). In fact, that change in outlook—from "I" to "us"—often signals the subtle but significant moment in a developing relationship when new partners first acknowledge their attachment to each other (Agnew et al., 1998). Indeed, researchers can assess the amount of intimacy in a close relationship by simply asking partners to rate the extent to which they "overlap." The Inclusion of Other in the Self Scale (see Figure 1.1) is a straightforward measure of mutuality that does a remarkably good job of distinguishing between intimate and more casual relationships (Aron et al., 2013).

Finally, intimate partners are ordinarily *committed* to their relationships. That is, they expect their partnerships to continue indefinitely, and they invest the time, effort, and resources that are needed to realize that goal. Without such commitment, people who were once very close may find themselves less and less interdependent and knowledgeable about each other as time goes by.

None of these components is absolutely required for intimacy to occur, and each may exist when the others are absent. For instance, spouses in a stale, unhappy marriage may be very interdependent, closely coordinating the practical details of their daily lives but living in a psychological vacuum devoid of much affection or responsiveness. Such partners would certainly be more intimate than mere acquaintances are, but they would undoubtedly feel less close to one another than they used to (for instance, when they decided to marry),

FIGURE 1.1. **The Inclusion of Other in the Self Scale.**
How intimate is a relationship? Just asking people to pick the picture that portrays a particular partnership does a remarkably good job of assessing the closeness they feel.

Please circle the picture below that best describes your **current** relationship with your partner.

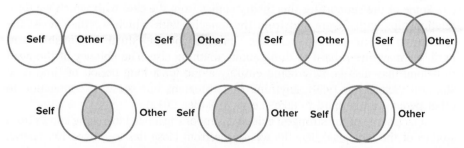

Source: Aron, A., Aron, E. N., & Smollan, D. "Inclusion of Other in the Self Scale and the structure of interpersonal closeness," Journal of Personality and Social Psychology, 63, 1992, 596–612.

when more of the components were present. In general, our most satisfying and meaningful intimate relationships include all seven of these defining characteristics (Fletcher et al., 2000). Still, intimacy can exist to a lesser degree when only some of them are in place. And as unhappy marriages demonstrate, intimacy can also vary enormously over the course of a long relationship.

So, there's no one kind of intimate relationship. Indeed, a fundamental lesson about relationships is a very simple one: They come in all shapes and sizes. This variety is a source of great complexity, but it can also be a source of endless fascination. (And that's why I wrote this book!)

The Need to Belong

Our focus on intimate relationships means that we will not consider the wide variety of the interactions that you have each day with casual friends and acquaintances. Should we be so particular? Is such a focus justified? The answers, of course, are yes. Although our casual interactions can be very influential (Sandstrom & Dunn, 2014), there's something special about intimate relationships. In fact, a powerful and pervasive drive to establish intimacy with others may be a basic part of our human nature. According to theorists Roy Baumeister and Mark Leary (1995), we *need* frequent, pleasant interactions with intimate partners in lasting, caring relationships if we're to function normally. There is a human **need to belong** in close relationships, and if the need is not met, a variety of problems follows.

Our need to belong is presumed to necessitate "regular social contact with those to whom one feels connected" (Baumeister & Leary, 1995, p. 501). In order to fulfill the need, we are driven to establish and maintain close relationships with other people; we require interaction and communion with those who know and care for us. But we only need a few close relationships; when the need to belong is satiated, our drive to form additional relationships is reduced. (Thus, when it comes to relationships, quality is more important than quantity.) It also doesn't matter much *who* our partners are; as long as they provide us stable affection and acceptance, our need can be satisfied. Thus, when an important relationship ends, we are often able to find replacement partners who—though they may be quite different from our previous partners—are nonetheless able to satisfy our need to belong (Spielmann et al., 2012).

Some of the support for this theory comes from the ease with which we form relationships with others and from the tenacity with which we then resist the dissolution of our existing social ties. Indeed, when a valued relationship is in peril, we may find it hard to think about anything else. The potency of the need to belong may also be why being entirely alone for a long period of time is so stressful (Schachter, 1959); anything that threatens our sense of connection to other people can be hard to take (Leary & Miller, 2012).

In fact, some of the strongest evidence supporting a need to belong comes from studies of the biological benefits we accrue from close ties to others. In general, people live happier, healthier, longer lives when they're closely connected to others than they do when they're on their own (Loving & Sbarra, 2015). Holding a lover's hand reduces the brain's alarm in response to threatening situations (Coan et al., 2006), and pain seems less potent when one simply looks at a photograph of a loving partner (Master et al., 2009). Wounds even heal faster when others accept and support us (Gouin et al., 2010). In contrast, people with insufficient intimacy in their lives are at risk for a wide variety of health problems (Valtorta et al., 2016). When they're lonely, young adults have weaker immune responses, leaving them more likely to catch a cold or flu (Pressman et al., 2005). Across the life span, people who have few friends or lovers—and even those who simply live alone— have much higher mortality rates than do those who are closely connected to caring partners (Holt-Lunstad et al., 2015b); in one extensive study, people who lacked close ties to others were *2 to 3 times* more likely to die over a 9-year span (Berkman & Glass, 2000). Married people in the United States are less likely to die from *any* of the 10 leading causes of cancer-related death than unmarried people are (Aizer et al., 2013). And losing one's existing ties to others is damaging, too: Elderly widows and widowers are much more likely to die in the first few months after the loss of their spouses than they would have been had their marriages continued (Elwert & Christakis, 2008), and a divorce also increases one's risk of an early death (Zhang et al., 2016).

A Point to Ponder

Why are married people less likely to die from cancer than unmarried people are? Are unhealthy people simply less likely to get married, or is marriage advantageous to our health? How might marriage be beneficial?

Our mental and physical health is also affected by the *quality* of our connections to others (Robles et al., 2014) (see Figure 1.2). Day by day, people who have pleasant interactions with others who care for them are more satisfied with their lives than are those who lack such social contact (Gerstorf et al., 2016), and this is true around the world (Galínha et al., 2013). In contrast, psychiatric problems, anxiety disorders, and substance abuse tend to afflict those with troubled ties to others (Whisman, 2013). On the surface (as I'll explain in detail in chapter 2), such patterns do not necessarily mean that shallow, superficial relationships *cause* psychological problems; after all, people who are prone to such problems may find it difficult to form loving relationships in the first place. Nevertheless, it does appear that a lack of intimacy can both cause such problems and make them worse (Eberhart & Hammen, 2006). In general, whether we're young or old (Allen et al., 2015), gay or straight (Wight et al., 2013), or married or just cohabiting (Kohn & Averett, 2014), our well-being seems to depend on how well we satisfy the need to belong.

Why should we need intimacy so much? Why are we such a social species? One possibility is that the need to belong *evolved* over eons, gradually becoming a natural tendency in all human beings (Baumeister & Leary, 1995). That argument goes this way: Because early humans lived in small tribal groups surrounded by a difficult environment full of saber-toothed tigers, people who were loners were less likely than gregarious humans to have children who would grow to maturity and reproduce. In such a setting, a tendency to form stable, affectionate connections to

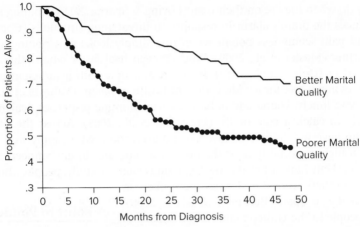

Source: Coyne, J. C., Rohrbaugh, M. J., Shoham, V., Sonnega, J. S., Nicklas, J. M., & Cranford, J. A. "Prognostic importance of marital quality for survival of congestive heart failure," American Journal of Cardiology, 88, 2001, 526–529.

FIGURE 1.2. **Satisfying intimacy and life and death.**
Here's a remarkable example of the manner in which satisfying intimacy is associated with better health. In this investigation, middle-aged patients with congestive heart failure were tracked for several years after their diseases were diagnosed. Forty-eight months later, *most* of the patients with less satisfying marriages had died whereas most of the people who were more happily married were still alive. This pattern occurred both when the initial illnesses were relatively mild and more severe, so it's a powerful example of the link between happy intimacy and better health. In another study, patients who were satisfied with their marriages when they had heart surgery were over *3 times* more likely to still be alive 15 years later than were those who were unhappily married (King & Reis, 2012). Evidently, fulfilling our needs to belong can be a matter of life or death.

others would have been evolutionarily *adaptive,* making it more likely that one's children would survive and thrive. As a result, our species slowly came to be characterized by people who cared deeply about what others thought of them and who sought acceptance and closeness from others. Admittedly, this view—which represents a provocative way of thinking about our modern behavior (and about which I'll have more to say later in this chapter)—is speculative. Nevertheless, whether or not this evolutionary account is entirely correct, there is little doubt that almost all of us now care deeply about the quality of our attachments to others. We are also at a loss, prone to illness and maladjustment, when we have insufficient intimacy in our lives. We know that food, water, and shelter are essential for life, but the need to belong suggests that intimacy with others is essential for a good, long life as well (Kenrick et al., 2010).

Now, let's examine the major influences that will determine what sort of relationships we construct when we seek to satisfy the need to belong. We'll start with a counterpoint to our innate need for intimacy: the changing cultures that provide the norms that govern our intimate relationships.

THE INFLUENCE OF CULTURE

I know it seems like ancient history—smart phones and Snapchat and AIDS didn't exist—but let's look back at 1965, which may have been around the time that your grandparents were deciding to marry. If they were a typical couple, they would have married in their early twenties, before she was 21 and before he was 23.[1] They probably would not have lived together, or "cohabited," without being married because almost no one did at that time. And it's also unlikely that they would have had a baby without being married; 95 percent of the children born in the United States in 1965 had parents who were married to each other. Once they settled in, your grandmother probably did not work outside the home—most women didn't—and when her kids were preschoolers, it's quite likely that she stayed home with them all day; most women did. It's also likely that their children—in particular, your mom or dad—grew up in a household in which both of their parents were present at the end of the day.

Now, however, things are very different. The last several decades have seen dramatic changes in the cultural context in which we conduct our close relationships. Indeed, you shouldn't be surprised if your grandparents are astonished by the cultural landscape that *you* face today. In the United States,

- Fewer people are marrying than ever before. Back in 1965, almost everyone (94 percent) married at some point in their lives, but more people remain unmarried today. Demographers now predict that fewer than 80 percent of young adults will ever marry (and that proportion is even lower in Europe [Perelli-Harris & Lyons-Amos, 2015]). Include everyone who is separated, divorced, widowed, or never married, and slightly less than *half* (49 percent) of the adult population of the United States is presently married. That's an all-time low.
- People are waiting longer to marry. On average, a woman is 27 years old when she marries for the first time, and a man is 29, and these are the oldest such ages in American history. That's much older than your grandparents probably were when they got married (see Figure 1.3). A great many Americans (43 percent) reach their mid-30s without marrying. Do you feel sorry for people who are 35 and single? Read the box on p. 9![2]
- People routinely live together even when they're not married. Cohabitation was very rare in 1965—only 5 percent of all adults ever did it—but it is now ordinary. Most young adults—nearly three-fourths of them—will at some time live with a lover before they ever marry (Lamidi & Manning, 2016).
- People often have babies even when they're not married. This was an uncommon event in 1965; only 5 percent of the babies born in the United States that

---

[1] These and the following statistics were obtained from the U.S. Census Bureau at www.census.gov, the U.S. National Center for Health Statistics at www.cdc.gov/nchs, the U.S. Bureau of Labor Statistics at bls.gov/data, the Pew Research Center at pewsocialtrends.org and the National Center for Family and Marriage Research at www.bgsu.edu/ncfmr.html.

[2] Please try to overcome your usual temptation to skip past the boxes. Many of them will be worth your time. Trust me.

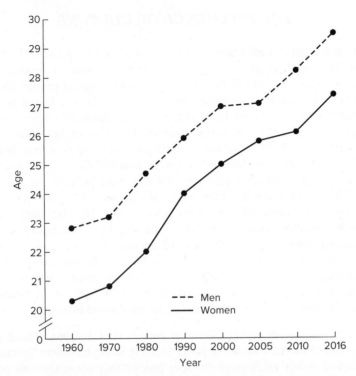

FIGURE 1.3. **Average age of first marriage in the United States.**
American men and women are waiting longer to get married than ever before.

year had unmarried mothers. Some children were *conceived* out of wedlock, but their parents usually got married before they were born. Not these days. In 2015, *40 percent* of the babies born in the United States had unmarried mothers (Hamilton et al., 2016). On average, an American mother now has her first child (at age 25.3) before she gets married (at 27.4).

- About one-half of all marriages end in divorce, a failure rate that's *2-and-a-half times* higher than it was when your grandparents married. In recent years, the divorce rate has been slowly decreasing for couples with college degrees—which is probably good news if you're reading this book!—but it remains high and unchanged for people with less education. In 2015 in the United States, there were more than half as many divorces as marriages (Anderson, 2016a). So because not all lasting marriages are happy ones, an American couple getting married this year is more likely to divorce sometime down the road than to live happily ever after.[3]

- Most preschool children have mothers who work outside the home. In 1965, three-quarters of U.S. mothers stayed home all day when their children were too young to go to school, but only 40 percent of them do so now.

---

[3] This is depressing, but your chances for a happy marriage (should you choose to marry) are likely to be better than those of most other people. You're reading this book, and your interest in relationship science is likely to improve your chances considerably.

Are You Prejudiced Against Singles?

Here's a term you probably haven't seen before: **singlism**. It refers to prejudice and discrimination against those who choose to remain single and opt not to devote themselves to a primary romantic relationship. Many of us assume that normal people want to be a part of a romantic couple, so we find it odd when anyone chooses instead to stay single. The result is a culture that offers benefits to married couples and puts singles at a disadvantage with regard to such things as Social Security benefits, insurance rates, and service in restaurants (DePaulo, 2014).

Intimacy is good for us, and married people live longer than unmarried people do. Middle-aged Americans who have never married are *two-and-half times* more likely than those who are married to die an early death (Siegler et al., 2013). Patterns like these lead some researchers to straightforwardly recommend a happy marriage as a desirable goal in life. And most single people *do* want to have romantic partners; only a few singles (4 percent) prefer being unattached to being in a steady romantic relationship (Poortman & Liefbroer, 2010), and a fear of being single can lead people to lower their standards and "settle for less" with lousy lovers (Spielmann et al., 2016). Still, we make an obvious mistake if we casually assume that singles are unhealthy, lonely loners. Many singles have an active social life and close, supportive friendships that provide them all the intimacy they desire, and they remain uncoupled because they celebrate their freedom and self-sufficiency. Not everyone, they assert, wants or needs a constant companion or soulmate (DePaulo, 2015). Indeed, on average, singles have *closer* relationships with their parents, siblings, neighbors, and friends than married people do (Sarkisian & Gerstel, 2016).

So, what do you think? Is there something wrong or missing in people who are content to remain single? If you think there is, you may profit by reading Bella DePaulo's blog defending singles at www.psychologytoday.com/blog/living-single.

These remarkable changes suggest that our shared assumptions about the role that marriage and parenthood will play in our lives have changed substantially in recent years. Once upon a time, everybody got married within a few years of leaving high school and, happy or sad, they tended to stay with their original partners. Pregnant people felt they *had* to get married, and cohabitation was known as "living in sin." But not so anymore. Marriage is now a *choice,* even if a baby is on the way (Hayford et al., 2014), and increasing numbers of us are putting it off or not getting married at all. If we do marry, we're less likely to consider it a solemn, life-long commitment (Cherlin, 2009). In general, recent years have seen enormous change in the cultural norms that used to encourage people to get, and stay, married.

Do these changes matter? Indeed, they do. Cultural standards provide a foundation for our relationships (Hefner & Wilson, 2013); they shape our expectations and define the patterns we think to be normal. Let's consider, in particular, the huge rise in the prevalence of cohabitation that has occurred in recent years. Most young adults now believe that it is desirable for a couple to live together before they get married so that they can spend more time together, share expenses, and test their compatibility (Anderson, 2016b). Such attitudes make cohabitation a reasonable choice—and indeed, most people now cohabit before they ever marry. However, when people do not already have firm plans to marry, cohabitation does not make it more likely that a subsequent marriage (if one occurs) will be successful; instead, such cohabitation *increases* a couple's risk that they will later divorce (Jose et al., 2010). There are probably several reasons for this. First, on average, those who cohabit begin living together at younger ages than their older—and possibly wiser—peers who get married (Kuperberg, 2014). But more importantly, couples who choose to cohabit are usually less committed to each other than are those who marry—they are, after all, keeping their options open (Wiik et al., 2012)—so they encounter more problems and uncertainties than married people do (Hsueh et al., 2009). They experience more conflict (Stanley et al., 2010), jealousy (Gatzeva & Paik, 2011), infidelity (Thornton et al., 2007), and physical aggression (Urquia et al., 2013), so cohabitation is more tumultuous and volatile than marriage usually is. As a result, the longer people cohabit, the less enthusiastic about marriage—and the more accepting of divorce—they become. Take a look at Figure 1.4: As time passes, cohabitating couples gradually become *less* likely to ever marry but no less likely to split up; 5 years down the road, cohabitating couples are just as likely to break up as they were when they moved in

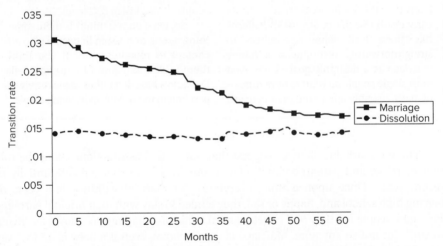

Source: Wolfinger, N. H. Understanding the divorce cycle: The children of divorce in their own marriages. *New York: Cambridge University Press, 2005.*

FIGURE 1.4. **The outcomes of cohabitation over time.**
Here's what became of 2,746 cohabiting couples in the United States over a span of 5 years. As time passed, couples were less likely to marry, but no less likely to break up. After living together for 5 years, cohabiting couples were just as likely to break up as they were when they moved in together. (The transition rate describes the percentage of couples who either broke up or got married each month. The numbers seem low, but they reflect the proportion of couples who quit cohabiting each month, so the proportions add up and become sizable as months go by.)

together. (Marriage is fundamentally different. The longer a couple is married, the less likely they are to ever divorce [Wolfinger, 2005]). Overall, then, casual cohabitation that is intended to test the partners' compatibility seems to undermine the positive attitudes toward marriage, and the determination to make a marriage work, that support marital success (Rhoades et al., 2009). Couples who are engaged to marry when they move in together typically fare better than those who cohabit without plans to marry (Willoughby & Belt, 2016), but even they tend to be less happy with their relationships than those who marry without cohabiting first (Brown et al., 2017). So casual cohabitation is corrosive, and these days, cohabiting partners are actually less likely to ever marry than in the past (Guzzo, 2014). Widespread acceptance of cohabitation as a "trial run" is probably one reason why, compared to 1965, fewer people get married and fewer marriages last.[4]

Sources of Change

So, the norms that currently govern our intimate relationships differ from those that guided prior generations, and there are several reasons why. One set of influences involves *economics*. Societies tend to harbor more single people, tolerate more divorces, and support a later age of marriage the more industrialized and affluent they become (South et al., 2001), and levels of socioeconomic development have increased around the world. Education and financial resources allow people to be more independent, so that women in particular are less likely to marry than they used to be (Dooley, 2010). And in American marriages, more than one of every three wives earns more than her husband (Cohn & Caumont, 2016), so "the traditional male breadwinner model has given way to one where women routinely support households and outearn the men they are married to, and nobody cares or thinks it's odd" (Mundy, 2012, p. 5).[5]

Over the years, the *individualism*—that is, the support of self-expression and the emphasis on personal fulfillment—that characterizes Western cultures has also become more pronounced (Grossman & Varnum, 2015). This isn't good news, but most of us are more materialistic (Twenge & Kasser, 2013), less trusting (Twenge et al., 2014), and less concerned with others (Twenge, 2013) than our grandparents were. And arguably, this focus on our own happiness has led us to expect more personal gratification from our intimate partnerships—more pleasure and delight, and fewer hassles and sacrifices—than our grandparents did (Finkel et al., 2015a). Unlike prior generations (who often stayed together for the "sake of the kids"), we

---

[4]Most people don't know this, so here's an example of an important pattern we'll encounter often: Popular opinion assumes one thing, but relationship science finds another. Instances such as these demonstrate the value of careful scientific studies of close relationships. Ignorance isn't bliss. Intimate partnerships are complex, and accurate information is especially beneficial when common sense and folk wisdom would lead us astray.

[5]Well, actually, some men, particularly those with traditional views of what it means to be a man (Coughlin & Wade, 2012), *are* troubled when they earn less than their wives. Their self-esteem suffers (Ratliff & Oishi, 2013), and they are more likely than other men to use drugs to treat erectile dysfunction (Pierce et al., 2013). Traditional masculinity can be costly in close relationships, a point to which we'll return on p. 26.

Zits: ©2007 Zits Partnership. Distributed by King Features Syndicate, Inc.

Modern technology is transforming the ways we interact with our partners. But is that always a good thing?

feel justified in ending our partnerships to seek contentment elsewhere if we become dissatisfied (Cherlin, 2009). Eastern cultures promote a more collective sense of self in which people feel more closely tied to their families and social groups (Wu et al., 2016), and the divorce rates in such cultures (such as Japan) are much lower than they are in the United States (Cherlin, 2009).

New *technology* matters, too. Modern reproductive technologies allow single women to bear children fathered by men picked from a catalog at a sperm bank whom the women have never met! Women can also control their fertility, having children only when they choose, and American women are having fewer children than they used to. The American birth rate is at an all-time low (Livingston, 2016), and almost one in every four American women aged 20–24 has used emergency contraception—a "morning-after" pill—to help keep it that way (Daniels et al., 2013).

Modern communication technologies are also transforming the ways in which we conduct our relationships. Your grandparents didn't have mobile phones, so they didn't expect to be able to reach each other anywhere at any time of day. They certainly didn't do any *sexting*—that is, sending sexually explicit images of themselves to others with a smartphone—as about 20 percent of young adults now have (Garcia et al., 2016, who also found that 23 percent of the time, those who receive a sext *share* it with two or three others). And they did not have to develop rules about how frequently they could text each other, how long they could take to respond, and whether or not they could read the messages and examine the call histories on the other's phone; these days, couples are happier if they do (Miller-Ott et al., 2012).

In addition, most of the people you know are on Facebook (Greenwood et al., 2016), connected to hundreds of "friends,"[6] and that can complicate our more

---

[6] Psychology students at Sam Houston State University (*n* = 298) do have hundreds of Facebook "friends"—562 each, on average—but that number doesn't mean much because most of them aren't real friends; 45 percent of them are mere acquaintances, and others (7 percent) are strangers they have never met (Miller et al., 2014). We'll return to this point in chapter 7, but for now, let me ask: How many people on your Facebook list are *really* your friends?

intimate partnerships. Facebook provides an entertaining and efficient way to (help to) satisfy our needs for social contact (Knowles et al., 2015), but it can also create dilemmas for lovers, who have to decide when to go "Facebook official" and announce that they're now "in a relationship" (Lane et al., 2016). (They also have to decide what that means: Women tend to think that this change in status signals more intensity and commitment than men do [Fox & Warber, 2013].) Thereafter, a partner's heavy use of Facebook (Clayton et al., 2013) and pictures of one's partner partying with others (Muscanell et al., 2013) can incite conflict and jealousy, and a breakup can be embarrassingly public (Fox & Moreland, 2015). Clearly, social media such as Facebook and Snapchat can be mixed blessings in close relationships (Utz et al., 2015).

Moreover, many of us are *permanently* connected to our social networks, with our smartphones always by our sides (Vorderer et al., 2016), and we are too often tempted to "give precedence to people we are not with over people we are with" (Price, 2011, p. 27). Modern couples have to put up with a lot of **technoference**, the frequent interruptions of their interactions that are caused by their various technological devices (McDaniel & Coyne, 2016), and **phubbing**—which occurs when one partner snubs another by focusing on a phone—is particularly obnoxious (Roberts & David, 2016). No one much likes to be ignored while you text or talk with someone else (Brown et al., 2016). In fact—and this is troubling—our devices can be so alluring (Lapierre & Lewis, 2017) that simply having a stray smartphone lying nearby reduces the quality of the conversation of two people who are just getting to know each other (Przybylski & Weinstein, 2013). Here's a suggestion: When you next go out to dinner with your lover, why don't you leave your phone in the car?

A Point to Ponder

Which of the remarkable changes in technology over the last 50 years has had the most profound effect on our relationships? Birth control pills? Smartphones? Online dating sites? Something else?

Finally, an important—but more subtle—influence on the norms that govern relationships is the relative numbers of young men and women in a given culture (Kandrik et al., 2015). Societies and regions of the world in which men are more numerous than women tend to have very different standards than those in which women outnumber men. I'm describing a region's **sex ratio,** a simple count of the number of men for every 100 women in a specific population. When the sex ratio is high, there are more men than women; when it is low, there are fewer men than women.

The baby boom that followed World War II caused the U.S. sex ratio, which had been very high, to plummet to low levels at the end of the 1960s. For a time after the war, more babies were born each year than in the preceding year; this meant that when the "boomers" entered adulthood, there were fewer older men than younger women, and the sex ratio dropped. However, when birthrates began to slow and fewer children entered the demographic pipeline, each new flock of women was smaller than the preceding flock of men, and the U.S. sex ratio crept higher in the 1990s. Since then, reasonably stable birthrates have resulted in fairly equal numbers of marriageable men and women today.

These changes may have been more important than most people realize. Cultures with high sex ratios (in which there aren't enough women) tend to support traditional, old-fashioned roles for men and women (Secord, 1983). After the men buy expensive engagement rings (Griskevicius et al., 2012), women stay home raising children while the men work outside the home. Such cultures also tend to be sexually conservative. The ideal newlywed is a virgin bride, unwed pregnancy is shameful, open cohabitation is rare, and divorce is discouraged. In contrast, cultures with low sex ratios (in which there are too few men) tend to be less traditional and more permissive. Women seek high-paying careers (Durante et al., 2012), and they are allowed (if not encouraged) to have sexual relationships outside of marriage. The specifics vary with each historical period, but this general pattern has occurred throughout history (Guttentag & Secord, 1983). Ancient Rome, which was renowned for its sybaritic behavior? A low sex ratio. Victorian England, famous for its prim and proper ways? A high sex ratio. The Roaring Twenties, a footloose and playful decade? A low sex ratio. And in more recent memory, the "sexual revolution" and the advent of "women's liberation" in the late 1960s? A very low sex ratio.

Thus, the remarkable changes in the norms for U.S. relationships since 1965 may be due, in part, to dramatic fluctuations in U.S. sex ratios. Indeed, another test of this pattern is presently unfolding in China, where limitations on family size and a preference for male children have produced a dramatic scarcity of young women. Prospective grooms will outnumber prospective brides in China by more than 50 percent for the next 30 years (Huang, 2014). What changes in China's norms should we expect? The rough but real link between a culture's proportions of men and women and its relational norms serves as a compelling example of the manner in which culture can affect our relationships. To a substantial degree, what we expect and what we accept in our dealings with others can spring from the standards of the time and place in which we live.

THE INFLUENCE OF EXPERIENCE

Our relationships are also affected by the histories and experiences we bring to them, and there is no better example of this than the global orientations toward relationships known as **attachment styles.** Years ago, developmental researchers (e.g., Bowlby, 1969) realized that infants displayed various patterns of attachment to their major caregivers (usually their mothers). The prevailing assumption was that whenever they were hungry, wet, or scared, some children found responsive care and protection to be reliably available, and they learned that other people were trustworthy sources of security and kindness. As a result, such children developed a **secure** style of attachment: They happily bonded with others and relied on them comfortably, and the children readily developed relationships characterized by relaxed trust.

Other children encountered different situations. For some, attentive care was unpredictable and inconsistent. Their caregivers were warm and interested on some occasions but distracted, anxious, or unavailable on others. These children thus developed fretful, mixed feelings about others known as **anxious-ambivalent** attachments. Being uncertain of when (or if) a departing caregiver would return, such children became nervous and clingy, and were needy in their relationships with others.

Finally, for a third group of children, care was provided reluctantly by rejecting or hostile adults. Such children learned that little good came from depending on others, and they withdrew from others with an **avoidant** style of attachment. Avoidant children were often suspicious of and angry at others, and they did not easily form trusting, close relationships.

The important point, then, is that researchers believed that early interpersonal experiences shaped the course of one's subsequent relationships. Indeed, attachment processes became a popular topic of research because the different styles were so obvious in many children. When they faced a strange, intimidating environment, for instance, secure children ran to their mothers, calmed down, and then set out to bravely explore the unfamiliar new setting (Ainsworth et al., 1978). Anxious-ambivalent children cried and clung to their mothers, ignoring the parents' reassurances that all was well.

These patterns were impressive, but relationship researchers really began to take notice of attachment styles when Cindy Hazan and Phillip Shaver (1987)

©237/Tom Merton/Getty Images

Children's relationships with their major caregivers teach them trust or fear that sets the stage for their subsequent relationships with others. How responsive, reliable, and effective was the care that you received?

demonstrated that similar orientations toward close relationships could also be observed among *adults*. They surveyed people in Denver and found that most people said that they were relaxed and comfortable depending on others; that is, they sounded secure in their intimate relationships. However, a substantial minority (about 40 percent) said they were *in*secure; they either found it difficult to trust and to depend on their partners, or they nervously worried that their relationships wouldn't last. In addition, the respondents reported childhood memories and current attitudes that fit their styles of attachment. Secure people generally held positive images of themselves and others, and remembered their parents as loving and supportive. In contrast, insecure people viewed others with uncertainty or distrust, and remembered their parents as inconsistent or cold.

With provocative results like these, attachment research quickly became one of the hottest fields in relationship science (e.g., Gillath et al., 2016). And researchers promptly realized that there seemed to be *four,* rather than three, patterns of attachment in adults. In particular, theorist Kim Bartholomew (1990) suggested that there were two different reasons why people might wish to avoid being too close to others. In one case, people could want relationships with others but be wary of them, fearing rejection and mistrusting them. In the other case, people could be independent and self-reliant, genuinely preferring autonomy and freedom rather than close attachments to others.

Thus, Bartholomew (1990) proposed four general categories of attachment style (see Table 1.1). The first, a **secure** style, remained the same as the secure style identified in children. The second, a **preoccupied** style, was a new name for anxious ambivalence. Bartholomew renamed the category to reflect the fact that, because they nervously depended on others' approval to feel good about

TABLE 1.1. **Four Types of Attachment Style**

Which of these paragraphs describes you best?

Secure	It is easy for me to become emotionally close to others. I am comfortable depending on others and having others depend on me. I don't worry about being alone or having others not accept me.
Preoccupied	I want to be completely emotionally intimate with others, but I often find that others are reluctant to get as close as I would like. I am uncomfortable being without close relationships, but I sometimes worry that others don't value me as much as I value them.
Fearful	I am uncomfortable getting close to others. I want emotionally close relationships, but I find it difficult to trust others completely or to depend on them. I worry that I will be hurt if I allow myself to become too close to others.
Dismissing	I am comfortable without close emotional relationships. It is very important to me to feel independent and self-sufficient, and I prefer not to depend on others or have others depend on me.

Source: Bartholomew, 1990.

themselves, such people worried about, and were preoccupied with, the status of their relationships.

The third and fourth styles reflected two different ways to be "avoidant." **Fearful** people avoided intimacy with others because of their fears of rejection. Although they wanted others to like them, they worried about the risks of relying on others. In contrast, people with a **dismissing** style felt that intimacy with others just wasn't worth the trouble. Dismissing people rejected interdependency with others because they felt self-sufficient, and they didn't care much whether others liked them or not.

It's also now generally accepted that two broad themes underlie and distinguish these four styles of attachment (Mikulincer & Shaver, 2016). First, people differ in their *avoidance of intimacy*, which affects the ease and trust with which they accept interdependent intimacy with others. People who are comfortable and relaxed in close relationships are low in avoidance, whereas those who distrust others, value their independence, and keep their emotional distance are high in avoidance (Ren et al., 2017). People also differ in their *anxiety about abandonment*, the dread that others will find them unworthy and leave them. Secure people take great comfort in closeness with others and do not worry that others will mistreat them; as a result, they gladly seek intimate interdependency with others. In contrast, with all three of the other styles, people are burdened with anxiety or discomfort that leaves them less at ease in close relationships. Preoccupied people want closeness but anxiously fear rejection. Dismissing people don't worry about rejection but don't like closeness. And fearful people get it from both sides, being uncomfortable with intimacy *and* worrying it won't last. (See Figure 1.5.)

FIGURE 1.5. **The dimensions underlying attachment.**

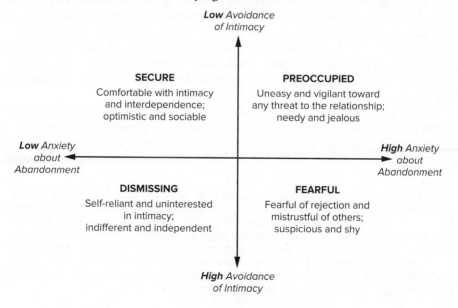

Importantly, the two themes of avoidance of intimacy and anxiety about abandonment are *continuous* dimensions that range from low to high. This means that, although it's convenient to talk about attachment styles as if they were discrete, pure categories that do not overlap, it's not really accurate to do so (Fraley et al., 2015). When they are simply asked to pick which one of the four paragraphs in Table 1.1 fits them best, most people in the United States—usually around 60 percent—describe themselves as being securely attached (Mickelson et al., 1997).[7] However, if someone has moderate anxiety about abandonment and middling avoidance of intimacy, which category fits him or her best? The use of any of the four categories is rather arbitrary in the middle ranges of anxiety and avoidance where the boundaries of the categories meet.

So don't treat the neat classifications in Figure 1.5 too seriously. The more sophisticated way to think about attachment is that there seem to be two important themes that shape people's global orientations toward relationships with others. (Samples of the items that are often used to measure anxiety and avoidance are provided on page 56 in chapter 2.) Both are important, and if you compare high scorers on either dimension to low scorers on that dimension, you're likely to see meaningful differences in the manner in which those people conduct their relationships. Indeed, most current studies of attachment (e.g., Ren et al., 2017) describe people with regard to their relative standing on the two dimensions of anxiety and avoidance instead of labeling them as secure, preoccupied, fearful, or dismissing.

Nevertheless, the four labels are so concise that they are still widely used, so stay sharp. Developmental researchers used to speak of only three attachment styles: secure, avoidant, and anxious-ambivalent. Now theorists routinely speak of four styles, but they treat them as convenient labels for sets of anxiety and avoidance scores, not as distinctly different categories that have nothing in common. The biggest distinction is between people who are "secure" and those who are not (being those who have high anxiety about abandonment or high avoidance of intimacy, or both) (Overall & Simpson, 2013). And for now, the important point is that attachment styles appear to be orientations toward relationships that are largely *learned* from our experiences with others. They are prime examples of the manner in which the proclivities and perspectives we bring to a new relationship emerge in part from our experiences in prior partnerships.

Let's examine this idea more closely. Any relationship is shaped by many different influences—that's the point of this chapter—and both babies and adults affect through their own behavior the treatment they receive from others. As any parent knows, for instance, babies are born with various temperaments and arousal

---

[7]This isn't true of American college students; only about 40 percent of them are secure. And that proportion has been *declining* over the last 30 years (Konrath et al., 2014). [Here's a Point to Ponder in a footnote! Why do you think that is?] Also, in many other countries, secure styles are more common than any of the other three styles but secure people are outnumbered by the other three groups combined. Thus, in most regions of the world, more people are insecure than secure (Schmitt, 2008). Nevertheless, there is some good news here: Around the world, people tend to become less anxious about abandonment as they age (Chopik & Edelstein, 2014). So, even if you're insecure now, time and experience may teach you to be more secure 30 years from now.

levels. Some newborns have an easy, pleasant temperament, whereas others are fussy and excitable, and inborn differences in personality and emotionality make some children easier to parent than others. Thus, the quality of parenting a baby receives can depend, in part, on the child's own personality and behavior; in this way, people's attachment styles are influenced by the traits with which they were born, and our genes shape our styles (Masarik et al., 2014).

However, our experiences play much larger roles in shaping the styles we bring to subsequent relationships (Fraley et al., 2013). The levels of acceptance or rejection we receive from our parents are huge influences early on (Bernier et al., 2014). Expectant mothers who are glad to be pregnant are more likely to have secure toddlers a year later than are mothers-to-be who are hesitant and uncertain (Miller et al., 2009). Once their babies are born, mothers who enjoy intimacy and who are comfortable with closeness tend to be more attentive and sensitive caregivers (Jones et al., 2015), so secure moms tend to have secure children whereas insecure mothers tend to have insecure children (Verhage et al., 2016). Indeed, when mothers with difficult, irritable babies are trained to be sensitive and responsive parents, their toddlers are much more likely to end up securely attached to them than they would have been in the absence of such training (van den Boom, 1994). And a mother's influence on the attachment styles of her children does not end in preschool (Raby et al., 2015). The parenting adolescents receive as seventh graders predicts how they will behave in their own romances and friendships when they become adults; those who have nurturing and supportive relationships with their parents will be likely to have richer relationships with their lovers and friends *60* years later (Waldinger & Schulz, 2016). There's no doubt that youngsters import the lessons they learn at home into their subsequent relationships with others (Simpson et al., 2014).

We're not prisoners of our experiences as children, however, because our attachment styles continue to be shaped by the experiences we encounter as adults (Haak et al., 2017). Being learned, attachment styles can be *un*learned, and over time, attachment styles can change (Fraley et al., 2011). A bad breakup can make a formerly secure person insecure, and a good relationship can gradually make an avoidant person less wary of intimacy (Arriaga et al., 2014). As many as a third of us may encounter real change in our attachment styles over a 2-year period (Davila & Cobb, 2004).

Nevertheless, once they have been established, attachment styles can also be stable and long-lasting as they lead people to create new relationships that reinforce their existing tendencies (Hadden et al., 2014). By remaining aloof and avoiding interdependency, for instance, fearful people may never learn that some people can be trusted and closeness can be comforting—and that perpetuates their fearful style. In the absence of dramatic new experiences, people's styles of attachment can persist for decades (Fraley, 2002).

Thus, our global beliefs about the nature and worth of close relationships appear to be shaped by our experiences within them. By good luck or bad, our earliest notions about our own interpersonal worth and the trustworthiness of others emerge from our interactions with our major caregivers and start us down a path of either trust or fear. But that journey never stops, and later obstacles or aid from fellow travelers may divert us and change our routes. Our learned styles of attachment to others may either change with time or persist indefinitely, depending on our interpersonal experiences.

THE INFLUENCE OF INDIVIDUAL DIFFERENCES

Once they are formed, attachment styles also exemplify the idiosyncratic personal characteristics that people bring to their partnerships with others. We're all individuals with singular combinations of experiences and traits, and the differences among us influence our relationships. In this section of the chapter, we'll consider four influential types of individual variation: sex differences, gender differences, personalities, and self-esteem.

Sex Differences

At this moment, you're doing something rare. You're reading an academic textbook about relationship science, and that's something most people will never do. This is probably the first serious text you've ever read about relationships, too, and that means that we need to confront—and hopefully correct—some of the stereotypes you may hold about the differences between men and women in intimate relationships.

This may not be easy. Many of us are used to thinking that men and women have very different approaches to intimacy—that, for instance, "men are from Mars, women are from Venus." A well-known book with that title asserted that

> men and women differ in all areas of their lives. Not only do men and women communicate differently but they think, feel, perceive, react, respond, love, need, and appreciate differently. They almost seem to be from different planets, speaking different languages and needing different nourishment. (Gray, 1992, p. 5)

Wow! Men and women sound like they're members of different species. No wonder heterosexual relationships are sometimes problematic!

But the truth is more subtle. Human traits obviously vary across a wide range, and (in most cases) if we graph the number of people who possess a certain talent or ability, we'll get a distinctive chart known as a *normal curve*. Such curves describe the frequencies with which particular levels of some trait can be found in people, and they demonstrate that (a) most people have talents or abilities that are only slightly better or worse than average and (b) extreme levels of most traits, high or low, are very rare. Consider height, for example: A few people are very short or very tall, but most of us are only two or three inches shorter or taller than the average for our sex.

Why should we care about this? Because many lay stereotypes about men and women portray the sexes as having very different ranges of interests, styles, and abilities. As one example, men are often portrayed as being more interested in sex than women are (see the box on page 23), and the images of the sexes that people hold often seem to resemble the situation pictured in Figure 1.6. The difference

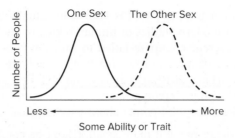

FIGURE 1.6. **An imaginary sex difference.**
Popular stereotypes portray the sexes as being very different, with almost no overlap
between the styles and preferences of the two sexes. This is *not* the way things really are.

between the average man and the average woman is presumed to be large, and
there is almost no overlap between the sexes at all. But, despite the "Mars" and
"Venus" stereotypes, this is *not* the way things really are. As we'll see in chapter 9,
men do tend to have higher sex drives, on average, than women do. Nevertheless,
actual sex differences take the form of the graphs shown in Figure 1.7, which
depict ranges of interests and talents that *overlap* to a substantial extent (Reis &
Carothers, 2014).

The three graphs in Figure 1.7 illustrate sex differences that are considered
by researchers to be small, medium, and large, respectively. Formally, they differ
with respect to a *d* statistic that specifies the size of a difference between two
groups.[8] In the realm of sexual attitudes and behavior, graph A depicts the different ages of men and women when they first have intercourse (men tend to be
slightly younger), graph B illustrates the relative frequencies with which they
masturbate (men masturbate more often), and graph C depicts a hypothetical

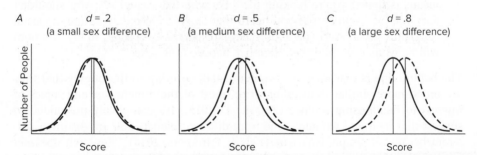

FIGURE 1.7. **Actual sex differences take the form of overlapping normal curves.**
The three graphs depict small, medium, and large sex differences, respectively. (To keep
them simple, they portray the ranges of attitudes or behavior as being the same for both
sexes. This isn't always the case in real life.)

[8] To get a *d* score in these cases, you compute the difference between the average man and the average
woman, and divide it by the average differences among the scores *within* each sex (which is the standard deviation of those scores). The resulting *d* value tells you how large the sex difference is compared
to the usual amount by which men and women differ among themselves.

difference that is larger than any that is known to actually exist. That's right. A sprawling analysis of modern studies of human sexuality involving 1,419,807 participants from 87 different countries failed to find *any* difference in the sexual attitudes and behavior of men and women that was as large as that pictured in graph C (Petersen & Hyde, 2010). Obviously, the real-life examples that do exist look nothing like the silly stereotype pictured in Figure 1.6. More specifically, these examples make three vital points about psychological sex differences:

- Some differences are real but quite small. (Don't be confused by researchers' terminology; when they talk about a "significant" sex difference, they're usually referring to a *"statistically* significant"—that is, numerically reliable—difference, and it may actually be quite modest in size.) Almost all of the differences between men and women that you will encounter in this book fall in the small to medium range.
- The range of behavior and opinions among members of a given sex is always *huge* compared to the average difference between the sexes. Men are more accepting of casual, uncommitted sex than women are (Petersen & Hyde, 2010), but that certainly doesn't mean that all men like casual sex. Some men like to have sex with strangers, but other men don't like that at all, and the sexual preferences of the two groups of men have less in common than those of the average man and the average woman do. Another way to put this is that despite this sex difference in sexual permissiveness, a highly permissive man has more in common with the average *woman* on this trait than he does with a low-scoring *man*.
- The overlap in behavior and opinions is so large that many members of one sex will always score higher than the average member of the other sex. With a sex difference of medium size (with men higher and a *d* value of .5), one-third of all women will still score higher than the average man. What this means is that if you're looking for folks who like casual sex, you shouldn't just look for *men* because you heard that "men are more accepting of casual sex than women are"; you should look for permissive *people,* many of whom will be women despite the difference between the sexes.

The bottom line is that men and women usually overlap so thoroughly that they are much more similar than different on most of the dimensions and topics of interest to relationship science (Zell et al., 2015). It's completely misguided to suggest that men and women come from different planets and are distinctly different because it simply isn't true (Reis & Carothers, 2014). "Research does *not* support the view that men and women come from different cultures, let alone separate worlds" (Canary & Emmers-Sommer, 1997, p. vi). According to the careful science of relationships you'll study in this book, it's more accurate to say that "men are from North Dakota, and women are from South Dakota" (Dindia, 2006, p. 18). (Or, as a bumper sticker I saw one day suggests: "Men are from Earth. Women are from Earth. Deal with it.")

Thus, sex differences in intimate relationships tend to be much less noteworthy and influential than laypeople often think. Now that you're reading a serious text on intimate relationships, you need to think more carefully about sex

---

Combating Simplistic Stereotypes

Here's a joke that showed up in my inbox one day:

<u>How to Impress a Woman</u>:
Compliment her. Cuddle her. Kiss her. Caress her. Love her. Comfort her. Protect her. Hug her. Hold her. Spend money on her. Wine and dine her. Listen to her. Care for her. Stand by her. Support her. Go to the ends of the earth for her.

<u>How to Impress a Man</u>:
Show up naked. Bring beer.

It's a cute joke. But it may not be harmless. It reinforces the stereotypes that women seek warmth and tenderness in their relationships whereas men simply seek unemotional sex. In truth, men and women differ little in their desires in close relationships; they're not "opposite" sexes at all (Hyde, 2014). Although individuals of both sexes may differ substantially from each other, the differences between the average man and the average woman are rather small. Both women *and* men generally want their intimate partners to provide them with lots of affection and warmth (Brumbaugh & Wood, 2013).

But so what? What are the consequences of wrongly believing that men are all alike, having little in common with women? Pessimism and hopelessness, for two (Metts & Cupach, 1990). People who really believe that the sexes are very different are less likely to try to repair their heterosexual relationships when conflicts occur (as they inevitably do). Thinking of the other sex as a bunch of aliens from another world is not just inaccurate—it can also be damaging, forestalling efforts to understand a partner's point of view and preventing collaborative problem solving. For that reason, I'll try to do my part to avoid perpetuating wrongful impressions by comparing men and women to the **other** sex, not the *opposite* sex, for the remainder of this book. Words matter (Sczesny et al., 2015), so I invite you to use similar language when you think and talk about the sexes.

---

differences and interpret them more reasonably.[9] There are interesting sex differences that are meaningful parts of the fabric of relationships, and we'll encounter several of them in the chapters that follow. But they occur in the context of even broader similarities between the sexes, and the differences are always modest when they are compared to the full range of human variation. It's more work, but also more sophisticated and accurate, to think of individual differences, not sex differences, as the more important influences on interpersonal interaction. People differ among themselves whether they are male or female (as in the case of attachment styles), and these variations are usually much more consequential than sex differences are.

---

[9] Has this discussion led you to think that men and women are perhaps not as different as you had thought they were? If so, you may be better off. Reading about the similarities of the sexes tends to reduce people's sexist beliefs that one sex is better than the other (Zell et al., 2016), and that's a good thing. Such beliefs have corrosive effects on relationships (Cross et al., 2017), and they're best avoided. We'll return to this point in chapter 11.

Gender Differences

I need to complicate things further by distinguishing between sex differences and *gender* differences in close relationships. When people use the terms carefully, the term *sex differences* refers to biological distinctions between men and women that spring naturally from their physical natures. In contrast, *gender differences* refer to social and psychological distinctions that are created by our cultures and upbringing (Muehlenhard & Peterson, 2011). For instance, when they are parents, women are mothers and men are fathers—that's a sex difference—but the common belief that women are more loving, more nurturant parents than men reflects a gender difference. Many men are capable of just as much tenderness and compassion toward the young as any woman is, but if we expect and encourage women to be the primary caregivers of our children, we can create cultural gender differences in parenting styles that are not natural or inborn at all.

Distinguishing sex and gender differences is often tricky because the social expectations and training we apply to men and women are often confounded with their biological sex (Eagly & Wood, 2012). For instance, because women lactate and men do not, people often assume that predawn feedings of a newborn baby are the mother's job—even when the baby is being fed formula from a bottle that was warmed in a microwave! It's not always easy to disentangle the effects of biology and culture in shaping our interests and abilities. Nevertheless, the distinction between sex and gender differences is meaningful because some influential differences between men and women in relationships—gender differences—are largely *taught* to us as we grow up.

The best examples of this are our **gender roles,** the patterns of behavior that are culturally expected of "normal" men and women. Men, of course, are supposed to be "masculine," which means that they are expected to be assertive, self-reliant, decisive, and competitive. Women are expected to be "feminine," or warm, sensitive, emotionally expressive, and kind. You and I aren't so unsophisticated, but they're the *opposite* sexes to most people, and to varying degrees men and women are expected to specialize in different kinds of social behavior all over the world (Löckenhoff et al., 2014). However, people inherit only about a quarter to a third of their tendencies to be assertive or kind; most of these behaviors are learned (Lippa & Hershberger, 1999). In thoroughgoing and pervasive ways, cultural processes of socialization and modeling (rather than biological sex differences) lead us to expect that all men should be tough and all women should be tender (Levant & Rankin, 2014).

Nevertheless, those stereotypes don't describe real people as well as you might think; only *half* of us have attributes that fit these gender role expectations cleanly (Donnelly & Twenge, 2017). Instead of being just "masculine" or "feminine," a sizable minority of people—about 35 percent—are both assertive *and* warm, sensitive *and* self-reliant. Such people possess both sets of the competencies that are stereotypically associated with being male and with being female, and are said to be **androgynous.** If androgyny sounds odd to you, you're probably just using a stereotyped vocabulary: On the surface, being "masculine" sounds incompatible with also being "feminine." In fact, because those terms can be confusing, relationship researchers often use alternatives, referring to the "masculine" task-oriented talents as **instrumental** traits and to the "feminine" social and emotional skills as **expressive** traits. And it's not all that remarkable to find both sets of traits in the same individual. An androgynous person would be one who could effectively, assertively stand up for himself or herself in a heated salary negotiation but who could then go home and sensitively, compassionately comfort a preschool child whose pet hamster had died. A lot of people, those who specialize in either instrumental *or* expressive skills, would feel at home in one of those situations but not both. Androgynous people would be comfortable and capable in both domains (Martin et al., 2017).

In fact, the best way to think of instrumentality and expressiveness is as two separate sets of skills that may range from low to high in either women or men (Choi et al., 2007). Take a look at Table 1.2. Traditional women are high in expressiveness but low in instrumentality; they're warm and kind but not assertive or dominant. Men who fulfill our traditional expectations are high in instrumentality but low in expressiveness and are stoic, "macho" men. Androgynous people are both instrumental and expressive. The rest of us—about 15 percent—are either high in the skills typically associated with the other sex (and are said to be "cross-typed") or low in both sets of skills (and are said to be "undifferentiated"). Equal proportions of men and women fall into the androgynous, cross-typed, and undifferentiated categories, so, as with sex differences, it's simplistic and inaccurate to think of men and women as wholly distinct groups of people with separate, different traits (Donnelly & Twenge, 2017).

In any case, gender differences are of particular interest to relationship researchers because, instead of making men and women more compatible, they "may actually be responsible for much of the *incompatibility*" that causes relationships to fail (Ickes, 1985, p. 188). From the moment they meet, for instance, traditional men and women enjoy and like each other less than androgynous people do. In a classic experiment, Ickes and Barnes (1978) paired men and women in couples in which (a) both partners fit the traditional gender roles or (b) one or both partners were androgynous. The two people were introduced to each other and then simply left alone for 5 minutes sitting on a couch while the researchers covertly videotaped their interaction. The results were striking. The traditional couples talked less, looked at each other less, laughed and smiled less, and

TABLE 1.2. Gender Roles

Instrumental Traits	Expressive Traits
Assertiveness	Warmth
Self-Reliance	Tenderness
Ambition	Compassion
Leadership	Kindness
Decisiveness	Sensitivity to Others

Our culture encourages men to be highly instrumental and women to be highly expressive, but which of these talents do you *not* want in an intimate companion?

Sally Forth ©1995 *Distributed by King Features Syndicate, Inc.*

Instrumental, masculine people often feel ill at ease when they are asked to provide warm, sensitive support to others.

afterward reported that they liked each other less than did the other couples. (Should this surprise us? Think about it: Stylistically, what do a masculine man and a feminine woman have in common?) When an androgynous man met a traditional woman, an androgynous woman met a traditional man, or two androgynous people got together, they got along much better than traditional men and women did.

More importantly, the disadvantage faced by traditional couples does not disappear as time goes by. Surveys of marital satisfaction demonstrate that marriages in which both spouses adhere to stereotyped gender roles are generally *less* happy than those enjoyed by nontraditional couples (Helms et al., 2006). With their different styles and different domains of expertise, masculine men and feminine women simply do not find as much pleasure in each other as less traditional, less stereotyped people do (Marshall, 2010).

Perhaps this should be no surprise. When human beings devote themselves to intimate partnerships, they want affection, warmth, and understanding (Reis et al., 2000). People who are low in expressiveness—who are not very warm, tender, sensitive people—do not readily provide such warmth and tenderness; they are not very affectionate (Miller et al., 2003). As a result, men or women who have spouses who are low in expressiveness are chronically less satisfied than are those whose partners are more sensitive, understanding, and kind. Around the world (Lease et al., 2013), across different ethnicities (Stanik & Bryant, 2012), and in both straight and gay partnerships (Wade & Donis, 2007), traditional men have romantic relationships of lower quality than more expressive men do. Thus, traditional gender roles do men a disservice, depriving them of skills that would make them more rewarding husbands.

On the other hand, people who are low in instrumentality—who are low in assertiveness and personal strength—tend to have low self-esteem and to be less well adjusted than those who have better task-oriented skills (Stake & Eisele, 2010). People feel better about themselves when they are competent and effective at "taking care of business" (Reis et al., 2000), so traditional gender roles also do women a disservice, depriving them of skills that would facilitate more accomplishments and achievements. Such roles also seem to cost women money; around the world, traditional women earn less on the job than their nontraditional co-workers do (Stickney & Konrad, 2007).

The upshot of all this is that both instrumentality and expressiveness are valuable traits, and the happiest, best-adjusted, most effective, mentally healthy people possess both sets of skills (Stake & Eisele, 2010). In particular, the most desirable spouses, those who are most likely to have contented, satisfied partners, are people who are both instrumental and expressive (Marshall, 2010). And in fact, when they ponder the partners they'd like to have, most people say that they'd prefer androgynous partners to those who are merely masculine or feminine (Thomae & Houston, 2016).

So, it's ironic that we still tend to put pressure on those who do not rigidly adhere to their "proper" gender roles. Women who display as much competitiveness and assertiveness as men risk being perceived as pushy, impolite, and uppity (Williams & Tiedens, 2016). If anything, however, gender expectations are stricter for men than for women (Steinberg & Diekman, 2016); girls can be tomboys and nobody frets too much, but if a boy is too feminine, people worry (O'Neil, 2015). U.S. gender roles are changing slowly but surely; in particular, U.S. women are becoming more instrumental (Donnelly & Twenge, 2017), and young adults of both sexes are gradually becoming more egalitarian and less traditional in their views of men and women (Donnelly et al., 2016). Nonetheless, even if they limit our individual potentials and are right only half the time, gender stereotypes persist (Haines et al., 2016). We still expect and too often encourage men to be instrumental and women to be expressive (Levant & Rankin, 2014), and such expectations are important complications for many of our close relationships.

A Point to Ponder

If you saw a YouTube video of a new father crying when he holds his newborn baby for the first time, would you admire him or disrespect him? Why?

Personality

Shaped by our experiences, some consequential differences among people (such as attachment styles and gender differences) may change over a few years' time, but other individual differences are more stable and lasting. Personality traits influence people's behavior in their relationships across their entire lifetimes (Vukasović & Bratko, 2015) with only gradual change over long periods of time (Milojev & Sibley, 2017).

The central traits known as the Big Five traits characterize people all over the world (McCrae & Costa, 2010), and they all affect the quality of the relationships people have. On the positive side, extraverted, agreeable, and conscientious people who are open to new experiences have happier relationships than do those who score lower on those traits (Schaffhuser et al., 2014). Extraverted people are outgoing and agreeable people are friendly, so they tend to be likable. Conscientious people work hard and tend to follow the rules, so they weren't very popular in high school (van der Linden et al., 2010)—but, once they grow up, they make dependable, trustworthy, desirable partners (Hill et al., 2014).

The Big Five Personality Traits

A small cluster of fundamental traits does a good job of describing the broad themes in behavior, thoughts, and emotions that distinguish one person from another (McCrae & Costa, 2010). These key characteristics are called the Big Five traits by personality researchers, and they differ in their influence on our intimate relationships. Which of these traits do you think matter most?

Openness to experience—the degree to which people are imaginative, curious, unconventional, and artistic versus conforming, uncreative, and stodgy.

Extraversion—the extent to which people are outgoing, gregarious, assertive, and sociable versus cautious, reclusive, and shy.

Conscientiousness—the extent to which people are industrious, dependable, responsible, and orderly versus unreliable, disorganized, and careless.

Agreeableness—the degree to which people are compassionate, cooperative, good-natured, and trusting versus suspicious, selfish, and hostile.

Neuroticism—the degree to which people are prone to fluctuating moods and high levels of negative emotion such as worry, anxiety, and anger.

The five traits are listed in order from the least important to the most influential (Malouff et al., 2010). People are happier when they have imaginative, adventurous, sociable partners, but what you *really* want is a lover who is responsible and reliable, generous and thoughtful, and optimistic and emotionally stable. And after you've been together for 30 years or so, you may find that conscientiousness becomes particularly important (Claxton et al., 2012); dependable partners who keep all their promises are satisfying companions.

"People who are less conscientious exceed their credit limit . . . cancel plans, curse, oversleep, and break promises" (Jackson et al., 2010, p. 507), so they tend to be unreliable companions.

The most influential Big Five trait, however, is the one that has a negative impact: neuroticism (Malouff et al., 2010). Neurotic people are prone to anger and anxiety, and those unhappy tendencies tend to result in touchy, pessimistic, and argumentative interactions with others (Jeronimus et al., 2014). In fact, a remarkable study that tracked 300 couples over a span of 45 years found that a full 10 percent of the satisfaction and contentment spouses would experience in their marriages could be predicted from measures of their neuroticism when they were still engaged (Kelly & Conley, 1987). The less neurotic the partners were, the happier their marriages turned out to be. Everyone has good days and bad days, but some of us chronically have *more* bad days (and fewer good ones) than other people (Hudson et al., 2017)—and those unlucky folks are especially likely to have unhappy, disappointing relationships. (Do take note of this when you're shopping for a mate!)

Working alongside the global influences of the Big Five traits are other more specific personal characteristics that regulate our relationships, and I'll mention several in later chapters. (Check out, for instance, whether or not we like casual sex [on page 283] and whether or not we can control ourselves [on page 425].) For now, let's note that although our personalities clearly have a genetic basis (Vukasović & Bratko, 2015), our enduring traits can be shaped to a degree by our relationships (Soto, 2015). Dissatisfying and abusive relationships can gradually make us more anxious and neurotic, and warm, rewarding partnerships may make us more agreeable over time. But these effects are subtle, and our relationships have much bigger effects on the last individual difference we will consider: the self-evaluations we bring to our transactions with others.

Self-Esteem

Most of us like ourselves, but some of us do not. Our evaluations of ourselves constitute our **self-esteem,** and when we hold favorable judgments of our skills and traits, our self-esteem is high; when we doubt ourselves, self-esteem is low. Because people with high self-esteem are generally happier and more successful than those with low self-regard (Orth & Robins, 2014), it's widely assumed that it's good to feel good about yourself (Swann & Bosson, 2010).

But how do people come to like themselves? A provocative, leading theory argues that self-esteem is a subjective gauge, a **sociometer,** that measures the quality of our relationships with others (Leary, 2012). When others like us, we like ourselves; when other people regard us positively and value their relationships with us, self-esteem is high. However, if we don't interest others—if others seem not to care whether or not we are part of their lives—self-esteem is low (Leary & Acosta, 2018). Self-esteem operates in this manner, according to sociometer theory, because it is an evolved mechanism that serves our need to belong. This argument suggests that, because their reproductive success depended on staying in the tribe and being accepted by others, early humans became sensitive to any signs of exclusion that might precede rejection by others. Self-esteem became a psychological gauge that alerted people to declining acceptance by others, and dislike or disinterest from others gradually caused people to dislike themselves (Kavanagh & Scrutton, 2015).

This perspective nicely fits most of what we know about the origins and operation of self-esteem. There's no question, for instance, that people feel better about themselves when they think they're attractive to the other sex (Bale & Archer, 2013). And the regard we receive from others clearly affects our subsequent self-evaluations (Reitz et al., 2016). In particular, events that involve interpersonal rejection damage our self-esteem in a way that other disappointments do not. Leary and his colleagues demonstrated this point in a clever study in which research participants were led to believe that they would be excluded from an attractive group either through bad luck—they had been randomly selected to be sent home—or because they had been voted out by the other members of the group (Leary et al., 1995). Even though the same desirable opportunity was lost in both situations, the people who had been personally rejected felt much worse about themselves than did those whose loss was impersonal. It's also interesting to note that public events that others witness affect our self-esteem more than do private events that are otherwise identical but are known only to us. In this and several other respects, whether we

An Individual Difference That's Not Much of a Difference: Sexual Orientation

I've mentioned gays and lesbians only twice so far, and that's because there hasn't been much to say. Sexual orientations are complex: Lots of people who consider themselves to be heterosexual have experienced attraction to, infatuation with, and fantasies involving others of the same sex (Savin-Williams, 2014). But fewer of us—about 8 percent of men and 9 percent of women—have had genital sex with a member of the same sex (Twenge et al., 2016), and smaller numbers of us—about 4 percent—consider ourselves to be lesbian, gay, or bisexual (LGB) (Bailey et al., 2016). As a result, most relationship studies have not included a focus on LGB partnerships—and that's not because researchers aren't interested, but because large samples of such couples are harder to obtain. (See our discussion of *convenience samples* on page 47.) However, when researchers *do* focus on LGB relationships, they find that the processes of intimacy don't depend much on sexual orientation at all.[10] Other than their relative numbers, heterosexuals and LGBs are resoundingly similar on most of the topics we encounter in this book (Frost et al., 2015). For instance, gays and lesbians exhibit the same attachment styles in the same proportions as heterosexual men and women do (Roisman et al., 2008), and they, too, are happier with romantic partners of high (rather than low) expressivity (Wade & Donis, 2007).

There *are* some potentially important differences between same-sex and other-sex

relationships. Gay men tend to be more expressive than heterosexual men, on average, and lesbians tend to be more instrumental than other women, so gays and lesbians are less likely than heterosexuals to adhere to traditional gender roles (Lippa, 2005). Gays and lesbians also tend to be better educated and to be more liberal (Grollman, 2017). But the big difference between same-sex and other-sex relationships is that a gay couple is composed of two people who identify as *men* and a lesbian couple is composed of two people who identify as *women*. To the extent that there are any differences in the way men and women conduct their relationships, same-sex couples may behave differently than heterosexual couples do, not because of their sexual orientations but because of the sexes of the people involved. For instance, when their relationships are new, gay men have sex more often than heterosexual couples do, and lesbian couples have sex less often than heterosexual couples do (Diamond, 2015). The more men there are in a partnership, the more often the couple has sex—but that's probably because men have higher sex drives than women do, *not* because there's anything special about gay men (Regan, 2015).

Except for the sex and gender differences that may exist, same-sex and other-sex partnerships operate in very similar manners (Manning et al., 2016). Gays and lesbians fall in love the same way, for instance, and they feel the same passions, experience the same doubts, and feel the same commitments as heterosexuals do (Kurdek, 2006). Where differences in relationship functioning do exist, they tend to be small, but gays and lesbians are the clear winners. They have *better* relationships than heterosexuals do, on average (Kurdek, 2005). They divide up household chores more fairly,

[10] Unfortunately, I won't be able to say anything about the relationships of transgendered people; although relationship science does not subscribe to cisnormativity, there isn't yet sufficient data for me to report. Personally, however, I'd be surprised if transgenders love their partners any differently than the rest of us do.

experience less conflict, and feel more compatible, more intimate, and more satisfied with their lovers (Balsam et al., 2008). (Given the social disapproval same-sex couples still get from some people (Fingerhut, 2016), their contentment is remarkable. But remember, there are no sex differences in same-sex relationships. How much do you think that contributes to the success of their relationships?)

Still, there's no reason to write two different books on *Intimate Relationships;* intimacy operates the same way in both same-sex and other-sex partnerships. We'll encounter sexual orientation several times in later chapters, but it won't be a major theme because the processes of close relationships are very similar in same-sex and heterosexual couples (Peplau & Fingerhut, 2007). Anyone who assumes otherwise is not well-informed.

realize it or not, our self-evaluations seem to be much affected by what we think others think of us (Lemay & Spongberg, 2015), and this is true around the world (Denissen et al., 2008).

Here is further evidence, then, that we humans are a very social species: It's hard to like ourselves (and, indeed, it would be unrealistic to do so) if others don't like us, too. In most cases, people with chronically low self-esteem have developed their negative self-evaluations through an unhappy history of failing to receive sufficient acceptance and appreciation from other people.

And sometimes, this is very unfair. Some people are victimized by abusive relationships through no fault of their own, and, despite being likable people with fine social skills, they develop low self-esteem as a result of mistreatment from others. What happens when those people enter new relationships with kinder, more appreciative partners? Does the new feedback they receive slowly improve their self-esteem?

Not necessarily. A compelling program of research by Sandra Murray, John Holmes, Joanne Wood, and Justin Cavallo has demonstrated that people with low self-esteem sometimes sabotage their relationships by underestimating their partners' love for them (Murray et al., 2001) and perceiving disregard when none exists (Murray et al., 2002). Take a look at Table 1.3. People with low self-regard find it hard to believe that they are well and truly loved by their partners and, as a result, they tend not to be optimistic that their loves will last. "Even in their closest relationships," people with low self-esteem "typically harbor serious (but unwarranted) insecurities about their partners' feelings for them" (Holmes & Wood, 2009, p. 250). This leads them to overreact to their partners' occasional bad moods (Bellavia & Murray, 2003); they feel more rejected, experience more hurt, and get more angry than do those with higher self-esteem. And these painful feelings make it harder for them to behave constructively in response to their imagined peril. Whereas people with high self-regard draw closer to their partners and seek to repair the relationship when frustrations arise, people with low self-esteem defensively distance themselves, stay surly, and behave badly (Murray, Bellavia et al., 2003). They also feel even worse about themselves (Murray, Griffin et al., 2003).

All of this occurs, say Murray and her colleagues (Cavallo et al., 2014), because we take large risks when we come to depend on others. Close ties to

TABLE 1.3. How My Partner Sees Me

Sandra Murray and her colleagues use this scale in their studies of self-esteem in close relationships. People with high self-esteem believe that their partners hold them in high regard, but people with low self-esteem worry that their partners do not like or respect them as much. What do you think your partner thinks of you?

In many ways, your partner may see you in roughly the same way you see yourself. Yet in other ways, your partner may see you differently than you see yourself. For example, you may feel quite shy at parties, but your partner might tell you that you really seem quite relaxed and outgoing on these occasions. On the other hand, you and your partner may both agree that you are quite intelligent and patient.

For each trait or attribute that follows, please indicate *how you think that your partner sees you*. For example, if you think that your partner sees the attribute "self-assured" as moderately characteristic of you, you would choose "5."

Respond using the scale below. Please enter your response in the blank to the left of each trait or attribute listed.

1	2	3	4	5	6	7	8	9
Not at All Characteristic		Somewhat Characteristic		Moderately Characteristic		Very Characteristic		Completely Characteristic

My partner sees me as . . .

_____	Kind and Affectionate	_____	Tolerant and Accepting
_____	Critical and Judgmental	_____	Thoughtless
_____	Self-Assured	_____	Patient
_____	Sociable/Extraverted	_____	Rational
_____	Intelligent	_____	Understanding
_____	Lazy	_____	Distant
_____	Open and Disclosing	_____	Complaining
_____	Controlling and Dominant	_____	Responsive
_____	Witty and Humorous	_____	Immature
_____	Moody	_____	Warm

an intimate partner allow us to enjoy rich rewards of support and care, but they also leave us vulnerable to devastating betrayal and rejection if our partners prove to be untrustworthy. Because they are confident about their partners' love and regard for them, people with high self-esteem draw closer to their partners when difficulties arise. In contrast, people with low self-esteem have lasting doubts about their partners' regard and reliability, so when times get tough, they withdraw from their partners in an effort to protect themselves. We all need to balance connectedness with self-protection, Murray's team suggests, but people with low self-esteem put their fragile egos before their relationships, and that's self-defeating when they have loving, devoted partners and there is nothing to fear (Murray et al., 2013).

As a result, the self-doubts and thin skins of people with low self-esteem lead them to make mountains out of molehills. They stay on alert for signs of rejection (H. Li et al., 2012), and they wrongly perceive small bumps in the road as worrisome signs of declining commitment in their partners. Then, they respond with obnoxious, self-defeating hurt and anger that cut them off from the reassurance they crave. Even their Facebook updates tend to be pessimistic and self-critical, and they receive fewer "likes" and comments than others do (Forest & Wood, 2012). By comparison, people with high self-esteem correctly shrug off the same small bumps and remain confident of their partners' acceptance and positive regard. The unfortunate net result is that once it is formed, low self-esteem may be hard to overcome (Kuster & Orth, 2013); even after 10 years of marriage, people with low self-esteem still tend to believe that their spouses love and accept them less than those faithful spouses really do (Murray et al., 2000), and that regrettable state of affairs undermines their—and their spouse's—satisfaction (Erol & Orth, 2013). Relationships are more fulfilling for both partners when they both have high self-esteem (Robinson & Cameron, 2012).

Thus, our self-esteem appears to both result from and then subsequently steer our interpersonal relationships (Luciano & Orth, 2017). What we think of ourselves seems to depend, at least in part, on the quality of our connections to others. And those self-evaluations affect our ensuing interactions with new partners, who provide us further evidence of our interpersonal worth. In fundamental ways, what we know of ourselves emerges from our partnerships with others and then matters thereafter (Mund et al., 2015).

THE INFLUENCE OF HUMAN NATURE

Now that we have surveyed some key characteristics that distinguish people from one another, we can address the possibility that our relationships display some underlying themes that reflect the animal nature shared by all humankind. Our concern here is with evolutionary influences that have shaped close relationships over countless generations, instilling in us certain tendencies that are found in everyone (Confer et al., 2010).

Evolutionary psychology starts with three fundamental assumptions. First, *sexual selection* has helped make us the species we are today. You've probably heard of *natural* selection, which refers to the advantages conferred on animals that cope more effectively than others with predators and physical challenges such as food shortages. Sexual selection involves advantages that result in greater success at reproduction. And importantly:

> Contrary to what many people have been taught, evolution has nothing to do with the survival of the fittest. It is not a question of whether you live or die. The key to evolution is reproduction. Whereas all organisms eventually die, not all organisms reproduce. Further, among those that do reproduce, some leave more descendants than others. (Ash & Gallup, 2008, p. 313)

This point of view holds that motives such as the need to belong have presumably come to characterize human beings because they were *adaptive,* conferring some sort of reproductive advantage to those who possessed them. As I suggested earlier, the early humans who sought cooperative closeness with others were probably more likely than asocial loners to have children who grew up to have children of their own. Over time, then, to the extent that the desire to affiliate with others is heritable (and it is; Tellegen et al., 1988), sexual selection would have made the need to belong more prevalent, with fewer and fewer people being born without it. In keeping with this example, evolutionary principles assert that any universal psychological mechanism exists in its present form because it consistently solved some problem of survival or reproduction in the past (Confer et al., 2010).

Second, evolutionary psychology suggests that men and women should differ from one another only to the extent that they have historically faced different reproductive dilemmas (Geary, 2010). Thus, men and women should behave similarly in close relationships except in those instances in which different, specialized styles of behavior would allow better access to mates or promote superior survival of one's offspring. Are there such situations? Let's address that question by posing two hypothetical queries:

> If, during one year, a man has sex with 100 different women, how many children can he father? (The answer, of course, is "lots, perhaps as many as 100.")

> If, during one year, a woman has sex with 100 different men, how many children can she have? (Probably just one.)

Obviously, there's a big difference in the minimum time and effort that men and women have to invest in each child they produce. For a man, the minimum requirement is a single ejaculation; given access to receptive mates, a man might father hundreds of children during his lifetime. But a woman can have children only until her menopause, and each child she has requires an enormous investment of time and energy. These biological differences in men's and women's obligatory **parental investment**—the time, energy, and resources one must provide to one's offspring in order to reproduce—may have supported the evolution of different strategies for selecting mates (Geary, 2000). Conceivably, given their more limited reproductive potential, women in our ancestral past who chose their mates carefully reproduced more successfully (with more of their children surviving to have children of their own) than did women who were less thoughtful and deliberate in their choices of partners. In contrast, men who promiscuously pursued every available sexual opportunity may have reproduced more successfully. If they flitted from partner to partner, their children may have been less likely to survive, but what they didn't offer in quality (of parenting) they could make up for in quantity (of children). Thus, today—as this evolutionary account predicts— women do choose their sexual partners more carefully than men do. They insist on smarter, friendlier, more prestigious, and more emotionally stable partners than men will accept, and they are less interested in casual, uncommitted sex than men are (N. Li et al., 2012). Perhaps this sex difference evolved over time.

Another reproductive difference between the sexes is that a woman always knows for sure whether or not a particular child is hers. By comparison, a man suffers **paternity uncertainty;** unless he is completely confident that his mate has been faithful to him, he cannot be absolutely certain that her child is his (Buss & Schmitt, 1993). Perhaps because of that, even though women cheat less than men do (Tsapelas et al., 2011), men are more preoccupied with worries about their partners' infidelity than women are (Schützwohl, 2006). This difference, too, may have evolved over time.

An evolutionary perspective also makes a distinction between *short-term* and *long-term* mating strategies (Buss & Schmitt, 1993). Men and women both seem to pursue different sorts of attributes in the other sex when they're having a brief fling than when they're entering a longer, more committed relationship. In particular, men have a greater desire than women do for sexual liaisons of short duration; they are more interested in brief affairs with a variety of partners, and when they enter new relationships, they're ready to have sex sooner than women are (Schmitt, 2016). As a result, when they're on the prowl, men are attracted to women who seem to be sexually available and "easy" (Schmitt et al., 2001). However, if they think about settling down, the same men who consider promiscuous women to be desirable partners in casual relationships often prefer chaste women as prospective spouses (Buss, 2000). Men also tend to seek wives who are young and pretty. When they're thinking long-term, men value physical attractiveness more than women do, and as men age, they marry women increasingly younger than themselves (Conway et al., 2015).

Women exhibit different patterns. When women select short-term mates—particularly when they have extramarital affairs (Greiling & Buss, 2000)—they seek sexy, charismatic, dominant men with lots of masculine appeal. But when they evaluate potential husbands, they look for good financial prospects; they seek men with incomes and resources who presumably can provide a safe environment for their children, even when those men aren't the sexiest guys in the pack (Gangestad & Simpson, 2000). In general, women care more than men do about the financial prospects and status of their long-term partners (Conroy-Beam et al., 2015).

The effort to delineate human nature by identifying patterns of behavior that are found in all of humanity is one of the compelling aspects of the evolutionary perspective. In fact, the different preferences I just mentioned—with men valuing good looks and women valuing good incomes—have been found in dozens of cultures, everywhere they have been studied around the world (Buss, 2015).[11] However, an evolutionary perspective does not imply that culture is unimportant.

---

[11] Here's a chance for you to rehearse what you learned earlier in this chapter about sex differences. On average, men and women differ in the importance they attach to physical attractiveness and income, but that doesn't mean that women don't care about looks and men don't care about money. And overall, as we'll see in chapter 3, men and women mostly want the *same* things, such as warmth, emotional stability, and generous affection, from their romantic partners. Despite the sex differences I just described, people do not want looks or money at the expense of other valuable characteristics that men and women both want (Li, 2008). Finally, before I finish this footnote, do you see how differences in parental investment may underlie men's interest in looks and women's interest in money? Think about it, and we'll return to this point in chapter 3.

Indeed, a third basic assumption of evolutionary psychology is that cultural influences determine whether evolved patterns of behavior are adaptive—and cultural change occurs faster than evolution does. Our ancient forebears were walking around on two legs *millions* of years ago,[12] facing challenges we can only imagine. A best guess is that more than one in every four infants failed to survive their first year of life, and about half didn't live long enough to reach puberty (Volk & Atkinson, 2013). Things are different now. Our species displays patterns of behavior that *were* adaptive eons ago, but not all of those inherited tendencies may fit the modern environments we inhabit today. For instance, cavemen may have reproduced successfully if they tried to mate with every possible partner, but modern men may not: In just the last two generations, we have seen (a) the creation of reproductive technologies—such as birth control pills—that allow women complete control of their fertility and (b) the spread of a lethal virus that is transmitted through sexual contact (the human immunodeficiency virus that causes AIDS). These days, a desire for multiple partners is probably less adaptive for men than it was millions of years ago. Conceivably, modern men may reproduce more successfully if they display a capacity for commitment and monogamy that encourages their partners to allow a pregnancy to occur. But the human race is still evolving. Sexual selection will ultimately favor styles of behavior that fit our new environment, but it will take several thousand generations for such adaptations to occur. (And how will our cultures have changed by then?)

Thus, an evolutionary perspective provides a fascinating explanation for common patterns in modern relationships (Eastwick, 2016): Certain themes and some sex differences exist because they spring from evolved psychological mechanisms that were useful long ago. We are not robots who are mindlessly enacting genetic directives, and we are not all alike (Boutwell & Boisvert, 2014), but we do have inherited habits that are triggered by the situations we encounter. Moreover, our habits may fit our modern situations to varying degrees. Behavior results from the interplay of both personal and situational influences, but some common reactions in people result from evolved human nature itself:

> The pressures to which we have been exposed over millennia have left a mental and emotional legacy. Some of these emotions and reactions, derived from the species who were our ancestors, are unnecessary in a modern age, but these vestiges of a former existence are indelibly printed in our make-up. (Winston, 2002, p. 3)

This is a provocative point of view that has attracted both acclaim and criticism. On the one hand, the evolutionary perspective has prompted intriguing new discoveries (Buss, 2015). On the other hand, assumptions about the primeval social environments from which human nature emerged are necessarily speculative. And importantly, critics assert, an evolutionary model is not the only reasonable

---

[12] I don't know about you, but this blows my mind. The bones of Lucy, the famous female *Australopithecus afarensis,* are estimated to be 3.2 million years old, a span of time I find to be incomprehensible. That's how long our predecessors have been adjusting, adapting, and reproducing. Is it so unlikely that, in the midst of huge individual idiosyncrasy, some behavioral patterns became commonplace?

explanation for many of the patterns at issue (Eagly & Wood, 2013a). Women may have to pick their mates more carefully than men do, for instance, not because of the pressures of parental investment but because cultures routinely allow women less control over financial resources (Wood & Eagly, 2007); arguably, women have to be concerned about their spouses' incomes when it's hard for them to earn as much money themselves. If women routinely filled similar roles and had social status as high as men's, women's greater interest in a mate's money might be much reduced (Zentner & Mitura, 2012).

Thus, critics of an evolutionary perspective emphasize the role of culture in shaping male and female behavior (Eagly & Wood, 2012), and they contend that patterns of behavior that are presumed to be evolved tendencies are both less noticeable and more variable across cultures than an evolutionary model would suggest (Eagly & Wood, 2013b). Proponents respond that, of course, cultures are hugely influential—after all, they determine which behaviors are adaptive and which are not—but there are differences in the mating strategies and behavior of men and women that can't be explained by social roles and processes (Buss, 2013; Schmitt, 2016). The contest between these camps isn't finished (Hagen, 2016), and we'll encounter it again later on. For now, one thing is certain: Right or wrong, evolutionary models have generated fascinating research that has been good for relationship science. And take note of the bottom line: Whether it evolved or was a social creation (or both), there may well be a human nature that shapes our intimate relationships.

THE INFLUENCE OF INTERACTION

The final building block of relationships is the interaction that the two partners share. So far, we've focused on the idiosyncratic experiences and personalities that individuals bring to a relationship, but it's time to acknowledge that relationships are much more than the sum of their parts. Relationships emerge from the *combination* of their participants' histories and talents (Mund et al., 2016), and those amalgamations may be quite different from the simple sum of the individuals who create them. Chemists are used to thinking this way; when they mix two elements (such as hydrogen and oxygen), they often get a compound (such as water) that doesn't resemble either of its constituent parts. In a similar fashion, the relationship two people create results from contributions from each of them but may only faintly resemble the relationships they share with other people.

Consider the levels of trust you feel toward others. Even if you're a secure and trusting person, you undoubtedly trust some people more than others because trust is a two-way street that is influenced both by your dispositions and those of your partners (Simpson, 2007). Moreover, it emerges from the dynamic give-and-take you and your partners share each day; trust is a fluid *process* rather than a static, changeless thing, and it ebbs and flows in all of your relationships.

Every intimate relationship is like this. Individually, two partners inevitably encounter fluctuating moods and variable health and energy; then, when they interact, their mutual influence on one another may produce a constantly changing variety of outcomes (Totenhagen et al., 2016). Over time, of course, unmistakable patterns of interaction will often distinguish one relationship from another (Heerey, 2015). Still, at any given moment, a relationship may be an inconstant entity, the product of shifting transactions of complex people.

Overall, then, relationships are constructed of diverse influences that may range from the fads and fashions of current culture to the basic nature of the human race. Working alongside those generic influences are various idiosyncratic factors such as personality and experience, some of them learned and some of them inherited. And ultimately, two people who hail from the same planet—but who may otherwise be somewhat different in every other respect—begin to interact. The result may be frustrating or fulfilling, but the possibilities are always fascinating—and that's what relationships are made of.

THE DARK SIDE OF RELATIONSHIPS

I began this chapter by asserting the value of intimacy to human beings, so, to be fair, I should finish it by admitting that intimacy has potential costs as well. We need intimacy—we suffer without it—but distress and displeasure sometimes result from our dealings with others. Indeed, relationships can be disappointing in so many ways that whole books can, and have been, written about their drawbacks (Spitzberg & Cupach, 2014)! When they're close to others, people may fear that their sensitive secrets will be revealed or turned against them. They may dread the loss of autonomy and personal control that comes with interdependency (Baxter, 2004), and they may worry about being abandoned by those on whom they rely. They recognize that there is dishonesty in relationships and that people sometimes confuse lust with love (Diamond, 2014). And in fact, most of us (56 percent) have had a troublesome relationship in the last 5 years (Levitt et al., 1996), so these are not empty fears.

Some of us fear intimacy (Mikulincer & Shaver, 2016). Indeed, some of us anxiously expect that others will reject us, and we live on edge waiting for the relational axe to fall (Kawamoto et al., 2015). But whether our fears are overstated or merely realistic, we're all likely to experience unexpected, frustrating costs in our relationships on occasion (Miller, 1997b). And the deleterious consequences for our physical health of disappointment and distress in our close relationships can be substantial (Liu & Waite, 2014).

So why take the risk? Because we are a social species. We need each other. We prematurely wither and die without close connections to other people. Relationships can be complex, but they are essential parts of our lives, so they are worth understanding as thoroughly as possible. I'm glad you're reading this book, and I'll try to facilitate your understanding in the chapters that follow.

FOR YOUR CONSIDERATION

Mark and Wendy met during their junior years in college, and they instantly found a lot to like in each other. Wendy was pretty and very feminine and rather meek, and Mark liked the fact that he was able to entice her to have sex with him on their second date. Wendy was susceptible to his charms because she unjustly doubted her desirability, and she was excited that a dominant, charismatic man found her attractive. They started cohabitating during their senior years and married 6 months after graduation. They developed a traditional partnership, with Wendy staying home when their children were young and Mark applying himself to his career. He succeeded in his profession, winning several lucrative promotions, but Wendy began to feel that he was married more to his work than to her. She wanted him to talk to her more, and he began to wish that she was eating less and taking better care of herself.

Having read this chapter, what do you think the future holds for Mark and Wendy? How happy will they be with each other in another 10 years? Why?

CHAPTER SUMMARY

The Nature and Importance of Intimacy

This book focuses on adult friendships and romantic relationships.

The Nature of Intimacy. Intimate relationships differ from more casual associations in at least seven specific ways: *knowledge, interdependence, caring, trust, responsiveness, mutuality,* and *commitment.*

The Need to Belong. Humans display a need to belong, a drive to maintain regular interaction with affectionate, intimate partners. Adverse consequences may follow if the need remains unfulfilled over time.

The Influence of Culture

Cultural norms regarding relationships in the United States have changed dramatically over the last 50 years. Fewer people are marrying than ever before, and those who do marry wait longer to do so. People routinely cohabit, and that often makes a future divorce more, not less, likely.

Sources of Change. Economic changes, increasing individualism, and new technology contribute to cultural change. So does the *sex ratio;* cultures with high sex ratios are characterized by traditional roles for men and women, whereas low sex ratios are correlated with more permissive behavior.

The Influence of Experience

Children's interactions with their caregivers produce different styles of attachment. Four styles—*secure, preoccupied, fearful,* and *dismissing*—which differ in *avoidance of intimacy* and *anxiety about abandonment*, are now recognized.

These orientations are mostly learned. Thus, our beliefs about the nature and worth of close relationships are shaped by our experiences within them.

The Influence of Individual Differences

There's wide variation in people's abilities and preferences, but individual differences are usually gradual and subtle instead of abrupt.

Sex Differences. Despite lay beliefs that men and women are quite different, most sex differences are quite small. The range of variation among members of a given sex is always large compared to the average difference between the sexes, and the overlap of the sexes is so substantial that many members of one sex will always score higher than the average member of the other sex. Thus, the sexes are much more similar than different on most of the topics of interest to relationship science.

Gender Differences. *Gender* differences refer to social and psychological distinctions that are taught to people by their cultures. Men are expected to be dominant and assertive, women to be warm and emotionally expressive—but a third of us are *androgynous* and possess both *instrumental,* task-oriented skills and *expressive,* social and emotional talents. Men and women who adhere to traditional gender roles do not like each other, either at first meeting or later during a marriage, as much as less stereotyped, androgynous people do.

Personality. Personality traits are stable tendencies that characterize people's thoughts, feelings, and behavior across their whole lives. Openness, extraversion, agreeableness, and conscientiousness help produce pleasant relationships, but neuroticism undermines one's contentment.

Self-Esteem. What we think of ourselves emerges from our interactions with others. The *sociometer* theory argues that if others regard us positively, self-esteem is high, but if others don't want to associate with us, self-esteem is low. People who have low self-esteem undermine and sabotage their close relationships by underestimating their partners' love for them and overreacting to imagined threats.

The Influence of Human Nature

An evolutionary perspective assumes that sexual selection shapes humankind, influenced, in part, by sex differences in *parental investment* and *paternity uncertainty.* The sexes pursue different mates when they're interested in a long, committed relationship than they do when they're interested in a short-term affair. The evolutionary perspective also assumes that cultural influences determine whether inherited habits are still adaptive—and some of them may not be.

The Influence of Interaction

Relationships result from the combinations of their participants' histories and talents, and thus are often more than the sum of their parts. Relationships are fluid processes rather than static entities.

The Dark Side of Relationships

There are potential costs, as well as rewards, to intimacy. So why take the risk? Because we are a social species, and we need each other.

CHAPTER 2

Research Methods

THE SHORT HISTORY OF RELATIONSHIP SCIENCE ◆ DEVELOPING A QUESTION ◆ OBTAINING PARTICIPANTS ◆ CHOOSING A DESIGN ◆ THE NATURE OF OUR DATA ◆ THE ETHICS OF SUCH ENDEAVORS ◆ INTERPRETING AND INTEGRATING RESULTS ◆ A FINAL NOTE ◆ FOR YOUR CONSIDERATION ◆ CHAPTER SUMMARY

I bet you dread a chapter on research methods. You probably regard it as a distraction to be endured before getting to "the good stuff." Love, sex, and jealousy probably appeal to you, for instance, but research designs and procedures are not at the top of your list.

Nevertheless, for several reasons, some basic knowledge of the methods used by researchers is especially valuable for consumers of relationship science. For one thing, more charlatans and imposters compete for your attention in this field than in most others. Bookstores and websites are full of ideas offered by people who don't really study relationships at all but who (a) base suggestions and advice on their own idiosyncratic experiences or (b) even worse, simply make them up (MacGeorge & Hall, 2014). Appreciating the difference between trustworthy, reliable information and simple gossip can save you money and disappointment. Moreover, misinformation about relationships is more likely to cause people real inconvenience than are misunderstandings in other sciences. People who misunderstand the nature of the solar system, for instance, are much less likely to take action that will be disadvantageous to them than are people who are misinformed about the effects of divorce on children. Studies of relationships often have real human impact in everyday life (Hawkins et al., 2013).

Indeed, this book speaks more directly to topics that affect you personally than most other texts you'll ever read. Because of this, you have a special responsibility to be an informed consumer who can distinguish flimsy whimsy from solid truths.

This isn't always easy. As we'll see in this chapter, there may be various ways to address a specific research question, and each may have its own particular advantages and disadvantages. Reputable scientists gather and evaluate information systematically and carefully, but no single technique may provide the indisputable answers they seek. A thoughtful understanding of relationships often requires us to combine information from many studies, evaluating diverse facts with judicious discernment. This chapter provides the overview of the techniques of relationship science that you need to make such judgments.

Only basic principles are described here—this is one of the shortest chapters in the book—but they should help you decide what evidence to accept and what to question. And trust me. There's a lot here that's worth thinking about even if you've read a Methods chapter before. Hopefully, when we're finished you'll be better equipped to distinguish useful research evidence from useless anecdotes or mere speculation. For even more information, don't hesitate to consult other sources such as Mehl and Conner (2012) and Leary (2017).

THE SHORT HISTORY OF RELATIONSHIP SCIENCE

Isaac Newton identified some of the basic laws of physics more than 400 years ago (back in 1687). Biology and chemistry have been around for just as long. The systematic study of human relationships, on the other hand, is a recent invention that is so new and so recent that you can actually talk, if you want, with most of the scientists who have ever studied human intimacy! This is no small matter. Because relationship science has a short history, it is less well known than most other sciences, and for that reason, it is less well understood. Very few people outside of colleges and universities appreciate the extraordinary strides this new discipline has made in the last 50 years.

Until the mid-twentieth century, relationships were pondered mainly by philosophers and poets. They had lots of opinions—doesn't everybody?—but those views were only opinions, and many of them were wrong. So, the first efforts of behavioral scientists to conduct empirical observations of real relationships were momentous developments. Relationship science can be said to have begun in the 1930s with a trickle of historically important studies of children's friendships (e.g., Moreno, 1934) and courtship and marriage (e.g., Waller, 1937). However, relatively few relationship studies were done before World War II. After the war, several important field studies, such as Whyte's (1955) *Street Corner Society* and Festinger, Schachter, and Back's (1950) study of student friendships in campus housing, attracted attention and respect. Still, as the 1950s drew to a close, a coherent science of relationships had yet to begin. The president of the American Psychological Association even complained that "psychologists, at least psychologists who write textbooks, not only show no interest in the origin and development of love and affection, but they seem to be unaware of its very existence" (Harlow, 1958, p. 673)!

That began to change, thank goodness, when an explosion of studies put the field on the scientific map in the 1960s and 1970s. Pioneering scientists Ellen Berscheid and Elaine Hatfield began systematic studies of attraction and love that were fueled by a new emphasis on laboratory experiments in social psychology (Reis et al., 2013). In a quest for precision that yielded unambiguous results, researchers began studying specific influences on relationships that they were able to control and manipulate. For instance, in a prominent line of research on the role of attitude similarity in liking, Donn Byrne and his colleagues (e.g., Byrne & Nelson, 1965) asked people to inspect an attitude survey that had supposedly been completed by a stranger in another room. Then, they asked the participants how much they liked the stranger. What the participants didn't know was that the researchers had prepared the survey either to agree or disagree with the participants' own attitudes (which had been assessed earlier). This manipulation of attitude similarity had clear effects: Apparent agreement caused people to like the stranger more than disagreement did.

The methodological rigor of procedures like these satisfied researchers' desires for clarity and concision. They legitimized and popularized the study of interpersonal attraction, making it an indispensable part of psychology textbooks for the first time. In retrospect, however, these investigations often did a poor job of representing the natural complexity of real relationships. The participants in many of Byrne's experiments never actually met that other person or interacted with him or her in any way. Indeed, in the procedure I've been describing, a meeting couldn't occur because the stranger didn't actually exist! In this "phantom stranger" technique, people were merely reacting to check marks on a piece of paper and were the only real participants in the study. The researchers were measuring attraction to someone who wasn't even there. Byrne and his colleagues chose this method, limiting their investigation to one carefully controlled aspect of relationship development, to study it conclusively. However, they also created a rather sterile situation that lacked the immediacy and drama of chatting with someone face-to-face on a first date.

But don't underestimate the importance of studies like these. They demonstrated that relationships could be studied scientifically and that such investigations had enormous promise, and they brought relationship science to the attention of fellow scholars for the first time (Reis, 2012). And in the decades since, through the combined efforts of family scholars, psychologists, sociologists, communication researchers, and neuroscientists, relationship science has grown and evolved to encompass new methods of considerable complexity and sophistication. Today, relationship science

- often uses diverse samples of people drawn from all walks of life and from around the world,
- examines varied types of family, friendship, and romantic relationships,
- frequently studies those relationships over long periods of time,
- studies both the pleasant and unpleasant aspects of relationships,
- often follows relationships in their natural settings, and
- uses sophisticated technology.

Here are some examples of how the field currently operates:

- At Northwestern University, Eli Finkel and his colleagues conduct "speed-dating" studies in which singles rotate through short conversations with 10 different potential romantic partners. Participants spend 4 minutes chatting with someone, record their reactions to the interaction, and then move on to someone new. The dating prospects are real; if both members of a couple indicate that they would like to see each other again, the researchers give them access to a website where they can exchange messages. But the researchers are also able to inspect the building blocks of real romantic chemistry as people pursue new mates (Vacharkulksemsuk et al., 2016). (Watch http://www.youtube.com/watch?v=4hOKtyQMZeE for further detail.)

- At the University of Texas at Arlington, William Ickes and his colleagues study spontaneous, unscripted interactions between people who have just met by leaving them alone on a comfortable couch for a few minutes while their conversation is covertly recorded. A camera is actually hidden in another room across the hall and can't be seen even if you're looking directly at it, so there's no clue that anyone is watching. Afterward, if the participants give their permission for their recordings to be used, they can review the tapes of their interaction in private cubicles where they are invited to report what they were thinking—and what they thought their partners were thinking—at each point in the interaction. The method thus provides an objective recording of the interaction (Babcock et al., 2014), and participants' thoughts and feelings and perceptions of one another can be obtained, too.
- In the Virtual Human Interaction Lab at Stanford University, two people play a game of 20 Questions—trying to guess someone's secret word (such as "ocean") by asking 20 yes or no questions—while their facial expressions are tracked and mapped onto avatars in a virtual environment. Each player can only see the other's avatar, and that allows Jeremy Bailenson and his colleagues to subtly manipulate the expressions each person sees (Oh et al., 2016). People enjoy their interaction more when they see smiles on the simulated faces of their partners that are slightly bigger and broader than the real smiles their partners are displaying (see Figure 2.1). Immersive virtual realities are allowing researchers to home in on the individual influences that underlie enjoyable interactions. (See what the Lab is doing at https://vhil.stanford.edu/.)

FIGURE 2.1. **Real versus "enhanced" facial expressions in virtual reality.**
Gesture tracking systems and modern modeling techniques allow researchers to manage and manipulate the expressions people see on the faces of their partners during interactions in virtual environments. Here, "enhanced" smiles that were augmented by the researchers made an interaction more enjoyable than the participants' real smiles did. (An avatar's mouth in an "open-close" face moved as the person talked, but the avatar never smiled even when its owner really did.)

Normal Smile Condition	Enhanced Smile Condition	Mouth Open-Close Condition

©Indeed/Getty Images	Accurate representation of smiling behavior	Enhanced representation of smiling behavior	Slight smile regardless of smiling behavior

Oh, S. Y., Bailenson, J., Krämer, N., & Li, B. "Let the avatar brighten your smile: Effects of enhancing facial expressions in virtual environments." PloS One, 2016, e0161794. Copyright ©2016 by Oh et al.

- At the University of Arizona, Matthias Mehl and his colleagues capture brief slices of social life by equipping people with small recorders that they carry with them during the day (Bollich et al., 2016). The tiny devices record all the sounds in the immediate vicinity for 30-second intervals about 70 times a day. The resulting soundtrack indicates how often people are alone, how frequently they interact with others, and whether their conversations are pleasant or argumentative. This technique allows researchers to listen in on real life as it naturally unfolds. (You can do some eavesdropping of your own at http://fun-research.netfirms.com/spsp/talks/Mehl.pdf.)
- For years in Seattle (http://www.gottman.com/research/family/), John Gottman and his colleagues (Gottman et al., 2015) invited married couples to revisit the disagreement that caused their last argument. They knew that their discussions were being recorded, but after a while they typically became so absorbed in the interaction that they forgot the cameras. The researchers often also took physiological measurements such as heart rate and electrodermal responses from the participants. Painstaking second-by-second analysis of the biological, emotional, and behavioral reactions they observed allowed the researchers to predict with 93 percent accuracy which of the couples would, and which would not, divorce years later (Gottman, 2011).
- At Stony Brook University, Art Aron and his colleagues (Acevedo & Aron, 2014) have asked people who have been married for more than 20 years to look at pictures of their beloved spouse or an old friend while the activity in their brains is monitored with functional magnetic resonance imaging (fMRI). The structures in the brain that regulate love, and the physical differences between love and friendship (Acevedo, 2015), are being mapped for the first time. (Watch http://www.youtube.com/watch?v=lDazasy68aU to get a feel for this work.)
- In Germany, as part of a Panel Analysis of Intimate Relationships and Family Dynamics (or "pairfam"), a team of researchers (e.g., Luciano & Orth, 2017) are conducting extensive interviews each year with over 12,400 people, their lovers, their parents, and their children (if any). The project began in 2008 and is designed to continue until at least 2023! (See for yourself at http://www.pairfam.de/en.)
- In the Early Years of Marriage Project run by Terri Orbuch and her colleagues (Fiori et al., 2017), 199 white couples and 174 black couples from the area surrounding Detroit, Michigan, have been interviewed every few years since they were married in 1986. The project is taking specific note of the influences of social and economic conditions on marital satisfaction, and it allows comparisons of the outcomes encountered by white and black Americans. In 2002, 16 years after the project began, 36 percent of the white couples and 55 percent of the black couples had already divorced (Birditt et al., 2012). Entire marriages are being tracked from start to finish as time goes by. (Visit the project at http://projects.isr.umich.edu/eym/.)

I hope that you're impressed by the creativity and resourcefulness embodied in these methods of research. (I am!) But as notable as they are, they barely scratch the surface in illustrating the current state of relationship science. It's still young, but the field is now supported by hundreds of scholars around the world who hail from diverse scientific disciplines and whose work appears in several different professional journals devoted entirely to personal relationships. If you're a student, you probably have access to the *Journal of Marriage and Family,* the *Journal of Social and Personal Relationships,* and the journal simply entitled *Personal Relationships.* You can visit the International Association for Relationship Research, the world's largest organization of relationship scientists, at http://www.iarr.org, and if you're enjoying this book, you *have* to check out the wonderful site, http://www.scienceofrelationships.com/.

DEVELOPING A QUESTION

How do these scholars study relationships? The first step in any scientific endeavor is to ask a question, and in a field like this one, some questions emerge from *personal experience.* Relationship researchers have an advantage over many other scientists because their own experiences in close relationships can alert them to important processes. Indeed, they may be hip deep in the very swamps they are trying to drain (Miller, 2008)! Broader *social problems* also suggest questions for careful study. For instance, the huge increase in the U.S. divorce rate from 1965 to 1985 resulted in a considerable amount of research on divorce as social scientists took note of the culture's changes.

Questions also come from *previous research:* Studies that answer one question may raise new ones. And still other questions are suggested by *theories* that strive to offer explanations for relational events. Useful theories both account for existing facts and make new predictions, and studies often seek to test those hypotheses. Relationship science involves questions that spring from all of these sources; scientists will put together their personal observations, their recognition of social problems, their knowledge of previous research, and their theoretical perspectives to create the questions they ask (Fiske, 2004).

The questions themselves are usually of two broad types. First, researchers may seek to *describe* events as they naturally occur, delineating the patterns they observe as fully and accurately as they can. Alternatively, researchers can seek to establish the *causal connections* between events to determine which events have meaningful effects on subsequent outcomes and which do not. This distinction is important: Different studies have different goals, and discerning consumers judge investigations with respect to their intended purposes. If an exploratory study seeks mainly to describe a newly noticed phenomenon, we shouldn't criticize it for leaving us uncertain about the causes and the effects of that phenomenon; those are different questions to be addressed later, after we specify what we're talking about. And more importantly, thoughtful consumers resist the temptation to draw causal connections from studies with descriptive goals. Only certain research designs allow any insight into the causal connections between events, and clever consumers do *not* jump to unwarranted conclusions that the research results do not support. This is a very key point, and I'll return to it later on.

OBTAINING PARTICIPANTS

So, whose relationships are studied? Relationship researchers usually recruit participants in one of two ways. The first approach is to use anyone who is readily available and who consents to participate; this is a **convenience sample** because it is (comparatively) convenient for the researcher to obtain. University professors often work with college students who are required to be research participants as part of their course work. Although some specific characteristics must sometimes be met (so that a study may focus, for instance, only on dating partners who have known each other for less than 2 months), researchers who use convenience samples are usually glad to get the help of everyone they can (McCormack, 2014).

In contrast, projects that use a **representative sample** strive to ensure that, collectively, their participants resemble the entire population of people who are of interest. A truly representative study of marriage, for example, would need to include married people of all sorts—all ages, all nationalities, and all socioeconomic levels. That's a tall order because, if nothing else, the people who voluntarily consent to participate in a research study may be somewhat different from those who refuse to participate (see the box on page 49). Still, some studies have obtained samples that are representative of (volunteers in) the adult population of individual countries or other delimited groups. And studies that are straightforward enough to be conducted over the Internet can attract very large samples that are much more diverse than those found on any one campus or even in any one country (Gosling & Mason, 2015).

On the one hand, there is no question that if we seek general principles that apply to most people, representative samples are better than convenience samples. A convenience sample always allows the unhappy possibility that the results we obtain are idiosyncratic, applying only to people who are just like our participants—students at a certain university, or people from a particular area of the country. And although relationship science is now conducted around the world, most of the studies we'll encounter in this book have come from cultures that are Western, well-educated, industrialized, relatively rich, and democratic—so their participants are a little *weird*. (Get it?) In fact, people from "weird" cultures do sometimes behave differently than those who live in less developed nations (Henrich et al., 2010). On the other hand, many processes studied by relationship researchers are basic enough that they don't differ substantially across demographic groups; people all over the world, for instance, share similar standards about the nature of physical beauty (see chapter 3). To the extent that research examines fundamental aspects of the ways humans react to each other, convenience samples may not be disadvantageous.

Let's consider a specific example. Back in 1978, Russell Clark sent men and women out across the campus of Florida State University to proposition members of the other sex. Individually, they approached unsuspecting people and randomly assigned them to one of three invitations (see Table 2.1); some people were simply asked out on a date, whereas others were asked to have sex! The notable results were that no woman accepted the offer of sex from a stranger, but 75 percent of the men did—and that was more men than accepted the date!

TABLE 2.1. "Would You Go to Bed with Me Tonight?"

In Clark and Hatfield's (1989) studies, college students walking across campus encountered a stranger of the other sex who said, "Hi, I've noticed you around campus, and I find you very attractive," and then offered one of the following three invitations. What percentage of the students accepted the various offers?

	Percentages Saying "Yes"	
Invitations	Men	Women
"Would you go out with me tonight?"	50	56
"Would you come over to my apartment tonight?"	69	6
"Would you go to bed with me tonight?"	75	0

This was a striking result, but so what? The study involved a small convenience sample on just one campus. Perhaps the results told us more about the men at FSU than they did about men and women in general. In fact, Clark had trouble getting the study published because of reviewers' concerns about the generality of the results. So, in 1982, he and Elaine Hatfield tried again; they repeated the study at FSU and got the same results (Clark & Hatfield, 1989).

Well, still so what? It was 4 years later, but the procedure had still been tried only in Tallahassee. If you give this example some thought, you'll be able to generate several reasons why the results might apply only to one particular time and one particular place.

I'd like to suggest a different perspective. Let's not fuss too much about the exact percentage of college men in Florida or elsewhere who would consent to sex with a stranger. That's the kind of specific attitude that you'd *expect* to vary some from one demographic group to another. Instead of endlessly criticizing—or, even worse, dismissing—the results of the Clark and Hatfield (1989) studies, let's recognize their limitations but not miss their point: Men were generally more accepting of casual sex than women were. When somebody actually asked, men were much more likely to accept a sexual invitation from a stranger than women were. Stated generally, that's exactly the conclusion that has now been drawn from subsequent investigations involving more than 20,000 participants from every major region of the world (Schmitt & the International Sexuality Description Project, 2003), and Clark and Hatfield were among the very first to document this sex difference. Their method was simple, and their sample was limited, but they were onto something, and their procedure detected a basic pattern that really does seem to exist.[1]

---

[1] For instance, in a study in May 2006 along the west coast of France, 57 percent of the men but only 3 percent of the women accepted invitations to have sex with an attractive stranger (Guéguen, 2011). In June 2009, 38 percent of the men but only 2 percent of the women in urban areas of Denmark did so (Hald & Høgh-Olesen, 2010). And in June 2013, 50 percent of the men and 4 percent of the women approached in a student nightclub in southwest Germany did so (Baranowski & Hecht, 2015). I detect a pattern here. These glaring differences are smaller, however, when men and women are asked to imagine offers for sex from celebrities such as Jennifer Lopez and Brad Pitt (Conley, 2011)!

The Challenge of Volunteer Bias in Relationship Research

Regardless of whether investigators use convenience or representative sampling, they still face the problem of **volunteer bias:** Of the people invited to participate, those who do may differ from those who don't. In one illustration of this problem, Karney et al. (1995) simply asked 3,606 couples who had applied for marriage licenses in Los Angeles County whether they would participate in a longitudinal study of their relationships. Only 18 percent of the couples said that they would, and that's a typical rate in procedures of this sort. But their marriage licenses, which were open to the public, provided several bits of information about them (e.g., their addresses, their ages, and their jobs). The volunteers differed from those who refused to participate in several ways; they were better educated, employed in higher-status jobs, and more likely to have cohabited. If the researchers had carried out a complete study with these people, would these characteristics have affected their results?

The answer may depend on what questions are asked, but volunteer bias can color the images that emerge from relationship research. People who volunteer for studies dealing with sexual behavior, for instance, tend to be younger, more sexually experienced, and more liberal than nonvolunteers (Wiederman, 2004). Subtle bias can occur even when people are *required* to be research participants, as college students often are. Conscientious students participate earlier in the semester than slackers do, and students who select face-to-face lab studies are more extraverted than those who stay home and participate online (Witt et al., 2011). Volunteer biases such as these can limit the extent to which research results apply to those who did not participate in a particular study.

The people in a representative sample reflect the demographic characteristics (sex, age, race, etc.) of the entire population of people that the researchers wish to study.
©Image Source/Digital Vision/Getty Images

So, it's absolutely true that the Clark and Hatfield (1989) studies were not perfect. That's a judgment with which Clark and Hatfield (2003) themselves agree! But as long as their results are considered thoughtfully and judiciously, even small studies using convenience samples like these can make important contributions to relationship science. Our confidence in our collective understanding of relationships relies on knowledge obtained with diverse methods. Any single study may have some imperfections, but those weaknesses may be answered by another study's strengths. With a series of investigations, each approaching a problem from a different angle, we gradually delineate the truth. To be a thoughtful consumer of relationship science, you should think the way the scientists do: No one study is perfect. Be cautious. Various methods are valuable. Wisdom takes time. But the truth is out there, and we're getting closer all the time.

CHOOSING A DESIGN

Okay, we've formulated a research question and obtained some participants. Now, we need to arrange our observations in a way that will answer our question. How do we do that?

Correlational Designs

Correlations describe patterns in which change in one event is accompanied to some degree by change in another. The patterns can be of two types. If the two events are *positively* correlated, they go up and down together—that is, as one goes up, so does the other, and as the other goes down, so does the one. In speed-dating studies, for instance, the more two strangers think they have in common after a brief interaction, the more they tend to like each other (Tidwell et al., 2013). Higher levels of perceived similarity are associated with greater liking.

In contrast, if two events are *negatively* correlated, they change in opposite directions: as one goes up, the other goes down, and as the one goes down, the other goes up. For example, people who are high in neuroticism[2] tend to be less satisfied with their marriages than others are; higher neuroticism is associated with lower marital satisfaction (Malouff et al., 2010). Positive and negative correlations are portrayed in Figure 2.2, which also includes an example of what we see when two events are *un*correlated: If events are unrelated, one of them doesn't change in any predictable way when the other goes up or down.

Patterns like these are often intriguing, and they can be very important, but they are routinely misunderstood by unsophisticated consumers. Please, always remember that correlations tell us that two events change together in some recognizable way, but, all by themselves, they do **not** tell us **why** that occurs. Correlational designs typically study naturally occurring behavior without trying to influence or control the situations in which it unfolds—and the correlations that are observed do not tell us about the causal connections between events. Be careful not to assume too much when you encounter a correlation; many different

---

[2] Take a look back at page 28 if you'd like to refresh your memory of what *neuroticism* is.

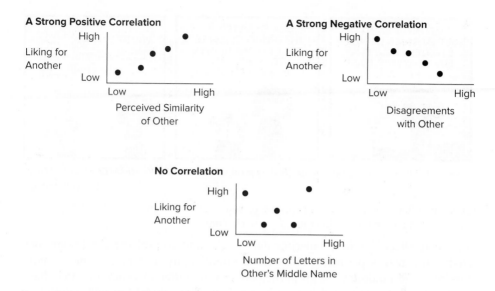

FIGURE 2.2. **Correlational patterns.**

plausible causal connections may all be possible when a correlation exists. Consider the fact that perceived similarity is positively related to liking; here are three straightforward possibilities:

- one of these two may cause the other—perceived similarity might lead to greater liking. *Or,*
- the other of these two could cause the one—so that liking others leads us to assume that we have a lot in common with them. *Or,*
- something else, a third variable, may explain why similarity and liking are related. Similarity may not lead to liking, and liking may not lead to perceived similarity; instead, something else, like really good looks, may cause us to like others and to assume (or hope?) that we're compatible with them.

Any of these three, along with many other more complex chains of events, may be possible when two events are correlated. If all we have is a correlation, all we know is that a predictable pattern exists. We don't know what causal connections are involved.[3]

Experimental Designs

When it's possible, the way to investigate causal connections is to use an experimental design. **Experiments** provide straightforward information about causes

[3]I should note, however, that if we have *lots* of correlations involving a number of variables, or if we have taken our measurements on several occasions over a span of time, sophisticated statistical analyses can usually rule out some of the possible causal connections that make correlational findings ambiguous. We should be careful not to assume that simple correlations involve causal connections, but advanced statistical techniques can make it possible to draw some defensible conclusions about cause and effect within correlational designs.

There are often several possible, plausible reasons why two events are related. If all you've got is a correlation, don't jump to conclusions!

and their effects because experimenters create and control the conditions they study. In a true experiment, researchers intentionally manipulate one or more variables and randomly assign participants to the different conditions they have created to see how those changes affect people. Thus, instead of just asking "Do two things change together?" experimenters ask "If we change one, what happens to the other?"

Let's illustrate the difference between an experiment and a correlational study by reconsidering Donn Byrne's classic work on attitude similarity and attraction (e.g., Byrne & Nelson, 1965). Had Byrne simply measured partners' perceptions of each other's attitudes and their liking for each other, he would have obtained a positive correlation between perceived similarity and liking, but he would *not* have been sure *why* they were related.

What Byrne did instead was an experiment. Once his participants arrived at his lab, he flipped a coin to determine randomly who would encounter a similar stranger and who would encounter one who didn't agree with them at all. He *controlled* that apparent agreement or disagreement, and it was the only difference between the two situations in which participants found themselves. With this procedure, when Byrne observed higher liking for the similar stranger, he could reasonably conclude that the greater agreement had *caused* the higher liking. How? Because the participants were randomly assigned to the two situations, the different degrees of liking could not be due to differences in the people who encountered each situation; on average, the two groups of participants were identical. Moreover, they all had identical experiences in the experiment except for the apparent similarity of the stranger. The only reasonable explanation for the different behavior Byrne observed was that similarity leads to liking. His experiment clearly showed that the manipulated cause, attitude similarity, had a noticeable effect, higher liking.

Experiments provide clearer, more definitive tests of causal connections than other designs do. Done well, they clearly delineate cause and effect. Why, then, do researchers ever do anything else? The key is that experimenters have to be able to control and manipulate the events they wish to study. Byrne could control the information that his participants received about someone they had never met, but he couldn't manipulate other important influences on intimate relationships. We still can't. (How do you create full-fledged experiences of romantic love in a laboratory?) You can't do experiments on events you cannot control.

So, correlational and experimental designs each have their own advantages. With correlational designs, we can study compelling events in the real world—commitment to a relationship, passionate love, unsafe sex—and examine the links among them. But correlational designs are limited in what they can tell us about the causal relationships among events. With experimental designs, we can examine causal connections, but we are limited in what we can study. Hopefully, you can see why different researchers may study the same topic in different ways, with different research designs—and why that's a good thing.

THE NATURE OF OUR DATA

Now, just what type of information will we actually be collecting? Are we recording others' judgments and perceptions of a relationship, or are we inspecting specific interactions ourselves? Two major types of research measures are described here: (a) people's own reports about their thoughts, feelings, and behaviors and (b) careful observations of others' behavior. We'll also examine some variations on these themes.

Self-Reports

The most common means of studying intimate relationships is to *ask* people about their experiences. Their responses are **self-reports,** and they can be obtained in a variety of formats: through written questionnaires, verbal interviews, or even diaries in which participants record the events of their day (Repetti et al., 2015). The common theme linking such techniques is that people are telling us about their experiences—we're not watching them ourselves.

Self-report data have important benefits. For one thing, they allow us to "get inside people's heads" and understand personal points of view that may not be apparent to outside observers. Self-report data are also inexpensive and easy to obtain. Consider, for instance, the short self-report measure provided in Table 2.2: Those 12 questions do a remarkably good job of assessing the extent to which a relationship is flourishing, being healthy, close, and rewarding. For most purposes, there's no reason to ask more elaborate questions or use other means to distinguish fulfilling partnerships from those that are less rich because this handful of straightforward questions works just fine (Fowers et al., 2016). Self-report measures can be both very efficient and very informative. Still (and by now, this probably isn't a surprise!), self-reports may also present potential problems. Here are three things to worry about.

Participants' Interpretations of the Questions

Self-reports always occur in response to a researcher's instructions or questions. If the participants misinterpret what the researcher means or intends, their

TABLE 2.2. The Relationship Flourishing Scale

Is your current relationship rich and rewarding? Does it offer you meaningful opportunities for self-expression, personal growth, and fulfillment both as an individual and as a supportive partner? This scale addresses those issues.

For the first four items, choose the response that best captures your agreement with the following statements about your relationship with your partner, using this scale:

1	2	3	4	5
strongly disagree	disagree	neutral	agree	strongly agree

_____ 1. I have more success in my important goals because of my partner's help.
_____ 2. We look for activities that help us grow as a couple.
_____ 3. My partner has helped me grow in ways that I could not have done on my own.
_____ 4. It is worth it to share my most personal thoughts with my partner.

Now, choose the response that best captures aspects of your relationship with your partner, using this scale:

1	2	3	4	5
never	rarely	sometimes	often	always

_____ 5. When making important decisions, I think about whether it will be good for our relationship.
_____ 6. It is natural and easy for me to do things that keep our relationship going.
_____ 7. Talking with my partner helps me to see things in new ways.
_____ 8. I make a point to celebrate my partner's successes.
_____ 9. I really work to improve our relationship.
_____ 10. My partner shows interest in things that are important to me.
_____ 11. We do things that are deeply meaningful to us as a couple.
_____ 12. I make time when my partner needs to talk.

Source: Fowers, B. J., Laurenceau, J., Penfield, R. D., Cohen, L. M., Lang, S. F., Owenz, M. B., & Pasipandoya, E. Enhancing relationship quality measurement: The development of the Relationship Flourishing Scale. Journal of Family Psychology, 30, 2016, 997-1007.

The average sum of all these ratings for both men and women is 46.4, and the standard deviation is 7.6. So, scores between 39 and 53 are average. But if your sum is 54 or higher, your relationship is richer and closer than most, and if it's 38 or lower, your partnership is less rich than most.

subsequent self-reports can be misleading. For instance, consider this question: "With how many people have you had sex?" It sounds straightforward, but about half of us consider oral-genital contact that brings us to orgasm to be "having sex," and the other half of us do not (Barnett et al., 2017). There are complexities here, and undetected problems with people's comprehension of terms describing sexual behavior—including what it means to be a "virgin" (Barnett et al., 2017)—add difficulty to sexuality research (Sewell & Strassberg, 2015).

Difficulties in Recall or Awareness

Even when people understand our questions, they may not be able to answer them correctly. For one thing, they may lack insight into their actions, so that what they think is going on isn't entirely accurate. For instance, women say the physical attractiveness of a mate is less important to them than men do. However, when they encounter and evaluate several potential partners at once in speed-dating studies, looks *do* matter just as much to women as they do to men (Eastwick & Finkel, 2008), and looks are the most important influence on who likes whom for both sexes (Luo & Zhang, 2009). On occasion, what people can tell us about their preferences and behavior doesn't accurately reflect what they actually say and do.

Faulty memories can also be a problem. Self-reports are most accurate when people describe specific, objective events that have occurred recently. They are more likely to be inaccurate when we ask them about things that happened long ago (Aicken et al., 2013). Specific details may be forgotten—in one study (Mitchell, 2010), 50 percent of a large sample of divorced people did not correctly report in which month they were divorced—and past feelings are especially likely to be misremembered. In particular, if a passionate romance ends in pain and discontent, the disappointed lovers are likely to have a very hard time remembering how happy and enthusiastic they felt months earlier when they had just fallen in love (Grote & Frieze, 1998).

Bias in Participants' Reports

A final worry—a big one—involves the possibility of systematic bias or distortion in people's reports. In particular, people may be reluctant to tell researchers anything that makes them look bad or that portrays them in an undesirable light. This can cause a **social desirability bias,** or distortion that results from people's wishes to make good impressions on others. For instance, studies that simply ask people how often they've cheated on (Schick et al., 2014), or beaten (Follingstad & Rogers, 2013), their partners are likely to get answers that underestimate the prevalence of both events. In one case, 4 percent of those who had been divorced a few years earlier—the researchers knew this because they had seen the divorce decrees on file at county courthouses—claimed that they had never been divorced (Mitchell, 2010)! In another instance, women reported having more sex partners and losing their virginity at younger ages when they were hooked up to lie detectors than when they were not (Fisher, 2013). Procedures that guarantee participants' anonymity—such as allowing them to take surveys online instead of face-to-face (Liu & Wang, 2016)—help reduce social desirability problems such as these, but bias is always a concern when studies address sensitive issues.

Observations

Another way to collect information about relationships is to observe behavior directly. Scientific observations are rarely casual undertakings. Researchers either measure behavior with sophisticated tools or carefully train their colleagues to make observations that are accurate, reliable, and often quite detailed.

Some studies involve direct observations of ongoing behavior whereas others use recordings from which observations are made at a later time. **Experience-sampling** is a method that uses intermittent, short periods of observation to capture samples

Assessing Attachment Styles

Studies of attachment have become a major theme in relationship science, and I'll mention attachment in every chapter to come. Where do all these findings come from? In most cases, research participants have described their feelings about close relationships on a questionnaire. Now that we've considered some of the nuances of self-report data, let's inspect the tool that's most often used to assess attachment.

The 12 items presented here are drawn from a longer questionnaire created by Kelly Brennan and her colleagues (1998), and they obtain results that are very similar to those obtained with the longer scale (Wei et al., 2007). I've labeled the two dimensions of attachment to which the items pertain, but those labels do not appear on the actual survey, and the items are mixed together. Respondents are asked to rate the extent of their agreement or disagreement with each item on a seven-point scale ranging from 1 (*disagree strongly*) to 7 (*agree strongly*). Note that you'd report high levels of anxiety or avoidance by agreeing with some items and disagreeing with others; this is a common tactic that is used to encourage thoughtful answers and to help researchers detect careless responses.

Researchers typically derive two scores, an *anxiety* score and an *avoidance* score, and then determine how they predict different relational outcomes. People with a secure style of attachment, as you may recall (from page 17), would have low scores on both dimensions.

Items measuring
Anxiety about Abandonment:

1. I worry that romantic partners won't care about me as much as I care about them.
2. My desire to be close sometimes scares people away.
3. I need a lot of reassurance that I am loved by my partner.
4. I find that my partner(s) don't want to get as close as I would like.
5. I get frustrated when romantic partners are not available when I need them.
6. I do not often worry about being abandoned.

Items measuring
Avoidance of Intimacy:

1. I want to get close to my partner, but I keep pulling back.
2. I am nervous when partners get too close to me.
3. I try to avoid getting too close to my partner.
4. I usually discuss my problems and concerns with my partner.
5. It helps to turn to my romantic partner in times of need.
6. I turn to my partner for many things, including comfort and reassurance.

To get your own score on these items, *reverse* your score on the sixth Anxiety item and on numbers 4, 5, and 6 of the Avoidance items. A score of 1 becomes a 7, a 3 becomes a 5, a 6 becomes a 2, and so on. An average score on the Anxiety items is 22; a score below 15 is pretty low, and a score above 29 is pretty high. Average Avoidance is 15, with 9 being noticeably low and 21 being notably high (Wei et al., 2007).

Do the answers that people give to questions such as these really matter? Yes, they do. There are other means of assessing attachment that involve extensive interviews, but they are not used as often because these items do such a fine job of identifying meaningful individual differences (Gillath et al., 2016). Despite possible biases, vocabulary problems, and all the other potential problems with self-reports, these items delineate different global orientations to intimate relationships that are very influential, as we will see throughout this book.

of behavior that actually occur over longer periods of time; investigators may randomly sample short spans of time when a target behavior is likely to occur, scattering periods of observation through different times on different days. The work being done by Matthias Mehl (Mehl & Robbins, 2012) with small recorders that fit in a pocket is a fine example of this technique. The devices are called electronically activated recorders, or EARs. (Get it?) They switch on for brief periods at regular intervals during the day and capture the sounds of whatever interactions participants are having at the time. And smartphone apps are being developed that will allow researchers to both hear and see what people are doing as they interact with others (Thomas & Azmitia, 2016).

The observations that result from procedures such as this can take several forms. Researchers sometimes make *ratings* that characterize the events they witness in relatively global terms. For example, an argument might be rated with regard to the extent to which it is "constructive and problem solving" or "argumentative and hostile." Alternatively, observers may employ *coding procedures* that focus on very specific behaviors such as the amount of time people speak during an interaction, the number of smiles they display, or the number of times they touch each other (Humbad et al., 2011). These perceptions are typically more objective than ratings are, and they can sometimes be mechanized to be even more impartial. For instance, James Pennebaker has developed software that codes the words people use, and it allows an automatic analysis of the content of people's conversations. (And it's bad news when partners use the word "you" too frequently; such people tend to be less satisfied with their relationships than those who use "you" less often [Tausczik & Pennebaker, 2010].)

Other technologies provide additional measures of behavior. In an eye-tracking study, for instance, participants don headgear that focuses tiny video cameras on their eyes. Then, when they inspect various images, their eye movements indicate what they're looking at, and for how long (Garza et al., 2016). We'd be able to tell, for instance, whether you prefer blondes or brunettes by presenting two images differing only in hair color side-by-side: You'd spend more time scrutinizing the image you find more alluring.

Observations such as these generally avoid the disadvantages of self-reports. On the other hand, we need self-reports if we're to understand people's personal perceptions of their experiences. Observational studies can also be expensive, sometimes requiring costly equipment and consuming hours and hours of observers' time. One remarkable study filmed every waking moment experienced by the members of 32 different families over the course of four days, and the 1,540 hours of resulting video required thousands of hours of careful inspection to code and categorize (Ochs & Kremer-Sadlik, 2013).

Observational research can also suffer from the problem of **reactivity:** People may change their behavior when they know they are being observed. (A camera in your living room would probably change some of your behavior—at least until you got used to it.) For that reason, researchers are always glad to conduct observations that cannot possibly alter the behaviors they're studying—and in one such investigation, relationship scientists monitored the Facebook profiles of 1,640 people—almost the entire freshman class at a particular university—as their college years went by (Wimmer & Lewis, 2010). They tracked the public information in the profiles to determine how the users' tastes and values influenced the friendships they formed. The researchers had specific, serious aims—this was not informal browsing—and they couldn't have unwanted influence on the behavior they were studying because the participants did not know that they were being watched! (There's actually some controversy over this tactic [Kosinski et al., 2015], but some studies continue to mine public information from profile pages without people's knowledge. Do you find this troubling? Why?)

Physiological Measures

We can also avoid any problems with reactivity if we observe behavior that people cannot consciously control, and physiological measures of people's autonomic and biochemical reactions often do just that. Physiological measures assess such responses as heart rate, muscle tension, genital arousal, brain activity, and hormone levels to determine how our physical states are associated with our social behavior.

Some investigations examine the manner in which physiology shapes our interactions with others. For instance, compared to those who are less content, satisfied spouses have higher levels of the neuropeptide oxytocin in their blood (Holt-Lunstad et al., 2015a). This may be, in part, because inhaling a dose of oxytocin leads people who avoid intimacy to feel warmer and kinder toward others (Bartz et al., 2015). It also leads people who are low in extraversion to feel closer and more trusting toward others (Human et al., 2016). Our biochemistry evidently shapes our affiliative motives.

Other studies seek to map the physiological foundations of social behavior (Beckes & Coan, 2015). For example, fMRI has identified the structures in our brains that seem to regulate love and lust (Tomlinson & Aron, 2012). fMRI images show which parts of the brain are consuming more oxygen and are therefore more active than others when certain states occur—and as it turns out, warm romantic affection and yearning sexual desire appear to be controlled by different parts of our brains. (Are you surprised?)

Physiological measures are often expensive, but their use is increasing because they allow researchers to explore the physical foundations of our relationships. They are a good example of the manner in which relationship science is becoming more complex and sophisticated all the time.

Archival Materials

Historical **archives** also avoid the problem of reactivity. Personal documents such as photographs and diaries, public media such as newspapers and websites, and governmental records such as marriage licenses and birth records can all be valuable sources of data about relationships, and when these are dated, they become "archival" information. In one study, researchers examined old university yearbook photos to determine if people's expressions as young adults could predict their chances of a future divorce (Hertenstein et al., 2009). (What did they find? See chapter 5!) Archival materials are "nonreactive" because inspection of archival data does not change the behaviors being studied. They can be limited, however, because they may not contain all the information a researcher would really like to have.

THE ETHICS OF SUCH ENDEAVORS

Studies using archival materials often run no risk at all of embarrassing anyone, but research on relationships does occasionally require investigators to ask questions about sensitive topics or to observe private behavior. Should we pry into people's personal affairs?

This is not an issue I pose lightly. Although it's enormously valuable and sorely needed, relationship science presents important ethical dilemmas. Just asking people to fill out questionnaires describing their relationships may have unintended effects on those partnerships. When we ask people to specify what they get out of a relationship or to rate their love for their partners, for instance, we focus their attention on delicate matters they may not have thought much about. We stimulate their thinking and encourage them to evaluate their relationships. Moreover, we arouse their natural curiosity about what their partners may be saying in response to the same questions. Researchers' innocent inquiries may alert people to relationship problems or frustrations they didn't know they had.

Some procedures may have even more impact. Consider John Gottman's (2011) method of asking spouses to revisit the issue that caused their last argument: He didn't encourage people to quarrel and bicker, but some of them did. Spouses who disagree sourly and bitterly are at much greater risk for divorce than are spouses who disagree with grace and humor, and Gottman's work illuminated the specific behaviors that forecast trouble ahead. This work was extremely important. But did it do damage? Is it ethical to actually invite couples to return to a disagreement that may erode their satisfaction even further?

The answer to that question isn't simple. Relationship scientists ordinarily are very careful to safeguard the welfare of their participants. Detailed information is provided to potential participants before a study begins so that they can make an informed decision about whether or not to participate. Their consent to participate is voluntary and can be withdrawn at any time. After the data are collected, the researchers provide prompt feedback that explains any experimental manipulations and describes the larger purposes of the investigation. Final reports regarding the outcomes of the study are often made available when the study is complete. In addition, when ticklish matters are being investigated, researchers may provide information about where participants can obtain couples' counseling should they wish to do so; psychological services may even be offered for free.

As you can see, relationship science begins with compassionate concern for the well-being of its participants. People are treated

A Point to Ponder

Relationship science studies sensitive issues and private behavior such as infidelity and partner abuse. Should it? Do you support such studies? Are you willing to participate in them?

with respect, thanked warmly for their efforts, and may even be paid for their time. They may also find their experiences to be interesting and enlightening. People who participate in studies of sexual behavior (Kuyper et al., 2014) and dating violence (Shorey et al., 2011), for instance, routinely have positive reactions and are distressed very rarely. And being asked to reflect and report on their experiences may even help people adjust to and recover from difficult situations. In one study, compared to those who were asked fewer questions, people bounced back from a breakup more quickly when they provided extensive self-reports about their feelings on several occasions (Larson & Sbarra, 2015); the introspection prompted by their participation was evidently good for them. That's reassuring. Still, should we be trying to study such private and intimate matters?

The answer from here is absolutely yes. There's another side to the issue of ethics I haven't yet mentioned: science's ethical imperative to gain knowledge that can benefit humanity. Ignorance can be wasteful. Since 2002, the U.S. Department of Health and Human Services has spent more than $800 million on a variety of marriage and relationship education programs that are intended to teach low-income families skills that will help them sustain their marriages. Families of modest means are targets of these marriage-enrichment programs because, compared to families with more resources, they are less likely to marry and more likely to divorce (Johnson, 2012). The programs all have good intentions, but on the whole, it's hard to say that they have done much, if any, good (Johnson, 2014); even their proponents admit that their outcomes have been "mixed" and "modest," sometimes actually making things worse (Hawkins, 2014). An enduring problem is that too many of these programs miss the point: They seek to teach low-income couples to value marriage more, but such couples *already* want to get married (Trail & Karney, 2012). They don't marry—and their marriages are more fragile if they do—because of their financial worries, which put enormous stress and strain on their relationships (Jackson et al., 2016). The relative fragility of low-income marriages seems to have more to do with social class than with the attitudes and skills of the spouses themselves (Emery & Le, 2014).

So it's pretty silly to expect that values education will change anything. A government program that seeks to improve relationships would probably do better to increase the minimum wage and to fund child care and effective training for better jobs than to try to teach people to respect marriage. And clearly, if we seek to promote human well-being, we need good information as well as good intentions. In a culture that offers us bizarre examples of "love" on TV shows such as *The Bachelor* and *The Bachelorette*—and in which real marriages are more likely to be failures than to be successes (Cherlin, 2009)—it would be unethical *not* to try to understand how relationships work. Intimate relationships can be a source of the grandest, most glorious pleasure human beings experience, but they can also be a source of terrible suffering and appalling destructiveness. It is inherently ethical, relationship scientists assert, to try to learn how the joy might be increased and the misery reduced.

INTERPRETING AND INTEGRATING RESULTS

This isn't a statistics text (and I know you're pleased by that), but there are a few more aspects of the way relationship scientists do business that the thoughtful consumer of the field should understand. Most relationship studies subject the data they obtain to statistical analysis to determine whether their results are statistically "significant." This is a calculation of how likely it is that the results (e.g., the observed correlations or the effects of the manipulated variables in an experiment) could have occurred by chance. If it's quite unlikely that the results could be due to chance, we have a "significant" result. All of the research results reported in this book are significant results. You can also be confident that the studies that have obtained these results have passed critical inspection by other scientists. This does not mean, however, that every single specific result I may mention is unequivocally, absolutely, positively true: Some of them might have occurred by chance, reflecting the influence of odd samples of people or unwanted mistakes of various sorts. Remember, too, that the results we'll encounter always describe patterns that are evident in the behavior of *groups* of people—and because of differences among individuals (see chapter 1), those patterns will apply to particular individuals to varying degrees. Please do not be so naïve as to think that research results that *do*, in fact, apply to most people must be wrong because you know someone to whom those results do not seem to apply. I'll need you to be more sophisticated and reasonable than that.

With those cautions in place, let's note that the data obtained in relationship studies can also present unique challenges and complexities. Here are two examples:

Paired, interdependent data. Most statistical procedures assume that the scores of different participants are independent of each other—that is, one person's responses are not influenced by anyone else's—but that's not true when both members of a couple are involved. Wilma's satisfaction with her relationship with Fred is very likely to be influenced by whether or not Fred is happy too, so her satisfaction is *not* independent of his. Responses obtained from relationship partners are often interdependent, and special statistical procedures are advisable for analyzing such data (e.g., Ackerman et al., 2015).

Three sources of influence. Furthermore, relationships emerge from the individual contributions of the separate partners *and* from the unique effects of how they combine as a pair. For example, imagine that Betty and Barney have a happy marriage. One reason for this may be the fact that Barney is an especially pleasant fellow who gets along well with everyone, including Betty. Alternatively (or, perhaps, in addition), Betty may be the one who's easy to live with. However, Betty and Barney may also have a better relationship with each other than they could have with anyone else because of the unique way their individual traits combine; the whole may be more than the sum of its parts. Relationship researchers often encounter phenomena that result from the combination of all three of these influences, the two individual partners and the idiosyncratic partnership they share. Sophisticated statistical analyses are required to study all of these components at once (Ackerman et al., 2015), another indication of the complexity of relationship science.

A Point to Ponder

What's your first thought when you encounter a fact in this book that you find surprising? Is it, "Wow, I didn't know that," or something more like, "This is wrong"? Where does your reaction come from?

So what's my point here? I've noted that studies of close relationships tackle intricate matters and that statistical significance testing involves probabilities, not certainties. Should you take everything I say with a grain of salt, doubting me at every turn? Well, yes and no. I want you to be more thoughtful and less gullible, and I want you to appreciate the complexities underlying the things you're about to learn. Remember to think like a scientist: No study is perfect, but the truth is out there. We put more faith in patterns of results that are obtained by different investigators working with different samples of participants. We are also more confident when results are replicated with diverse methods.

For these reasons, scientists now do frequent **meta-analyses,** which are studies that statistically combine the results from several prior studies (e.g., Robles et al., 2014). In a meta-analysis, an investigator compiles all existing studies of a particular phenomenon and combines their results to identify the themes they contain. If the prior studies all produce basically the same result, the meta-analysis makes that plain; if there are discrepancies, the meta-analysis may reveal why.

With tools like this at its disposal, relationship science has made enormous strides despite its short history and the complexity of its subject matter. And despite my earlier cautions, (nearly all of) the things I'll share with you in this text are dependable facts, reliable results you can see for yourself if you do what the researchers did. Even more impressively, most of them are facts that had not been discovered when your parents were born.

A FINAL NOTE

In my desire to help you be more discerning, I've spent a lot of this chapter noting various pros and cons of diverse procedures, usually concluding that no single option is the best one in all cases. I hoped to encourage you to be more thoughtful about the complexities of good research. But in closing, let me reassure you that relationship science is in better shape than all of these uncertainties may make it seem. When relationship science began, the typical study obtained self-reports from a convenience sample of college students, and many studies are still of that sort. However, researchers are now routinely studying more diverse samples with sophisticated designs that employ more complex measures, and the variety of methods with which researchers now study relationships is a *strength,* not a weakness (Ickes, 2000). Furthermore, the field's judicious ability to differentiate what it does and does not yet know is a mark of its honesty and its developing maturity and wisdom.

People like easy answers. They like their information cut-and-dried. Many people actually prefer simple nonsense—such as the idea that men come from Mars and women come from Venus—to the scientific truth, if the truth is harder to grasp. However, as a new consumer of the science of relationships, you have an obligation to prefer facts to gossip, even if you have to work a little harder to make sense of their complexities. Don't mistake scientific caution for a lack of quality. To the contrary, I want to leave you with the thought that it demonstrates scientific respectability to be forthright about the strengths and weaknesses of one's discipline. It's more often the frauds and imposters who claim they are always correct than the cautious scientists, who are really trying to get it right.

FOR YOUR CONSIDERATION

Chris and Kelsey had to participate in research studies if they wanted to pass the Introductory Psychology course they were taking together, so they signed up for a study of "Relationship Processes." They had been dating for 2 months, and the study was seeking "premarital romantic couples," and they liked the fact that they would be paid $5 if they both participated. So, they attended a session with a dozen other couples in which they were separated and seated on opposite sides of a large room. They read and signed a permission form that noted they could quit anytime they wanted and then started to work on a long questionnaire.

Some of the questions were provocative. They were asked how many different people they had had sex with in the last year and how many people they wanted to have sex with in the next 5 years. Then, they were asked to answer the same questions again, this time as they believed the other would. Chris had never pondered such questions before, and he realized, once he thought about it, that he actually knew very little about Kelsey's sexual history and future intentions. That night, he was a little anxious, wondering and worrying about Kelsey's answers to those questions.

Having read this chapter, do you think this research procedure was ethical? Why?

CHAPTER SUMMARY

The Short History of Relationship Science

The scientific study of relationships is a recent endeavor that has come of age only in the last 35 years. The field has now grown to include the study of all types of relationships in their natural settings around the world.

Developing a Question

Research questions come from a number of sources, including personal experience, recognition of social problems, the results of prior research, and theoretical predictions. The questions usually seek either to describe events or to delineate causal connections among variables.

Obtaining Participants

Convenience samples are composed of participants who are easily available. *Representative samples* are more costly, but they better reflect the population of interest. Both types of samples can suffer from *volunteer bias*.

Choosing a Design

Correlational Designs. A *correlation* describes the strength and direction of an association between two variables. Correlations are inherently ambiguous because events can be related for a variety of reasons.

Experimental Designs. Experiments control and manipulate situations to delineate cause and effect. Experiments are very informative, but some events cannot be studied experimentally for practical or ethical reasons.

The Nature of Our Data

Self-Reports. With self-reports, participants describe their own thoughts, feelings, and behavior, but they may misunderstand the researchers' questions, have faulty memories, and be subject to *social desirability biases*.

Observations. In *experience-sampling,* brief observations are made intermittently. Observations avoid the problems of self-reports, but they are expensive to conduct, and *reactivity* can be a problem.

Physiological Measures. Measurements of people's biological changes indicate how our physical states are associated with our social interactions.

Archival Materials. Historical records are nonreactive and allow researchers to compare the present with the past.

The Ethics of Such Endeavors

Participation in relationship research may change people's relationships by encouraging them to think carefully about the situations they face. As a result, researchers take pains to protect the welfare of their participants.

Interpreting and Integrating Results

Statistical analysis determines the likelihood that results could have occurred by chance. When this likelihood is very low, the results are said to be *significant*. Some such results may still be due to chance, however, so the thoughtful consumer does not put undue faith in any one study. *Meta-analysis* lends confidence to conclusions by statistically combining results from several studies.

A Final Note

Scientific caution is appropriate, but it should not be mistaken for weakness or imprecision. Relationship science is in great shape.

CHAPTER 3

Attraction

THE FUNDAMENTAL BASIS OF ATTRACTION ◆ PROXIMITY: LIKING THOSE NEAR US ◆ PHYSICAL ATTRACTIVENESS: LIKING THOSE WHO ARE LOVELY ◆ RECIPROCITY: LIKING THOSE WHO LIKE US ◆ SIMILARITY: LIKING THOSE WHO ARE LIKE US ◆ SO, WHAT DO MEN AND WOMEN WANT? ◆ FOR YOUR CONSIDERATION ◆ CHAPTER SUMMARY

You're alone in a classroom, beginning to read this chapter, when the door opens and a stranger walks in. Is this someone who appeals to you? Might you have just encountered a potential friend or lover? Remarkably, you probably developed a tentative answer to those questions more quickly than you were able to read this sentence (Willis & Todorov, 2006). What's going on? Where did your judgment come from? This chapter considers these issues. Psychologically, the first step toward a relationship is always the same: interpersonal *attraction,* the desire to approach someone. Feelings of attraction don't guarantee that a relationship will develop, but they do open the door to the possibility. I'll examine several major influences that shape our attraction to others, starting with a basic principle about how attraction works.

THE FUNDAMENTAL BASIS OF ATTRACTION

A longstanding assumption about interpersonal attraction is that we are attracted to others whose presence is rewarding to us (Clore & Byrne, 1974). And two different types of **rewards** influence attraction: noticeable *direct* rewards we obviously receive from our interaction with others, and more subtle *indirect* benefits of which we're not always aware and that are merely associated with someone else. Direct rewards refer to all the evident pleasures people provide us. When they shower us with interest and approval, we're usually gratified by the attention and acceptance. When they are witty and beautiful, we enjoy their pleasing characteristics. And when they give us money or good advice, we are clearly better off. Most of the time, the more direct rewards that people provide us, the more attracted we are to them.

But attraction also results from a variety of subtle influences that are only indirectly related to the obvious kindness, good looks, or pleasing personalities of those we meet. For instance, anything about new acquaintances that resembles us, however tangentially, may make them seem more likable. Consider a fellow named Dennis who is fond of his name; because of the shared first letter, "it might not be too far-fetched [for] Dennis to gravitate toward cities such as Denver, careers such as dentistry, and romantic partners such as Denise" (Pelham et al., 2005, p. 106). In fact, that's what happens: People are disproportionately likely to fall in love with someone who has a name that resembles their own (Jones et al., 2004). Rewards like these are indirect and mild, and we sometimes don't even consciously notice them—but they do illustrate just how diverse and varied the rewards that attract us to others can be.

Indeed, most of us simply think that we're attracted to someone if he or she is an appealing person, but it's really more complex than that. Attraction does involve the perceived characteristics of the person who appeals to us, but it also depends on our current needs, goals, and desires, all of which can fluctuate over time and from one situation to the next. Given that, theorists Eli Finkel and Paul Eastwick (2015) assert that the fundamental basis of attraction is **instrumentality,** the extent to which someone is able to help us achieve our present goals.[1] Simply put, we're attracted to others who can help us get what we currently want. An instrumentality perspective acknowledges that attraction can be idiosyncratic, differing from person to person according to one's present goals, and changing over time as needs are fulfilled. But we're most attracted, as you'd expect, to others whose company is consistently rewarding, those who routinely fulfill *several* chronic and important desires—such as those whose company is pleasurable and who fulfill our need to belong.[2] And as those desires are pervasive, some specific influences on attraction are rather ubiquitous, clearly influencing most people most of the time. We'll consider them in this chapter, beginning our survey with one that's more important than most of us think.

PROXIMITY: LIKING THOSE NEAR US

We might get to know someone online, but isn't interaction more rewarding when we can hear others' voices, see their smiles, and actually hold their hands? Most of the time, relationships are more rewarding when they involve people who are near one another (who are physically, as well as psychologically, close). Indeed, our physical **proximity** to others often determines whether or not we ever meet them in the first place. More often than not, our friendships and romances grow out of interactions with those who are nearby.

In fact, there is a clear connection between physical proximity and interpersonal attraction, and a few feet can make a big difference. Think about your Relationships classroom: Who have you gotten to know since the semester started? Who is a new friend? It's likely that the people you know and like best sit near you in class. When they are assigned seats in a classroom, college students are much more likely to become friends with those sitting near them than with those sitting across the room, even when the room is fairly small (Back et al., 2008a).

---

[1] This is the second time I've introduced the term "instrumentality," which we used to describe traits such as assertiveness and self-reliance back on page 25. The idea remains the same. Our "instrumental" traits promote our own accomplishments and achievements, and as Finkel and Eastwick use the term, "instrumentality" describes the extent to which someone else can offer us help in accomplishing our present goals.

[2] Remember? A *really* fundamental goal that characterizes the human race. See page 4.

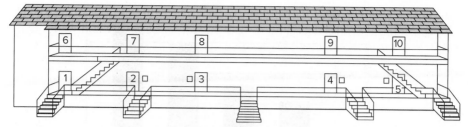

Source: *Myers, D.* Social Psychology, *9th Edition. McGraw-Hill, 1993.*

FIGURE 3.1. **A student apartment building at MIT.**
In the study by Festinger et al. (1950), residents were randomly assigned to rooms in buildings like these.

TABLE 3.1. Friendship Choices in Campus Housing at MIT

Two hundred seventy people living in buildings like that pictured in Figure 3.1 were asked to list their three closest companions. Among those living on the same floor of a given building, here's how often the residents named someone living:

1 door away	41% of the time
2 doors away	22%
3 doors away	16%
4 doors away	10%

Only 88 feet separated residents living four doors apart, at opposite ends of the same floor, but they were only one-quarter as likely to become friends as were people living in adjacent rooms. Similar patterns were obtained from one floor to the next, and from building to building in the housing complex, so it was clear that small distances played a large part in determining who would and who would not be friends.

A similar phenomenon occurs in student housing complexes. In a classic study, Festinger, Schachter, and Back (1950) examined the friendships among students living in campus housing at the Massachusetts Institute of Technology. Residents were randomly assigned to rooms in 17 different buildings that were all like the one in Figure 3.1. People who lived close to each other were much more likely to become friends than were those whose rooms were further apart. Indeed, the chances that residents would become friends were closely related to the distances between their rooms (see Table 3.1). And the same result was also obtained from one building to the next: People were more likely to know and like residents of other buildings that were close to their own. Obviously, even small distances have a much larger influence on our relationships than most people realize. Whenever we choose the exact place where we will live or work or go to school, we also take a major step toward determining who the significant others in our lives are likely to be.

Familiarity: Repeated Contact

Why does proximity have such influence? For one thing, it increases the chances that two people will cross paths often and become more familiar with each other. Folk wisdom suggests that "familiarity breeds contempt," but research evidence

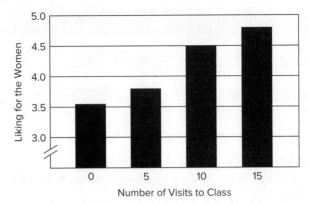

Source: Data from Moreland, R. L., & Beach, S. R. "Exposure effects
in the classroom: The development of affinity among students,"
Journal of Experimental Social Psychology, 28, 1992, 255–276.

FIGURE 3.2. **The mere exposure effect in college classrooms.**
Even though they never interacted with anyone, other students liked the women more
the more often they visited a class.

generally disagrees. Instead of being irritating, repeated contact with—or **mere exposure** to—someone usually increases our liking for him or her (Zajonc, 2001). Even if we have never talked to them, we tend to like people whose faces we recognize more than those whose faces are unfamiliar to us.

Moreland and Beach (1992) provided an interesting example of the mere exposure effect when they had college women attend certain classes either 15 times, 10 times, or 5 times during a semester. These women never talked to anyone and simply sat there, but they were present in the room frequently, sometimes, or rarely. Then at the end of the semester, the real students were given pictures of the women and asked for their reactions. The results were very clear: The more familiar the women were, the more the students were attracted to them. And they were all liked better than women the students had never seen at all. (See Figure 3.2.)

The proximity that occurs in college classrooms influences real relationships, too. An intriguing analysis of a whole year's worth of the millions of e-mail messages passed among the tens of thousands of students at a large university—back before texting became commonplace—demonstrated that, among students who did not already share an acquaintance, taking a class together made it *140* times more likely that they would message each other (Kossinets & Watts, 2006). And small distances matter; students who are assigned seats next to each other are *much* more likely to become friends than are those who are given seats a couple of rows apart (Segal, 1974).[3]

---

[3] This effect is so striking, I keep thinking that I should insist that my own students change seats halfway through the semester and sit next to a whole new bunch of potential friends. They would probably leave the course knowing—and liking—more people. But, because they'd probably also be annoyed to move, I've never done it.

Of course, familiarity has it limits. As we gain information about others, we may find that they are obnoxious, disagreeable, or inept, and increasing exposure to such people may lead us to like them *less*, not more (Norton et al., 2013). Indeed, a study in a condominium complex in California (Ebbesen et al., 1976) found that although most of the residents' friends lived nearby, most of their enemies did, too! Only rarely did people report that they really disliked someone who lived several buildings away from them. Instead, they despised fellow residents who were close enough to annoy them often—by playing music too loudly, letting their dogs bark, and so on.

Proximity can also be disadvantageous when people who have come to know each other online—see the box on page 70—meet in person for the first time. People put their best foot (and face) forward when they're writing personal profiles and posting pictures, so what you see on the Web is not necessarily what you get when you finally meet someone face-to-face (J. A. Hall et al., 2010). In particular, men often claim that they're taller and richer, and women claim that they're lighter and younger, than they really are ("Online Dating Statistics," 2017). They've also typically been careful and selective in describing their attitudes and tastes, so there's still a lot to learn about them. Thus, on average, when people who have met online get together in person for the first time, they're mildly disappointed; the knowledge they have about each other goes up, but their perceived similarity to, and their liking for, each other goes *down* (Norton et al., 2007). When we find out who our online partners actually are—as opposed to who we *thought* they were—our attraction to them often declines (Ramirez et al., 2015).

Proximity can also be surprisingly problematic when partners in long-distance relationships are reunited after some time apart. When partners have to separate— for instance, when one of them is called to military service—"out of sight" does not inevitably lead to "out of mind." A separation *can* destroy a relationship, particularly if the partners start dating other people who are close at hand (Sahlstein, 2006). But the more committed partners are to their relationship, the more they miss each other, and the more they miss each other, the harder they work to express their continued love and regard for each other across the miles (Le et al., 2011). Their conversations tend to be longer and more personal than those they would ordinarily have face-to-face, and they also tend to stay positive and steer clear of touchy topics (Rossetto, 2013). As a result, they're likely to construct idealized images of their partnership that portray it as one that's worth waiting for (Kelmer et al., 2013), and absence can indeed (at least temporarily) make the heart grow fonder (Jiang & Hancock, 2013). Unfortunately, reunions are often more stressful than people expect. When soldiers return home, for instance, the reunited lovers lose some of their autonomy and have to relearn how to comfortably depend on one another; they have to renegotiate their roles and rhythms, and confront the things (which they have often forgotten) that they didn't like about each other (Knobloch & Wehrman, 2014). So perhaps it isn't surprising that one-third of the long-distance dating partners—and remember, commitment is a key influence on all of this—who get back together break up within 3 months of their reunion (Stafford et al., 2006).

So, the effects of familiarity depend both on what we learn about someone else and on the amount of interdependence we are forced to share. It is certainly

Digital Distance

Where Almost Everybody Is Just a Click or Two Away

Proximity matters, but we also have astounding reach to others online, where we can encounter potential mates that we'd never meet any other way (Hamilton, 2016) "Today, if you own a smartphone, you're carrying a 24-7 singles bar in your pocket" (Ansari, 2015, p. 42), and it's now commonplace for romances to begin online on dating apps or websites, or on Facebook, in chat rooms, online communities, multiplayer games, and other online locales. Online encounters are now the second-most-common way (after meeting through friends) that heterosexual couples get started, and they are the *most* frequent way gays and lesbians find each other; about one in every four (23 percent) heterosexual couples and most gay and lesbian couples (61 percent) now meet online (Rosenfeld & Thomas, 2012). Eighty percent of those who have tried dating apps and websites think that they are "a good way to meet people" (Smith, 2016), and there's something for everyone. Do you have a passion for pets? Try *YouMustLove-DogsDating.com*.* Are you looking for another vegetarian? *VeggieDate.org*. A sugar daddy? *SugarDaddie.com*. A hookup? *On-lineBootyCall.com*, which features the "Booty Call˚ Commandment" "Thou shalt kiss anything except my mouth." An extramarital affair? *AshleyMadison.com* in the United States, and *IllicitEncounters.com* in the United Kingdom. And if you're in a hurry, apps can show you interested others who, at the moment, happen to be nearby; download *Tinder* if you're heterosexual, *Grindr* if you're a gay man, and *HER* if you're a lesbian or bisexual woman.

So, there's amazing access to others online, and when we're actively seeking others, expectations are often high. But the outcomes people experience with dating apps and on dating sites can be disappointing, for several reasons. For one thing, most users encounter a lot of ambiguous rejection. They "swipe right" to like some others but don't get any interest in return. What does that mean? Have potential partners considered you closely and found you unworthy? Or are they simply otherwise engaged and unaware of your interest? Either way, users can begin to doubt themselves, and Tinder users tend to have lower levels of satisfaction with their faces and bodies than non-users do (Strübel & Petrie, 2016). For another thing, there are fewer partners out there than it may seem; in order to make their pages more impressive, dating websites may be slow to remove inactive profiles of ex-subscribers who have left the service. By one estimate in 2010, only 7 percent of the profiles that were visible on *Match.com* belonged to people who were still seeking partners (Slater, 2013). And the (apparent) abundance of choices isn't necessarily conducive to relationship success. Overwhelmed by hundreds of profiles, people can become sloppy and less exacting in their choices, homing in, for instance, on particularly attractive people with whom they have absolutely nothing in common (Kreager et al., 2014). Distracted by their many options, they may also be less likely to commit to any one partner; most users (53 percent) have dated more than one person simultaneously ("Online Dating Statistics," 2017). And finally, it's unlikely that a dating site that offers to identify people who will be particularly perfect partners for their subscribers will be able to actually fulfill that promise;

*I am **not** recommending any of these sites! Buyer beware. They're mentioned here only to illustrate the remarkable reach of the Web. They're just examples, and there are plenty more where they came from.

unique compatibility is so complex, it's hard to predict before two people have actually met (Finkel et al., 2012).

Nevertheless, more than one-third of American marriages now result from meetings of the spouses that occurred on-line. (Only 45 percent of those meetings occur on dating sites; most occur else-where.) The data regarding the long-term outcomes that result from online meetings are mixed; compared to partnerships that begin offline, couples who meet online are sometimes more lasting (Cacioppo et al., 2013) and sometime less (Paul, 2014). But one thing is certain: Technology influ-ences relationships, and there's no more dramatic example than the advent of online dating and mating. It introduces us to a much larger variety of people than we would ever meet otherwise (Potarca, 2017), and in some respects, "the Internet may be altering the dynamics and out-comes of marriage itself" (Cacioppo et al., 2013, p. 10135).

possible to reach a point of saturation at which additional time with, and more information about, other people begins to *reduce* our liking for them (Finkel et al., 2015b). But in general, when people first meet, we prefer others we recognize to those who are total strangers (Zajonc, 2001)—and one reason proximity is usually profitable is that it increases the chances that others will be recognizable to us.

Convenience: Proximity Is Rewarding and Distance Is Costly

Another reason why proximity promotes most partnerships is that when others are nearby, it's easy to enjoy whatever rewards they offer. Everything else being equal, a partner who is nearby has a big advantage over one who is far away: The expense and effort of getting to a distant partner—such as expensive airfares or hours on the road—make a distant relationship more costly overall than one that is closer to home. Distant relationships are less rewarding, too; an expression of love over a video feed is less delightful than an actual soft kiss on the lips.

The only notable thing about this is that anyone should find it surprising. However, lovers who have to endure a period of separation may blithely believe, because their relationship has been so rewarding up to that point, that some time apart will not adversely affect their romance. If so, they may be surprised by the difference distance makes. When a relationship that enjoys the convenience of proximity becomes inconvenient due to distance, it may suffer more than either partner expects. Lovers who are deeply committed to their relationship often sur-vive a separation (Kelmer et al., 2013), but other partnerships may ultimately be doomed by distance (Sahlstein, 2006).

The Power of Proximity

The bottom line is that proximity makes it more likely that two people will meet and interact. What follows depends on the people involved, of course, but the good news is that most of the time, when two strangers begin chatting, they like each other more the more they chat (Reis et al., 2011). This does not occur with everyone we meet (Norton et al., 2013), and over time, constant contact with someone also carries the possibility that unrewarding monotony will set in

(Finkel et al., 2015b). Nevertheless, when we come to know others and our goal is simply to get along and to have a good time, familiarity and convenience increase our attraction to them. And that's the power of proximity.

PHYSICAL ATTRACTIVENESS: LIKING THOSE WHO ARE LOVELY

After proximity brings people together, what's the first thing we're likely to notice about those we meet? Their looks, of course. And, although we all know that we shouldn't "judge books by their covers," looks count. Physical attractiveness greatly influences the first impressions that people form of one another. In general, right or wrong, we tend to assume that good-looking people are more likable, better people than those who are unattractive (Brewer & Archer, 2007).

Our Bias for Beauty: "What Is Beautiful Is Good"

Imagine that you're given a photograph of a stranger's face and, using only the photo, are asked to guess at the personality and prospects the person possesses. Studies of judgments such as these routinely find that physically attractive people are presumed to be interesting, sociable people who are likely to encounter personal and professional success in life and love (see Table 3.2). In general, we seem to think that *what is beautiful is good;* we assume that attractive people—especially those who share our own ethnic background (Agthe et al., 2016)—have desirable traits such as agreeableness, extraversion, and conscientiousness that complement their desirable appearances (Segal-Caspi et al., 2012). And we seem to make these judgments automatically, without any conscious thought; a beautiful face triggers a positive evaluation the instant we see it (Olson & Marshuetz, 2005).

TABLE 3.2. **What Is Beautiful Is Good**

Both male and female research participants judged that physically attractive people were more likely than unattractive people to be:

Kind	Interesting
Strong	Poised
Outgoing	Sociable
Nurturant	Exciting date
Sensitive	Good character
Sexually warm and responsive	

These same judges also believed that, compared to those who were unattractive, physically attractive people would have futures that involved

More prestige	Happier marriages
More social and professional success	More fulfilling lives

Source: Dion, K. K., Berscheid, E., & Walster, E. "What is beautiful is good." Journal of Personality and Social Psychology, 24, 1972, 285–290.

We don't expect good-looking strangers to be wonderful in every respect; the more attractive they are, the more promiscuous we think them to be (Brewer & Archer, 2007). (Is this just wishful thinking? It may be. One reason that we like to think that pretty people are outgoing and kind is because we're attracted to them, and we want them to like us in return [Lemay et al., 2010]. Hope springs eternal.) Still, there's no question that attractive people make better overall impressions on us than less attractive people do, and this tends to be true all over the world. In Korea, for example, pretty people are presumed to be sociable, intelligent, and socially skilled, just as they are in the United States. However, in keeping with Korea's collectivist culture (which emphasizes group harmony), attractive people are also presumed to be concerned with the well-being of others, a result that is not obtained in the West (Wheeler & Kim, 1997). What is beautiful is desirable around the world, but the specific advantages attributed to lovely people depend somewhat on the specific values of a culture.

The bias for beauty may also lead us to confuse beauty with talent. In the workplace, physically attractive people make more money and are promoted more often than are those with average looks. On average, good-looking folks earn $230,000 more during their lifetimes than less lovely people do (Hamermesh, 2013). On campus, attractive professors get better teaching evaluations than unattractive instructors do, and students attend their classes more frequently (Wolbring & Riordan, 2016). The more attractive U.S. politicians are, the more competent they are judged to be (Olivola & Todorov, 2010a). Attractive people even make better impressions in court; good-looking culprits convicted of misdemeanors in Texas get lower fines than they would have received had they been less attractive (Downs & Lyons, 1991).

But are the interactions and relationships of beautiful people really any different from those of people who are less pretty? I'll address that question shortly. First, though, we need to assess whether we all tend to agree on who is pretty and who is not.

Who's Pretty?

Consider this: On the first day of a college class, researchers invite you to join a circle that, including you, contains four men and four women. All of the others are strangers. Your task is to take a close look at each person and to rate (secretly!) his or her physical attractiveness while they all judge you in return. What would you expect? Would all four members of the other sex in your group agree about how attractive you are? Would you and the other three people of the same sex give each of the four others exactly the same rating? David Marcus and I did a study just like this to determine the extent to which beauty is in the "eye of the beholder" (Marcus & Miller, 2003). We did find some mild disagreement among the observers that presumably resulted from individual tastes. Judgments of beauty were somewhat idiosyncratic—but not much. The take-home story of our study was the overwhelming consensus among people about the physical beauty of the strangers they encountered. Our participants clearly shared the same notions of who is and who isn't pretty.

Moreover, this consensus exists across ethnic groups: Asians, Hispanics, and black and white Americans all tend to agree with each other about the attractiveness of women from all four groups (Cunningham et al., 1995). Even more striking is the finding that newborn infants exhibit preferences for faces like those that adults find attractive, too (Slater et al., 2000); when they are much too young to be affected by social norms, babies spend more time gazing at attractive than unattractive faces.

What faces are those? There's little doubt that women are more attractive if they have "baby-faced" features such as large eyes, a small nose, a small chin, and full lips (Jones, 1995). The point is not to look childish, however, but to appear feminine and youthful; beautiful women combine those baby-faced features with signs of maturity such as prominent cheekbones, narrow cheeks, and a broad smile (Cunningham et al., 2002). Women who present all these features are thought to be attractive all over the world (Jones, 1995).

Male attractiveness is more complex. Men who have strong jaws and broad foreheads—who look strong and dominant—are usually thought to be handsome (Rhodes, 2006). (Envision George Clooney.) On the other hand, when average male faces are made slightly more feminine and baby-faced through computer imaging, the "feminized" faces—which look warm and friendly—are attractive, too. (Envision Tobey Maguire.) Remarkably, which facial style is more attractive to women is influenced by their menstrual cycles; if they are not using hormonal contraception and are cycling naturally, they tend to find rugged, manly features somewhat more appealing when they are fertile, just before they ovulate, but they're more attracted to youthful boyishness the rest of the month (Little et al., 2002).

In any case, good-looking faces in both sexes have features that are neither too large nor too small. Indeed, they are quite average. If you use computer

Which of these two faces is more appealing to you? They are composite images of the *same* face that have been altered to include feminine or masculine facial features, and if you're a woman, your answer may depend on the current phase of your menstrual cycle. Women tend to find the more masculine face on the right to be more attractive when they are fertile, but they consider the more feminine face on the left to be more appealing during the rest of the month. This is a subtle effect—the differences in preference are not large (Gildersleeve, Haselton, & Fales, 2014)—but the fact that they exist at all is interesting. I'll have more to say about this phenomenon a few pages from now. Picture A is a 50% feminized male composite; B is a 50% masculinized male composite.

A   B

©Little et al., 2002 Anthony Little (www.alittlelab.com)

imaging software to create composite images that combine the features of individual faces, the *average* faces that result are more attractive than nearly all of the faces that make up the composite (Little, 2015). This is true not only in the United States but also in China, Nigeria, India, and Japan (Rhodes et al., 2002). (For a delightful set of examples from Germany, go to www.beautycheck.de.)

However, this doesn't mean that gorgeous people have bland, ordinary looks. The images that result from this averaging process are actually rather unusual. Their features are all proportional to one another; no nose is too big, and no eyes are too small, and there is nothing about such faces that is exaggerated, underdeveloped, or odd. Averaged faces are also *symmetrical* with the two sides of the face being mirror images of one another; the eyes are the same size, the cheeks are the same width, and so on. Facial symmetry is attractive in its own right, whether or not a face is "average" (Fink et al., 2006). In fact, if you take a close look at identical twins, whose faces are very similar, you'll probably think that the twin with the more symmetric face is the more attractive of the two (Lee et al. 2016). Both symmetry and "averageness" make their own contribution to facial beauty, so beautiful faces combine the best features of individual faces in a balanced, well-proportioned whole.

Of course, some bodies are more attractive than others, too. Men find women's shapes most alluring when they are of normal weight, neither too heavy nor too thin, and their waists are noticeably narrower than their hips (Lassek & Gaulin, 2016). The most attractive **waist-to-hip ratio,** or WHR, is a curvy 0.7 in which the waist is 30 percent smaller than the hips (see Figure 3.3 on the next page); this "hourglass" shape appeals to men around the world (Valentova et al., 2017).[4] In

Look what happens when 2, 8, or 32 real faces are morphed together into composite images. When more faces are combined, the resulting image portrays a face that is not odd or idiosyncratic in any way and that has features and dimensions that are more and more typical of the human race. The result is a more attractive image. Averaged faces are attractive faces.

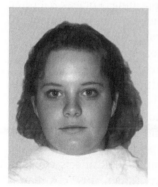 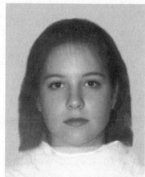 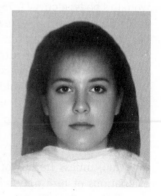

a. 2-Face Composite   b. 8-Face Composite   c. 32-Face Composite

©*Langlois Social Development Lab*

[4]If you want to measure your own WHR, find the circumference of your waist at its narrowest point and divide that figure by the circumference of your hips at their broadest point, including your buttocks. Your butt is included in your "waist-to-hip" ratio.

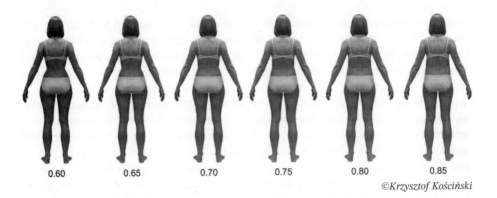

| 0.60 | 0.65 | 0.70 | 0.75 | 0.80 | 0.85 |

©Krzysztof Kościński

FIGURE 3.3. **Waist-to-hip ratios.**
These figures portray the range of different waist-to-hip ratios that are typically found in young women. When men study a variety of images that present all of the possible WHRs from 0.6 to 0.85, they find an average WHR of 0.7 to be most attractive.

the Czech Republic, for instance, the slimmer a woman's waist is, the more often she and her man have sex and the better his erectile function is (Brody & Weiss, 2013). This appears to be a fundamental preference, too; even men who have been blind from birth prefer a low WHR in women's bodies when they assess their shapes by touch (Karremans et al., 2010). Women who are overweight are usually judged to be less attractive than slender and normal-weight women are (Faries & Bartholomew, 2012), and marriages are more satisfying to both spouses, on average, when wives are thinner than their husbands (Meltzer et al., 2011), but thin women are *not* more attractive to men than women of normal weight (Swami et al., 2007). Around the world, men like medium-sized breasts more than small breasts—and larger breasts do not make a woman any more attractive (Havlíček et al., 2017)— but in any case, their size is less important than their proportion to the rest of a woman's body; a curvy 0.75 waist-to-bust ratio is very appealing (Voracek & Fisher, 2006). In addition, a woman's WHR has more influence on men's judgments of her attractiveness than her breast size does (Dixson et al., 2011).[5]

Once again, male attractiveness is more complex. Men's bodies are most attractive when their waists are only slightly narrower than their hips, with a WHR of 0.9. Broad shoulders and muscles are also attractive; men with higher shoulder-to-hip ratios (around 1.2) and bigger muscles have sex with more women and at earlier ages than do men who have narrower shoulders (Hughes & Gallup, 2003) or smaller muscles (Lassek & Gaulin, 2009)—and this, too, is true around the world (Frederick et al., 2011). However, a nice shape doesn't attract a woman to a man unless he has other resources as well; a man's WHR affects women's evaluations of him only when he earns a healthy salary (Singh, 1995). A man is not all that attractive to women if he is handsome but poor.

---

[5] I can also report that when men get 5 seconds to inspect full-body frontal images of naked women, the first things they look at are the breasts and waist (Garza et al., 2016). The face comes later. (But if you're a woman, you already knew that.)

Judgments of physical attractiveness are evidently multifaceted, and several other characteristics also influence those perceptions. Both men and women tend to prefer heterosexual partnerships in which he is taller than she is (Stulp et al., 2013), but height matters more to women than to men (Yancey & Emerson, 2016). So, tall men get more responses from women to their online profiles than short men do. A guy who's short—say, 5' 4"—can get as many responses on a dating website as a fellow who's much taller—say, 6' 1"—but only if he earns more money. A lot more. In this particular case, the shorter man would have to earn $221,000 more each year to be as interesting to women (Hitsch et al., 2010).

A potential partner's smell also matters more to women than to men (Herz & Inzlicht, 2002), and remarkably, they prefer the smells of guys who have been eating a healthy diet full of fruits and vegetables to the smells of guys who've been consuming a lot of carbohydrates (Zuniga et al., 2017). But men are sensitive to smell, too, preferring the natural scents of pretty women to those of women who are less attractive (Thornhill et al., 2003). In a typical study of this sort, people shower using unscented soap before they go to bed and then sleep in the same T-shirt for several nights. Then, research participants who have never met those people take a big whiff of those shirts and select the scents that are most appealing to them. Symmetrical, attractive people evidently smell better than asymmetrical, less attractive people do, because strangers prefer the aromas of attractive people to the smells of those who are more plain (Thornhill et al., 2003). What's more, heterosexual men don't much like the smell of gay men, who have aromas that are more attractive to other gay guys than to straight men (Martins et al., 2005). I am not making this up, so there are evidently subtle influences at work here.

Women are also more attractive to men when they have longer rather than shorter hair. In studies of this sort, men evaluate a woman whose hair—through the magic of computer imaging—varies in length from picture to picture. They're more interested in dating women who (appear to) have long hair, in part because they think that the women are less likely to be engaged or married and more willing to have sex on a first date (Boynton, 2008). Long hair doesn't work as well on a man's chest or scalp; women prefer men with smoother, less hairy chests to those who are more hirsute (Dixson et al., 2010), and a man seems taller and more dominant with a shaved head than he does with a full head of hair (Mannes, 2013).

Women also like smart guys (which should be good news for most of the men reading this book) (Karbowski et al., 2016). In one intriguing study, researchers gave men intelligence tests and then filmed them throwing a Frisbee, reading news headlines aloud, and pondering the possibility of life on Mars. When women watched the videos, the smarter the men were, the more appealing they were (Prokosch et al., 2009). This may be one reason that, when they are trying to impress a woman, men use a more elaborate vocabulary—that is, bigger words—than they do in ordinary discourse (Rosenberg & Tunney, 2008).

Finally, there's a particular power to the color red. Both men and women find strangers of the other (but not the same) sex to be more attractive and sexually appealing when they are pictured in red rather than green or blue shirts (Elliot et al., 2010)—and this effect is so universal, it is found even in Burkina Faso, an African nation in which the color actually carries negative connotations of bad luck and illness (Elliot et al., 2013b). Red has this effect because a woman seems more sexually receptive when she's wearing red than when she's not (Pazda et al., 2014). So, men are more likely to ask women for dates when they're wearing red (Elliot & Niesta, 2008), and, if a relationship develops, they're more likely to keep track of their partners' whereabouts when she's wearing red (Prokop & Pazda, 2016). All of this may not be accidental: Women choose to wear more red when they expect to meet attractive (but not unattractive) men (Elliot et al., 2013a), and they're more likely to wear red on days they're fertile than on other days of the month (Eisenbruch et al., 2015). Valentines are red for a reason.

An Evolutionary Perspective on Physical Attractiveness

I've just mentioned a lot of details, so you may not have noticed, but people's preferences for prettiness generally fit the assumptions of an evolutionary perspective. Consider these patterns:

- Cultures differ in several respects, but people all over the world still tend to agree on who is and who is not attractive (Cunningham et al., 1995; Jones, 1995). That's one reason why the winners of international beauty pageants are usually gorgeous no matter where they're from.
- Babies are born with preferences for the same faces that adults find attractive (Slater et al., 2000). Some reactions to good looks may be inherited.
- People with attractive symmetrical faces also tend to have symmetrical bodies and to enjoy better mental and physical health—and therefore make better mates—than do people with asymmetrical faces (Nedelec & Beaver, 2014; Perilloux et al., 2010). Symmetric women have higher levels of estradiol, which probably makes them more fertile (Jasieńska et al., 2006), and symmetric people of both sexes are smarter (Luxen & Buunk, 2006) and get sick less often (Van Dongen & Gangestad, 2011) than do those whose faces and bodies have odd proportions.
- Hormones influence waist-to-hip ratios by affecting the distribution of fat on people's bodies. With their particular mix of estradiol and progesterone, women with WHRs near the attractive norm of 0.7 get pregnant more easily and tend to enjoy better physical health than do women with fewer curves (Jasieńska et al., 2004). A man with an attractive WHR of 0.9 is likely to be in better health than another man with a plump belly (Payne, 2006). So, both sexes are most attracted to the physical shapes that signal the highest likelihood of good health in the other sex (Singh & Singh, 2011).
- Everybody likes good looks, but physical attractiveness matters most to people who live in equatorial regions of the world where there are many parasites and pathogens that can endanger good health (Gangestad & Buss, 1993). In such areas, unblemished beauty may be an especially good sign that someone is in better health—and will make a better mate—than someone whose face is in some way imperfect.

- Ultimately, all things considered, attractive people in the United States reproduce more successfully—they have more children—than do those who are less attractive (Jokela, 2009).
- There are subtle but provocative changes in women's preferences that accompany their monthly menstrual cycles. Women are only fertile for the few days that precede their ovulation each month (see Figure 3.4), and during that period, women find some characteristics in men to be more appealing than they seem during the rest of the month. When they are fertile, women prefer deeper voices, the scents of more symmetrical men, and bolder, more arrogant, more charismatic behavior than they do when they are infertile (Gildersleeve, Haselton, & Fales, 2014), and they are better able to judge whether a guy is gay or straight (Rule et al., 2011b). They also find the scents of men with high testosterone to be more pleasing (Thornhill et al., 2013). Thus, women are attracted to assertive, cocky men—that is, those who are "more likely to behave like cads than be good dads" (Perrett, 2010, p. 104)—when they are most likely to conceive a child, but they prefer warmer, kinder, less pushy men the rest of the month (Aitken et al., 2013). These cyclic changes do not occur if women are taking birth control pills (and therefore are not ovulating) (Alvergne & Lummaa, 2010).

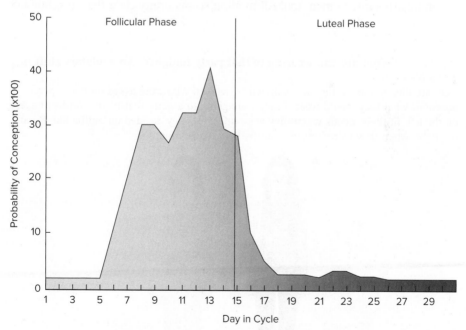

Source: Jöchle, W. "Coitus-induced ovulation," Contraception, 7, 1973, 523–564.

FIGURE 3.4. **Women's probability of conception during the menstrual cycle.**
Women are fertile during the few days just before they ovulate at the end of the follicular phase of their menstrual cycles. During that period, they prefer the smells of symmetrical men and bolder, more cocky behavior from men than they do during the rest of the month.

A Point to Ponder

Are you intrigued or are you annoyed by the data that suggest that women's behavior toward men changes when they're fertile? Why?

• Women's behavior toward men also changes when they're fertile. They wear more cosmetics (Guéguen, 2012), and dress more provocatively, wearing sexier clothes that show more skin (Schwarz & Hassebrauck, 2008). They're 3 times more likely to wear red (Beall & Tracy, 2013). They're more flirtatious toward attractive (but not drab) men (Cantú et al., 2014), their dancing is more enticing (Fink et al., 2012a), and they're more willing to accept an invitation to slow dance with a stranger (Guéguen, 2009). And they become more interested in sex with attractive men, even ones they do not know well (Roney & Simmons, 2016). Evidently, when they're fertile for a few days each month, women act more alluringly than they do when they're infertile (Little, 2015). See Figure 3.5.

• All of this is not lost on men, who think women smell better when they're about to ovulate than at other times of the month (Gildersleeve et al., 2012). Smelling the T-shirts of such women causes men to experience a surge of testosterone (Miller & Maner, 2010) and to start thinking sexy thoughts (Miller & Maner, 2011). When women are fertile, their voices (Pipitone et al., 2016), faces (Bobst & Lobmaier, 2014), and bodies (Grillot et al., 2014) are all more attractive to men, too. All in all, it seems pretty clear that in subtle but

FIGURE 3.5. **"What are you wearing to that party tonight?" An ovulatory shift in women's outfits.**
Here are illustrations of the outfits drawn by women who were asked on two separate occasions what they would wear if they were going to a party that night. Outfits like **A**, on the left, fit their moods when they were infertile. They decided on outfits like **B**, on the right, when they were infertile, shortly before ovulation.

real ways—and without necessarily being aware of it—men can tell there's something slightly different and desirable about a woman when she's about to ovulate (Haselton & Gildersleeve, 2011).[6]

These patterns convince some theorists that our standards of physical beauty have an evolutionary basis (Eastwick & Tidwell, 2013). Presumably, early humans who successfully sought fertile, robust, and healthy mates were more likely to reproduce successfully than were those who simply mated at random. As a result, the common preferences of modern men for symmetrical, low-WHR partners and of modern (fertile) women for symmetrical, masculine, and dynamic men may be evolved inclinations that are rooted more in their human natures than in their particular cultural heritage.

Culture Counts, Too

On the other hand, evolutionary theorizing doesn't sit well with everyone. Some of the findings I recounted above regarding an *ovulatory shift* in women's preferences and behavior have been questioned by other researchers (Wood & Carden, 2014) who argue either that these patterns are very subtle and hard to replicate (Harris, 2013) or that they are the result of a mishmash of procedures that make them hard to interpret (Harris et al., 2013). No, say the folks with an evolutionary perspective, these results are not quirks and these patterns truly exist (Gildersleeve et al., 2013), and meta-analyses say so (Gildersleeve et al., 2014).

Still, as the contest between these camps continues (Wood, 2016), there's no doubt that standards of attractiveness are also affected by changing economic and cultural conditions. Have you seen those Renaissance paintings of women who look fat by modern standards? During hard times, when a culture's food supply is unreliable and people are hungry, slender women are actually *less* desirable than heavy women are (Nelson & Morrison, 2005). Around the world, only during times of plenty are slender women considered to be attractive (Swami et al., 2010). Indeed, as economic prosperity spread through the United States during the twentieth century, women were expected to be slimmer and slimmer so that the average *Playboy* Playmate is now so slender she meets the weight criterion for having an eating disorder (Owen & Laurel-Seller, 2000).

Norms can differ across ethnic groups as well (influenced in part, perhaps, by different patterns of economic well-being). Black and Latina women in the United States are more accepting of some extra weight than white women are, and indeed, black and Latino men like heavier women than white men do

---

[6]Once again, and as always, I am not making any of this up. More importantly, aren't these findings remarkable? Keep in mind that if a woman is changing the normal ebb and flow of her hormones by taking birth control pills, none of this happens (Alvergne & Lummaa, 2010). But when women are cycling normally, these patterns support the possibility that estrous cycles exist in humans just as they do in other animals. The actual frequency with which heterosexual women have sex with their men does not fluctuate with ovulation (Grebe et al., 2013), so such cycles are more subtle in humans, to be sure—but they may exist nonetheless (Gangestad, 2012).

(Glasser et al., 2009). (But watch out: They still prefer the same curvaceous 0.7 WHR that is universally appealing to men [Singh & Luis, 1995]. In fact, even those Renaissance paintings depicted women with 0.7 WHRs.)

Collectively, these findings suggest that human nature and environmental conditions work together to shape our judgments of who is and who isn't pretty (Eastwick, 2013). We're usually attracted to people who appear to be good mates, but what looks good depends somewhat on the conditions we inhabit. Still, beauty is not just in the eye of the beholder. There is remarkable agreement about who's gorgeous and who's ugly around the world.

Looks Matter

When a stranger walks into the room, you'll know with a glance how attractive he or she is (Willis & Todorov, 2006). Does that matter? Indeed, it does. During speed dates—in which people meet a variety of potential partners and get a chance to exchange any information they want—the biggest influence on their liking for others is outward appearance. "Participants are given 3 minutes in which to make their judgments, but they could mostly be made in 3 seconds" (Kurzban & Weeden, 2005, p. 240). Men are attracted to women who are slender, young, and physically attractive, and women are attracted to men who are tall, young, and physically attractive. Of all the things people could learn about each other in a few minutes of conversation, the one that matters most is physical attractiveness (Li et al., 2013). Take someone's Big 5 personality traits, attachment style, political attitudes, and other values and interests into account, and the best predictor of interest in him or her after a brief first meeting remains physical attractiveness. As you'd expect, friendly, outgoing people tend to be well liked, and nobody much likes people who are shy or high in anxiety about abandonment (McClure & Lydon, 2014), but nothing else about someone is as important at first meeting as his or her looks (Luo & Zhang, 2009).

Of course, speed-dating events can be a bit hectic—have you ever introduced yourself to 25 different potential partners in a busy hour and a half?—and people may shop for partners more thoughtfully when they're able to take their time (Lenton & Francesconi, 2010). In particular, when they ponder the question, men all over the world report higher interest in having a physically attractive romantic partner than women do (Conroy-Beam et al., 2015; see Figure 3.6). This is true of gays and lesbians, too (Ha et al., 2012). And indeed, 4 years into a marriage, a man's satisfaction is correlated with his spouse's attractiveness, but a woman's contentment is unrelated to her partner's looks (Meltzer et al., 2014). Both sexes even spend more time inspecting the profile photos of women on Facebook than they do examining the pictures posted by men (Seidman & Miller, 2013). Women know that men are judging them by their looks, which may be why 87 percent of the cosmetic surgery

A Point to Ponder

Modern culture is full of images of tall, slender, shapely women and tall, muscular, handsome men. How are these idealized images of the two sexes subtly influencing your real-life relationships?

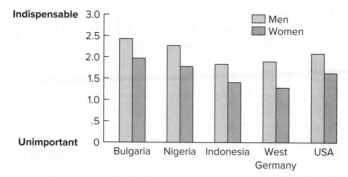

Source: Data from Buss, D. M., & Schmitt, D. P. "Sexual strategies theory:
An evolutionary perspective on human mating," Psychological Review,
100, 1993, 204–232.

FIGURE 3.6. **Desire for physical attractiveness in a romantic partner.**
Around the world, according to their self-reports, men care about a partner's looks more
than women do.

performed in the United States in 2015 was done on women (American Society
of Plastic Surgeons, 2016).

But remember, despite the different emphasis men and women (say they) put
on good looks, physical attractiveness influences both sexes when people get
together (Eastwick et al., 2014). Looks matter. They're the most potent influence
on how much the two sexes will initially like each other.

The Interactive Costs and Benefits of Beauty

So, what effects do our looks have on our interactions with others? Notably,
despite men's interest in women's looks, there is actually no correlation overall
between a woman's beauty and the amount of time she spends interacting with
men (Reis et al., 1982). Attractive women get more dates, but plain women spend
plenty of time interacting with men in group settings where others are present.
In contrast, men's looks *are* correlated with the number and length of the interactions they have with women. Unattractive men have fewer interactions of any sort
with fewer women than good-looking guys do. In this sense, then, physical attractiveness has a bigger effect on the social lives of men than it does on women.

Being more popular, attractive people tend to be less lonely, more socially
skilled, and a little happier than the rest of us (Feingold, 1992), and they're able to
have sex with a wider variety of people if they want (Weeden & Sabini, 2007).
Physical attractiveness may even account for as much as 10 percent of the variability in people's adjustment and well-being over their lifetimes (Burns & Farina, 1992).
But being attractive has disadvantages, too. For one thing, others lie to pretty people
more often. People are more willing to misrepresent their interests, personalities,
and incomes to get close to an attractive person than they are to fabricate an image
for a plain partner (Rowatt et al., 1999). As a result, realizing that others are often
"brown-nosing," or trying to ingratiate themselves, gorgeous people may cautiously
begin mistrusting or discounting some of the praise they receive from others.

Consider this clever study: Attractive or unattractive people receive a written evaluation of their work from a person of the other sex who either does or does not know what they look like (Major et al., 1984). In every case, each participant receives a flattering, complimentary evaluation. (Indeed, everyone gets exactly the same praise.) How did the recipients react to this good news? Attractive men and women trusted the praise more and assumed that it was more sincere when it came from someone who *didn't* know they were good-looking. They were evidently used to getting insincere compliments from people who were impressed by their looks. On the other hand, unattractive people found the praise more compelling when the evaluator *did* know they were plain; sadly, they probably weren't used to compliments from people who were aware of their unappealing appearances.

So, gorgeous people are used to pleasant interactions with others, but they tend not to trust other people as much as less attractive people do (Reis et al., 1982). In particular, others' praise may be ambiguous. If you're very attractive, you may never be sure whether people are complimenting you because they respect your abilities or because they like your looks.

Matching in Physical Attractiveness

I've spent several pages discussing physical attractiveness—which is an indication of its importance—but there is one last point to make about its influence at the beginning of a relationship. We all may want gorgeous partners, but we're likely to end up paired off with others who are only about as attractive as we are (Hitsch et al., 2010). Partners in established romantic relationships tend to have similar levels of physical attractiveness; that is, their looks are well matched, and this pattern is known as **matching.**

The more serious and committed a relationship becomes, the more obvious matching usually is. People may pursue others who are better-looking than they, but they are unlikely to go steady with, or become engaged to, someone who is "out of their league" (Taylor et al., 2011). What this means is that, even if everybody wants a physically attractive partner, only those who are also good-looking are likely to get them. None of the really good-looking people want to pair off with us folks of average looks, and we, in turn, don't want partners who are "beneath us," either (Lee et al., 2008).

Thus, it's not very romantic, but similarity in physical attractiveness seems to operate as a screening device. If people generally value good looks, matching will occur as they settle for the best-looking partner who will have them in return (Montoya, 2008). There is, however, a heartwarming exception to this rule: Matching is less obvious—and mismatches in attractiveness are more likely to occur—in partners who were platonic friends before a romance developed between them (Hunt et al., 2015). Evidently, matching matters less if people grow close before the issue of relative attractiveness rears its ugly head (so to speak). Husbands and wives do tend to be noticeably similar in physical attractiveness (Little et al., 2006), and some relationships never get started because the two people don't look enough alike (van Straaten et al., 2009)—but that needn't always be the case.

RECIPROCITY: LIKING THOSE WHO LIKE US

The matching phenomenon suggests that, to enjoy the most success in the relationship marketplace, we should pursue partners who are likely to return our interest. In fact, most people do just that. When we ponder possible partners, most of us rate our realistic interest in others—and the likelihood that we will approach them and try to start a relationship—using a formula like this (Shanteau & Nagy, 1979):

$$\begin{array}{c} \text{A Potential} \\ \text{Partner's Desirability} \end{array} = \begin{array}{c} \text{His/Her} \\ \text{Physical Attractiveness} \end{array} \times \begin{array}{c} \text{His/Her Probability} \\ \text{of Accepting You} \end{array}$$

Everything else being equal, the better-looking people are, the more desirable they are. However, this formula suggests that people's physical attractiveness is multiplied by our judgments of how likely it is that they will like us in return to determine their overall appeal. Do the math. If someone likes us a lot but is rather ugly, that person probably won't be our first choice for a date. If someone else is gorgeous but doesn't like us back, we won't waste our time. The most appealing potential partner is often someone who is moderately attractive and who seems to offer a reasonably good chance of accepting us (perhaps *because* he or she isn't gorgeous) (Montoya & Horton, 2014).

Our expectations regarding the probability of others' acceptance have much to do with our **mate value,** or overall attractiveness as a reproductive partner. People with high mate values are highly sought by others, and as a result, they're able to insist on partners of high quality. And they do (Hughes & Aung, 2017). For instance, women who are very good-looking have very high standards in men; they don't just want a kind man who would be a good father, or a sexy man who has good economic prospects; they want *all* of those desirable characteristics in their partners (Buss & Shackelford, 2008). If their mate values are high enough, they might be able to attract such perfect partners (Conroy-Beam & Buss, 2016)— but if they're overestimating their desirability and overreaching, they're likely to remain frustrated (Bredow, 2015).

In general, our histories of acceptance and rejection from others have taught us what to expect when we approach new potential partners (Kavanagh et al., 2010). Compared to the rest of us, for instance, people who are shy (Wenzel & Emerson, 2009) or who have low self-esteem (Bale & Archer, 2013) nervously expect more rejection from others, so they pursue less desirable partners. But it's common to be cautious when we are unsure of others' acceptance. A clever demonstration of this point emerged from a study in which college men had to choose where to sit to watch a movie (Bernstein et al., 1983). They had two choices: squeeze into a small cubicle next to a very attractive woman, or sit in an adjacent cubicle—alone—where there was plenty of room. The key point is that some of the men believed that the *same* movie was playing on both monitors, whereas other men believed that *different* movies were showing on the two screens. Let's consider the guys' dilemma. Presumably, most of them wanted to become acquainted with the beautiful woman. However, when only one movie was available, squeezing in next to her entailed some risk of rejection; their intentions

What's a Good Opening Line?

You're shopping for groceries, and you keep crossing paths with an attractive person who smiles at you warmly when your eyes meet. You'd like to meet him or her. What should you say? You need to do more than just say, "Hi," and wait for a response, don't you? Perhaps some clever food-related witticism is the way to go: "Is your dad a baker? You've sure got a nice set of buns."

Common sense suggests that such attempts at humor are good opening lines. Indeed, the Web is full of sites with lists of funny pickup lines that are supposed to make a good impression. Be careful, though; serious research has compared the effectiveness of various types of opening lines, and a cute or flippant remark may be among the *worst* things to say.

Let's distinguish cute lines from innocuous openers (such as just saying, "Hi" or "How're you doing?") and direct lines that honestly communicate your interest (such as "Hi, I'd like to get to know you"). When women evaluate lines like these by watching tapes of men who use them, they like the cute lines much less than the other two types (Kleinke & Dean, 1990). More importantly, when a guy actually uses one of these lines on a woman in a singles bar, the innocuous and direct openers get a favorable response 70 percent of the time compared to a success rate of only 24 percent for the cute lines (Cunningham, 1989). A line that is sexually forward (such as "I may not be Fred Flintstone, but I bet I can make your bed rock") usually does even worse (Cooper et al., 2007). There's no comparison: Simply saying hello is a much smarter strategy than trying to be cute or forward (Weber et al., 2010).

Why, then, do people create long lists of flippant pickup lines? Because they're men. When a *woman* uses a cute line on a *man* in a singles bar, it usually works—but that's because any opening line from a woman works well with a man; in Cunningham's (1989) study, saying "Hi" succeeded every time. Men don't seem to care what opening lines women use—and this may lead them to overestimate women's liking for cute openers in return.

would be obvious, and there was some chance that the woman would tell them to "back off." However, when two different movies were available, they were on safer ground. Sitting next to the woman could mean that they just wanted to see that particular movie, and a rebuff from her would be rude. In fact, only 25 percent of the men dared to sit next to the woman when the same movie was on both monitors, but 75 percent did so when two movies were available and their intentions were more ambiguous. Moreover, we can be sure that the men were taking advantage of the uncertain situation to move in on the woman—instead of really wanting to see that particular movie—because the experimenters kept changing which movie played on which screen. Three-fourths of the men squeezed in with the gorgeous woman no matter which movie was playing there!

In general, then, people seem to take heed of the likelihood that they will be accepted and liked by others, and they are more likely to approach those who offer acceptance than rejection. Our judgments of our mate values can vary from one relationship to another, as we assess our compatibility—and appeal—to particular partners (Eastwick & Hunt, 2014). But the *best* acceptance usually comes from potential partners who are selective and choosy and who don't offer acceptance to everyone. In speed-dating situations, for example, people who are eager to go out with everyone they meet are liked less by others—and make fewer matches—than those who are more discriminating; people who say "yes" to everybody get few "yesses" in return, whereas those who record interest in only a select few are more enticing to those they pick (Eastwick et al., 2007). These results jive nicely, by the way, with classic studies of what happens when people play "hard to get." Because people like to be liked, pretending to be aloof and only mildly interested in someone is a dumb way to try to attract him or her. Playing hard to get doesn't work. What does work is being *selectively* hard to get—that is, being a difficult catch for everyone *but* the person you're trying to attract (Walster et al., 1973). Those who can afford to say "no" to most people but who are happy to say "yes" to us are the most alluring potential partners of all.

Still, everything else being equal, it's hard *not* to like those who like us (Curtis & Miller, 1986). Imagine that the first thing you hear about a new transfer student is that he or she has noticed you and really likes you; don't you feel positively toward him or her in return? Liking and acceptance from others is powerfully rewarding, and we're attracted to those who provide it.

SIMILARITY: LIKING THOSE WHO ARE LIKE US

So, it's rewarding to meet people who like us. It's also enjoyable to find others who are *just* like us and who share the same background, interests, and tastes. Indeed, when it comes to our attitudes, age, race (and, to some degree, our personalities), the old cliché that "birds of a feather flock together" is absolutely correct (Bahns et al., 2017; Montoya & Horton, 2013). Like attracts like. Consider these examples:

- At the University of Michigan, previously unacquainted men were given free rooms in a boardinghouse in exchange for their participation in a study of developing friendships (Newcomb, 1961). At the end of the semester, the men's closest friendships were with those housemates with whom they had the most in common.
- At the University of Texas, researchers intentionally created blind dates between men and women who held either similar social and political attitudes or dissimilar views (Byrne et al., 1970). Each couple spent 30 minutes at the student union getting to know each other over soft drinks. After the "dates," similar couples liked each other more than dissimilar couples did.
- At Kansas State University, 13 men spent 10 days jammed together in a simulated fallout shelter, and their feelings about each other were assessed along the way (Griffitt & Veitch, 1974). The men got along fine with those with whom they had a lot in common, but would have thrown out of the shelter, if they could, those who were the least similar to themselves.

As these examples suggest, similarity is attractive.

What Kind of Similarity?

But what kinds of similarities are we talking about? Well, lots. Whether they are lovers or friends, happy relationship partners resemble each other more than random strangers do in several ways. First, there's *demographic* similarity in age, sex, race, education, religion, and social class (Hitsch et al., 2010). Most of your best friends in high school were probably of the same age, sex, and race (Hartl et al., 2015). People are even more likely than you'd expect to marry someone whose last name begins with the same last letter as their own (Jones et al., 2004)!

Then there's similarity in *attitudes and values.* There is a straightforward link between the proportion of the attitudes two people think they share and their attraction to each other: the more agreement, the more liking. Take note of the pattern in Figure 3.7. When people were told that they agreed on a lot of issues, attraction didn't level off after a certain amount of similarity was reached, and there was no danger in having "too much in common." Instead, where attitudes are concerned, the more similar two people are, the more they like each other. For whom did you vote in the last election? It's likely you and your best friend cast similar ballots.

Finally, to a lesser degree, partners may have similar *personalities*—but this pattern is a bit complex. When it comes to me being happy with you, it's not vital that you and I have similar personalities; what matters is that *you* are agreeable, conscientious, and emotionally stable, and so are easy and pleasant to live with (Watson et al., 2014). My contentment will have more to do with your desirable

Attraction is influenced by similarity. People who are similar in background characteristics, physical attractiveness, and attitudes are more likely to be attracted to each other than are those who are dissimilar.

©*Asia Images Group/Getty Images*

FIGURE 3.7. **The relationship between attraction and perceived similarity in attitudes.**

People expected to like a stranger when they were led to believe that the stranger shared their attitudes.

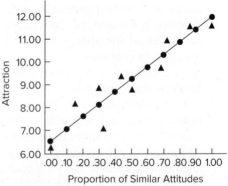

Source: Adapted from Byrne, D., & Nelson, D. "Attraction as a linear function of proportion of positive reinforcements," Journal of Personality and Social Psychology, *1, 1965, 659–663.*

qualities than with how similar we are (Becker, 2013). Of course, if I have a congenial, dependable personality, too, then you're also happy, and our personalities are fairly similar—but it's not our similarity per se that's promoting our satisfaction (Wood & Furr, 2016). The key here is that the link between similarity and attraction is stronger for attitudes than for personalities (Watson et al., 2004), and it actually varies some from country to country (Gebauer et al., 2012). In China, a country that values group harmony, for instance, the personalities of husbands and wives are typically more similar than those of spouses in the United States, a country that celebrates individualism (Chen et al., 2009). (And that sounds like a point to ponder.)

In any case, people with similar styles and traits usually get along well when they encounter each other; for instance, the first meetings of two gregarious people or two shy people are typically more enjoyable than the first conversation of a gregarious person and a shy person is (Cuperman & Ickes, 2009). People even like others better, when they meet online, if they have similar avatars (van der Land et al., 2015).

A Point to Ponder

Husbands and wives in China typically have personalities that are more similar to one another than spouses in the United States do. When it comes to marital satisfaction, is that a good or a bad thing?

Do Opposites Attract?

So, in general, the more two people have in common, the more they like each other. "Relationships are formed, in part, by the selection of partners who *share* important attitudes, values, prejudices, activities, and some personality traits" (Bahns et al., 2017, p. 341).[7] Why, then, do some of us believe that "opposites attract"? Are people really more attracted to each other when they are less alike? The simple answer is no. There are some nuances at work, but people are not routinely more content with dissimilar, rather than similar, partners. However, there *are* several important subtleties in the way similarity operates that may mislead people into thinking that opposites do sometimes attract.

How Much Do We *Think* We Have in Common? Perceived Similarity Matters

The first subtlety is that our *perceptions* of how much we have in common affect our attraction to each more than our actual similarity does. For instance, 4 minutes after people have met in a speed-dating study, their interest in each other has little to do with how much they really have in common; instead, to the extent their liking for each other is influenced by their personalities and interests, it depends on how similar they *think* they are (Tidwell et al., 2013). And perceived similarity remains important even if a relationship develops and the partners come to know each other better. After years of friendship—or marriage!—partners still routinely think that they have more in common with each other than they really do (Goel et al., 2010). They overestimate the similarities they share (de Jong & Reis, 2014)—and

---

[7] I added the italics to this quote.

Interethnic Relationships

Most of our intimate relationships are likely to be with others of the same race. Nevertheless, marriages between spouses from different ethnic groups are occurring at a record pace in the United States, with 17 percent of newlyweds marrying someone of a different race (Bialik, 2017). Those couples raise an interesting question: If similarity attracts, what's going on? The answer is actually straightforward: nothing special. If you ignore the fact of their dissimilar ethnicity, interethnic couples appear to be influenced by the same motives that guide everyone else. The partners tend to be similar in age, education, and attractiveness, and their relationships, like most, are based on common interests and personal compatibility (Brummett, 2017). A few things distinguish people who date partners from other cultural groups: Compared to their peers, they've had closer contact with other ethnicities and they're more accepting of other cultures (Brooks & Neville, 2017). They also tend to live in areas where potential partners of the same race are relatively scarce (Choi & Tienda, 2017). In general, however, interethnic partners are just as satisfied as other couples (Troy et al., 2006) and they have the same chances for marital success as their peers (Zhang & Van Hook, 2009). Their relationships operate the same way: Two people who consider each other to be good-looking and smart (Wu et al., 2015)—and who are more alike than different—decide to stay together because they're happy and they've fallen in love.

discovering how wrong they are (if they ever do) can take some time. Meanwhile, interested onlookers—friends, family, co-workers—may correctly observe that the partners are two very different people and infer, therefore, that opposites must attract. No, the partners aren't together because their differences are desirable, they're together because they think they're *not* very different, and they're wrong (Sprecher, 2014).

Discovering Dissimilarities Can Take Time

If we like others when we meet them (perhaps simply because they're good-looking), we tend to expect (or is it hope?) that they have attitudes and values that are similar to our own (Morry et al., 2011)—and of course, sometimes we're mistaken. If we get to know them better, the interests and attitudes we actually share are likely to become influential (Luo, 2009), but it may take a while for us to figure that out.

A process like this was evident in Newcomb's (1961) study of developing friendships among men sharing a boardinghouse. Soon after they met, the men liked best the housemates who they thought were most like them; thus, at first, their friendships were influenced mostly by *perceived* similarity. As the semester progressed, however, the actual similarities the men shared with each other played a larger and larger role in their friendships. When they got to know each other better, the men clearly preferred those who really were similar to them, although this was not always the case at first.

Then, even when we do know our partners well, there may still be surprises ahead. According to Bernard Murstein's (1987) **stimulus-value-role** theory, we gain three different broad types of information about our partners as a new relationship develops. When we first meet, our attraction to each other is primarily based on "stimulus" information involving obvious attributes such as age, sex, and, of course, looks. Thereafter, during the "value" stage, attraction depends on similarity in attitudes and beliefs as we learn whether we like the same kinds of pizzas, movies, and politics (see Figure 3.8). Only later does "role" compatibility become important, when we finally find out if we agree on the basics of parenting, careers, and housecleaning, among other life tasks. The point is that partners can be perfectly content with each other's tastes in music (for instance) without ever realizing that they disagree fundamentally about where they'd like to live and how many kids—if any!—they want to have. Important dissimilarities sometimes become apparent only after couples have married; such spouses may stay together despite their differences, but it's not because opposites attract.

The influence of time and experience is also apparent in **fatal attractions** (Felmlee, 2001). These occur when a quality that initially attracts one person to another gradually becomes one of the most obnoxious, irritating things about that partner. For instance, partners who initially seem spontaneous and fun may later seem irresponsible and foolish, and those who appear strong and assertive may later seem domineering. Those who initially welcome a partner's high level of attention and devotion may come to resent such behavior when it later seems too possessive. In such cases, the annoying trait is no secret, but people fail to appreciate how their judgments of it will change with time. Importantly, such fatal qualities are often different from one's own; they may seem admirable and desirable at first—so that a spendthrift who's always broke may initially admire a tightwad who counts every penny—but over time people realize that such opposites aren't attractive (Rick et al., 2011).

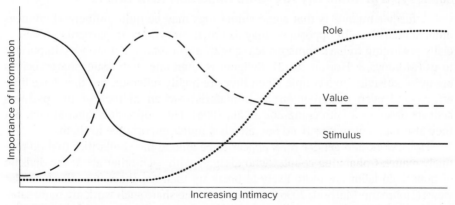

Source: Data from Murstein, B. I. "A clarification and extension of the SVR theory of dyadic pairing," Journal of Marriage and the Family, *49, 1987, 929–933.*

FIGURE 3.8. **Three different phases of relationship development.**
Murstein's (1987) *stimulus-value-role* theory suggests that developing relationships are influenced by three different types of information that differ in importance and influence as time goes by and the partners learn more about each other.

You May Be the Person I Want to Become

Along those lines, people also admire those who possess skills and talents they wish they had. Another nuance in the operation of similarity lies in our attraction to others who are similar to our *ideal selves,* that is, who exhibit desirable qualities that we want to, but do not yet, possess (Strauss et al., 2012). This tendency is complex because it's threatening and unpleasant when people surpass us and make us look bad by comparison (Herbst et al., 2003). However, if others are only a little better than us—so that they offer us implicit encouragement instead of humiliation—we may be attracted to those who are actually a little different from us (for now) (Klohnen & Luo, 2003). Let's not overstate this subtlety. The most appealing partners of all are those who are similar to us in most dimensions but who fit our attainable ideals in others (Figueredo et al., 2006). Such people are hardly our "opposites." But as long as the differences are not too great, we may prefer a partner who is someone we'd like to become to one who more closely resembles who we really are now.

Dissimilarity May Decrease over Time

Moreover, relationships can change people (Hafen et al., 2011). Their personalities don't change much (Rammstedt et al., 2013), but as time goes by, the members of a couple often come to share more similar attitudes (Gonzaga et al., 2010). Some of this decrease in dissimilarity probably occurs automatically as a couple shares compelling experiences, but some of it also occurs as the partners consciously seek compatibility and contentment (Becker & Lois, 2010). Thus, opposites don't attract, but some opposites may gradually fade if a couple stays together for some other reason.

Some Types of Similarity Are More Important than Others

A further nuance is that some similarities may be quite influential whereas other similarities—or opposites—may be rather innocuous. In particular, it's especially rewarding to have someone agree with us on issues that are very important to us (Montoya & Horton, 2013). Religion is often one such issue; shared beliefs are quite satisfying to a couple when they are highly religious, but they have little effect—and even disagreement is immaterial—when neither of the partners actively observes a faith (Lutz-Zois et al., 2006). Thus, opposites don't attract, but they also may not matter if no one attaches much importance to them.

Housework and gender roles appear to be among the similarities that *do* routinely matter. Cohabiting couples who disagree with each other about the division of household labor are more likely to break up than are those who share similar views (Hohmann-Marriott, 2006), and spouses who share such work are more satisfied than those who divide it unequally (Amato et al., 2007). And husbands and wives who are more similar in their gender roles—not less, as a traditional outlook would lead us to expect—are more happily married than those who differ from one another in their styles and skills (Gaunt, 2006). In particular, compared to spouses who are more alike, macho husbands and feminine wives (who clearly have different gender roles) feel less understood, share less companionship, and experience less love and contentment in their marriages as time goes by (Helms et al., 2006).

Matching Is a Broad Process

Another source of confusion arises when people pair off with others who are obviously very different but who nevertheless have a similar mate value—as may be the case when an old rich guy marries a lovely young woman. In such cases, the partners are clearly dissimilar, and "opposites" may seem to attract. That's a rather unsophisticated view, however, because such partners are really just *matching* in a broader sense, trading looks for money and vice versa. They may have different assets, but such partners are still seeking good matches with others who have similar standing overall in the interpersonal marketplace. People usually end up with others of similar mate value, but the specific rewards they offer each other may be quite different.

This sort of thing goes on all the time. A study of 6,485 users of an online dating service found that very homely—okay, ugly—men (those in the bottom 10 percent of attractiveness among men) needed $186,000 more in annual income in order to attract as much attention from women as fine-looking fellows (i.e., those in the top 10 percent); nevertheless, if they did make that much more money, ugly guys received just as many inquiries as handsome men did (Hitsch et al., 2010).

Indeed, it's not very romantic, but fame, wealth, health, talent, and looks all appear to be commodities that people use to attract more desirable partners than they might otherwise entice. If we think of matching as a broad process that involves both physical attractiveness and various other assets and traits, it's evident that people usually pair off with others of similar status, and like attracts like.

In fact, trade-offs like these are central ideas in evolutionary psychology. Because men are more likely to reproduce successfully when they mate with healthy, fertile women, sexual selection has presumably promoted men's interest in youthful and beautiful partners (Buss, 2015). Youth is important because women are no longer fertile after they reach menopause in middle age. Beauty is meaningful because, as we've already seen, it is roughly correlated with some aspects of good health (Van Dongen & Gangestad, 2011). Thus, men especially value good looks in women (see Figure 3.6), and, as they age, they seek partners who are increasingly younger than they are (Antfolk et al., 2015). They pay more for prostitutes in their teens and early 20s than for women in their 30s (Sohn, 2016), and if they *purchase* a bride (as may happen in South Korea), they never buy one older than 25 even when they're in their 40s or 50s (Sohn, 2017). Around the world, men who marry in their twenties pair off with women who are 2 years younger than they are, on average, but if a man marries in his fifties, he's likely to seek a wife 15 years younger than he (Dunn et al., 2010).

Women don't need to be as concerned about their partners' youth because men normally retain their capacity for reproduction as long as they live. Instead, given their vastly greater parental investment in their offspring,[8] women should seek mates with resources who can provide for the well-being of mother and child during the long period of pregnancy and nursing. In fact, as Figure 3.9 illustrates, women *do* care more about their partners' financial prospects than men do, and men who flash their cash attract more sexual partners than stingy men do (Sundie et al., 2011). When he asks a woman who is walking by, for instance, a guy climbing out of a luxury car (an Audi A5) is more likely to get

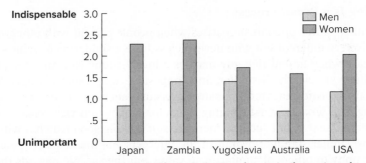

Source: Data from Buss, D. M., & Schmitt, D. P. "Sexual strategies theory: An evolutionary perspective on human mating," Psychological Review, 100, 1993, 204–232.

FIGURE 3.9. **Desire for good financial prospects in a romantic partner.**
Around the world, women care more about a partner's financial prospects than men do.

her phone number than he would be if he had a cheap car (a Renault Mégane) (Guéguen & Lamy, 2012). Furthermore, women's preferences for the age of their mates do not change much as they age (Antfolk et al., 2015); women don't start seeking younger men as mates until they (the women) are around 75 years old (Alterovitz & Mendelsohn, 2011).

Thus, matching based on the exchange of feminine youth and beauty for masculine status and resources is commonplace (Conroy-Beam et al., 2015). Sure enough, when they advertise for partners on Craig's List, women get the most interest from men when they say they're "lovely, slim, and very attractive," but men get the most interest from women when they describe themselves as "financially independent and successful" (Strassberg & English, 2015). Still, is all this the result of evolutionary pressures? Advocates of a cultural perspective argue that women pursue desirable resources through their partners because they are so often denied direct access to political and economic power of their own (Wood & Eagly, 2007). Indeed, in the United States—a culture in which smart women have access to career opportunities—the more intelligent a woman is, the lower her desire is for wealth and status in a romantic partner (Stanik & Ellsworth, 2010). And around the world, the extent to which women care more about a mate's money is reduced in countries that support and promote female equality (Conroy-Beam et al., 2015). Still, even in such countries (such as Finland, Germany, and the United States), women care a lot more about a mate's financial prospects, on average, than men do (Zentner & Mitura, 2012).

So, the origins of the feminine-beauty-for-masculine-money trade-off remain uncertain. But in any case, the bottom line here is that matching is a broad process that involves multiple resources and traits. When "opposites" seem to attract, people may be trading one asset for another in order to obtain partners of similar social status, and it's their similar mate values, not any desired differences, that make them attractive to each other.

---

[8] If a reminder regarding *parental investment* will be welcome, look back at pages 34.

Not everyone agrees that women's interest in a man's resources is a result of evolutionary pressures. Nevertheless, whereas 78 percent of American women say that finding a partner with a steady job is very important to them, only 46 percent of American men say the same thing (Livingston & Caumont, 2017).

One Way "Opposites" May Attract Now and Then: Complementarity

Finally, there are times when different types of behavior can fit together well. In keeping with the principle of *instrumentality* (back on page 66), we like responses from others that help us reach our goals (Fitzsimons et al., 2015). When two partners have different skills, each is usually happy to allow the other to take the lead on those tasks at which the other is more talented (Beach et al., 2001). Such behavior is said to *complement* our own, and **complementarity**—reactions that provide a good fit to our own—can be attractive. Most complementary behaviors are actually similar actions; people who are warm and agreeable, for instance, are happiest when they are met with warmth and good humor in return.

However, some profitable forms of complementarity involve different behaviors from two partners. Consider a couple's sexual interactions; if one of them enjoys receiving oral sex, their satisfaction is likely to be higher when the other enjoys giving it (de Jong & Reis, 2014). Divisions of labor that suit our talents in pursuit of shared goals are often advantageous: If I'm a dreamer who comes up with great ideas and you're a details person who's a careful planner, we can enjoy some terrific vacations if we like to go to the same places (Bohns et al., 2013). And when we really want something, it's nice when our partners let us have our way. When we feel very sure of ourselves, we want our partners to heed our advice; on other occasions, when we need help and advice, we want our partners to give it (Markey et al., 2010).

Do these examples of rewarding complementarity sound like "opposites attract" to you? I hope not. In general, patterns of behavior in others that are genuinely opposite to our own—such as cool aloofness instead of our warmth, or submissive passivity instead of our assertion and self-confidence—are annoying and frustrating (Hopwood et al., 2011). Dominant people like to get their way, but they like other assertive folks more than they like those who are chronically servile (Markey & Markey, 2007)—and in any case, there's not a lot of one spouse bossing the other around in happy marriages (Cundiff et al., 2015). And trust me, if you're an impulsive person who tends to act without thinking, you do *not* want to pair off with a partner who is cautious and planful (why? to keep you out of trouble?); you'll be happier if you partner with some-one who is just as impetuous and reckless as you are (Derrick et al., 2016).

The bottom line appears to be that we like partners who entertain and support us but we don't like partners who frustrate or impede us, and a partnership is fulfilling when we desire the same goals and are able to work together to successfully achieve them. So, the blend of similarities and differences that form an optimal mix may vary from couple to couple (Baxter & West, 2003). Personal growth and novel activities are also rewarding, so we like people with interests that are different from (but not incompatible with) our own when they introduce us to things we'll both like (Aron et al., 2006). The important thing to remember is that similar partners are more likely than others to share our goals (Gray & Coons, 2017), so they supply us what we want more often than anyone else can.

Add it all up, and opposites may sometimes seem to attract, but birds of a feather are more likely to flock together. Similarity is usually rewarding; opposition is not.

SO, WHAT DO MEN AND WOMEN WANT?

We are nearly at the end of our survey of major influences on attraction, but one important point remains. As we've seen, men and women differ in the value they place on a partner's physical attractiveness and income (Li et al., 2013). I don't want those results to leave you with the wrong impression, however, because despite those differences, men and women generally seek the same qualities in their relational partners (Li et al., 2011). Let's look more closely at what men and women want.

Around the world, there are three themes in the criteria with which people evaluate potential mates (Lam et al., 2016). If we had our way, almost all of us would have partners who offered

- *warmth and loyalty,* being trustworthy, kind, supportive, and understanding;
- *attractiveness and vitality,* being good-looking, sexy, and outgoing; and
- *status and resources,* being financially secure and living well.

All of these characteristics are desirable, but they're not of equal importance, and their prominence depends on whether we're seeking a relatively casual, short-term fling or a more committed long-term romance.

Men and women have the same (relatively low) standards when they're pursu-ing short-term flings (Eastwick et al., 2014). They both want a casual lover to be good-looking (Li et al., 2013), and both sexes are less picky when they're evaluating partners for short-term liaisons than for lasting unions (Fletcher et al., 2004). For instance, both sexes will accept lower intelligence, warmth, and earning potential in a lover with whom they have a casual fling than they would require in a spouse (Buunk et al., 2002). In particular, when they are contemplating short-term affairs, women will accept men who aren't especially kind, dependable, or understanding as long as their lovers are muscular, sexy, and "hot" (Frederick & Haselton, 2007).

But women clearly recognize that attractive, dominant, masculine men who might make compelling lovers often make unreliable long-term mates (Boothroyd et al., 2007). When they are picking husbands, women consider a man's good character to be more important than his good looks. They attach more importance to the criteria of warmth and loyalty and status and resources than to the criterion of attractiveness and vitality when they are thinking long term (Fletcher et al., 2004). Prestige and accomplishments become more important than dominance and daring (Kruger & Fitzgerald, 2011). When she finds she can't have it all, the average woman prefers a man who is kind, understanding, and well to do—but not particularly handsome—to a good-looking but poor one, or a rich and good-looking but cold and disloyal one (Li, 2008).

Men have different priorities. Like women, they value warmth and loyalty, but unlike women, they attach more importance to attractiveness and vitality in a long-term partner than to status and resources (Fletcher et al., 2004). The average guy prefers a kind, beautiful woman without any money to wealthy women who are gorgeous grouches or women who are sweet but ugly (Li, 2008).

Of course, we typically have to accept some trade-offs like these when we're seeking intimate partners. Fulfilling all of our diverse desires by finding (and winning!) the perfect mate is hard to do. If we insist that our partners be kind and understanding *and* gorgeous *and* rich, we're likely to stay frustrated for a long time. So, when they're evaluating potential mates, men typically check first to make sure that a woman has at least average looks, and then they seek as much warmth, kindness, honesty, openness, stability, humor, and intelligence as they can get (Li et al., 2002). Great beauty is desirable to men, but it's not as important as high levels of warmth and loyalty are (with status and resources coming in a distant third). Women usually check first to make sure that a man has at least some money or prospects, and then they, too, seek as much warmth, kindness, honesty, openness, stability, humor, and intelligence as they can get (Li et al., 2002). Wealth is desirable to women, but it's not as important as high levels of warmth and loyalty, and looks are in third place.

Gays and lesbians behave similarly, wanting the same things that heterosexual men and women do (Lawson et al., 2014). And although most of the research results described in this chapter were obtained in the United States, people all over the world concur; a global sample of 218,000 Internet users ranked intelligence, humor, kindness, and dependability as the top four traits they sought in a relationship partner (Lippa, 2007), and studies in Brazil (Castro & de Araújo Lopes, 2010), Russia (Pearce et al., 2010), Singapore (Li et al., 2011), and China (Chen et al., 2015) have all yielded similar results.

Men and women generally agree on the things they *don't* want in a mate, too. When they are asked to identify *dealbreakers,* the characteristics that would lead them to reject someone as a partner, both sexes put objectionable traits (such as being untrustworthy, unfeeling, or abusive), ill-health (STDs or alcoholism), and poor hygiene ("smells bad") at the top of their lists (Jonason et al., 2015). Women are a bit more cautious and choosy (Fletcher et al., 2014), having more dealbreakers than men, and as you would expect (given our discussion back on page 85), people with higher mate value have more dealbreakers, too (Jonason et al., 2015).

So, add all this up, and attraction isn't so mysterious after all. Men attend to looks and women take note of resources, but everybody seems to want partners who are amiable, agreeable, loving, and kind. Men and women do not differ in this regard and their preference for warmth and kindness in a mate grows stronger as they get older (and wiser?) (Brumbaugh & Wood, 2013). As long as she's moderately pretty and he has some money, both sexes want as much warmth and loyalty as they can get. To the extent there is any surprise here, it's in the news that women don't simply want strong, dominant men; they want their fellows to be warm and kind and capable of commitment, too (Jensen-Campbell et al., 1995). If you're an unemotional, stoic, macho male, take note: Women will be more impressed if you develop some affectionate warmth to go with your strength and power.

FOR YOUR CONSIDERATION

Rasheed introduced himself to Rebecca because she was really hot, and he was mildly disappointed when she turned out to be a little suspicious, self-centered, and vain. On the other hand, she was really hot, so he asked her out anyway. Because she was impressed with his designer clothes and bold style, Rebecca was intrigued by Rasheed, but after a few minutes she thought him a little pushy and arrogant. Still, he had tickets to an expensive concert, so she accepted his invitation to go out on a date.

Having read this chapter, what do you think the date—and the future—hold for Rebecca and Rasheed? Why?

CHAPTER SUMMARY

The Fundamental Basis of Attraction

We are attracted to people whose presence is rewarding because they offer us *instrumentality*, assistance in achieving our goals.

Proximity: Liking Those Near Us

We select our friends, and our enemies, from those around us.

Familiarity: Repeated Contact. In general, familiarity breeds attraction. Even brief, *mere exposure* to others usually increases our liking for them.

Convenience: Proximity Is Rewarding, Distance Is Costly. Relationships with distant partners are ordinarily less satisfying than they would be if the partners were nearby.

The Power of Proximity. Close proximity makes it more likely that two people will meet and interact, for better or for worse.

Physical Attractiveness: Liking Those Who Are Lovely

Our Bias for Beauty: "What Is Beautiful Is Good." We assume that attractive people have other desirable personal characteristics.

Who's Pretty? Symmetrical faces with average features are especially beautiful. *Waist-to-hip ratios* of 0.7 are very appealing in women whereas a WHR of 0.9 is attractive in a man if he has money.

An Evolutionary Perspective on Physical Attractiveness. Cross-cultural agreement about beauty, cyclical variations in women's preferences and behavior, and the link between attractiveness and good health are all consistent with the assumptions of evolutionary psychology.

Culture Counts, Too. Standards of beauty also fluctuate with changing economic and cultural conditions.

Looks Matter. When people first meet, nothing else affects attraction as much as their looks do.

The Interactive Costs and Benefits of Beauty. Physical attractiveness has a larger influence on men's social lives than on women's. Attractive people doubt the praise they receive from others, but they're still happier than unattractive people are.

Matching in Physical Attractiveness. People tend to pair off with others of similar levels of beauty.

Reciprocity: Liking Those Who Like Us

People are reluctant to risk rejection. Most people calculate others' overall desirability by multiplying their physical attractiveness by their probability of reciprocal liking. People who are desirable partners—that is, those with high *mate value*—insist that their partners be desirable, too.

Similarity: Liking Those Who Are Like Us

Birds of a feather flock together. People like those who share their attitudes.

What Kind of Similarity? Happy relationship partners resemble each other in demographic origin, attitudes, and, to a lesser degree, in personalities.

Do Opposites Attract? Opposites do not attract, but they may seem to for several reasons. First, we are attracted to those who we think are like us, and we can be wrong. Then, it takes time for *perceived similarity* to be replaced by more accurate understanding of the attributes we share with others. People may be attracted to those who are mildly different from themselves but similar to their ideal selves. People also tend to become more similar over time, and some types of similarity are more important than others. Matching is also a broad process; fame, wealth, talent, and looks can all be used to attract others. Finally, we may appreciate behavior from a partner that differs from our own but that complements our actions and helps us to reach our goals.

So, What Do Men and Women Want?

People evaluate potential partners with regard to (a) warmth and loyalty, (b) attractiveness and vitality, and (c) status and resources. For lasting romances, women want men who are warm and kind and who are not poor, and men want women who are warm and kind and who are not unattractive. Thus, everybody wants intimate partners who are amiable, agreeable, and loving.

©*Monkey Business Images/Shutterstock*

When we meet others for the first time, stereotypes and primacy effects influence our interpretations of the behavior we observe. Confirmation biases and overconfidence may follow.

tentative. Armed with only some of the facts—those that tend to support our case—we put misplaced faith in our judgments of others, being wrong more often than we realize.

Now, of course, we come to know our partners better with time and experience, and first impressions can certainly change as people learn more about each other (Brannon & Gawronski, 2017). However—and this is the fundamental point I wish to make—*existing beliefs are influential* at every stage of a relationship, and when it comes to our friends and lovers, we may see what we want to see and hold confident judgments that aren't always right (Leising et al., 2014).

For instance, who are the better judges of how long your current romantic relationship will last, you or your parents? Remarkably, when university students, their roommates, and their parents were all asked to forecast the future of the students' dating relationships, the parents made better predictions than the students did, and the roommates did better still (MacDonald & Ross, 1999). You'd think that people would be the best judges of their own relationships, but the students focused on the strengths of their partnerships and ignored the weaknesses, and as a result, they confidently and optimistically predicted that the relationships would last longer than they usually did. Parents and roommates were more dispassionate and evenhanded, and although they were less confident in their predictions, they were more accurate in predicting what the future would hold. In fact, the most accurate predictions of all regarding the future of a heterosexual relationship often come from the friends of the woman involved (Loving, 2006). If her friends approve of a partnership, it's likely to continue, but if they think the relationship is doomed, it probably is (Etcheverry & Agnew, 2004).

Thus, the same overconfidence, confirmatory biases, and preconceptions that complicate our perceptions of new acquaintances operate in established relationships as well. Obviously, we're not clueless about our relationships, and when we're deliberate and cautious, we make more accurate predictions about their futures than we do when we're in a romantic mood. But it's hard to be dispassionate when we're devoted to a relationship and want it to continue; in such

We Don't Always Know Why We Think What We Do

Consider this: When you show up for a psychology study, the researcher asks you to hold her cup of hot coffee for about 20 seconds while she records your name on a clipboard. Then, you're asked to form an impression of a stranger who is described in a brief vignette. Would your warm hands lead you to intuit that the stranger is a warm and generous person? Would you have liked the stranger less if you had been holding a cup of iced coffee instead? Remarkably, the answer to both of those questions is yes. Warm hands lead research participants to think warmer thoughts about a stranger than cool hands do (Williams & Bargh, 2008).

How about this? Would sitting at a wobbly table on a wobbly chair increase your desire for stability (such as trustworthiness and reliability) in a mate? The answer is yes, again (Kille et al., 2013), and there are two aspects of these phenomena that are intriguing. First, our impressions of others can be shaped by a variety of influences, and some of them have nothing to do with the person who's being judged. Second, the people in these studies were completely unaware that current conditions such as the temporary temperature of their hands were swaying their judgments. We don't always know *why* we hold the opinions we do, and on occasion, our impressions of others are unwarranted. Both points are valuable lessons for a discerning student of social cognition.

cases, we are particularly prone to confirmation biases that support our optimistic misperceptions of our partners (Gagné & Lydon, 2004).

So, our perceptions of our relationships are often less detached and completely correct than we think they are. And, for better or for worse, they have considerable impact on our subsequent feelings and behavior, as we'll see next.

THE POWER OF PERCEPTIONS

Our judgments of our relationships and our partners seem to come to us naturally, as if there were only one reasonable way to view them. Little do we realize that we're often *choosing* to adopt the perspectives we use, and we facilitate or inhibit our satisfaction with our partners by the choices we make.

Idealizing Our Partners

What are you looking for in an ideal romantic relationship? As we saw in chapter 3, most of us want a partner who is warm and trustworthy, loyal and passionate, and attractive and rich, and our satisfaction depends on how well our lovers approach those ideals (Tran et al., 2008). What we usually get, however, is something less. How, then, do we ever stay happy with the real people we attract?

One way is to construct charitable, generous perceptions of our partners that emphasize their virtues and minimize their faults. People often judge their lovers with **positive illusions** that portray their partners in the best possible light (Fletcher et al., 2013). Such "illusions" are a mix of realistic knowledge about our partners and idealized perceptions of them. They do not ignore a partner's faults; they just consider them to be circumscribed, specific drawbacks that are less important and influential than their many assets and advantages are (Neff & Karney, 2003). They have all the facts, but they interpret them differently than everyone else—so they judge their partners more positively than other people do, and even more positively than the partners judge themselves (Solomon & Vazire, 2014).

Isn't it a little dangerous to hold a lover in such high esteem? Won't people inevitably be disappointed when their partners fail to fulfill such positive perceptions? The answers may depend on just how unrealistic our positive illusions are (Neff & Karney, 2005). If we're genuinely fooling ourselves, imagining desirable qualities in a partner that he or she does not possess, we may be dooming ourselves to disillusionment (Niehuis et al., 2011). It's not so great for our partners, either, when we put them on a pedestal and expect them to be perfect (Tomlinson et al., 2014). On the other hand, if we're aware of all the facts but are merely interpreting them in a kind, benevolent fashion, such "illusions" can be very beneficial (Fletcher, 2015). When we idealize our partners, we're predisposed to judge their behavior in positive ways, and we are more willing to commit ourselves to maintaining the relationship (Luo et al., 2010). And we can slowly convince our partners that they actually are the wonderful people we believe them to be because our high regard improves their self-esteem (Murray et al., 1996). Add it all up, and idealized images of romantic partners are associated with greater satisfaction as time goes by (Murray et al., 2011).

In addition, there's a clever way in which we protect ourselves from disillusionment: Over time, as we come to know our partners well, we tend to revise our opinions of what we want in an ideal partner so that our standards fit the partners we've got (Fletcher & Kerr, 2013). To a degree, we conveniently decide that the qualities our partners have are the ones we want.

Thus, by choosing to look on the bright side—perceiving our partners as the best they can be—and by editing our ideals and hopes so that they fit the realities we face, we can increase the chances that we'll be happy with our present partners. Indeed, our partners generally know that we're idolizing them, and they usually want us to, within reason (Boyes & Fletcher, 2007)—and if we receive such positive, charitable perceptions in return, everybody wins.

Attributional Processes

Our delight or distress is also affected by the manner in which we choose to explain our partners' behavior. The explanations we generate for why things happen—and in particular why a person did or did not do something—are called **attributions.** An attribution identifies the causes of an event, emphasizing the impact of some influences and minimizing the role of others. Studies of such judgments are important because there are usually several possible explanations for most events in our lives, and they can differ in meaningful ways. We can emphasize influences that are either *internal* to someone, such as the person's personality, ability, or effort, or *external*, implicating the situation or circumstances the person faced. For instance (as you've probably noticed), students who do well on exams typically attribute their success to internal causes (such as their preparation and talent) whereas those who do poorly blame external factors (such as a tricky test) (Forsyth & Schlenker, 1977). The causes of events may also be rather *stable* and lasting, as our abilities are, or *unstable* and transient, such as moods that come and go. Finally, causes can be said to be *controllable*, so that we can manage them, or *uncontrollable*, so that there's nothing we can do about them. With all of these distinctions in play, diverse explanations for a given event may be plausible. And in a close relationship in which interdependent partners may *both* be partly responsible for much of what occurs, judgments of cause and effect can be especially complicated.

Nevertheless, three broad patterns routinely emerge from studies of attributions in relationships. First, despite their intimate knowledge of each other, partners are affected by robust **actor/observer effects:** They generate different explanations for their own behavior than they do for the similar things they see their partners do (Malle, 2006). People are often acutely aware of the external pressures that have shaped their own behavior, but they overlook how the same circumstances affect others; as a result, they acknowledge external pressures when they explain their own actions, but they make internal attributions (for instance, to others' personalities) when other people behave exactly the same way. What makes this phenomenon provocative in close relationships is that it leads the partners to overlook how *they* often personally provoke the behavior they observe in each other. During an argument, if one partner thinks, "she infuriates me so when she does that," the other is likely to be thinking, "he's so temperamental. He needs to learn to control himself." This bias is so pervasive that two people in almost any interaction are reasonably likely to agree about what each of them did but to disagree about why each of them did it (Robins et al., 2004). And to complicate things further, the two partners are unlikely to be aware of the discrepancies in their attributions; each is likely to believe that the other sees things his or her way. When partners make a conscious effort to try to understand the other's point of view, the actor/observer discrepancy gets smaller (Arriaga & Rusbult, 1998), but it rarely vanishes completely (Malle, 2006). The safest strategy is to assume that even your closest partners seldom comprehend all your reasons for doing what you do.

Second, despite genuine affection for each other, partners are also likely to display **self-serving biases** in which they readily take credit for their successes but try to avoid the blame for their failures. People like to feel responsible for the good things that happen to them, but they prefer external excuses when things go wrong. Thus, although they won't tell their partners (Miller & Schlenker, 1985), they usually think that they personally deserve much of the credit when their relationships are going well, but they're not much to blame if a partnership is doing poorly (Thompson & Kelley, 1981). One quality that makes this phenomenon interesting is that most of us readily recognize overreaching ownership of success and flimsy excuses for failure when they come from other people, but we think that our own similar, self-serving perceptions are sensible and accurate (Pronin et al., 2002). This occurs in part because we are aware of—and we give ourselves credit for—our own good intentions, even when we fail to follow through on them, but we judge other people only by what they do, not what they may have intended to do (Kruger & Gilovich, 2004).

This is a provocative pattern, so let's consider how it works. Imagine that Fred goes to sleep thinking, "I bet Wilma would like breakfast in bed in the morning." He intends to do something special for her, and he proudly gives himself credit for being a thoughtful partner. But when he oversleeps and has to dash off to work without actually having done anything generous, he's likely to continue feeling good about himself: After all, he had kind intentions. In contrast, Wilma can only judge Fred by his actions; she's not a party to what he was thinking, and she has no evidence in this instance that he was thoughtful at all. Their different sources of information may lead Fred to consider himself a better, more considerate partner than Wilma (or anyone else) perceives him to be (Lemay, 2014). (Remember those thank-you notes you were intending to write but never did? You probably give yourself some credit for wanting to get around to them, but all your disappointed grandmother knows is that you never thanked her, and you're behaving like an impolite ingrate!)

Subtle processes like these make self-serving explanations of events routine in social life. It's true that loving partners are less self-serving toward each other than they are with other people (Sedikides et al., 1998). Nevertheless, self-serving biases exist even in contented relationships. In particular, when they fight with each other, spouses tend to believe that the argument is mostly their partner's fault (Schütz, 1999). And if they have extramarital affairs, people usually consider their own affairs to be innocuous dalliances, but they consider their spouse's affairs to be grievous betrayals (Buunk, 1987).

> **A Point to Ponder**
>
> To what extent are you able to comprehend your partner's perceptions of the role *you* played in escalating your last argument with him or her?

Thus, partners' idiosyncratic perspectives allow them to feel that they have better excuses for their mistakes than their friends and lovers do. They also tend to believe that their partners are the source of most disagreements and conflict. Most of us feel that *we're* pretty easy to live with, but *they're* hard to put up with sometimes. Such perceptions are undoubtedly influential, and, indeed, a third important pattern is that the general pattern of a couple's attributions helps determine how satisfied they will be with their relationship (Osterhout et al., 2011). Happy people make attributions for their partners' behavior that are *relationship enhancing*. Positive actions by the partner are judged to be intentional, habitual, and indicative of the partner's fine character; that is, happy couples make controllable, stable, and internal attributions for each other's positive behavior. They also tend to discount one another's transgressions, seeing them as accidental, unusual, and circumstantial; thus, negative behavior is excused with attributions to external, unstable, and uncontrollable causes.

Through such attributions, satisfied partners magnify their partner's kindnesses and minimize their missteps, and, as long as a partner's misbehavior really *is* just an occasional oversight, these benevolent explanations keep the partners happy (McNulty, 2011). But dissatisfied partners do just the opposite, exaggerating the bad and minimizing the good (Fincham, 2001). Unhappy people make *distress-maintaining* attributions that regard a partner's negative actions as deliberate and routine and positive behavior as unintended and accidental. (See Figure 4.3.) Thus, whereas satisfied partners judge each other in generous ways that are likely to keep them happy, distressed couples perceive each other in an unforgiving fashion that can keep them dissatisfied no matter how each behaves (Durtschi et al., 2011). When distressed partners *are* nice to one another, each is likely to write off the other's thoughtfulness as a temporary, uncharacteristic lull in the negative routine. When kindnesses seem accidental and hurts seem deliberate, satisfaction is hard to come by (Hook et al., 2015).

Where does such a self-defeating pattern come from? Attachment styles are influential. People with secure styles tend to tolerantly employ relationship-enhancing attributions, but insecure people—particularly those who are high in anxiety about abandonment—are more pessimistic (Kimmes et al., 2015). And disappointments of various sorts may cause anyone to gradually adopt a pessimistic perspective (Karney & Bradbury, 2000). But one thing is clear: Maladaptive attributions can

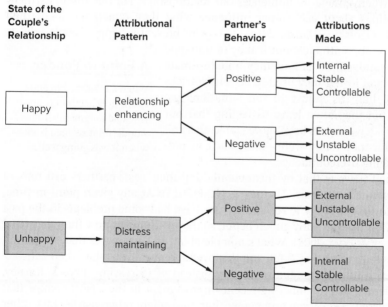

Source: *Data from Brehm, S., & Kassin, S. M. Social Psychology (6th ed.),*
New York: Houghton Mifflin, 1990.

FIGURE 4.3. **Attributions made by happy and unhappy couples.**
Relationship-enhancing attributions give partners credit for thoughtful, generous actions and excuse undesirable behavior as a temporary aberration. Distress-maintaining attributions do just the opposite; they blame partners for undesirable conduct but give them no credit for the nice things they do.

lead to cantankerous behavior and ineffective problem solving (Hrapczynski et al., 2011), and they can cause dissatisfaction that would not have occurred otherwise (Kimmes et al., 2015). With various points of view at their disposal, people can choose to explain a partner's behavior in ways that are endearing and forgiving, or pessimistic and pejorative—and the success of their relationship may ultimately hang in the balance.

Memories

Our perceptions of the current events in our relationships are obviously influential. So are our memories of the things that have happened in the past.

We usually assume that our memories are faithful representations of past events. In particular, we're likely to trust vivid memories because they seem so certain and detailed. But years of research (see Della Sala, 2010) have clearly demonstrated that we edit and update our memories—even seemingly vivid ones—as new events unfold, so that what we remember about the past is always a mix of what happened then and what we know now. Psychologists use the term **reconstructive memory** to describe the manner in which our memories are continually revised and rewritten as new information is obtained.

Reconstructive memory influences our relationships. For one thing, partners' current feelings about each other influence what they remember about their shared past (Ogolsky & Surra, 2014). If they're presently happy, people tend to forget past disappointments; but if they're unhappy and their relationship is failing, they underestimate how happy and loving they used to be. These tricks of memory help us adjust to the situations we encounter, but they often leave us feeling that our relationships have always been more stable and predictable than they really were—and that can promote damaging overconfidence.

> ### A Point to Ponder
>
> When a relationship ends badly, how accurately are you able to remember how wonderful it seemed back when it was going well?

The good news is that by misremembering their past, partners can remain optimistic about their future (Lemay & Neal, 2013). At any given point in time, contented lovers are likely to recall that they have had some problems in the past but that things have recently gotten better, so they are happier now than they used to be (Karney & Frye, 2002). What's notable about this pattern is that, if you follow couples over time, they'll tell you this over and over even when their satisfaction with each other is gradually eroding instead of increasing (Frye & Karney, 2004). Evidently, by remembering recent improvement in their partnerships that has not occurred, people remain happier than they might otherwise be. Like other perceptions, our memories influence our subsequent behavior and emotions in our intimate relationships (Lemay, 2014).

Relationship Beliefs

People also enter their partnerships with established beliefs about how relationships work. For instance, Brian Willoughby and his colleagues (2015a) suggest that we have a collection of beliefs about getting and being married that take the forms of *marital paradigms,* which are broad assumptions about whether, when, and under what circumstances we should marry that are accompanied by beliefs about what it's like to *be* married. About one-third of a sizable sample of students at Ball State University in Indiana were enthusiastic about marriage and eager to get married, but a greater number of them (58 percent) were more cautious: They attached less priority to being married, wanted to wait longer to get married, and were more accepting of divorce. And the remaining 10 percent of the group judged marriage to be even less important, thinking they'd be 35 years old when (or if) they married (Willoughby & Hall, 2015).

Underpinning such broad outlooks are a variety of more specific beliefs such as **romanticism,** the view that love should be the most important basis for choosing a mate (Weaver & Ganong, 2004). People who are high in romanticism believe that (a) each of us has only one perfect, "true" love; (b) true love will find a way to overcome any obstacle; and (c) love is possible at first sight. These beliefs apparently provide a rosy glow to a new relationship—romantic people experience more love, satisfaction, and commitment in the first few months of their romantic partnerships than unromantic people do—but these beliefs tend to erode as time goes by (Sprecher & Metts, 1999). Real relationships rarely meet such lofty expectations.

At least romantic beliefs appear to be fairly benign (Leising et al., 2014). The same cannot be said for some other specific beliefs that are clearly disadvantageous. Certain beliefs that people have about relationships are *dysfunctional;* that is, they appear to have adverse effects on the quality of relationships, making it less likely that the partners will be satisfied (Goodwin & Gaines, 2004). What ideas could people have that could have such deleterious effects? Here are six:

- *Disagreements are destructive.* Disagreements mean that my partner doesn't love me enough. If we loved each other sufficiently, we would never disagree.
- *"Mindreading" is essential.* People who really care about each other ought to be able to intuit each other's needs and preferences without having to be told what they are. My partner doesn't love me enough if I have to tell him or her what I want or need.
- *Partners cannot change.* Once things go wrong, they'll stay that way. If a lover has faults, he or she won't improve.
- *Sex should be perfect every time.* Sex should always be wonderful and fulfilling if our love is pure. We should always want, and be ready for, sex.
- *Men and women are different.* The personalities and needs of men and women are so dissimilar, you really can't understand someone of the other sex.
- *Great relationships just happen.* You don't need to work at maintaining a good relationship. People are either compatible with each other and destined to be happy together or they're not.

Most of these beliefs were identified by Roy Eidelson and Norman Epstein (1982) years ago, and since then, studies have shown that they put people at risk for distress and dissatisfaction in close relationships (Wright & Roloff, 2015). They're unrealistic. When disagreements do occur—as they always do—they seem momentous to people who hold these views. Any dispute implies that their love is imperfect. Worse, people with these perspectives don't exert much effort to nurture and maintain their relationships (Weigel et al., 2016)—after all, if you're made for each other, you shouldn't have to break a sweat to live happily ever after—and they don't behave constructively when problems arise. Believing that people can't change and that true love just happens, such people don't strive to solve problems; they report more interest in ending the relationship than in working to repair it (Knee & Petty, 2013).

In their work on relationship beliefs, Chip Knee and his colleagues refer to perspectives like these as **destiny beliefs** because they assume that two people are either well suited for each other and destined to live happily ever after, or they're not (Knee & Petty, 2013). Destiny beliefs take an inflexible view of intimate partnerships (see Table 4.1). They suggest that if two people are meant to be happy, they'll know it as soon as they meet; they'll not encounter early doubts or difficulties, and once two soulmates find each other, a happy future is ensured. This is the manner in which

TABLE 4.1. Destiny and Growth Beliefs

Chip Knee (1998) measured destiny and growth beliefs with these items. Respondents were asked to rate their agreement or disagreement with each item using this scale:

1	2	3	4	5	6	7
strongly disagree						*strongly agree*

1. Potential relationship partners are either compatible or they are not.

2. The ideal relationship develops gradually over time.

3. A successful relationship is mostly a matter of finding a compatible partner right from the start.

4. Challenges and obstacles in a relationship can make love even stronger.

5. Potential relationship partners are either destined to get along or they are not.

6. A successful relationship is mostly a matter of learning to resolve conflicts with a partner.

7. Relationships that do not start off well inevitably fail.

8. A successful relationship evolves through hard work and resolution of incompatibilities.

Source: Knee, C. R. "Implicit theories of relationships: Assessment and prediction of romantic relationship initiation, coping, and longevity," Journal of Personality and Social Psychology, 74, 1998, 360–370.

As you undoubtedly surmised, the odd-numbered items assess a destiny orientation and the even-numbered items assess a growth orientation. A scale with these items and 14 more is now used in destiny and growth research (Knee & Petty, 2013), but these classic items are still excellent examples of the two sets of beliefs. Do you agree with one set of ideas more than the other?

"I thought we were soul mates, too, so imagine my surprise to find that my actual soul mate is Nicole in accounting."

©Barbara Smaller/The New Yorker Collection/The Cartoon Bank.

The belief that all you have to do to live happily ever after is to find the right, perfect partner is *not* advantageous.

Hollywood often portrays love in romantic comedies—and people who watch such movies do tend to believe that true loves are meant to be (Hefner & Wilson, 2013).

Different views, which you rarely see at the movies, assume that happy relationships are the result of hard work (Knee & Petty, 2013). According to **growth beliefs**, good relationships are believed to develop gradually as the partners work at surmounting challenges and overcoming obstacles, and a basic presumption is that with enough effort, almost any relationship can succeed.

As you might expect, these different perspectives generate different outcomes when difficulties arise (and as it turns out, Hollywood isn't doing us any favors). When couples argue or a partner misbehaves, people who hold growth beliefs remain more committed to the relationship and more optimistic that any damage can be repaired than do those who do not hold such views. And those who hold growth beliefs can discuss their lovers' imperfections with equanimity; in contrast, people who hold destiny beliefs become hostile when they are asked to confront their partners' faults (Knee & Petty, 2013). "It may be romantic for lovers to think they were made for each other, but it backfires when conflicts arise and reality pokes the bubble of perfect unity. Instead, thinking of love as a journey, often involving twists and turns but ultimately moving toward a destination, takes away some of the repercussions of relational conflicts" (Lee & Schwarz, 2014, p. 64).

Thus, some relationship beliefs are more adaptive than others (Cobb et al., 2013). These perspectives can gradually change over time as our romances wax

Attachment Styles and Perceptions of Partners

Relationship beliefs can vary a lot from person to person, and another individual difference that's closely tied to the way people think about their partnerships is attachment style (Gillath et al., 2016). People with different styles are thought to have different "mental models" of relationships; they hold different beliefs about what relationships are like, expect different behavior from their partners, and form different judgments of what their partners do. I've already noted that secure people are more likely than those with insecure styles to employ relationship-enhancing attributions (Kimmes et al., 2015); they're also less likely to hold maladaptive relationship beliefs (Stackert & Bursik, 2003). Secure people trust their partners more (Mikulincer, 1998), believe that their partners are more supportive (Collins & Feeney, 2004), and have more positive expectations about what the future holds (Birnie et al., 2009). They're also more likely than insecure people to remember positive things that have happened in the past (Miller & Noirot, 1999). Even their dreams are different; compared to those who are insecure, secure people portray others in their dreams as being more available and supportive and as offering greater comfort (Mikulincer et al., 2011). In general, then, people with secure styles are more generous, optimistic, and kindly in their judgments of others than insecure people are.

Attachment styles *can* change, as we saw in chapter 1, but no matter what style people have, they tend to remember the past as being consistent with what they're thinking *now* (Feeney & Cassidy, 2003). Happily, if positive experiences in a rewarding relationship help us gradually develop a more relaxed and trusting outlook on intimacy with others, we may slowly forget that we ever felt any other way.

and wane (Willoughby et al., 2015b), but they can also change with education and insight (Sharp & Ganong, 2000). Indeed, if you recognize any of your own views among the dysfunctional beliefs three pages back, I hope that these findings are enlightening. Unrealistic assumptions can be so idealistic and starry-eyed that no relationship measures up to them, and distress and disappointment are certain to follow.

Expectations

When relationship beliefs are wrong, they may *stay* wrong. In contrast, people can also have more specific expectations about the behavior of others that are initially false but that become true (Rosenthal, 2006). I'm referring here to **self-fulfilling prophecies,** which are false predictions that become true because they lead people to behave in ways that make the erroneous expectations come true. Self-fulfilling prophecies are extraordinary examples of the power of perceptions because the events that result from them occur only because people expect them to, and then act as if they will.

Let's examine Figure 4.4 together to detail how this process works. As a first step in a self-fulfilling prophecy, a person whom we'll call the *perceiver forms an*

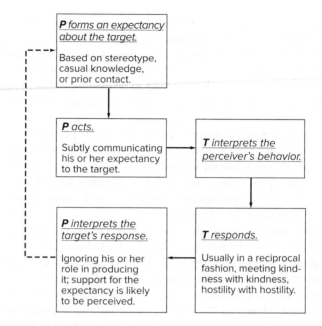

FIGURE 4.4. **A self-fulfilling prophecy.**
Originally false expectations held by a perceiver (*P*) can seem to come true when he or she interacts with someone else, his or her target (*T*).

expectancy about someone else—the *target*—that predicts how the target will behave. Various information about the target, such as his or her age, sex, race, physical attractiveness, or social class may affect the perceiver's judgments in ways of which the perceiver is unaware.

Then, in an important second step, the *perceiver acts,* usually in a fashion that is in accord with his or her expectations. Indeed, it may be hard for the perceiver to avoid subtly communicating what he or she really thinks about the target. People with favorable expectations, for instance, interact longer and more often with their targets, sharing more eye contact, sitting closer, smiling more, asking more questions, and encouraging more responses than do perceivers who have less positive expectations (Rosenthal, 2006).

The recipient of the perceiver's behavior is likely to notice all of this, and the *target's interpretation* will influence his or her response (Stukas & Snyder, 2002). In most cases, however, when the *target responds* in the fourth step, it will be in a manner that is similar to the perceiver's behavior toward him or her. Enthusiasm is usually met with interest (Snyder et al., 1977), hostility with counterattacks (Snyder & Swann, 1978a), and flirtatiousness with allurement (Lemay & Wolf, 2016b). Thus, the perceiver usually elicits from the target the behavior he or she expected, and that may be nothing like the way the target would have behaved if the perceiver hadn't expected it.

But such is the nature of a self-fulfilling prophecy that, as the *perceiver interprets the target's response,* the perceiver is unlikely to recognize the role that

The Power of Perceptions

Partners' perceptions can be very consequential.

Idealizing Our Partners. Happy partners construct *positive illusions* that emphasize their partners' virtues and minimize their faults.

Attributional Processes. The explanations we generate for why things happen are called *attributions.* Partners are affected by *actor/observer effects* and *self-serving* biases, and they tend to employ either *relationship-enhancing* or *distress-maintaining* patterns of attribution.

Memories. We edit and update our memories as time goes by. This process of *reconstructive memory* helps couples stay optimistic about their futures.

Relationship Beliefs. Our assumptions about the role marriage will play in our lives take the form of *marital paradigms. Dysfunctional relationship beliefs* such as *destiny beliefs* are clearly disadvantageous. *Growth beliefs* are more realistic and profitable.

Expectations. Our expectations about others can become *self-fulfilling prophecies,* false predictions that make themselves come true.

Self-Perceptions. We seek reactions from others that are self-enhancing and complimentary *and* that are consistent with what we already think of ourselves— with *self-verification* leading people to seek intimate partners who support their existing self-concepts.

Impression Management

We try to influence the impressions of us that others form.

Strategies of Impression Management. Four different strategies of impression management—*ingratiation, self-promotion, intimidation,* and *supplication*—are commonplace.

Impression Management in Close Relationships. High *self-monitors* are less committed to their romantic partners, but all of us work less hard to present favorable images to our intimate partners than to others.

So, Just How Well Do We Know Our Partners?

We generally don't understand our partners as well as we think we do.

Knowledge. As a relationship develops and partners spend more time together, they typically do understand each other better.

Motivation. The interest and motivation with which people try to figure each other out help to determine how insightful and accurate they will be.

Partner Legibility. Some personality traits, such as extraversion, are more visible than others.

Perceiver Ability. Some judges are better than others, too. *Emotional intelligence* is important in this regard.

Threatening Perceptions. However, when accurate perceptions would be worrisome, intimate partners may actually be motivated to be inaccurate.

Perceiver Influence. Perceptions that are initially inaccurate may become more correct as we induce our partners to become the people we want them to be.

Summary. Right or wrong, our judgments matter.

CHAPTER 5

Communication

NONVERBAL COMMUNICATION
♦ VERBAL COMMUNICATION ♦ DYSFUNCTIONAL
COMMUNICATION AND WHAT TO DO ABOUT IT
♦ FOR YOUR CONSIDERATION ♦ CHAPTER SUMMARY

Imagine that you and your romantic partner are seated alone in a comfortable room, revisiting the topic of your last disagreement. Your conversation is more structured than most because before you say anything to your partner, you record a quick rating of what you intend to say next. You rate the intended impact of your message by pushing one of five buttons with labels ranging from *super negative* through *neutral* to *super positive.* Then, after you speak, your partner quickly rates his or her perception of your message in the same way before replying to you. This process continues as you take turns voicing your views and listening to what your partner says in return. You're engaging in a procedure called the *talk table* that allows researchers to get a record of both your private thoughts and your public actions. The notable point is that if you're currently unhappy with your relationship, you may not *intend* to annoy or belittle your lover, but you're likely to do so, anyway. Unhappy couples don't differ on average from happy, contented couples in what they are trying to say to each other, but the impact of their messages—what their partners think they hear—is more critical and disrespectful nonetheless (Gottman et al., 1976). And this is consequential because this single afternoon at the talk table predicts how happy the two of you will be later on; spouses whose communications are frustrating will be less happily married 5 years later (Markman, 1981).

Communication is incredibly important in intimate relationships. And it's more complex than we usually realize (Vangelisti, 2015). Let's consider the simple model of communication shown in Figure 5.1. Communication begins with the sender's intentions, the message that the sender wishes to convey. The problem is that the sender's intentions are private and known only to him or her; for them to be communicated to the listener, they must be encoded into verbal and non-verbal actions that are public and observable. A variety of factors, such as the sender's mood or social skill, or noisy distractions in the surrounding environment, can influence or interfere with this process. Then, the receiver must decode the speaker's actions, and interference can occur here as well (Albright et al., 2004). The final result is an effect on the receiver that is again private and known only to him or her.

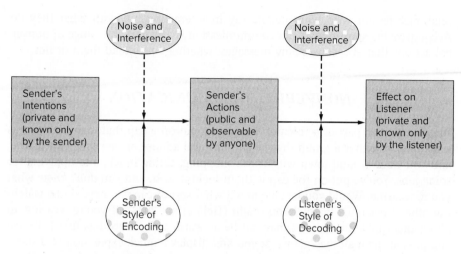

Source: Adapted from Gottman, J. M., Notarius, C., Gonso, J., & Markman, H. A couple's guide to communication. Champaign, IL: Research Press, 1976.

FIGURE 5.1. **A simple model of interpersonal communication.**
There is often a discrepancy—an *interpersonal gap*—between what the sender intends to say and what the listener thinks he or she hears.

The point here is that getting from one person's intentions to the impact of that person's message on a listener involves several steps at which error and mis-understanding may occur (Puccinelli, 2010). We usually assume that our messages have the impact that we intended, but we rarely *know* that they do. More often than we realize (Vangelisti, 2015), we face an **interpersonal gap** in which the sender's intentions differ from the effect on the receiver. Indeed, such gaps are actually *more* likely to occur in close relationships than they are among strangers (Savitsky et al., 2011). We don't expect our partners to misunderstand us, so we don't work as hard as we do with strangers to check that we're on the same page.

Interpersonal gaps are frustrating. And not only are they related to dissatisfac-tion, they can even prevent rewarding relationships from ever beginning! Consider what happens when a shy man has a chance to make his interest in dating a woman known to her. Chatting after class, he may make a timid, innocent inquiry—"What are you doing this weekend?"—thinking that his romantic intentions are transparent and hoping for an enthusiastic reply. Unfortunately, he probably thinks that his amorous aims are more obvious to his potential partner than they really are (Cameron & Vorauer, 2008). If she fails to notice that he's hinting about a date and makes a bland, noncommittal response, he may perceive an explicit rejection of a clear-cut invitation that she never actually received. Wounded, he may then keep his distance, and she may never realize what has transpired.

This sort of thing actually happens (Vorauer et al., 2003). I don't want it to happen to you, however, so I'll do what I can in this chapter to help you close your own interpersonal gaps. But we'll start our survey of communication in relationships not with what people say in interaction but with what they *do*. Accompanying spoken words in communication is a remarkable range of nonverbal actions that also carry many messages, whether you intend them or not.

NONVERBAL COMMUNICATION

Imagine that as part of a research study, you put on a cap that identifies you as a member of either a group that people like and admire or one that they loathe, and you walk around town with it on, shopping, eating lunch, and applying for some jobs. You've put on the cap without looking at it, and you *don't know* what you're wearing. Would you be able to tell what sort of cap you have on by watching others' reactions to you? You might (Hebl et al., 2002). If you're wearing an obnoxious cap, your waitress may not be as warm and cheerful as usual. People you pass at the mall may glance at you and display a quick expression of distaste or disgust. Even if no one mentions your cap, others' behavior may clearly indicate that they don't like what they see. In fact, because you'd be curious and alert to how others responded, their sentiments might be unmistakably plain.

In such a situation, you'd probably notice the remarkable amount of information carried by nonverbal behavior, which includes all of the things people do in their interactions except for their spoken words and syntax. Indeed, nonverbal behavior can serve several functions in our transactions with others. Table 5.1 lists five such functions, and I'll emphasize three of them.

First, nonverbal behavior **provides information** about people's moods or meaning. If you playfully tease someone, for instance, your facial expression and the sound of your voice may be the only way listeners can tell that you don't intend to be antagonistic. This function is so important that we have had to invent emojis, the imitation facial expressions people put in text messages, to sometimes show what we mean.

Second, nonverbal behavior also plays a vital part in **regulating interaction.** Non-verbal displays of interest often determine whether or not a conversation ever begins, and, thereafter, subtle nonverbal cues allow people to take turns as they talk seamlessly and gracefully.

Finally, by expressing intimacy and carrying signals of power and status, nonverbal behavior helps to **define** the **relationships** we share with others. People who are intimate with each other act differently toward one another than acquaintances do, and dominant, high-status people act differently than subordinates do. Without a word being spoken, observers may be able to tell who likes whom and who's the boss.

How are these functions carried out? The answer involves all of the diverse components of nonverbal communication, so we'll survey them next.

Components of Nonverbal Communication

One clue to the enormous power of nonverbal communication is the number of different channels through which information can be transmitted. I'll describe seven: facial expressions, gazing behavior, body movement, touch, interpersonal distances, smells, and paralanguage.

TABLE 5.1. Functions of Nonverbal Behavior in Relationships

Category	Description	Example
Providing information	A person's behavior allows others to make inferences about his or her intentions, feelings, traits, and meaning	A husband's facial expression leads his wife to judge that he is upset
Regulating interaction	Nonverbal behavior provides cues that regulate the efficient give-and-take of smooth conversations and other interactions	A woman starts looking steadily at her partner as the tone of her voice drops on her last word, and he starts speaking because he knows she's finished
Defining the nature of the relationship	The type of partnership two people share may be evident in their nonverbal behavior	Lovers stand closer to each other, touch more, and look at each other more than less intimate partners do
Interpersonal influence	Goal-oriented behavior designed to influence someone else	As a person requests a favor from his friend, he leans forward, touches him on the arm, and gazes intently
Impression management	Nonverbal behavior that is managed by a person or a couple to create or enhance a particular image	A couple may quarrel on the way to a party but then hold hands and pretend to be happy with each other once they arrive

Source: Data from Patterson, M. L. More than words: The power of nonverbal communication. *Barcelona, Spain: Aresta, 2011.*

Facial Expression

People's facial expressions signal their moods and emotions in a manner you'll recognize anywhere you go (Hwang & Matsumoto, 2016). Even if you don't speak the language in a foreign country, for example, you'll be able to tell if others are happy: If they are, the muscles in their cheeks will pull up the corners of their mouths, and the skin alongside their eyes will crinkle into folds. Obviously, they're *smiling,* and happiness, like several other emotions—sadness, fear, anger, disgust, surprise, and contempt—engenders a unique facial expression that's the same all over the world. In fact, the universality of these expressions suggests that they are hardwired into our species. People don't *learn* to smile when they're happy—they're born to do it. People who have been blind all their lives, for instance, display the same facial expressions all the rest of us do (Hwang & Matsumoto, 2016).

Compelling information is often available in facial expressions. Are you displaying a big smile in your Facebook profile photo, or do you look like a sourpuss? The bigger the smiles college students posted during their first semester at school, the more satisfied they were with their social lives and their college careers when they were seniors 4 years later (Seder & Oishi, 2012). In fact, the smiles people display in their college yearbooks predict their chances of being divorced later in

Nonverbal Behavior and Sexual Orientation
Or, "Don't Ask, Don't Tell"? Who Has To Ask?

For 17 years, from 1994 to 2011, the U.S. Armed Forces maintained a "don't ask, don't tell" policy toward the sexual orientation of their personnel. Fearing that open same-sex sexuality would undermine the cohesion of its troops—something that, as it turned out, didn't happen (Belkin et al., 2013)—the military asked its gays and lesbians not to advertise their orientations. Of course, the policy assumed that someone's sexual orientation wasn't already obvious— but often it is. "Gaydar" exists: Nonverbal channels of information allow attentive observers to assess the orientations of others very quickly with reasonable accuracy. A 10-second video of a person's body movements is all observers need to make correct judgments 72 percent of the time (Ambady et al., 1999).

What's visible in the videos? The patterns of a person's gestures and movement are key. Heterosexual men tend to swagger, swinging their shoulders when they walk, and heterosexual women tend to sway, moving their hips. People whose behavior includes the motions that are typical of the other sex are likely to be judged to be homosexual, and those perceptions are often correct (Johnson et al., 2007). Differences in posture and gazing are evident when people are just sitting and chatting, too (Knöfler & Imhof, 2007).

But the most remarkable result of these studies is the finding that people who get a glimpse of men's faces that lasts for only *half a second* can accurately judge whether they are gay or straight about 60 percent of the time, and they do almost as well when the faces are turned upside down (Tabak & Zayas, 2012)! How? The differences are subtle, but gay men tend to have shorter, rounder noses and more feminine faces than straight men do (Rule, 2017). So, an attentive observer often has some idea of whether someone shares his or her sexual orientation before a single word is said, and this is true around the world (Rule et al., 2011a).

shakes your hand. People with firm, full, long handshakes tend to be more extraverted and open to experience, and less neurotic, than people with wimpy handshakes are (Chaplin et al., 2000).

So, touch may be informative from the moment two people meet. Thereafter, different types of touches have distinctly different meanings. Positive, supportive feelings such as love (which, for instance, might lead you to stroke someone's arm) and sympathy (with you patting it) engender touches that are quite different from those that communicate disgust (pushing) or anger (hitting). The emotions communicated by touch are often so distinct, both the recipient of the touch and bystanders watching it can tell what feelings are at work even when the touch is all they see (Hertenstein, 2011).

Two people also tend to touch each other more when their relationship is more intimate (Debrot et al., 2013), and that's a good thing. Loving touches are actually good for our health: Kissing your partner more often can reduce your cholesterol (Floyd et al., 2009), affectionate touch from your partner reduces your production of stress hormones (Burleson et al., 2013), and getting a lot of hugs makes it less likely that you'll catch a cold (Cohen et al., 2015). Touch can clearly convey closeness and affection, and it can have healing properties, too.[1]

Interpersonal Distance

One aspect of touching that makes it momentous is that people have to be near each other for touching to occur. That means that the two partners are typically in a region of *interpersonal distance*—the physical space that separates two people—that is usually reserved for relatively intimate interactions. The **intimate zone** of interpersonal distance extends out from the front of our chests about a foot-and-a-half (Hall, 1966). (See Figure 5.2.) If two people are standing that close to each other face-to-face, their interaction is probably either quite loving or quite hostile. More interactions occur at greater distances in a **personal zone** that ranges from 1½ to 4 feet away from us. Within this range, friends are

FIGURE 5.2. **Zones of interpersonal distance.**
There are four discrete regions of space in which different kinds of social interaction are likely to occur.

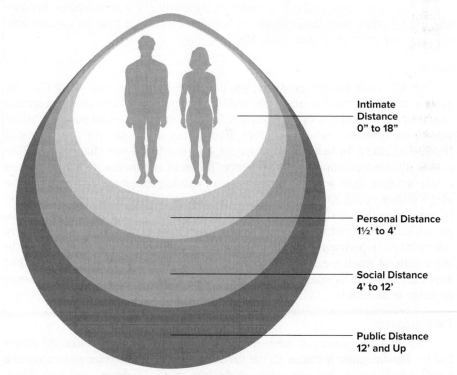

Intimate
Distance
0" to 18"

Personal Distance
1½' to 4'

Social Distance
4' to 12'

Public Distance
12' and Up

---

[1] But not everyone likes a lot of touching. People who are high in avoidance of intimacy (see page 17) don't like to cuddle with either their lovers or their children as much as the rest of us do (Chopik et al., 2014), and they take less comfort in being touched by a friend or lover, too (Jakubiak & Feeney, 2016). Evidently, compared to those with secure styles of attachment, they're less comfortable with both psychological *and* physical closeness.

likely to interact at smaller distances and acquaintances at larger ones, so distancing behavior helps to define the relationships people share. Even further away, in a **social zone** (4 to 12 feet), interactions tend to be more businesslike. When you sit across a desk from an interviewer or a professor, you're in the social zone, and the distance seems appropriate; however, it would seem quite odd to stand 5 feet away from a good friend to hold a personal conversation. Beyond 12 feet, interactions tend to be quite formal. This is the **public zone,** which is used for structured interaction like that between an instructor and his or her students in a lecture class.

These distances describe the general patterns of interactions among North Americans, but they tend to be larger than those used by many other peoples of the world (Matsumoto et al., 2016). French, Latin, and Arabic cultures prefer distances smaller than these. A person's sex and status also affect distancing behavior (Holland et al., 2004). Men tend to use somewhat larger distances than women do, and people usually stand further away from others of high status than from those of lower power and prestige. Whatever one's preferences, however, spacing behavior is a subtle way to calibrate the desired intimacy of an interaction, and it may even be an indirect measure of the quality of a relationship: Spouses who are unhappy keep larger distances between each other than do spouses who are currently content (Crane et al., 1987).

Smell

If you're near enough to others, you can *smell* them, too, and you'll likely be gaining more information than you realize. Different emotions cause people to emit different chemicals, or *chemosignals,* from their bodies—and people who are scared, for instance, have a different aroma than do those who are disgusted (Pazzaglia, 2015). In fact, the atmosphere in a movie theater changes as a film evokes different emotions in its audience; different chemicals are exhaled when a film is funny than when it is suspenseful, causing measurable changes in the air (Williams et al., 2016). And whether or not we realize it, we can be affected by chemosignals like these: When people are exposed to the armpit odors of others who are happy, they feel happier, too (de Groot et al., 2015)! Smells carry information, so perhaps it should be no surprise that people who were born without a sense of smell are at an interpersonal disadvantage; such men, for example, have only one-fifth as many sexual relationships during their lives as normal men do (Croy et al., 2013).

Paralanguage

The final component of nonverbal communication isn't silent like the others can be. *Paralanguage* includes all the variations in a person's voice other than the actual words he or she uses, such as rhythm, pitch, loudness, and rate. Thus, paralanguage doesn't involve *what* people say, but *how* they say it (Frank et al., 2013). Good examples of distinctive paralanguage are the sounds we make—without using any words at all—that can tell people what we're feeling. If you wanted to show someone with just a brief sound that you were scared, or angry, or sad, could you do it? How about relieved, amused, or awed? Research participants are indeed able to reliably communicate these emotions and several more to listeners without using words, and this is true around the world (Cordaro et al., 2016).

Paralanguage helps define relationships because lovers tend to talk to each other differently than friends do. When they start a phone call by saying "how are you?," men use a lower pitch with their lovers than with their friends, but women use a higher pitch—and strangers listening in can usually tell whether a friend or lover is on the other end of the call (Farley et al., 2013). Moreover, listeners who hear brief clips of simultaneous laughter (but nothing else) taken from the conversations of various couples can tell with 61 percent accuracy whether the two people are friends or strangers who have just met—and this, too, is true all over the world (Bryant et al., 2016). Laughter appears to be a nonverbal language we all understand. (Friends sound more spontaneous and relaxed, with shorter bursts of laughter that have more irregular volumes and pitch; listen for yourself at http://www.pnas.org/content/suppl/2016/04/05/1524993113.DCSupplemental)

Some voices are routinely more beguiling than others as well. Women like their men to have deep, low-pitched voices (O'Connor et al., 2014), and around the world, winners of presidential elections typically have lower-pitched voices than the losers do (Banai et al., 2017). And voices *are* a cue to a partner's mate value because people with appealing voices tend to have alluring faces and bodies, too (Smith et al., 2016). Even more intriguingly, if you listen to tapes of a variety of women counting from 1 to 10 at various times during their menstrual cycles, you'll hear that a woman's voice becomes more attractive just before she ovulates each month (Pipitone & Gallup, 2008). This is probably due to the effects of her changing hormones on her larynx, and it doesn't happen in women who are on the pill—but when nature is allowed to run its course, this is a fine example of the subtlety with which nonverbal channels communicate important information from one person to another.

Combining the Components

I've introduced the components of nonverbal communication as if they are independent, discrete sources of information, and, in one sense, they are: Each of them can have its own effects on interaction. Usually, however, they reinforce each other, working together to convey consistent information about a person's sentiments and intentions. When you're face-to-face with someone, all of these components are in play, and together, they'll tell you what people really mean by what they say. Consider *sarcasm*, for instance, when people say one thing but mean another: Their true intent is conveyed not in their words but in their actions and paralanguage. Most of the time, our nonverbal behavior communicates the same message as our words, and we like people better when that's the case (Weisbuch et al., 2010). But when there *is* a discrepancy between people's words and actions, the truth behind their words usually lies in their nonverbal, not their verbal, communication (Vrij, 2006).

Furthermore, all the channels may be involved in the nonconscious behavioral **mimicry** that occurs during a conversation when the participants adopt similar postures and mannerisms, display comparable expressions, and use similar paralanguage. If they're enjoying their interaction, people tend to synchronize

Zits ©2008 Zits Partnership. Distributed by King Features Syndicate, Inc.

Our facial expressions and our paralanguage usually combine to make our feelings and meanings plain to attentive audiences.

their nonverbal behavior automatically without thinking about it; if one of them scratches his or her nose, the other is more likely to do so as well. When this occurs, the conversation tends to flow smoothly, and, more importantly, they tend to like each other even when they don't notice the mutual imitation taking place (Chartrand & Lakin, 2013). Indeed, it seems to be rewarding to be met with nonverbal behavior from others that resembles our own. In one demonstration of this effect, participants watched a persuasive argument from an avatar in a virtual reality that either used the recorded movements of a real person or simply mimicked the participant's own actions with a 4-second delay. People were not consciously aware of the mimicry, but they attributed more positive traits to the avatar and were more convinced by its argument when it duplicated their own actions than when it behaved like someone else (Bailenson & Yee, 2005). (Is this the future of high-tech advertising?) We are evidently charmed and more at ease when nonverbal mimicry takes place, and it can be surprisingly stressful to interact with someone who does not imitate us at all (Kouzakova et al., 2010).

The various components of nonverbal behavior also allow us to fine-tune the intimacy of our interactions to establish a comfortable level of closeness (Patterson, 2011). Imagine that you're seated next to an acquaintance on a two-person couch when the conversation takes a serious turn and your acquaintance mentions an intimate personal problem. If this development makes you uncomfortable—if you've just received too much information—you can adjust the perceived intimacy of your interaction by nonverbally "backing off." You can turn away and lean back to get more distance. You can avert your gaze. And you can signal your discomfort through less animated paralanguage and a less pleasant facial expression, all without saying a word (Andersen et al., 2006). Nonverbal communication serves several important functions in interaction and is the source of useful subtlety in social life.

Nonverbal Sensitivity

Given all this, you might expect that it's advantageous for couples to do well at nonverbal communication, and you'd be right. The sensitivity and accuracy with which couples read, decode, and correctly interpret each other's nonverbal behavior predict how happy their relationship will be (Fitness, 2015). Husbands and wives who do poorly tend to be dissatisfied with their marriages, and, moreover, when such problems occur, it's usually the husband's fault (Noller, 2006).

What? How do we arrive at such a conclusion? Well, when nonverbal exchanges fail, there may be errors in encoding or decoding, or both (Puccinelli, 2010): The sender may enact a confusing message that is difficult to read (that's poor encoding), or the receiver may fail to correctly interpret a message that is clear to everyone else (and that's poor decoding). Women typically start with an advantage at both tasks because, if no deception is involved, women are both better encoders and more astute decoders than men are on average (Brody & Hall, 2010). (Men and women don't differ in their abilities to detect deception, as we'll see in chapter 10.) Thus, stereotypes about "women's intuition" (Gigerenzer et al., 2014) actually have a basis in fact; more than men, women tend to attentively use subtle but real nonverbal cues to discern what's going on. Do women possess more skill at nonverbal communication, or are they just working harder at it? That's a good question, and I'll answer it shortly.

Researchers can assess the quality of husbands' and wives' encoding and decoding by asking them to send specific nonverbal messages that are then decoded by the other spouse. The messages are statements that can have several different meanings, depending on how they are nonverbally enacted; for instance, the phrase, "I'm cold, aren't you?" could be either an affectionate invitation ("Come snuggle with me, you cute thing") or a spiteful complaint ("Turn up the damn heat, you cheapskate!"). In research on nonverbal sensitivity, a spouse is assigned a particular meaning to convey and is filmed sending the message. Then, impartial strangers are shown the film. If they can't figure out what the spouse is trying to communicate, the spouse's encoding is assumed to be faulty. On the other hand, if they *can* read the message but the other spouse *can't,* the partner's decoding is implicated.

In the first ingenious study of this sort, Patricia Noller (1980) found that husbands in unhappy marriages sent more confusing messages and made more decoding errors than happy husbands did. There were no such differences among the wives, so the poorer communication that Noller observed in the distressed marriages appeared to be the husbands' fault. Men in troubled marriages were misinterpreting communications from their wives that were clearly legible to total strangers. Even worse, such husbands were completely clueless about their mistakes; they assumed that they were doing a fine job communicating with their wives, and they were confident that they understood their wives and that their wives understood them (Noller & Venardos, 1986). The men were doing a poor job communicating and didn't know it, and that's why they seemed to be at fault.

On the other hand, to be fair, nonverbal marital miscommunication is not entirely due to husbands' shortcomings. In another study, Noller (1981) compared spouses' accuracy in decoding the other's messages to their accuracy in decoding communications from strangers. In unhappy marriages, *both* the husbands and wives understood strangers better than they understood each other. When they were dissatisfied, everyone was communicating poorly, despite being capable of adequate nonverbal communication with others.

This is a key point because, now that you're becoming a more sophisticated consumer of relationship science, you've probably already realized that a correlation between nonverbal miscommunication and relationship dissatisfaction is consistent with several possibilities. On the one hand, the partners' nonverbal skills may determine how satisfying their relationships are; poor skills may result in poor relationships, but good skills may promote pleasurable partnerships. On the other hand, the partners' satisfaction may determine how hard they work to communicate well; poor relationships may engender lazy (mis)communication, and good relationships may foster good communication.

Actually, both of these propositions are correct. Nonverbal insensitivity makes someone a less rewarding partner than he or she otherwise would be (Määttä & Uusiautti, 2013). But once partners grow dissatisfied for any reason, they tend to start tuning each other out, and that causes them to communicate less adeptly than they could if they really tried (Noller, 2006). In this fashion, nonverbal insensitivity and dissatisfaction can become a vicious cycle, with each exacerbating the other.

In any case, people's problems with communication may stem from either skill deficits or performance deficits, and the distinction is an important one. Some people simply aren't very talented at nonverbal communication, and their deficits are provocative (and a little eerie). For instance, men who beat their wives have more trouble than nonviolent men figuring out what their wives are feeling (Marshall & Holtzworth-Munroe, 2010). And abusive mothers have trouble identifying signs of distress in infants; they tend not to know when their babies are scared and unhappy (Wagner et al., 2015). It's possible, then, that skill deficits give some people blind spots that make them less likely to realize just how much harm they are doing to others.

So, why is it that women do better at nonverbal communication than men do? Skill and motivation both seem to be involved: Men's performance improves when they're motivated to pay close attention and to judge others correctly, but they never do better than women (Hall & Mast, 2008), who naturally seem to judge others' emotions more quickly and accurately than men do (Thompson & Voyer, 2014). Given the frustrating impact of nonverbal miscommunication, men's poorer performances can be a nuisance, so here's a tip: Watch someone's eyes. Women spend more time watching others' eyes than men do, and that appears to be one reason why they read others' expressions more accurately (J. K. Hall et al., 2010). And as this tip suggests, training and practice *can* improve one's skills (Blanch-Hartigan et al., 2012). The good news is that both men and women do better at nonverbal communication when they look and listen and put their minds to it, and we're usually more adept at reading our intimate partners' nonverbal cues than those of acquaintances or strangers (Zhang & Parmley, 2011). The bad news is that lazy inattention from either partner is likely to lead to more misunderstanding and less happiness and satisfaction than a couple would otherwise enjoy (Fitness, 2015).

VERBAL COMMUNICATION

If nonverbal communication is so important, what about the things we actually say to each other? They are probably even more consequential, of course (Solomon & Theiss, 2013). Verbal communication is a vital part of close relationships, and it is extensively involved in the development of intimacy in the first place.

Self-Disclosure

Imagine that as part of a psychology experiment, you meet a stranger and answer questions that lead you to gradually reveal more and more personal information about yourself (Aron et al., 1997). The questions aren't intimate at first—"Given the choice of anyone in the world, whom would you want as a dinner guest?"— but they slowly get more personal: "If you could go back in your life and change any one experience, what would it be and why?" "When did you last cry in front of another person? By yourself?" The stranger answers similar questions, and 45 minutes later, you know a lot of personal details about each other. What would happen? Would you like the stranger more than you would have if the two of you had just shared small talk for the same amount of time? In most cases, the answer is definitely "yes." Experiences such as these usually generate immediate closeness between the participants. People who open up to each other, even when they're just following researchers' instructions, like each other more than do couples who do not reveal as much (Slatcher, 2010).

The process of revealing personal information to someone else is called **self-disclosure.** It is one of the defining characteristics of intimacy: Two people cannot be said to be intimate with each other if they do not share some personal, relatively confidential information with one another (Laurenceau et al., 2004).

How Self-Disclosure Develops

Of course, in real life, meaningful self-disclosure takes longer than 45 minutes. Most relationships begin with the exchange of superficial information—"small talk"—and only gradually move to more meaningful revelations. The manner in which this occurs is the subject of **social penetration theory,** which holds that relationships develop through systematic changes in communication (Altman & Taylor, 1973). People who have just met may feel free to talk with each other about only a few relatively impersonal topics: "Where are you from?" "What's your major?" But if this superficial conversation is rewarding, they're likely to move closer to each other by increasing two aspects of their communication:

1. Its *breadth:* the variety of topics they discuss, and
2. Its *depth:* the personal significance of the topics they discuss.

According to the theory, if we diagram all the things there are to know about someone, self-disclosure at the beginning of a new relationship is likely to take the form of a wedge that's both narrow (only a few different topics are being discussed) and shallow (only impersonal information is being revealed). (See Figure 5.3.) As the relationship develops, however, the wedge should become broader (with more topics being discussed) and deeper (with more topics of personal significance being revealed).

In general, that is what happens (Derlega et al., 2008). In addition, early encounters between acquaintances usually involve obvious *reciprocity* in self-disclosure. New partners tend to match each other's level of openness, disclosing more as the other person does, and disclosing less if the other person's self-disclosure declines. Just how much people reveal about themselves, then, tends to depend on the specific partner and may vary considerably from relationship to relationship (Dindia, 2002). This also tends to be a gradual process, with new

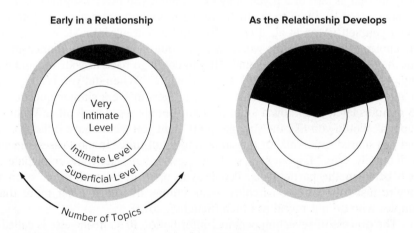

FIGURE 5.3. **Altman and Taylor's wedge of social penetration.**
If information about someone exists in several layers, self-disclosure increases in both *breadth* and *depth* as a relationship develops.

Are You a High "Opener"?

Some people are especially good at eliciting self-disclosure from others. Lynn Miller, John Berg, and Rick Archer (1983) developed the Opener Scale to assess this ability, and people who get high scores really do draw out more intimate information from others than do people who receive low scores on the scale. They do this through both verbal and nonverbal channels: High openers appear more attentive during conversation—gazing and nodding more, and looking interested—and they verbally express more interest in what others are saying (Purvis et al., 1984). They seem to be absorbed by what others have to say, so they tend to be very good interviewers (Shaffer et al., 1990).

Women tend to be better openers than men (Miller et al., 1983). The average score for women on the Opener Scale is 31, whereas 28 is typical for men. If your own score is 5 points higher than average, you're a fairly high opener, but if it's 5 points lower, your score is rather low. You can figure your score by rating yourself on each item using this scale:

0	1	2	3	4
Strongly disagree	Disagree	Neither agree nor disagree	Agree	Strongly agree

The Opener Scale

1. People frequently tell me about themselves.
2. I've been told that I'm a very good listener.
3. I'm very accepting of others.
4. People trust me with their secrets.
5. I easily get people to "open up."
6. People feel relaxed around me.
7. I enjoy listening to people.
8. I'm sympathetic to people's problems.
9. I encourage people to tell me how they are feeling.
10. I can keep people talking about themselves.

partners moving toward deeper topics by stages rather than all at once. Saying too much too soon can be risky; it violates others' expectations and often makes a poor impression (Buck & Plant, 2011). The best strategy is usually to be patient. Take turns instead of engaging in long monologues, and allow measured reciprocity to gradually increase the intimacy of your interactions (Sprecher & Treger, 2015).

However, an **interpersonal process model of intimacy** proposed by Harry Reis and Phillip Shaver (1988) argues that genuine intimacy is likely to develop between two people only when certain conditions have been met. When we open up to others, we want our disclosures to be received with apparent interest, sympathy, and respect. That is, we want *responsiveness* from others that indicates that they understand us and care about us. If they are suitably responsive, trust builds, disclosures deepen, and intimacy increases; alternatively, if they seem disinterested or uncaring, we back off and our disclosures decrease. So, for two people to become close, three things have to happen. First, they have to engage in meaningful self-disclosure. Relationships that are characterized by authenticity, openness, and honesty involve more commitment and are generally more satisfying than superficial partnerships are (Wickham et al., 2015). Then, they have to respond to each other's personal information with interest and empathy—and in heterosexual relationships, it's particularly valuable when men do this (Mitchell et al., 2008). Finally—and this is important—they each have to recognize that the other *is* being responsive. The judgment that one's partner is understanding and caring, which is known as *perceived partner responsiveness*, is a key part of the ongoing process by which intimacy develops (Laurenceau et al., 2005). If we don't perceive our partners to be caring, understanding, and respectful, we'll not tell them our secrets.

Secrets and Other Things We Don't Want to Talk About

Even when a relationship becomes quite intimate, we'll probably keep some things to ourselves. Social penetration is almost never total, and it probably shouldn't be because partners like and need some privacy, too (Petronio 2010). Both intimate self-disclosure *and* selective secrecy contribute to marital satisfaction (Finkenauer et al., 2009), and some privacy is desirable even in a close, intimate relationship. In general, "the value of openness should be balanced against other values, such as politeness, respectfulness, and discretion" (Caughlin & Basinger, 2015, p. F2). (I'm reminded of a cover story in *Cosmopolitan* magazine that asked, if you've had an affair, "Should You Ever Tell?" Their answer, after much discussion, was "probably not.")

Of course, it's not always easy to keep a secret, especially in an intimate relationship. Doing so is often quite stressful (Larson et al., 2015), and it's risky, too: Relationships are undermined when people learn that their partners are concealing something (Aldeis & Afifi, 2015). Why go to the trouble? There are several possible reasons. When they intentionally withhold information from others, "people generally long to protect themselves, protect their relationships, or protect others" (Afifi et al., 2007, p. 79). It's pretty straightforward, really: When people believe that keeping a secret is more trouble than it's worth, they usually reveal it to others after a while (Caughlin & Vangelisti, 2009). On the other hand, if they worry that they or others may be harmed by an unwanted truth, they may strive to conceal it forever.

There may also be important issues that both partners simply don't want to talk about. Explicitly or implicitly, partners may agree to steer clear of **taboo topics,** sensitive matters that, in their opinion, may threaten the quality of their relationship. Curiously, the most common taboo topic is the state of the relationship itself; in one survey, 68 percent of the respondents acknowledged that the current or future state of their romantic relationships was a subject that was better off not being mentioned (Baxter & Wilmot, 1985). (Other common taboos involved current relationships with *other* partners, avoided by 31 percent of the respondents, and past relationships [25 percent]. Discussion of past sexual experiences is also

Cautious Communication: Coming Out

You probably know someone who's openly gay or lesbian. LGBs (lesbians, gays, and bisexuals) are much more likely to announce their sexual identities to friends and family, and to do so at earlier ages, than was the case a generation ago (Hunter, 2007). Public acknowledgments of their identities are still important milestones for most LGBs, however, and it's an action they usually take thoughtfully and cautiously (if they do so at all).

LGBs typically know for sure that they are gay, lesbian, or bisexual when they are teenagers, but they don't tell anyone until three years later (at age 18 for gay men, 20 for bisexuals, and 21 for lesbian women, on average) (Martos et al., 2015). Their first disclosures usually go well, resulting in supportive, positive reactions because the confidant is commonly a trusted friend (Savin-Williams, 2005). But it's a year later when they first tell a parent, usually their mothers, and some parents never learn the truth; about two-thirds of gays and lesbians have come out to their mothers, but only half have told their fathers. Overall, about three-fourths of gays and lesbians have told most of the important people in their lives of their sexual orientations, but only

28 percent of bisexuals have done so (Pew Research Center, 2013).

So, although concealing one's true sexual identity is stressful (Riggle et al., 2017), LGB teens usually live with a big secret for several years before telling anyone (and a few never do). Why so long? It's usually because they correctly recognize that their disclosure will be a turning point in their relationships with their families. And they rarely wish to injure anyone; instead, they seek to be honest and authentic rather than secretive and distant (Hunter, 2007). They disclose the truth to be closer to the ones they love, and the good news is that they usually succeed: They usually receive support from their friends, and over time most parents come to accept their same-sex orientation with either equanimity or encouragement (Legate et al., 2012). Nevertheless, coming out is often a mixed blessing: Compared to their peers who are still closeted, lesbians who have recently come out are less likely to be depressed, but gay men are *more* likely to be depressed (Pachankis et al., 2015). Regrettably, announcing one's authentic identity can still make one a target of discrimination. How will you react if a friend comes out to you?

routinely avoided [Anderson et al., 2011].) People are often keenly interested in the likely future of their partnerships and are eager to learn their partners' expectations and intentions—but they don't ask (Knobloch et al., 2013). Instead, romantic partners may create *secret tests* of their lovers' fidelity and devotion (Baxter & Wilmot, 1984). They watch closely to see how their lovers respond to other attractive people (that's a "triangle test"); they contrive difficulties that the lover must overcome in order to demonstrate his or her devotion (an "endurance test"); and they find reasons to be apart to see how enthusiastically their lovers welcome their return (a "separation test"). This all seems like a lot of trouble when they could simply ask the partner what he or she is thinking—and they *do* often ask the partner's *friends*—but in many relationships, such matters seem too delicate to be discussed openly. But watch out: The more taboo topics there are in a relationship, the less satisfied the partners are unless they feel that they're avoiding touchy topics to promote and protect their relationship (Dillow et al., 2009). Ducking discussions because of cowardice or incompetency erodes partners' satisfaction, but politely working together to maintain the partnership rarely has ill effects.

Self-Disclosure and Relationship Satisfaction

The bottom line is that the more self-disclosure romantic couples share, the happier they tend to be. Self-disclosure that fits the situation breeds liking and contentment in close relationships, and that occurs for several reasons (Collins & Miller, 1994). First, we tend to reveal more personal information to those we like. If we're attracted to others, we tend to be more open with them. However, we also tend to like others *because* we have self-disclosed to them. Everything else being equal, opening up to others causes us to like them more. Finally, and perhaps most importantly, it's rewarding to be entrusted with self-disclosures from others. People who engage in intimate disclosures are liked more by others than are those who say less about themselves (Sprecher et al., 2013b). So, it feels good to give and to receive self-disclosures, and this aspect of verbal communication is an essential building block of close relationships. Try it yourself for 45 minutes, and you'll probably make a new friend (Slatcher, 2010).

Finally, self-disclosure is not only good for our relationships, it's good for *us*. Compared to those who engage in more superficial small talk, people who have substantive, deep conversations and who make themselves known to others enjoy better health (Sloan, 2010) and more satisfaction with life (Mehl et al., 2010). And there's a particular sort of self-disclosure that you should absolutely, positively engage in more often: Tell those you love that you love them. Your honest expressions of fondness, regard, affection, and care are powerful rewards for those who want to be close to you (Hesse & Mikkelson, 2017), and it's not enough just to have such feelings; you have to *communicate* them in a way that makes them plain (Burleson et al., 2013). But here's the real point of this paragraph: Affectionate communication is not just affirming and pleasing to your partner; it also can be remarkably beneficial to you. In lab studies, people who get randomly assigned to write love letters that express their affection for their partners experience improved neuroendocrine responses to stress (Floyd et al., 2007b) and, over time, lower cholesterol levels, heart rates, and blood pressures (Floyd et al., 2007a). Tell your partners of your affection for them. It'll be good for both of you.[2]

Gender Differences in Verbal Communication

People have made a lot of money writing books that describe men and women as different species that come from different planets and speak different languages. I'm trying to combat that simple-minded way of thinking throughout this book because the sexes really are more similar than they are different. However, there are some gender differences in verbal communication that can influence our interactions. For instance, men and women don't speak different languages, but they do sometimes talk about different things.

---

[2]There's no need to tell them I put you up to it.

Attachment Styles and Communication

Attachment styles are evident in communicative behavior. Compared to those who are insecure, people with secure styles generally exhibit warmer, more expressive nonverbal behavior involving more laughter, smiling, gazing, and touching; their lower concern about acceptance from others and their greater comfort with closeness is apparent in their actions (Tucker & Anders, 1998). Secure people are also more affectionate (Hesse & Trask, 2014) and keep fewer secrets (Merrill & Afifi, 2015) than insecure people do.

In particular, people who are high in avoidance of intimacy tend to be especially closelipped; they engage in less self-disclosure (Bradford et al., 2002) and express their emotions less openly (Kafetsios, 2004) than less avoidant people do. They also decode others' expressions of positive emotions less accurately (Kafetsios et al., 2014) and judge others' negative emotions to be more intense and hostile than they really are (Overall et al., 2015). (Do you see how such misperceptions can lead people to keep a defensive distance from others?) By comparison, people with secure styles are more open and accurate with their intimate partners than avoidant people are, and those are two reasons why their partnerships are more satisfying as the years go by (Tan et al., 2012).

People who are high in anxiety about abandonment are more talkative; if anything, in their nervous quest for intimacy and acceptance, they routinely self-disclose too much, too soon (Mikulincer & Shaver, 2013). In general, though, the most relaxed and responsive communicators are those who are low in both avoidance and anxiety—that is, those who are secure. They're the most desirable confidants (Mikulincer & Shaver, 2013).

Topics of Conversation

If you read a transcript of a conversation between two friends, would you be able to tell if the participants were men or women? You might. Among themselves, women are more likely than men to discuss their feelings about their close relationships and other personal aspects of their lives. Feelings and people figure prominently in both the conversations and text messages of women (Fox et al., 2007). In contrast, men tend to stick to more impersonal matters, discussing objects and actions such as cars and sports, gossiping about celebrities and politicians instead of friends, and seeking a few laughs instead of support and counsel (McHugh & Hambaugh, 2010). As a result, the conversations men have with each other tend to be less intimate and personal than the conversations women share (Reis, 1998).

However, when men and women interact with each other, these differences are less apparent than you might think. When young adults chatted with strangers online using written messages, they were generally *un*able to correctly guess the sex of the person they were chatting with if the researchers didn't tell them. The sorts of things that distinguish men's and women's conversations (such as the latest sports results) rarely came up, so there was usually no way to determine

Texts, Tweets, and Status Updates: Modern (Mis?)Communication

We send a lot of text messages these days, and they offer us great convenience, global reach, and the opportunity for even more confusion in our communication with others. Texts, tweets, and other forms of computer-mediated communication (or CMC) differ in important ways from actually talking to someone. For one thing, we can take our time to consider what we want to say if we wish. Also, no "leaky" nonverbal behavior is involved, so we have more control over the messages we send. These qualities make CMC seem safer and more manageable to some people than actual conversation is, so that, for instance, shy people are more comfortable chatting online than they are face-to-face (Van Zalk et al., 2011).

Text is a more pallid form of communication than talking, however, so we often go to some trouble to specify how a statement is meant to be read. *Most* of our e-mails contain at least one phrase that should not be taken literally (Whalen et al., 2009), so we offer instructions such as emojis that clarify our meaning. Hi, out there in textbook land, by the way: {*_*} The problem is that we usually think that we've resolved any doubt and that our messages are more exact and unambiguous than they really are. Because we know what we mean, we typically fail to appreciate how easily others can take our words differently (Kruger et al., 2005). Interpersonal gaps abound online.

Still, despite frequent misunderstandings, there's an amazing amount of information about people available in CMC. For instance, strangers get some insight into our personalities from the Twitter handles and e-mail addresses we choose (Back et al., 2008b), and if we use lots of exclamation points in our messages, they'll probably think we're female (McAndrew & De Jonge, 2011). We also seem extraverted when we expand instead of abbreviate words and use a lot more characters than we need (as in "bitchhhhhhhhhhhh") (Holtgraves, 2011). But those stylistic nuances pale by comparison to the wealth of personal details that many of us intentionally self-disclose on social networking sites. Almost everybody posts their birthdays, and most people post their hometowns—key bits of info that are hugely valuable to identity thieves—and of course, that just scratches the surface of the personal data people put out there. People aren't entirely heedless of their privacy on Facebook, but they manage it less attentively online than they do in face-to-face communication.

Overall, though, the most important aspect of CMC for our relationships is the manner in which it provides us private *access* to others (Vanden Abeele et al., 2017). Texting provides a way to be in (almost) continuous contact, and young adults typically exchange texts with those they're dating every single day (Boyle & O'Sullivan, 2016). Notably, however, a constant stream of superficial and trivial messages seems to result in *lower* satisfaction with a relationship (Rains et al., 2016); contented partners send high proportions of more meaningful messages that contain thoughtful self-disclosures, affirmations and assurances, and other useful news (McEwan & Horn, 2016).

Still, CMC doesn't provide the same rewards we routinely gain from talking to people in person (Goodman-Deane et al., 2016). Our connection with, and focus on, others is shallower when we're typing out a message (Lipinski-Harten & Tafarodi, 2012). So, when we're troubled, we get more comfort from talking to others than from texting them (Iacovelli & Johnson,

2012), in part because the familiar sound of a partner's voice reduces the stress hormones in our blood (Seltzer et al., 2012).

So, CMC certainly isn't perfect, and it can be disadvantageous if it begins to interfere with rich face-to-face interaction with others (Roberts & David, 2016). But most of us are clearly at home with our keypads, and CMC is here to stay. And that's the end of this box. Thanks for reading it. TTFN. LUMTP.

with whom one was chatting (Williams & Mendelsohn, 2008). What differences there are in men's and women's discourse are clearly rather subtle.[3]

Styles of Conversation

Women speak somewhat less forcefully than men do, being more indirect and seeming less certain (Leaper & Robnett, 2011). It's a style of conversation in which one uses hedges to soften assertions and asks questions instead of making straightforward statements, as in this wry example: "Women are sort of more tentative than men, aren't they?" (Palomares, 2009, p. 539). It's not clear, however, that this tentativeness stems from a lack of assertion; it may just reflect greater concern for others' feelings (Leaper & Robnett, 2011). Supporting that possibility, women are also less profane (McHugh & Hambaugh, 2010).

There are also hackneyed stereotypes that suggest that women are more talkative than men, but that is not the case. Portable recordings of their interactions demonstrate that college women speak 16,215 words a day, on average, whereas men speak 15,559. It's a trivial difference (Mehl et al., 2007). What's more striking is that men speak up and say something less often than women do, but when they do get started, they talk longer, brooking no interruption (Leaper & Ayres, 2007). Women speak more often but produce fewer monologues.

So, despite some stereotypes to the contrary, there aren't sizable global differences in the way men and women talk. However, there *are* meaningful differences in language use from one person to the next, and the words we use are so informative that strangers can get accurate impressions of us by overhearing a few minutes of our conversation (Holleran et al., 2009). Our personalities are apparent in the words we use. For example, a careful analysis of the writings of almost 700 bloggers found that words such as *awful, worse, horrible,* and *annoying* were used more often by people who were high in neuroticism than by those who were less prone to fretfulness and worry. *Drinks* and *dancing* characterized extraverts, and *visiting, together, hug,* and other such friendly terms were related to agreeableness (Yarkoni, 2010).[4] Our vocabulary really does tell others who we are, and, notably, two people are likely to be more attracted to each other at first meeting if they use language the same way (Ireland et al., 2011).

---

[3] And seriously, isn't it a little ridiculous to suggest that men and women come from different planets and speak different languages when, if we don't already know who they are, we can't even tell them apart?

[4] If you don't quite recall what these traits are, take a look back at page 28.

Self-Disclosure

So far, we haven't encountered big differences in men's and women's verbal communication. But here's a difference that matters: In established relationships, women are more self-disclosing than men are, and in keeping with their higher scores on the "Opener" scale (on page 153), they elicit more self-disclosure from others, too (Dindia, 2002). Indeed, men tend to offer their female partners more intimate self-disclosures than they provide their male best friends—and the result is that interactions that include a woman tend to be more intimate and meaningful than are interactions that involve only men (Reis, 1998). Men open up to women, and women are open among themselves, but men disclose less to other men.

An important consequence of all this is that men often depend more on women for emotional warmth and intimacy than women do on them in return (Wheeler et al., 1983): Whereas women may have intimate, open, supportive connections with partners of both sexes, heterosexual men are likely to share their most meaningful intimacy only with women. Consequently, a man may need a woman in his life to keep him from being lonely, but women don't usually need men this way in return.

Instrumentality versus Expressivity

Importantly, however, this difference between men and women in self-disclosure is a *gender* difference that is more closely associated with people's gender roles than with their biological sex. Women engage in intimate verbal communication with trusted partners because they tend to be high in expressivity[5] and are comfortable talking about their feelings. This also comes naturally to men who are high in expressivity, as androgynous men are, and such men tend to have meaningful, intimate interactions with both sexes just as women do (Aubé et al., 1995). So, to refine the point I just made, it's really just traditional, macho men who have superficial conversations with their best friends (Shaffer et al., 1996) and who need relationships with women to keep from being lonely (Wheeler et al., 1983). In contrast, androgynous men (who are both assertive *and* warm) self-disclose readily to both sexes and enjoy meaningful interactions with all their friends; as a result, they tend not to be lonely, and, as a bonus, they spend more time interacting with women than less expressive, traditional men do (Reis, 1986).

Given this, it's silly to think that men and women speak different languages and come from different planets. Many men *are* more taciturn than the average woman, but there are also men who are more open and self-disclosing than most women are. The typical intimacy of a person's interactions is tied to his or her level of expressivity, and once you take that into account, it doesn't matter whether the person is a man or woman. Moreover, expressivity is a trait that ranges from low to high in both women and men, so it makes more sense to take note of individual differences in communicative style than to lump all men together and treat them as a group distinct from women.

Indeed, people also vary in how loquacious and effusive they are. Some of us put our thoughts and feelings into words quickly—we blurt out whatever we're

---

[5] *Expressivity, instrumentality,* and *androgyny?* See pages 24–27.

thinking and thereby engage in animated, rapid-fire conversation—whereas others of us are slower, more deliberate, and more hesitant in verbalizing our feelings. The word is a bit goofy, but these differences in verbal style are said to be individual differences in **blirtatiousness** (Swann & Rentfrow, 2001). A talkative, highly blirtatious woman and a taciturn, close-mouthed man may get along fine when they meet (Swann et al., 2006)—he doesn't have to say much because she's happy to do all the talking—but they make a precarious match if they settle down together (Swann et al., 2003). She's likely to dominate the discussion of the conflicts that arise (as they always do; see chapter 11), and that pattern violates traditional expectations that make men the heads of their households. This doesn't bother progressive, androgynous men, but it does frustrate traditional guys, who tend to be dissatisfied in the long run when they are paired with assertive, talkative women (Angulo et al., 2011). Gender role stereotypes obviously influence what we take for granted in heterosexual interaction.

Indeed, men value instrumental communication skills such as the ability to give clear instructions and directions more than women do. And women value expressive communication skills such as expressing affection and feelings more than men do. Still, both men and women consider expressive skills to be more important in close relationships than instrumental skills are (Burleson et al., 1996). They are sometimes caricatured as speaking different languages, but men and women agree that the ability to adequately communicate one's love, respect, and regard for one's partner is indispensable in close relationships (Floyd, 2006).

DYSFUNCTIONAL COMMUNICATION AND WHAT TO DO ABOUT IT

As we've seen, the more self-disclosing partners are, the more satisfied they tend to be. But not all our efforts to speak our minds and communicate with our partners have positive results. More often than we realize, an interpersonal gap causes misunderstanding in those who hear what we have to say. And the nature and consequences of miscommunication are very apparent in relationships in which the partners are distressed and dissatisfied. The verbal communications of unhappy partners often just perpetuate their discontent and make things worse instead of better.

Miscommunication

Indeed, we can gain valuable insights into what we shouldn't do when we talk with others by carefully comparing the communicative behaviors of happy lovers to those of unhappy partners. John Gottman and his colleagues at the University of Washington did this for over 30 years, and they observed several important patterns. First, unhappy people do a poor job of *saying what they mean* (Gottman, 1994b). When they have a complaint, they are rarely precise; instead, they're prone to **kitchen-sinking,** in which they tend to address several topics at once (so that everything but the "kitchen sink" gets dragged into the conversation). This usually causes their primary concern to get lost in the barrage of frustrations that are announced at the same time. If they're annoyed by overdrawn fees on a debit card, for instance, they may say, "It's not just your carelessness; it's about your drinking and your lousy attitude about helping out around the house." As a result, their conversations frequently drift **off-beam,** wandering from topic to topic so that the conversation never stays on one problem long enough to resolve it: "You never do what I ask. You're just as hard-headed as your mother, and you always take her side." Flitting from problem to problem on a long list of concerns makes it almost certain that none of them will get fixed.

Second, unhappy partners do a poor job of *hearing each other.* They rarely try to patiently double-check their understanding of their partners' messages. Instead, they jump to conclusions (often assuming the worst) and head off on tangents based on what they presume their partners really mean. One aspect of this is **mindreading,** which occurs when people assume that they understand their partners' thoughts, feelings, and opinions without asking. All intimate couples mindread to some extent, but distressed couples do so in critical and hostile ways; they tend to perceive unpleasant motives where neutral or positive ones actually exist: "You just said that to make me mad, to get back at me for yesterday." Unhappy partners also **interrupt** each other in negative ways more than contented couples do. Not all interruptions are obnoxious. People who interrupt their partners to express agreement or ask for clarification may actually be communicating happily and well. But people who interrupt to express disagreement or to change the topic are likely to leave their partners feeling disregarded and unappreciated (Daigen & Holmes, 2000).

Distressed couples also listen poorly by finding something wrong or un-workable with anything their partners say. This is **yes-butting,** and it communicates constant criticism of the others' points of view: "Yeah, we could try that, but it won't work because. . . ." Unhappy partners also engage in **cross-complaining** that fails to acknowledge others' concerns; instead of expressing interest in what their partners have to say, they just respond to a complaint with one of their own:

"I hate the way you let the dishes pile up in the sink."
"Well, I hate the way you leave your clothes lying around on the floor."

Finally, unhappy partners too often display *negative affect* when they talk with each other (Gottman & Levenson, 1992). They too often react to their partner's complaints with sarcastic disregard that is demeaning and scornful, and instead of mending their problems, they often make them worse. Damaging interactions like these typically begin with clumsy **criticism** that attacks a partner's personality or character instead of identifying a specific behavior that is causing concern. For instance, instead of delineating a particular frustration ("I get annoyed when you leave your wet towel on the floor"), a critic may inflame the interaction by making a global accusation of a character flaw ("You are such a slob!"). **Contempt** in the form of insults, mockery, or hostile humor is often involved as well. The partners' common response to such attacks is **defensiveness;** instead of treating the clumsy complaint as legitimate and reasonable, the partners seek to protect themselves from the unreasonable attack by making excuses or by cross-complaining, hurling counterattacks of their own. **Stonewalling** may follow as a partner "clams up" and reacts to the messy situation by withdrawing into a stony silence (Eldridge & Baucom, 2012). People may believe they're helping the situation by refusing to argue further, but their lack of responsiveness can be infuriating (Arriaga et al., 2014b). Instead of demonstrating appropriate acknowledgment and concern for a partner's complaints, stonewalling typically communicates "disapproval, icy distance, and smugness" (Gottman, 1994b, p. 94). Ultimately, destructive **belligerence** may occur with one partner aggressively rejecting the other altogether ("So what? What are you gonna do about it?").

When communication routinely degenerates into these contentious patterns, the outlook for the relationship is grim (Lannin et al., 2013). Surly, churlish communication between spouses predicts discontent and distress down the road (Markman et al., 2010). In fact, videotapes of just the first 3 minutes of a marital conflict enable researchers to predict with 83 percent accuracy who will be divorced 6 years later (Carrère & Gottman, 1999). Couples whose marriages are doomed display noticeably more contempt, defensiveness, and belligerence than do those who will stay together. And among those who stay together, spouses who communicate well are happier and more content than those who suffer frequent misunderstanding (Lavner et al., 2016).

The challenge, of course, is that it's not always easy to avoid these problems. When we're angry, resentful, or anxious, we may find ourselves cross-complaining, kitchen-sinking, and all the rest. How can we avoid these traps? Depending on the situation, we may need to send clearer, less inflammatory messages, listen better, or stay polite and calm, and often we need to do all three.

Saying What We Mean

Complaints that criticize a partner's personality or character disparage the partner and often make mountains out of molehills, portraying problems as huge, intractable dilemmas that cannot be easily solved. (Given some of the broad complaints we throw at our partners, it's no wonder that they sometimes get defensive.) It's much more sensible—and accurate—to identify as plainly and concretely as possible a specific behavior that annoyed us. This is **behavior description,** and it not only tells our partners what's on our minds but also focuses the conversation on discrete, manageable behaviors that, unlike personalities, can often be readily changed. A good behavior description specifies a particular event and does not involve generalities; thus, words such as *always* or *never* should never be used. This is *not* a good behavior description: "You're always interrupting me! You never let me finish!"

We should also use **I-statements** that specify our feelings. I-statements start with "I" and then describe a distinct emotional reaction. They force us to identify our feelings, which can be useful both to us and to our partners. They help us to "own" our feelings and to acknowledge them instead of keeping the entire focus on the partner. Thus, instead of saying, "You really piss me off," one should say, "I feel pretty angry right now."

Communicating Sympathy and Concern

Few of us know what to say when we encounter bereaved others who are suffering from the loss of a loved one. We want to express sympathy and support, but our words often seem inadequate to the task. However, grief, and others' reactions to it, have been studied by relationship researchers (Wortman & Boerner, 2007), and I can offer some advice about this important kind of communication. First, you *should* mention the person's loss (Toller, 2011). The death of a beloved is a huge loss, something that the person will never forget (Carnelley et al., 2006). Assuming that the person's pain has ended or is no longer salient to him or her, even months later, is simply insensitive. Talking about the lost partner acknowledges the person's distress and communicates caring and concern. It may not be easy for you to do (Lewis & Manusov, 2009), but it's kind.

What should you say? Something simple. Try "I'm so sorry," or "I feel so sad for you" and then *stop*. Do not mention any of your own tales of woe. Do not imply that the loss is not the most tragic, awful thing that has ever happened. Do not try to comfort the person with optimistic projections about the future. And do not offer advice about how the person can put his or her life back together. Such efforts may spring from good intentions, but each of them ultimately demeans the person's current suffering. Offer heartfelt sympathy and nothing more. Just nod your head and be a good listener and be nonjudgmental.

Thus, offering welcome comfort to others is more straightforward than you may have thought, as long as you avoid the pitfalls of saying too much. With this in mind, can you see what's wrong with the following dumb remarks? Each is a quote from someone who was probably trying—and failing—to be helpful (Wortman & Boerner, 2007):

"The sooner you let go, the better."

"Crying won't bring him back."

"He should have been wearing a seat belt."

"God needed her more than you did."

"You're young, you can have other children."

"You have many good years left."

A handy way to use both behavior descriptions and I-statements to communicate more clearly and accurately is to integrate them into **XYZ statements.** Such statements follow the form of "When you do **X** in situation **Y**" (that's a good behavior description), "I feel **Z**" (an I-statement). Listen to yourself next time you complain to your partner. Are you saying something like this:

"You're so inconsiderate! You never let me finish what I'm saying!"

Or, are you being precise and accurate and saying what you mean:

"When you interrupted me just now, I felt annoyed."

There's a big difference. One of those statements is likely to get a thoughtful, apologetic response from a loving partner, but the other probably won't.

Zits ©2007 Zits Partnership. Distributed by King Features Syndicate, Inc.

This interaction would be going better if Mom had used a reasonable behavior description and Jeremy wasn't cross-complaining defensively. Do you see how both of them are communicating poorly?

Active Listening

We have two vital tasks when we're on the receiving end of others' messages. The first is to accurately understand what our partners are trying to say, and the second is to communicate that attention and comprehension to our partners so that they know we care about what they've said. Both tasks can be accomplished by **paraphrasing** a message, repeating it in our own words and giving the sender a chance to agree that that's what he or she actually meant. When people use paraphrasing, they don't assume that they understood their partners and issue an immediate reply. Instead, they take a moment to check their comprehension by rephrasing the message and repeating it back. This sounds awkward, but it is a terrific way to avoid arguments and conflict that would otherwise result from misunderstanding and mistakes. Whenever a conversation begins to get heated, paraphrasing can keep it from getting out of hand. Look what's wrong here:

WILMA: (sighing) I'm so glad your mother decided not to come visit us next week.
  FRED: (irate) What's wrong with my mother? You've always been on her case, and I think you're an ungrateful witch!

Perhaps before Fred flew off the handle, some paraphrasing would have been helpful:

WILMA: (sighing) I'm so glad your mother decided not to come visit us next week.
  FRED: (irate) Are you saying you don't like her to be here?
WILMA: (surprised) No, she's always welcome. I just have my paper due in my relationships class and I won't have much time then.
  FRED: (mollified) Oh.

Another valuable listening skill is **perception checking,** which is the opposite of mindreading. In perception checking, people assess the accuracy of their inferences about a partner's feelings by asking the partner for clarification. This communicates one's attentiveness and interest, and it encourages the partner to be more open: "You seem pretty upset by what I said, is that right?"

Listeners who paraphrase and check their perceptions make an *active* effort to understand their partners, and that care and consideration is usually much appreciated (Bodie et al., 2015). In terms of the interpersonal process model of intimacy, they are being *responsive*, and that's a good thing. Active listening like this is likely to help smooth the inevitable rough spots any relationship encounters. Indeed, people who practice these techniques typically report happier marriages than do those who simply assume that they understand what their partners mean by what they say (Markman et al., 1994).

> **A Point to Ponder**
>
> When was the last time you asked your partner if your perception of his or her feelings was accurate? Have you ever done that?

Being Polite and Staying Cool

Still, even the most accurate sending and receiving may not do much good if our conversations are too often crabby and antagonistic. It's hard to remain mild and relaxed when we encounter contempt and belligerence from others, and people who deride or disdain their partners often get irascible, irritated reactions in return. Indeed, dissatisfied spouses spend more time than contented lovers do locked into patterns of *negative affect reciprocity* in which they're contemptuous of each other, with each being scornful of what the other has to say (Levenson et al., 1994). Happy couples behave this way, too—there are probably periods of acrimonious disregard in most relationships—but they break out of these ugly cycles more quickly than unhappy partners do (Bloch et al., 2014).

In fact, defusing cycles of increasing cantankerousness when they begin is very beneficial, but it may not be easy. Although XYZ statements and active listening skills can help prevent surly interactions altogether, Gottman and his colleagues argue that people rarely have the presence of mind to use them once they get angry (Gottman et al., 2000). It can be difficult or even "impossible to make 'I-statements' when you are in the 'hating-my-partner, wanting revenge, feeling-stung-and-needing-to-sting-back' state of mind" (Wile, 1995, p. 2).

Thus, being able to stay cool when you're provoked by a partner and being able to calm down when you begin to get angry are very valuable skills. (And given that, you may want to skip ahead to page 343.) Anger results from the perception that others are causing us illegitimate, unfair, avoidable grief. Use a different point of view to reduce or prevent anger altogether (Finkel et al., 2013). Instead of thinking, "S/he has no right to say that to me!," it's more adaptive to think, "Hmm. Contrary statements from someone who loves me. I wonder why?"

Of course, it can be hard to maintain such a placid stream of thought when we're provoked. So, it's also a good idea to (try to) reduce the number of provocations you encounter by agreeing in advance to be polite to each other when you disagree (Gottman, 1994b). You may wish to schedule regular meetings at which you and your partner (politely) air your grievances; knowing that a problem will

©*Stuart Jenner/Getty Images*

Unhappy partners often have difficulty saying what they mean, hearing each other, and staying polite and calm when disagreements arise.

be addressed makes it easier to be pleasant to your partner the rest of the week (Markman et al., 1994). And under no circumstances should the two of you continue an interaction in which you're just hurling insults and sarcasm back and forth at each other. If you find yourself in such a pattern of negative affect reciprocity, take a temporary *time out* to stop the cycle. Ask for a short break—"Honey, I'm too angry to think straight. Let me take 10 minutes to calm down"—and then return to the issue when you're less aroused. Go off by yourself and take no more than six long, slow, deep breaths per minute, and you will calm down, faster than you think (Tavris, 1989).

The Power of Respect and Validation

The key ingredients in all of these components of good communication—our conscious efforts to send clear, straightforward messages, to listen carefully and well, and to be polite and nonaggressive even when disagreements occur—are the indications we provide that we care about and respect our partners' points of view. We expect such concern and regard from our intimate partners, and distress and resentment build when we think we're disrespected. Thus, **validation** of our partners that acknowledges the legitimacy of their opinions and communicates respect for their positions is always a desirable goal in intimate interaction (Kellas et al., 2013).

Validation does not require you to agree with someone. You can communicate appropriate respect and recognition of a partner's point of view without agreeing with it. Consider the following three responses to Barney's complaint:

	BARNEY: I hate it when you act that way.
Cross-complaining	BETTY: And I hate it when you get drunk with Fred.
Agreement	BETTY: Yeah, you're right. I'll stop.
Validation	BETTY: Yeah, I can see how you'd feel that way. You've got a point. But I'd like you to try to understand what I'm feeling, too.

Only the last response, which concedes the legitimacy of Barney's point of view but allows Betty her own feelings, invites an open, honest dialogue. We need not be inauthentic or nonassertive to respect our partners' opinions, even when we disagree with them.

Indeed, validating our partners will often make disagreement much more tolerable. All of the skills I have mentioned here support an atmosphere of responsive care and concern that can reduce the intensity and impact of disputes with our partners (Verhofstadt et al., 2005). You may even be able to set a troubled relationship on a more promising path by rehearsing these skills and pledging to be polite and respectful to one another when difficulties arise (Stanley et al., 2000).

FOR YOUR CONSIDERATION

James loved deer hunting season. He liked to sit shivering in a deer blind in the chill before dawn, sipping coffee, and waiting for what the day would bring. But his wife, Judy, always dreaded that time of year. James would be gone for several weekends in a row, and each time he returned he'd either be grumpy because he was empty-handed or he would have lots of venison—and extra work—for her to handle. The costs of his gas, permit, and lease were also substantial, and the expense kept them from enjoying an occasional weekend at that bed-and-breakfast at the lake she liked so much.

So, when Judy handed James a thermos of hot coffee and walked with him to the door at 4:30 in the morning on the first day of deer season, she was already feeling melancholy and lonely. She looked at him and tried to be cheerful, but her smile was forced and her expression downcast as she said in a plaintive tone, "Have a nice time, dear." James happily replied, "Okay, thanks, hon. See you Sunday night!" and was gone.

Having read this chapter, what do you think the future holds for James and Judy? Why?

CHAPTER SUMMARY

When a sender's intentions differ from the impact that a message has on the recipient, a couple faces an *interpersonal gap*.

Nonverbal Communication

Nonverbal communication serves vital functions, *providing information, regulating interaction,* and *defining the nature of the relationship* two people share.

Components of Nonverbal Communication. Nonverbal communication includes

- *Facial expression.* Facial expressions are good guides to others' moods, but cultural norms influence expressive behavior.
- *Gazing behavior.* The direction and amount of a person's looking is important in defining relationships and in regulating interaction. In addition, our pupils dilate when we're seeing something that interests us.
- *Body movement.* Gestures vary widely across cultures, but the posture and motion of the entire body are informative as well.
- *Touch.* Different types of touch have distinctly different meanings.
- *Interpersonal distance.* We use different zones of personal space—the *intimate, personal, social,* and *public* zones—for different kinds of interactions.
- *Smell.* Information about one's emotions is transmitted to others by one's smell.
- *Paralanguage.* Paralanguage involves all the variations in a person's voice—such as rhythm, rate, and loudness—other than the words he or she uses.
- *Combining the components.* Mimicry occurs when people use similar nonverbal behavior without realizing it. Nonverbal actions allow us to fine-tune the intimacy of our interactions in subtle but real ways.

Nonverbal Sensitivity. Unhappy spouses, especially husbands, do a poor job at nonverbal communication.

Verbal Communication

Self-Disclosure. Intimacy involves sharing personal information about oneself to one's partner.

- *How self-disclosure develops.* As a relationship develops, both the breadth and depth of self-disclosure increase. Intimacy develops when we perceive *responsiveness* in others that indicates that they understand us and care about us.
- *Secrets and other things we don't want to talk about.* Couples avoid *taboo topics,* and some secrecy is routine even in intimate partnerships.
- *Self-disclosure and relationship satisfaction.* Appropriate self-disclosure breeds liking and contentment, and expressions of affection are good for us.

Gender Differences in Verbal Communication. Women are more likely than men to discuss feelings and people, but men and women are equally talkative. However, macho men self-disclose relatively little to other men even when they are friends, and thus are likely to share their most meaningful intimacy only with women. A woman who is high in *blirtatiousness* is a precarious match for a taciturn man.

Dysfunctional Communication and What to Do About It

Miscommunication. Distressed couples have trouble saying what they mean, and they engage in destructive verbal behavior characterized by *kitchen-sinking*, drifting *off-beam*, *mindreading*, *interruptions*, *yes-butting*, and *complaining*, and involving *criticism, contempt, stonewalling*, and *belligerence*.

Saying What We Mean. Skillful senders use *behavior description, I-statements*, and *XYZ statements* to focus on specific actions and make their feelings clear.

Active Listening. Good listeners use *paraphrasing* and *perception checking* to understand their partners.

Being Polite and Staying Cool. Happy couples also avoid extended periods of *negative affect reciprocity*.

The Power of Respect and Validation. Partners should communicate respect and recognition of the other's point of view even when they disagree.

CHAPTER 6

Interdependency

SOCIAL EXCHANGE ◆ THE ECONOMIES OF RELATIONSHIPS
◆ ARE WE REALLY THIS GREEDY? ◆ THE NATURE OF COMMITMENT
◆ FOR YOUR CONSIDERATION ◆ CHAPTER SUMMARY

If you've been in a relationship for a while, why are you *staying* in that relationship? Are you obligated to continue it for some reason? Are you simply waiting for something better to come along? Or have you carefully shopped around, examined your options, and decided that you can't do better than your present partner? Hopefully, your current relationships have been so rewarding that you've never given much thought to any of these questions. However, they're just the sort of things we'll consider in this chapter, which will take an *economic* view of our dealings with others.

Our subject will be *interdependency,* which exists when we need others and they need us in order to obtain valuable interpersonal rewards. If I rely on you to provide me affection, support, and acceptance that I'm not getting anywhere else, and you similarly rely on me in return, we need each other and are thus "interdependent." Studies of interdependency yield fascinating explanations of why we stay in some relationships and leave others but we won't say anything about love; that's another chapter. Instead, our focus will be the spreadsheets with which we tally the profits and losses of our interactions with others. You may not yet have thought of yourself as an interpersonal accountant, but doing so provides powerful insights into the workings of close relationships.

SOCIAL EXCHANGE

Interdependency theories assume that we're all like shoppers in an interpersonal marketplace: We're all seeking the most fulfilling relationships that are available to us. And from this perspective, relationships begin when two people offer each other rewards that entice them to begin a process called **social exchange** in which they each provide to the other benefits and rewards that the other wants. When you give me (some of) what I want and I give you (some of) what you want, we engage in social exchange, the mutual exchange of desirable rewards. There are several different social exchange theories, but the ideas introduced by John Thibaut and Harold Kelley (1959; Kelley & Thibaut, 1978)—now known as *interdependence theory*—are most often used by

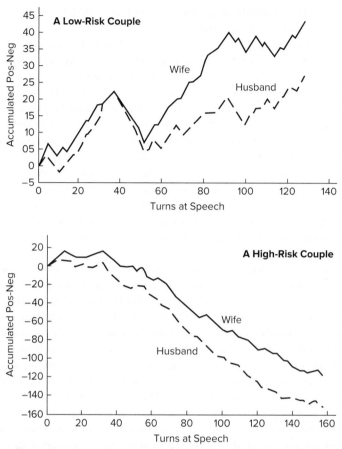

Source: Gottman, J. M., & Levenson, R. W. "Marital processes predictive of later dissolution: Behavior, physiology, and health," Journal of Personality and Social Psychology, 63, 1992, 221–233.

FIGURE 6.3. **The arguments of couples at low and high risk of divorce.**
These are the actual charts of the conversations of two couples who had returned to the topics of their last arguments. During their discussions, one couple remained (mostly) polite and collaborative whereas the other was more disrespectful, sour, and sarcastic. Which of these couples was much more likely to be separated or divorced 4 years later?[2] (Pos-Neg = number of positive vs. negative exchanges.)

notice all of the loving and affectionate behaviors their lovers provide; a study that tracked partners' perceptions for 4 weeks found that both men and women failed to notice about one-fourth of the positive behaviors that their partners said they performed (Gable et al., 2003). Husbands and wives with dismissing or fearful attachment styles are especially likely to miss some of the positive, loving things their spouses do for them. In fact, it appears that one reason such people

[2]Okay, I admit that's a dumb question. Isn't the answer obvious?

are less comfortable with interdependent intimacy is that they don't fully realize how pleasant it can be (Spielmann et al., 2013a)!

Another complication is that partners may disagree about the meaning and value of the rewards they exchange. Judgments of what favors are worth, for example, routinely differ for those who provide the favors and those who receive them (Zhang & Epley, 2009), and gender differences complicate things further. So, when spouses are asked what they would change if they could, wives say they desire more emotion and affection from their husbands whereas the husbands say they want more sex (Heyman et al., 2009). What matters to you may not be quite the same as what matters to your partner, and those differing perceptions add intricacy to your quest for mutually satisfying interaction.

Rewards and Costs Are Different

Another more subtle influence is that rewards and costs have different, separate effects on our well-being in relationships, and this causes complexity. According to research by Shelly Gable and her colleagues (Gable & Gosnell, 2013), we try to do two things in our close relationships. First, we try to obtain rewards, and second, we try to avoid costs—and importantly, these are *not* the same things. In seeking rewards, we try to satisfy an appetite for desirable experiences that is known as an **approach motivation.** That is, we pursue pleasure and our motivation for doing something is to feel good, and when we draw near to—or *approach*—desired experiences, we feel positive emotions such as enthusiasm and excitement. Approach motivations for having sex, for instance, would be to feel close to our partners and to enjoy the physical experience (Cooper et al., 2011). Our desire to avoid costs is a different drive known as an **avoidance motivation.** That is, we also seek to elude or escape punishment and pain, so we strive to *avoid un*desired experiences and to reduce negative feelings such as anxiety and fear. Avoidance motivations for having sex would be to avoid rejection or to end a peevish partner's pouting.

The key point is that our approach and avoidance motives are not just two different sides of the same coin. They don't cancel each other out. Pleasure results from fulfilling our approach goals, and pain results from failing to fulfill our avoidance goals, but—and here's where this gets really interesting—pleasure and pain are different processes. They operate independently, involving different brain mechanisms and causing distinct emotions and behaviors (Cacioppo et al., 2012). The provocative result is that pleasure and pain can coexist, or both may be absent, in any relationship. Moreover, because pleasure and pain are unrelated, safe and secure relationships in which nothing bad happens are not necessarily satisfying, and satisfying relationships are not always safe and secure.

Let's explore this more fully with a look at Figure 6.4, which shows the approach and avoidance dimensions arranged at right angles. Every relationship you have lies somewhere along both of those lines, and its current status is defined by how well you are fulfilling both your approach and avoidance goals. For instance, the vertical line is the approach dimension; relationships that are full of positive events are exciting and invigorating—so they would lie near the top of the line—whereas those that offer few positive outcomes are unfulfilling and stagnant (and they would land near the bottom). Importantly, dull relationships aren't actually painful, they're just not fun. The horizontal line is the avoidance dimension. Whether or not they're rewarding, some relationships are full of conflict and danger (which would put them on the left side of the line), whereas others are more placid (which is on the right); however, just because a partnership is safe and has no negatives doesn't necessarily mean it is fun. As Reis and Gable (2003, p. 142) asserted, "the absence of conflict and criticism in a relationship need not imply the presence of joy and fulfillment, just as the presence of joy and fulfillment need not denote the absence of conflict and criticism."

So, why do we care, exactly? There are several reasons. First, in a really great relationship, we're able to fulfill both motivations at the same time. Such relationships are full of delights and aggravations are absent, and the partnership can be said to be *flourishing* (Fincham & Beach, 2010). (Take a good long look at Figure 6.4.) And clearly, in contrast, if neither motivation is being fulfilled so that costs are high and rewards are low, a relationship is *distressed*. But because our approach and avoidance motivations operate independently, one motivation may also be fulfilled while the other is not, and that allows some interesting possibilities. Consider a relationship that offers compelling attractions—so that it is

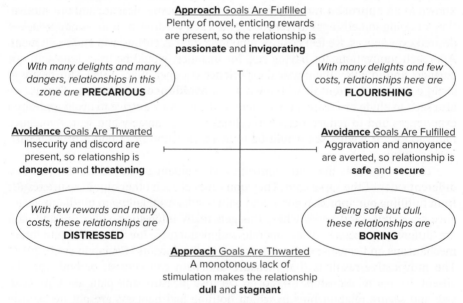

Approach Goals Are Fulfilled
Plenty of novel, enticing rewards
are present, so the relationship is
passionate and **invigorating**

With many delights and many
dangers, relationships in this
zone are **PRECARIOUS**

With many delights and few
costs, relationships here are
FLOURISHING

Avoidance Goals Are Thwarted
Insecurity and discord are
present, so relationship is
dangerous and **threatening**

Avoidance Goals Are Fulfilled
Aggravation and annoyance
are averted, so relationship is
safe and **secure**

With few rewards and many
costs, these relationships are
DISTRESSED

Being safe but dull,
these relationships are
BORING

Approach Goals Are Thwarted
A monotonous lack of
stimulation makes the relationship
dull and **stagnant**

Source: Figure based on the insights of Reis & Gable, 2003, and Fincham & Beach, 2010.

FIGURE 6.4. **Approach and avoidance processes in relationships.**
People seek rewards and want to avoid costs, but these are two different motivations that combine to influence our feelings in close relationships. When avoidance goals are fulfilled, people avoid costs but are not necessarily happy. When approach goals are fulfilled, people feel engaged and excited but may not feel safe and secure. Only when both motivations are fulfilled simultaneously are people wholly content.

passionate and exciting—but that is also replete with doubts and discord: There'd be a lot of drama, and the potent pleasures of the partnership would be infused with danger and uncertainty in a perilous and *precarious* mix. There'd be a lot to like, but one's costs would be too high, so the partners' feelings about the relationship might vacillate widely, depending on which motivation was salient to them at the time (Gable & Poore, 2008).

The interplay of the two motivations also presents a fourth possibility that's important enough to get its own paragraph. Consider what results when our avoidance goals are fulfilled and our costs and annoyances are very low—so there's really nothing to *dis*like about the relationship—but our approach motivation is unfulfilled, so there's not much to *like* about the relationship either. The partnership would have few negatives, but it would lack novelty and stimulation; it would be dull, stale, and stagnant and, in a word, *boring*. Boredom is characterized by tedium, disinterest, and a lack of energy, and it occurs when nothing enticing, intriguing, or new is occurring in an intimate relationship. There are no sparks, no excitement, no arousal, and no fun (Harasymchuk & Fehr, 2013). And, of course, this is not a good place to be: Boredom now is linked to dissatisfaction later. In the Early Years of Marriage Project,[3] spouses who thought that their marriages were becoming monotonous after a few years were less happy 9 years later than were spouses who weren't getting bored (Tsapelas et al., 2009). So, what does all this suggest we do to live happily ever after? Let me return to that in just a moment.

A second reason to note the roles of approach and avoidance motivations in our relationships is that the chronic strength of these motives differs from person to person (Gable, 2006). Bad is generally stronger than good, for instance, but some people are very sensitive to negative events that wouldn't much ruffle others (Boyce et al., 2016)—and such people may feel especially threatened by disagreements or conflict with their partners. Indeed, a strong motive to avoid costs leads people to notice all of the annoying things their partners do whereas, in contrast, a strong motive to approach rewards leads them to focus on all the thoughtful and generous things their partners do (Strachman & Gable, 2006). (Which point of view do you think leaves people more satisfied?) When they make small sacrifices to benefit their partners (such as going to a movie they don't much want to see), people with approach motives are pursuing greater intimacy with their partners; so, they feel good about their actions, and their relationships profit. In contrast, people with avoidance motives are trying to avoid conflict; they begrudge the sacrifice, and their relationships suffer (Impett et al., 2014a). And over time, people who have high approach motivations are generally less lonely and more content (Gable, 2006). They enter social situations eager to make new friends whereas people with high aversive motivations just want to avoid annoying, offending, or upsetting anybody. Evidently, it may be more beneficial to focus on obtaining rewards, rather than cutting costs, in our close relationships (Impett et al., 2013).

Finally, and perhaps most importantly, the independent operation of approach and avoidance motivations means that being happy may involve different strategies than those that are involved in *not* being *un*happy. We want to avoid painful conflict

[3]See pages 45 and 399.

and other costs, of course, but if we wish our relationships to prosper and to be fulfilling, we need to do more than simply avoid any unpleasantries. We need to combat boredom: We must strive to meet our partners' approach goals by providing them joyous, interesting, and exciting experiences (Strong & Aron, 2006).

This conclusion is also at the heart of a **self-expansion model** of human motivation that holds that we are attracted to partnerships that expand the range of our interests, skills, and experiences (Aron et al., 2013). Novel activities, the development of new talents, and the acquisition of new perspectives are all thought to be inherently gratifying (Sheldon et al., 2013), and that's why new loves are often so exhilarating: Newfound intimacy typically involves increases in knowledge and changes in mutuality that enhance and expand our self-concepts (Aron et al., 2013).

But self-expansion usually slows once a new partner becomes familiar, and that's when many partnerships begin to feel more bland and ordinary than they initially seemed (Sheets, 2014). The key to staying happy, according to the self-expansion model, is to combat boredom by creatively finding ways to continue your personal growth (Fivecoat et al., 2015). Thus, as well as continually seeking out novel activities and challenges, consider the value of intentionally inventing new ways to play and have fun and laugh together during your daily routine (Sheldon et al., 2013). Seek and invent "activities that are adventurous, passionate, playful, romantic, sexual, and spontaneous" (Malouff et al., 2015, p. 234). Monotony can make any relationship seem stale, but innovation and novelty may keep boredom at bay. (And I'll have more to say about this in chapter 14.)

So, rewards and costs are different, and minimizing our costs isn't the same thing as increasing our rewards. And as our discussion of boredom suggests, relationships begin when a couple's interactions are rewarding, but that can change with time. Indeed, despite the partners' best intentions, many relationships gradually become less satisfying as time goes by. Let's take a closer look at how rewards and costs change as relationships develop.

Rewards and Costs as Time Goes By

Here's the situation: You've started dating a new person and things are going great. Your satisfaction is rising fast, and the two of you are quickly growing closer. Does continual bliss lie ahead? *Probably not.* After a period of initial excitement that is characterized by a rapid increase in satisfaction, most relationships— even those that are destined to succeed and prosper—hit a lull in which the partners' pleasure stalls for a time (see Figure 6.5). This can be disconcerting, but it shouldn't be surprising; according to a model of **relational turbulence** created by Leanne Knobloch and Denise Solomon (2004), we should *expect* a period of adjustment and turmoil as new partners become accustomed to their increasing interdependence. In particular, as the partners spend more and more time together, they disrupt each others' routines. Instead of waiting to be asked out on a date, for instance, one of the partners may start *assuming* that they'll spend the weekend together, and that may interfere with the other's plans. The partners may also encounter some resistance from their friends as the new relationship absorbs

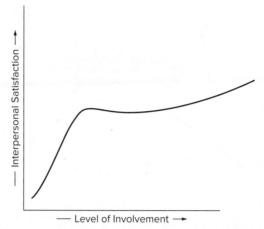

Source: Adapted from Eidelson, R. J. "Interpersonal satisfaction
and level of involvement: A curvilinear relationship," Journal of
Personality and Social Psychology, 39, 1980, 460–470.

FIGURE 6.5. **Satisfaction in beginning relationships.**
After a rapid rise in satisfaction at the very beginning of their relationships, many couples encounter a lull as they adjust to their increasing interdependence. Successful relationships survive this period of re-evaluation and become even more satisfying, but at a more gradual rate.

more of their time and they see less of their old companions. Uncertainty and doubt can also accompany emerging commitment; both partners may wonder where the relationship is going and what the future holds, and the more uncertain they are, the more turbulent the situation is likely to be (Knobloch & Theiss, 2010). Altogether, the turbulence model suggests that an unsettled period of adjustment and reevaluation often occurs at moderate levels of intimacy in a developing relationship as the partners learn to coordinate their needs and to accommodate each other.

The turbulence model in beginning relationships is depicted in Figure 6.6. When intimacy levels are low, interdependence is minimal and there is negligible interference from one's partner and few concerns about the future of the partnership. However, as the partners draw closer, they need to adjust to increasing limitations to their autonomy, rising uncertainty, and, perhaps, mounting ambivalence from their friends, and this phase—the transition from casual dating to more serious involvement in the relationship—can be tumultuous. If the relationship becomes more established and intimacy increases further, things settle down as doubts diminish, friends adjust, and the partners grow more adept at being interdependent. Successful relationships survive the turbulent transition to the partners' new status as a recognized couple, and a new but more gradual increase in satisfaction may occur as the relationship continues to develop. (Take another look at Figure 6.5.)

Turbulence may also occur down the road if a relationship undergoes a major transition, as when, for instance, babies are born (Theiss et al., 2013), a soldier

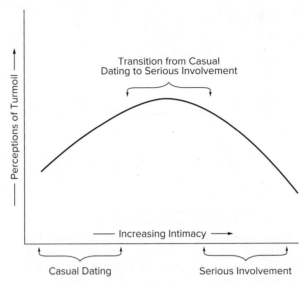

Source: Adapted from Knobloch, L. K., & Donovan-Kicken, E. "Perceived involvement of network members in courtships: A test of the relational turbulence model," Personal Relationships, *13, 2006, 281–302.*

FIGURE 6.6. **The relational turbulence model.**
The amount of turmoil and turbulence in a new relationship increases as the partners spend more time together and begin to interfere with each other's routines and to wonder where the relationship is headed. This turmoil reaches a peak when the couple decides to become more seriously involved, but it then declines as they adjust to their new interdependency.

returns home from a tour of duty (Theiss & Knobloch, 2014), or the last kid leaves home and the parents have an "empty nest" (King & Theiss, 2016). Renegotiation of old roles and expectations—and some resulting uncertainty and turmoil—are common in such situations (Solomon et al., 2016). Hopefully, however, such turbulence is temporary, because marriages are more fragile when they result from courtships in which the partners are too often uncertain about where they're heading (Ogolsky et al., 2016). And it's particularly worrisome when people have lasting doubts about whether they *should* get married in the first place; women with reservations about marrying are about 2.5 times more likely to divorce later on than are those who have no doubts (Lavner et al., 2012). (Men have such doubts more often, but they're only 1.5 times more likely to divorce as a result.)

So, periods of uncertainty can be problematic, and it's customary for new partners to experience a lull in their increasing satisfaction as they adjust to their new interdependency. Are there predictable changes in satisfaction over longer stretches of time in established relationships? There are, and I've got good news and bad news for you. Let's begin with the bad news, which starts with Figure 6.7. Pictured there are the annual reports of marital satisfaction from 538 newlywed couples, many of whom were tracked for 10 years (if they stayed married that

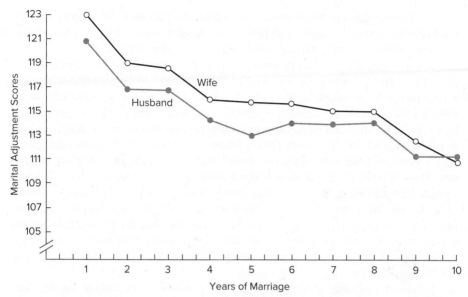

Source: Data from Kurdek, L. A. (1999). "The nature and predictors of the trajectory of change in marital quality for husbands and wives over the first 10 years of marriage," Developmental Psychology, 35, 1999, 1283–1296.

FIGURE 6.7. **The average trajectory of marital satisfaction.**
Some couples experience decreases in satisfaction that are steeper than this, but others don't experience any decline at all. In addition, on average, gay and lesbian couples experience milder decreases in satisfaction than heterosexual couples do (Kurdek, 2008b).

long). As you can see, the typical trajectory of marital bliss involved a gradual erosion of delight that resulted in people becoming less satisfied as the years rolled by (Kurdek, 1999). Even worse, recent studies that probed carefully for different trajectories of marital satisfaction over 4 (Lavner & Bradbury, 2012), 16 (Birditt et al., 2012), 20 (Anderson et al., 2010), and 35 years (James, 2015) found that in a number of couples—about one in every six—the declines in contentment were much more severe. Some newlyweds find their dreams dashed rather quickly.

The good news from the recent studies is that, despite the general trend pictured in Figure 6.7, a number of couples—about one in every four—don't experience large declines in their delight. Most American marriages don't last as long as 21 years (Elliott & Simmons, 2011), but some do, and clearly, it really is possible for some couples to live happily ever after.

What distinguishes those who stay happy from the majority who become less content? There are several influences, and none of them will surprise a careful reader of our prior chapters. Spouses who stay happy tend to be low in neuroticism and high in self-esteem, and they start their marriages being happier together than most other couples are. They discuss touchy issues with affection and humor and without anger, and they luckily encounter relatively few stressors such as economic hardship or ill health (Birditt et al., 2012). Over time, then, the outcomes of their interactions are undoubtedly more positive than those of couples who are more fretful, insecure, surly, and beset with hassles and burdens—and interdependency theory argues that that's why they stay more content.

It also turns out that happy couples keep their expectations in check so that their CLs don't get too high. Remember that it's hard to be satisfied when you expect things to be magnificent, and sure enough, on average, people who begin their marriages with the highest expectations of how special and wonderful wedlock will be are the least happy spouses a few years down the road. Justin Lavner, Ben Karney, and Tom Bradbury (2013) followed 251 newlywed couples across the first 4 years of their marriages and found that, over time, the happiest couples were those who had had the most realistic outlooks about what wedded life would be like. In contrast, spouses who had unrealistically positive expectations tended to be disappointed once the honeymoon was over. It's not a good idea to expect that "my partner and I will always be able to resolve our disagreements" or "my partner and I will always communicate well" or even that "my partner will always be interested in how my day went" (Neff & Geers, 2013, p. 60) because it's just not likely to be true.

Indeed, I can offer several reasons why prudent and cautious expectations about the futures of your intimate relationships are more reasonable and sensible than romantic idealism is. First, we all know how to be polite and thoughtful, and we can behave that way when we want to, but it takes effort. Relationships are more satisfying when people work at them (Shafer et al., 2014), but once a courtship is over and a partner is won, we usually stop trying so hard to be consistently charming. The same people who would never fart noisily on a first date may become spouses who fart at will at the dinner table, perhaps dismissing their lack of propriety by saying, "Sorry, I couldn't help it." The point is that they *could* help it if they wanted to—they just didn't go to the trouble to do so (Miller, 2001).

Second, interdependency magnifies conflict and friction. We spend lots of time with our intimate partners and depend on them for unique, especially valuable rewards, and that means that they are certain to cause us more frustration— even inadvertently—than anyone else can. For instance, we're more affected by the moods (Caughlin et al., 2000) or work stress (Karney & Neff, 2013) of intimate partners than by the similar difficulties of others. Frequent interaction also means that trivial annoyances may gradually cause real grief through sheer repetition— in much the same way that the light tapping of a slowly dripping faucet can drive you mad when you're trying to sleep at night (Cunningham et al., 2005).

Third, intimacy means that others know your secrets, foibles, and weaknesses. That gives them ammunition with which to wound and tease us when conflict occurs. But even when they have no wish to do us harm, their access to sensitive information practically guarantees that they will accidentally reveal some secret (Petronio, 2010), hurt our feelings (Malachowski & Frisby, 2015), or embarrass us (Miller, 1996) sometime or other. They can unintentionally hurt us in ways others can't.

Fourth, even if people are usually aware of most of their incompatibilities and problems before they marry, there will almost always be some surprises ahead. These tend to be of two general types. First, there's learning the truth about things we thought we knew. Good examples of this are the *fatal attractions* I mentioned in chapter 3. You may like the fact that your lover is fun-loving and spontaneous, but you may not appreciate how irresponsible, flighty, and unreliable that same behavior may seem after a few years of marriage when you have babies and a mortgage to contend with. Speaking of babies, the other type of unwelcome surprise is learning undesired things that you didn't know at all, and the real facts of parenthood are often good examples. If you don't have kids, you might assume that parenthood will be fun, your kids will be invariably adorable, and raising children will bring you and your partner closer together. The reality, however (as you know if you do have kids), is that "after the birth of a child the prognosis for the course of the marital relationship is unequivocally grim" (Stafford & Dainton, 1994, p. 270). I can safely say that parenthood is an extraordinary and often marvelous adventure, and children usually bring people more joy than misery (Nelson et al., 2013). Nevertheless, parenthood is unquestionably hard on the relationship between the parents (Luhmann et al., 2012), and although outcomes certainly vary from couple to couple (Don & Mickelson, 2014), most "people are better off without having children" (Hansen, 2012, p. 29). Kids are expensive and they're endless work, and most parents experience a steep and unexpected decline in the time they spend having fun together (Dew & Wilcox, 2011). When babies arrive, conflict increases, and satisfaction with the marriage (and love for one's partner) decrease (Doss et al., 2009), and this occurs around the world (Wendorf et al., 2011) in both gay (Huebner et al., 2012) and straight relationships. If the parents don't expect such difficulties, they're going to be surprised.

Finally, all of this means that close relationships are often much different from the blissful, intimate idylls we want them to be, and the difference between what we expected and what we get can leave us feeling cheated and disappointed, sometimes unnecessarily so (Niehuis et al., 2015). To the extent that even great relationships involve hard work and sacrifice, people with misplaced, glorified expectations about relationships may end up disappointed in their outcomes even when they're doing better than everyone else (Stoeber, 2012).

So, through (a) **lack of effort**; because (b) **interdependency is a magnifying glass;** and through (c) **access to weaponry,** (d) **unwelcome surprises,** and (e) **unrealistic expectations,** people usually encounter unanticipated costs, even in good relationships (Miller, 1997b), and most spouses' satisfaction actually declines during the first years of marriage. These are all normal processes in close relationships, so it's naïve to think that you won't encounter them. More annoyances and nuisances lie ahead than you may have thought.

This may seem gloomy, but it isn't meant to be. Indeed, I don't want this analysis to seem pessimistic at all! To the contrary, knowledge is power, and I suspect that being aware of the usual trajectory of marital satisfaction and thoroughly understanding these issues can help people avoid needless disappointment— and it may even help them to forestall or avoid a creeping decline in outcomes that would otherwise occur. If informed caution leads you to form reasonable expectations, you *should* be optimistic that your close relationships will succeed; a positive outlook that is rooted in good sense is likely to make lasting satisfaction more, rather than less, attainable (Neff & Geers, 2013).

And importantly, if nothing else, this perspective reminds us of our constant responsibility to be as pleasant as possible to those whose company we value. We want great outcomes, but so do they, and even if they like us, they'll go elsewhere if we don't provide them enough reward. This is a consequential idea, and it leads to some subtleties of the social exchange perspective that we have yet to consider.

ARE WE REALLY THIS GREEDY?

So far in this chapter, we've been portraying people as greedy hedonists who are concerned only with their own outcomes. That's not a complimentary portrayal, but it *is* useful because rewards and costs matter enormously in close relations. Research supports the basic precepts of interdependence theory quite well (Le et al., 2010). Nevertheless, our portrait so far is incomplete. There are good reasons why people will usually want their partners to prosper as well.

The Nature of Interdependency

Okay, you've got the idea: According to interdependence theory, we want maximum reward at minimum cost, and we want the best interpersonal deals we can get. Everybody behaves this way. But what happens when we get a good deal? Then we become dependent on our partners and don't want to leave them. That's significant because it means that we have an important stake in *keeping our partners happy,* so that our partners will continue providing those desired rewards. If you want to keep valued relationships going, it's to your advantage to ensure that your partners are just as dependent on you as you are on them, and a straightforward way to do that is to provide them great outcomes that make them want to stick around (Murray et al., 2009).

Pursuing this strategy can influence the value of many transactions with a desired partner. Actions that would be costly if enacted with a stranger can actually be rewarding in a close relationship because they give pleasure to one's partner and increase the likelihood that one will receive valuable rewards in return (Kelley, 1979). Providing good outcomes to one's partner, even when it involves effort and sacrifice, can ultimately be self-serving if it causes a desirable relationship to continue. Indeed, even greedy people should be generous to others if it increases their own profits! As a writer to an advice column reported, "It is heaven to be with someone who enjoys making sure I'm taken care of in every way. And it makes me want to do everything I can to see that he's happy in return" (Mitchell & Sugar, 2007, p. A6).

So, interdependence theory suggests that in the quest for good outcomes, individuals will often be magnanimous to those on whom they depend because it is reasonable (and valuable) to do so. And if both partners in a relationship want it to continue, both of them should thoughtfully protect and maintain the other's well-being. If people need each other, it can be advantageous to be positively philanthropic to each other, increasing the partner's profits to keep him or her around. Thus, even if people are greedy, there is likely to be plenty of compassionate thoughtfulness and magnanimity in interdependent relationships.

Exchange versus Communal Relationships

Indeed, when people seek closeness with others, they are often rather generous, offering more to others than they seek in return (Beck & Clark, 2009). We seem to realize that rewarding interdependency is more likely to develop when we're *not* greedily pursuing instant profit. With this in mind, Margaret Clark and Judson Mills (2012) proposed a distinction between partnerships that are clearly governed by explicit norms of even exchange and other, more generous, relationships that are characterized by obvious concern for the partner's welfare. In **exchange relationships,** people do favors for others expecting to be repaid by receiving comparable benefits in return. If they accept a kindness from someone, people feel obligated to return a similar favor to even the scales. Thus, as Table 6.1 shows, people in exchange relationships don't like to be in one another's debt; they track each other's contributions to joint endeavors; they monitor the other person's needs only when they think there's a chance for personal gain; and they don't feel bad if they refuse to help the other person. As you might expect, exchange relationships are typified by superficial, often brief, relatively task-oriented encounters between strangers or acquaintances.

In contrast, in **communal relationships,** the partners feel a special concern for the other's well-being, and they provide favors and support to one another without expecting repayment (Clark & Aragón, 2013). As a result, people who seek a communal relationship avoid strict cost accounting, and they'd rather *not* have their kindnesses quickly repaid; they monitor their partners' needs even

TABLE 6.1. Differences between Exchange and Communal Relationships

Situation	Exchange Relationships	Communal Relationships
When we do others a favor	We prefer those who pay us back immediately.	We prefer those who *don't* repay us immediately.
When others do us a favor	We prefer those who request immediate repayment.	We prefer those who do *not* request immediate repayment.
When we are working with others on a joint task	We seek to distinguish our contributions from those of others.	We don't make any clear distinction between others' work and our own.
When we help others	Our moods and self-evaluations change only slightly.	Our moods brighten and our self-evaluations improve.
When we don't help others	Our moods do not change.	Our moods get worse.
When we feel vulnerable or anxious	We are unwilling to tell others what we are feeling.	We are willing to tell others about our true feelings.
When we're married	We are less satisfied.	We are more satisfied.

Source: Beck & Clark, 2010b; Clark & Aragón, 2013; Clark et al., 2010.

when they see no opportunity for personal gain; and they feel better about themselves when they help their partners (Xue & Silk, 2012). In communal relationships, people often make small sacrifices on behalf of their partners and do costly favors for each other, but they enjoy higher quality relationships as a result (Clark & Grote, 1998). Indeed, people like marriages to operate this way, and the more generosity and communal concern spouses display toward each other, the happier they are (Clark et al., 2010).

Clearly, the extent of our generosity in response to our partners' needs can vary from relationship to relationship, and Mills and Clark and their colleagues (Mills et al., 2004) have developed a short scale to measure *communal strength,* the motivation to be responsive to a particular partner's needs (see Table 6.2). As their feelings of communal strength increase, people *enjoy* making small sacrifices for their partners (Kogan et al., 2010)—for instance, they're more willing to have sex with their partners even when their own desire is low (Muise & Impett, 2016)—and both they and their partners are happier as a result (Day et al., 2015). Thoughtful concern for the well-being of one's partner is clearly connected to closeness and contentment in intimate partnerships (Le et al., 2012).

But does the lack of apparent greed in communal relationships indicate that the principles of exchange we've been discussing do not apply there? Not at all. In businesslike relationships, debts are repaid quickly with comparable benefits, and tit-for-tat exchanges are the norm. In contrast, in close communal relationships, both partners expect that the other will be attentive and responsive to one's needs when they arise, whatever they are, and more diverse rewards are exchanged by the partners over a longer span of time. What we do to meet a partner's needs may involve very different actions from what the partner did to meet our own needs, and the reciprocity that results involves broad concern for each other instead of an exchange of specific favors (Clark & Aragón, 2013).

In addition, the partners in a profitable communal relationship may not seem to be keeping track of their specific rewards and costs because they're happy and they know they're doing well, so there's no need to fuss with the details. Being generous to each other may simply become a habit that doesn't require much thought or effort (Kammrath et al., 2015) and the partners stop scrutinizing their personal profits. However, if their outcomes start falling and their heady profits evaporate, even intimate partners in (what had been) communal relationships may once again begin paying close attention to the processes of exchange (Grote & Clark, 2001). When dissatisfaction sets in, people in (what had been) communal

TABLE 6.2. A Measure of Communal Strength (Mills et al., 2004): Some Example Items

Place a partner's initials in the blank in each item and ask yourself: How far would you be willing to go in each case?

1. How far would you go out of your way to do something for _____?

2. How much would you be willing to give up to benefit _____?

3. How high a priority for you is meeting the needs of _____?

relationships often become very sensitive to minute injustices in the outcomes they receive (Jacobson et al., 1982).

So, a distinction between exchange and communal relationships isn't incompatible with interdependence theory at all. Communal relationships don't involve the same explicit this-for-that exchange of specific benefits that occurs in exchange relationships, but they still require the profitable transfer of valuable rewards between the partners. And when they begin, the workings of communal relationships demonstrate how quickly people begin to take others' welfare into consideration and how readily people provide benefits to those with whom they wish to develop close relationships (Beck & Clark, 2009). Most people seem to recognize, as interdependence theory suggests, that if you want others to be nice to you, you've got to be nice to them.

Equitable Relationships

Another point of view argues that you not only have to be nice but also to be *fair.* **Equity** theorists extend the framework of social exchange to assert that people are most satisfied in relationships in which there is *proportional justice,* which means that each partner gains benefits from the relationship that are proportional to his or her contributions to it (Hatfield & Rapson, 2012). A relationship is equitable when the ratio of your outcomes to your contributions is similar to that of your partner, or when

$$\frac{\text{Your outcomes}}{\text{Your contributions}} = \frac{\text{Your partner's outcomes}}{\text{Your partner's contributions}}$$

Now, because this pattern involves a bit of algebra, you may already wish that I was done talking about it. But give this idea a chance! It's interesting: Relationships are fair only when both partners are getting what they deserve, given their contributions to their partnership. A relationship is fair, according to equity theory, only when a partner who is working harder to maintain the relationship is getting more out of it as well.

Let's look at some examples. Here are three equitable relationships, with outcomes and contributions rated on a 0-to-100-point scale:

	Fred		Wilma
(a)	80/50	=	80/50
(b)	20/100	=	20/100
(c)	50/25	=	100/50

In relationships (a) and (b), both partners are receiving equal outcomes and making equal contributions, but the quality of outcomes is much higher for the partners in relationship (a) than for those in relationship (b). Equity theory emphasizes fairness, not the overall amount of rewards people receive, and because both (a) and (b) are fair, they should both be satisfying to the partners. (Do you think they would be? I'll return to this point later.) Relationship (c) is also equitable even though the partners do not make equal contributions or derive equal outcomes. Wilma is working harder to maintain the relationship than Fred is, but both of them are receiving outcomes that are proportional to their contributions; each is getting two units of benefit for every unit he or she contributes, so Wilma's better outcomes are fair.

In contrast, in inequitable relationships, the two ratios of outcomes to contributions are not equal. Consider these examples:

	Fred		Wilma
(d)	80/50	≠	60/50
(e)	80/50	≠	80/30

In relationship (d), the partners are working equally hard to maintain the relationship, but one of them is receiving better outcomes than the other. That's not fair. If you and I are making similar contributions to our relationship but I'm getting more from it, you're likely to be annoyed. In (e), the partners' outcomes are the same, but their contributions are different. That, too, isn't fair. If you and I are getting similar benefits from our relationship but I'm working harder to keep it going, then *I'm* likely to be annoyed. And in fact, a notable prediction of equity theory is that in both of these cases, *both* of the partners are likely to be distressed— even if they're getting good outcomes—because neither relationship is fair. In such situations, one partner is **overbenefited**, receiving better outcomes than he or she deserves, and the other is **underbenefited**, receiving less than he or she should. Does that matter? Interdependence theory says it shouldn't, much, as long as both partners are prospering, but equity theory says it does.

The Distress of Inequity

One of the most interesting aspects of equity theory is its assertion that everybody is nervous in inequitable relationships. It's easy to see why underbenefited partners would be unhappy; they're being exploited, and they may feel angry and resentful. On the other hand, overbenefited partners are doing too well, and they may feel somewhat guilty (Guerrero et al., 2008). It's better to be over- than underbenefited, of course, but people are presumed to dislike unfairness, being motivated to change or escape it. So, equity theory proposes that the most satisfactory situation is an equitable division of outcomes; the theory expects overbenefited people to be somewhat less content than those who have equitable relationships, and underbenefited people to be *much* less satisfied (Hatfield & Rapson, 2012).

What's More Important? Being Treated Fairly or Excellent Outcomes?

A Point to Ponder

If you're treated well by your partner and are happy in your relationship, would it bother you to realize that your partner is profiting even more than you are?

Several studies that have assessed the satisfaction of spouses and other romantic couples have obtained results that fit the predictions of equity theory very nicely (e.g., Sprecher, 2017): Partners who were overbenefited were less relaxed and content than were those whose outcomes were equitable, and people who were underbenefited were less happy still. However, few of these studies took note of just how good the participants' outcomes were. (Remember, you can be over-benefited relative to how your partner is doing and still be getting crummy out-comes that could cause some dissatisfaction.) Other investigations that have assessed the quality of partners' outcomes have found that—just as interdependence theory asserts—the overall amount of reward that people receive is a better predictor of their satisfaction than is the level of equity they encounter (e.g., Cate et al., 1988). In these studies, it didn't matter what one's partner gave or got as long as one's own benefits were high enough, and the more rewards people said they received from a relationship, the better they felt about it.

There's complexity here. Some studies suggest that fairness is an important factor in the workings of intimate relationships, and some do not. One reason for these conflicting results may be that some people are more concerned with fair-ness in interpersonal relations than other people are. Across relationships, some people consistently value equity more than others do, and they, unlike others, are more satisfied when equity exists than when it does not (Woodley & Allen, 2014).

In addition, no matter who we are, equity may be more important in some domains than in others. Two sensitive areas in which equity appears to be advis-able are in the allocation of *household tasks* and *child care*. When these chores are divided equally, both spouses tend to be satisfied with their marriages: "When the burden of housework is shared, each spouse is likely to appreciate the other spouse's contribution, and there may be more leisure time for shared activities" (Amato et al., 2007, p. 166). In contrast, when one of the partners is doing most of the work, "bad feelings spill over and affect the quality of the marriage" (Amato et al., p. 166). Unfortunately, equitable allocation of these duties is often difficult for married women to obtain; even when they have similar job responsibilities outside the home, working wives in the United States provide more child care (Yavorsky et al., 2015) and do about twice as many household chores as their husbands do (Pew Research Center, 2015a). Cohabiting couples and gay and les-bian couples usually divide these tasks more fairly (Coltrane & Shih, 2010), so there may be something about heterosexual partnerships that leads husbands to expect to do less around the house. Whenever it occurs, however, this inequity clearly reduces women's satisfaction (Britt & Roy, 2014). Indeed, one general

Your parents may not have done things this way, but couples are usually happier these days when household tasks and child care are shared by the partners.

Baby Blues © 2013 Baby Blues Partnership. Distributed by King Features Syndicate, Inc.

Feminism Is Bad for Romance, Right?

Back in chapter 1, I reported that women married to traditional, masculine men are less content, on average, than are women with warmer, more expressive husbands. Now we've seen that unequal divisions of household chores breed resentment and distress. Both of these points suggest that (if you choose to marry), your chances for lasting marital bliss will be higher if you *don't* adhere to rigid, traditional expectations about what it means to be husband and wife (Stanik et al., 2013). In fact, in the United States, women enjoy happier, healthier, and more stable romantic relationships when they are partnered with men who are feminists—that is, who believe in the equality of the sexes—than they do when their men are more traditional. They enjoy better sex, too (Rudman & Mescher, 2012a).

Okay, women like their men to think of them as equals. But what about the guys? The old norms are clearly changing—24 percent of American wives who work now earn noticeably higher incomes than their husbands do (Pew Research Center, 2015)—but a lot of people still think that women who believe in the equality of the sexes are likely to be homely, pushy, unromantic harpies who are lousy in bed (Rudman & Mescher, 2012a). However, to the contrary, female feminists are *less* hostile toward men than other women are (Anderson et al., 2009), and men who are partnered with feminist women enjoy more stable relationships and more sexual satisfaction than do men with traditional partners (Rudman & Mescher, 2012a). Clearly, it's absurd to think that feminism is incompatible with romance. Thinking of one's lover as an equal partner may help create a relationship that is actually more rewarding and robust than a partnership that is based on the last century's old, outmoded expectations (Carlson et al., 2016).

admonition offered by marriage researchers to modern couples is for men "to do more housework, child care, and affectional maintenance if they wish to have a happy wife" (Gottman & Carrère, 1994, p. 225). (And desirable outcomes may follow: Men who do their fair share of housework have more frequent and more satisfying sexual interactions with their wives [Johnson et al., 2016].) Equity in these conspicuous domains may be much more influential than similar fairness applied to other areas of a couple's interactions.

A third and perhaps most important reason why research results are mixed may be that equity is a salient issue when people are dissatisfied, but it's only a minor issue when people are content (Holmes & Levinger, 1994). When rewards are ample, equity may not matter much. People who are prospering in their relationships may spend little time monitoring their exchanges and may not be concerned by any imbalances they do notice. (They might also tend to report that their partnerships are "fair" when researchers ask.) But if costs rise and rewards fall, people may begin tracking their exchanges much more carefully, displaying concern about who deserves to get what. And no matter what the truth is, people who are very dissatisfied are likely to perceive that they are being underbenefited by their partners (Grote & Clark, 2001). In this sense, then, inequity may not cause people to become dissatisfied; instead, being dissatisfied could lead people to think they're being treated unfairly.

Overall, the best conclusion appears to be that both the global quality of outcomes people receive *and* underbenefit, when it occurs, play important roles in predicting how satisfactory and enduring a relationship will be (Dainton, 2017). Being overbenefited doesn't seem to bother people much, and equity doesn't seem to improve a relationship if it is already highly rewarding. In contrast, the inequity that accompanies deprivation and exploitation—underbenefit—routinely causes distress (Kuijer et al., 2002), and selfishness is disliked wherever it's encountered (Allen & Leary, 2010). But the bottom line is that outcome level matters more than inequity does; if our outcomes are poor and unsatisfactory, it isn't much consolation if they're fair, and if our outcomes are wonderful, inequity isn't a major concern.

Summing Up

So, what's the final answer? Is simple greed a good description of people's behavior in intimate relationships? The answer offered by relationship science is a qualified "yes." People are happiest when their rewards are high and their costs (and expectations) are low. But because we depend on others for the rewards we seek in intimate relationships, we have a stake in satisfying them, too. We readily protect the well-being of our intimate partners and rarely exploit them if we want those relationships to continue. Such behavior may be encouraged by selfish motives, but it is still thoughtful, generous, and often loving. So, even if it is ultimately greedy behavior, it's not undesirable or exploitative.

THE NATURE OF COMMITMENT

The good news is that happy dependence on an intimate partner leads to **commitment,** a desire for the relationship to continue and the willingness to work to maintain it. People who both need their partners and who are currently content associate the concept of commitment with positive qualities such as sharing, supportiveness, honesty, faithfulness, and trust (Hampel & Vangelisti, 2008); they are affectionate, attentive, and respectful, and they happily plan to be together in the future (Weigel & Ballard-Reisch, 2014). (You can see why these people are staying put.) The bad news is that unhappy people can be committed to their relationships, too, not because they want to stay where they are but because they feel they *must.* For these people, commitment can be experienced more as burdensome entrapment than as a positive feeling (Weigel et al., 2015).

Different components of commitment are apparent in a handy commitment scale developed by Ximena Arriaga and Christopher Agnew (2001) that contains three themes. First, committed partners expect their relationship to continue. They also hold a long-term view, foreseeing a future that involves their partners. And finally, they are psychologically attached to each other so that they are happier when their partners are happy, too. Each of these themes is represented by

TABLE 6.3. **Arriaga and Agnew's Commitment Scale**

Answer each of the questions that follow using this scale:

| 1 not at all true | 2 slightly true | 3 moderately true | 4 very true | 5 extremely true |

1. I feel very strongly linked to my partner—very attached to our relationship.
2. It pains me to see my partner suffer.
3. I am very affected when things are not going well in my relationship.
4. In all honesty, my family and friends are more important to me than this relationship.
5. I am oriented toward the long-term future of this relationship (e.g., I imagine being with my partner several years from now).
6. My partner and I joke about what things will be like when we are old.
7. I find it difficult to imagine myself with my partner in the distant future.
8. When I make plans about future events in my life, I think about the impact of my decisions on our relationship.
9. I intend to stay in this relationship.
10. I want to maintain our relationship.
11. I feel inclined to keep our relationship going.
12. My gut feeling is to continue in this relationship.

Source: Arriaga, X. B., & Agnew, C. R. "Being committed: Affective, cognitive, and conative components of relationship commitment," Personality and Social Psychology Bulletin, *27, 2001, 1190–1203.*

To determine your total commitment score, reverse the rating you used for questions 4 and 7. If you answered 1, change it to 5; 2 becomes 4; 4 becomes 2; and so on. Then add up your ratings. The higher your score, the greater your commitment.

---

four questions on the commitment scale; take a look at Table 6.3 and you'll be able to tell which theme applies to each question.

This portrayal of commitment as a multifaceted decision is consistent with a well-known conceptualization of commitment developed by Caryl Rusbult and her colleagues known as the **investment model.** According to the investment model, commitment emerges from all of the elements of social exchange that are associated with people's CLs and CL$_{alt}$s (e.g., Rusbult et al., 2012). First, satisfaction increases commitment. People generally wish to continue the partnerships that make them happy. However, alternatives of high quality are also influential, and they *decrease* commitment. People who have tempting alternatives enticing them away from their present partners are less likely to stay in their existing relationships. But people don't always pursue such alternatives even when they're available, if the costs of leaving their current relationships are too high. Thus, a third determinant of commitment is the size of one's investments in the existing relationship. High investments increase commitment regardless of the quality of one's alternatives and whether or not one is happy.

Altogether, then, the investment model suggests that people will wish to remain with their present partners when they're happy, or when there's no other desirable place for them to go, or when they won't leave because it would cost too much (see Figure 6.8). These influences are presumed to be equally important,

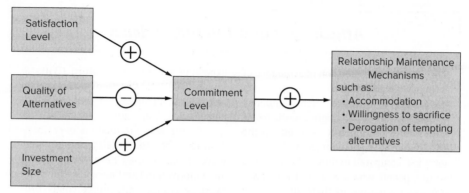

Source: Adapted from Rusbult, C. E., Martz, J. M., & Agnew, C. "The Investment Model Scale:
Measuring commitment level, satisfaction level, quality of alternatives, and investment size,"
Personal Relationships, 5. 1998, 357–391.

FIGURE 6.8. **The investment model of commitment.**
Satisfaction and investments are both positively related to commitment. The happier we
are and the more we would lose by leaving, the greater our commitment to our present
partners. However, high-quality alternatives undermine commitment; the more alluring
our other options, the less committed we are.

and commitment emerges from the complex combination of all three. Thus, as
people's circumstances change, relationships often survive periods in which one
or both partners are dissatisfied, tempted by alluring alternatives, or free to walk
out at any time. Episodes such as these may stress the relationship and weaken
the partners' commitment, but the partnership may persist if the other components of commitment are holding it together.

In general, research results support the investment model quite well (Le et al.,
2010). Satisfaction, the quality of one's alternatives, and the size of one's investments all tell us something useful about how committed a person is likely to be
(Lemay, 2016), and the model applies equally well to men and women, heterosexual and same-sex couples (Kurdek, 2008), and to Eastern (Lin & Rusbult, 1995),
as well as Western, cultures. Moreover, the usefulness of the investment model
provides general support for an exchange perspective on intimate relationships.
The economic assessments involved in the investment model do a very good job
of predicting how long relationships will last (Le et al., 2010), whether or not the
partners will be faithful to each other (Drigotas et al., 1999), and even whether
battered wives will try to escape their abusive husbands (Rusbult & Martz, 1995).

However, there are some nuances in the nature of commitment that aren't
explicated by the investment model. For one thing, another major influence on
your current commitment to a relationship is your *forecast* of how satisfying the
partnership will be *in the future* (Lemay, 2016). Commitment is enhanced not just
by current contentment but also by the expectation that a relationship will be
prosperous and fulfilling in the years to come.

In addition, the investment model treats commitment as a unitary concept—
that is, there's really only one kind of commitment—and other theorists argue

Attachment and Interdependency

The attachment dimension of avoidance of intimacy describes the comfort with which people accept intimate interdependency with others. So, as you might expect, avoidance figures prominently in several of the patterns we have encountered in this chapter. First, compared to those who are more secure, people who are high in avoidance are more attentive to their alternatives; they keep track of the other romantic options open to them (Miller, 2008) and they are more attracted to the newcomers they meet (Overall & Sibley, 2008). As a result, their CL_{alt}s tend to be higher than those of other people, and that leaves them less committed to their present partners (Etcheverry et al., 2013b). Avoidant people also value their independence and self-sufficiency, so their approach motivations are weaker; they perceive intimate connections to others to be less rewarding than secure people do, so they are less highly motivated to pursue fulfillment from their partnerships with others (Gere et al., 2013). They are also less attracted to others who use communal norms; they prefer people who do *not* do favors for them without expecting something in return (Bartz & Lydon, 2008), and they think that others do favors for them out of obligation, not kindness (Beck & Clark, 2010a).

People who are anxious over abandonment fret that their partners may leave them, so they have strong avoidance motivations and nervously focus on averting conflict and other costly outcomes (Gere et al., 2013). But that's not a recipe for contentment, and anxious people tend to be less satisfied with their relationships than more relaxed and trusting—that is, secure—people are (Etcheverry et al., 2013b).

Thus, both anxiety about abandonment and avoidance of intimacy are associated—albeit for somewhat different reasons—with lower satisfaction and commitment in close relationships as time goes by (Hadden et al., 2014). Your chances of living happily ever after will be greater if you settle down with someone who is comfortable and secure needing and depending on you and who is happy to accept your dependence on him or her in return (Waldinger et al., 2015).

that commitment not only springs from different sources, it comes in different forms (Knopp et al., 2015). For instance, sociologist Michael Johnson (1999) asserted that there are actually three types of commitment. The first, **personal commitment,** occurs when people *want* to continue a relationship because they are attracted to their partners and the relationship is satisfying. In contrast, the second type, **constraint commitment,** occurs when people feel they *have* to continue a relationship because it would be too costly for them to leave. In constraint commitment, people fear the social and financial consequences of ending their partnerships, and they continue them even when they wish they could depart. Finally, the third type of commitment, **moral commitment,** derives from a sense of moral obligation to one's partner or one's relationship. Here, people feel they *ought* to continue the relationship because it would be improper to end it and break their promises or vows. Spouses who are morally committed tend to believe in the sanctity of marriage and may feel a solemn social or religious responsibility to stay married no matter what (Stafford et al., 2014).

Research using this scheme demonstrates that the three types of commitment do feel different to people, and there is value in distinguishing them in studies of relationships (Knopp et al., 2015). Personal commitment is often the strongest of the three, but constraint commitment and moral commitment can be influential, too. Even when people are unhappy and their personal commitment is low, for instance, they may stay in a partnership if constraint commitment is high because of financial or family pressures (Rhoades et al., 2012). And when people embark on a long-distance romantic relationship, moral commitment does a better job of predicting whether or not the partnership will survive the period of separation than personal commitment does (Lydon et al., 1997). Evidently, moral commitment can keep a relationship going even when one's enthusiasm for the relationship wanes.

The Consequences of Commitment

Nevertheless, whatever its origins or nature, commitment substantially affects the relationships in which it occurs (Rusbult et al., 2012). The long-term orientation that characterizes commitment reduces the pain that would otherwise accompany rough spots in the relationship. When people feel that they're in a relationship for the long haul, they may be better able to tolerate episodes of high cost and low reward in much the same way that investors with a long-range outlook will hold on to shares of stock during periods of low earnings (Arriaga et al., 2007). In addition, commitment can lead people to think of themselves and their partners as a single entity, as "us" instead of "him" and "me" (Agnew et al., 1998). This may substantially reduce the costs of sacrifices that benefit the partner, as events that please one's partner produce indirect benefits for oneself as well.

Perhaps the most important consequence of commitment, however, is that it leads people to take action to protect and maintain a relationship even when it is costly for them to do so. Committed people engage in a variety of behavioral and cognitive maneuvers that both preserve and enhance the relationship and reinforce their commitment to it (Ogolsky & Bowers, 2013). We'll consider these *relationship maintenance mechanisms* in detail in chapter 14—but to close this chapter, let's briefly preview that material.

As one example, commitment promotes **accommodation** in which people refrain from responding to provocation from their partners with similar ire of their own (Häfner & IJzerman, 2011). Accommodating people tolerate destructive behavior from their partners without fighting back; they swallow insults, sarcasm, or selfishness without retaliating. By so doing, they avoid quarrels and help dispel, rather than perpetuate, their partners' bad moods. That's usually good for the relationship. Such behavior may involve considerable self-restraint, but it is not motivated by weakness; instead, accommodation often involves a conscious effort to protect the partnership from harm.

Committed people also display greater **willingness to sacrifice** their own self-interests for the good of the relationship (Totenhagen et al., 2013). They do things they wouldn't do if they were on their own, and they do not do things they would have liked to do in order to benefit their partners and their partnerships.

As a final example, commitment leads us to judge other potential partners to be less attractive than they would seem to be if we were single and unattached (Petit & Ford, 2015). This **derogation of tempting alternatives** reduces the allure of those who might otherwise entice us away from our present partners, and that helps protect our partnerships.

People maintain their relationships with other mechanisms, but these three sufficiently illustrate the manner in which commitment motivates thoughts and actions that preserve partnerships. People seek maximum reward at minimum cost in their interactions with others, but dependency on a partner leads them to behave in ways that take the partner's well-being into account. As a result, committed partners often make sacrifices and accommodate their partners, doing things that are not in their immediate self-interest, to promote their relationships.

If people did these things indiscriminately, they would often be self-defeating. However, when they occur in interdependent relationships and when both partners behave this way, such actions provide powerful means of protecting and enhancing desired connections to others (Ramirez, 2008). In this manner, even if we are basically greedy at heart, we are often unselfish, considerate, and caring to those we befriend and love.

FOR YOUR CONSIDERATION

One of the things Gregg liked about Gail was that she was a great cook. When she would have him over to dinner, she would serve elaborate, delicious meals that were much more appealing than the fast food he often ate on his own. He liked to keep things tidy and neat, and he noticed that her apartment was always disheveled and cluttered, but he didn't much care because she was an exciting, desirable companion. However, once they were married, Gail cooked less often; they both worked, and she frequently called him before he came home to ask him to pick up take-out meals for dinner. He also became annoyed by her slovenly housekeeping. He did his fair share of housework, but a pile of unfolded laundry constantly occupied their living room couch, and they had to push it aside to sit together to watch television. She seemed not to notice just how scattered and disorganized her belongings were, and Gregg began to feel resentful.

What do you think the future holds for Gail and Gregg? Why?

CHAPTER SUMMARY

Social Exchange

Interdependence theory offers an economic view of relationships that involves *social exchange* in which partners provide each other desirable rewards.

Rewards and Costs. Rewards are gratifying and costs are punishing. The net profit or loss from an interaction is its *outcome.*

What Do We Expect from Our Relationships? People have *comparison levels* (CLs) that reflect their expectations for their interactions with others. When the outcomes they receive exceed their CLs, they're satisfied, but if their outcomes fall below their CLs, they're discontent.

How Well Could We Do Elsewhere? People also judge the outcomes available elsewhere using a *comparison level for alternatives* (CL_{alt}). When the outcomes they receive exceed their CL_{alt}s, they can't do better elsewhere, and they're dependent on their current partners.

Four Types of Relationships. Comparing people's CLs and CL_{alt}s with their outcomes yields four different relationship states: happy and stable; happy and unstable; unhappy and stable; and unhappy and unstable.

CL and CL_{alt} as Time Goes By. People adapt to the outcomes they receive, and relationships can become less satisfying as the partners' CLs rise. Cultural influences shape both our expectations and our CL_{alt}s.

The Economies of Relationships

Counting up the rewards and costs of a relationship provides extraordinary information about its current state and likely future.

Rewards and Costs Are Different. An *approach motivation* leads us to seek rewards, an *avoidance motivation* leads us to avoid costs, and the extent to which each is fulfilled defines different relationship states.

Rewards and Costs as Time Goes By. A *relational turbulence model* suggests that new relationships usually encounter a lull when partners adjust to their new status as an established couple. Thereafter, marital satisfaction usually decreases over the first years of marriage. This may be due to the partners' *lack of effort* and to the manner in which *interdependence magnifies small irritations,* and to other routine influences such as *unwelcome surprises* and *unrealistic expectations.* Insight may forestall or prevent these problems.

Are We Really This Greedy?

The Nature of Interdependency. Interdependent partners have a stake in keeping each other happy. As a result, generosity toward one's partner is often beneficial to oneself.

Exchange versus Communal Relationships. *Exchange relationships* are governed by a desire for immediate repayment of favors, whereas *communal relationships* involve selfless concern for another's needs.

Equitable Relationships. *Equity* occurs when both partners gain benefits from a relationship that are proportional to their contributions to it.

According to equity theory, people dislike inequity. However, *overbenefit* is not always associated with reduced satisfaction with a relationship—but *underbenefit* is.

Summing Up. Both the quality of outcomes one receives and underbenefit, when it occurs, determine how happy and stable a relationship will be.

The Nature of Commitment

Commitment is a desire to continue a relationship, and the willingness to maintain it. The *investment model* asserts that satisfaction, the quality of one's alternatives, and the size of one's investments influence commitment. However, there may be three kinds of commitment: *personal, constraint,* and *moral.*

The Consequences of Commitment. Committed people take action to protect and maintain their relationships, being accommodating, making sacrifices willingly, and derogating others who might lure them away from their relationships.

CHAPTER 7

Friendship

THE NATURE OF FRIENDSHIP ◆ FRIENDSHIP
ACROSS THE LIFE CYCLE ◆ DIFFERENCES IN FRIENDSHIP
◆ FRIENDSHIP DIFFICULTIES ◆ FOR YOUR CONSIDERATION
◆ CHAPTER SUMMARY

I get by with a little help from my friends. *John Lennon*

Take a moment and think about your two best friends. Why are they such close companions? You probably *like* but don't *love* them. (Or, at least, you're not "in love" with them, or you'd probably think of them as more than just "friends.") You've probably shared a lot of good times with them, and you feel comfortable around them; you know that they like you, too, and you feel that you can count on them to help you when you need it.

Indeed, the positive sentiments you feel toward your friends may actually be rather varied and complex. They annoy you sometimes, but you're fond of them, and because they're best friends, they know things about you that no one else may know. You like to do things with them, and you expect your relationship to continue indefinitely. In fact, if you look back at the features that define *intimacy* (way back on page 2), you may find that your connections to your best friends are quite intimate, indeed. You may have substantial knowledge of them, and you probably feel high levels of trust and commitment toward them; you may not experience as much caring, interdependence, responsiveness, and mutuality as you do with a romantic partner, but all four are present, nonetheless.

So, are friendships the same as but just less intimate than our romantic partnerships? Yes and no. Friendships are based on the same building blocks of intimacy as romances are, but the mix of components is usually different. Romances also have some ingredients that friendships typically lack, so their recipes do differ. But many of the elements of friendships and romances are quite similar, and this chapter will set the stage for our consideration of love (in chapter 8) by detailing what it means to *like* an intimate partner. Among other topics, I'll describe various features of friendship and question whether men and women can be "just friends."

happiness than to those who respond to our good fortune with apathy or indifference (Reis et al., 2010), and relationships in which capitalization routinely occurs are more satisfying and longer lasting than those in which it is infrequent (Logan & Cobb, 2016).

Social Support

Enthusiastic celebration of our good fortune is one way in which our intimate partners uplift us and provide us aid, or *social support* (Gable et al., 2012). We also rely on friends to help us through our difficulties, and there are four ways in which they can provide us help and encouragement (Barry et al., 2009). We rely on our partners for *emotional support* in the form of affection, acceptance, and reassurance; *physical comfort* in the form of hugs and cuddling; *advice support* in the form of information and guidance; and *material support*, or tangible assistance in the form of money or goods. A partner who tries to reassure you when you're nervous about an upcoming exam is providing emotional support whereas a friend who loans you her car is providing material support. But don't take these distinctions too seriously, because these types of aid can and do overlap; because her generous concern would be touching, a friend who offers a loan of her car as soon as she learns that yours is in the shop could be said to be providing emotional as well as material support.

Social support can be of enormous value, and higher amounts of all four types of support are associated with higher relationship satisfaction and greater personal well-being as time goes by (Barry et al., 2009). Indeed, warm, attentive support from one's partners matters more than money when it comes to being happy; your income is likely to have less effect on your happiness than your level of social support does (North et al., 2008). But there are several complexities involved in the manner in which social support operates in close relationships. Consider these points:

- *Emotional support has real physiological effects.* People who have affectionate partners have chronically lower blood pressures, cholesterol levels, and stress hormone levels than do those who receive lesser amounts of encouragement and caring from others (Seeman et al., 2002). They recover faster from stress, too (Meuwly et al., 2012), and in lab procedures, they even experience less pain when they submerge their arms in ice-cold water (Brown et al., 2003). When people are under stress, just thinking about a supportive friend tends to reduce their heart rates and blood pressures (Smith et al., 2004).
- *Effective social support also leads people to feel closer to those who provide it.* Sensitive, responsive support from others increases our happiness, self-esteem, and optimism about the future (Feeney & Collins, 2015), and all of these have beneficial effects on our relationships. In marriages, happy spouses provide each other more support than distressed couples do (Verhofstadt et al., 2013), and higher levels of support when the partners are newly married are associated with a lower likelihood of divorce 10 years later (Sullivan et al., 2010).

Friends Matter More Than We Think

You're aware of the pleasures to be found in a close friendship, but it's likely that your friends are influencing you even more than you realize. One way our friends often matter is in making or breaking our romantic relationships. They routinely help new romances get started by introducing us to potential new partners and running interference for us (Ackerman & Kenrick, 2009). And thereafter, they come to approve or disapprove of our ongoing romances, and their opinions count (Keneski & Loving, 2014). Our romances are imperiled when our friends disapprove of them: Even when they're (initially) satisfied with their relationships, young lovers are more likely to have broken up 7 months later when their friends disapprove of their partnerships (Lehmiller & Agnew, 2007). One reason this occurs, of course, is that our friends are more dispassionate—and thus often more discerning—about our romances than we are. They tend to disapprove of our romances when they judge us to be less happy than we ought to be (Etcheverry et al., 2013a), and they sometimes see trouble coming before we do. But it's also hard to swim upstream against a tide of disapproval (Rosenthal & Starks, 2015), and even when we would otherwise be genuinely happy with a lover, disregard of the relationship from others can be very burdensome. We're more committed to our romantic partners when our friends like them, too (Sinclair et al., 2015).

Our friends also have surprising influence on whether we're happy or sad (or fat or thin!). A remarkable 30-year study of the health of more than 12,000 people found that having happy friends makes it more likely that you'll be happy as well (Christakis & Fowler, 2009). Each friend we have who possesses good cheer increases the chance that we will also be happy by 15 percent. And our friends' friends also matter; each happy friend our friends have increases our chances of being happy by 10 percent even if we've never met that person! The norms supported and the experiences offered by our social networks are surprisingly potent, and they can work against, as well as for, us. For instance, if a friend gets heavy, the chance that you will also begin gaining too much weight goes up by 57 percent. Each *unhappy* friend we have decreases the likelihood that we're happy by 7 percent. And loneliness is contagious: We're 52 percent more likely to become lonely if a friend gets lonely first, and 25 percent more likely if a friend's friend becomes lonely (Cacioppo et al., 2009). We're typically more connected to others than we realize, and our friends usually matter more than we think.

- But *some people are better providers of social support than others are.* For instance, attachment styles matter. Secure people, who readily accept interdependent intimacy with others, tend to provide effective support that reassures and bolsters the recipient, and they do so for altruistic, compassionate reasons (Davila & Kashy, 2009). In contrast, insecure people are more self-serving, and their support tends to be less effective, either because (in the case of avoidant people) they provide less help than secure people do (Farrell et al., 2016) or because (in the case of anxious people) their help is intrusive and controlling (Jayamaha et al., 2017). People are generally more satisfied

TABLE 7.1. The Perceived Responsiveness Scale

Here are items with which Harry Reis measures the extent to which friends and lovers judge their partners to be responsive. To use the scale, identify a particular person and rate your agreement with all 12 items while you are thinking of him or her. As will be apparent, the higher the sum of your combined ratings, the more responsive you perceive your partner to be.

Compared to most experiences I've had meeting somebody new, I get the feeling that this person:

1	2	3	4	5	6	7
not at all true		somewhat true		very true		completely true

_____	1.	... sees the "real" me.
_____	2.	... "gets the facts right" about me.
_____	3.	... esteems me, shortcomings and all.
_____	4.	... knows me well.
_____	5.	... values and respects the whole package that is the "real" me.
_____	6.	... understands me.
_____	7.	... really listens to me.
_____	8.	... expresses liking and encouragement for me.
_____	9.	... seems interested in what I am thinking and feeling.
_____	10.	... values my abilities and opinions.
_____	11.	... is on "the same wavelength" with me.
_____	12.	... is responsive to my needs.

Source: Reis, H. T., Maniaci, M. R., Caprariello, P. A., Eastwick, P. W., & Finkel, E. J. "Familiarity does indeed promote attraction in live interaction," Journal of Personality and Social Psychology, *101, 2011, 557–570.*

2016). They sleep better, too; we're less restless and our sleep is more efficient when we feel cared for and understood (Selcuk et al., 2017). Perceived partner responsiveness may even be a key influence on our health: Life seems more meaningful (Selcuk et al., 2016) and the levels of our stress hormones are lower (Slatcher et al., 2015) when we feel appreciated and cared for. There's enormous value in the understanding, respect, and regard that's offered by a responsive partner, and it's clear that friends can supply us with potent interpersonal rewards.

The Rules of Friendship

Good friends can also be counted on to play by the rules. We don't often explicate our expectations about what it means to be a friend, but most of us nevertheless have **rules for relationships** that are shared cultural beliefs about what behaviors friends should (and should not) perform. These standards of conduct help relationships operate more smoothly. We learn the rules during childhood, and one of the things we learn is that when the rules are broken, disapproval and turmoil result. For instance, in a seminal study, British researchers generated a large set of possible friendship rules and asked adults in England, Italy, Hong Kong,

Responsiveness in Action

One of the most successful relationship self-help books of all time is over 80 years old and still going strong. Dale Carnegie published *How to Win Friends and Influence People* in 1936, long before relationship scientists began studying the interactive effects of responsiveness. Carnegie firmly believed that the road to financial and interpersonal success lay in behaving toward others in a manner that made them feel important and appreciated. He suggested six straightforward ways to get others to like us, and the enduring popularity of his homespun advice helps demonstrate why responsiveness from a friend is so uplifting. Here are Carnegie's rules (1936, p. 110):

1. Become genuinely interested in other people.
2. Smile.
3. Remember that a man's name is to him the sweetest and most important sound in any language.
4. Be a good listener. Encourage others to talk about themselves.
5. Talk in terms of the other man's interest.
6. Make the other person feel important—and do it sincerely.

All of these actions help communicate the attention and support that constitute responsiveness, and modern research supports Carnegie's advice. To favorably impress people you've just met, for instance, offer them genuine smiles (Miles, 2009), and then focus on them, being warm, interested, and enthusiastic (Eastwick et al., 2010). It also helps to be Latin American. Latinos generally endorse a cultural norm of *simpático* that values friendly courtesy and congeniality, and sure enough, when they are left alone with a stranger in Texas, Mexican Americans talk more, look more, smile more, and enjoy the interaction more than American whites or blacks do. The people who meet them enjoy the interactions more, too (Holloway et al., 2009). Carnegie was on to something. People like to receive warm, attentive interest and support from others, and being responsive is a good way to make—and keep—friends.

and Japan which of the rules they would endorse (Argyle & Henderson, 1984). Several rules for conducting friendships appeared to be universal, and they're listed on the next page in Table 7.2. As you can see, they involve trust, capitalization, and support as well as other desirable aspects of intimacy.

In general, then, we expect good friends to be (Hall, 2012):

- trustworthy and loyal, having our best interests at heart;
- confidants with whom we can share our secrets;
- enjoyable and fun companions;
- similar to us in attitudes and interests; and
- helpful, providing material support when we need it.

(It's also nice when a friend is attractive and financially well-off, but those are lesser considerations.) Women, in particular, have high standards for their friends (Felmlee et al., 2012); they expect more loyalty, self-disclosure, enjoyment, and similarity than men do (Hall, 2012). But all of us expect more from our friends

TABLE 7.2. The Rules of Friendship

Don't nag
Keep confidences
Show emotional support
Volunteer help in time of need
Trust and confide in your partner
Share news of success with your partner
Don't be jealous of each other's relationships
Stand up for your partner in his/her absence
Seek to repay debts and favors and compliments
Strive to make him/her happy when you're together

Source: Argyle, M., & Henderson, M. "The rules of friendship," Journal of Social and Personal Relationships, 1, 1984, 211–237.

than from less intimate companions, and the more closely we adhere to these rules, the closer and more satisfying our relationships are (Kline & Stafford, 2004). Romances are richer, too, involving more love, commitment, and sexual gratification, when the lovers value their friendship (VanderDrift et al., 2013b). So, people profit when they follow the rules of friendship, and in most cases when friendships fail, somebody hasn't been following the rules (Perlman et al., 2015).

A Point to Ponder

How rich a friendship do you have with your romantic partner? How would your romance be different if you were even better friends?

FRIENDSHIP ACROSS THE LIFE CYCLE

We change as we grow and age, and our friendships do, too. For one thing, our attachment styles continue to be shaped by the experiences we encounter, and for most of us that's a good thing: We're likely to experience less anxiety about abandonment later in life than we do now (Chopik et al., 2013). And here's more good news: You're likely to be (even) more satisfied with your friendships in your elder years than you are now (Luong et al., 2011). Why is that? Let's survey friendships over the life span to find out.

Childhood

Preschool children have rudimentary friendships in which they have favorite playmates. Thereafter, the enormous changes that children encounter as they grow and mature are mirrored in their friendships, which gradually grow richer and more complex (Howes, 2011). One important change involves children's cognitive development; as they age, children are increasingly able to appreciate others' perspectives and to understand their wishes and points of view. And accompanying this increasing cognitive sophistication are changes in the inter-personal needs that are preeminent as children age. According to Duane Buhrmester and Wyndol Furman (1986), these key needs are *acceptance* in the early elementary years, *intimacy* in preadolescence, and *sexuality* during the teen years. The new needs are added on top of the old ones at each stage, so that older children have more needs to satisfy than younger children do. And the success-ful resolution of each stage requires the development of specific competencies that affect the way a child handles later stages; if those skills aren't acquired, problems occur.

For instance, when children enter elementary school, the companionship of, and *acceptance* by, other children is important; those who are not sufficiently accepted by their peers feel excluded. Later, in preadolescence, children develop a need for *intimacy* that typically focuses on a friend who is similar to them in age and interests. This is when full-blown friendships characterized by extensive self-disclosure first emerge, and during this period, children develop the skills of perspective taking, empathy, and generosity that are the foundation for close adult relationships. Children who were not previously accepted by others may overcome their sense of isolation, but if they cannot, they experience true loneliness for the first time. Thereafter, *sexuality* erupts, and the typical adolescent develops an interest in the other sex. Most adolescents initially have difficulty satisfying their new emerging needs, but most manage to form sensitive, caring, and open sexual relationships later on.

Overall, then, theorists generally agree that our relationships change as we grow older. The rich, sophisticated ways in which adults conduct their friend-ships are years in the making. And to some degree, success in childhood relation-ships paves the way for better adult outcomes. For instance, infants who are securely attached to their caregivers tend to be well liked when they start school; as a result, they form richer, more secure childhood friendships that leave them secure and comfortable with intimacy when they fall in love as young adults (Oriña et al., 2011). On the other hand, children who are rejected by their peers tend to encounter a variety of difficulties—such as dropping out of school, crim-inal arrests, and psychological maladjustment—more often than those who are well-liked (Wong & Schonlau, 2013). Peer rejection doesn't necessarily cause such problems, but it might: Interventions that teach social skills enhance children's acceptance by their peers, and that reduces their risk of later maladjustment (Waas & Graczyk, 1998).

Adolescence

There are other ways in which friendships change during the teen years. First, teens spend less and less time with their families and more and more time with their peers. An experience-sampling study in Chicago found that children in fifth grade spent 35 percent of their time with family members whereas high school seniors were with their families only 14 percent of the time (Larson et al., 1996).

A second change is that adolescents increasingly turn to their friends for the satisfaction of important attachment needs (Fraley & Davis, 1997). Attachment theorists identify four components of attachment (Hazan & Zeifman, 1994): (a) *proximity seeking*, which involves approaching, staying near, or making contact with an attachment figure; (b) *separation protest*, in which people resist being separated from a partner and are distressed by separation from him or her; (c) *safe haven*, turning to an attachment figure as a source of comfort and support in times of stress; and (d) *secure base*, using a partner as a foundation for exploration of novel environments and other daring exploits. All of these components of attachment can be found in the relationships young children have with their parents, but, as they grow older, they gradually shift their primary attachments from their parents to their peers in a component-by-component fashion.

For instance, around the ages of 11 to 14, young adolescents often shift the location of their safe haven from their parents to their peers; if something upsets them, they'll seek out their friends before they approach their parents. Indeed, about a third of older teens identify a peer (who is usually a romantic partner rather than a friend), not a parent, as their primary attachment figure (Rosenthal & Kobak, 2010). Peers gradually replace parents in people's lives.

Young Adulthood

During their late teens and twenties, people enter young adulthood, a period in which a central task—according to Erik Erikson (1950), a historically prominent theorist—is the development of "intimacy versus isolation." It's at this age, Erikson believed, that we learn how to form enduring, committed intimate relationships.

You may be undertaking your quest for intimacy in a novel environment: a college some distance from home. Leaving home to go to school has probably influenced your friendships (Roberts & Dunbar, 2011), and you're not alone if you haven't seen much of your old high school friends lately. A year-long survey of a freshman class at the University of Denver found that the friendships the students had at home tended to erode and to be replaced by new relationships on campus as the year went by (Shaver et al., 1985). This didn't happen immediately, and the students' satisfaction with their social networks was lowest in the fall after they arrived at college. But by the end of that first year, most people were again content with their social networks; they had made new friends, but it had taken some time.

What happens after college? In one impressive study, 113 young adults kept diaries of their social interactions on two separate occasions, once when they were still in college and again 6 years after they had graduated (Reis et al., 1993). Overall, the participants saw less of their friends each week once they were out of school; in particular, the amount of time spent with same-sex friends and groups of three or more people declined. The total amount of time spent with friends or lovers increased, but the number of those partners decreased, especially for men. Still, just as developmental theory suggests, the average intimacy levels of the participants' interactions increased during their twenties. After college, then, people tend to interact with fewer friends, but they have deeper, more interdependent relationships with the friends they have.

What's a Best Friend?

People usually have a lot of friendly acquaintances, a number of casual friends, a few close friends, and just one or two *best* friends with whom they share especially rich relationships. What's so special about a best friend? What distinguishes a best friend from all of the other people who are important to us?

The simple answer is that it's all a matter of degree (Fehr, 1996). Best friendships are more intimate than common friendships are, and all of the components of intimacy are involved. Consider *knowledge*: Best friends are usually our closest confidants. They often know secrets about us that are known to no one else, including our spouses! Consider *trust:* We typically expect a very high level of support from our best friends, so that a best friend is "someone who is there for you, no matter what" (Yager, 1997, p. 18). Consider *interdependence:* When our best friends are nearby and available to us, we try to see more of them than our other friends; we interact with them more often and in a wider range of situations than we do with lesser buddies. And finally, consider *commitment:* We ordinarily expect that a best friend will be a friend forever. Because such a person "is *the* friend, before all others," best friendships routinely withstand "the tests of time and conflict, major changes such as moving, or status changes, such as marrying or having a child" (Yager, 1997, p. 18).

In general, then, best friendships are not distinctly different relationships of some unique type (Fehr, 1996). Instead, they are simply more intimate than other friendships—involving richer, more rewarding, and more personal connections to others—and that's why they are so prized.

Midlife

What happens when people settle down with a romantic partner? It's very clear: When people gain romantic partners, they spend less time with their families and friends. A pattern of **dyadic withdrawal** occurs; as people see more and more of a lover, they see less and less of their friends (Burton-Chellew & Dunbar, 2015). One study found that people spent an average of 2 hours each day with good friends when they were casually dating someone, but they saw their friends for less than 30 minutes per day once they became engaged (Milardo et al., 1983). Romantic couples do tend to have more contact with friends they have in common, but this doesn't offset declines in the total number of friends they have and the amount of time they spend with them (Wrzus et al., 2013).

The erosion of people's friendships doesn't stop once they get married. Friendships with members of the other sex are especially affected; people tend to see much less of friends who could be construed by a spouse to be potential romantic rivals (Werking, 1997). Still, even though they see less of their friends, spouses often have larger social networks than they did when they were single because they see a lot more of their in-laws (Milardo et al., 1983). (Make no mistake about this, and beware if you don't like your lover's family: You will see a lot more of them if you marry!)

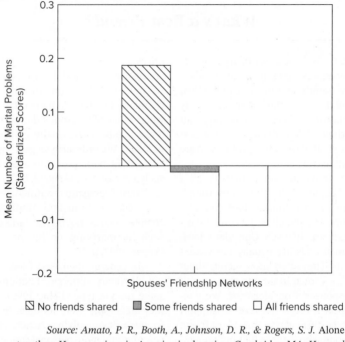

Source: Amato, P. R., Booth, A., Johnson, D. R., & Rogers, S. J. Alone together: How marriage in America is changing. *Cambridge, MA: Harvard University Press, 2007.*

FIGURE 7.1. **Friendship networks and marital adjustment.**
Spouses encounter more frustrations and difficulties when they have no friends in common.

Thus, people's social lives don't wither away completely when they commit themselves to a spouse and kids, but the focus of their socializing does shift from their personal friends to family and friends they share with their spouses. In fact, it appears to be hard on a marriage when a husband and wife have no friends in common (Barton et al., 2014). As you can see in Figure 7.1, couples have more marital problems when none of their personal friendships involve their spouses (Amato et al., 2007). Having some friends of one's own does no harm, but having only exclusive friendships seems to be risky.

Old Age

Ultimately, elderly people have smaller social networks and fewer friends than younger people do (Gillespie et al., 2015). They're not unsociable, they're just more selective: They have just as many close friends as they did when they were younger, but they spend less time with casual friends and other peripheral social partners (Fung et al., 2001).

A **socioemotional selectivity theory** argues that this change occurs because seniors have different interpersonal goals than younger people do (Löckenhoff & Carstensen, 2004). With a long life stretching out before them, young adults are presumed to pursue future-oriented goals aimed at acquiring information that will be useful later in life. (That's presumably what you're doing now if you're in college.) With such ends in mind, young people seek relatively large social networks that include diverse social partners (and, often, hundreds of Facebook "friends"!). However, when people age and their futures seem more and more finite, they become oriented more toward the present than toward the future, and they emphasize emotional fulfillment to a greater extent (Fung & Carstensen, 2004). The idea is that as their time perspective shrinks, seniors aim for quality not quantity; they focus on a select group of satisfying friendships that are relatively free of conflict (Fingerman & Charles, 2010), work harder to maintain and enrich them (Lang et al., 2013), and let more casual partnerships lapse. Indeed, the theory predicts that anyone who considers his or her future to be limited will also choose to spend more time with a small number of close friends instead of a wider variety of more casual buddies—and that's exactly what happens in younger adults whose time orientation is changed by contracting a fatal illness (Carstensen et al., 1999). In general, socioemotional selectivity theory seems to be a reasonable explanation for age-related changes in sociability.

Finally, let's note that—reflecting the vital role of intimacy in our lives—elderly people who have good friends live longer, healthier, happier lives than do those who are less connected to others (Gerstorf et al., 2016). Friendships are invaluable for as long as we live.

DIFFERENCES IN FRIENDSHIP

Friendships don't just differ across the life cycle; they also differ from person to person and from partner to partner. In this section of the chapter, we'll consider how the nature of friendships is intertwined with gender and other individual differences.

Gender Differences in Same-Sex Friendships

Consider these descriptions of two same-sex friendships:

Wilma and Betty are very close friends. They rely on each other for support and counsel, and if they experience any problems in their romantic relationships, they immediately call each other, asking for, and getting, all the advice and consolation they need. Wilma and Betty feel that they know everything about each other.

Fred and Barney are very close friends. Often, they stay up half the night playing cards or tinkering with Fred's beloved 1966 Chevy, which is constantly breaking down. They go everywhere together—to the bars, to ball games, and to work out. Barney and Fred feel they are the best of friends.

Do these two descriptions sound familiar? They might. Lots of research shows that women's friendships are usually characterized by **emotional sharing** and self-disclosure, whereas men's friendships revolve around **shared activities,** companionship, and competition (Marshall, 2010; McGuire & Leaper, 2016). It's an

ZITS © 2006 Zits Partnership. Distributed by King Features, Inc.

Of course, there are fewer differences in guys' and girls' friendships than are shown here. Nevertheless, women's friendships do tend to be more intimate than men's. That's important, as we'll see on page 234.

oversimplification, but a pithy phrase coined years ago by Wright (1982) is still service-able today: Women's friendships are *"face-to-face,"* whereas men's are *"side-by-side."*[3]

This difference emerges from several specific patterns in same-sex friendships (Fehr, 1996):

- women spend more time talking to friends on the phone;
- men and women talk about different topics: Women are more likely to talk about relationships and personal issues, whereas men are more likely to talk about impersonal interests such as sports;
- women self-disclose more than men do;
- women provide their friends more emotional support than men do; and
- women express more feelings of affection in their friendships than men do.

Add all this up, and women's same-sex friendships tend to be closer and more intimate than men's are. The net result is that—although adult men and women have the same number of friends, on average (Gillespie et al., 2015)—women typically have partners outside their romantic relationships to whom they can turn for sensitive, sympathetic understanding and support, but men often do not. For instance, ponder this provocative question (Rubin, 1986, p. 170): "Who would you turn to if you came home one night and your wife [or husband or lover] announced she [or he] was leaving you?" When research participants actually considered this question, nearly every woman readily named a same-sex friend, but only a few

[3]This clever statement is oversimplified because it implies that women just talk and men just play, and of course that isn't true. Women share enjoyable activities with their friends about as often as men do (Fehr, 1996). However, men are more reluctant than women to share their feelings and fears with their friends, so emotional sharing does distinguish women's friendships from those of men, on average (Marshall, 2010).

Can Pets Be Our Friends?

We've all heard that "a dog is a man's best friend." Really? Can a pet be a *friend*?

People certainly behave as if that's the case: The presence of a beloved pet can help someone manage stressful situations even better than a human friend can. Pets generally improve the autonomic and cardiovascular health of their owners (Beetz & Bales, 2016), and in a study that compared pets to people (Allen et al., 2002), participants were asked to work a mental math problem for 5 minutes—rapidly counting backward by threes from 7,654—when they were (a) alone, (b) with their spouses, or (c) with their pets but no one else. The presence of a pet was soothing; the difficult task caused only slight arousal when people were with their pets, but their heart rates and blood pressures went up substantially when they were alone, and their cardiovascular readings soared when their spouses were present. A human audience, even a loving partner, made the potentially embarrassing task more stressful, but a companion animal made it less taxing.

These results are intriguing, but they could be due to idiosyncrasies in the people who choose to have pets. So, in another test of this effect (Allen et al., 2001), businessmen who lived alone were *randomly assigned* either to adopt pets from an animal shelter or to continue to live alone. When they were then put under stress, the new pet owners displayed increases in blood pressure that were only half as large as those that occurred among those without pets. Moreover, the fewer friends the men had, the greater the benefits of owning a pet.

Now, let's not overstate this "friend" business. Animals can soothe us even when they are strangers to us; people who were excluded by others in a lab procedure found the experience less painful when the *experimenter's* dog was in the room than when it was not (Aydin et al., 2012). And pet ownership isn't beneficial for some people: There appear to be differences from person to person in attachment to pets that mirror the anxiety and avoidance seen in human relationships (Zilcha-Mano et al., 2011). And of course, a pet cannot supply the same respect, responsiveness, or trust that human friends can.

Still, people often imagine that their pets have human traits and qualities (Epley et al., 2008), and they can feel that their relationships with their pets are just as close as their partnerships with other humans (Kurdek, 2008b). When they're distressed, pet owners are even more likely to turn to their pets for solace than they are to seek out their (human) friends (Kurdek, 2009). And if they had to choose one or the other, one of every seven pet owners would discard their spouses rather than lose their pets (Italie, 2011)! So, given the pleasure and genuine support that pets provide, sure, as long as we use the term loosely, pets can be our friends.

men did (Rubin, 1986). (In fact, most men could not come up with *anyone* to whom they could turn for solace if their lovers left them.)

Why are men's same-sex friendships less intimate than women's? Are men less capable of forming close friendships with each other, or are they just less willing? Usually, they are less willing (Flannery & Smith, 2017). Men seem to be fully capable of forming intimate friendships with other men when the circumstances support such closeness—but they generally choose not to do so because such intimacy is less socially acceptable among men than among women (Reis, 1998). And why is that? Cultural norms and gender roles appear to be the main culprits (Bank & Hansford, 2000). A traditional upbringing encourages men to be instrumental, but not expressive,[4] and (as we found in chapter 5), a person's expressivity predicts how self-disclosing he or she will be. Androgynous men tend to have closer friendships than traditional, sex-typed men do, but more men are sex-typed than androgynous. Also, in keeping with typical gender roles, we put pressure on men to display more *emotional constraint* than we put on women. Cultural norms lead men to be more reluctant than women to express their worries and emotions to others, and gender differences in the intimacy of friendship disappear in societies (such as the Middle East) where expressive male friendships are encouraged (Reis, 1998).

Thus, the lower intimacy of men's friendships usually isn't due to an inability to share meaningful, close attachments to other men. Instead, it's a choice that is supported by cultural pressures. Many men would probably have closer same-sex friendships if Western cultures did not discourage psychological intimacy with other men.

Can Men and Women Be Close Friends?

Of course. They often are. Most people have had a close friendship with a member of the other sex, and such relationships are commonplace among college students. However, once they leave college, most people no longer maintain intimate cross-sex friendships (Marshall, 2010). Why? What's going on?

The first thing to note is that men and women become friends for the same reasons they grow close to their same-sex friends; the same responsiveness, trust, and social support are involved (Fuhrman et al., 2009). And because they are dealing with women instead of other men, men are often more open and expressive with their female friends than with their male companions (Fehr, 1996). Indeed, men who have higher levels of expressivity and women who have higher levels of instrumentality are more likely than their peers to have close friendships with the other sex (Lenton & Webber, 2006). In particular, 10th-grade boys who understand emotions well have 1.8 more female friends, on average, than less empathic boys do; "females

clearly want to befriend empathic males" (Ciarrochi et al., 2017, p. 499). As always, perceived similarity attracts.

However, cross-sex friendships face a hurdle that same-sex partnerships do not ordinarily encounter: determining whether the relationship is a friendship or a romance. Friendships are typically nonexclusive, nonsexual, equal partnerships, and people may find themselves in unfamiliar territory as they try to negotiate an intimate friendship with someone of the other sex. A big question is whether the partners— who, after all, are very close—will have sex. Men are more likely than women to think that sex would be a fine idea (Lehmiller et al., 2011), and they typically think their female friends are more interested in having sex than they really are (Lemay & Wolf, 2016b). In turn, women usually *under*estimate how much their male friends would like to sleep with them, so some misunderstanding often occurs: "Most women do not reciprocate their male friend's sexual yearnings, despite the fact that men sometimes delude themselves that their female

---

[4]Would you like a quick reminder about the nature of instrumentality and expressivity? Look back at page 25 in chapter 1.

friends do" (Buss, 2003, p. 262). As a result, "sexual tension" is often mentioned as the thing people dislike most about their cross-sex friendships (Marshall, 2010).

Most cross-sex friendships never become sexual (Halatsis & Christakis, 2009). But when they do, they take a variety of forms (Mongeau et al., 2013). Some partners are genuinely close friends who trust and respect each other and who share a variety of activities in addition to the sex—and who are thus true "friends with benefits," or FWBs (Lehmiller et al., 2014)—whereas others get together solely to have sex and so are really just engaging in a series of casual "booty-calls" (Jonason et al., 2011). Moreover, the partners may be on their way from being just friends to conducting a romance or, conversely, transitioning out of a romance that has failed. Either trajectory can be complex, but there *are* differences between FWB relationships and romances, so the partners may know where they stand. More commitment is involved in romances (VanderDrift et al., 2012); FWB partners are less likely to be monogamous, having sex with a wider variety of other people, and although more of the time they spend together is devoted to sex, they tend to be less satisfied than romantic lovers are with both the sex they have and their relationship (Collibee & Furman, 2016).

Notably, most FWBs continue their friendship when the sex ends, especially if they were genuine friends and weren't just in it for the sex (Owen et al., 2013). But even when they're not sexual, cross-sex friendships can be tricky to maintain if the partners marry others. Spouses are often threatened by a partner's close connection to a potential rival, and sometimes with good reason: When people are attracted to a current cross-sex friend, they tend to be less satisfied with their romantic relationships (Bleske-Rechek et al., 2012). As a result, married people are less likely than singles to have close cross-sex friendships, and that's a major reason that such relationships become less common after people finish their schooling.

Individual Differences in Friendship

Another personal characteristic that influences our social networks is *sexual orientation*. In a convenience sample[5] of 1,415 people from across the United States, most heterosexual men and women did *not* have a close friend who was gay, lesbian, or bisexual, but most lesbians, gays, and bisexuals (or LGBs) *did* have friends who were straight (Galupo, 2009). Only about one in every six heterosexuals (knew that they) had LGB buddies, but about 80 percent of LGBs had close heterosexual friends. So, the friendship networks of straight people tend to be less diverse with regard to sexual orientation than those of LGBs. If heterosexuals are actually steering clear of LGBs, they may be making a mistake: The friendships of LGBs with heterosexuals are just as close and rewarding, on average, as their friendships with other LGBs (Ueno et al., 2009), and the more contact heteros have with LGBs, the more they like them (Lytle & Levy, 2015).

Our self-concepts influence our friendships, too. Some of us think of ourselves mostly as independent, autonomous agents, and the qualities that are foremost in our self-concepts are the traits that distinguish us from others. In contrast, others of us define ourselves to a greater extent in terms of our relationships to others,

[5]Chapter 2: the gift that keeps on giving. See p. 47.

and intriguing individual differences known as **relational self-construals** describe the extent to which we think of ourselves as interdependent, rather than independent, beings. For those of us with a highly relational self-construal, relationships are central features in our self-concepts, and we "tend to think and behave so as to develop, enhance, and maintain harmonious and close relationships" with others (Cross & Morris, 2003, p. 513). A relational self-construal makes someone a desirable friend (Morry et al., 2013); compared to those who are more independent, highly relational people better understand others' opinions and values, and they strive to behave in ways that benefit others as well as themselves. Motivations supporting both individuality and interdependence with others tend to be present in everyone, but Western cultures such as that of the United States tend to celebrate and emphasize independence and autonomy. So, highly relational self-construals are more common in other parts of the world (Cross et al., 2011).

Finally, there are other personality traits that—unlike relational self-construals—have corrosive and deleterious effects on our friendships. We've already touched on *narcissism,*[6] the arrogant self-importance, entitlement, and selfishness that can make a good first impression but that quickly wears thin (Jauk et al., 2016); let's add *Machiavellianism* and *psychopathy* to the list. People who are high in Machiavellianism[7] think that there's a sucker born every minute and that it's smart to take advantage of gullible fools (Jones, 2016); they're cynical, duplicitous, and manipulative, and they readily lie to others if it helps them get what they want (Azizli et al., 2016). Those who are high in psychopathy tend to be impulsive thrill-seekers who sometimes seem charming but who callously disregard others' feelings and well-being; they're rarely remorseful when they do others harm (O'Boyle et al., 2015). Narcissism, Machiavellianism, and psychopathy are often collectively called the **Dark Triad** because they have features in common—they all involve low levels of the Big 5 trait of agreeableness (DeShong et al., 2017)—and they all tend to result in behavior toward others that is disadvantageous, being arrogant, manipulative, exploitative, cold, and hostile (Southard et al., 2015). When disagreements arise, for instance, you can expect to encounter more counterproductive criticism, contempt, defensiveness, and stonewalling from those who have higher levels of the Dark Triad traits (Horan et al., 2015). So, we may initially be attracted to the self-confidence and cleverness of these folks (Qureshi et al., 2016) but it's best to beware: In the end, they make pretty lousy friends.

FRIENDSHIP DIFFICULTIES

Now, in this last section of the chapter, let's examine some of the more common states and traits that interfere with rewarding friendships. We'll focus on two problems, *shyness* and *loneliness,* that most of us have experienced at one time or

---

[6] Back on page 124.

[7] The trait is named for an Italian fellow, Niccolò Machiavelli, who advocated such tactics way back in 1512.

another. As we'll see, shy or lonely people usually want to develop close friendships, but they routinely behave in ways that make it difficult to do so.

These days, we may need every friend we've got. More than one out of every eight adult Americans lives alone—a proportion that's doubled since 1960 (Wilson & Lamidi, 2013)—and intimate friendships are less common in the United States than they used to be, too (McPherson et al., 2006). The number of people who say they have no close confidant of any sort has soared from only 10 percent in 1985 to 25 percent today. One of every four adult Americans has no one to whom to turn for intimate counsel and support. Another 19 percent say they have only one confidant (who is often a spouse or a sibling), and, overall, the average number of intimate partners people have, including both close friends and lovers, has plummeted from three (in 1985) to two. Many of us have hundreds of "friends" on Facebook, but only rarely are they companions who offer the rich rewards of real intimacy. And once they leave school, only slightly more than half of all Americans (57 percent) have a close confidant to whom they are not related. Many Americans have none. And shyness and loneliness make things even worse.

Shyness

Have you ever felt anxious and inhibited around other people, worrying about what they thought of you and feeling awkward in your conversations with them? Most of us have. Over 80 percent of us have experienced **shyness,** the syndrome that combines social reticence and inhibited behavior with nervous discomfort in social settings (Miller, 2009). Take a look at Table 7.3 on the next page; when people are shy, they fret about social disapproval and unhappily anticipate unfavorable judgments from others. They feel self-conscious, uncomfortable, and inept (Arroyo & Harwood, 2011). As a result, they interact with others in an impoverished manner. If they don't avoid an interaction altogether, they behave in an inhibited, guarded fashion; they look at others less, smile less, speak less often, and converse less responsively (Ickes, 2009). Compared to people who are not shy, they manage everyday conversation poorly.

Shyness may beset almost anyone now and then. It's especially common when we're in unfamiliar settings, meeting attractive, high-status strangers for the first time, and it's less likely when we're on familiar turf interacting with old friends (Leary & Kowalski, 1995). However, some people are *chronically* shy, experiencing shyness frequently, and three characteristics distinguish them from people who are shy less often. First, people who are routinely shy *fear negative evaluation* from others. The possibility that others might dislike them is rarely far from their minds, and the threat of derision or disdain from others is more frightening to them than it is to most people. They worry about social disapproval more than the rest of us do (Miller, 2009). Second, they tend to doubt themselves. *Poor self-regard* usually accompanies chronic shyness, and shy people tend to have low self-esteem (Tackett et al., 2013). Finally, they feel less competent in their interactions with others, and sometimes with good reason: Overall, they have lower levels of *social skill* than do people who are not shy (Ickes, 2009).

- *Capitalization.* Friends usually respond eagerly and energetically to our happy outcomes, sharing our delight and reinforcing our pleasure.
- *Social support.* This comes in various forms, including affection, advice, and material assistance. Some people are better providers of social support than others are, and the best support fits our needs and preferences. Invisible support that goes unnoticed by the recipient is sometimes very beneficial, but perceived support is very important; it's not what people do for us but what we *think* they do for us that matters in the long run.
- *Responsiveness.* Friends provide attentive and supportive recognition of our needs and interests, and *perceived partner responsiveness* is powerfully rewarding.

The Rules of Friendship. Friendships also have rules, shared beliefs within a culture about how friends should (and should not) behave.

Friendship across the Life Cycle

Childhood. As children grow and mature, their friendships gradually grow richer and more complex. The sophisticated ways in which adults conduct their friendships are years in the making.

Adolescence. During the teen years, adolescents increasingly turn to their friends for the satisfaction of important attachment needs.

Young Adulthood. After college, people tend to interact with fewer friends, but they have deeper relationships with the friends they have.

Midlife. *Dyadic withdrawal* occurs as people see more of a lover; they see less of their friends (but a lot more of their in-laws).

Old Age. *Socioemotional selectivity theory* suggests that seniors aim for quality, not quantity, in their friendships.

Differences in Friendship

Gender Differences in Same-Sex Friendships. Women's friendships are usually characterized by *emotional sharing* and self-disclosure, whereas men's friendships revolve around *shared activities,* companionship, and competition.

Individual Differences in Friendship. Most gays and lesbians have heterosexual friends, but most heterosexuals do not (think that they) have gay or lesbian friends. *Relational self-construals* lead people to emphasize their relationships rather than their independence. And it's best to beware of people with high levels of the *Dark Triad* traits of narcissism, Machiavellianism, and psychopathy; they're usually callous and manipulative.

Friendship Difficulties

Shyness. Shy people fear social disapproval and behave timidly, often making the negative impressions that they were hoping to avoid. Many shy people interact comfortably with others when they are given an excuse for things to go poorly, so they need increased self-confidence instead of better social skills.

Loneliness. Dissatisfaction and distress occur when we want more, or more satisfying, connections with others, and both *social loneliness* and *emotional loneliness* may be involved. Loneliness results from genetic influences, insecure attachment, low self-esteem, and low expressivity. It is associated with negative attitudes and drab interactions that are unappealing to others. Hopeful attributions and reasonable expectations are helpful in overcoming loneliness.

CHAPTER 8

Love

A BRIEF HISTORY OF LOVE ◆ TYPES OF LOVE
◆ INDIVIDUAL AND CULTURAL DIFFERENCES IN LOVE
◆ DOES LOVE LAST? ◆ FOR YOUR CONSIDERATION
◆ CHAPTER SUMMARY

Here's an interesting question: If someone had all the other qualities you desired in a spouse, would you marry that person if you were not in love with him or her? Most of us reading this book would say no: Huge majorities of American men and women consider romantic love to be necessary for marriage (Sprecher & Hatfield, 2017). Along with all the other characteristics people want in a spouse—such as warmth, good looks, and dependability—young adults in Western cultures insist on romance and passion as a condition for marriage (Livingston & Caumont, 2017). What makes this remarkable is that it's such a new thing. Throughout history, the choice of a spouse has usually had little to do with romantic love (Ackerman, 1994); people married each other for political, economic, practical, and family reasons, but they did not marry because they were in love with each other. Even in North America, people began to consider love to be a requirement for marriage only a few decades ago. In 1967, 76 percent of women and 35 percent of men *would* have married an otherwise perfect partner whom they did not love (Kephart, 1967). These days, most people would refuse such a marriage.

In a sense, then, we have embarked on a bold experiment. Never before, until now, have people considered love to be an essential reason to marry (Coontz, 2005). People experience romantic passion all over the world, but there are still many places where it has little to do with their choice of a spouse. North Americans use romance as a reason to marry to an unprecedented degree (Hatfield & Rapson, 2008). Is this a good idea? If there are various overlapping types of "love" and different types of lovers—and worse, if passion and romance decline over time—marriages based on love may often be prone to confusion and, perhaps, disappointment.

Consideration of these possibilities lies ahead. I'll start with a brief history of love and then ponder different varieties of love and different types of lovers. Then, I'll finish with a key question: Does love last? (What do you think the answer is?)

A BRIEF HISTORY OF LOVE

Our modern belief that spouses should love one another is just one of many perspectives with which different cultures have viewed the experience of love (Hunt, 1959). Over the ages, attitudes toward love have varied on at least four dimensions:

- *Cultural value.* Is love a desirable or undesirable state?
- *Sexuality.* Should love be sexual or nonsexual?
- *Sexual orientation.* Should love involve heterosexual or same-sex partners?
- *Marital status.* Should we love our spouses, or is love reserved for others?

Different societies have drawn upon these dimensions to create some strikingly different patterns of what love is, or should be.

In ancient Greece, for instance, passionate attraction to another person was considered a form of madness that had nothing to do with marriage or family life. Instead, the Greeks admired platonic love, the nonsexual adoration of a beloved person that was epitomized by love between two men.

In ancient Egypt, people of royal blood often married their siblings, and in ancient Rome, "the purpose of marriage was to produce children, make favorable alliances, and establish a bloodline . . . it was hoped that husband and wife would be friends and get on amiably. Happiness was not part of the deal, nor was pleasure. Sex was for creating babies" (Ackerman, 1994, p. 37).

Heterosexual love took on more positive connotations in the concept of "courtly love" in the twelfth century. Courtly love required knights to seek love as a noble quest, diligently devoting themselves to a lady of high social standing. It was very idealistic, very elegant, and—at least in theory—nonsexual. It was also explicitly adulterous: In courtly love, the male partner was expected to be unmarried and the female partner married to someone else! In the Middle Ages, marriage continued to have nothing to do with romance; in contrast, it was a deadly serious matter of politics and property. Indeed, passionate, erotic desire for someone was thought to be "dangerous, a trapdoor leading to hell, which was not even to be condoned between husband and wife" (Ackerman, 1994, p. 46).

Over the next 500 years, people came to believe that passionate love could be desirable and ennobling but that it was usually doomed. Either the lovers would be prevented from being with each other (often because they were married to other people), or death would overtake one or the other (or both) before their love could be fulfilled. It was not until the seventeenth and eighteenth centuries that Europeans, especially the English, began to believe that romantic passion could occasionally result in a happy ending. Still, the notion that one *ought* to feel passion and romance for one's husband or wife was not a widespread idea; indeed, in the late 1700s, defenders of "traditional marriage" were generally horrified by the emergence of love as a reason for marriage (Coontz, 2015).

Even now, the assumption that romantic love should be linked to marriage is held only in some regions of the world (Merali, 2012). Nevertheless, you probably do think love and marriage go together. Why should your beliefs be different from those of most people throughout history? Why has the acceptance of and enthusiasm for marrying for love been most complete in North America (Hatfield & Rapson, 2008)? Probably because of America's individualism and economic prosperity (which allow most young adults to live away from home and choose their own marital partners) and its lack of a caste system or ruling class. The notion that individuals (instead of families) should choose marriage partners because of emotional attachments (not economic concerns) makes more sense to Americans than it does to many other peoples of the world. In most places, the idea that a young adult should leave home, fall in love, decide to marry, and then bring the beloved home to meet the family seems completely absurd (Buunk et al., 2010). This is slowly changing, as technology and socioeconomic development spread around the world (Manglos-Weber & Weinreb, 2017), but for now, the marital practices of North Americans strike most folks as odd.

In any case, let's consider all the different views of love we just encountered:

- Love is doomed.
- Love is madness.
- Love is a noble quest.
- Love need not involve sex.
- Love and marriage go together.
- Love can be happy and fulfilling.
- Love has little to do with marriage.
- The best love occurs among people of the same sex.

Some of these distinctions simply reflect ordinary cultural and historical variations (Eastwick, 2013). However, these different views may also reflect an important fact: There may be diverse forms of love. Let's ponder that possibility.

TYPES OF LOVE

Advice columnist Ann Landers was once contacted by a woman who was perplexed because her consuming passion for her lover fizzled soon after they were married. Ms. Landers suggested that what the woman had called "the love affair of the century" was "not love at all. It was one set of glands calling to another" (Landers, 1982, p. 2). There was a big distinction, Ms. Landers asserted, between horny infatuation and real love, which was deeper and richer than mere passion. Love was based in tolerance, care, and communication, Landers argued; it was "friendship that has caught fire" (p. 12).

Does that phrase characterize your experiences with romantic love? Is there a difference between romantic love and infatuation? According to a leading theory of love experiences, the answer to both questions is probably "yes."

The Triangular Theory of Love

Robert Sternberg (1987, 2006) proposed that three different building blocks combine to form different types of love. The first component of love is **intimacy,** which includes the feelings of warmth, understanding, trust, support, and sharing that often characterize loving relationships. The second component is **passion**, which is characterized by physical arousal and desire, excitement, and need. Passion often takes the form of sexual longing, but any strong emotional need that is satisfied by one's partner fits this category. The final ingredient of love is **commitment,** which includes feelings of permanence, stability, and the decisions to devote oneself to a relationship and to work to maintain it. Commitment is mainly cognitive in nature, whereas intimacy is emotional and passion is a motive, or drive. The "heat" in loving relationships is assumed to come from passion, and the warmth from intimacy; in contrast, commitment can be a cool-headed decision that is not emotional or temperamental at all.

In Sternberg's theory, each of these three components is said to be one side of a triangle that describes the love two people share. Each component can vary in intensity from low to high, so triangles of various sizes and shapes are possible. In fact, countless numbers of shapes can occur, so to keep things simple, we'll consider the relatively pure categories of love that result when one or more of the three ingredients is plentiful but the others are very low. As we proceed, you should remember that pure experiences that are this clearly defined may not be routine in real life.

Nonlove. If intimacy, passion, and commitment are all absent, love does not exist. Instead, you have a casual, superficial, uncommitted relationship between people who are probably just acquaintances, not friends.

Liking. Liking occurs when intimacy is high but passion and commitment are very low. Liking occurs in friendships with real closeness and warmth that do not arouse passion or the expectation that you will spend the rest of your life with that person. If a friend *does* arouse passion or is missed terribly when he or she is gone, the relationship has gone beyond liking and has become something else.

Infatuation. Strong passion in the absence of intimacy or commitment is infatuation, which is what people experience when they are aroused by others they barely know. Sternberg (1987) admits that he pined away for a girl in his 10th-grade biology class whom he never got up the courage to get to know. This, he now acknowledges, was nothing but passion. He was infatuated with her.

Empty love. Commitment without intimacy or passion is empty love. In Western cultures, this type of love may occur in burned-out relationships in which the warmth and passion have died, and the decision to stay together is the only thing that remains. However, in other cultures in which marriages are arranged, empty love may be the first, rather than final, stage in the spouses' lives together.

None of the categories I've mentioned so far may seem much like love to you. That's probably because each is missing some important ingredient that we associate with being in love—and that is precisely Sternberg's point. Love is a multifaceted experience, and that becomes clear when we combine the three components of love to create more complex states.

© Comstock/PunchStock/Getty Images

Love can last a lifetime. But what *kind* of love do you think this couple shares?

Romantic love. When high intimacy and passion occur together, people experience romantic love. Thus, one way to think about romantic love is as a combination of liking and infatuation. People often become committed to their romances, but Sternberg argues that commitment is not a defining characteristic of romantic love. A summer love affair can be very romantic, for instance, even when both lovers know that it is going to end when the summer is over.

Companionate love. Intimacy and commitment combine to form love for a close companion, or companionate love. Here, closeness, communication, and sharing are coupled with substantial investment in the relationship as the partners work to maintain a deep, long-term friendship. Companionate love is epitomized by a long, happy marriage in which the couple's youthful passion has gradually died down.

Fatuous love. Passion and commitment in the absence of intimacy create a foolish experience called *fatuous love.* ("Fatuous" means "stupid" and "lacking substance.") This type of love can occur in whirlwind courtships in which two partners marry quickly on the basis of overwhelming passion but don't know (or necessarily like) each other very well. In a sense, such lovers invest a lot in an infatuation—and that's a risky business.

Consummate love. Finally, when intimacy, passion, and commitment are all present to a substantial degree, people experience "complete," or consummate, love. This is the type of love many people seek, but Sternberg (1987) suggests that it's a lot like losing weight: easy to do for a while, but hard to maintain over time.

TABLE 8.1. The Triangular Theory of Love: Types of Relationships

	Intimacy	Passion	Commitment
Nonlove	Low	Low	Low
Liking	**High**	Low	Low
Infatuation	Low	**High**	Low
Empty love	Low	Low	**High**
Romantic love	**High**	**High**	Low
Companionate love	**High**	Low	**High**
Fatuous love	Low	**High**	**High**
Consummate love	**High**	**High**	**High**

Source: Based on Sternberg, R. J. "A duplex theory of love." In R. J. Sternberg & K. Weis (Eds.), The new psychology of love *(pp. 184–199). New Haven, CT: Yale University Press, 2006.*

Thus, according to the triangular theory of love, diverse experiences can underlie the simple expression "I love you" (as you can see in Table 8.1). Another complication that makes love tricky is that the three components can change over time, so that people may encounter various types of love in a given relationship (Ahmetoglu et al., 2010). Of the three, however, passion is assumed to be the most variable by far. It is also the least controllable, so that we may find our desire for others soaring and then evaporating rapidly in changes we cannot consciously control (Sternberg, 1987).

Is the theory right? Are these assertions accurate? Consider that, if the triangular theory's characterization of romantic love is correct, one of its key ingredients is a high level of passion that simply may not last. There's much to consider in wondering whether love lasts, however, so I'll put that off for a while. For now, I'll note that the three components of intimacy, passion, and commitment do all appear to be important aspects of loving relationships; in particular, each of the three components makes a loving relationship more satisfying, and the most rewarding romances contain big servings of all three ingredients (Fletcher et al., 2015).

A Physiological Perspective

Studies of the physical foundations of love also suggest that passion and intimacy are distinct experiences. The regions of the brain that regulate our sexual desire for others appear to be different from those that manage our feelings of attachment and commitment to our lovers (Cacioppo & Cacioppo, 2016). In some state-of-the-art studies of love, researchers are using fMRI technology to examine the activity in people's brains as they look at pictures of their lovers (as opposed to other people), and passion activates different areas of the brain than affection and commitment do, both in the United States (Acevedo & Aron, 2014) and in China (Xu et al., 2011). Thus, it really is possible to feel strong desire for those we do not love and to feel little passion for those to whom we are happily attached (Diamond, 2014). (But you probably already knew that.)

Indeed, theorist Helen Fisher (2006) argued that it makes evolutionary sense for there to be three interrelated but distinct biological systems that control components of love experiences. First, there's *lust,* or the sex drive, which is regulated by the sex hormones. Lust drives successful reproduction by providing us the motivation to mate with others. Then there's *attraction,* which promotes the pursuit of a particular preferred romantic partner. Attraction drives pair-bonding by fueling romantic love, which is regulated by the neurotransmitter dopamine in specific regions of the brain that control feelings of reward (Acevedo & Aron, 2014). Increased levels of dopamine may be responsible for the excitement and exhilaration that occur when we fall in love, explaining "why lovers feel euphoric, rejuvenated, optimistic, and energized, happy to sit up talking all night or making love for hours on end" (Ackerman, 1994, p. 165). Indeed, when people have just fallen in love, a look at their lovers makes pain not hurt as much. Romantic love also activates the areas of the brain that are affected by pain-relieving drugs, and sure enough, when they see their sweethearts, young lovers can shrug off pain (produced by a computer-controlled heating pad attached to a hand) that would be quite troubling under other circumstances (Younger et al., 2010). Finally, there's *attachment,* a term used here to describe the feelings of comfort, security, and connection to a long-term mate that keep a couple together long enough to protect and sustain their very young children (Fletcher et al., 2015). Attachment drives companionate love, which is regulated by the neuropeptide oxytocin. (More on that later.)

Thus, we may be equipped with three different physiological systems that each evolved to facilitate some component of successful reproduction—and they support the triangular theory's proposition that the related experiences of passion, intimacy, and commitment can vary separately and range from weak to strong at any given time. On the other hand, intimacy, passion, and commitment are clearly interrelated in many loving relationships (Whitley, 1993). For instance, if men become sexually aroused by inspecting porn, they report more love for their romantic partners than they do when they're not turned on (Dermer & Pyszczynski, 1978).

As a result, as I warned you earlier, the clearly defined categories offered by the triangular theory may not seem so distinct in real life. People's actual experiences of love are complex. For instance, a father's love for his son is likely to resemble his love for his own father, but the two feelings are also likely to differ in meaningful ways that the triangular theory does not readily explain. Different types of love probably overlap in a messier, more confusing way than the theory implies (Fehr, 2015).

Nevertheless, the theory offers a very useful framework for addressing different types of love, and whether or not it is entirely correct, it identifies two types of love that may be especially likely to occur in most romantic relationships over the long haul. Let's examine each of them more closely.

Romantic, Passionate Love

Has anyone ever told you, "I love you, but I'm not *in* love with you"? If so, it was probably bad news. As you probably knew, he or she was trying to say, "I like you, I care about you, I think you're a marvelous person with wonderful qualities and so forth, but I don't find you sexually desirable" (Myers & Berscheid, 1997, p. 360).

Just as the triangular theory of love proposes, sexual attraction (or *passion*) appears to be one of the defining characteristics of romantic love (Fehr, 2015). So, it's disappointing if a romantic partner implies, "I just want us to be friends."

The fact that romantic love involves passion is important. Passion involves activation and arousal, and remarkably, *any* form of strong arousal, good or bad, can influence our feelings of romantic love.

Arousal

A classic analysis of romantic love by Elaine Hatfield and Ellen Berscheid proposed that passionate attraction is rooted in two factors: (1) physiological arousal such as a fast heart beat that is coupled with (2) the belief that another person is the cause of your arousal (Berscheid & Walster, 1974). According to this two-factor perspective, romantic love is produced, or at least intensified, when feelings of arousal are associated with the presence of another attractive person.

Now, imagine this: You're in a park in North Vancouver, British Columbia, starting across a long, narrow bridge made of wooden planks that are suspended by wire, hanging hundreds of feet over a deep gorge. The bridge bounces and tilts and sways as you walk across it, and it has a low wire railing that comes up only to your waist. Far, far below is a rocky creek, and (because you're just like all the rest of us) you can't help but feel some nervous excitement (or perhaps outright fear) as you make your way across. But, then, right in the middle of the precarious bridge, you encounter an attractive person of the other sex who asks you to answer a few questions. You're shown a picture and asked to make up a story, and your interviewer thanks you warmly and invites you to call later if you have any questions. How attracted would you be to the person you met on the bridge?

This is just the question that was asked in a famous experiment by Dutton and Aron (1974), who sent attractive women to interview unaccompanied young men (between 19 and 35 years of age) either in the middle of the spooky suspension bridge or on another bridge that was stable and just a few feet off the ground in another part of the park. The stories that the men wrote were scored for sexual imagery, and Dutton and Aron found that the men on the swaying suspension bridge were thinking sexier thoughts than other men. In addition, those men were more likely to call the woman later at her home. They were more attracted to her, and the arousal—or fear—caused by the dangerous bridge had evidently fueled their interest in her. Other men who encountered the same woman in a less dramatic place found her less compelling. On the precarious bridge, fear had apparently fueled attraction.

Or had it? Could nervous excitement caused by a shaky bridge really be mistaken, at least in part, for romantic attraction to a stranger? Well, try this procedure: You're a young man who runs in place for either 2 minutes or 15 seconds, so your pulse rate is high and you're breathing hard, or you're just a little more aroused than normal. Flushed with more or less arousal, you move to another room and inspect a video of a young woman whom you think you're about to meet. You and other men all see the same woman, but, through some clever makeup, she looks either quite becoming or rather unattractive. What do you think of her? When real research participants reported their reactions, it was clear that high

TABLE 8.2. Arousal and Attraction

	Attractiveness of the Woman	
Arousal of the Men	High	Low
Low	26.1	15.1
High	32.4	9.4

Source: Data from White, G. L., Fishbein, S., & Rutstein, J. "Passionate love: The misattribution of arousal," Journal of Personality and Social Psychology, 41, 1981, 56–62.

The higher the scores, the more desirable the men judged the woman to be. The lovely woman was always judged to be more desirable than the unattractive woman, but a faster heart beat accentuated this effect: When their pulses were racing, men thought that an attractive woman was *more* compelling and an unattractive woman was even less desirable.

---

arousal intensified the men's responses to the woman (White et al., 1981). The attractive version of the woman was always preferred to the unattractive version, of course, but as you can see in Table 8.2, the men liked the attractive model even more—and liked the unattractive model even less—when they were aroused than when they were calm. High arousal magnified the guys' responses, so that men who encountered an attractive woman when their pulses were racing thought that she was *really* hot.

Moreover, the effects of arousal on attraction do not depend on the type of arousal that is produced. In another procedure (White et al., 1981), men listened to one of three tapes:

- *Negatively arousing.* A description of the brutal mutilation and killing of a missionary while his family watched.
- *Positively arousing.* Selections from Steve Martin's Grammy Award-winning comedy album, *A Wild and Crazy Guy.*[1]
- *Neutral.* A boring description of the circulatory system of a frog.

Thereafter, as before, the men viewed a video of a lovely or plain woman and provided their impressions of her. Arousal again fueled attraction, and it didn't matter what type of arousal it was. When the men had experienced either type of strong emotion—whether by laughing hard at the funny material or by being disgusted by the gory material—they were more attracted to the appealing woman and less attracted to the unappealing woman than they were when they had listened to the boring biology tape.

Taken together, these studies demonstrate that adrenaline fuels love. High arousal of various types, including simple exertion and amusement, all seem to be able to enhance our feelings of romantic attraction to desirable potential partners. Consider the implications: Have you ever had a screaming argument with a lover and then found that it was especially sweet to "kiss and make up" a few

[1]You've probably never heard this. You should.

minutes later? Might your anger have fueled your subsequent passion? Is that what being "in love" is like?

To some degree, it is. One useful measure of the passion component of romantic love is a Passionate Love Scale created by Elaine Hatfield and Susan Sprecher (1986). The short form of the scale is reprinted in Table 8.3; as you can see, the scale assesses fascination and preoccupation with, high desire for, and strong emotions about the object of one's love. Scores on the Passionate Love Scale increase as someone falls deeper and deeper into romantic love with someone else, only leveling off when the partners become engaged or start living together. (Note that—as I mentioned earlier—American couples decide to marry or live

---

TABLE 8.3. The Short Form of the Passionate Love Scale

This questionnaire asks you to describe how you feel when you are passionately in love. Please think of the person whom you love most passionately *right now*. Keep this person in mind as you complete this questionnaire.

Answer each item using this scale:

1	2	3	4	5	6	7	8	9
Not at all true				Moderately true				Definitely true

1. I would feel deep despair if _____ left me.
2. Sometimes I feel I can't control my thoughts; they are obsessively on _____.
3. I feel happy when I am doing something to make _____ happy.
4. I would rather be with _____ than anyone else.
5. I'd get jealous if I thought _____ was falling in love with someone else.
6. I yearn to know all about _____.
7. I want _____ physically, emotionally, mentally.
8. I have an endless appetite for affection from _____.
9. For me, _____ is the perfect romantic partner.
10. I sense my body responding when _____ touches me.
11. _____ always seems to be on my mind.
12. I want _____ to know me—my thoughts, my fears, and my hopes.
13. I eagerly look for signs indicating _____'s desire for me.
14. I possess a powerful attraction for _____.
15. I get extremely depressed when things don't go right in my relationship with _____.

Hatfield, E., & Sprecher, S. "Measuring passionate love in intimate relationships," Journal of Adolescence, 9, 1986, 383–410. Copyright 1986 by Elsevier. All rights reserved. Used with permission.

Higher scores on the PLS indicate greater passionate love. Across all 15 items, the average rating per item—add up all your ratings and divide by 15—for both men and women is 7.15. If your average is 9 (the highest possible), you're experiencing more passionate love than most people, and if your average is 5.25 or lower, you're experiencing less.

together when their passion is at a peak.) The vision of romantic love that emerges from the Passionate Love Scale is one of need and desire—ecstasy when one is loved in return and agony when one is not—and these are clearly responses that burn brighter when one is aroused than when one is calm and relaxed.

So, one aspect of romantic love is the exhilaration and euphoria of high arousal, and various events that excite us may increase our feelings of love for our partners. Romance is more than just passion, however. It also involves our thoughts.

Is Romantic Love an Emotion?

I'll confess up front: The issue is still in doubt, so I don't have a definite answer to the question posed by the title of this box. Romantic love certainly involves fervent feelings and strong motives, but theorists in affective science typically reserve the term *emotion* for an organized response with particular characteristics (Lamy, 2016). Many (but not all) researchers consider emotions to result from specific events that cause discrete physiological reactions and that elicit distinct patterns of expressive behavior and goal-oriented responses (Keltner et al., 2014). Emotions exist, theorists argue, because they promote effective, adaptive responses to important, recurring tasks (Ekman & Cardaro, 2011). Thus, if it is unequivocally an emotion, romantic love should have a concrete, useful function, and it should occur in response to particular stimuli, cause distinctive physical changes, be visible to others, and engender recognizable behavioral responses. (If you pause for a moment and consider these last few criteria, you may see why the issue is in doubt.)

In focusing our attention and energies on particular partners, romantic love promotes commitment that can increase our reproductive success (Fletcher et al., 2015). It is also elicited by others who we think would make compelling mates. But it doesn't activate specific, delimited areas of the brain as many other emotions do; regions regulating reward switch on, but so do several other areas, so romantic love has more diffuse effects than other discrete emotions (Xu et al., 2011). People who are in love display enthusiastic interest in their partners, with lots of nodding, smiling, and close interpersonal distances (Gonzaga et al., 2006), but the extent to which these cues are definitive signals of love per se is arguable. And people find it more difficult to talk themselves into feeling in love than they do some other emotions. If you vividly envision the provocation that last made you angry, you can bring back some of your anger—but people have less success reigniting the preoccupied passion of romantic love on command (Aron, 2010). The existing evidence leads most observers to think that romantic love is more a mood with particular motives than a discrete emotion (Diamond, 2014).

And why should you care, exactly? Well, consider that emotions are rather *brief* events (Keltner et al., 2014). Every other potent emotion you've ever experienced flared up quickly, burned brightly, and then faded away. Moods last longer, but they're more diffuse events that have more variable effects on our behavior; if romantic love is a mood, it may have different effects on different people.

So, exactly what sort of affective experience romantic love is remains undecided. But whatever it is, there's another question that now looms large: Other emotions, moods, and motives don't last forever, so does love last? Can our romantic, passionate attraction to a particular partner continue indefinitely? Keep this key question in the back of your mind as you continue reading, and we'll return to it at the end of the chapter.

Thought

The two-factor theory of passionate love emphasizes the role of our thoughts and beliefs in accounting for arousal. Our judgments are also linked to romance in other ways, with lovers thinking about each other in ways that differ from the ways they think about their friends. Some of these distinctions are apparent in the contents of a Love Scale and a Liking Scale created by Zick Rubin in 1973. Years before Hatfield and Sprecher created the Passionate Love Scale, Rubin created dozens of statements that reflected a wide range of interpersonal attitudes and asked people to use them to describe both a lover and a friend. The handful of items that epitomized people's romances ended up on a Love Scale that gives a partial indication of what lovers are thinking.

One theme in the items on the Love Scale is *intimacy*, just as the triangular theory of love defines it. Romance is characterized by openness, communication, and trust (see item 1 in Table 8.4). A second theme is needy *dependence* (see item 2 in Table 8.4). The dependence items describe ardent longing for one's partner that has much in common with the passion we've discussed. A last theme on the Love Scale, however, describes feelings that are not mentioned by the triangular theory: *caring*. Romantic lovers report concern for the welfare and well-being of their partners (see item 3). They want to take care of their partners and keep them happy.

Thus, like other efforts to characterize love (e.g., Fehr, 2015), the Love Scale portrays romantic love as a multifaceted experience that involves both giving (i.e., caring) and taking (i.e., dependence). If you're in love with someone, it's probably partly selfish—you love your partner because of how that person makes you feel—and partly generous; you genuinely care for your partner and will work to satisfy and protect him or her. (In fact, compassionate concern for those we love may define yet another type of love, as we'll see on page 256.) In addition, these diverse sentiments are experienced with relative intensity and urgency: You'd do *anything* for your partner and be *miserable* without him or her.

TABLE 8.4. Rubin's (1973) Love and Liking Scales: Some Example Items

Rubin's Love Scale

1. I feel that I can confide in my partner about virtually anything.
2. If I could never be with my partner, I would be miserable.
3. I would do almost anything for my partner.

Rubin's Liking Scale

1. My partner is one of the most likable people I know.
2. My partner is the sort of person that I would like to be.
3. I think that my partner is unusually well-adjusted.

Romantic love is a complex state that emerges from multifaceted feelings and high arousal. It's a combination of intimacy and passion.

Compare those thoughts and feelings to the sorts of things people say about their friends. As you can see in Table 8.4, the Liking Scale seems bland by comparison. People say they like their friends because their friends are nice, well-adjusted, likable people. But they love their lovers because they need them and would do anything the lover asks. There's a fervor to the thoughts that characterize romantic love that is lacking when we just like someone.

The specific judgments people make of their partners are important, too. As we saw in chapter 4, people tend to hold rosy views of their relationship partners, and their tendency to idealize and glorify their lovers is probably at a peak when they are most in love. In fact, the moment romance enters the picture, people start ignoring or reinterpreting undesirable information about potential partners. Imagine that you're a male college student who is asked to play the role of a restaurant owner who is evaluating the work of a woman who is pitching you an advertising campaign (Goodwin et al., 2002). You watch a video of her presentation, which is either coherent and clever or clumsy and inept. Would you be able to tell the difference between the competent and incompetent work? Of course you would. But what if you knew that you'd be going out on a date with the woman on Friday? Would the possibility of a romance influence your judgment? You may not think so, but when men really participated in a procedure like this, a romantic orientation had a big effect, as Figure 8.1 illustrates. The upcoming date obviously contaminated the men's judgment, magically transforming a lousy performance into one of much higher quality. Any distinction between good and bad work disappeared entirely when the possibility of romance was in play.

As these results suggest, in a real way, "love is blind": People underestimate or ignore their lovers' faults. They hold idealized images of their lovers that may differ in meaningful ways from the concrete realities they face. In fact, a major difference between love and friendship may be our imaginations: Our lovers are fascinating, mysterious, and appealing in ways our friends are not (Langeslag et al., 2015).

Romantic love also makes it easier to put tempting alternatives to our present partners out of our minds. When we're fascinated and preoccupied with a lover, we may have difficulty focusing and concentrating on anyone—or anything—else

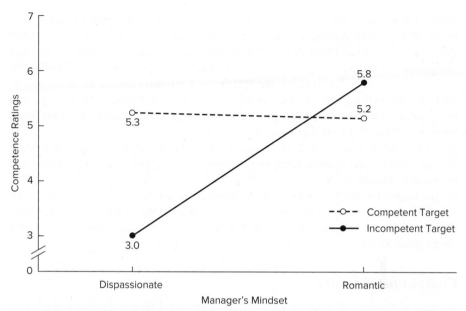

Source: Data from Goodwin, S. A., Fiske, S. T., Rosen, L. D., & Rosenthal, A. M. "The eye of the beholder: Romantic goals and impression biases," Journal of Experimental Social Psychology, *38,* 2002, 232–241.

FIGURE 8.1. **Love is blind.**
When men expected to date a woman, they thought her lousy work was much better than it really was.

(van Steenbergen et al., 2014). Here's another provocative procedure: Imagine yourself inspecting photos of attractive members of the other sex, picking the best-looking one of the bunch, and then writing essays on (a) why that person is attractive and (b) what a perfect first meeting with that person would be like. Clearly, the researchers have you pondering a compelling alternative to your current romantic partner (Gonzaga et al., 2008). But the plot thickens; you're now asked to put the fantasy alternative out of mind and to stop thinking about him or her while you write another essay about (a) your love for your partner, (b) your sexual desire for your partner, or (c) just your current stream of thought. Can you do it? *Can* you ignore the alluring alternative? You can if you're mentally rehearsing your love for your current partner. People were better able to distract themselves from the alternative—and they remembered less about the alternative's looks—when they envisioned their love for their partners than in the other two conditions. Evidently, love keeps our attention on one preferred partner; rehearsing our romantic love for our partners even makes us less likely to notice other attractive people in the first place (Maner et al., 2008).

Finally, even our thoughts about ourselves can change when we fall in love. Arthur and Elaine Aron's *self-expansion model* suggests that love causes our self-concepts to expand and change as our partners bring us new experiences and new roles, and we gradually learn things about ourselves that we didn't know before (Aron et al., 2013). Indeed, a study that tracked young adults for 10 weeks while they fell in love found that their self-concepts become more diversified and their self-esteem went up, which were two reasons why falling in love was so delightful (Aron et al., 1995). The passion we feel for our partners seems to be fueled, in part, by the self-expansion they provide us—and over time, if a relationship becomes routine, both our self-expansion and our passion gradually simmer down (Sheets, 2014). (More on this a bit later, too.)

All of this is potent stuff. The arousal and cognition that characterize romantic, passionate love involve surging emotion, imagination and idealization, and occasional obsession (Aron et al., 2008). And it is the presence of this complex, hectic state that leads most North Americans to consider marriage. However, romantic passion may not be the reason they *stay* married in the years that follow. Whether or not a relationship lasts may have more to do with companionate love (Berscheid, 2010).

Companionate Love

Because it does not depend on passion, companionate love is a more settled state than romantic love is. The triangular theory suggests that it is a combination of intimacy and commitment, but I can characterize it more fully as a "comfortable, affectionate, trusting love for a likable partner, based on a deep sense of friendship and involving companionship and the enjoyment of common activities, mutual interests, and shared laughter" (Grote & Frieze, 1994, p. 275). It takes the form of a rich, committed friendship with someone with whom our lives are intertwined.

Sounds pleasant, but isn't it a bit bland compared to the ecstasies of romantic passion? Perhaps so, but you may want to get used to it. When hundreds of couples who had been married at least 15 years were asked why their marriages had lasted, they *didn't* say that they'd do anything for their spouses or be miserable without them, like romantic lovers do (Lauer & Lauer, 1985). Instead, for both men and women, the two most frequent reasons were (a) "My spouse is my best friend," and (b) "I like my spouse as a person." Long-lasting, satisfying marriages seem to include a lot of companionate love.

A useful measure of companionate love is the Friendship-Based Love Scale created by Nancy Grote and Irene Frieze (1994). As you can see in Table 8.5, the feelings described by the scale are very different than those that accompany passionate love; friendship and companionship are much more in evidence on the Friendship-Based Love Scale than they are on measures of romantic love.

Of course, deep friendships also occur often in the context of romantic love. In one study, 44 percent of the young adults in premarital relationships reported that their romantic partners were also their closest friends (Hendrick & Hendrick, 1993). However, when they are a part of romantic love, friendships are combined (and sometimes confused) with sexual arousal and passion. The predominant importance of friendship in creating the experience is easier to detect in companionate love, when intimacy is paired with commitment, than in romantic love, when intimacy is paired with passion.

TABLE 8.5. The Friendship-Based Love Scale

Think about your closest current relationship, and then rate your agreement or disagreement with each of these questions on the following scale:

1	2	3	4	5
strongly disagree				strongly agree

1. I feel our love is based on a deep and abiding friendship.
2. I express my love for my partner through the enjoyment of common activities and mutual interests.
3. My love for my partner involves solid, deep affection.
4. An important factor in my love for my partner is that we laugh together.
5. My partner is one of the most likable people I know.
6. The companionship I share with my partner is an important part of my love for him or her.

Source: Adapted from Grote, N. K., & Frieze, I. H. "The measurement of friendship-based love in intimate relationships," Personal Relationships, 1, 1994, 275–300.

The average total score for married men is 25.2, and the average total for married women is 26.4. Scores ranging between 21 and 30 are typical for men, and scores between 22 and 30 are routine for women. Scores on the scale are more highly correlated with relationship satisfaction and duration than scores on the Passionate Love Scale are.

A Physiological Foundation

Companionate love also has a physiological foundation that differs from that of romantic love. Experiences of romantic, passionate love stimulate the release of the neurotransmitter *dopamine,* which works in reward and pleasure centers of our brains (Acevedo & Aron, 2014). Companionate love, on the other hand, seems to involve *oxytocin,* a neuropeptide that promotes relaxation and reduces stress (Diamond, 2014). Oxytocin is released by mothers during childbirth and breastfeeding (and in fact, a synthetic form of oxytocin, pitocin, is used to induce labor), and the more oxytocin a young mother has in her blood, the more she'll cuddle and coo, look, and smile at her baby (Feldman et al., 2007). Among adults, a lot of it is produced during orgasm; oxytocin may be one of the causes of the relaxed lethargy that couples often experience after lovemaking (Floyd, 2006). Moreover—and this is interesting—research participants who snort a spray of oxytocin seem to become more motivated to seek social connection with others (Bartz, 2016). People who are low in extraversion become more friendly (Human et al., 2016), and those who are avoidant of intimacy feel more kind and warm toward others (Bartz et al., 2015).

Because of patterns like these, journalists sometimes call oxytocin the "love and cuddle hormone," but it doesn't always lead us to be nice to strangers. It seems to arouse affiliative motives, but if we encounter barriers to closeness—such as antagonistic provocation from an opponent in a lab procedure (Ne'eman et al.,

2016)—it can make us meaner, too (Bartz, 2016). Oxytocin has variable effects on our social behavior.

Nevertheless, in a close, comfortable relationship, oxytocin seems to promote a soothing sense of well-being. People who have higher levels of oxytocin in their blood tend to be warmer and kinder when they discuss touchy topics with their spouses (Gouin et al., 2010), and they're more satisfied with their marriages (Holt-Lunstad et al., 2015a). And oxytocin may encourage enduring attachments to those who become associated with its presence in the bloodstream (Floyd, 2006)—so, in short, the production of oxytocin may provide a biological basis for feelings of companionate love.

Still, even if dopamine is a key player in romantic love and oxytocin a central ingredient in companionate love, both agents are always present in the body in some amount, so we rarely encounter pure experiences of romantic and companionate love in which one is present and the other is not. Companionate lovers can and do experience passion, and romantic lovers can and do feel commitment. As we experience them, the distinctions between romantic and companionate love are much fuzzier than this discussion may have implied (Graham, 2011). Nevertheless, if we're willing to tolerate some ambiguity, we can conclude that there appear to be at least two major types of love that frequently occur in American romance: a love that's full of passion that leads people to pair off with each other, and a love that's full of friendship that underlies relationships that last. Over time, companionate love is typically stronger in enduring relationships than romantic, passionate love is (Ahmetoglu et al., 2010), and it is more highly correlated with the satisfaction people enjoy (Langeslag et al., 2013). We'll return to this point at the end of the chapter.

Compassionate Love

There's a third type of love that occurs in successful romances (Fehr, 2015) that is not delineated by the triangular theory of love because the theory does not assert that considerate caring for other people is a specific component of love. Perhaps it should. An altruistic care and concern for the well-being of one's partner is a defining characteristic of **compassionate love**, a type of love that combines the trust and understanding of *intimacy* with compassion and *caring* that involves empathy, selflessness, and sacrifice on behalf of the beloved (Fehr et al., 2014). (Now before we go any further, let's take a moment and examine the label "compassionate" love. It sounds like a combination of romantic, passionate love [which obviously involves passion] and companionate love [which includes the word "companion"], but it is different from either one. Compassion involves empathy for others and the benevolent wish to aid those who are in need of help. Don't confuse companionate love with compassionate love.[2])

People who feel compassionate love tend to share the pain or joy that their loved ones experience (Collins et al., 2014), and they would rather suffer themselves than to allow someone close to them to be hurt. They are attentive, empathic,

---

[2] And don't blame me for the similarity of the terms. It's not my fault.

TABLE 8.6. Items from the Compassionate Love Scale

To what extent are these statements true about you?

1. I spend a lot of time concerned about the well-being of those people close to me.
2. If a person close to me needs help, I would do almost anything I could to help him or her.
3. I would rather suffer myself than see someone close to me suffer.

and generous, and their care and concern for their loved ones are evident in a Compassionate Love Scale created by Susan Sprecher and Beverley Fehr (2005). (See Table 8.6.) As you might expect, compassionate lovers provide their partners more support—and take more pleasure in doing so—than do those who are less compassionate (Sprecher et al., 2007).

The thoughtful, benevolent, and generous behaviors that compassionate lovers offer their partners are good for their relationships. Each night for two weeks, Harry Reis and his colleagues (2017) asked 175 newlywed couples from across the United States and Canada to report which of the specific behaviors in Table 8.7 had occurred that day. The young lovers did these things often, but not *that* often; on average, a new spouse performed at least one of these kind acts on only about 60 percent of all days. But when they did occur, *both* spouses were more satisfied with their relationship the next day, and it was actually better to give than to

TABLE 8.7. A Compassionate Love Acts Diary

Which of these things have you done today? Both you and your lover will be more satisfied with your relationship if you up your game and intentionally behave this way more frequently. And just how pleasant and profitable will your partnership be if you *both* behave this way?

Today, I voluntarily did something special for my partner.

Today, I went out of my way to "be there" for my partner.

Today, I said or did something to show that I value my partner.

Today, I expressed a lot of tenderness and caring for my partner.

Today, I willingly put my partner's goals or wishes ahead of my own.

Today, I really tried to understand my partner's thoughts and feelings.

Today, I willingly modified my plans or activities for my partner's sake.

Today, I was genuinely open and receptive to things my partner said or asked of me.

Today, I really tried to be accepting rather than judging of something about my partner.

Today, I did something to show my partner that I respect and admire him/her as a person.

Source: Reis, H. T., Maniaci, M. R., & Rogge, R. D. "The expression of compassionate love in everyday compassionate acts," Journal of Social and Personal Relationships, *31, 2014, 651–676.*

receive: The donors of these generous actions experienced even better moods than the recipients did. You probably won't be surprised, then, to read that greater compassionate love for one's partner, which is evident when compassionate acts like these occur often, is associated with more relationship satisfaction and commitment over time, too (Fehr et al., 2014).

Compassionate love is highly correlated with experiences of romantic love and companionate love—they all have intimacy in common—but there are still differences among them that are worth noting (Fehr, 2015). Whereas romantic love is "blind," compassionate love is rooted in more accurate understanding of our partners' strengths and weaknesses; we recognize their deficiencies, but we love them anyway (Neff & Karney, 2009). And the selfless concern that defines compassionate love may be invaluable in protecting and maintaining a relationship if the partners become infirm with age or if a "malevolent fate plunges one of the partners from 'better' to a permanent 'worse'" (Berscheid, 2010, p. 17). Is compassionate love necessary for continued satisfaction in long-term relationships? We don't yet know: Those studies are just beginning to be done (e.g., Sabey et al., 2016). Nevertheless, along with passion and friendship, compassionate caring for one's partner may be another key ingredient in the very best experiences of love.

> ### A Point to Ponder
>
> Imagine that you're developing the recipe for the perfect love that you'd like to get from a perfect lover. What would that love include? What would your lover feel about you?

Styles of Loving

Another scheme for distinguishing different types of love experiences was offered by sociologist John Alan Lee (1988), who used Greek and Latin words to describe six styles of love that differ in the intensity of the loving experience, commitment to the beloved, desired characteristics of the beloved, and expectations about being loved in return. (See Table 8.8.) One style is **eros,** from which the word *erotic* comes. Eros has a strong physical component, and erotic lovers are likely to be heavily influenced by physical appearance and to believe in love at first sight.

TABLE 8.8. Styles of Loving

Eros	The erotic lover finds good looks compelling and seeks an intense, passionate relationship.
Ludus	The ludic lover considers love to be a game and likes to play the field.
Storge	The storgic lover prefers friendships that gradually grow into lasting commitments.
Mania	The manic lover is demanding, possessive, and excitable.
Agape	The agapic lover is altruistic and dutiful.
Pragma	The pragmatic lover is practical, careful, and logical in seeking a mate.

Source: Based on Lee, J. A. "Love-styles," in R. J. Sternberg & M. L. Barnes (Eds.), The psychology of love (pp. 38–67). New Haven, CT: Yale University Press, 1988.

A Type of Love You Probably Don't Want to Experience
Unrequited Love

Have you ever loved someone who did not love you back? You probably have. Depending on the sample, 80 percent (Aron et al., 1998) to 90 percent of young adults (Baumeister et al., 1993) report that they have experienced unrequited love: romantic, passionate attraction to someone who did not return that interest. It's a common experience that may involve a mere acquaintance, a past partner, or even a current partner who's less immersed in the relationship than we would wish (Bringle et al., 2013).

Why do we experience such loves? Several factors may be involved. First, would-be lovers are very attracted to their unwilling targets, and they assume that relationships with them are worth working and waiting for. Second, they optimistically overestimate how much they are liked in return (Aron et al., 1998). And third, perhaps most importantly, unre- quited love often offers the hope of future rewards; people cling to the illusion that they will win their targets' love in the end (Bringle et al., 2013).

It's painful when that doesn't happen, but it's actually worse to be the target of someone's undesired adoration. Sure, it's nice to be wanted, but those on the receiving end of unrequited love often find their pursuers' persistence to be intrusive and annoying, and they usually feel guilty when they turn their ardent pursuers down (Joel et al., 2014). They are usually nice, "well-meaning people who find themselves caught up in another person's emotional whirlwind and who themselves often suffer acutely as a result" (Baumeister & Wotman, 1992, p. 203). As distressing as it was to gradually realize that the objects of our affection would not become our steady partners, we may have made it harder on them when we fell into unrequited love.

A second style, **ludus** (pronounced "loo-dus"), treats love as an uncommitted game. Ludic lovers are often fickle and (try to) have several different partners at once. In contrast, a third style, **storge**, ("store-gay") leads people to de-emphasize strong emotion and to seek genuine friendships that gradually lead to real commitment.

A fourth style, **mania,** is demanding and possessive and full of vivid fantasy and obsession. A fifth style, **agape** ("ah-gaa-pay"), is giving, altruistic, and selfless, and treats love as a duty. Finally, the last style, **pragma**, is practical and pragmatic. Pragma leads people to dispassionately seek partners who will logically be a good match for them.

How useful are these distinctions? Instead of thinking of them as six additional types of love, it makes more sense to consider them as six themes in love experiences that overlap and are differentially related to the types of love we've considered so far. In particular, storge, mania, and pragma have little in common with romantic love, companionate love, or compassionate love; the obsession of mania and the cool, friendly practicality of storge and pragma differ noticeably from the loving intimacy at the heart of all three types of love (Graham, 2011). However, all of the components of love described by the triangular theory—that

CHAPTER 9

Sexuality

SEXUAL ATTITUDES ◆ SEXUAL BEHAVIOR
◆ SEXUAL SATISFACTION ◆ SEXUAL COERCION
◆ FOR YOUR CONSIDERATION ◆ CHAPTER SUMMARY

I have two questions for you. First, if a mischievous genie offered you a constant supply of compelling orgasms but required that you experience them alone and never again have sex with another person, would you accept the offer? Second, if you discovered on your honeymoon that your new spouse had been secretly taking a drug like Viagra to enhance his or her sexual response to you, would you be hurt?

Different people will undoubtedly answer these questions in different ways. Those who have not had sex with an intimate romantic partner for a long time may find compelling orgasms, even solitary ones, an attractive option. But I suspect that most people would be reluctant to give up a potential future of physical connections with a lover or lovers. Orgasms are more fulfilling when they are shared with someone (Bensman, 2012), and most of us would be disappointed were we no longer able to share sex with someone we love. And we want our lovers to find *us* compelling and to want us in return. So, it may be hurtful to learn that a partner's apparent desire for us is the result, at least in part, of some drug (Morgentaler, 2003).

As these questions may imply, there's a lot more to human sexuality than great orgasms. For some of us, sex need not always involve romantic intimacy, but for most of us, romantic intimacy involves sex. Our close romantic relationships often have a sexual component, and our sexual behavior and sexual satisfaction are often dependent on the nature, and health, of those relationships. As we'll see in this chapter, there's a close connection between sexuality and intimate relationships.

SEXUAL ATTITUDES

Attitudes about Casual Sex

Times have changed, and it's likely that you're more accepting of nonmarital sexual intercourse than your grandparents were. Fifty years ago, most people disapproved of sex "before marriage," but these days, fewer than 25 percent of us think that nonmarital sex is "always or almost always wrong" (Twenge et al., 2015). The circumstances matter. Most of us hold a *permissiveness with affection standard* (Daugherty & Copen, 2016): We believe that sex between unmarried partners is fine as long as it occurs in the context of a committed, caring relationship. We're more ambivalent about **hookups**—sexual interactions with nonromantic partners that usually last one night and do not involve any expectation of a lasting relationship (Kuperberg & Padgett, 2016). On the one hand, both men and women usually have more positive than negative feelings after a hookup, but mixed feelings are common, and the event is mostly confusing or disappointing about 40 percent of the time (Strokoff et al., 2015). (Unhappy reactions are especially likely when people have hookups that were unintended or undesired [Vrangalova, 2015].) And hookups aren't actually as popular as they seem to be: Both sexes enjoy hookups less than they think other people do (Reiber & Garcia, 2010), and big majorities of both men and women, as it turns out, prefer dating someone to just hooking up (Bradshaw et al., 2010).

Do men and women differ in their sexual opinions? On average, they do: Men hold more permissive sexual values and attitudes, although the difference is shrinking over time, and how big it is depends on the particular attitude being measured (Hyde, 2014). One of the larger sex differences is in attitudes toward casual nonmarital sex; men are more likely than women to think that sex without love is okay, so they usually feel better the morning after a hookup than women do (Strokoff et al., 2015). This difference undoubtedly influences the things that men and women *regret* about their past sexual behavior: Whereas women are more likely than men to regret things they've done (such as having a hookup), men are more likely than women to regret things they *didn't* do (such as not having sex when they had the chance). When it comes to casual sex, women tend to regret their actions, but men regret their *in*actions (Galperin et al., 2013).

A person's sex may be involved in other sexual attitudes, as well. Traditionally, women have been judged more harshly than men for being sexually experienced or permissive. Whereas men who have multiple sexual partners may be admired as "studs," women with the same number of partners may be dismissed as "sluts." This asymmetry is known as the *sexual double standard,* and years ago it was quite obvious, but it appears to be more subtle today: We tend to disapprove of anyone, male or female, who hooks up "a lot" (Allison & Risman, 2013). But a double standard still exists, especially among men (Rudman et al., 2013). Women expect more disregard than men do if they accept an offer of casual sex (Kettrey, 2016), a woman with a sexually transmitted infection (or STI) is judged more harshly than a man is (Smith et al., 2008), and a woman who participates in a threesome is liked less than a man is (Jonason & Marks, 2009).[1] These days, once they become young adults, people generally like their potential partners to have *some* sexual experience—being a virgin doesn't enhance your attractiveness (Gesselman et al., 2017)—but if they've had more than two or three lovers, potential mates (both women *and* men) seem less and less desirable as their number of past

---

[1] And no, it didn't matter if the three participants were two women and one man or two men and one woman; female participants were judged more negatively in both cases.

partners goes up (Stewart-Williams et al., 2017). So, a strong sexual double standard no longer seems to exist, but a person's sex can still have some influence on others' evaluations of his or her sexual experiences.

Attitudes about Same-Sex Sexuality

A person's sexual orientation matters to some people, too. A noticeable minority of adult Americans—about 34 percent—feel that sexual relations between adults of the same sex are "morally wrong." However, most Americans do *not* hold that view; almost two-thirds of them—63 percent—consider same-sex relations to be "morally acceptable" (Jones, 2015). This hasn't always been true, of course, but our attitudes about same-sex sexuality have changed dramatically in recent years. Back in 2001, for instance, 57 percent of Americans opposed the prospect of legal marriage between same-sex partners, and such marriages were impossible to obtain—but 62 percent now *approve* of "gay marriage," and it's the law of the land (Pew Research, 2017). Similar sizable shifts have also occurred in several other areas of the world (such as Scotland, Uruguay, New Zealand, and Brazil; see Pew Research, 2015).

Why has this occurred? I'll touch on two contributing reasons. First, gays and lesbians are more visible in public life than ever before—consider the influence over the years of very popular TV shows such as *Will and Grace, Glee,* and *Modern Family*—and the more contact people have with gays and lesbians, the more favorable their feelings toward them tend to be (Cunningham & Melton, 2013; Lytle & Levy, 2015). Young adults in the United States have much more favorable attitudes toward gays and lesbians than elderly people do (Pew Research, 2017), but they're much more likely to know (and like) openly gay or lesbian people, too.

A second stimulus is that we *understand* same-sex sexuality much better than we used to. For instance, our judgments of same-sex relationships have much to do with our beliefs about *why* someone is gay or lesbian, as Figure 9.1 shows. By a very large margin, people consider homosexuality to be acceptable when they believe that sexual orientation results from biological influences that occur before we are born. On the other hand, by a substantial margin, people find homosexuality unacceptable if they believe that it is a lifestyle one chooses to adopt. So, it's important that for the last 20 years the number of people who believe that one's sexuality is already set at birth has been gradually increasing and the number of those who believe that people choose to be gay or lesbian has declined (Jones, 2015). It's important because—particularly with regard to gay men—the first group is *right* and the second bunch is *wrong*. In just the last few years, psychological and biological science has determined that "preference in sexual identity and partnerships is apparently irrevocably etched in the developing fetal brain and cannot be changed. Who we are sexually, and who and how we love sexually, seem in most cases to be hardwired, beginning even before birth" (Horstman, 2012, p. 60).

Sexual orientation is complex, involving one's emotional and sexual attractions to others, one's actual behavior, and one's identity, and we humans aren't just gay or straight: Researchers are finding that at least *five* categories of sexual orientation—heterosexual, mostly heterosexual, bisexual, mostly gay/lesbian, and gay/lesbian—are needed to capture the range of sexual behavior people display

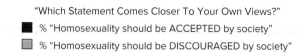

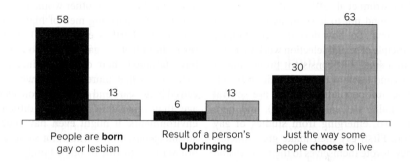

Respondents' Beliefs about the Origins of Sexual Orientation

Source: Data from Pew Research Center. "In gay marriage debate, both supporters and opponents see legal recognition as 'inevitable.'" June 2013.

FIGURE 9.1. **Tolerance of same-sex sexuality depends on one's beliefs about its origins.** Here are the results of a poll conducted by the Pew Research Center that surveyed a representative national sample of Americans in May 2013. People were much more likely to be tolerant of homosexuality—saying that it should be accepted by society—if they believed that sexual orientation was something that people are born with. On the other hand, if they believed that people *choose* to be gay or lesbian, they were intolerant of such behavior. The poll's margin of error was 3 points. $N = 1,504$.

(Savin-Williams, 2014). And to some degree (more for women than for men), our behavior and self-concepts can change over time (Diamond, 2015). But we don't "catch" same-sex attractions from our friends (Brakefield et al., 2014), and our upbringing doesn't teach us to be gay (Långström et al., 2010). Most gays and lesbians feel that they've had no choice whatsoever about their orientations (Herek et al., 2010), and there are a variety of physical differences between straight and gay men (Myers, 2013). The bottom line is that there's no longer any doubt that same-sex sexual behavior is based, in part, in one's genes (Långström et al., 2010), and "clearly, sexual orientation is not a matter of conscious, moral choice" (Myers, 2013, p. 90). Slowly but surely, more of us are coming to understand that—and greater tolerance often follows.

Relationship science has demonstrated that there was never any empirical justification for denying gays and lesbians access to the legal benefits (involving, for instance, taxation, health insurance, pensions, and property rights) that marriage provides (Myers, 2013). Indeed, the American Psychological Association resolved that because (a) same-sex relationships operate in much the same manner as heterosexual partnerships (Rostosky & Riggle, 2017), (b) sexual orientation has nothing to do with a person's ability to be a loving, nurturing, and successful parent (Goldberg & Smith, 2013), and (c) marriage is good for people, including gays and

Men Report More Sexual Partners than Women Do. How?

The best, most comprehensive surveys of sex in the United States paint somewhat different pictures of the sexual behavior of men and women. In particular, the National Center for Health Statistics determined that the average middle-aged American man has had seven sexual partners during his lifetime whereas the average woman has had only four. Men in their young twenties have had an average of 4.1 partners, and women 2.6 (Copen et al., 2016). Men also report having sex more often than women do. Why aren't these figures the same? One would think that each time a man has sex with a new partner, that partner does, too, and most of the sex men have is with women, not other men. So, why are these different rates routinely found?

There are several possible reasons, and one is procedural. Despite their careful sampling techniques, surveys usually fail to include representative numbers of those particular women—prostitutes—who have sex with many men (if for no other reason than that they're not home at night when the surveys are usually conducted). When researchers make special efforts to include prostitutes in their samples, the average numbers of partners reported by men and women are more similar (Brewer et al., 2000).

Also, men and women occasionally define "sex" differently. If a heterosexual couple engages only in oral sex, for instance, he may be more likely to say that they've had "sex" than she is (Gute et al., 2008). The sexes generally agree about whether "sex" has occurred (Sewell & Strassberg, 2015), but men are somewhat more likely than women to count as "sex partners" lovers with whom intercourse did not occur (Barnett et al., 2016).

However, the most important source of the discrepancy is the tendency for men to exaggerate, and for women to minimize, the number of partners they've had. When they are connected to (what they think are effective) lie detectors, men report having had fewer sex partners, and women report having had more (Fisher, 2013). (In fact, when they thought any lies could be detected, these women—who were students at a large university in the midwestern United States—reported having had more partners than the men did.) So, self-reports like these are clearly prone to social desirability biases like those we covered back in chapter 2 (Schick et al., 2014), and they speak to some of the difficulties researchers face in studying intimate behavior.

One more point: When college students are asked how many sex partners they would like to have during the next year, the typical response from a majority of women is "one," and from most men, "two" (Fenigstein & Preston, 2007). Only tiny minorities hope to have lots of partners. So, there is a sex difference of note here—men want to have more partners than women do—but very few people want to be promiscuous.

I discuss sexual desire a few pages from now.) After 10 years together, everybody has sex less often, but the drop in frequency is greater for gays, and they end up having sex less frequently than heterosexual couples do. On the other hand, regardless of the duration of the relationship, lesbians have sex less often than any other relationship group (Diamond, 2015). When it's just up to them, women have sex much less frequently than they do when there is a man involved.

Infidelity

Most people around the world strongly disapprove of someone who is in a committed relationship engaging in **extradyadic sex** (that is, having sex outside the dyad, or couple, with someone other than one's partner) (Buunk et al., 2018).[2] Thus, we might expect that sexual infidelity would be rather rare. But is it? A compilation of 47 different investigations involving more than 58,000 participants, most of them in the United States and most of them married, found that 21 percent of the women and 32 percent of the men had been sexually unfaithful to their romantic partners at least once. Most husbands and wives never have sex with other people after they marry, but about one out of every five wives and one out of three husbands do (Tafoya & Spitzberg, 2007). Rates of cheating are higher in couples that are dating or cohabiting. We usually think that it's very unlikely that our partners will cheat (Watkins & Boon, 2016), but a national survey in the U.S. found that someone in a cohabiting couple—and sometimes it was both of them—had cheated 31 percent of the time (Frisco et al., 2017). And in another sample that focused on dating partners (Graham et al., 2016), when someone had extradyadic sex the other partner usually didn't know it, and the cheating partner didn't use a condom 22 percent of the time.[3]

As you may have noticed, men are more likely to cheat on their partners than women are. They hold more positive attitudes toward casual sex, and they often pursue extradyadic sex simply for the sake of sexual variety (whereas women are more likely to seek an emotional connection; Impett et al., 2014b). Indeed, these sex differences are particularly pronounced in the same-sex relationships of gay and lesbian couples, where male and female fidelity operate free of the influence of the other sex. Gay men have a lot more extradyadic sex than both lesbian women and heterosexual men do (Peplau et al., 2004), as you can see in Figure 9.3, which depicts the results of a large survey of Americans back in the early 1980s that obtained data on spouses, cohabitating couples, and gay and lesbian couples (Blumstein & Schwartz, 1983). In many cases, the gay men had such sex with the permission of their partners, who wanted the same freedom (Mitchell et al., 2016), and some observers have speculated that many heterosexual men would also behave this way if their female lovers would let them get away with it (Diamond, 2015)!

Certainly, however, not all men are promiscuous and not all women are chaste, and there is an influential individual difference that makes both men and women more likely to engage in extradyadic sex. For some of us, sex is connected to love and commitment: It's not especially rewarding to have sex with people we don't know well or don't care much about, and we have casual sex with

---

[2] The "sex" I'll be referring to in this section will be vaginal intercourse. Extradyadic behavior takes a variety of forms ranging from erotic texting and cybersex to kissing, heavy petting, oral sex, and intercourse, but people differ in their definitions of which of these are "cheating" (Kruger et al., 2013). So that we'll all be on the same page, I'll focus on behavior that almost everybody considers to be unfaithful.

[3] Yikes.

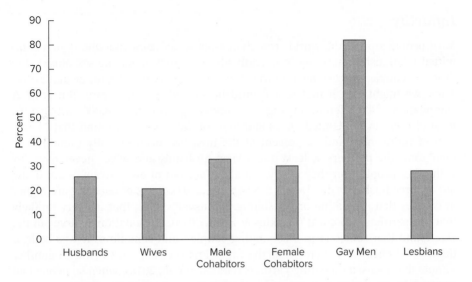

Source: Blumstein, P., & Schwartz, P. American couples: Money, work, sex. New York: William
Morrow, 1983.

FIGURE 9.3. **Percentages of individuals reporting any instance(s) of extradyadic
sex since the beginning of their relationships.**
Gay men clearly have more extradyadic sex than anyone else, but in many cases they are
not "cheating" on their partners. Note, too, that men and women who are cohabiting are
more likely to have sex with other people than husbands and wives are. Marriage
involves more thoroughgoing commitment than cohabiting does.

acquaintances or strangers rarely, if at all. For others of us, however, sex has less
to do with love and commitment; we think that "sex without love is OK," and
we're content to have sex with people for whom we have no particular feelings.
These different approaches to sex emerge from our **sociosexual orientations,**
the traitlike collections of beliefs and behaviors that describe our feelings about
sex (Simpson et al., 2004). Individual differences in *sociosexuality* were discovered
by Jeff Simpson and Steve Gangestad (1991), who used the measure in the box
on the next page to measure respondents' sociosexual orientations. People who
were generally willing to have sex only in the context of a committed and affectionate relationship were said to have a "restricted" sociosexual orientation,
whereas those who did not seek much closeness or commitment before pursuing
sex were said to have "unrestricted" sociosexuality. As it turns out, people with
unrestricted orientations tend to be dynamic, flirtatious people who are always on
the prowl for new partners (Simpson et al., 2004). And around the world, men
are more unrestricted on average than women are (Schmitt, 2005).

You probably won't be surprised, then, to learn that sociosexuality is associated with the likelihood that people will have extradyadic sex. Over their lifetimes,
compared to those with more restricted orientations, unrestricted people have

Measuring Sociosexuality

Sociosexuality describes the degree to which a person is comfortable having sex in the absence of any love or commitment. Jeff Simpson and Steve Gangestad (1991) developed this brief measure, the Sociosexual Orientation Inventory, to assess sociosexuality. Respondents are asked to answer these questions as honestly as possible:

1. With how many different partners have you had sex (sexual intercourse) within the past year?

   _____

2. How many different partners do you foresee yourself having sex with during the next five years? (Please give a *specific, realistic* estimate). _____

3. With how many different partners have you had sex on *one and only one* occasion? _____

4. How often do you fantasize about having sex with someone other than your current dating partner? (Circle one).

   a. never
   b. once every 2 or 3 months
   c. once a month
   d. once every 2 weeks
   e. once a week
   f. a few times each week
   g. nearly every day
   h. at least once a day

5. Sex without love is OK.

1	2	3	4	5	6	7	8	9

   I strongly   I strongly
   disagree   agree

6. I can imagine myself being comfortable and enjoying "casual" sex with different partners.

1	2	3	4	5	6	7	8	9

   I strongly   I strongly
   disagree   agree

7. I would have to be closely attached to someone (both emotionally and psychologically) before I could feel comfortable and fully enjoy having sex with him or her.

1	2	3	4	5	6	7	8	9

   I strongly   I strongly
   disagree   agree

Responses to the last item (#7) are reverse scored, and a total score is computed by weighing the scores of some items more heavily than others. In general, higher numbers on each question (and for the total score) reflect an *unrestricted* sexual orientation, and lower numbers reflect a *restricted* orientation. Compared to those with a lower score, people with an unrestricted orientation "typically engage in sex earlier in their romantic relationships, are more likely to engage in sex with more than one partner at a time, and tend to be involved in sexual relationships characterized by less expressed investment, less commitment, and weaker affectional ties" (Simpson & Gangestad, 1991, p. 879). Sociosexuality is a good example of how characteristics of individuals have a powerful impact on the nature of sexual interactions.

more sexual partners and are more likely to cheat on their primary lovers (Rodrigues et al., 2017). David Seal and his colleagues (1994) shed light on this pattern in a clever study of heterosexual college students who were currently in dating relationships but who were asked to evaluate a computer dating video of an attractive member of the other sex. After viewing the tape, participants were told they could enter a drawing to win a free date with the person in the video, and they were invited to indicate how willing they would be—if they went on the date and had a good time—to engage in a series of physically intimate behaviors with the date. The researchers found that 36 percent of those who were unrestricted in their sociosexuality entered the drawing for the date whereas only 4 percent of those who were restricted did. (Remember, all the participants were currently involved in existing relationships!) Unrestricted individuals were also more interested in having sex with their new dates than restricted individuals were. Sociosexuality is clearly a meaningful characteristic that distinguishes those who are likely to cheat from those who are not.

It's intriguing, then, that when their faces are presented side-by-side, observers can generally distinguish people with unrestricted orientations (who tend to be on the prowl) from those with restricted orientations (who are more likely to be faithful) (Boothroyd et al., 2011). Unrestricted women tend to have facial features that are somewhat more masculine than those of other women—and remarkably, although their faces are more attractive, men consider them to be less desirable as long-term mates. They're lovely, but they seem less trustworthy than other women do (Campbell et al., 2009). Unrestricted men look more masculine, too, but women prefer the faces of restricted men for long-term mates (Boothroyd et al., 2008); they seem to sense that unrestricted men would make riskier husbands.

An evolutionary perspective has an interesting spin on all this. With their lower parental investment,[4] men can afford to engage in relatively casual sex, and, arguably, sexual selection[5] has historically favored men who mated with as many women as possible. But why would evolution encourage a woman to cheat? Given the potentially violent costs she might incur if her actions are discovered (Buss, 2000), what reproductive advantage would there be? One provocative answer is that she'd not be able to produce more children by having extradyadic sex, but she might be able to have *better* (that is, healthier and more attractive) children. A **good genes hypothesis** suggests that some women—in particular, those with less desirable mates—can profit from a *dual mating* strategy in which they (a) pursue long-term partners who will contribute resources to protect and feed their offspring while (b) surreptitiously seeking good genes for their children from other men (Pillsworth & Haselton, 2006). By obtaining commitment and security from one man and having taller, stronger, healthier children with another, women could bear offspring who were especially likely to survive and thrive.

Some modern patterns of behavior are consistent with the good genes hypothesis. First, as we noted in chapter 3, women find sexy, symmetrical men—those who display visible markers of masculine fitness—to be especially compelling each month when they are fertile and can conceive a child (Gildersleeve et al., 2014). And wives with dominant, assertive, masculine husbands are more satisfied with their marriages when they're fertile than when they're not—but wives with less masculine husbands don't display this pattern (Meltzer, 2017). Second, children have more robust immune systems when their parents each give

---

[4]This key concept was introduced way back in chapter 1 on p. 34.

[5]Ditto. Chapter 1, p. 33.

them different sets of genes of the type that regulate immune responses—and women whose partners have *similar* genes are more likely than those whose partners have *different* genes to have sex with other men, particularly when they're fertile (Garver-Apgar et al., 2006). If women were pursuing extradyadic sex simply for the sake of variety, it would be foolhardy to entertain other lovers during the few days they're fertile each month, but that's exactly what they do; women are more attracted to extradyadic mates when they're fertile than when they're not, and this tendency is more pronounced when their primary partners are relatively unattractive (Larson et al., 2013).

If our ancient female ancestors behaved this way, they often would have had children who were healthier and more attractive than those who would have been fathered by the women's usual mates (and thus, their extradyadic sex would have offered some advantages). Does this sort of thing happen today? It does. Meta-analyses of several dozen studies of paternity find that 2 percent of the world's children, on average, are being raised by men who don't know that someone else is the child's biological father (e.g., Larmuseau et al., 2016). Moreover, in the United States, about 1 out of every 400 pairs of fraternal twins involves simultaneous siblings who were fathered by two different men (Blickstein, 2005).

These results suggest that, historically, men have occasionally encountered situations involving **sperm competition,** which occurs when the sperm of two or more men occupy a woman's vagina at the same time (Pham & Shackelford, 2015). Some researchers contend that in response to such situations, evolution has equipped men with a penis that is ideally shaped to scoop any semen from other men away from their partner's cervix (Gallup & Burch, 2006). Common sense might expect that a second lover would only push an earlier lover's ejaculate through the cervix and into the woman's uterus, but that's not what happens: Deep thrusts force any sperm that is already present behind the head of the penis, which then pulls the sperm out of the woman. Indeed, consistent with this notion, when men know that their partners are spending a lot of time with other men (such as coworkers and friends), they tend to have intercourse in a manner—involving a higher number of unusually deep thrusts over a longer period of time—that is particularly likely to displace any sperm that might be present (Pham et al., 2017).

Thus, an evolutionary perspective argues that extradyadic sex can have reproductive benefits for some women, and that in response to such challenges, men have adapted. An entirely different perspective on infidelity focuses on the current quality of a couple's relationship. In general, as you'd expect, people are more likely to cheat when they become dissatisfied with their present partners (Scott et al., 2017) and the quality of their alternatives is high (Tsapelas et al., 2011). Unhappy lovers who have tempting alternatives available to them are less likely to remain faithful. If they do cheat in such situations, women are more likely than men to break up with their old partners and begin a new long-term relationship with the new mate (Impett et al., 2014b); thus, women are more likely to switch mates as a result of an affair (Buss et al., 2017). However, if you're shopping around, you may want to steer clear of someone who's cheating on his or her current partner to be with you. Compared to the rest of us, cheaters tend to be callous, manipulative people (Jones & Weiser, 2014) who are low in agreeableness and conscientiousness (Schmitt & Shackelford, 2008) but relatively high in anxiety about abandonment (Russell et al., 2013). You can probably do better.

Sexual Desire

Men's higher sociosexuality scores and more frequent infidelity may be results, in part, of another, broader difference between the sexes. On average, men have higher **sex drives** than women do. They experience more frequent and more intense sexual desires and are routinely more motivated to engage in sexual activity than women are (Regan, 2015). One study of young adults found that men reported episodes of sexual desire 37 times per week whereas women reported only 9 (Regan, 2013). Because you're being a thoughtful consumer of relationship science, you should remember that there are sizable individual differences at work here, and there are certainly many men who are chronically less horny than many women are. Nevertheless, a wide array of facts demonstrates that on average, and around the world (Lippa, 2009), men have higher sex drives than women do:

- Throughout their lives, men masturbate more often (Das et al., 2011), perhaps because their sexual impulses are stronger and harder for them to control (Tidwell & Eastwick, 2013). Almost half of all men who have a regular sex partner still masturbate more than once a week, whereas only 16 percent of women who are in sexual relationships masturbate as frequently (Klusmann, 2002). In England, it's likely that 73 percent of the men between the ages of 16 and 44 have masturbated in the past month, but only 37 percent of the women have (Gerressu et al., 2008).
- Men want sex more often than women do, and they are more likely than women to feel dissatisfied with the amount of sex they get (Sprecher, 2002).
- In developing relationships, men typically want to begin having sex sooner than women do (Sprecher et al., 1995). As a result, women are usually the "gatekeepers" who decide when sex begins in a new relationship. On average, when he first wants to have sex, he has to wait, but when she wants to have sex, they do.
- Men think about sex more often than women do. When young adults carry clickers with which to count their thoughts, sex-related thoughts enter men's minds 34 times a day, women's only 19 (Fisher et al., 2012).
- Men spend more money on sex, buying more sex toys and porn (Laumann et al., 1994). In particular, men sometimes pay to obtain sex—in one study in Australia, 23 percent of men had paid for sex at least once—but women almost never do (Pitts et al., 2004).
- Finally, as we've already seen, men are more accepting of casual sex, on average, than women are (Sprecher et al., 2013a). They'd like to have sex with more people, too (Schmitt et al., 2012).

Add up these patterns, and the sex difference in sex drive may be no small matter. To a greater or lesser degree, each of these patterns may lead to misunderstanding or annoyance as heterosexual couples negotiate their sexual interactions.

Some husbands may be chronically frustrated by getting less sex than they want at the same time that their wives are irritated by their frequent insistence for more. (I'm reminded, in this regard, of a clever bit in the movie *Annie Hall,* which beat *Star Wars* to win the Academy Award for Best Picture for 1977: On a split screen, both members of a romantic couple are visiting their therapists, who have asked how often they have sex; he laments, "Hardly ever, maybe three times a week," as she complains, "Constantly, I'd say three times a week.") The typical sex difference in sex drive means that some couples will encounter mismatches in sexual desire, and difficulty may result (Willoughby et al., 2014b). And the mismatch may get only worse with time; most women experience a drop in desire after they go through menopause (McCabe & Goldhammer, 2012), so perhaps we shouldn't be surprised that a study of 60-year-olds in Germany didn't find *any* couple in which she wanted as much sex as he did (Klusmann, 2006).

There may be further consequences of men wanting more sex than women do. As the gatekeepers who decide when sex occurs, women may find men willing to offer various concessions in exchange for sex (Kruger, 2008). Men's greater interest in sex may put the principle of lesser interest[6] in action: Women's control over access to something that they have and that men want may give them power with which to influence their men (Rasmussen & Boon, 2016). In some relationships, sex may be "a valued good for which there is a marketplace in which women act as sellers and men as buyers" (Baumeister & Vohs, 2004, p. 359).

This sounds "decidedly unromantic" (Vohs & Baumeister, 2015) because it can promote an adversarial view of sexual interactions (Fetterolf & Rudman, 2017). But partners need not endorse or even be consciously aware of this pattern for it to affect their interactions. Instead, without ever thinking about it, people may just take it for granted that a woman who, over a period of time, accepts a series of gifts from a man—such as expensive dates and other desirable entertainments—should feel some obligation to offer sex in return (or else she should stop accepting the gifts). Advice columnists acknowledge this: "Women do not owe sexual favors for a free dinner, but when men bear the entire cost of dating, they believe the woman is interested in a romantic, eventually intimate relationship. They otherwise feel used and resent it" (Mitchell & Sugar, 2008, p. B2). A dark consequence of this pattern is that some men may feel justified in pressuring or coercing women to have sex when they feel that the women "owe it" to them (Basow & Minieri, 2011).

Safe, Sensible Sex

There's a lot of casual sex going on, and only some of it is safe. Most college students—about three-fourths—have had hookups, with about half of them having had one in the past year (LaBrie et al., 2014). Most hookups involve partners with whom one is well acquainted—much of the time, the partner is a friend—but a lot of hookups (37 percent) involve others who are either strangers or who are not well known (Grello et al., 2006). Some hookups just involve kissing

[6]Would you like to refresh your understanding of the principle of lesser interest? It's back on page 178.

The Ins and Outs of Cybersex

There's a lot of real and imagined sexual activity taking place online these days. The Web offers a unique mix of characteristics that allow us to have rather personal contact with others cheaply and easily: *accessibility* to large numbers of people, *affordability* that makes a cyber-date inexpensive, and *anonymity* that lowers inhibitions and prevents our partners from following us home (Subotnik, 2007). The interactions that result often take place in "a sexual space midway between fantasy and action" (Ross, 2005, p. 342); they may fulfill our fantasies when we're only sitting at home typing, and they can feel very intimate even when we have very little, if any, factual information about our partners.

Is cybersex innocuous? Those who engage in cybersex generally think so (Grov et al., 2011), but it's a complex issue; sex takes three broad forms online, and they have different implications for face-to-face relationships (Henline et al., 2007). First, people pursue porn. Most of us don't disapprove of a partner's occasional consumption of pornography, but a quarter of us do, considering it to be either undesirable or unacceptable when one is in a committed relationship (Olmstead et al., 2013). And the critics of porn may have a point. Most porn portrays women in a demeaning manner—as horny sluts who are always ready to serve and please men— and there's a lot of gagging, slapping, and name-calling in porn (Bridges et al., 2013), so it may teach lessons that can have an adverse effect on close relationships. In particular, teens who consume a lot of porn tend to endorse casual, recreational attitudes toward sex, to hold more favorable views of extradyadic sex, and to think of women as sex objects, that is, devices to be used for men's pleasure (Wright & Bae, 2016). They have more frequent hookups with more people, too (Braithwaite et al., 2015). And because porn is full of (imaginary) gorgeous alternative partners who

seem eager and willing, people who watch porn alone tend to be less satisfied with, and less committed to, their current partners than are people who watch porn *with* their partners—or not at all (Rasmussen, 2016). The larger the discrepancy in partners' use of porn, the more obnoxious porn use becomes (Willoughby et al., 2016)—but porn's adverse effects disappear when the partners consume it with similar frequencies (Kohut et al., 2017).

Visits to porn sites usually don't involve interactions with others online, but other forms of online sex do. Sometimes it's just sexy flirting and talking dirty, but an interaction becomes **cybersex** when it involves sexual chat for the purpose of sexual gratification (Daneback et al., 2005) with, as one example, the participants sharing explicit descriptions of sexual activities while they each masturbate. Cybersex is often shared anonymously by strangers who never meet (and who may not be who they say they are), but many of us, 45 percent, would find it to be a serious type of infidelity (Henline et al., 2007).

Even more consequential, however, may be the last form of online sex, which involves emotional involvement with someone at the other end of an Internet connection. People can and do form intimate connections with others they have never actually met, and such liaisons seem unfaithful to 39 percent of us. But because these partnerships are usually much more personal than the typical episode of cybersex—often involving deep self-disclosure— they are often more problematic for existing face-to-face relationships. People who become emotionally involved online are more likely to arrange a way to meet offline, and then real extradyadic sex sometimes occurs (Henline et al., 2007). Online sex can be a playful flight of fancy or a serious search for a new partner, and we sometimes don't know which until some damage has been done to our current relationships.

and heavy petting, but about half of them include oral sex or intercourse (especially if people have been drinking), and when sex occurs, condoms are used only about half the time (Lewis et al., 2012).

Sex is no safer off-campus. A survey of 740 women (most of them in their 30s and 40s) who were seeking new partners on dating Web sites found that the women were generally very careful when they met a new guy face-to-face for the first time; they had long conversations, ran background checks, and negotiated boundaries before agreeing to a meeting, and then they met in a public place, carried pepper spray, or had a friend nearby. But all of that caution did not translate into safe sex. Perhaps because they already (believed that they) knew so much about each other, 30 percent of the women had sex with their new partners when they first met. And, overall, whenever it occurred, 77 percent of the women who met online partners did not use a condom when they first had sex (Padgett, 2007).

Thus, many people do not use condoms when they have sex with a new or temporary partner, and they forgo safe sex in an environment in which 42 percent of American men are infected with HPV (Han et al., 2017) and the number of cases of sexually transmitted diseases in the United States is at an all-time high (Barton et al., 2016). What's going on? Why is it that so many smart people are having so much unsafe sex? There are several reasons:

- *Underestimates of risk.* First, a lot of us are lousy at math. For instance, the chance that a woman will be infected with human immunodeficiency virus (HIV) in a single unprotected sexual encounter with an infected male is actually quite low, less than 1 percent. But of course, if you give a low-frequency event several chances to occur, the probability that it *will* occur at least once goes up. If a woman has unprotected sex with an infected man a few dozen times, it becomes very likely that she will be infected, too; her chance of infection becomes substantial (Linville et al., 1993).

    In a similar manner, almost all of us underestimate the cumulative overall risk that a new partner who has been sexually active in the past is carrying a sexually transmitted infection (Knäuper et al., 2005), and that false sense of security deters condom use. (A lot of us never even *ask* if a new partner has an STI, either [Manning et al., 2012].) Someone who has had several prior sexual partners is more likely to be infected than we think, even if the individual risk encountered with each of those other partners was low. And we are particularly likely to underestimate a partner's risk when he or she is attractive; the better looking someone is, the lower the risk we perceive, and the less likely we are to use a condom if sex occurs (Knäuper et al., 2005).

    A particular bias known as the **illusion of unique invulnerability** can also influence our estimates of risk. Many of us believe that bad things are generally more likely to happen to others than to us, so we fail to take sensible precautions that would prevent foreseeable dangers (Burger & Burns, 1988). The irony here, of course, is that those who consider themselves relatively invulnerable to STIs are less likely to use condoms, and that makes them *more* likely to catch one. People even think they're unlikely to catch an STI *after* they've already got one. A representative national survey of young adults in the United

States found that only 22 percent of those who tested positive for chlamydia, gonorrhea, or trichomoniasis had noticed any symptoms in the past year, so most people didn't know they were carrying an STI—and only 28 percent of those who *already had* one of these STIs believed that they were at risk of becoming infected (Wildsmith et al., 2010). There's a lot of biased—or simply ignorant—assessment of risk out there (Syme et al., 2017).

- *Faulty decision making.* When we intend to use condoms, we sometimes change our minds in the heat of the moment and then regret our decisions afterward. What causes us to make poor decisions? *Sexual arousal,* for one. When we get turned on, we see things differently than we do when we're not aroused: Diverse sexual behaviors (such as spanking, a threesome, and sex with a 60-year-old) seem more appealing (Imhoff & Schmidt, 2014); morally questionable behavior (such as slipping someone a drug to get sex) seems more acceptable (Ariely & Loewenstein, 2006); and condoms seem less desirable (Skakoon-Sparling et al., 2016). We really can get "carried away" when we get turned on.

  Intoxication can also alter our decision making, particularly when we're sexually aroused (Ebel-Lam et al., 2009). When people get drunk, they're less likely to use condoms when they're having sex with someone for the first time, in part because intoxication leads them to ignore the potential consequences and to think that having sex is a great idea (Davis et al., 2016). This is an example of a phenomenon known as **alcohol myopia,** which involves the reduction of people's abilities to think about and process all of the information available to them when they are intoxicated (Giancola et al., 2010). This limited capacity means that they are able to focus only on the most immediate and salient environmental cues. When they're drunk, people may not be able to think of anything but how attractive their partners are, and they completely forget their prior intentions to use the condoms they're carrying in a pocket or purse (T. MacDonald et al., 2000). Alcohol and arousal are evidently a recipe for high-risk sexual behavior. In particular, a lot of hookups would never have happened if the participants hadn't been drinking (Kuperberg & Padgett, 2017).

- *Pluralistic ignorance.* One of the striking things about hookups is that they are not as popular as most people, including the participants, think they are. Both men and women overestimate their peers' approval of, enthusiasm for, and frequency of hooking up (Barriger & Vélez-Blasini, 2013). Women tend to regret hookups that involve intercourse or oral sex (Garcia et al., 2012), but because they believe that *other* people generally approve of such behavior, they can feel some social pressure to engage in it, too (Lewis et al., 2014).

  This is an example of **pluralistic ignorance,** which occurs when people wrongly believe that their feelings and beliefs are different from those of others. By misperceiving each other's true preferences, a group of people can end up following norms that everyone thinks are prevalent but that almost no one privately supports. Thus, young adults may wisely want to have safe sex but fail to pursue it because they wrongly believe that it's unpopular. Indeed, women think that men hold more negative attitudes toward condoms than they really do (Edwards & Barber, 2010), and both sexes underestimate how often their peers

sho
pos
exp
ner
200
lon;
tho:
ship
inte
201·
new
sex-
sure
sati:

find
crea
follc
grov
a si
conc
succ
striv
to h
com
Our
have
espe
et al
to be

Sex

Here
own
too c
with
moai
signa
2011
fearlc
one
satisf
have
grun

⁹The ¡

use condoms, and overestimate how frequently they have casual sex (Lewis et al., 2014). Facebook isn't helpful in this regard; when people browse others' sexy, playful photos, they come to believe that their friends are having more hookups and using fewer condoms than they really are (Young & Jordan, 2013).

- *Inequalities in power.* As we'll see in chapter 12, *power* is the ability to get a partner to do what you want. When two partners possess different levels of power, they are unlikely to use condoms if the more powerful partner opposes them (Woolf & Maisto, 2008). In general, the more powerful the woman is (Pulerwitz et al., 2000), and the more honest and forthright she is (Impett et al., 2010), the more likely she and her partner are to use condoms when they have sex.

- *Abstinence education.* In order to convince teens that abstinence is the only way to go, some abstinence education programs teach their students that condoms don't work (which, of course, is nonsense) (Lin & Santelli, 2008). The undesired result is that when those teens have sex—and most of them do—they are less likely than other adolescents to use condoms (Hall et al., 2016).

- *Low self-control.* We'll find in chapter 14 that *self-control* is the ability to manage our impulses, practice self-restraint, and generally do the right thing even when it requires perseverance and effort. As you might expect, those of us with higher chronic levels of self-control (and who, therefore, are less impulsive and less likely to take unnecessary risks) are more likely to have used condoms and other forms of contraception the last time we had intercourse (Moilanen, 2015).

- *Decreased intimacy and pleasure.* The most important deterrent of all, however, may be that people enjoy sex more, on average, when they don't use condoms than when they do. Both men and women find intercourse more pleasurable when condoms are not involved, with men being particularly likely to prefer unprotected sex (Randolph et al., 2007), and people who don't use condoms consider their sex to be more intimate and emotionally satisfying (Smith et al., 2008). Consequently, lots of people—30 percent of men and 41 percent of women—have had a partner try to talk them out of using a condom. Remarkably, the more sex partners people have had—and, therefore, the higher their cumulative risk of having an STI—the *more* likely they are to try to dissuade their new lovers from using condoms (Ashenhurst et al., 2017).

Clearly, condom use is subject to diverse influences. Education can counteract some of the misunderstandings that deter condom use, but changing the perception that condoms are impersonal and unpleasant may be more difficult. So, I have two suggestions. Condoms are less likely to "break the mood" when they're treated as a part of sexy foreplay (Scott-Sheldon & Johnson, 2006). Don't treat condoms as if they're a nuisance that interrupts your love-making; when it's time, help your partner put one on in a manner that creatively and deliberately enhances, rather

A Point to Ponder

Have you ever wanted to use a condom but didn't? Why? Do you think that you'll ever allow that to happen again? Why?

The famous sex researchers William Masters and Virginia Johnson (1970) highlighted the importance of good sexual communication in a provocative study that compared the sexual experiences of heterosexuals and gays and lesbians. Masters and Johnson observed couples having sex and interviewed them extensively, and they concluded that the subjective quality of the sexual experience— including psychological involvement, responsiveness to the needs and desires of the partner, and enjoyment of each aspect of the sexual experience—was actually greater for gays and lesbians than it was for heterosexuals. Same-sex sex was better sex. One advantage of the sexual interactions shared by gays and lesbians was that both participants *were* of the same sex; knowing what they liked themselves, gays and lesbians could reasonably predict what their partners might like, too. However, Masters and Johnson argued that the primary foundation for more rewarding same-sex relations was good communication. Gays and lesbians talked more easily and openly about their sexual tastes than heterosexuals did. They would ask each other what was desired, provide feedback on what felt good, and generally guide their lovers on how to please them. In contrast, heterosexual couples exhibited a "persistent neglect" of open communication and a "potentially self-destructive lack of intellectual curiosity about the partner" (Masters & Johnson, p. 219).

Importantly, if heterosexuals honestly tell each other what they like and don't like and how each of them is doing, they're more likely to have superb sex, too. This sort of discussion is very intimate, and couples who engage in a lot of it not only enjoy more sexual satisfaction but feel more contented overall in their relationships as well (Coffelt & Hess, 2014).

Better communication can also help us manage situations in which we do not want to have sex and our intentions are being misunderstood. You may have already learned the hard way that women and men often interpret sexual situations differently (Ambrose & Gross, 2016), and frustration or antagonism can result. Men have stronger sexual desires than women do, and they're literally thinking about sex more often than women are, so they tend to read sexual interest into innocent behavior from women who have no sexual intentions (Galperin & Haselton, 2013). This was first demonstrated in a classic study by Antonia Abbey (1982), who invited men and women to get acquainted with each other, chatting one-on-one, while another man and another woman observed their conversation. Both the men participating in the interactions and those watching them tended to interpret friendliness from the women as signs of sexual interest, even when the women doing the talking had no wish to be sexually provocative and the women looking on saw no such conduct. The men literally perceived signs of sexual flirtatiousness that were not intended and that probably did not exist.

This sort of thing isn't rare; most men (54 percent) have misperceived a woman's intentions at least once (Jacques-Tiura et al., 2007). Undoubtedly, some of these errors were innocent mistakes; sometimes, a woman's behavior may be reasonably taken to be *either* flirtatious or just friendly (Hall, 2016), and because men are less sensitive than women to nonverbal nuance, they can easily form the wrong impression in such cases (Lindgren et al., 2012). Along those lines, it's interesting that when men tried to judge the sexual interests of 81 different women and received *feedback* about their accuracy along the way, they started attending more to the women's facial expressions (and less to their physical attractiveness), and the quality of their judgments improved (Treat et al., 2016).

Importantly, though, misperceptions of women's interests are more likely from some men than from others. Men who reject traditional gender roles and value equality of the sexes make fewer of these mistakes (Farris et al. 2008), whereas macho men who consider sex to be an exploitative contest make more of them (Wegner & Abbey, 2016). These latter guys, who actually don't like women very much, are the men who are most likely to engage in sexual coercion (Casey et al., 2017), particularly when they're drunk (Cowley, 2014) and/or horny (Bouffard & Miller, 2014). Explicit, unambiguous communication is sometimes needed to set such men straight—and the best refusals are assertive, consistent, and persistent (Yagil et al., 2006). Don't be coy or playful when it's time to make your feelings known; plainly state your disinterest, and repeat as necessary.

Notably, once a couple starts living together, overestimates of women's sexual interest are less common. In fact, in a Canadian study, husbands tended to *under-*estimate the sexual desire of their wives—and instead of being a nuisance, this pattern was associated with greater marital satisfaction for the wives (Muise et al., 2016b). There could be several things going on here—it's another interesting point to ponder—but if husbands routinely feel that they need to woo their wives, their wives may be more content.

Sexual Satisfaction and Relationship Satisfaction

Finally, let's note that sexual satisfaction does not occur in a vacuum; we're unlikely to be satisfied with our sex lives if we're *dis*satisfied with our relationships with our partners. Sexual satisfaction and relationship satisfaction go hand-in-hand (McNulty et al., 2016). Whether they are married or cohabiting, heterosexual or not, the most gratifying sex is enjoyed by couples who are satisfied with, and committed to, their relationships (Byers & Cohen, 2017).

One reason sexual satisfaction and relationship satisfaction are linked is that they are subject to similar influences. Similarity and perceived partner responsiveness[10] are two examples. We generally like those who are similar to us, and spouses are more content when they (think that they) share similar levels of sexual desire (de Jong & Reis, 2015) and similar sexual histories. The larger the difference in the number of past sexual partners a husband and wife have had, for instance, the less happily married they are likely to be (Garcia & Markey, 2007). Furthermore, being valued and accepted by an attentive partner is associated with increased desire for that partner (Birnbaum et al., 2016); responsiveness from one's partner is not only deeply rewarding, it's sexy, too.

Most importantly, however, we tend to be more satisfied in intimate relationships in which there's good sex because fulfilling sex makes a partnership more gratifying, and love for a partner makes sex more rewarding in turn (Yucel & Gassanov, 2010). Pleasing sex with a partner reduces stress and improves one's mood in a way in which a solitary orgasm through masturbation does not. Then,

[10] This one's on page 213.

Attachment and Sexuality

People who are anxious about abandonment are needy, and people who want to avoid intimacy keep their distance, and both of these dimensions of attachment are closely tied to sexual behavior. Perhaps because sex is often a very intimate act, avoidant people have less frequent sex with their romantic partners (Favez & Tissot, 2017), and more frequent sex with casual, short-term partners (Schmitt & Jonason, 2015), than secure people do. They tend not to have sex to foster closeness with, and to celebrate their intimacy with, their lovers. On the contrary, in order to "get some space" and to maintain their freedom, men with a dismissing attachment style are more likely than secure men to cheat on their partners (Schmitt & Jonason, 2015).

By comparison, people who are high in attachment anxiety have more passionate, needier sex that springs from their desire to feel accepted by their partners (Davis et al., 2004). Passion is great, but it's tinged with desperation in anxious people; to avoid displeasing their partners, they are also less likely to use condoms and to refuse to do things they don't want to do (Strachman & Impett, 2009). And with their endless appetites for reassurance, people who are high in anxiety also have more extramarital affairs than secure people do (Fish et al., 2012).

Moreover, people with high levels of either anxiety or avoidance are less likely than secure people are to be honest and open in discussing their needs and desires with their partners (Davis et al., 2006). It shouldn't surprise us, then, that they're less satisfied with their sex lives. And their partners often are, too; people with avoidant spouses wish their sex was less detached and distant (Butzer & Campbell, 2008).

All things considered, whether they're gay or straight (Starks & Parsons, 2014), the greatest sexual self-confidence, best communication, and most satisfaction with sex are enjoyed by people with secure attachment styles. Secure people are more playful and open to exploration in bed, and they more happily and readily commit themselves to faithful, monogamous intimacy (Mikulincer & Shaver, 2013). Great lovers tend to be secure lovers.

that positive mood and a happy outlook increase the levels of physical affection and sexual activity that follow (Burleson et al., 2007). Sexual satisfaction thus increases relationship satisfaction, and vice versa.

What's more, this pattern persists throughout life. A study of elderly couples married for an average of 43 years found that, even though they had less of it than they used to, sex continued to be an influential component of their marital satisfaction (Hinchliff & Gott, 2004). Overall, then, studies of sexual satisfaction find that it emerges from a rewarding *partnership* (Fisher et al., 2015). Sex isn't some kind of magical ingredient that automatically makes a relationship fulfilling. The best sex seems to depend on:

- each person having his or her needs met by a partner who understands and respects one's specific sexual desires,
- valuing one's partner and being devoted to the relationship, and
- enjoying being with each other, in bed and out of it.

SEXUAL COERCION

These desirable ingredients are absent when one partner intentionally cajoles, induces, pressures, or even forces another to engage in sexual activities against his or her will. These actions can take various forms (DeGue & DiLillo, 2005). The *type of pressure* that is applied can range from (a) mildly coercive verbal persuasion (that may involve false promises, guilt induction, or threats to end the relationship); to (b) plying someone with alcohol or drugs to weaken his or her resistance; and on to (c) the threat of—or actual use of—physical force to compel someone's submission. The *unwanted sexual behavior* that results can range from touching and fondling to penetration and intercourse.

Take a look at Figure 9.4, which portrays these two dimensions. Together, they depict four different broad types of sexual violation. The boundaries between them are not exact—they blend from one to the other depending on the specific circumstances—but they still make useful distinctions. The first category, in quadrant 1, includes interactions in which one person coaxes and cons another to submit to touching that he or she doesn't want. Because the violations that result are relatively less severe, you may not consider them to be a

FIGURE 9.4. **Four broad types of sexual violation.**
Two different dimensions—the type of pressure that is applied and the behavior that results—combine to delineate four different broad types of sexual misconduct. In all cases, the sexual contact is unwanted, and consent is either coerced or never given—and thus, a violation occurs.

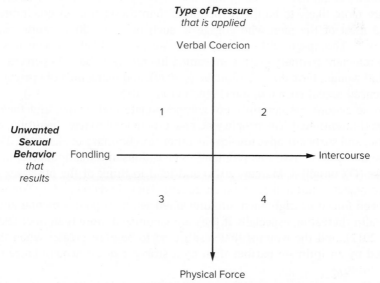

Source: Adapted from DeGue, S., & DiLillo, D. "'You would if you loved me':
Toward an improved conceptual and etiological understanding of nonphysical
male sexual coercion." Aggression and Violent Behavior, 10, 2005, 513–532.

form of sexual coercion; many of us still expect sex to be a competition in which men and women are adversaries—with women holding a prize that men seek to win through guile, persistence, and superior might—so interactions in which men ignore women's disinterest and "cop a feel" whenever possible may seem unremarkable (Krahé et al., 2007). However, because they are unwanted, these actions are not innocuous. They disrespect one's partner, and when they are directed at women, they are most likely to be enacted by men who quietly hold hostile attitudes toward women and who believe that all women would secretly like to be raped (Hoyt & Yeater, 2011). They also have a corrosive effect on relationships, being associated with lower sexual and relationship satisfaction (Katz & Myhr, 2008).

In quadrant 2, verbal manipulation and/or intentional intoxication lead to penetration of the genitals. If a woman does not actively and strenuously protest this behavior, a lot of people will consider her to share the responsibility for the act (Cohn et al., 2009), so these behaviors are rarely prosecuted. Quadrants 3 and 4 involve various degrees of physical force (or a drug-induced stupor that leaves the victim unable to resist), and the behaviors there are more likely to seem patently illegal. Many legal jurisdictions would prosecute the actions in quadrant 4 as "forcible rape" if they became known.

Most men and women never direct any of these forms of sexual coercion toward the other sex (Spitzberg, 1999). Nevertheless, they are scarily common. Specific counts depend on the precise definitions employed, but most American women (73 percent) have encountered some form of sexual victimization since they turned 16 (Turchik & Hassija, 2014), and ten percent of the women in Great Britain have, through pressure or force, had sex with someone against their will (Macdowall et al., 2013). Overall, men use more physical force than women do—they are more likely to be the perpetrators than the victims in quadrants 3 and 4—and most of the men who engage in such behavior do so more than once (Zinzow & Thompson, 2015). But women are just as likely as men to verbally coerce reluctant partners to have unwanted intercourse; about 25 percent of both men and women have done so (Spitzberg, 1999), and many men (43 percent) have experienced sexual coercion, too (French et al., 2015).

These actions are certainly not compassionate and loving, and they're not even well-intentioned. The people who enact them tend to have belittling, unsympathetic, and surly attitudes toward the other sex (Bouffard et al., 2016). The men and women who behave this way tend to be callous and manipulative; they lack remorse (O'Connell & Marcus, 2016) and tend to think of the other sex as animals or objects (Rudman & Mescher, 2012b). They do damage, too: Women who have been forced or frightened into unwanted sex have poorer mental and physical health thereafter, especially if they are victimized more than once (Perilloux et al., 2012), and the wounds that result tend to be even greater when they are inflicted by an intimate partner than by a stranger or an acquaintance (Impett et al., 2014b).

So the prevalence of sexual coercion, whatever its form, is very distressing. What can be done to reduce its frequency? I have several suggestions. First, beware of potential partners who view sex as a contest. They are unlikely to have your best interests at heart. Second, beware of intoxication in either you or your partner; it increases the chances that one will behave inappropriately, and indeed, most episodes of sexual coercion involve alcohol or drugs (Cleere & Lynn, 2013). Third, resolve to assertively resist unwanted advances; women who decide in advance to rebuff sexual misconduct are less likely to passively submit if such a situation develops (Gidycz et al., 2008). Fourth, reduce the need for such assertion by setting sexual boundaries with frank, direct discussion before you start an intimate interaction. (At a minimum, tell your partner, "If I say no, I'm gonna *mean* no.") Miscommunication and misunderstanding are often at work in interactions involving sexual coercion, and the distinction between right and wrong is clearer when the ground rules are laid out in advance (Winslett & Gross, 2008). Finally, consider the value of thinking of your lover as an equal partner whose preferences and pleasure are as important as your own. Not only is such respect and thoughtfulness incompatible with sexual coercion, if you and your lover both feel that way, you're likely to have great sex (Fisher et al., 2015).

FOR YOUR CONSIDERATION

Chad was in love with Jennifer. He felt a lot of sexual desire for her, and he always enjoyed having sex with her, but he still felt something was missing. She was usually glad to have sex, and she seemed to enjoy it, too, but she rarely took any initiative and he typically did all the work. She usually just lay there, and he wanted her to be more active and take the lead now and then. He wished that she would be more inventive, and he wanted her to work him over occasionally. Nevertheless, he didn't say anything. Their sex was good, if not great, and he worried that any complaints would make things worse, not better, between them.

Having read this chapter, what do you think the future holds for Chad and Jennifer? Why?

CHAPTER SUMMARY

Sexual Attitudes

Attitudes about Casual Sex. People's attitudes about sex have become more permissive over time. Today, most people tolerate unmarried sex if the partners care for each other, but a *sexual double standard* may still lead us to judge women's sexuality more harshly than men's.

Attitudes about Same-Sex Sexuality. Americans dislike gays or lesbians if they think sexual orientation is a choice. Nevertheless, times have changed, and most Americans now approve of gays' and lesbians' marriages.

Cultural Differences in Sexual Attitudes. Sexual attitudes in the United States are relatively conservative compared to those in many other countries.

Sexual Behavior

Sex for the First Time. Almost all of us have sex before we marry, and the first time usually involves a steady close relationship. If the partners aren't close, some regret typically follows.

Sex in Committed Relationships. People have sex for diverse reasons, and their relationship status, age, and sexual orientation all influence the frequency with which sex occurs. Couples who have sex once a week are just as happy, on average, as those who have sex more often.

Infidelity. Men cheat more than women do, and they are more likely than women to have an unrestricted *sociosexual orientation*. The *good genes hypothesis* suggests that women cheat in order to have healthy offspring, and *sperm competition* may have evolved to counteract such behavior.

Sexual Desire. Men have higher *sex drives* than women do. This may lead to annoyance as heterosexual couples negotiate their sexual interactions.

Safe, Sensible Sex. Most college students have had *hookups,* sometimes having intercourse without condoms. Condom use is influenced by underestimates of risk, faulty decision making, pluralistic ignorance, inequalities of power, abstinence education, low self-control, and concerns about intimacy and pleasure.

Sexual Satisfaction

The best sex is motivated by approach goals and fulfills basic needs, but traditional gender roles tend to undermine women's choice and control in bed. Endorsement of *sexual growth beliefs* is desirable when challenges arise.

Sexual Communication. Direct and honest sexual communication is associated with greater sexual satisfaction. Because gays and lesbians discuss their preferences more openly than heterosexuals do, they enjoy better sex. Good communication may also avoid misperceptions of sexual intent.

Sexual Satisfaction and Relationship Satisfaction. Partners who are satisfied with their sex lives tend to be more satisfied with their relationships, with each appearing to make the other more likely.

Sexual Coercion

Various forms of pressure and behavioral outcomes describe four broad types of sexual violations. These are distressingly prevalent, but several strategies may make them less common.

CHAPTER 10

Stresses and Strains

PERCEIVED RELATIONAL VALUE ◆ HURT FEELINGS ◆ OSTRACISM
◆ JEALOUSY ◆ DECEPTION AND LYING ◆ BETRAYAL ◆ FORGIVENESS
◆ FOR YOUR CONSIDERATION ◆ CHAPTER SUMMARY

Let's take stock. In previous chapters, we have encountered adaptive and maladaptive cognition, good and bad communication, and rewarding and unrewarding social exchange. We've been evenhanded in considering both beneficial and disadvantageous influences on close relationships. But that won't be true here. This chapter focuses on various pitfalls, stumbling blocks, and hazards that cause wear and tear in relationships (with just one bright spot at the end). And importantly, the stresses and strains I cover here—hurt feelings, ostracism, jealousy, lying, and betrayal—are commonplace events that occur in most relationships somewhere along the way. We've all had our feelings hurt (Malachowski & Frisby, 2015), and sooner or later, almost everyone lies to their intimate partners (DePaulo et al., 2009). Even outright betrayals of one sort or another are surprisingly widespread and hard to avoid (Baxter et al., 1997).

However, the fact that these incidents are commonplace doesn't mean they are inconsequential. Negative events like these can be very influential. They help explain why most of us report having had a very troublesome relationship within the last 5 years (Levitt et al., 1996). And despite their idiosyncrasies, all of these unhappy events may share a common theme (Leary & Miller, 2012): They suggest that we are not as well liked or well respected as we wish we were.

PERCEIVED RELATIONAL VALUE

Fueled by our need to belong,[1] most of us care deeply about what our intimate partners think of us. We want them to want us. We want them to value our company and to consider their partnerships with us to be valuable and important. As a result, according to theorist Mark Leary (Leary & Acosta, 2018), it's painful to perceive that our **relational value**—that is, the degree to which others consider their relationships with us to be valuable and important—is lower than we would like it to be.

When our relational value is high, others value our company and prioritize their partnerships with us, and we feel appreciated, respected, and accepted by

---

[1] Need a reminder about the human need to belong? Revisit page 4, way back in chapter 1.

them. In contrast, when our relational value is low, others do not seek us out or choose us for their teams, and they're not much interested in who we are and what we have to say; so, we feel unwanted.

Some of the people in our lives value us more than others do, so we routinely encounter various degrees of acceptance and rejection in our dealings with others. Take a look at Table 10.1. Sometimes we enjoy the strongest possible acceptance, called *maximal inclusion*: Others are eager to be with us, and if they want to host a party (for instance), they'll change the date or just cancel if we can't come; we are that important to them. (Maximal inclusion may be pretty rare; when was the last time you were *that* important to someone?) More often, we encounter *active inclusion*, which occurs when others make sure to invite us to their parties and are disappointed if we can't come, but have the parties anyway if we're unavailable. We're important to them, but not so important that they can't go on without us. We experience *passive inclusion* when others don't invite us to their parties but are content to let us in the door if we hear about the gatherings and just show up; they don't dislike us and it's nice to see us, but we're a low priority for them, and we can join their parties only when there's room.

And then there's *ambivalence*, which occurs when others are neither accepting nor rejecting; they genuinely don't care one way or the other whether we show up or not. If we want others to like us and value their relationships with us, noncommittal ambivalence from them may be bad enough, but things can get worse. We encounter *passive exclusion* when others ignore us and wish we were elsewhere, and we suffer *active exclusion* when others go out of their way to avoid us altogether. However, the most complete rejection occurs when, in *maximal exclusion*, others order us to leave their parties when they find us there. In such instances, merely avoiding us won't do; they want us gone.

Our emotional reactions to such experiences depend on how much we want to be accepted by particular others, and just what their acceptance or rejection of us means. On occasion, people exclude us because they regard us positively, and such rejections are much less painful than are exclusions that result from our deficiencies or faults. Consider the game show *Survivor:* Contestants sometimes

TABLE 10.1. Degrees of Acceptance and Rejection

Being accepted or rejected by others is not an all-or-nothing event. People can desire our company to greater or lesser degrees, and researchers use these labels to describe the different extents to which we may be included or excluded by others.

Maximal inclusion	Others seek us out and go out of their way to interact with us.
Active inclusion	Others want us and welcome us but do not go to lengths to be with us.
Passive inclusion	Others allow us to be included.
Ambivalence	Others do not care whether we are included or not.
Passive exclusion	Others ignore us but do not avoid us.
Active exclusion	Others avoid us, tolerating our presence only when necessary.
Maximal exclusion	Others banish us, sending us away, or abandon us.

Source: Adapted from Leary, M. R. "Toward a conceptualization of interpersonal rejection." In M. R. Leary (Ed.),
Interpersonal rejection. *New York: Oxford University Press, 2001, 3–20.*

try to vote the most skilled, most able competitors off the island to increase their personal chances of winning the game. Being excluded because you're better than everyone else may not hurt much, but rejection that suggests that you're inept, insufficient, or inadequate usually does (Çelik et al., 2013).

In addition, it's not much of a blow to be excluded from a party you didn't want to attend in the first place. Exclusion is much more painful when we want to be accepted by others than when we don't much care what they think of us (Vanhalst & Leary, 2014). Indeed, it's also possible to be accepted and liked by others but be hurt because they don't like us as much as we want them to. This is what unrequited love is often like (see p. 259). Those for whom we feel unrequited love may be fond of us in return, but if we want to be loved instead of merely liked, their mildness is painful.

All of these possibilities suggest that there is only a rough connection between the objective reactions we receive from others and our *feelings* of acceptance or rejection that result, so we will focus on the *perception that others value their relationships with us less than we want them to* as a core ingredient of the stresses and strains that we will inspect in this chapter (Leary & Miller, 2012). We feel hurt when our **perceived relational value** for others—that is, the apparent importance that others attach to their relationships with us—is lower than we want it to be.

HURT FEELINGS

In fact, the feelings of acceptance or rejection we experience in our dealings with others are related to their evaluations of us in a complex way: Maximal exclusion doesn't feel much worse than simple ambivalence does (Buckley et al., 2004). Take a careful look at Figure 10.1 on the next page. The graph depicts people's reactions to evaluations from others that vary across a 10-point scale. Maximal *ex*clusion is described by the worst possible evaluation, a 1, and maximal *in*clusion is described by the best possible evaluation, a 10; ambivalence, the point at which others don't care about us one way or the other, is the 5 at the midpoint of the scale. The graph demonstrates that once we find that others don't want us around, it hardly matters whether they dislike us a little or a lot: Our momentary judgments of our self-worth bottom out when people reject us to *any* extent (that is, when their evaluations range from 4 down to 1).

On the other hand, when it comes to acceptance, being completely adored doesn't improve our self-esteem beyond the boost we get from being very well-liked. Instead, we appear to be very sensitive to small differences in regard from others that range from ambivalence at the low end to active inclusion at the high end. As people like us more and more, we feel better and better about ourselves until their positive regard for us is fully ensured. This all makes sense from an evolutionary perspective (Leary & Cottrell, 2013); carefully discerning degrees of acceptance that might allow access to resources and mates is more useful than monitoring the enmity of one's enemies. (After all, when it comes to reactions from potential mates, there are usually few practical differences between mild distaste and outright disgust!)

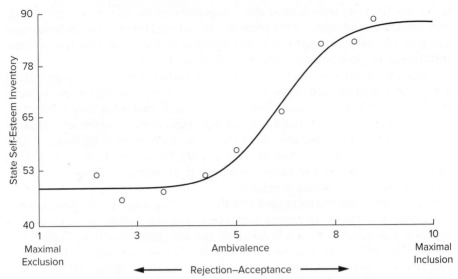

Source: Data from Leary, M. R., Haupt, A. L., Strausser, K. S., & Chokel, J. T. "Calibrating the sociometer: The relationship between interpersonal appraisals and state self-esteem," Journal of Personality and Social Psychology, 74, 1998, 1290–1299.

FIGURE 10.1. **Reactions to acceptance and rejection.**
This curve describes how our momentary feelings about ourselves map onto the treatment we receive from others. Self-esteem increases sharply as people move from being ambivalent about us to wanting us around, but any rejection at all causes our self-esteem to bottom out. When people prefer to ignore us, we feel nearly as bad about ourselves as we do when they order us to leave or throw us out.

So, mild rejection from others usually feels just as bad as more extreme rejection does. But *decreases* in the *acceptance* we receive from others may be even worse, particularly when they occur in that range between ambivalence and active inclusion—that is, when people who liked us once appear to like us less now. Leary and his colleagues demonstrated the potent impact of decreases in acceptance when they manipulated the evaluations that research participants received from new acquaintances (Buckley et al., 2004). As young adults talked about themselves to another person over an intercom system, they received intermittent approval ratings on a computer screen (see Figure 10.2); the ratings supposedly came from their conversation partner, but they were actually controlled by the experimenters, who provided one of four patterns of feedback. Some people received consistent acceptance, receiving only 5's and 6's, whereas others encountered constant rejection, receiving only 2's and 3's. It's painful to be disliked by others, so of course, those who were accepted by the unseen acquaintance were happier and felt better about themselves than those who were rejected. But other people received evaluations that changed over time, starting poorly and getting better, or starting well and getting worse. In the latter case, over a span of 5 minutes, the research participants received successive ratings of 6, 5, 3, 3, and 2. Apparently, as the new acquaintance got to know them better, the less the acquaintance liked them.

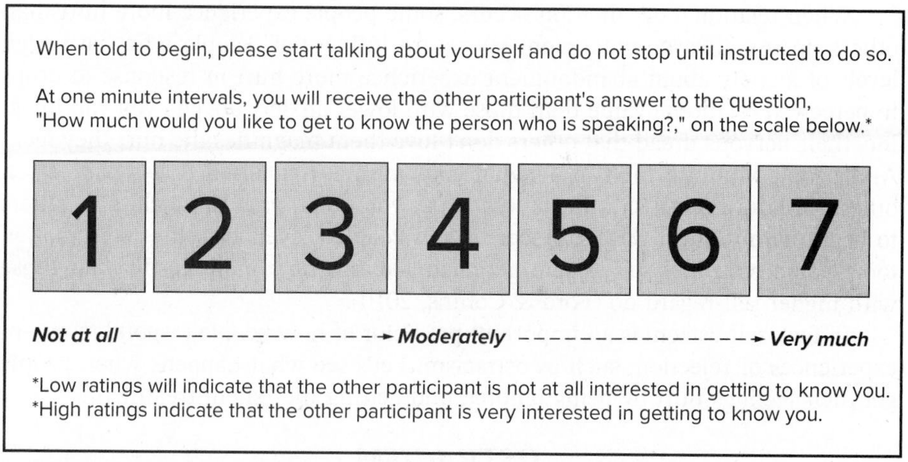

When told to begin, please start talking about yourself and do not stop until instructed to do so.

At one minute intervals, you will receive the other participant's answer to the question, "How much would you like to get to know the person who is speaking?," on the scale below.*

| 1 | 2 | 3 | 4 | 5 | 6 | 7 |

Not at all – – – – – – – – – – – – –➤ *Moderately* – – – – – – – – – – – – –➤ *Very much*

*Low ratings will indicate that the other participant is not at all interested in getting to know you.
*High ratings indicate that the other participant is very interested in getting to know you.

Source: Buckley, K. E., Winkel, R. E., & Leary, M. R. (2004). *"Reactions to acceptance and rejection: Effects of level and sequence of relational evaluation."* Journal of Experimental Social Psychology, *40, 14–28.*

FIGURE 10.2. **Relational devaluation in the lab.**
Imagine that as you describe yourself to someone in another room, one of these numbers lights up every 60 seconds, and you receive evaluations that start high but get worse and worse over time. After 5 minutes, the other person is giving you a "2" that indicates that he or she is quite uninterested in meeting you. How would you feel?

The pattern of decreasing acceptance was particularly painful, causing more negative reactions than even constant rejection did (Buckley et al., 2004). Evidently, it's especially awful to experience drops in our perceived relational value— that is, **relational devaluation,** or apparent decreases in others' regard for us—and it causes a variety of unhappy emotions. When their partners turned against them, people felt sad, angry, and *hurt,* with the latter emotion being a particular sensation that is uniquely associated with losses of relational value (Leary & Leder, 2009). Hurt feelings have much in common with real pain; when people suffering from romantic rejection are placed in fMRI scanners and asked to study pictures of the ex-lovers who broke up with them, their brains respond as if they were experiencing physical pain (Eisenberger, 2013). Rejection really hurts. And remarkably, the pain reliever acetaminophen reduces the pain of social rejection just as it does a headache:[2] After a week-and-a-half of daily doses of acetaminophen, college students had fewer hurt feelings at the end of the day than did other students who were taking a placebo (DeWall et al., 2010). Marijuana blunts[3] social pain, too (Deckman et al., 2014). Obviously, psychological wounds can cause real distress, and the sense of injury that characterizes hurt feelings— the feeling that relationship rules have been broken (Malachowski & Frisby, 2015) and that one has been damaged, shattered, cut, or stabbed—makes hurt feelings a distinct emotional experience (Feeney, 2005).

[2] Acetaminophen, the active ingredient in the product known to Americans as Tylenol, is called *paracetamol* in most places outside North America.
[3] No pun intended.

When relational devaluation occurs, some people experience more hurt than others do. As always, attachment styles are influential. People who have high levels of anxiety about abandonment experience more hurt in response to drops in perceived relational value than those with lower anxiety do. (As you can imagine, their nervous dread that others don't love them magnifies the hurt they feel.) And people who are high in avoidance of intimacy experience less pain when others withdraw; exclusion hurts less when you don't want to be close to others to begin with (Shaver & Mikulincer, 2013). People's levels of self-esteem matter, too: People with low self-esteem get their feelings hurt more easily than those with higher self-regard do (Ford & Collins, 2010).

In fact, self-esteem is an important predictor of how people respond to potent experiences of rejection, such as ostracism. Let's see what happens when people get their feelings hurt by being ignored and getting the "silent treatment."

OSTRACISM

A specific form of rejection that often occurs even in close relationships is **ostracism,** in which people are given the "cold shoulder" and ignored by those around them. When the silent treatment is intentional, ostracizers deliberately refrain from responding to others, sometimes pretending that their targets are not even present. Most of us have experienced this unpleasant treatment; in one broad survey, 67 percent of Americans admitted that they had given an intimate partner the cold shoulder, and 75 percent reported that they had been ostracized by a loved one (Williams, 2001).

Why do people sometimes intentionally ignore their partners? Ostracizers usually justify their actions as an effective way to punish their partners, to avoid confrontation, or to calm down and cool off following a conflict, and they usually believe that the ostracism was beneficial in helping them achieve their goals (Sommer et al., 2001). But by its very nature, ostracism often leaves its targets wondering why they are being ignored. Only rarely is an explanation offered when a partner remains silent, and the victims of ostracism often have no idea why it is happening. As a result, the targets of ostracism typically do not consider their partners' withdrawal to be a kind or effective way to behave, and they usually believe that the ostracism has damaged their relationships (Arriaga et al., 2014b).

Ostracism can be potent and painful because it threatens basic social needs (Wesselmann & Williams, 2013). It's dehumanizing (Bastian & Haslam, 2010). The silent treatment threatens our need to belong, damages our feelings of self-worth, and reduces our perceived control over our interactions. And our initial reactions to such threats usually involve confused, unhappy disarray (Wesselmann et al., 2012). A "cold shoulder" *feels* cold: When people feel excluded, they think the room is cooler and that warm food and drink are more desirable than they do when they have not been rejected (Zhong & Leonardelli, 2008). Our bodies show signs of stress; our adrenal glands dump cortisol, a stress hormone, into our blood (Dickerson & Zoccola, 2013). Time seems to pass more slowly, too; in one study in which they were asked to estimate how much time had passed during a 40-second interval, people who felt accepted by others offered an average (and quite accurate) estimate of 42 seconds, whereas those who were rejected believed that 64 seconds had passed (Twenge et al., 2003).

©Iakov Filimonov/Shutterstock

Ostracism is confusing and obnoxious, but it can elicit compliance from others on occasion. But it may also engender hostility instead.

What happens next seems to depend on which of a person's needs are in the most peril (Wesselmann & Williams, 2013). When belongingness is threatened, people who are being ostracized may work hard to regain their partners' regard, being compliant and doing what their tormentors want, especially when they think the relationship—and their relational value—can be repaired (Richman & Leary, 2009). However, they may also start looking for new, less punishing partners. After an experience with exclusion, people are often especially eager to make new, kinder friends (Maner et al., 2007).

More antagonistic reactions may occur when ostracism seems illegitimate and unjust and threatens people's feelings of control or self-worth (Tuscherer et al., 2015). When ostracized people get angry, they dismiss the opinions of those who are ignoring them as unfounded, unfair, and dim-witted, and they become more surly and aggressive (even toward innocent bystanders) than cowed and compliant (DeWall et al., 2009). In fact, instances of ostracism or romantic rejection precede most of the awful cases in which students take guns to school and shoot innocent classmates (Leary et al., 2006). Those who ostracize others are just as likely to frustrate and anger them as to shame or instruct them (Hales et al., 2016).

Researchers who study ostracism have developed a variety of ingenious procedures to create potent experiences of rejection in the lab. After short introductions to strangers, people have learned that no one wanted to work with them (Leary, 2005), and others have been ignored in face-to-face discussions or Internet chat rooms run by research assistants (Williams, 2001). But an inspired procedure created by Kipling Williams and his colleagues that involves a simple game of catch is especially nefarious. If you encounter this procedure, you'll find yourself sitting for 5 minutes with two other people who begin playfully tossing and bouncing a racquetball back and forth. You've all just met, and you're all just passing time, waiting for an experimenter to return; so, the first minute of play, in which you frequently receive the ball, is pretty lighthearted. But then things change. Over the next 4 minutes, nobody tosses you the ball. The two other people gleefully toss the ball between themselves and completely ignore you, neither looking your way nor acknowledging any protest. It's as if you have ceased to exist.

Researchers have even conducted studies of ostracism online, and thousands of people around the world have now encountered a variation of the ball-tossing procedure on the Web (Hartgerink et al., 2015). In this version, people believe that they are online with two other people represented by screen icons who are sending a Cyberball back and forth by clicking each other's icons. What happens next is all controlled by the computer program and there really aren't any other people involved, but as in real life, after a few warm-up throws, participants are partially or fully excluded from the "tossing" of the ball. What's striking is that this Internet ostracism is quite painful even when it is (apparently) dispensed by strangers one will never meet. In fact, even after people learn that their exclusion is controlled by the computer and that no real interpersonal evaluation is even remotely involved, they still get their feelings hurt when the computer program fails to toss them the ball (Zadro et al., 2004)! Ostracism even hurts when it is dispensed by groups we despise, such as the Ku Klux Klan (Gonsalkorale & Williams, 2007). Our species seems to be quite sensitive to even the merest hint of social rejection.

So, ostracism is an obnoxious, unpleasant experience that can be just as likely to engender hostility as compliance. And people with high self-esteem are relatively unlikely to put up with it. When they are ignored by others, people with high self-regard are more likely than those with lower self-esteem to end their relationships with their ostracizers and to seek new partners who will treat them better—and perhaps as a result, they get the silent treatment less often. In comparison, people with low self-esteem experience more ostracism, and they are more likely to carry a grudge and to ostracize others in return (Sommer & Rubin, 2005). Instead of leaving those who ostracize them, people with low self-regard are more likely to hang around but be spiteful.

In sum, then, we are likely to feel sadness, anger, and hurt when others ostracize us, and a core ingredient in such experiences seems to be the perception that those others do not value their relationships with us as much as we wish they did. Let's turn now to the special kind of threat to our relational value that occurs when we believe that a romantic rival is luring a beloved partner away.

JEALOUSY

A different kind of negative emotional experience results from the potential loss of a valued relationship to a real or imagined rival. **Jealousy** can involve a variety of feelings, ranging all the way from sad dejection to actual pride that one's partner is desirable to others, but the three feelings that define jealousy best are *hurt, anger,* and *fear* (Guerrero et al., 2005).[4]

Hurt follows from the perception that our partners do not value us enough to honor their commitments to our relationships, and fear and anxiety result from

---

[4] Jealousy is sometimes confused with envy, but the two are quite different (DelPriore et al., 2012). We envy someone when we wish we had what they have; envy is characterized by a humiliating longing for another person's possessions. In contrast, jealousy is the confused state of hurt, anger, and fear that results from the threat of losing what we already have, a relationship that we do not wish to give up.

the dreadful prospect of abandonment and loss. But the unique element in jealousy is the romantic rival who threatens to lure a partner away: "To be jealous, one must have a relationship to lose and a rival to whom to lose it" (DeSteno & Salovey, 1994, p. 220). It's being cast aside for someone else that gets people angry, and that anger is usually directed both at the meddlesome rival and at the partner who is beginning to stray (Schützwohl, 2008b). Sometimes that anger turns violent; 13 percent of all the murders in the United States result from one spouse killing another, and when that occurs, jealousy is the most common motive (Buss, 2000).

Obviously, jealousy is an unhappy experience. But here's an interesting question: How would you feel if you *couldn't* make your lover jealous? Would you be disappointed if nothing you did gave your partner a jealous twinge? Most people probably would be, but whether or not that's a sensible point of view may depend on what type of jealousy we're talking about, why your partner is jealous, and what your partner does in response to his or her jealousy. Let's explore those issues.

> **A Point to Ponder**
>
> Is getting your partner just a little jealous every now and then an acceptable thing to do? Why or why not?

Two Types of Jealousy

Reactive jealousy occurs when someone becomes aware of an actual threat to a valued relationship (Buunk & Dijkstra, 2006). The troubling threat may not be a current event; it may have occurred in the past, or it may be anticipated in the near future (if, for instance, your partner expresses the intention to date someone else), but reactive jealousy always occurs in response to an actual, realistic danger. A variety of behaviors from one's partner can cause concern; just fantasizing about or flirting with someone else is considered "cheating" by most young adults in the United States (Kruger et al., 2013). Unfortunately, there may be a lot to be jealous about. In one sample of American adults, 98 percent of the men and 80 percent of the women said they had had extradyadic sexual fantasies in the past two months (Hicks & Leitenberg, 2001). And in two surveys of over 800 American college students, lots of young adults reported having dated, kissed, fondled, or slept with a third party while they were in a serious dating relationship with someone else (Brand et al., 2007). Half of the women and two-fifths of the men said they had kissed or fondled an extradyadic interloper, and a fifth of both men and women said they had had intercourse with that person (most of them more than once).

In contrast, **suspicious jealousy** occurs when one's partner *hasn't* misbehaved and one's suspicions do not fit the facts at hand (Buunk & Dijkstra, 2006). Suspicious jealousy results in worried and mistrustful vigilance and snooping as the jealous partner seeks to confirm his or her suspicions, and it can range from a mildly overactive imagination to outright paranoia. In all cases, however, suspicious jealousy can be said to be unfounded; it results from situations that would not trouble a more secure and more trusting partner.

The distinction between the two types of jealousy is meaningful because almost everybody feels reactive jealousy when they realize that their partners have been unfaithful (Buss, 2000), but people vary a lot in their tendencies to feel suspicious jealousy in the absence of any provocation. Nevertheless, the distinction

Bizarro ©2008 Dan Piraro, Distributed by King Features Syndicate, Inc.

Suspicious jealousy does not fit the facts at hand.

between the two isn't quite as sharp as it may seem. A jealous reaction to a partner's affair may linger on as suspicious jealousy years later when trust, once lost, is never fully regained (Zandbergen & Brown, 2015). And people may differ in their judgments of what constitutes a real threat to their relationship (Guerrero, 1998). Knowledge that a partner is merely fantasizing about someone else may not trouble a secure partner who is not much prone to jealousy, but it may cause reactive jealousy in a partner who is insecure. So, the boundary between them can be vague, and as we explore individual differences in susceptibility to jealousy in our next section, I'll ask a generic question that refers to both types of jealousy.

Who's Prone to Jealousy?

On the whole, men and women do not differ in their jealous tendencies (Buunk, 1995), but some people nevertheless feel jealous more readily and more intensely than other people do. One obvious precursor of jealousy is *dependence* on a relationship (Rydell et al., 2004). When people feel that they need a particular partner because their alternatives are poor—that is, when people have a low CL_{alt}—any threat to their relationship is especially menacing. In contrast, people who have desirable alternatives tend to be less jealous because they have less to lose if the relationship ends.

Jealousy also increases with feelings of *inadequacy* in a relationship (White, 1981). People who worry that they can't measure up to their partners' expectations or who fret that they're not what their lovers are looking for are less certain that their relationships will last, and they are more prone to jealousy than are people who feel certain they can keep their partners satisfied (Redlick, 2016). Self-confidence in a relationship is undoubtedly affected by a person's global sense of self-worth, and people with high self-esteem do tend to be less prone to jealousy than those with low self-esteem (DeSteno et al., 2006). However, a person's perceptions of his or her adequacy as a partner in a specific relationship are especially important, and even people with generally high self-esteem can be prone to jealousy if they doubt their ability to fulfill a particular partner.

One of the ingredients in such doubt is a discrepancy in the mate value each person brings to the relationship (Redlick, 2016). If one partner is more desirable than the other, possessing (for example) more physical attractiveness, wealth, or talent, the less desirable partner is a less valuable mate, and that's a potential problem. The less desirable partner is likely to be aware that others could be a better match for his or her lover, and that may cause a sense of inadequacy that does not exist in other areas of his or her life (or with other partners). Here is another reason, then, why *matching* occurs with people pairing off with others of similar mate value (see chapter 3): Most of us want the most desirable partners we can get, but it can be threatening to realize that our partners could do better if they really wanted to.

In any case, consider the perilous situation that faces people who feel both dependent on and inadequate in their current relationships: They need their partners but worry that they're not good enough to keep them. It's no wonder that they react strongly to real or imagined signs that a romantic rival has entered the scene.

Of course, *attachment styles* influence jealousy, too. To some extent, people with a preoccupied style routinely find themselves in a similar fix: They greedily seek closeness with others, but they remain chronically worried that their partners don't love them enough in return. That's a recipe for jealousy, and sure enough, preoccupied people experience more jealousy than do those with the other three styles (Miller et al., 2014). The folks who are least affected when a relationship is threatened are typically those with a dismissing style of attachment. Feeling self-sufficient and trying not to depend on others is apparently one way to stay relatively immune to jealousy (Guerrero, 1998).

Finally, *personality traits* are also involved. People who are high in neuroticism, who tend to worry about a lot of things, are particularly prone to jealousy. On the other hand, agreeable people, who tend to be cooperative and trusting, are less likely than others to become jealous (Buunk & Dijkstra, 2006). And through no fault of their own (except, perhaps, in their poor choice of mates), the partners of people who are high in the Dark Triad traits of narcissism, Machiavellianism, and/or psychopathy are probably jealous more often than the rest of us: High scorers on each trait tend to be faithless cheaters (Jones & Weiser, 2014), and psychopaths, in particular, are more likely to *try* to get their partners jealous in order to increase their power and control over their partners (Massar et al., 2017). (See what I mean about a poor choice of mates?)

Who Gets Us Jealous?

We become jealous when our partners are interested in someone else, but not all rivals are created equal. It's particularly obnoxious when our friends start horning in on our romantic relationships; rivalry from a friend is more upsetting than is similar behavior from a stranger (Bleske & Shackelford, 2001). It's also especially painful when our partners start expressing renewed interest in their former lovers (Cann & Baucom, 2004). But no matter who they are, romantic rivals who have high mate value and who make us look bad by comparison are worrisome threats to our relationships, and they arouse more jealousy than do rivals who are milder competition.

And what kind of rivals are those? It depends on what our partners like. As you'll recall from chapter 3, women care more than men do about a mate's resources, so men are more jealous of other men who are self-confident, dominant, assertive, and rich than they are of rivals who are simply very handsome (Buunk et al., 2011). On the other hand, a handsome rival is bad enough: Everybody likes lovely lovers (Eastwick & Finkel, 2008), so attractive competitors evoke more jealousy in both men and women than homely rivals do (Massar & Buunk, 2009). The good news is that our rivals are usually not as attractive to our partners as we think they are, so our fears are usually overblown—but the bad news is that we do make such mistakes, overestimating the desirability of our competition and thereby suffering more distress than is warranted (Hill, 2007).

What Gets Us Jealous?

Evolutionary psychology has popped up here and there in this book, and here's another place it's pertinent. In this case, an evolutionary perspective suggests that jealousy evolved to motivate behavior designed to protect our close relationships from the interference of others. Presumably, early humans who reacted strongly to interlopers—being vigilant to outside interference, fending off rivals, and working hard to satisfy and fulfill their current partners— maintained their relationships and reproduced more successfully than did those who were blasé about meddlesome rivals. This perspective thus suggests that because it offered reproductive advantages in the past, jealousy is now a natural, ingrained reaction that is hard to avoid (Buss, 2000). More provocatively, it also suggests that men and women should be especially sensitive to different sorts of infidelity in their romantic partners.

Remember (from chapter 1) that men face a reproductive problem that women do not have: *paternity uncertainty*. A woman always knows whether or not a particular child is hers, but unless he is completely confident that his mate hasn't had sex with other men, a man can't be certain (without using some advanced technology) that he is a child's father. And being cuckolded and raising another man's offspring is an evolutionary dead end; the human race did not descend from ancestors who raised other people's children and had none of their own! Indeed, the potential evolutionary costs of failing to detect a partner's infidelity are so great that sexual selection may have favored men who were *too* suspicious of their partners' faithfulness over those who were not suspicious enough (Haselton & Galperin, 2013). Unwarranted doubt about a partner's fidelity is divisive and painful, but it may not be as costly and dangerous to men in an evolutionary sense as being too trusting and failing to detect infidelity when it occurs. Thus, today, men have more extramarital affairs than women do (Tafoya & Spitzberg, 2007), but it's men, not women, who are more accurate at detecting sexual infidelity in a cheating partner (Andrews et al., 2008). And vigilance is sometimes sensible; as we saw in chapter 9, about 2 percent of the world's children are being raised by men who do not know that the children were fathered by another man (Larmuseau et al., 2016).

For their part, women presumably enjoyed more success raising their children when they were sensitive to any signs that a man might withdraw the resources that were supporting the care and feeding of their children. Assuming that men were committed to them when the men in fact were not would have been risky

Stresses and Strains on Facebook

Along with its amazing reach to friends near and far, Facebook also makes possible an impressive variety of new ways to get our feelings hurt. Sooner or later, we're likely to be disappointed or stung when others ignore or deny a friend request, remove our messages or photo tags, or simply don't "like" our clever comments with the frequency they deserve (Tokunaga, 2011). We also learn of gatherings we missed (or to which we weren't invited) and see a lot of conclusive photographic proof that everybody else is having more fun than we are (Krasnova et al., 2015). Because it connects us to a lot of acquaintances who, in truth, don't value their relationships with us all that much (Miller et al., 2014), threats to perceived relational value abound on Facebook.

Difficulties don't disappear in our more intimate partnerships. In developing relationships, the partners have to decide when (if?) to go "Facebook official" by announcing their relationship to the world. Everybody assumes that a new status of "in a relationship" signals that the members of a couple now feel some commitment to each other (Lane et al., 2016), but women tend to assume that that status is more meaningful, entailing stronger

feelings and more exclusivity, than men do (Fox & Warber, 2013). Annoyance and dissatisfaction can result, particularly when one partner feels that he or she is "in a relationship" and the other does not (Papp et al., 2012). This is not a problem your grandparents faced forty or fifty years ago.

Finally, if you're prone to suspicious jealousy, Facebook can be a place of torment and peril. You can find old photos of your partner smiling alongside a prior partner, fret that there aren't enough pictures of *you* on his or her profile page, and stew over any of his or her new friends who are unfamiliar to you (Muscanell et al., 2013). Indeed, when they're feeling jealous, women spend more time snooping—monitoring their partner's Facebook activity—particularly when they're anxious about abandonment (Muise et al., 2014). (Men are less likely to do this, but then they tend to respond to jealousy differently than women do, as we'll see on page 321). Overall, despite its wonderful capabilities, Facebook has its hazards. If you find yourself snooping a lot, and worrying needlessly as a result, you may want to step away from your screen.

for women, so sexual selection may have favored those who were usually skeptical of men's declarations of true love. Unfairly doubting a man's commitment may be obnoxious and self-defeating, but believing that a mate was devoted and committed when he was not may have been more costly still. In our ancestral past, women who frequently and naïvely mated with men who then abandoned them probably did not reproduce as successfully as did women who insisted on more proof that a man was there to stay. Thus, modern women are probably the "descendants of ancestral mothers who erred in the direction of being cautious," who tended to prudently underestimate the commitment of their men (Haselton & Buss, 2000, p. 83).

As a result of all this, an evolutionary perspective suggests that men should experience more jealousy than women do at the thought of *sexual* infidelity in their mates, whereas women should react more than men do to the threat of *emotional* infidelity, the possibility that their partners are falling in love with someone else. Either type of infidelity can provoke jealousy in either sex, of course, but they differ in their evolutionary implications. For a man, it's not a partner's love for someone else that's the bigger threat to his reproductive success, it's the *sex;* his children may still thrive if his mate loves another man, but he certainly does not want to raise the other man's children. For a woman, it's not a partner's intercourse with someone else that's more dangerous, it's the *love;* as long as he continues to provide needed resources, her children may still thrive even if he impregnates other women—but if he falls in love and moves out entirely, her kids' future may be imperiled.

This reasoning led David Buss and his colleagues (Buss et al., 1992, p. 252) to pose this compelling question to research participants:

> *Please think of a serious committed romantic relationship that you have had in the past, that you currently have, or that you would like to have. Imagine that you discover that the person with whom you've been seriously involved became interested in someone else. What would distress or upset you more (please pick only one):*
> (A) Imagining your partner forming a deep emotional attachment to that person.
> (B) Imagining your partner enjoying passionate sexual intercourse with that other person.

Which one would you pick? Most of the men—60 percent—said the sex would upset them more, but only 17 percent of the women chose that option; instead, a sizable majority of the women—83 percent—reported that they would be more distressed by a partner's emotional attachment to a rival. Moreover, a follow-up study demonstrated that men and women differed in their physiological reactions to these choices (Buss et al., 1992). Men displayed more autonomic changes indicative of emotional arousal when they imagined a partner's sexual, rather than emotional, infidelity, but the reverse was true for women.

These results are consistent with an evolutionary perspective, but they have engendered controversy (Carpenter, 2012; Sagarin et al., 2012) with critics suggesting that they are less convincing than they seem. One straightforward complaint is methodological. The use of a "forced-choice" question in which research participants have to pick one option or the other can exaggerate a subtle and relatively minor difference between the sexes (DeSteno, 2010). If men find sexual infidelity only slightly more threatening than women do, a forced-choice question could yield the striking results Buss et al. (1992) obtained even if the actual difference in men's and women's outlooks is rather trivial. And in fact, when they are allowed to simply indicate that they would find both types of infidelity equally upsetting, most people—both men and women—do (Lishner et al., 2008).

More subtly, the two types of infidelity may mean different things to women than they do to men (DeSteno & Salovey, 1996). Because men are more accepting of casual sex, women may routinely assume that a man's sexual infidelity is just that: casual sex. His emotional infidelity, however, may mean that he's having sex with someone else *and* is in love with her, which would make emotional infidelity the more serious

Mate Poaching

The good news with regard to romantic rivalries is that huge majorities—99 percent!—of American college students say that they want to settle down with a mutually monogamous sexual partner at some point in their lives (Pedersen et al., 2002). Most of us expect to (try to) be faithful to one special person sometime down the road. However, the bad news is that *mate poaching,* behavior that is intended to lure someone away from an existing relationship at least for one night, is commonplace. Around the world, most men (54 percent) and quite a few women (34 percent) have tried to poach someone else's partner (Davies et al., 2007), and about four-fifths of them have succeeded at least once (Schmitt et al., 2004). Moreover, about 70 percent of us have encountered a poacher's efforts to lure us away from our partners (or just into bed), and most men (60 percent) and half of all women who have been pursued have succumbed to a poaching attempt (Schmitt et al., 2004). And on average, poachers who are already our friends usually succeed in undermining our commitment to our existing relationships (Lemay & Wolf, 2016a).

What sort of person pursues someone else's mate? In general, mate poachers are horny, extraverted people who are low in agreeableness and conscientiousness and who approve of adulterous promiscuity (Schmitt & Buss, 2001); they also tend to be high in all three of the Dark Triad traits (Kardum et al., 2015), so they are callous, manipulative, and disinterested in trusting intimacy with others. Instead, they're motivated to poach by the challenge and the ego boosts they experience when they're successful (Davies et al., 2010). None of this is very loving, and poachers sound like lousy long-term

mates! Nevertheless, the more attractive they are, the more successful their poaching attempts tend to be (Sunderani et al., 2013), and their success may lie in the fact that those who succumb to poaching attempts tend to resemble their pursuers; they also do not much value sexual fidelity (Schmitt et al., 2004), and if they're men, they score higher on the Dark Triad traits, too (Kardum et al., 2015).

The poaching tactics used by men and women tend to differ. When they are trying to entice someone else's mate, women advertise their good looks and sexual availability, whereas men publicize their power and their willingness to provide their lovers desirable resources (Schmitt & Buss, 2001). Similar strategies are used when people *want* to be poached and wish to communicate their availability to potential poachers. In such cases, women flaunt their beauty, promise access to sex, and complain about their current partners, whereas men offer compliments and are overly generous to their targets (Schmitt & Shackelford, 2003).

In the long run, those who succumb to poaching usually don't do themselves any favors. Relationships that result from mate poaching inevitably begin with betrayal, and the partnerships that follow are not as satisfying and committed, on average, as those in which poaching does not occur. Poachers are untrustworthy, and to some degree, people get poached because they are looking around for something better, and everybody involved tends to *keep* looking around even after they start a new relationship. Having been unfaithful once, they tend to be unfaithful again (Foster et al., 2014). Poachers certainly aren't perfect partners.

threat. For their part, men may assume that women often love someone without having sex, but usually love those with whom they *do* have sex, and that would make her sexual infidelity more momentous. In fact, men and women do generally hold such views (Whitty & Quigley, 2008). We tend to think that a cheating spouse is more likely to be emotionally attached to the illicit lover when the cheater is a woman rather than a man (Sprecher et al., 1998). Thus, because we assume that sex and love are more closely connected for women than for men,[5] a choice between the two types of infidelity probably does mean different things for men than for women.

So, consider this: You've discovered that your partner has fallen in love with someone else *and* is having great sex with him or her. *Both* emotional and sexual infidelity have occurred. Which aspect of your partner's faithlessness, the sex or the love, bothers you more? This scenario answers the criticism that, individually, they mean different things to the different sexes, and in the United States, Korea, and Japan, more men than women chose sexual infidelity as the more hurtful insult (Buss et al., 1999). (In the United States, 61 percent of the men chose sexual infidelity as the more alarming threat, but only 13 percent of the women did.) In addition, the same sex difference is usually (Sagarin et al., 2012)—but not always (Zengel et al., 2013)—obtained when people rate their distress in response to the two infidelities instead of just picking the one that bothers them most, so the pattern doesn't depend much on how you ask the question.

Various other research results are also consistent with the evolutionary perspective. Men and women show different patterns of neural activity when they think about jealousy-evoking situations; regions of the brain controlling sex and aggression are more active in men when they think about sexual infidelity than when they imagine emotional infidelity, but no such difference appears in women (Takahashi et al., 2006). And sex differences disappear when parents are asked to envision the infidelity of a daughter-in-law or son-in-law. Grandmothers face the same challenges to their reproductive success as grandfathers do, so an evolutionary perspective suggests that they should not differ in their reactions to infidelity from a child's partner. And indeed, when they imagine their sons or daughters having a cheating spouse, both mothers and fathers regard sexual infidelity to be more worrisome when it is committed by a daughter-in-law, and emotional infidelity to be more distressing when it is committed by a son-in-law (Shackelford et al., 2004). Siblings feel the same way about their sisters- and brothers-in-law (Michalski et al., 2007).

At bottom, men and women appear to be differentially sensitive to the two types of threat. When the possibility exists, men are quicker to assume that sexual infidelity is occurring than women are, whereas women decide that emotional infidelity is occurring faster than men do (Schützwohl, 2005). If they discover incriminating text messages on their partner's phone, men spend more time studying the sexual messages than women do, and women spend more time inspecting the emotional messages than men do (Dunn & McLean, 2015). Then, after suspicions arise, men ruminate more about the threat of their mate's sexual infidelity whereas women fret more about their partner's emotional infidelity (Schützwohl, 2006). And if they interrogate their partners, men are more likely than women to inquire about the

---

[5] This assumption, you'll recall, is correct. On average, sex and love *are* more closely connected for women than for men. Look back at our discussion of sociosexual orientation that begins on page 282.

sexual nature of the illicit relationship, whereas women are more likely than men to ask about its emotional nature (Kuhle et al., 2009). This pattern is evident on the TV show *Cheaters,* which allows viewers to eavesdrop as unfaithful partners are confronted with evidence of their infidelity by their jealous partners; careful coding of 55 episodes of the show revealed that jealous men were usually more keen to find out if sex had happened, whereas women more often wanted to know if their men had fallen in love with their rivals (Kuhle, 2011; see Figure 10.3). And if their suspicions turn out to be unfounded, men are more relieved to learn that sexual infidelity has not occurred, whereas women are more relieved to find that their partners do not love someone else (Schützwohl, 2008a).

Finally, the sex difference disappears, and men dread sexual infidelity only as much as women do when the cheating carries no risk of conceiving a child—that is, when their partners cheat with someone of the *same* sex in a gay or lesbian affair (Sagarin et al., 2003). Paternity uncertainty is irrelevant when a romantic rival is of the same sex as one's partner, and sure enough, men and women are equally threatened by the two types of infidelity in such situations. (And which kind of rival is worse? Someone of a different sex from one's partner. The thought of a partner's affair with someone of the same sex causes less emotional upset for both men and women [although women do think they'd be more likely to end the relationship if their fellows had sex with other men; Denes et al., 2015].) In addition, gays, lesbians,

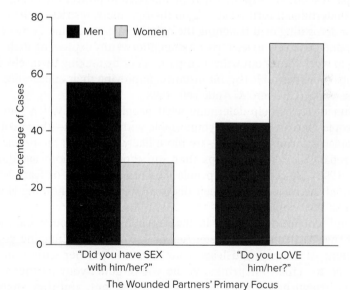

The Wounded Partners' Primary Focus

Source: Kuhle, B. X. "Did you have sex with him? Do you love her?
An in vivo test of sex differences in jealous interrogations,"
Personality and Individual Differences, *51, 2011, 1044–1047.*

FIGURE 10.3. **What do jealous victims of infidelity want to know?**
When they confronted their cheating partners, men were more likely than women to ask if their partners had had sex with an interloper. Women were more interested in whether their partners had fallen in love with someone else.

and bisexuals suffer the same upset to either sexual or emotional infidelity; only heterosexual men and women differ in their judgments of the two types of injury (Frederick & Fales, 2016).

In the end, our responses to the dreadful prospect of a partner's infidelity are complex, and men and women don't differ much: All of us tend to get angry at the thought of a lover's sexual infidelity, and we're hurt by the prospect of an emotional affair (Green & Sabini, 2006). Clearly, the most reasonable conclusion from all of these studies is that everybody hates both types of infidelity, and here, as in so many other cases, the sexes are more similar to each other than different. Still, to the extent that they differ at all, women are likely to perceive a partner's emotional attachment to a rival as more perilous than men do, whereas men are more threatened by extradyadic sex—and evolutionary psychology offers a fascinating, if arguable, explanation of these reactions.

Responses to Jealousy

People may react to the hurt, anger, and fear of jealousy in ways that have either beneficial or destructive effects on their relationships (Dindia & Timmerman, 2003). On occasion, jealous people lash out in ways that are unequivocally harmful, retaliating against their partners with violent behavior or verbal antagonism, or with efforts to make them jealous in return (Guerrero et al., 2005). On other occasions, people respond in ways that may be intended to protect the relationship but that often undermine it further: spying on their partners, restricting their partners' freedom, or derogating or threatening their rivals. There are times, however, when people respond positively to jealousy by straightforwardly expressing their concerns and trying to work things out with their partners or by making themselves or their relationships more desirable (by, for instance, improving their appearance or doing more housework) (Guerrero & Andersen, 1998).

Attachment styles help determine what people will do. When they become jealous, people who are relatively comfortable with closeness—those with secure or preoccupied attachment styles—are more likely to express their concerns and to try to repair their relationships than are those with more avoidant styles (Guerrero, 1998). By comparison, people who are dismissing or fearful are more likely to avoid the issue or deny their distress by pretending nothing is wrong or by acting like they don't care.

Men and women often differ in their responses to jealousy, too, with consequences that can complicate heterosexual relationships. Imagine yourself in this situation: At a party, you leave your romantic partner sitting on a couch when you go to refill your drinks. While you're gone, your partner's old boyfriend or girlfriend happens by and sits for a moment, and they share a light kiss of greeting just as you return with the drinks. What would you do? When researchers showed people videotapes of a scenario like this and measured their intentions, men and women responded differently (Shettel-Neuber et al., 1978). Women said they would react to the rival's interference by seeking to *improve the relationship;* they intended to put on a show of indifference but compete with the rival by making themselves more attractive to their partners. In contrast, men said they would strive to *protect their egos;* they planned to get drunk, confront and threaten the rival, and pursue other women. Whereas women seemed to focus on preserving the existing relationship (Aylor & Dainton, 2001), men considered leaving it and salving their wounded pride with conquests of new partners.

Sex differences such as these have also been obtained in other studies (Miller & Maner, 2008), and one thing that makes them worrisome is that women are more likely than men to *try* to get their partners jealous (White, 1980). When they induce jealousy—usually by discussing or exaggerating their attraction to other men, sometimes by flirting with or dating them—they typically seek to test the relationship (to see how much he cares) or try to elicit more attention and commitment from their partners (Fleischmann et al., 2005). They evidently want their men to respond the way women do when they get jealous, with greater effort to protect and maintain the relationship. The problem, of course, is that that's not the way men typically react. Women who seek to improve their relationships by inducing jealousy in their men may succeed only in driving their partners away.

Coping Constructively with Jealousy

An unhappy mixture of hurt, anger, and fear occurs when you want your partner but aren't sure you can keep him or her from preferring a rival. It may be a natural thing for humans to feel, but it's often an ugly, awful feeling that results in terribly destructive behavior (Buss, 2000). Someday you may find yourself wishing that you could feel it less intensely and limit its effects. What can be done?

When jealousy is justified and a rival is real, the experts suggest that we work on reducing the connection between the exclusivity of a relationship and our sense of self-worth (Salovey & Rodin, 1988). Finding that someone we love is attracted to a rival can be painful—but we react irrationally when we act as though our self-worth totally depended on a particular relationship. Endless rumination about the injustice that's been done is useless (Elphinston et al., 2013); we should strive instead to maintain a sense of self-confidence about our abilities to act and to survive independently, with or without our present partners.

When people are unable to do that on their own, formal therapy can help. Clinical approaches to the treatment of jealousy usually try to (a) reduce irrational, catastrophic thinking that exaggerates either the threat to the relationship or the harm that its loss would entail; (b) enhance the self-esteem of the jealous partner; (c) improve communication skills so the partners can clarify their expectations and agree on limits that prevent jealous misunderstandings; and (d) increase satisfaction and fairness in the relationship (Pines, 1998). Most of us don't need therapy to cope with jealousy. But it might help some of us if romantic relationships came with a warning label:

> *WARNING: It may be dangerous to your and your partner's health if you do not know beyond doubt that you are a valuable and worthwhile human being with or without your partner's love.*

DECEPTION AND LYING

Other sources of stress and strain occur much more often than jealousy does. Indeed, the hazards I'll consider next, lying and other forms of deception, occur so often in social life that they are commonplace (whether we realize it or not). As we'll see, deception of some sort or another occurs regularly even in intimate relationships that are based on openness and trust.

Deception is intentional behavior that creates an impression in the recipient that the deceiver knows to be untrue (Vrij et al., 2010). Outright lying in which people fabricate information and make statements that contradict the truth is the most straightforward example of deceptive behavior, but there are various other ways to convey misleading impressions without coming right out and saying things that are untrue (Buller & Burgoon, 1994). For instance, people may simply *conceal* information and not mention details that would communicate the truth, or they may *divert attention* from vital facts, abruptly changing topics to avoid the discussion of touchy subjects. On other occasions, they may mix truthful and deceptive information into *half-truths* that are misleading. I'll focus on lies because they have been studied much more extensively than other forms of deception, but we'll only be scratching the surface of the various ways intimate partners mislead each other.

Lying in Close and Casual Relationships

There's a lot of lying in everyday life. On any given day, lots of us—60 percent in the U.S., but only 24 percent in the United Kingdom—tell no lies at all. And most of the lies we do tell are small white lies of convenience, so it's fair to say that most of us are pretty honest most of the time. Nevertheless, on average, most of us tell one meaningful big lie each week, and about seven percent of us are prolific liars who tell three big lies each *day*[6] (Serota & Levine, 2015).

Most lies are self-serving, benefitting the liar and warding off embarrassment, guilt, or obligation, or seeking approval or material gain. For instance, we expect others to lie online about their appearance—and even their gender—at least occasionally (Drouin et al., 2016), and most of us have, at one time or another, lied about the number of people with whom we've had sex (Horan, 2016). Men are more likely than women to misrepresent their ambition and income, and women are more likely than men to cry out in fake pleasure (Brewer & Hendrie, 2011) and to fake orgasms during sex (Cooper et al., 2014). Both men and women, as you can see, tell lies that are designed to appeal to the other sex (Haselton et al., 2005).

Still, one-fourth of all lies are told to benefit others, protecting their feelings or advancing their interests, and we're especially likely to misrepresent the truth when brutal honesty would hurt the feelings of someone who is highly invested

[6] Watch out for these folks. Compared to the rest of us, they are nine times more likely to have been fired from a job and four times more likely to have lost a relationship as a result of their dishonest behavior. And yet they keep lying (Serota & Levine, 2015).

in the issue at hand. For instance, imagine that you really dislike a painting but are describing your feelings about it to an art student who may have painted it. Would you be totally honest? In just such a situation, no one was (DePaulo & Bell, 1996). People typically admitted that the painting wasn't one of their favorites, but they were much less critical than they had been in prior written evaluations of the piece.

Lies that are undertaken to promote polite, friendly interaction with others seem less deceptive and more acceptable to most of us than greedy, consequential lies do (Dunbar et al., 2016), and they can even seem more ethical than admissions of painful truths would be (Levine & Schweitzer, 2014). And most lies in close relationships are benevolent, small lies like these (DePaulo & Kashy, 1998). Partners may (try to) communicate more affection to each other than they really feel (Horan & Booth-Butterfield, 2013), and claim that they find each other more attractive than they really do (Lemay et al., 2013). Fewer self-serving, greedy lies—and fewer lies overall—are told to lovers and friends than to acquaintances and strangers.

This may make lying sound rather innocuous in close relationships. But people still tell a lot of lies to their intimate partners—in one study, 97 percent of the participants admitted that they had lied to their lovers within the last week (Guthrie & Kunkel, 2013)[7]—and when they do tell serious lies about topics that could destroy their reputations or relationships, they tell them more often to their closest partners than to anyone else (DePaulo et al., 2004). The biggest deceptions we undertake occur more often in our intimate relationships than anywhere else.

In addition, lies can be consequential even when they go undetected. In general, people consider interactions in which they tell a lie for any reason to be less pleasant and less intimate than interactions in which they are totally honest, and lying to a close partner makes them particularly uncomfortable (DePaulo & Kashy, 1998). Moreover, lying in close relationships undermines the liar's trust in the partner who receives the lie (Sagarin et al., 1998). This is a phenomenon known as **deceiver's distrust:** When people lie to others, they often begin to perceive the recipients of the lies as less honest and trustworthy as a result. This seems to occur both because liars assume that other people are just like them—so they assume that others share their own deceitful motives—and because they feel better about themselves when they believe their faults are shared by others (Sagarin et al., 1998). In either case, lying can sully a relationship even when the liar is the only one who knows that any lying has taken place.

Liars are also likely to think that their lies are more harmless and inoffensive than the recipients do (Kaplar & Gordon, 2004). This is a common pattern when someone misbehaves in a partnership, and we'll see it again a few pages from now in our discussion of betrayals: The recipient (or victim) of a partner's wrongdoing almost always considers it more informative and influential than the perpetrator does (Feeney & Hill, 2006). Thus, what liars consider to be a small fib may be considered to be a harmful and duplicitous deceit by others if the lie becomes known. But that begs the question, how often do liars get caught? As we'll see, the answer is, "it depends."

---

[7] And the other 3 percent may have been lying when they said they hadn't. That's ironic, isn't it?

Lies and Liars

Even if we aren't prolific liars, some of us do lie more than others do. Those of us with insecure attachment styles, for instance, tell more lies than secure people do (Gillath et al., 2010). But practice does not make perfect; frequent liars are not necessarily more successful liars. A liar's performance depends, in part, on the level of motivation (and guilt and fear) with which he or she enacts the lie. Lies are typically shorter and less detailed than truths are (Hauch et al., 2015) unless the lie is important and the liar can prepare in advance and is highly motivated to get away with the lie; when liars care enough to send their very best, they create scripts that are more convincing than those authored by liars who are less highly motivated (DePaulo et al., 1983). However, when they deliver their lies, motivated liars do a poorer, more suspicious job than do those who have less to lose and who are more spontaneous and relaxed (Forrest & Feldman, 2000). People who really want to get away with a lie tend to be more obvious than they would be if they didn't care so much because strong emotions are harder to conceal than mild feelings are (Porter et al., 2012).

What goes wrong when lies are detected? Most of us assume that liars look shifty, avoiding eye contact, fidgeting, and generally looking nervous, but that's not necessarily true at all. If anything, people are more animated when they're telling the truth than when they're lying and preoccupied, trying to keep their story straight and working hard to seem sincere (Burgoon et al., 2015). With the exception of a few folks who are just very transparent, really lousy liars (Levine, 2016), those who are lying can appear to be cool and calm, and those telling the truth can fidget, and there's no reliable relation between any particular pattern of nonverbal behavior and lying (Levine et al., 2011). Really, there is nothing that people do, "not a single verbal, non-verbal, or physiological cue [that is] uniquely related to deception" (Vrij, 2007, p. 324); "there are no clear-cut guaranteed clues to deceit" (Frank & Svetieva, 2013, p. 139). However, careful attention to what people are saying—not just how they are saying it—can alert us to inconsistencies in their statements (Reinhard et al., 2011), and there may be discrepancies between their verbal and nonverbal behavior that give them away. A fascinating frame-by-frame analysis of television coverage of people who were emotionally pleading for the return of a missing relative was able to distinguish the liars (who, as it turned out, had actually murdered the missing person!) from those who were telling the truth (and who were genuinely upset); these were high-stakes lies, and the liars could not fake entirely convincing sadness and completely conceal their secret pleasure (ten Brinke & Porter, 2012). Their faces didn't seamlessly match what they were saying, but the discrepancies were subtle and hard to detect. And there wasn't any particular thing that the liars were always doing that indicated that they weren't telling the truth.

So, How Well Can We Detect a Partner's Deception?

The problem is that the specific reactions that indicate that a person is lying can be quite idiosyncratic. People differ in their mannerisms. Some of us speak hesitantly most of the time, whereas others are more verbally assertive; some people engage in frequent eye contact, whereas others rarely look us in the eye. Lying is usually apparent in *changes* in a person's ordinary demeanor, but to notice those changes, one may need some prior familiarity with the person's style (Vrij et al., 2010). People can learn to detect deception in others: When research participants get repeated opportunities to judge whether or not someone is lying— and are given continuing feedback about the accuracy of their judgments[8]—they do become better judges of that person's truthfulness. However, their improvement is limited to that particular person, and they're no better at detecting lying in anyone else (Zuckerman et al., 1984)!

Intimate partners have personal, idiosyncratic knowledge of each other that should allow them to be sensitive judges of each other's behavior. But they also *trust* each other (or their relationship probably isn't very intimate), and that leads them to exhibit a **truth bias** in which they assume that their partners are usually telling the truth (Park & Levine, 2015). As a result, intimate partners often make very confident judgments of each other's veracity, but their confidence has nothing whatsoever to do with how accurate they are (DePaulo et al., 1997). This means that people are sometimes certain that their partners are telling the truth when their partners are actually lying.

Now, if anyone routinely knows when your intimate partner is lying, you probably do. But any belief that our partners are completely transparent to us is probably misplaced. People tend not to be very skilled lie detectors: A sprawling meta-analysis of studies involving 24,483 research participants demonstrated that we correctly distinguish truths from lies 54 percent of the time (Bond & DePaulo, 2006)—but because we'd be right 50 percent of the time just by flipping a coin, that's not very good. So, despite our considerable experience with our close friends and lovers, we usually do a poorer job of distinguishing their fact from fancy than we realize (Elaad et al., 2012). In fact, if the listener doesn't actively interrogate the liar (Levine et al., 2014), not many lies in close relationships are detected at the time they're told; if the truth comes out, it's usually later on, when information from others, physical evidence, and the occasional confession come into play (von Hippel et al., 2016).

Thus, people tell lots of lies, even in close relationships, and they get away with most of them. However, don't pat yourself on the back if you're currently deceiving a partner. You're probably not as good at it as you think you are (Grieve & Hayes, 2013). And consider the big picture. People tell fewer lies in the relationships they find most rewarding, in part because lying violates shared expectations of honesty and trust. Keeping secrets isn't easy. And even if your lies go undetected, they may poison the atmosphere in your relationship, contributing to unwarranted suspicion and doubt. And you run the risk that if they are detected, your lies may seem to your partner to be a despicable example of our next topic: betrayal of an intimate partner.

---

[8] Researchers can provide feedback like this in a lab procedure, but it doesn't often happen in real relationships. How often do *you* get exact and accurate feedback about your judgments of a lover's truthfulness?

BETRAYAL

People don't always do what we want or expect them to do. And even our intimate partners occasionally do harmful things (or fail to do desirable things) that violate the expectations we hold for close confidants. Such acts are **betrayals,** disagreeable, hurtful actions by people we trusted and from whom we reasonably did not expect such treachery. Sexual and emotional infidelity and lying are common examples of betrayal, but any behavior that violates the norms of benevolence, loyalty, respect, and trustworthiness that support intimate relationships may be considered treasonous to some degree. People who reveal secrets about their partners, gossip about them behind their backs, tease in hurtful ways, break important promises, fail to support their partners, spend too much time elsewhere, or simply abandon a relationship can all be considered to have betrayed their partners (Fitness, 2012).

All of these actions involve painful drops in perceived relational value. When we are victimized by intimate partners, their betrayals demonstrate that they do not value their relationships with us as much as we had believed, or else, from our point of view, they would not have behaved as they did (Fitness, 2012). The sad irony is that for losses of relational value of this sort to occur, we must have (or think we have) a desired relationship that is injured; thus, casual acquaintances cannot betray us as thoroughly and hurtfully as trusted intimates can (Jones & Burdette, 1994). We're not always hurt by the ones we love, but the ones we love *can* hurt us in ways that no one else can (Miller, 1997b).

In fact, when our feelings get hurt in everyday life, it's usually our close friends or romantic partners who cause us distress (Leary & Leder, 2009). Those partners are rarely being intentionally malicious—which is fortunate because it's very painful to believe that our partners meant to hurt us (Vangelisti & Hampel, 2010)—but they often disappoint us anyway. Almost all of us have betrayed someone and have been betrayed by someone else in a close relationship at some time or another.

Because caring and trust are integral aspects of intimacy, this may be surprising, but perhaps it shouldn't be. Most of us are close in some way to more than one person, and when people try to be loyal simultaneously to several different relationships, competing demands are inescapable. And when obligations overlap, occasional violations of the norms in a given relationship may be unavoidable (Baxter et al., 1997). If two of your close friends schedule their weddings in different cities on the same day, for instance, you'll have to disappoint one of them, even without wanting to. Moreover, we occasionally face competing demands within a given relationship, finding ourselves unable to appropriately honor all of the responsibilities of a caring friend or lover. I once learned that the ex-wife of a good friend was now sleeping with my friend's best friend. Honesty and openness required that I inform my friend of his other friend's—and, arguably, his ex-wife's—betrayal. However, caring and compassion suggested that he not be burdened with painful, embarrassing news he could do nothing about. It was a no-win situation. Seeking to protect my friend's feelings, I decided not to tell him about his other friend's betrayal—but a few months later, when he learned the truth (and realized that I had known), he was hurt and disappointed that I had kept such a secret from him. Perceived betrayals sometimes occur when people have the best intentions but simply cannot honor all of the overlapping and competing demands that intimacy and interdependency may make (Peetz & Kammrath, 2011).

A Point to Ponder

Imagine that you discover your lover cheating on you with your best friend. Who do you think has committed the greater betrayal? Why?

Individual Differences in Betrayal

Nevertheless, some of us betray our partners more often than others do. Using an Interpersonal Betrayal Scale (see Table 10.2), Warren Jones found that betrayal is less frequent among those who are older, better educated, and religious (Jones & Burdette, 1994). More importantly, those who report repeated betrayals of others tend to be unhappy, resentful, vengeful, and suspicious people. They're prone to jealousy and cynicism, have a higher incidence of psychiatric problems, and are more likely than others to come from broken homes. Overall, betrayers do not trust others much, perhaps because they wrongly attribute to others the same motives they recognize in themselves (Couch & Jones, 1997).

Men and women do not differ in their tendencies to betray others, but they do differ in the targets of their most frequent betrayals (Jones & Burdette, 1994). Men are more likely than women to betray their romantic partners and business associates, whereas women betray their friends and family members more often than men do. Whether one is at particular risk for betrayal from a man or woman seems to depend on the part one plays in his or her life.

The Two Sides to Every Betrayal

Those who betray their intimate partners usually underestimate the harm they do. As we saw in chapter 4, it's normal for people to be self-serving when they consider their actions, but when it comes to betrayal, this tendency leads people to excuse and minimize actions that their partners may find quite harmful (Foster & Misra, 2013). Betrayers often consider their behavior to be inconsequential and

---

TABLE 10.2. An Interpersonal Betrayal Scale: Some Example Items

How often have you done these things?

1. Snubbed a friend when you are with others you want to impress.

2. Gossiped about a friend behind his or her back.

3. Told others information given to you in confidence.

4. Lied to a friend.

Source: Data from Jones, W. H., & Burdette, M. P. "Betrayal in relationships." In A. L. Weber & J. H. Harvey (Eds.), Perspectives on close relationships. Boston: Allyn & Bacon, 1994, 243–262.

A Practical Guide to Getting Away with It

Deception is corrosive and forgiveness is good for people, so I hesitate to offer advice about how to get away with betraying someone. Nevertheless, I'm here to present relationship science to you as objectively as possible, so here goes. Relationships are more adversely affected, and forgiveness is harder to obtain, if our partners catch us in an act of betrayal or learn of it from some third party than if we tell them of it ourselves when they ask (Afifi et al., 2001). (The least damaging mode of discovery, if our partners do learn of our betrayal, is for us to admit our wrongdoing without being asked, but that's not the point of this box.)

So, admitting a wrong is better than being caught red-handed, but just what we say is important, too. When you're asked about a transgression you've committed, you shouldn't deny it outright, because your bold lie will compound your sins if (when?) the truth comes out. Instead,

equivocate (Rycyna et al., 2009). Make your response as truthful as possible, and don't contradict the truth. A crafty strategy is to confess to a less serious offense; a partial confession often seems more trustworthy than a claim of complete innocence, and it avoids the harsher consequences of admitting the more serious wrong (Peer et al., 2014).

I'm *not* encouraging you either to betray or to deceive your partners. If you follow the guidelines presented here, you will be behaving disreputably. And you may not be doing yourself a favor. We continue to maintain guilty secrets when we offer only partial confessions, and we may end up feeling worse than we would have if we'd made a full confession. In the end, "true guilt relief requires people to fully come clean" (Peer et al., 2014, p. 215). Seems to me, though, the best thing to do is to not misbehave in the first place.

---

innocuous, and they are quick to describe mitigating circumstances that vindicate their actions (Stillwell et al., 2008). However, their victims rarely share those views. Those who are betrayed routinely judge the transgression to be more severe than the betrayers do (Feeney & Hill, 2006).

These two different perspectives lead to disparate perceptions of the harm that is done. People who are betrayed almost never believe that such events have no effect on their relationships; 93 percent of the time, they feel that a betrayal damages the partnership, leading to lower satisfaction and lingering suspicion and doubt (Jones & Burdette, 1994). In contrast, the perpetrators acknowledge that their behavior was harmful only about half the time. They even think that the relationship has *improved* as a result of their transgression in one of every five cases. Such judgments are clearly ill-advised. We may feel better believing that our occasional betrayals are relatively benign, but it may be smarter to face the facts: Betrayals almost always have negative, and sometimes lasting, effects on a relationship. Indeed, they are routinely the central complaint of spouses seeking therapy or a divorce (Amato & Previti, 2003).

Why Revenge Isn't Such a Good Idea

When they've been wronged, victims of both sexes may feel that they want to get some payback and exact a little revenge (Chester & DeWall, 2017), doing some intentional harm to those who have harmed them (Elshout et al., 2015). But that's ordinarily a destructive motive and a bad idea, for several reasons. A first problem with revenge stems from the different perspectives of perpetrator and victim, who rarely agree on the amount of retribution that's just: When victims inflict reciprocal injury that seems to them to be equal to the harm they suffered, their retribution seems excessive to the original perpetrators (who are now the new victims). And if I seem to you to have been meaner to you than you were to me, you then need to hurt me *again* to balance the scales, and a cycle of vengefulness continues (Stillwell et al., 2008). We also tend to excuse actions of our own that we judge to be blameworthy in others. Self-serving perceptions like these were evident in a remarkable study (Buunk, 1987) of dozens of Dutch couples in which *both* partners had cheated, having extradyadic sex: Almost everybody thought that their faithlessness had been relatively innocuous and meaningless but that their partner's infidelity had been a gross betrayal. If it's okay when I do it but wrong when you do it, revenge is impossible to calibrate so that genuine justice is served.

A second problem is that we routinely expect revenge to be more satisfying than it turns out to be. When you nurse a grudge, rehearsing an injury and plotting your revenge, you keep your wounds fresh and delay any healing. As it turns out, those who are given an opportunity for revenge stay distressed and surly longer than those who are wronged but then just have to move on and get over it (Carlsmith et al., 2008). We do ourselves no favors when we prolong an injury by thirsting for revenge. In addition, retaliation is usually fulfilling only when those who have wronged us connect the dots, understand why they're now being

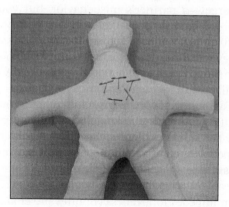

©*Stephen Yoshimura*

Here's a handy measure of vengeful inclinations: the Voodoo Doll Task. People are asked to imagine that the doll is a partner who has wronged them; then, they're provided a basket of pins and invited to "discharge negative energy" by stabbing the doll with as many pins as they wish. The number of pins people use does a good job of assessing their motivations to do real harm to their partners (DeWall et al., 2013). Think back to the last time someone upset you and consider: How many pins would *you* use? Where would you stick them?

harmed, and see the error of their ways; revenge is actually less satisfying than doing nothing at all when the original perpetrator fails to see that he or she had it coming (Funk et al., 2014). And how often does *your* partner say, "Yes, dear, you're right, I see that I deserved that because of my prior misbehavior"?

Finally, people who are prone to vengeance tend to be pretty sour folks who are high in neuroticism, low in agreeableness, and generally less happy with life than those of us who are less vengeful (Rey & Extremera, 2014). All three of the Dark Triad traits are associated with higher vengefulness, too (Brewer et al., 2015). So, they're greedy and manipulative and definitely not a fun bunch.

So, when partners have been betrayed, they do sometimes take hurtful action by, for instance, destroying a partner's possessions, cheating, and defaming their partners to others (Yoshimura & Boon, 2014). But spite is costly, both to one's partnership and to oneself. So, let's end our look at painful stresses and strains by considering the alternative: the healing process that can help a relationship survive a partner's wrongdoing.

FORGIVENESS

If a relationship is to continue to thrive after a painful betrayal, forgiveness may be necessary (McCullough, 2008). Forgiveness is "a decision to give up your perceived or actual right to get even with, or hold in debt, someone who has wronged you" (Markman et al., 1994, p. 217). It's a process in which "harmful conduct is acknowledged" and "the harmed partner extends undeserved mercy" to the one who has misbehaved (Waldron & Kelley, 2008, p. 19). When you forgive someone, you give up your grudge and discard the desire to retaliate; you don't condone—or forget—a partner's misbehavior, but you do communicate your "willingness to exit from a potential cycle of abuse and recrimination" (Fincham & Beach, 2002, p. 240). Forgiveness doesn't necessarily mean that you regain positive feelings toward the offender—getting past your negative feelings and letting go of your ire and antipathy is the key (Fincham & Beach, 2013)—but it does make reconciliation more likely.

It's not always easy to forgive someone, and it comes more readily to some of us than to others. Attachment style matters: Anxiety about abandonment and avoidance of intimacy both make people less forgiving (Kachadourian et al., 2004). In particular, secure people are more forgiving because they engage in less angry rumination that keeps an injury fresh in their minds (Burnette et al., 2007). Those who are high in agreeableness also forgive others relatively easily (Riek & Mania, 2012), but neuroticism impedes forgiveness (Braithwaite et al., 2016); people who are prone to negative emotions can sometimes maintain grudges for years (Maltby et al., 2008). And finally, self-control promotes forgiveness (Burnette et al., 2014). Those of us who are better able to manage our motives and control our impulses find it easier to set aside a desire for retribution.

Still, no matter who we are, forgiveness comes more readily when some important ingredients exist. The first is genuine, sincere *contrition*. Victims are more likely to forgive those who betray them when the offenders offer a meaningful apology by acknowledging their wrongs, accepting responsibility for their actions, offering genuine atonement by expressing shame, regret, and remorse for their misbehavior, and promising better conduct in the future (Lewicki et al., 2016). Forgiveness is less likely to occur when excuses are given or when an apology seems half-hearted. If you have misbehaved and a relationship is suffering, you might do well to recognize that your behavior was harmful, and apologize—and to do so sincerely (Ebesu Hubbard et al., 2013).

A second component to forgiveness is *empathy* on the part of the victim (Adams & Inesi, 2016). People who can take their partners' perspectives and grasp how guilty they are—and in particular, those who can admit that they're not perfect, either (Exline et al., 2008)—are much more likely to forgive them than are those in whom empathy is lacking.

Finally, forgiveness is less likely to occur when victims brood about their partners' transgressions and remain preoccupied with the damage done by their misbehavior (McCullough et al., 2007). We let go of anger and resentment when we forgive someone, but rumination about our hurt or our partners' flaws tends to keep our umbrage alive, and that makes forgiveness harder to attain (Ysseldyk et al., 2007).

Fortunately, around the world, forgiveness is more likely to occur in close, committed relationships than in those that are less committed (Karremans et al., 2011), because empathy occurs more easily and because the betrayers are more likely to apologize (Ohtsubo & Yagi, 2015). Partners in (what were) satisfying relationships are also more likely to employ lenient, sympathetic attributions that explain the offenders' misconduct as benevolently as possible—as circumstantial events that do not mean that the offender is a bad, unloving person (Hook et al., 2015)—and that, too, makes forgiveness more feasible (Friesen et al., 2005).

And importantly, forgiveness can protect the relationships in which it occurs (Kato, 2016). Retribution rarely gets our partners to reform and behave better, but forgiveness can; when people are forgiven, they are often grateful and, as a result, more repentant and less likely to repeat the offense (Mooney et al., 2016). Forgiveness also reduces conflict and encourages communication that can decrease declines in satisfaction and commitment (Braithwaite et al., 2011).

But perhaps even more significantly, people who are able to forgive their intimate partners usually enjoy more personal well-being—that is, more self-esteem, less hostility, less distress and tension, and more satisfaction with life—than do those from whom forgiveness is less forthcoming (Hojjat & Ayotte, 2013). They also enjoy better physical health (Weir, 2017). Forgiveness reduces our hurt and pain, replacing anger with equanimity, and whereas vengefulness increases our blood pressure, forgiveness reduces it (Hannon et al., 2012). There's no question that, within intimate relationships, forgiveness is more desirable and beneficial to those who wield it than is vengeance.

Forgiveness has its limits. It won't transform a selfish scoundrel into a worthy partner, and no one is suggesting that you doggedly continue to forgive a faithless partner who repeatedly takes advantage of you. Forgiveness that is offered in the absence of genuine contrition may be perceived to be a license to offend again; after all, why should I behave better if I'm certain to be forgiven

Betrayal

Betrayals are hurtful actions by people we trusted and from whom we did not expect such misbehavior.

Individual Differences in Betrayal. Frequent betrayers tend to be unhappy and maladjusted people who are resentful, vengeful, and suspicious of others.

The Two Sides to Every Betrayal. Betrayers often consider their behavior to be inconsequential and innocuous, but their victims rarely share those views.

Why Revenge Isn't Such a Good Idea. Revenge is usually less satisfying than people think it will be, and it usually seems excessive to its targets, thus engendering further dispute.

Forgiveness

Forgiveness entails giving up the right to retaliate for others' wrongdoing. It occurs more readily when the betrayers apologize and the victims are empathic. When one's partner is repentant, forgiveness usually improves the relationships in which it occurs.

CHAPTER 11

Conflict

THE NATURE OF CONFLICT ♦ THE COURSE OF CONFLICT
♦ THE OUTCOMES OF CONFLICT ♦ FOR YOUR CONSIDERATION
♦ CHAPTER SUMMARY

Do your friends and lovers always do everything you want, when you want it? Of course not. There's no such thing as an intimate relationship that does not involve occasional friction and incompatibility in the desires, opinions, and actions of the two partners. No matter how much two people care for each other, no matter how well-suited they are to each other, dispute and disagreement will occur (Canary & Lakey, 2013). And the more interdependent they are—the more time they spend together and the wider the variety of activities and tasks they try to coordinate—the more likely occasional conflict becomes (Miller, 1997b). Conflict is inevitable in close relationships.

It's also very influential. Over time, the manner in which two partners manage their conflicts may either enhance or erode their love and regard for each other. In this chapter, then, we'll examine the nature and sources of this sometimes frustrating, sometimes fulfilling, but ultimately unavoidable aspect of intimate relationships. We'll look at how conflicts unfold, how they escalate, and how people can respond to them more effectively. We'll also consider whether conflict can be beneficial to relationships. (What do you think the answer will be? Can conflict be advantageous?)

THE NATURE OF CONFLICT

What Is Conflict?

Interpersonal conflict can result whenever one person's motives, goals, beliefs, opinions, or behavior interfere with, or are incompatible with, those of another. Conflict is born of dissimilarity, which may be passing in the form of moods, or lasting in the form of beliefs and personality. Two people always differ in important ways, but I'll employ a definition of conflict that involves active interference with another's goals: **Conflict** occurs when one's wishes or actions actually obstruct or impede those of someone else. When two partners are both able to do as they wish, no conflict exists. On the other hand, if one or both of them have to give up something that they want because of the other's influence, conflict occurs. Anger and hostility aren't necessary; we make some sacrifices to accommodate our partners generously and happily. And not all conflicts are overt; we are sometimes unaware of the difficulties we are causing our partners. It's enough that someone knowingly or unknowingly prevents another from getting or doing everything he or she wants.

Conflict is inescapable for two reasons. First, the moods and preferences of any two people will occasionally differ. Intermittent incompatibilities between two partners' goals and behaviors will inevitably arise. For instance, even if both members of a couple are extraverted, hard-partying social animals, one of them will occasionally be disappointed by the other's wish to leave a party before it's over; a case of the flu or an upcoming exam in a close relationships class will make one of them, but not the other, unwilling to stay late.

Second, conflict is unavoidable because there are certain tensions that are woven into the fabric of close relationships that will, sooner or later, always cause some strain. When they devote themselves to an intimate relationship, people often experience opposing motivations called **dialectics** that can never be entirely satisfied because they contradict each other (Baxter, 2004). Fulfilling one goal may endanger another, so partners must engage in a delicate balancing act that leaves them drawn in different directions at different times. And with each partner vacillating between the pursuit of these opposing goals, occasional conflict between their predominant individual motives is inescapable (Erbert, 2000).

For instance, one potent dialectic in close relationships is the continual tension between personal *autonomy and connection* to others. On one hand, people often want to be free to do what they want, so they value their independence and autonomy. On the other hand, they also seek warm, close connections to others that can make them dependent on particular partners. So, which do they pursue? Intimacy or freedom? Independence or belonging? It's reasonable to assume that most people want some of both, but embracing one of them can mean denying the other. Commitment to a romantic relationship can bring us great pleasure, but it can also leave us feeling "stuck," "stifled," and "confined" (Weigel et al., 2015). So people's preferences may swing back and forth as they come to be more influenced by whichever motive has lately been less fulfilled. Maintaining an equilibrium between the two desires is a tricky balancing act (Slotter et al., 2014), and we can't simultaneously maintain high *indep*endence from a romantic partner and high *inter*dependence with him or her, so something's got to give. Conflict between the partners is likely to occur as they strive to fulfill opposing motives at different rates and at different times.

A Point to Ponder

Does your primary partner respond to your texts as quickly and consistently as you wish? Might you be infringing on his or her autonomy by expecting too much constant contact?

Another powerful dialectic is the tension between *openness and closedness*. Intimacy involves self-disclosure, and intimate partners are expected to share their thoughts and feelings with one another. However, people also like their privacy, and there are some things that prudent partners want to keep to themselves (Petronio, 2010). On the one hand, there's candor and transparent authenticity, and on the other hand, there's discretion and restraint.

There's also friction between *stability and change*. People with pleasant partnerships will want to maintain and protect them, keeping things the way they are. But people also relish novelty and excitement (Sheldon et al., 2013). Too much stagnant predictability becomes mundane and monotonous (Harasymchuk & Fehr, 2013). So, people are attracted to both the familiar and the new, and occasional indecision and conflict may result.

Finally, there's dialectic tension between *integration* with *and separation* from one's social network. Would you rather go to that party with your friends or stay home and snuggle with your sweetheart tonight? Will you travel to your in-law's home for Thanksgiving again this year or stay home and begin your own family tradition? When you're out to dinner with your lover, do you keep your phone by your side so your friends can reach you? Or do you leave it in the car (as I suggested way back on page 13)? These can be genuine dilemmas (Miller-Ott & Kelly, 2016), and our motives to stay involved with other people are sometimes at odds with the wish to devote ourselves to a romantic partnership. People see less of their friends when they invest time and effort into a romantic relationship (Burton-Chellew & Dunbar, 2015), and finding a satisfying ratio of time spent with and time apart from other people can be difficult.

Altogether, these four dialectics—autonomy versus connection, openness versus closedness, stability versus change, and integration versus separation—accounted for more than one-third of the recent fights and arguments reported by married couples in one study (Erbert, 2000). And what's important is that these tensions typically continue to some degree throughout the entire life of a relationship (Baxter, 2004). The dilemmas posed by fluctuating, opposing motives in close relationships never end. Sooner or later, conflict occurs.

The Frequency of Conflict

How often do partners engage in conflict? Frequently, but the answer varies with the population studied and the way in which conflict is defined and assessed. Little children and their parents are often at odds; one study determined that some conflict occurred every 3.6 minutes in conversations between 4-year-olds and their mothers (Eisenberg, 1992)! Dating couples report 2.3 conflicts per week when they keep diaries of their interactions (Lloyd, 1987), and spouses report seven memorable "differences of opinion" every 2 weeks (Papp et al., 2009); spouses also experience one or two "unpleasant disagreements" each month (McGonagle et al., 1992). And, importantly, many conflicts are never addressed; in one investigation, Northwestern University students didn't mention to their partners 40 percent of the conflicts and irritations they identified in their dating relationships (Roloff & Cloven, 1990). Conflict not only is common in close relationships, it also probably occurs more often than we realize.

However, as you might expect, some people experience more conflict than other people do. Various influences are correlated with the amount of conflict we encounter:

Personality. People who are high in neuroticism are impulsive and irascible, and they have more unhappy disagreements with others than people of low neuroticism do (Heaven et al., 2006). In contrast, people high in agreeableness are good natured, cooperative, and generally easy to get along with, and they have fewer conflicts; if conflict does occur, they also react more constructively than people of low agreeableness do (Jensen-Campbell & Graziano, 2001).

Attachment style. Secure people encounter less conflict—and manage it better when it does occur—than insecure people do (Mikulincer & Shaver, 2013). In particular, because they fret that their partners may leave them, people who are anxious about abandonment nervously perceive dissension and difficulty where it does not exist, and then respond with greater hurt and distress than others would (Overall et al., 2014). A married couple comprising an anxious wife and an avoidant husband is especially combustible: Her exaggerated fears chase him away, and his withdrawal then further fuels her worries (Barry & Lawrence, 2013). In the lab, both members of such couples evidence elevated levels of stress before a discussion of a disagreement even begins (L. Beck et al., 2013).

Stage of life. If you're a young adult, you may be experiencing more conflict with your partners than you used to. It's typical for people to develop lasting romances and to begin professional careers in their mid-20s, and according to a longitudinal study of young adults in New York state, these life changes are routinely associated with increased conflict (Chen et al., 2006). As you can see in Figure 11.1, conflict with romantic partners increases steadily from our late teens to our mid-20s, but things settle down somewhat thereafter.

Relationships get even more placid in our elder years. Older couples usually have fewer disagreements about children and money and other touchy topics than middle-aged couples do (Smith & Baron, 2016), and they tend to shy away from talking about the things they do disagree about (Holley et al., 2013).

Similarity. Conflict emerges from incompatibility, so it's not surprising that the less similar dating partners are, the more conflict they experience (Surra & Longstreth, 1990). This pattern continues if people marry; spouses who share similar tastes and expectations encounter less conflict and enjoy happier marriages than do those who have less in common (Huston & Houts, 1998). Indeed, those who really believe that "opposites attract" are likely to learn some hard lessons if they start living with someone who is notably different from them. Dissimilarity fuels friction, not smooth sailing.

Stress. People who have had hard, stressful days tend to be irritable and ornery when they get home, and the greater the combined stress two partners have experienced during the day, the more likely they are to encounter conflict that evening (Timmons et al., 2017).

Sleep. Partners tend to sleep poorly after they quarrel, and that leaves them grumpy and irritable the next day (El-Sheikh et al., 2013). As a result—and whenever either of them has slept poorly—romantic couples encounter more conflict that day (Gordon & Chen, 2014). Sleeplessness breeds conflict, so if you and your partner are getting testy and tetchy, try to get a good night's sleep.

Alcohol. Finally, lest there be any doubt, alcohol does not make people more agreeable and courteous; instead, intoxication exacerbates conflict. An intriguing study of alcohol's effects invited men who were either sober or intoxicated to revisit a recent romantic conflict (G. MacDonald et al., 2000). Drunkenness made

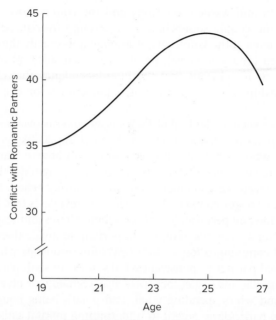

Source: Data from Chen, H., Cohen, P., Kasen, S., Johnson, J. G., Ehrensaft, M., & Gordon, K. "Predicting conflict within romantic relationships during the transition to adulthood," Personal Relationships, 13, 2006, 411–427.

Note. On the rating scale used by the researchers, a score of 0 indicated "no conflict," a score of 25 indicated "occasional mild disagreements," and 50 meant "some arguing and bickering with infrequent flare-ups."

FIGURE 11.1. **Romantic conflict in young adulthood.**
The many changes accompanying passage into adulthood—which often include graduation from college and entry into new careers—are associated with increased conflict in our romantic relationships. But things settle down after a while.

the men more sour and surly; in response to events of the same average intensity, intoxicated men were more hostile and blaming than sober men were. Adding alcohol to a frustrating disagreement is a bit like adding fuel to a fire.

THE COURSE OF CONFLICT

Instigating Events

So, what events cause conflict? A wide-ranging review of conflict studies by Donald Peterson (2002, p. 367) concluded that couples may disagree about almost any issue: "how to spend time together, how to manage money, how to deal with in-laws, frequency and mode of sexual intercourse, who did which chores, insufficient expressions of affect (not enough affection), exaggerated expressions of affect (moodiness, anger), personal habits, political views, religious beliefs, jealousies toward other men and women, relatives, and the couples' own children." You name it, and some couple somewhere is quarreling over it. After David Buss (1989) asked students at the University of Michigan to specify things that men do that upset women (and vice versa), he grouped their answers into 147 distinct sources of conflict. It's obvious that the interdependency that characterizes an intimate relationship provides "abundant opportunities for dispute" (Peterson, 2002, p. 367).

When spouses keep track of all of their disagreements over a span of 15 days, some topics recur more often than others (Papp et al., 2009). As you can see in Table 11.1, those who are parents disagree more about how to manage, discipline, and care for their children—and when—than about anything else. (Remember that people who haven't read chapter 6 sometimes naïvely believe that having kids will make their marriages happier—but in fact, the reverse is true [Wendorf et al., 2011].) The division and performance of household chores and responsibilities are next on the list (remember, it's hard, but important, to divide them fairly [Britt & Roy, 2014]), and communication is third (involving problems with interpersonal gaps and perceived partner responsiveness). It's down in sixth place, but the most enduring, contentious, and sometimes surly disagreements revolve around money: who's earning and who's spending what, and what's being bought. Arguments about money are particularly potent in undermining marital satisfaction (Britt & Huston, 2012). But all of these topics are frequent sources of conflict all over the world (Dillon et al., 2015), and what's striking is that (at least during the first four

TABLE 11.1. Issues That Produce Marital Conflict

Each night, husbands and wives made notes about any disagreements they had had that day. The topics they listed are presented in order of the frequency with which they were mentioned. Because a particular episode of conflict could—and often did—touch on more than one topic, the frequencies exceed 100%.

Topic	Issues	Proportion of Conflicts
Children	Care for and discipline of the kids	38%
Chores	Allocation of and performance of household duties	25
Communication	Paying attention, listening, misunderstandings	22
Leisure	Choice of and time spent in recreation	20
Work	Time spent at work; co-workers	19
Money	Bills, purchases, spending, wages	19
Habits	Annoying behaviors	17
Relatives	Family, in-laws, stepchildren, ex-spouses	11
Commitment	The meaning of commitment; infidelity	9
Intimacy	Displays of affection; sex	8
Friends	Time spent and activities with friends	8
Personality	A partner's or one's own traits	7

Source: Data from Papp, L. M., Cummings, E. M., & Goeke-Morey, M. C. "For richer, for poorer: Money as a topic of marital conflict in the home," Family Relations, 58, 2009, 91–103.

years of marriage) they *don't stop* being points of contention; the rates with which they cause frustrating disagreements remain remarkably stable over time (Lavner et al., 2014). Clearly, many conflicts are not readily resolved.

To make sense of this variety, Peterson (2002) classified the events that instigate conflicts into four common categories: criticism, illegitimate demands, rebuffs, and cumulative annoyances. **Criticism** involves verbal or nonverbal acts that are judged to communicate unfair dissatisfaction with a partner's behavior, attitude, or trait (Cupach, 2007). It doesn't matter what the actor intends by his or her remark or behavior; what matters is that the target interprets the action as being unjustly critical. A mild suggestion about how to load the dishwasher to fit in more stuff may injure one's partner and engender conflict if the suggestion is judged to be needless criticism.

Illegitimate demands involve requests that seem unjust because they exceed the normal expectations that the partners hold for each other. Even when one partner is frantically completing a major project (like writing a textbook, for instance), the other may be upset by being asked to fix dinner *and* do the dishes three nights in a row.

Rebuffs involve situations in which "one person appeals to another for a desired reaction, and the other person fails to respond as expected" (Peterson, 2002, p. 371). Someone whose partner rolls over and goes to sleep after receiving an implicit invitation to have sex is likely to feel rebuffed.

Finally, **cumulative annoyances** are relatively trivial events that become irritating with repetition. Such events often take the form of *social allergies:* Through repeated exposure to small recurring nuisances, people may develop hypersensitive reactions of disgust and exasperation that seem out of proportion to any particular provocation. Women are especially likely to become annoyed with men's uncouth habits, such as belching at the dinner table, and men are likely to grow irritated with women's lack of consideration, such as being late for appointments and shopping too long (Cunningham et al., 2005).

Evolutionary psychology makes its own intriguing predictions about conflict between intimates (Buss, 2015). From an evolutionary perspective, some conflict in heterosexual relationships flows naturally from differences in the partners' reproductive interests. Presumably, given their lower parental investment in any babies that may result, men can afford to be more interested in casual, uncommitted sex than women are; by comparison, women should be more prudent, offering access to sex only in return for meaningful commitment from a man. And in fact, the frustrations that men and women usually encounter early in a romantic relationship run right along these lines: "Women, far more than men, become angry and upset by those who want sex sooner, more frequently, and more persistently than they want. Men, far more than women, become angry and upset by those who delay sex or thwart their sexual advances" (Buss, 2000, p. 38). The question of whether to have sex is usually answered when people settle into established relationships, but the question of how often to have sex may persist for decades. Differences in sexual desire cause conflict for *most* couples, requiring negotiation, tradeoffs, and adjustment, and in most cases the difficulty never disappears completely (Elliott & Umberson, 2008). Individual differences in sexual neutral point of view. How might this person think about the disagreement?" (Finkel et al., 2013, p. 1597). Not only will your negotiation go more smoothly when you return to it (Harinck & De Dreu, 2011), continued use of this "third party" perspective is likely to leave you with a happier relationship a whole year later (Finkel et al., 2013).

Obviously, then, some responses to conflict are destructive, undermining a relationship, and others are constructive, helping to sustain it. Add this distinction to the difference between engaging a conflict and avoiding it that we encountered earlier, and you've got four different types of responses to conflict and dissatisfaction in a relationship that were introduced to relationship science by Caryl Rusbult and her colleagues (1982). Take a look at Figure 11.3; the four categories differ in being either *active* or *passive* and in being either *constructive* or *destructive:*

1. **Voice** is behaving in an active, constructive manner by trying to improve the situation by discussing matters with the partner, changing one's behavior in an effort to solve the problem, or obtaining advice from a friend or therapist.
2. **Loyalty** is behaving in a passive but constructive manner by optimistically waiting and hoping for conditions to improve.
3. **Neglect** is behaving in a passive but destructive manner by avoiding discussion of critical issues and reducing interdependence with the partner. When one is neglectful, one stands aside and just lets things get worse.

FIGURE 11.3. **A typology of responses to dissatisfaction in close relationships.**

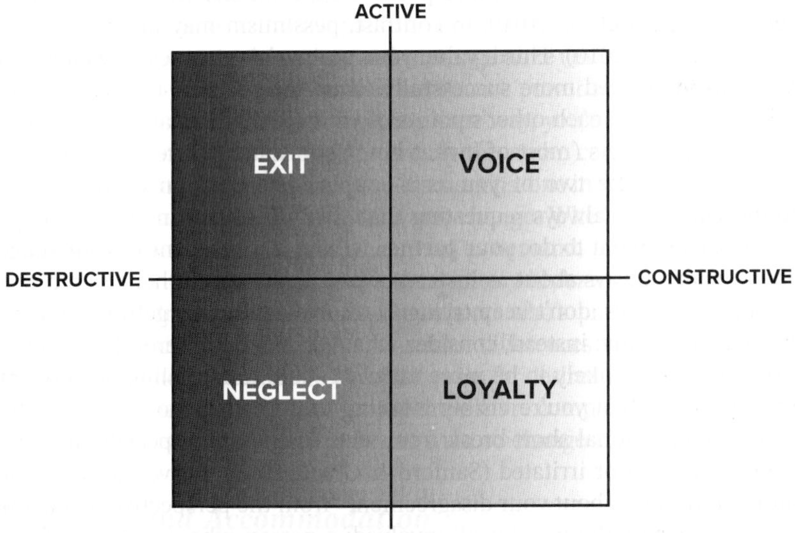

Source: Based on Rusbult, C. E., Zembrodt, I. M., & Gunn, L. K. "Exit, voice, loyalty, and neglect: Responses to dissatisfaction in romantic involvements," Journal of Personality and Social Psychology, 43, 1982, 1230–1242.

4. **Exit** is behaving in an actively destructive manner by leaving the partner, threatening to end the relationship, or engaging in abusive acts such as yelling or hitting.

If a relationship has been satisfying and their investments in it are high, people are more likely to employ the constructive responses of voice and loyalty than to neglect the relationship or exit from it (Weiser & Weigel, 2014). We typically seek to maintain relationships to which we are committed. And when that's the case, voice is more beneficial and productive than loyalty: Unlike voice, which communicates interest and concern and typically gets a positive, productive response from one's partner, loyalty often just goes unnoticed and does no good (Overall et al., 2010b). Exit is even worse, of course, and it's more frequently employed when attractive alternative partners are available; people are more likely to bail out of a struggling relationship than to work to sustain it when tempting alternatives exist (Rusbult et al., 1982).

When both partners choose destructive responses to conflict, a relationship is at risk (Rusbult et al., 1986), so the ability to remain constructive in the face of a lover's temporary disregard, which I identified as **accommodation** back in chapter 6 (on page 203), is a valuable gift. When partners behave destructively, accommodation involves inhibiting the impulse to fight fire with fire and striving to react instead with calm forbearance. I'll mention accommodation again in chapter 14; for now, I'll simply note that couples who are able to swallow occasional provocation from each other without responding in kind tend to be happier than are those who are less tolerant and who always bite back (Rusbult et al., 1998).

Dealing with Conflict: Four Types of Couples

Does the desirability of accommodation mean that you and your partner should avoid arguing with each other? Not at all. Even heated arguments can be constructive, and some couples who engage in forceful, robust arguments have stable, satisfying marriages. Arguments support or erode a couple's satisfaction depending on the manner in which they are conducted.

Marriage researcher John Gottman (1993, 1994a, 1999) studied conflict for years. In a typical procedure, he had couples discuss a continuing disagreement and then carefully inspected recordings of the resulting interactions. His results led him to suggest that there are three discrete approaches to conflict that can lead to stable and enduring marriages. (Does one of them fit you well? Before you read further, I invite you to assess your own conflict type using the box on the next page. Really, stop here, and head over to the box.)

Volatile couples have frequent and passionate arguments. They plunge into fiery efforts to persuade and influence each other, and they often display high levels of negative affect, but they temper their anger with plenty of wit and evident fondness for each other.

Validators fight more politely. They tend to be calmer than volatile couples are, and they behave more like collaborators than like antagonists as they work through their problems. Their discussions may become heated, but they frequently

Other conflicts end in conquest. In **domination,** one partner gets his or her way when the other capitulates. This happens routinely when one person is more powerful than the other, and the more powerful partner will typically be pleased with the outcome. Domination is aversive for the loser, however, often breeding ill will and resentment (Zacchilli et al., 2009).

Compromise occurs when both parties reduce their aspirations so that a mutually acceptable alternative can be found. As Peterson suggested (2002, p. 380), the partners' "interests are diluted rather than reconciled"; neither partner gets everything he or she wants, but neither goes empty handed. This may be the best outcome available when one person's gain can come only at the expense of the other, but in other situations, better solutions are usually available.

Integrative agreements satisfy both partners' original goals and aspirations, usually through creativity and flexibility. They're not easy to reach and typically take some work; partners may need to refine and prioritize their wishes, make selective concessions, and invent new ways of attaining their goals that do not impose upon their partners. Nevertheless, through determination, ingenuity, imagination, and generous cooperation, partners can often get the things they really want.

Finally, on occasion, the partners not only get what they want but also learn and grow and make desirable changes to their relationship. This pleasant outcome, **structural improvement,** isn't frequent, and when it occurs, it may result from significant turmoil and upheaval. Partners may have encountered perilous stress and serious conflict to reach a point that leads them to rethink their habits and to muster both the courage and the will to change them. Still, structual improvement leaves a couple better off. As Peterson (2002, p. 382) wrote:

> Some change will take place in one or more of the causal conditions
> governing the relationship. Each person will know more about the other
> than before. Each person may attribute more highly valued qualities to
> the other than before. Having weathered the storm of previous conflict,
> each person may trust the other and their relationship more than before,
> and thus be willing to approach other previously avoided issues in a more
> hopeful and productive way. With these changes, the quality of the
> relationship will be improved over many situations and beyond the
> time of the immediate conflict with which the process began.

Can Fighting Be Good for a Relationship?

Is Peterson right? Can fighting sometimes yield beneficial results? Perhaps. As we near the end of this chapter, you may still feel that it would be better not to have quarrels, disagreements, and arguments in your intimate relationships. Some people certainly feel that way, believing that "disagreement is destructive" and that an argument is a sure sign that one's love is flawed (Eidelson & Epstein, 1982). But (as we noted back in chapter 4) that's a *dys*functional belief that is correlated with *dis*satisfaction, and relationship scientists generally take a different view. They recognize that the more unexpressed nuisances and irritants partners have, the less satisfied with their relationships they tend to be

(Liu & Roloff, 2016). Newlyweds who withdraw from conflict without resolving their disagreements tend to be less happy years later (Noller, 2012). And even more remarkably, middle-aged women who fail to speak up when something about their marriages is bothering them are four times more likely than their more vocal neighbors to *die* within the next 10 years (Eaker et al., 2007). "Conflict in couples is common, normal, and necessary" (Gottman et al., 2014, p. 919), and it should not be ignored.

Indeed, the prevailing view among conflict researchers is that, for all the dilemmas it creates, conflict is an essential tool with which to promote intimacy. (John Gottman [1994b, p. 159] counseled, "The most important advice I can give to men who want their marriages to work is to try not to avoid conflict.") Conflict brings problematic issues and incompatibilities into the open, allowing solutions to be sought, and romantic partners are usually happier when they address their problems readily and openly (Jensen & Rauer, 2014). In particular, romantic illusions that idealize a relationship and minimize its flaws help us stay happy when the partnership is sound and its problems are minor—but they're treacherous when a relationship has major defects and they keep us from understanding the truth (McNulty, 2010). Recognizing real problems and being critical of them is the right thing to do when the problems are severe (McNulty & Russell, 2010). And handled well, conflict can defuse situations that would only fester and cause bigger problems later on. If you confront conflict head-on, there's no guarantee that your difficulties will be resolved and that contentment will follow. Nevertheless, it is usually the deft and skillful management of conflict—not the absence of conflict—that allows relationships to grow and prosper (Whitton et al., 2018).

Of course, for many of us, this is easier said than done. We tend to bring the lessons we learned at home as teenagers with us into our adult romances (Whitton et al., 2018), and people clearly differ in the sensitivity and dexterity with which they manage conflict (Zeidner & Kloda, 2013). In particular, boys who witness violent conflict between their parents tend to become men who handle conflict poorly, being more surly and sarcastic than their peers (Halford et al., 2000).

However, couples who are fighting badly do sometimes clean up their act. A study that followed couples as they became parents found that most of them maintained the same style of conflict over a span of 2 years; about half of them fought constructively, using plenty of validation and positive affect, and a quarter of them fought poorly, wallowing in antagonism and sour dissension for the full 24 months. In most cases, once you and your partner develop a style for managing conflict, it's likely to last (Kamp Dush & Taylor, 2012). Still, about 20 percent of the young parents who had been fighting destructively *changed* their styles and became less cantankerous—and more satisfied with their relationships—over that span of time (Houts et al., 2008).

If you're fighting unpleasantly now, you can probably change, too, and I have some suggestions in this regard. First, for most of us, successful conflict management involves *self-control*. To the extent that you work at remaining optimistic, avoiding blaming attributions, and mastering your anger, you're more likely to be tolerant, flexible, and creative, and integrative agreements are more likely to be reached (Canary & Lakey, 2013). Self-control may also be required for you to successfully execute this list of *don'ts* drawn from Gottman's (1994b) work:

- *Don't* withdraw when your partner raises a concern or complaint. Defensively avoiding a discussion of conflict is obnoxious and it doesn't fix anything. It's fair to ask that a difficult discussion be rescheduled for a more convenient time, but you should then feel obligated to honor that appointment.
- *Don't* go negative. Stifle your sarcasm, contain your contempt, and discard your disgust. Churlish, surly, and sour behavior has very corrosive effects on close relationships because (as you'll recall from chapter 6)[4] bad is stronger than good.

•*Don't* get caught in a loop of negative affect reciprocity. This is essential. Pay attention, and when you realize that you and your partner are hurling stronger and stronger insults and accusations back and forth, *stop.* Take a 10-minute break, gather yourself, calm down, and return to your discussion with an apology for the last disagreeable thing you said.

A Point to Ponder

What's the meanest and most venomous thing you've ever said to a romantic partner when you were angry? Will you ever say anything like that to him or her again? Why or why not?

A very good way to steer clear of bad-tempered, ill-mannered interaction is to employ a technique that's taught by marriage therapists to help couples manage conflict constructively (Markman et al., 1994). The **speaker-listener technique** provides a structure for calm, clear communication about contentious issues that promotes the use of active listening skills and increases the chances that partners will understand and validate each other despite their disagreement. In particular, the speaker-listener technique is designed to interrupt the cycle of misperception that too often occurs when partners respond quickly to one another without checking their understanding of the other's intent.

To use the technique, the partners designate a small object as the *floor.* (See Table 11.2.) Whoever has the floor is the speaker. That partner's job is to concisely describe his or her feelings using "I-statements"; the listener's job is to listen without interrupting and then to paraphrase the speaker's message. When the speaker is satisfied that his or her feelings have been understood, the floor changes hands and the partners switch roles. This patient pattern of careful communication allows the partners to demonstrate their concern and respect for each other's feelings without falling into a noxious cycle of self-justification, mind reading, interruption, and defensiveness—and of course, that's a good thing (Gordon & Chen, 2016). It can be "hard relational work," managing a conflict in a manner that allows your partners to "tell you their minds openly and honestly" (Epley, 2014, p. 183), but it's worth it.

If you strive to follow these suggestions, you'll probably manage conflict well. And when a conflict discussion is complete, you can grade your collaboration using a scorecard developed by George Bach and Peter Wyden (1983) known as the "Fight

[4] Page 181.

TABLE 11.2. The Speaker-Listener Technique

Want to stay cool when a discussion gets heated? Consider following these rules:

Rules for Both of You

1. *The Speaker has the floor.* Use a real object, such as a book or TV remote control, as the floor. Whoever holds the floor is the only person who gets to say anything until he or she is done.

2. *Share the floor.* When you're Speaker, don't go on and on. Keep each turn brief, and switch roles often as the floor changes hands.

3. *No problem solving.* The point of the technique is to delineate a disagreement, not to solve it. Collaborative brainstorming to solve the problem comes later.

Rules for the Speaker

4. *Speak for yourself. Don't try to be a mind reader.* Use "I" statements to describe your own thoughts, feelings, and concerns. Do not talk about your perceptions of your partner's motives or point of view.

5. *Stop and let the Listener paraphrase.* After a short time, stop and allow the Listener to paraphrase what you've just said. If he or she is not quite accurate, politely restate any points of confusion. The goal is to help the Listener really understand you.

Rules for the Listener

6. *Paraphrase what you hear.* Show the Speaker that you are listening by repeating back in your own words what you heard him or her say. The point is to make sure that you understood what was said.

7. *Focus on the Speaker's message. Don't rebut.* You should not offer your thoughts and opinions on the issue until you have the floor. Your job as Listener is to speak only in the service of understanding your partner.

Source: Adapted from Markman, H., Stanley, S., & Blumberg, S. L. Fighting for your marriage: Positive steps for preventing divorce and preserving a lasting love. *San Francisco: Jossey-Bass, 1994.*

Does this sound awkward? Perhaps, but it has its uses. As its creators suggest, the speaker-listener technique "isn't a normal way to communicate, but it is a relatively safe way to communicate on a difficult issue. Each person will get to talk, each will be heard, and both will show their commitment to discussing the problems constructively" (Markman et al., 1994, p. 67).

Effects Profile." (See Table 11.3.) If you have a "good" fight that has the positive effects listed in the table, your fight is likely to be good for your relationship.

I'm not underestimating how hard it is to fight fair and to have a "good" fight. It requires self-discipline and genuine caring about one's partner. But the positive outcomes are usually worth the effort. From this perspective, instead of being a dreadful problem, conflict is a challenging opportunity—a chance to learn about one's partner and oneself, and a possibility for one's relationship to become more satisfying and more intimate. Strive to fight fairly, and consider using the Fight Effects Profile to grade your efforts the next time conflict puts your communication skills to the test.

TABLE 11.3. The Fight Effects Profile

Each fight is scored by each person from his or her point of view. In a good fight, both partners win. That is, both partners have considerably more positive outcomes than negative ones.

Category	Positive Outcome	Negative Outcome
Hurt	You feel less hurt, weak, or offended.	You feel more hurt, weak, or offended.
Information	You gain more information about your partner's feelings.	You learn nothing new.
Resolution	The issue is now more likely to be resolved.	Possibility of a solution is now less likely.
Control	You have gained more mutually acceptable influence over your partner's behavior.	You now have less mutually acceptable influence over your partner.
Fear	Fear of fighting and/or your partner is reduced.	Fear has increased.
Trust	You have more confidence that your partner will deal with you with goodwill and with positive regard.	You have less confidence in your partner's goodwill.
Revenge	Vengeful intentions are not created by the fight.	Vengeful intentions are created by the fight.
Reconciliation	You make active efforts to undo any harm you have caused.	You do not attempt or encourage reconciliation.
Relational Evaluation	You feel you are more central to the other's concern and interest.	You feel you "count less" with your partner.
Self-Evaluation	You feel better about yourself: more confidence and more self-esteem.	You feel worse about yourself.
Cohesion-Affection	Closeness with and attraction to your partner have increased.	Closeness with and attraction to your partner have decreased.

Source: Adapted from Bach, G. R., & Wyden, P. The intimate enemy: How to fight fair in love and marriage. New York: Avon Books, 1983.

FOR YOUR CONSIDERATION

John's wife, Tina, is a bit hot headed. When something bothers her, she wants to drop everything else and work on the problem, but she tends to do so with high emotion. She has a volatile temper; she gets angry easily, but she cools off just as fast. John is more placid, and he dislikes conflict. When he gets angry, he does so slowly, and he simmers rather than erupts. When there's something bothering him, he prefers to just go off by himself and play video games instead of beginning a discussion that could turn into a fight.

Lately, Tina has become very frustrated because John is close-lipped and unresponsive when she brings up a complaint. His reluctance to discuss her grievances is just making her annoyance and dissatisfaction worse. Having read this chapter, what do you think the future holds for Tina and John? Why?

CHAPTER SUMMARY

The Nature of Conflict

What Is Conflict? Interpersonal *conflict* occurs when people have to give up something that they want because of their partners' influence. Conflict is inescapable. There are tensions known as *dialectics* that are woven into the fabric of close relationships that will, sooner or later, always cause some strain.

The Frequency of Conflict. Conflict occurs often. Its frequency is associated with neuroticism and agreeableness, attachment styles, one's stage of life, incompatibility between partners, stress, poor sleep, and alcohol use.

The Course of Conflict

Instigating Events. Four different categories of events cause most conflicts; these are *criticism, illegitimate demands, rebuffs,* and *cumulative annoyances.*

Attributions. Actor/observer effects and self-serving biases contribute to *attributional conflict,* with partners fighting over whose explanation is right.

Engagement and Escalation. Once an instigating event occurs, partners must decide either to engage in conflict or to avoid the issue and let it drop. If escalation occurs and the conflict heats up, the nasty things that partners say to each other may be either direct or indirect. Surly interaction becomes especially fractious when the partners fall into a pattern of *negative affect reciprocity.*

The Demand/Withdraw Pattern. A frustrating demand/withdraw cycle occurs when one person approaches the other about a problem, and the partner responds by avoiding the issue. Women tend to be the demanders and men the withdrawers more often than not.

Negotiation and Accommodation. Negotiation finally occurs when a couple works toward a solution in a sensible manner. *Voice, loyalty, neglect,* and *exit* are other responses to dissatisfaction in close relationships. *Accommodation* occurs when partners react with calm forbearance to the other's provocation.

Dealing with Conflict: Four Types of Couples. *Volatile* couples have frequent and passionate arguments. *Validators* have calmer, more relaxed discussions, and *avoiders* avoid confrontation. In contrast, the conflicts of *hostiles* are marked by negativity, and their marriages are relatively fragile.

The Outcomes of Conflict

Ending Conflict. There are five ways conflicts can end: *separation, domination, compromise, integrative agreement,* and *structural improvement.*

Can Fighting Be Good for a Relationship? Yes. Deft management of conflict allows relationships to grow and prosper. The *speaker-listener technique* provides a structure for calm, clear communication about touchy topics.

CHAPTER 12

Power and Violence

POWER AND INTERDEPENDENCE
◆ VIOLENCE IN RELATIONSHIPS ◆ FOR YOUR CONSIDERATION
◆ CHAPTER SUMMARY

Who calls the shots in your relationship? Do you usually get your way? Or do you and your partner trade the lead, with each of you getting some of what you want? Most people say that an ideal relationship would be an equal partnership, with both partners sharing the ability to make important decisions and to influence one another; when the 21st century began, for instance, 90 percent of young women and 87 percent of young men said they believed that dating partners should have "exactly equal say" in the relationship (Thornton & Young-DeMarco, 2001). That probably doesn't surprise you, but this preference for sharing power is nevertheless an enormous departure from the traditional model endorsed by previous generations, in which men were the dominant partners in heterosexual relationships, making all the important decisions and calling all the shots. These days, few people explicitly announce that they want to emulate this old-fashioned model, but figuring out how to achieve equality in a relationship can be much more complicated than it sounds. How should decision-making work in an egalitarian relationship? Should the partners make all decisions together? Or does each partner take responsibility for making exactly half the decisions? Does it matter which decisions are important and which ones aren't? Endorsing equality in a relationship is a simple matter, but making it a reality is a much greater challenge.

This chapter will explore the ways in which social power operates in intimate relationships. Social **power** is the ability to influence or change the thoughts, feelings, or behavior of others to suit our purposes and to resist their influence on us (Simpson et al., 2015). I'll identify some of the sources of power in relationships and consider the consequences of power for individuals and couples. Some of them, unfortunately, can be unpleasant: Too often, people use violence to try to get what they want.

POWER AND INTERDEPENDENCE

There are different ways to analyze social power, but a foremost perspective is that of interdependence theory (Thibaut & Kelley, 1959), which we examined in chapter 6. In this first half of the chapter, I'll use interdependency ideas to describe the bases on which power is built, the processes by which power is wielded, and the outcomes that are produced by its use.

Sources of Power

From an interdependency perspective, power is based on the control of valuable resources. If I control access to something you want, you'll probably be motivated to comply with my wishes (within reason) so that I'll let you get it. I'll then have power over you; I'll be able to get you to do what *I* want, at least for a while. This is a simple idea, but (as you might expect) there are various subtleties involved in this view of social power.

First, the person who has power does not have to possess the desired resources; it is enough that he or she controls access to them. Imagine that you're shopping with a friend at a flea market and you discover the rare imported bootleg concert DVD that you've wanted for months, but that you keep losing to higher bidders on eBay. Better yet, it's cheap, but you don't have enough cash with you, and you need a loan from your friend to buy the elusive disc. Your friend doesn't have the object you desire, but his or her power in this situation will come from controlling your ability to get it. In a similar fashion, relationship partners can control our access to valuable interpersonal rewards—such as physical affection—and thereby have power over us.

Of course, one derives power from controlling a resource only if other people want it, and the greater their need or desire, the greater one's power. The example of the rare DVD is an illustration of this: If you have only a mild interest in the disc, a friend with the money to buy it has only a little power over you. But if you want the disc desperately, your friend has more power and will be able to ask for a sizable favor in return. Whenever we want something badly (be it a rare DVD or interpersonal intimacy) and believe we cannot get it elsewhere, the person who has what we want is able to exert control over us.

We encountered an example of one person's desire fueling another person's power back in the box on page 178. The **principle of lesser interest** holds that in any partnership, the person who has less interest in continuing and maintaining the relationship has more power in that partnership (Waller & Hill, 1951). If your partner loves and needs you more than you love him or her, you'll get to do what you want more often than not. This sounds cold blooded, but it's true; in romantic relationships, the partner who is less committed to the relationship usually has more power (Lennon et al., 2013). We saw another example of this pattern in chapter 9 when I noted that men desire more sex, on average, than women do. Men's greater interest in sex gives women power; it's quite unromantic but rather enlightening to think of sex as a valuable resource that women can exchange for various benefits from men (Kruger, 2008). This arrangement is explicit in the case of prostitution when women trade sex for money, but it often also operates in more subtle ways in many romantic relationships. It's not uncommon, for instance, for a woman to wait for a declaration of affection and emerging commitment from a man before allowing him access to sex.

Of course, if something we want is readily available elsewhere, we can just go there to get it, and the availability of alternative sources of desired resources is another critical factor in an interdependency perspective on power. If there is another friend at the flea market who can lend you the money you need, the first friend has less power over you. And if there are many people who would loan you the money, then you are not very dependent on any one of them, and not one of them has much power over you at all.

In the same fashion, the availability of alternatives influences the balance of power in an intimate relationship. Those with few alternatives to their existing partnerships (who therefore have low CL_{alt}s) will be more dependent on their relationships than will those with many other other potential partners (who thereby have high CL_{alt}s). And as we have just seen, being more dependent means having less power. If one partner has few alternatives and the other has many, there will be a larger imbalance of power than would be the case if they needed each other to similar degrees (Lennon et al., 2013).

In fact, differences in available alternatives may be one reason that men are typically more powerful than women in traditional marriages. When husbands work outside the home and their wives do not, they often have higher CL_{alt}s for at least two important reasons. First, they may encounter larger numbers of other potential partners, and second, they're more likely to have the money to pursue them if they wish. In contrast, stay-at-home wives may not meet many other interesting men, and even if they do, they're likely to be economically dependent on their husbands, having little money of their own. Thus, the balance of power in a marriage sometimes changes when a wife enters the work force and gains new friends and money of her own (Fitch & Ruggles, 2000).

There are two more points to make about the interdependence perspective on power. First, interdependence theory recognizes two different broad types of power. On occasion, one can control a partner's outcomes no matter what the partner does; in such cases, one has a form of power known as **fate control:** One can autocratically determine what outcomes a partner receives, thereby controlling the other's fate. When she is his only option, a woman who refuses to have sex with her husband is exercising fate control; she can unilaterally determine whether or not sex occurs. A second, more subtle, type of power is **behavior control.** This occurs when, by changing one's own behavior, one encourages a partner to alter his or her actions in a desirable direction, too. If a woman offers to provide a special backrub if her partner cleans the garage, she's engaging in behavior control.

Of course, in almost all relationships, *both* partners have power over each other, and the last, and perhaps most essential, point of an interdependency perspective is that the interactions of two partners emerge from their mutual influence on one another. "Power dynamics in a relationship are likely to be fluid processes in which both partners, as well as their unique, interactive characteristics, affect one another's outcomes" (Simpson et al., 2015, p. 414). In many cases, one partner's power over the other will be matched by the other's *counterpower* over the one, so that both partners are able to get each other to do what they want some of the time. For instance, a woman may have fate control over whether or not her husband has sex, but he probably has some behavior control over her in return; by cajoling her, pleasing her, or worse, threatening her, he may be able to get her to do what he wants. Two partners' abilities to influence one another may be diverse and variable, being strong in some situations and weak in others, but both of them will routinely have some control over what the other does.

Types of Resources

So, power is based on the resources we control—but what kinds of resources are involved? Table 12.1 lists six bases of power first identified by French and Raven (1959); this scheme has been applied to all kinds of interactions, including those that occur in intimate relationships. The first two types, **reward power** and **coercive power,** refer to a person's ability to bestow various rewards and punishments on someone else. The benefits and costs involved can be physical or material goods, such as a pleasant gift or a painful slap, or intangible, interpersonal gains and losses, such as reassuring approval or hurtful disdain (Raven, 2001). For example, if a husband craves a shoulder massage from his wife, she has reward power over him: She can rub his back or not, supplying or withholding a physical reward. But in return, he may have coercion power over her: If he doesn't get his massage, he may sulk and be less affectionate, imposing intangible costs.

TABLE 12.1. Resources that Grant One Power

Type of Power	Resource	Gets People to Do What You Want Because
Reward power	Rewards	You can give them something they like or take away something they don't like.
Coercive power	Punishments	You can do something to them they don't like or take away something they do like.
Legitimate power	Authority or norms of equity, reciprocity, or social responsibility	They recognize your authority to tell them what to do.
Referent power	Respect and/or love	They identify with you, feeling attracted and wanting to remain close.
Expert power	Expertise	You have the broad understanding they desire.
Informational power	Information	You possess some specific knowledge they desire.

Source: Based on Raven, B. H. "Power/interaction and interpersonal influence: Experimental investigations and case studies." In A. Y. Lee-Chai & J. A. Bargh (Eds.), The use and abuse of power: Multiple perspectives on the causes of corruption (pp. 217–240). Philadelphia: Psychology Press, 2001.

The capabilities to provide desired benefits or to impose aversive costs on our partners are very important and very influential, but there are other ways to influence people, too. **Legitimate power** exists when our partners believe that we have a reasonable right to tell them what to do, and they have an obligation to comply. In some cultures, for instance, a husband really is thought to be the boss, and a wife is supposed not only to love and honor him, but to *obey* him as well, doing whatever he asks. This form of legitimate power comes from being in a position of authority, but potent social norms can also impart legitimate power to requests that come from anyone (Raven, 2001). For instance, the norm of *reciprocity* encourages us to do unto others as they have done unto us, and if someone who has already done you a favor asks for some kindness in return, the norm obligates you to repay the good deed. *Equity* is also normative, and if your partner has done extra housework lately, an invitation to fold some laundry might be difficult to decline. Finally, a norm of *social responsibility* urges us to be generous to those who depend on us—to help those who cannot help themselves—and if your partner is sick in bed with the flu, a request for some juice may be hard to turn down. Any of these norms can impart power to a partner's desires, making them very influential, at least temporarily.

We have **referent power** over our partners when they adore us and wish to do what we want because they feel connected to us. Our wishes may change our partners' preferences about what they want to do when they love us and want to stay close to us. **Expert power** exists when our partners recognize our superior knowledge and experience and are influenced by us because we know more than they do. When a wife is a better cook than her husband, for instance, he'll often follow her advice and instructions without question when it's his turn to prepare dinner. Finally, we have **informational power** when we have specific pieces of information that influence our partners' behavior; our partners may do what we want if we offer to share a juicy bit of gossip with them.

Men, Women, and the Control of Resources

How are these resources used in your relationships? What goes on between you and your partner is largely up to both of you, but you may be influenced to a greater extent than you realize by the broad cultural patterns that surround you. Many of us applaud the notion of equal partnerships but still conduct relationships in which "there is an imbalance of power, with one person making more decisions, controlling more of the joint activities and resources, winning more arguments and, in general, being in a position of dominance" (Impett & Peplau, 2006, p. 283). And in most heterosexual relationships, the dominant partner is the man. Indeed, this isn't good news for most of us (but perhaps it really isn't news at all): "In no known societies do women dominate men. In all societies that accumulate wealth, men, on average, enjoy more power than women, on average, and this appears to have been true throughout human history" (Pratto & Walker, 2004, p. 242). Heterosexual couples who seek to share power equally are swimming upstream against long-standing tradition, and there are three reasons for this.

First, men and women generally face a disparity in *relative resources.* Men get paid more than women for the work they do (even when it's the same work): In the United States, women with full-time jobs presently earn only 80 percent as much as men do (AAUW, 2017). Men are also far more likely to hold the reins of governmental, judicial, and corporate power; in 2017, for instance, only 19 percent of the members of the U.S. Congress were women (CAWP, 2017), and, even worse, only 6 percent of the chief executive officers of America's 500 largest companies were women (Catalyst, 2017). Money and status confer reward power and legitimate power on those who possess them, and men often have more of both than women do. Indeed, it's much more common than it used to be for wives to earn more than their husbands, but in about two-thirds of American marriages, he still makes more money than she does (Cohn & Caumont, 2016). And money is a source of power that can be used more flexibly than most other resources. Theorists describe some resources (such as money) as *universalistic* and others (such as love) as *particularistic* (Foa et al., 1993). Universalistic resources can be exchanged with almost anyone in a wide variety of situations, and whoever controls them has considerable freedom in deciding what to do with them (and with whom to do it). Particularistic resources are valuable in some situations but not in others, and they may confer power to their owner only with particular partners. A partner's love for you may give you referent power over him or her and no one else whereas a large pile of cash may provide you reward power over almost everyone you meet.

The second reason equality is hard to attain is related to the first: *Social norms* support and maintain male dominance. We expect husbands to be less satisfied with their marriages when they have lower professional status than their wives (Hettinger et al., 2014). And worldwide, most cultures are still governed by a norm of patriarchy that confers higher levels of expert and legitimate power on men than on women (Carli, 2001). Americans actually tend to think that women have skills that should make them more effective leaders than men; women are thought to be more honest, intelligent, compassionate, and creative and just as ambitious and hardworking as men (Pew Research Center, 2015b). But legitimate power still seems "unladylike" to some people, and when a woman seeks political office, the fact that she's seeking power undermines her appeal to voters; a man seeking office pays no such penalty (Okimoto & Brescoll, 2010). And if a woman does attain a position of leadership, she's likely to be evaluated more harshly than a man would be when she straightforwardly tells others what to do (Rudman et al., 2012). Cultural norms still keep women in their place, so Americans tend to prefer that their surgeons, lawyers, and airline pilots be men rather than women (Morin & Cohn, 2008). Women are preferred as elementary school teachers.

Thus, cultural tradition suggests that it's ordinary and natural for men to make more money and to be in charge most of the time. And that underlies the third reason equality is elusive: We're not sure what it looks like. Women usually get their way when it comes to decisions regarding household matters and the kids, and they get to pick the things the couple does on the weekend more often than men do (Shu et al., 2012). So, women can rightly feel that they're influential at home. But just how much? Married Americans still report that wives buy most of the groceries, fix most of the meals, and wash most of the dishes; they also do most of the laundry and clean more of the house (Aassve et al., 2014). Husbands do yard work and take care of the cars, but—and here's my point—that division of labor cannot possibly value wives' and husbands' time equally: The wives' duties are constant, and the husbands' are intermittent (Lachance-Grzela & Bouchard, 2010). Dinner gets eaten every night, but the cars' oil gets changed only every now and then. So, whereas an American woman does 18 hours of housework each week, on average, a man does only 10 (Pew Research Center, 2015a). And when it comes to fundamental, central decisions regarding the relationship—such as "are we going to get married or just keep cohabiting?"—men usually get to call the shots (Sassler & Miller, 2011). Wives do control most household routines, but because their husbands are more likely to get their way when it really matters, the husbands are more powerful. This still tends to be true, although to a lesser extent, even when women's disadvantage in relative resources is erased—that is, when they earn more than their husbands. For instance, wives with higher incomes do a smaller proportion of the household chores, but they still do most of them (Carlson & Lynch, 2017).

> ### A Point to Ponder
>
> It's 3:23 A.M., the baby's hungry, and nobody's had much sleep lately. Who's going to get up and give the baby her bottle, you or your partner? Why?

So, despite their expressed interests in equal partnerships (Sells & Ganong, 2017), most heterosexual couples still tolerate substantial inequality (Ponzi et al., 2015)—and they may not realize just how one-sided their partnerships are. In a culture that takes male dominance for granted, genuine equality that honors both parties' interests equally is certainly unfamiliar, and it may even seem peculiar or excessive. But, if you're interested, Table 12.2 may help you judge your own partnerships more evenhandedly; it offers several considerations that may be eye-opening.

Finally, I'll also note that men often have a lot of coercive power due to their typically larger size and greater strength. But coercion is a clumsy, corrosive way to get what one wants. Fear and punishment are aversive, and they breed discontent. They also foster resistance, so partners who are coerced are actually *less* compromising than they would have been had gentler power been employed (Oriña et al., 2002). I'll return to this point later in the chapter when we examine violence in close relationships, but for now I'll simply note that coercion is usually an inept, counterproductive way to influence an intimate partner.

The Process of Power

Power feels good. Powerful people are used to getting what they want, so they experience a lot of positive moods and feelings of well-being (Kifer et al., 2013). They feel in control of things. In fact, compared to the rest of us, they tend to think that they can control events that are uncontrollable, such as the outcome of a roll of some dice (Fast et al., 2009). They also tend to do what they want (Guinote et al., 2012); if there's just one cookie left on the plate, they'll take it without asking if anyone else wants it (Keltner et al., 2010). Indeed, they are relatively unlikely to realize that someone else was hoping to share the cookie because they're not very good at comprehending others' points of view. If you ask

TABLE 12.2. Elements of Equality in Close Relationships

These are four dimensions with which to judge how close you're coming to true equality in your relationships. They are suggested for your consideration by Anne Rankin Mahoney, a sociologist, and Carmen Knudson-Martin, a marital and family therapist (2009).

Relative Status

Whose interests matter more?
Who defines what's important to the two of you?
How are low-status chores around the house handled?

Attention to the Other

Who is more likely to notice and attend to the feelings of his or her partner?
Who is more likely to notice and attend to the needs of his or her partner?
Do both of you give and receive care and concern?

Patterns of Accommodation

Whose accommodations are noticed and acknowledged, and whose are taken for granted?
Who arranges more of his or her daily activities around the other's life?

Well-Being

Whose economic success is valued more?
Who's better off psychologically and physically?
Does one person's well-being come at the expense of the other's good health?

Source: Mahoney, A. R., & Knudson-Martin, C. "Gender equality in intimate relationships." In C. Knudson-Martin & A. Mahoney (Eds.), Couples, gender, and power: Creating change in intimate relationships (pp. 3–16). New York: Springer, 2009.

powerful people to quickly draw an "E" on their foreheads, they are much more likely than people of low power to draw the letter as if they were reading it, which makes it backward and illegible for anyone else—like this: Ǝ (Galinsky et al., 2015).

The self-importance of powerful people is also evident in their self-perceptions of their mate value.[1] People who are randomly assigned to lead work groups in lab studies expect that their subordinates will find them sexually interesting, and if they approve of casual sex, they both judge their subordinates to be more sexually available and stage more flirtatious interactions with them than those of lesser power do (Kunstman & Maner, 2011). Those perceptions apparently persist in the workplace: Compared to mid-level managers, more powerful professionals are more adulterous, being 50 percent more likely to cheat on their current partners (Lammers & Maner, 2016). And they may not think they're misbehaving; powerful people judge others' moral transgressions more harshly than their own, so that, compared to less powerful people, they're more strict in condemning others' cheating while cheating more often themselves (Lammers et al., 2010).

By comparison, being powerless isn't so great. Those who find themselves in positions of low power suffer more depression, behave more cautiously, and

---

[1]We first encountered *mate value* back on page 85.

timidly fear more punishment than powerful people do (Keltner et al., 2010), and day by day, they're more likely to be doing things their partners want to do than vice versa (Laurin et al., 2016). And, in keeping with these patterns, power differentials affect the behavior of people toward their intimate partners too. Let's inspect some of the ways in which power is expressed.

Conversation

The conversations two people share are likely to be influenced by the balance of power between them, and, for better or worse, women tend not to speak to men with the same implicit strength and power that they display toward other women. In particular, they allow themselves to be interrupted by men more often than they interrupt men in return.

In one of the first studies of this pattern, researchers surreptitiously recorded conversations of college students in public places (obtaining permission to analyze the recordings after the conversations were done) and then compared the conversations of same-sex dyads to those in which men and women conversed (Zimmerman & West, 1975). Women and men behaved similarly when they were talking to others of the same sex, but distinctive patterns emerged in interactions with the other sex. Men interrupted their female partners much more often than their female partners interrupted them (and they did most of the talking, too). That's important because people who get interrupted are judged to have lower status and to be less powerful than those who do the interrupting (Farley, 2008).

Now, fast-forward to this century and imagine that you and your lover have to decide how to spend a gift of $1,000. You each develop a personal list of your top five priorities and then get together to negotiate your options. If one of you frequently succeeds in interrupting the other, both of you are likely to judge him or her to be the more powerful partner (see Figure 12.1). And men still complete more of these interruptions than women do (Dunbar & Burgoon, 2005).

FIGURE 12.1. **Interruptions and perceived power.**
During discussions of personal priorities, the more often someone successfully interrupted his or her partner, the more powerful he or she was perceived to be.

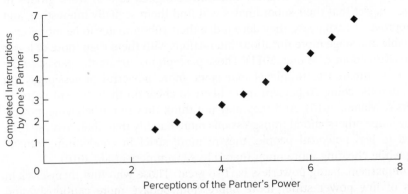

Source: Dunbar, N. E., & Burgoon, J. K. "Perceptions of power and interactional dominance in interpersonal relationships," Journal of Social and Personal Relationships, 22, 2005, 207–233.

FIGURE 12.2. **Low- and high-power postures.**
People of high status and power assume postures that are asymmetric and that take up a lot of space. It's a safe bet that someone who assumes the posture on the right feels (or will soon feel) more powerful than someone who assumes the posture on the left. By the way, if you were told that one of these silhouettes is a man and the other is a woman, which would you say is which?

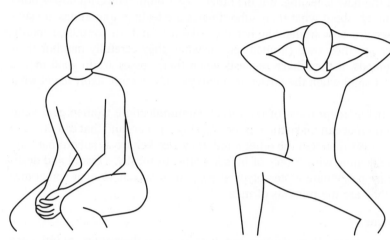

Source: Adapted from Frieze, I. H., Parsons, J. E., Johnson, P. B., Ruble, D. N., & Zellman, G. L. Women and sex roles: A social psychological perspective. New York: Norton, 1978.

Nonverbal Behavior

Power is also communicated to others nonverbally, and powerful people use larger interpersonal distances, display more intense facial expressions, and assume postures that are less symmetrical and that take up more space than those of people who are less powerful (Hall et al., 2005). Take a look at the two poses in Figure 12.2. They exemplify my postural point: The one on the right typifies someone of higher status. (That's obvious, isn't it?) Indeed, when people are posed in these positions by researchers, those who assume more space may *feel* more powerful; male or female, their testosterone levels rise, and they take bolder risks in a gambling game (Carney et al., 2015). The pose on the right is clearly more powerful—and interestingly, it's more masculine, too. Men tend to take up more space with their postures than women do—one certainly ought not assume the pose on the right if one is wearing a dress—and they use distances and postures that are typical of high-status people more often than women do (Kalbfleisch & Herold, 2006).

Nonverbal Sensitivity

Remember, too, from chapter 5, that women are generally more accurate judges of others' emotions and meaning than men are. Women decode others' nonverbal communications more accurately than men do, and they are usually more aware of what others are feeling (Thompson & Voyer, 2014). This skill is a tremendous asset because the sensitivity and accuracy with which a couple communicates nonverbally predicts how satisfied with each other they are likely to be (Fitness, 2015).

On the other hand, a person's nonverbal sensitivity also has something to do with how powerful and dominant he or she is. Powerful people recognize emotion in others' voices (Uskul et al., 2016) and facial expressions (Nissan et al., 2015) less acccurately than those with lower power do. And that shouldn't surprise us: When two people differ in status, it's typically the job of the subordinate to keep track of what the boss is feeling, not the other way around. Powerful bosses don't have to care much about what their subordinates are feeling; underlings are supposed to do what a boss wants whether they like it or not. In contrast, subordinates can increase their own (limited) power when they carefully monitor their supervisors' moods; if they make requests when their bosses are in good moods (and stay out of sight when the bosses are cranky), they're more likely to get what they want.

Thus, in being adept users of nonverbal communication, women gain valuable information that can make them more pleasing partners and that can increase their influence over men. On the other hand, they also behave as subordinates do when they are dealing with people of higher status. Ironically, a useful and desirable talent may perpetuate a stereotypical pattern in which women sometimes behave as if they are the minions of men.

Styles of Power

Just what strategies, then, do men and women use in their efforts to influence each other? Toni Falbo and Anne Peplau (1980) addressed this question in a classic study that asked 50 lesbians, 50 gay men, 50 heterosexual women, and 50 heterosexual men to describe "how I get [my partner] to do what I want." Two themes characterized the participants' replies. First, they sometimes explicitly asked for what they wanted, straightforwardly announcing their wishes or making unambiguous requests. Their efforts to influence their partners were overt and *direct,* and their preferences were plain. On other occasions, however, people's actions were more *indirect;* they hinted at what they wanted or pouted when their wishes were unfulfilled, but they never came right out and said what they wanted. Importantly, the more satisfied people were with their relationships, the more likely they were to use direct strategies. This could mean that when people have rewarding partnerships, they feel safe enough to be honest and forthright with their partners; on the other hand, it could also mean that people whose desires are expressed indirectly and ambiguously are less adept at getting what they want, and they're likely to be dissatisfied as a result. What's your guess? Does indirectness lead to dissatisfaction or follow from it? (Remember, it could be both.)

The second theme that distinguished different strategies described the extent to which people sought their goals through interaction with their partners (as opposed to doing what they wanted by themselves). Sometimes people reasoned or bargained with their partners in efforts to persuade them to provide some desired outcome; in such cases, people sought cooperation or collaboration from their partners, and their strategies were *bilateral,* involving both members of the couple. In contrast, on other occasions, people took independent *unilateral* action, doing what they wanted without involving their partners. Importantly, people who reported that they were more powerful than their partners said that they frequently

Influencing a Partner to Use a Condom

You'd think that it'd be taken for granted these days that people would expect to have safe sex when they begin having sex in a new relationship. Unfortunately, too often, one partner still needs to convince the other to use a condom. How do such negotiations proceed? The most common strategy is a direct one: People straightforwardly announce their wish to use a condom (Lam et al., 2004). That's a good thing because softer, more indirect requests are more likely to be ignored, particularly if everyone's been drinking (Wegner et al., 2017).

In most cases, though, the partner who is less committed to the relationship gets what he or she wants; it's another example of the principle of lesser interest at work (VanderDrift et al., 2013a). So, if you're the less powerful partner, you may want to make your wishes known in a manner that does not involve explicit discussion (Lam et al., 2004). One effective tactic is to simply produce a condom and begin putting it on. Without saying a word, you can demonstrate that condom use is expected and appreciated. A reluctant partner may protest that such precautions aren't needed, but his or her objections probably won't last long if you persist.

Indeed, when people *don't* want to use a condom, they usually don't mention their preference. Instead, they typically try to seduce their partners, getting them so turned on that sex proceeds without a pause for protection (De Bro et al., 1994). Thus, it may be useful, if you seek safe sex, to keep your wits about you and to remember that, with the force of supportive social norms behind you, you should be able to get what you want. Don't fall into the trap of thinking that your partner has more control over the situation than you do; that will make it harder for you to do the right thing and get what you want (Woolf & Maisto, 2008).

used bilateral strategies whereas those who were less powerful were more likely to use unilateral strategies. Thus, people who were able to influence their partners successfully did just that, reasoning and negotiating with them to gain their compliance. In contrast, those possessing low power were less likely to seek their partners' cooperation; they just went off and did their own thing.

Falbo and Peplau (1980) found that, overall, gays and lesbians employed similar strategies, but there were differences in the strategies used by heterosexual men and women. On average, heterosexual men reported more extensive use of direct and bilateral styles whereas heterosexual women used more indirect and unilateral strategies. Thus, when they were dealing with their romantic partners, heterosexual men tended to use styles of influence that are characteristic of people who are satisfied and powerful whereas women adopted styles typically used by those who are powerless and discontent.

Wow. Did heterosexual men typically behave in a mature and assertive fashion in their romantic partnerships, asking for what they want and reasoning logically with their lovers while their partners pouted and got moody without ever saying what they wanted? Well, yes, to a degree, but that's less likely to happen today. These days, when heterosexual couples engage in discussions in which each partner describes something about the other that they wish would change,[2] women use direct strategies just as often as men do (Overall et al., 2009). (And direct strategies are more successful in actually getting the partner to change, too.) Each new generation of American women is higher in instrumentality—that is, decisiveness and assertiveness—than the one before (Donnelly & Twenge, 2017), and couples have become more egalitarian in their expectations for marriage (Sells & Ganong, 2017).

Men probably have less automatic authority in their intimate relationships than they used to, and—here comes an important point—that appears to be a good thing: Disparities in power are linked to lower satisfaction in close relationships (Worley & Samp, 2016b). People who have to hint and pout to get (some of) what they want tend to be less content than are those who can come right out and ask for what they desire.

The Outcome of Power

Altogether, then, most of us say we want to have equal partnerships with our lovers, but we're surrounded by a culture that takes male dominance for granted, and we often unwittingly perpetuate gender inequalities through our day-to-day interactions. The outcome of these influences in many cases is subtle asymmetry in partners' influence on one another, with a partnership seeming fair or even entirely equal when in reality he has more influence than she does. Here's an example. When spouses are interviewed together about their political opinions, wives agree more with their husbands' answers, if the men answer the questions first, than husbands agree with their wives when their wives go first—and this occurs even when the wives earn higher salaries and are more expert on the issues (Zipp et al., 2004). Male autonomy and assertion and female conformity and compliance seem so natural to many people that imbalances of power that fit this pattern can pass without notice.

Nevertheless, the latest data on marital equality suggest that we should strive to create romantic partnerships in which both partners' wishes and preferences are given equal weight (Worley & Samp, 2016b). Things have changed in the 21st century (Sells & Ganong, 2017). Spouses are much more likely to share decision-making than they used to be, and those who do enjoy marriages that are happier, less contentious, and less prone to divorce than those in which one of the partners calls most of the shots (Amato et al., 2007). Take a look at Figure 12.3. The results portrayed there combine the outcomes experienced by husbands and wives, but the differences between equal and unequal partnerships are in the same direction for both men and women: Women are a *lot* happier when they're

---

[2]This is an intriguing procedure. You're seated in a comfortable room with your lover, just the two of you, and your assignment is to tell your partner what you would most like to change about him or her. How would you approach this touchy topic? Would you announce your issue straight away and explain why change was needed? Or would you compliment your partner's many good qualities, describe yourself as undeserving, and suggest your issue was trivial? (This latter approach is a more indirect strategy!)

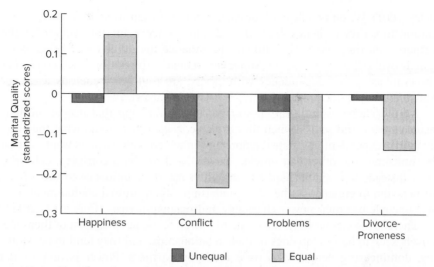

Source: Data from Amato, P. R., Booth, A., Johnson, D. R., & Rogers, S. J. Alone together: How marriage in America is changing. Cambridge, MA: Harvard University Press, 2007.

FIGURE 12.3. **Marital outcomes and the balance of power.**
Modern couples are happier, and they have less conflict, fewer problems, and are less prone to divorce when they share their decision-making equally. Much less advantageous outcomes occur when one of the partners calls most of the shots. Compared to those with equalitarian marriages, couples are less happy, and they experience more conflict, have more problems, and are more prone to divorce when one partner is more powerful than the other.

as powerful as their husbands, and notably, their husbands are a little happier, too. Everybody wins when power is shared. The bottom line is that our modern relationships appear to be more stable and happier on the whole when both partners matter to the same extent (Worley & Samp, 2016a). These days, husbands and wives who adhere to traditional divisions of labor and power are less satisfied with their marriages than are those who construct more equal partnerships (Ogolsky et al., 2014).

The Two Faces of Power

Our discussion thus far may have left you with the impression that power has caustic effects on close relationships, but if that's the case, it's time to correct that view. Imbalances of power can be problematic (Righetti et al., 2015), but power itself is not inherently undesirable at all. It does not always lead to the greedy exploitation of one's partners. Indeed, when people adopt communal orientations[3] in committed romantic relationships, they typically use their power for the benefit of their partners and their relationships, not for selfish ends (Gardner &

---

[3] A reminder is available on page 193.

Seeley, 2001). When people care for each other and want to maintain a rewarding relationship, they're benevolent; they display concern for the welfare of their partners, and they use their influence to enhance the other's well-being as well as their own (Chen et al., 2001). Moreover, people with relational self-construals,[4] who emphasize interdependency with others, are routinely generous when they resolve disputes with others of lower power (Howard et al., 2007).

An old cliché asserts that "power corrupts," implying that people inevitably become greedy and selfish when they are able to get others to do what they want. But in interdependent, intimate relationships in which both partners want the desirable outcomes the other can provide, power need not be a corrosive, deleterious force. Instead, committed, happy lovers often use their influence to benefit their partners and to enhance, rather than undermine, their mutual contentment. Kind, loving people use their power charitably and magnanimously (Côté et al., 2011).

There is also, however, a dark side to power. Some people, most of them men, actively seek to be the top dogs in their relationships, and they tend to be controlling, domineering people who have unhappy partners. Power is important to them, and when they are unable to get what they want through more legitimate influence, they may use violence in a sad but sometimes effective effort to exert control (Vescio et al., 2010). It is to this grimmest aspect of intimacy, the potential for intimate violence, to which we now turn.

VIOLENCE IN RELATIONSHIPS

We commit **violence** when we behave in a manner that is intended to do physical harm to others (Arriaga et al., 2018). The harm we intend may be rather minor or quite severe, and violent actions range from those that do little harm, such as grabbing or pushing, to others that inflict atrocious injury, such as beatings and burnings (see Table 12.3). And sadly, intimate violence of all types is more common than most people think.

The Prevalence of Violence

The Centers for Disease Control and Prevention are conducting a multiyear study of relationship violence in the United States, and the first wave of results (Black et al., 2011) is pretty grim. Almost one of every four women (24 percent) and one in seven men (14 percent) in America have encountered severe physical violence—being beaten, kicked, choked, burned, and more—by an intimate partner, both in heterosexual and same-sex (Nicholls & Hamel, 2015) relationships. And the rates of such violence are even higher elsewhere in the world. The World Health Organization (2013) reports that 30 percent of the world's women have been assaulted by a domestic partner, with the highest rates of such victimization—37 percent—occurring in Africa, the Middle East, and Southeast Asia.

When a couple has a history of angry disputes, rates of violence are higher still. Of several hundred cases of divorcing couples in Tucson, Arizona, who had

[4] Page 226.

TABLE 12.3. A Kick Is Worse Than a Slap

Magda Osman and her colleagues (2017) asked people in the United Kingdom and in Bosnia to put a price on the compensation they would feel they were owed if they experienced particular acts of violence. The rankings below demonstrate that violent acts vary considerably, and some are much more consequential than others. If you were the victim, what would each of these be worth to you?

Being spit upon	$8,929	Threatened with a knife	$11,631
Being slapped	$9,876	Hit with a head-butt	$19,636
Being punched	$10,354	Being choked	$118,119
Being kicked	$10,499	Being stabbed	$125,596

Source: Data from Osman, M., Pupic, D., & Baigent, N. "How many slaps is equivalent to one punch? New approaches to assessing the relative severity of violent acts," Psychology of Violence, 7, 2017, 69-81.

child-custody disputes, 75 percent had involved some form of physical abuse (C. Beck et al., 2013). And psychological aggression—such as screaming, ridicule, and threats—had occurred in almost all (95 percent) of those couples.

Psychological aggression is no small matter. It occurs at one time or another in *most* relationships (Fergusson et al., 2005), and it is clearly detrimental to marital satisfaction and personal well-being (Lorber et al., 2015). But as bad as it is, verbal aggression seems less worrisome to most of us than physical violence does (Arriaga & Schkeryantz, 2015), so I'll focus on violence here. And concern about intimate partner violence (or IPV) is warranted; in the United States, the Centers for Disease Control and Prevention (2014) estimate that IPV will cost nearly $9 billion in medical care, psychological services, and lost time from work this year.

Types of Couple Violence

It's one thing to describe the specific acts of violence that occur in close relationships, and another to explain why they occur. Michael Johnson (2008) has suggested that there are three major, distinct types of violence in romantic couples, and they spring from different sources. The most familiar type is **situational couple violence** (or SCV), which typically erupts from heated conflicts that get out of hand. It occurs when both partners are angry and is tied to specific arguments, so it is only occasional and is usually mild, being unlikely to escalate into serious, life-threatening forms of aggression. Often, it is also mutual, with both partners angrily and impulsively flying out of control.

A notably different kind of violence is **intimate terrorism** (or IT) in which one partner uses violence as a tool to control and oppress the other. The physical force and coercion that occurs in intimate terrorism may be just one tactic in a general pattern of threats, isolation, and economic subordination (see Table 12.4 on the next page), and when it is present in a relationship, it occurs more often than situational couple violence does (Hardesty et al., 2015). Indeed, compared to SCV, intimate terrorism is more likely to be one-sided, to escalate over time, and to involve serious injury to its target. It's also

Correlates of Violence

Careful consideration of intimate partner violence recognizes the distinction between situational couple violence and intimate terrorism (Arriaga et al., 2018). Most acts of violence in close relationships result from impetuous, impulsive failures of self-control (that's SCV), but some violence is part of a program of ruthless subjugation of one's partner (and that's IT). And importantly, SCV and IT seem to spring from somewhat different sources.

Situational Couple Violence

Both types of intimate partner violence are complex, emerging from various overlapping influences. A useful model of situational couple violence, the I^3 (or "I-cubed") **model** created by Eli Finkel (2014), organizes influences on SCV into *instigating triggers* that cause one or both partners to be frustrated or on edge, *impelling influences* that make it more likely that the partners will experience violent impulses, and *inhibiting influences* that encourage the partners to refrain from acting on those impulses. When we've been angry, *most* of us have experienced violent impulses, but most of us didn't act on them (Finkel et al., 2009), and Finkel's model suggests that we refrained from violence either because the impelling influences stimulating us to lash out were too weak or because the inhibiting forces dissuading us from physical action were too strong.

What sort of influences are these? Finkel (2008) suggested that both impelling and inhibitory influences could be distal, dispositional, relational, or situational. *Distal* influences emerge from one's background; they include cultural norms, economic conditions, and family experiences. *Dispositional* influences include personality traits and long-standing beliefs. *Relational* influences involve the current state of the couple's relationship, and *situational* influences include the immediate circumstances. These are all listed with some examples in Figure 12.4. The figure may seem intimidating at first, but don't fret; I'll walk you through it.

Instigating Triggers.   The path to situational couple violence begins with instigating influences that cause one or both of the partners to become cantankerous or angry. Anything about a couple's interaction that causes frustration or aggravation can set the model in motion: Jealousy-evoking events, remembered or discovered betrayals, real or imagined rejection (Giordano et al., 2010), or any of the exasperating events that exacerbate conflict[5] will suffice (Timmons et al., 2017). A particularly potent instigator, though, is verbal or physical abuse from one's partner: People are especially likely to become antagonistic when their partners curse or hit them first (Nicholls & Hamel, 2015).

Impelling Influences.   Then, when someone's fired up, the impelling influences that are at work become important. Some of the influences that predispose one to violence are events from much earlier in life. For instance, people who witnessed violence between their parents (Smith-Marek et al., 2015) or were

---

[5] Pages 339–341 in chapter 11.

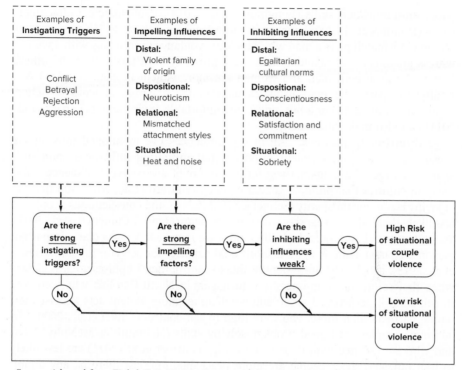

Source: Adapted from Finkel, E. J. "Intimate partner violence perpetration: Insights from the science of self-regulation." In J. P. Forgas & J. Fitness (Eds.), Social relationships: Cognitive, affective and motivational processes (pp. 271–288). New York: Psychology Press, 2008.

FIGURE 12.4. **The I³ model of SCV perpetration.**
If the answers to the three questions posed in the model are all "yes," situational couple violence is likely to occur. If any of the answers is "no," violence is unlikely. Examples of the influences that bear on each question are provided, but they are illustrative rather than exhaustive. Violence is the result of many sources, and the examples provided were chosen because of their relevance to relationship science.

abused when they were children (Elmquist et al., 2016), and those who consumed a lot of aggressive media (such as violent movies and video games) over the years (Coyne et al., 2010) are more likely than others to engage in IPV. Other impelling influences are enduring personal characteristics. People with sour dispositions who are prone to anger (Maldonado et al., 2015) or who are low in agreeableness (Carton & Egan, 2017) are also prone to intimate violence. So are men with traditional, sex-typed gender roles (Herrero et al., 2018) and those with attitudes that condone a little force now and then as a normal way of doing things (Casey et al., 2017). (Thus, here's a bit of good news in this grim landscape: Some of the personal characteristics that predispose people to violence are *attitudes* that may be comparatively easy to change [Neighbors et al., 2010].) Still other impelling influences emerge from the partners' patterns of interaction; for example, couples with poor communication skills (Longmore et al., 2014) or mismatched attachment styles (Doumas et al., 2008) engage in more IPV than others do.[6] (The most troublesome mismatch pairs a man who's high in avoidance of intimacy with a woman who is anxious about abandonment; they probably both push all of the other's buttons because both men and women are more violent in such couples.) And finally, the particular circumstances matter: Recent stress at work or school (Timmons et al., 2017) or a hot, noisy, uncomfortable environment (Larrick et al., 2011) can also make one touchy.

Inhibiting Influences.   All of the influences I've mentioned thus far are presumed to fuel one's violent impulses, but inhibiting influences counteract aggressive urges. Once again, these influences are of diverse types. Violence is less likely in cultures that promote gender equality (Herrero et al., 2017) and that are enjoying economic prosperity (Schneider et al., 2016), and conscientious people are less likely than others to aggress when they're angry (Jensen-Campbell et al., 2007). So, both cultural and individual differences are involved. A particularly important personal characteristic is one's dispositional capacity for self-control (Finkenauer et al., 2015). People who are generally able to control their impulses are less violent when they're provoked; in one study, teenagers in North Carolina who were low in self-control perpetrated seven-and-a-half *times* more violent acts against their dating partners than those who were high in self-control (Finkel et al., 2009).[7] In addition, couples with good problem-solving skills (Hellmuth & McNulty, 2008) and who are satisfied with their relationship (Fournier et al., 2011) are less likely to lash out, and sober people are more peaceable, too; lest there be any doubt, alcohol use does fuel IPV (Cafferky et al., 2017). The role of relationship commitment in SCV is also noteworthy: Commitment to one's partner makes violence less likely (Slotter et al., 2012), so spouses are less violent, on average, than cohabiting couples are (Brownridge, 2010). Otherwise, the various influences we've touched on here appear to operate similarly in both marriages and dating relationships, and in heterosexual and same-sex partnerships as well (Lewis et al., 2017).

Thus, the I[3] model holds that instigating triggers and impelling influences work together to create urges to be aggressive, but that people will nevertheless behave nonviolently when inhibiting influences are strong. However, if inhibiting influences are weak, violence may occur, and if inhibiting influences are *very*

---

[6] The I[3] model's distinction between distal, dispositional, relational, and situational influences is a helpful way to organize the variety of influences that shape IPV, but don't take it too seriously. The categories overlap, and to some degree, the placement of a particular influence in a specific category is arbitrary. For example, kids who grow up in violent homes are more likely than the rest of us to have insecure attachment styles, and certain combinations of insecure styles in a marriage—such as an anxious wife paired with an avoidant husband—are especially tricky (Godbout et al., 2009). So, the distal influence of a violent childhood home produces a dispositional characteristic, attachment insecurity, that becomes particularly problematic when it's combined with a partner's style in a way that produces a trying relationship that's full of annoying vexations. All four types of influences are involved in this sequence of events, and there's no need for you to fuss too much about what influences on IPV belong in which category. Instead, just note the wide variety of experiences and traits that are associated with violence in intimate relationships. IPV has complex origins. It results from multiple influences.

[7] Make a mental note about the value of *self-control*, will you? I'll have more to say about it in chapter 14.

weak, relatively small provocations may be enough to elicit intimate violence. What's more, situational couple violence originates in circumstances that are shaped both by temporary passing influences and by dispositional and distal influences that are stable and lasting. Couples may have some bouts of SCV when tempers run high even when neither partner is particularly prone to violence.

But here's a key question: If IPV happens once, will it happen again? Regrettably, the smartest answer to that question is "yes." In a large national study in the United States, only 30 percent of those who had been violent in one romantic relationship were violent again within the next 5 years in a *different*, second relationship; most people who engaged in SCV—sometimes because they were fighting back after their partners threw the first punch—did not continue to be violent once they changed partners (Whitaker et al., 2010). On the other hand, once violence starts in a particular relationship, it tends to recur. In one study involving newlyweds, *76 percent* of the men who were physically aggressive when they were engaged perpetrated violence again in the first 30 months after the wedding—and much of their violence was severe (Lorber & O'Leary, 2004). Intimate violence is occasionally an isolated event—but more often it continues, at least sporadically, once it starts. This is especially true of the more chronic, even more dangerous form of IPV: intimate terrorism.

Intimate Terrorism

The I^3 model also helps to explain intimate terrorism (Finkel, 2014), but the mix of influences is different. Intimate terrorism seems to be rooted in influences that are more enduring than those that may trigger SCV, with people who terrorize their partners coming from two camps (Holtzworth-Munroe & Meehan, 2005). Some of them may resort to violence because they are rather clumsy and pathetic, and threats of harm are their wretched efforts to keep their partners from leaving. Others seem to be more malevolent; they are antisocial or narcissistic, and violence is just another tool with which to get what they want (Fowler & Westen, 2011).

Men who are intimate terrorists do not become brutal overnight. They have often witnessed violent conflict between their parents and have been sexually abused themselves (Afifi et al., 2009), growing up in homes that taught them traditional gender roles and rather hostile, misogynistic attitudes (Liebold & McConnell, 2004); they are much more likely than other men to think of women as adversaries to be used for one's satisfaction and pleasure. As a result, they engage in more surveillance and violence than most men even when a relationship has just begun (Williams & Frieze, 2005), and they may be generally aggressive, abusing their pets as well as their partners (Simmons & Lehmann, 2007). The signs that suggest that a man may be an abuser are often evident from the start.

A Point to Ponder

What will you do if your lover ever slaps, hits, or kicks you? Why?

This set of surly attitudes is often combined with feelings of inadequacy that make violence seem to be one of the terrorist's few resources of power (Bosson & Vandello, 2011). Terrorists often feel intellectually inferior to their partners (Moore et al., 2008) and have low self-esteem (Cowan & Mills, 2004), often because they are plagued by poverty; violence is much more common in homes with low annual incomes than in homes that are affluent (Kaukinen & Powers, 2015). Certainly, some spouse abusers are well-to-do people with plenty of self-respect who are just flat out mean; nevertheless, on average, intimate terrorists are not well off, and they appear to turn to coercive power because they control few other resources.

One of the most dreadful aspects of all this is the manner in which intimate aggression is transmitted from one generation to the next, with children who are raised in violent homes being more likely to be violent themselves (Smith-Marek et al., 2015). However, this cycle is not inevitable. Indeed, none of the contributing risk factors I've described here guarantee that violence will occur. Sons of the most violent American parents are 10 times more likely than the sons of nonviolent parents to beat their wives. Yet even in this extreme group, only 20 percent of those studied had committed severe acts of violence in the past 12 months; the other 80 percent had not recently engaged in any severe violence in their intimate relationships (Johnson, 2008). Thus, children from violent homes are more likely than others to misbehave, but many never do. Still, their increased risk for such behavior is disturbing; in the cycle of family violence, the evil that people do may, in fact, outlive them.

The Rationales of Violence

Overall, then, men who engage in intimate terrorism often subscribe to masculine codes that promote a man's authority over women, but many of them feel inadequate to the task; they "often feel, or fear, that they do not measure up to those codes. Attempting to shore up their masculine self-concept, they may try to control others, particularly those who are physically weaker than they are" (Wood, 2004, p. 558). Do such men even realize that they are being abusive, or do they consider their use of force to be customary treatment of women by men?

Julia Wood (2004) provided insight into the minds of such men when she interviewed 22 incarcerated men who had abused their female partners. All of the men felt that their behavior had been a legitimate response to the disrespect they had faced from their partners, and all mentioned their partners' provocation as the genesis of their abuse. They also felt that men were supposed to be dominant and superior to women and so were entitled to use violence to control and discipline them. On the other hand, most believed that they were not "real" wife abusers because they did not enjoy hurting women and they had limited their level of abuse, doing less harm than they could have. One man had stabbed his wife only once, and another had brutally beaten his wife but argued that he hadn't hit her as hard as he could. Perhaps as a result of these rationalizations, only about half of the men expressed regret and remorse about their actions. They understood that their actions were illegal, but they didn't necessarily believe that their actions were wrong.

What do women feel in response to such treatment? In a broad review of the intimate violence literature, Sally Lloyd and Beth Emery (2000) noted that women are ordinarily surprised when they encounter intimate aggression, and they often

---

Stalking
Unwanted Intrusion

Another undesirable behavior that occurs in some relationships is intrusive pursuit of someone—often an ex-partner—who does not wish to be pursued. Legal definitions of *stalking* in most of the United States involve repeated, malicious following and harassing of an unwilling target that may include (depending on the state) unwanted phone calls, letters, and text messages, surveillance, and other invasions of privacy that scare those who are pursued (Spitzberg, 2017).

All of the United States have laws against stalking, and with good reason: 16 percent of American women and 5 percent of men have been targets of a frightening stalker (Black et al., 2011). And studies that focus more broadly on unwanted communications and other intrusions converge on the estimate that almost two-fifths of all women, and one-seventh of all men, have experienced unwelcome harassment from a persistent pursuer. Most of the victims of stalking (75 percent) are women, and their stalkers are usually male (Spitzberg et al., 2010).

Why do people pursue others who want nothing to do with them? There are several reasons because there are various kinds of stalkers; as Finch (2001) colorfully put it, stalkers may be bad, mad, or sad. They may be motivated by desires for revenge or jealous possessiveness and may wish either to intimidate or to exert control over their targets (Davis et al., 2012). Indeed, about half of all stalkers are people who pursue an ex-partner after the

end of a romantic relationship, and they generally tend to be insecure, disagreeable, hostile men with low self-esteem who are very sensitive to rejection (De Smet et al., 2015). Alternatively, stalkers may be a little crazy (McEwan et al., 2009), being obsessed with someone who is a mere acquaintanace or whom they don't even know; stalkers are complete strangers to their targets about one-fifth of the time. Or, finally, they may be lonely and possessed of poor social skills and may be seeking to form a relationship in an inept and hopeless way (Duntley & Buss, 2012). One-quarter of all stalkers are neighbors, co-workers, or other acquaintances such as teachers, bank tellers, or car mechanics, and they often wrongly believe that their victims are interested in them in return, even when they're told to "get lost" (Sinclair & Frieze, 2005).

Stalking is no trivial matter. Escape can be difficult, especially if modern technology is involved; in one case, a stalker hid a global positioning unit in a victim's car so he always knew where she was (Southworth et al., 2007). Victims are also often harassed on Facebook (Dardis & Gidycz, 2017). Faced with such persecution, victims often become anxious and fearful, and, even worse, some form of physical violence occurs in about one-third of all cases. The police are consulted half of the time (Spitzberg et al., 2010). Thus, another dark cost of some relationships is that they don't fully end when one partner tries to exit them.

---

struggle to make sense of it. They are influenced by romantic norms that encourage them to "forgive and forget" and they labor under cultural norms that blame victims for their difficulties, so they "consistently ask themselves why they went out with the wrong kind of man, why they made him angry when they knew he had a violent temper, or why they were in the wrong place at the wrong time"

(Lloyd & Emery, 2000, p. 508). As a result of these influences, women feel betrayed, but they sometimes also blame themselves for their partners' aggression (Lim et al., 2015) and, due to shame, naïveté, or ignorance, they often remain silent about their plight. Moreover, if they are committed to their partnership, they may work to excuse their partner's behavior, minimizing its offensiveness (Gilbert & Gordon, 2017) and coming to see it as tolerable (Arriaga et al., 2016).

Overall, intimate terrorism exacts a fearsome toll on its victims. Physical injuries are bad enough, but victims may also suffer negative psychological consequences ranging from lowered self-esteem and mistrust of men to depression and post-traumatic stress disorder (Watkins et al., 2014). There are also substantial social costs; battered women are often absent from work, and some become homeless when violence forces them to flee their homes. And at its most basic level, intimate violence makes a partnership much less desirable than it otherwise might be. The end of the relationship may follow (Lawrence & Bradbury, 2007).

Why Don't They All Leave?

Indeed, intimate violence causes many people to leave their partners. One study (Campbell et al., 1994) that followed battered women over two-and-a-half years found that at the end of that period,

> 43 percent of the participants had left their original partners, either remaining unattached (20 percent) or entering new, nonabusive relationships (23 percent),

> 23 percent remained with their partners but had successfully ended the violence for at least a year, and

> 33 percent were still in an abusive relationship, either as victims (25 percent) or as both victims and perpetrators of violence (8 percent).

Thus, in this sample, only one-third of the women stayed in an abusive partnership for an extended period. Perseverance and determination are often required to escape an abusive relationship, but most people do, one way or the other. But why don't all victims run from their persecutors?

There's a simple answer to that question. They don't leave because, despite the abuse, they don't think they'll be better off if they go (Edwards et al., 2011).[8] They're often wrong in thinking so: People are usually happier when they get away from an abusive partner than they think they will be (Arriaga et al., 2013). But a decision to leave is complex. Some violent partners are sweet and loving part of the time, and intermittent violence may be one's only complaint about the relationship (Marshall et al., 2000). The costs of leaving may also seem too high; whatever investments one has made in the relationship will be lost, and one's alternatives may seem bleak (Young & Furman, 2013). One's economic status is crucial in this regard; the financial expense of departing one's home may be too momentous to overcome if one is unemployed. Finally, unfortunately, the fear of

---

[8] This is an excellent example of the impact of our judgments of the outcomes awaiting us outside our current relationships, which we labeled as our *comparison level for alternatives* back in chapter 6. I invite you to look back at pages 173–175 for more discussion of these ideas.

even greater violence can also prevent the victims of intimate terrorism from exiting the relationship. Some aggressive, controlling partners may react with extreme anger against their lovers if they try to leave (Tanha et al., 2010)—and the threat of such retaliation suggests that we should do all we can to assist and protect those who are trying to escape the coercive power of an abusive partner.

Finally, I need to acknowledge the unfortunate truth that some people don't leave because they don't want to go. Women who have high anxiety about abandonment are sometimes drawn to possessive, controlling men. A man's intrusive jealousy and surveillance reassures an anxious partner that he still cares, and, perversely, the more psychological abuse a woman has encountered in the past, the stronger her preference for abusive men (Zayas & Shoda, 2007). Moreover, such men prefer anxious women in return, probably because they're willing to tolerate the men's abuse. Thus, an arrangement in which a man is clearly controlling and dominant to a subservient partner, which would be intolerable to most of us, suits some couples. It's likely, however, that if the women involved in such relationships come to value themselves more, they will find their partners' harsh, inequitable behavior toward them to be less acceptable. Power is all about getting what one wants, but violence should not be part of that equation.

FOR YOUR CONSIDERATION

During their first year of marriage, Britni and Jonathon fell into a pattern in which he kept track of their debit account and paid all their bills each month. She was still a senior in college and didn't have a job, but he was working and earning just enough money for them to live on each month if they were careful. He took pride in his prudent management of money, but both of them were glad when she graduated and got a great job that actually paid her a little more than Jonathon's did.

He was surprised, however, when she announced that she wanted to maintain her own checking and savings accounts. She suggested that they each put half of their earnings into a joint account that would pay the bills and then keep the rest of their money for their own use. He was hurt that she did not want to merge their monies and join financial forces, and he was annoyed when he realized that, if they each kept half their money, she would have a lot more money than he would after a few years. But she argued that she wanted to be allowed to do what she wanted with her extra earnings, spending or investing them as she saw fit, and she thought that separate accounts would actually avoid disagreements and conflict.

Having read this chapter, what do you think the future holds for Britni and Jonathon? Why?

CHAPTER SUMMARY

Power is the ability to influence the behavior of others and to resist their influence on us.

Power and Interdependence

Sources of Power. From an interdependency perspective, power is based on the control of valuable resources that are desired by others. The *principle of lesser interest* states that the partner who is less interested in continuing a relationship has more power in it.

There are two different broad types of power, *fate control* and *behavior control*. In almost all relationships, both partners have some power over each other, with each being able to influence the other some of the time.

Types of Resources. There are six resources that provide people power. *Reward power* and *coercive power* refer to one's ability to bestow rewards and punishments, respectively, on someone else. *Legitimate power* exists when one partner has a reasonable right—by dint of authority, reciprocity, equity, or social responsibility—to tell the other what to do. A partner's love and affection provides the other *referent power*, knowledge and expertise creates *expert power*, and specific pieces of information lend one *informational power*.

Men, Women, and the Control of Resources. Men tend to control more resources than women do, in part because social norms maintain male dominance. The balance of power in close relationships is also affected by the universalistic or particularistic nature of the resources one controls.

The Process of Power. Powerful people interrupt others and tend to be unaware of others' feelings. The specific influence tactics people use may be direct or indirect and bilateral or unilateral.

The Outcome of Power. Spouses are much more likely to share decision-making than they used to be, and those who do enjoy happier marriages than those who have marriages in which one partner is dominant.

The Two Faces of Power. When they are committed to a relationship, many people use power benevolently, generously enhancing their partners' well-being as well as their own. Unfortunately, this does not always occur.

Violence in Relationships

Violence is behavior that is intended to hurt someone else.

The Prevalence of Violence. Violence among intimates is common around the world, and it occurs in one of every four couples in the United States.

Types of Couple Violence. There are three distinct types of violence in romantic couples: *situational couple violence, intimate terrorism,* and *violent resistance.* Men and women are equally likely to engage in situational couple violence, but a huge majority of those who employ intimate terrorism are men.

Gender Differences in Intimate Violence. Women are violent as often as men, but men are more likely to inflict injury.

Correlates of Violence. Situational couple violence springs from impelling and inhibiting influences that are distal, dispositional, relational, or situational. Intimate terrorism is committed by men who are hostile toward women and who are plagued by feelings of inadequacy.

The Rationales of Violence. Wife-abusing men feel superior to women and believe that their aggression is a legitimate response to their wives' disrespect. Women sometimes blame themselves for their abuse.

Why Don't They All Leave? Most victims of abuse leave their relationships, but they stay when they don't believe they'll be better off if they go. A few don't leave because they don't want to go.

CHAPTER 13

The Dissolution and Loss of Relationships

THE CHANGING RATE OF DIVORCE ◆ THE PREDICTORS OF
DIVORCE ◆ BREAKING UP ◆ THE AFTERMATH OF BREAKUPS
◆ FOR YOUR CONSIDERATION ◆ CHAPTER SUMMARY

Sometimes the stresses and strains two partners experience catch up with them. Perhaps their conflict is too constant and too intense. Perhaps their partnership is inequitable, with one of them exploiting the other. Perhaps their passion has waned, and new attractions are distracting them. Or perhaps they are merely contented with each other, instead of delighted, so they are disappointed that the "magic" has died.

There are myriad reasons why relationships may fail, and the deterioration of any particular partnership may involve events and processes that are unique to that couple. On the other hand, there are also personal and cultural influences that can have generic, widespread effects on the stability of intimate relationships, and relationship scientists have been identifying and studying them for years. In this chapter, we'll consider the correlates and consequences of the decline and fall of satisfaction and intimacy. I'll have a lot to say about divorce because a decision to end a marriage is often more deliberate and weighty, and the consequences more complicated, than those that emerge from less formal partnerships. There's also been more research on divorce than on non-marital breakups. Nevertheless, the dissolution of any intimate relationship—such as a cohabiting partnership, dating relationship, or friendship—can be momentous, so we'll examine how people adjust to the end of those partnerships, too. Let's start with a reminder that the cultural landscape we face today is quite different from the one our grandparents knew.

THE CHANGING RATE OF DIVORCE

The Prevalence of Divorce

As you recall, current divorce rates are much higher than they were when your grandparents married. In the United States, there are currently half as many divorces as marriages each year (Anderson, 2016a), so the chance that a recent marriage will ultimately end in separation or divorce still hovers around 50 percent. This is remarkable because it suggests that despite all the good intentions and warm feelings with which people marry, the chances that they will succeed in living out their lives together are about the same as the chance of getting "heads" when you flip a coin.

Indeed, a typical American marriage won't last nearly as long as people think it will. Only about two-thirds (64 percent) of married couples stay together for 10 years, and fewer than half reach their twenty-first wedding anniversary, so the average length of a marriage in the United States is just over 18 years (Elliott & Simmons, 2011). That figure counts all marriages, including those that end with the death of a spouse, but the leading cause of death of a marriage in its first 20 years is, of course, divorce. Lots of people don't turn 30 without having been divorced; the median age at which men encounter their (first) divorce is 31.8, and for women, it's 29.4 (Cohn, 2010).

Two other patterns that result, in part, from the high divorce rate are noteworthy. First, only about *half* (49 percent) of the adult U.S. population is presently married (Perelli-Harris & Lyons-Amos, 2015). That's an all-time low. Second, 26 percent of American children—1 out of every 4 people under the age of 18—now live in single-parent homes, most of them run by their mothers (Cohn & Caumont, 2016). That rate is 3 times higher than it was in 1965.

Any way you look at it, divorce is now commonplace in America. Even our grandparents divorce more often than they used to; people over 50 are less likely to divorce than younger adults are, but their rate of divorce has *doubled* over the last 25 years (Stepler, 2017). Other countries have also seen big increases in their divorce rates in recent decades, but the United States has had the dubious distinction of being one of the leaders of the pack. The divorce rate in the United States is noticeably higher than in nearly all of Europe, Canada, or Japan (OECD, 2016). Marriages are less likely to end than other romantic relationships are, but they're also less likely to last than they used to be.

Why Has the Divorce Rate Increased?

There are no certain reasons why the second half of the twentieth century saw such a huge increase in U.S. rates of divorce. But there are several possibilities, and all of them may (or may not) be contributing influences.

One possibility is that we hold different, more demanding expectations for marriage than people used to. Our great-grandparents generally believed that if you wanted to live with a romantic partner, if you wanted to have children, and if you wanted to pay the bills and live well, you had to get married. Nowadays, however, cohabitation is widespread, there are lots of single parents, and most women have entered the workforce. As a result, marriage is no longer the practical necessity it used to be. Instead, in the opinion of some observers, people are more likely than ever before to pursue marriage as a path to personal fulfillment (Finkel et al., 2015a). Marriage is supposed to be play, not work; it's supposed to be exciting, not routine, and passionate, not warm (Amato, 2009). Thus, our expectations for marriage may be too high. A happy, warm, rewarding partnership may seem insufficient if it is measured against over-glorified and unrealistic expectations.

For instance, decades ago, Slater (1968, p. 99) warned:

Spouses are now asked to be lovers, friends, and mutual therapists in a society which is forcing the marriage bond to become the closest, deepest, most important and most enduring relationship of one's life. Paradoxically, then, it is increasingly likely to fall short of the emotional demands placed upon it and be dissolved.

We marry for love and passion and think that they won't change, and we expect our spouses to be soulmates who will never disappoint us. But these are lofty, perhaps impossibly high standards, and indeed, recent cultural history suggests that "no sooner had the ideal of the love match and lifelong intimacy taken hold than people began to demand the right to divorce" (Coontz, 2005, p. 8).

People may simply be expecting too much of marriage. The percentage of U.S. spouses who report that their marriages are "very happy" is lower now than it was 25 years ago (Wilcox & Marquardt, 2010), and the numbers of conflicts and problems that spouses report are higher (Hostetler et al., 2012). On the whole, the average perceived quality of American marriages has declined since 1970.

But the broader culture has changed, too, and several societal influences may be affecting not only the expectations with which we begin our marriages but also the situations we encounter once we are wed. For instance, most women in the United States now work outside the home, and their entry into the workforce has had several effects. First, spouses report more conflict between work and family than they used to, and the more hours a wife works during the week, the lower the quality of her marriage tends to be (Hostetler et al., 2012). Car repairs, child care, and the scheduling and cooking of meals (to name just a few examples) are more problematic when both spouses are employed, and the amount of time spouses spend together tends to decline. Both spouses are also affected by their problems at work, so that decreases in job satisfaction are associated with increases in marital discord (Amato et al., 2007). Participation in the labor force also increases spouses' access to interesting, desirable, alternative partners, and divorce is more frequent when women work in occupations that surround them with men (McKinnish, 2007).

Furthermore, women earn more money than they used to, and, around the world, divorce rates are higher when women are financially independent of men (Barber, 2003). People who are able to support themselves have more freedom to choose divorce when a marriage deteriorates, and in the United States there is a straightforward, positive correlation between a woman's income and her odds of divorce: The more money she makes, the more likely it is that she will someday be divorced (Mundy, 2012). But don't think that your marriage will be more stable if you just do without money; poverty has even more impact on marital quality. In general, couples with money troubles are less content with their marriages than are those who are better off (Barton & Bryant, 2016); in particular, couples with rather low incomes (under $25,000 per year) are twice as likely to divorce as are couples with higher incomes (over $50,000 per year) (Wilcox & Marquardt, 2010). Having money may make it easier to divorce, but being poor can cause stress that undermines a marriage, too.

Overall, then, women's increased participation in the labor force has plausibly increased conflict at home, made alluring, new romantic partners more available, and decreased wives' economic dependence on their husbands. Perhaps for all of these reasons, the trend is clear: As the proportion of American women employed outside the home increased during the twentieth century, so, too, did the divorce rate (Fitch & Ruggles, 2000).[1]

Our gender roles, the behaviors we expect from men and women, are changing, too. Women are gradually becoming more assertive and self-reliant (Donnelly & Twenge, 2017), and the partners in many marriages are dividing household responsibilities more equitably (Amato et al., 2007). Over the last 25 years, less traditional gender roles and increases in the equality of family decision-making have been associated with higher marital quality for both husbands and wives (Worley & Samp, 2016b). However, the new division of household labor has had different effects on men than on women; husbands are less happy now that they're doing more housework, but their wives are much more content (see Figure 13.1).

By some accounts, Western culture is also becoming more individualistic, with people being less connected to the others around them than they used to be (Amato, 2009). Indeed, most of us are less tied to our communities than our grandparents were (Ren, 2011). We're less likely to live near our extended families and less likely to know our neighbors; we participate in fewer clubs and social organizations, entertain at home less frequently, and move more often. As a result, we receive less social support and companionship from friends and acquaintances than our grandparents did (Talhelm & Oishi, 2014), and we rely on our spouses for more (Campbell et al., 2012), and this may affect divorce rates in two different ways. First, as I've already noted, we ask more of our spouses than ever before. We expect them to fulfill a wider variety of interpersonal needs, and that increases the probability that they will disappoint us in some manner. In addition, people who are less connected to their communities are less affected by community norms that might discourage them from divorcing. And as it turns out, people who move often from place to place really are more willing to cut ties with their friends and lovers (Gillath & Keefer, 2016) and are more prone to divorce (Magdol & Bessel, 2003) than are those who stay in one place and put down roots.

Our shared perceptions of divorce are also less negative than they used to be. In many circles, a divorce used to be considered a shameful failure, and the event itself was often a messy, lurid, embarrassing spectacle in which blame had to be assigned to someone. The advent of no-fault divorce laws in the United States

---

[1] As I describe these various patterns, do remember, please, that all of these links between social changes and divorce rates are *correlations* that allow diverse possibilities to exist. A connection between women's working and divorce does not necessarily mean that employment undermines women's commitment to their marriages. To the contrary, women are more likely to seek employment when there is preexisting discord and strife in their marriages, so it is just as likely that marital dissatisfaction causes women to find work as it is that women's work causes marital dissatisfaction (Rogers, 1999). Keep an open mind as you consider the implications of societal change.

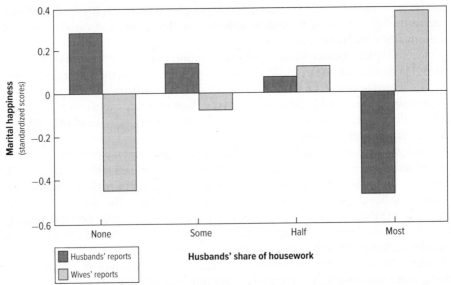

Source: *Data from Amato, P. R., Booth, A., Johnson, D. R., & Rogers, S. J.* Alone together: How marriage in America is changing. *Cambridge, MA: Harvard University Press, 2007.*

FIGURE 13.1. **Happiness and housework.**
The graph shows the average levels of marital happiness experienced by wives and husbands as the men do larger proportions of the household chores. Husbands grow less content, but their wives become more satisfied as the husbands do more housework. Two other facts are interesting: Somebody is always *really* unhappy when men do either most of the housework or none at all, and the only time both partners have above average happiness is when the housework is split 50–50. Is there news you can use here?

during the 1970s made a divorce much easier to obtain; for the first time in most jurisdictions, once they had agreed on the division of property and childcare, spouses merely had to certify that they faced "irreconcilable differences," and their marriage was dissolved. No-fault laws helped make the procedure more socially acceptable (Wolfers, 2006). On average, we feel that a divorce is a more reasonable and more desirable response to a bad marriage than our parents did, and more favorable attitudes toward divorce appear to reduce the quality of our marriages as time goes by (Amato & Rogers, 1999). We may be less likely to work hard to rescue a faltering relationship when divorce seems an expedient alternative (Whitton et al., 2013).

Most couples also cohabit before they marry these days, and as we saw in chapter 1, people who cohabit encounter an increased risk of divorce later on. Despite the widespread belief that cohabitation is a valuable trial run that allows people to avoid later problems, cohabitation is *positively* associated with the probability of divorce (Jose et al., 2010). The good news is that couples who start living together after they become engaged to marry and who cohabit for a shorter, rather than longer, period of time do not divorce much more frequently than do those who marry without living together (Willoughby & Belt, 2016). Brief cohabitation that is limited to one's fiancé doesn't seem to put a subsequent marriage at much risk. On the other hand, people who cohabit before they become engaged (or who ever cohabit with more than one partner) are more likely to later divorce (Tach & Halpern-Meekin, 2012), probably because cohabitation changes their beliefs and expectations about marriage. Casual cohabitation seems to lead to (a) less respect for the institution of marriage, (b) less favorable expectations about the outcomes of marriage, and (c) increased willingness to divorce (Rhoades et al., 2009), and all of these make divorce more likely.

In addition, as more parents divorce, more children witness family conflict and grow up in broken homes. Common sense may suggest that youngsters who suffer family disruption might be especially determined to avoid making the same mistakes, but, in reality, divorce is passed down from one generation to the next: Children who experience the divorce of their parents are more likely to be divorced themselves when they become adults (Amato & Patterson, 2017). Various processes may underlie this pattern. For one thing, children from divorced homes have less favorable views of marriage, and they report less trust in their partners when they begin their own romantic relationships; thus, compared to children from intact homes, they have less faith that their marriages will last (Lachance-Grzela & Bouchard, 2016). Furthermore, to some degree, children learn how to behave in intimate relationships from the lessons provided by their parents, and those who remember a childhood home full of strife and discord tend to have more acrimonious marriages of poorer quality themselves (Dennison et al., 2014). Thus, as divorce becomes more commonplace, more children become susceptible to divorce later on.

Finally, because divorce is now so commonplace, more of us have friends who will someday divorce—and remarkably, that will mean that *we* face an increased risk of divorcing, too. For 70 years, an extraordinary investigation, the Framingham Heart Study, has been tracking the health of more than 10,000 individuals—two generations of people—in a large town in Massachusetts. Compared to the average participant in the study, those who had a friend or family member (that is, a parent, child, or sibling) who divorced were 75 percent more likely—that's *much* more likely—to divorce as well. If a friend of a friend or relative divorced, people were 33 percent more likely to divorce (McDermott et al., 2013). (And that's where the effect stopped. If someone with three degrees of separation—for instance, the friend of a friend of a friend—divorced, people were at no greater risk of themselves also divorcing.) This provocative pattern may spring from several sources—and it makes a fine point to ponder—but the end result is clear: We're more likely to divorce when others in our social network do (Hogerbrugge et al., 2012).

A Point to Ponder

People are more likely to divorce when others in their close social network do. Why?

So, why has the divorce rate increased? There are reasons to believe that, compared to our grandparents' day:

- We expect more out of marriage, holding it to higher standards.
- Working women have more financial freedom and better access to attractive alternatives, and they experience corrosive conflict between work and family.

- Creeping individualism and social mobility leave us less tied to, and less affected by, community norms that might discourage divorce.
- New laws have made divorce more socially acceptable and easier to obtain.
- Casual cohabitation weakens commitment to marriage.
- Children of divorce are more likely to divorce when they become adults.
- More of us have friends who are divorced.

All of these possible influences are merely correlated with the increasing prevalence of divorce in the United States, so they all may be symptoms rather than causes of the social changes that have promoted divorce. It's a rather long list of possibilities, however, and it provides another good example of the manner in which cultural influences shape intimate relationships. Arguably, our culture supports lasting marriages less effectively than it did 40 or 50 years ago. But even with such changes, at least half of the marriages that begin this year will not end in divorce. (Not all of them will be happy, but at least they won't end in divorce.) What individual and relational characteristics predict who will and who will not ultimately separate? Let's turn to those next.

THE PREDICTORS OF DIVORCE

Whatever the cultural context, some marriages succeed and others fail, and as you'd expect, the differences between marital winners and losers have long been of interest to relationship scientists. Diverse models that explicate some of the sources of divorce have been proposed, and impressive studies have now tracked some marriages for decades. In this section, we'll inspect both theories and research results that identify some of the predictors of divorce.

Levinger's Barrier Model

George Levinger (1976), a proponent of interdependence theory, used concepts like those I described in chapter 6 in identifying three elements that influence the breakup of relationships. The first of these is *attraction*. For Levinger, attraction is enhanced by the rewards a relationship offers (such as enjoyable companionship, sexual fulfillment, security, and social status), and it is diminished by its costs (such as irritating incompatibility and the investment of time and energy). The second key influence on breakups is the *alternatives* one possesses. The most obvious of these are other partners, but any alternative to a current relationship, such as being single or achieving occupational success, may lure someone away from an existing partnership. Finally, there are the *barriers* around the relationship that make it hard to leave; these include the legal and social pressures to remain married, religious and moral constraints, and the financial costs of obtaining a divorce and maintaining two households.

A major contribution of Levinger's approach was to highlight the fact that unhappy partners who would like to break up may stay together because it would cost them too much to leave. He also persuasively argued that many barriers to divorce are psychological rather than material; distressed spouses may certainly stay married because they do not have enough money to divorce, but they may also stay together (even when they have sufficient resources to leave) because of the guilt or embarrassment they would feel—or cause others, especially their children (Poortman & Seltzer, 2007)—if they divorced.

Indeed, spouses report that there are several meaningful costs that would deter them from seeking a divorce (Previti & Amato, 2003). A survey of people married for 12 years demonstrated that the worry that their children would suffer, the threat of losing their children, religious norms, dependence on their spouses, and the fear of financial ruin were all perceived to be influential barriers that discouraged divorce (Knoester & Booth, 2000). However, over that 12-year span, once other risk factors such as low education and parental divorce were taken into account, only two of those perceived barriers, dependence on one's spouse and religious beliefs, actually distinguished couples who divorced from those who did not. And if people had grown genuinely dissatisfied with their marriages, even those two barriers seemed insignificant: Once they wanted out of their marriages, there was no stopping them (Knoester & Booth, 2000).

Thus, people are usually aware of several obstacles that they would have to overcome in order to divorce, but once a marriage is on the rocks, those barriers may not keep people from leaving. Levinger's model helpfully reminds us of deterrents to divorce that run through people's minds, but it may not fully recognize how ineffective those deterrents may become once marital misery sets in.

Karney and Bradbury's Vulnerability-Stress-Adaptation Model

Benjamin Karney and Thomas Bradbury (1995) developed a general model of marital instability that highlights another three influences that can contribute to divorce. According to this view, some people enter marriage with *enduring vulnerabilities* that increase their risk of divorce. Such vulnerabilities might include adverse experiences in one's family of origin, poor education, maladaptive personality traits, bad social skills, or dysfunctional attitudes toward marriage. None of these characteristics makes divorce inevitable, but all of them can shape the circumstances a couple encounters, and all of them influence the *adaptive processes* with which people respond to stress (e.g., Maisel & Karney, 2012). If a couple gets lucky and encounters only infrequent and mild difficulties, even those with poor coping and communication skills may live happily ever after.

However, almost every marriage must face occasional *stressful events* that require the partners to provide support to one another and to adjust to new circumstances. Some stressors (such as a period of unemployment or a major illness) befall some marriages and not others, whereas other stressors (such as pregnancy, childbirth, and parenting) are commonplace. The little ups and downs of daily life can combine to be surprisingly stressful, too (Afifi et al., 2016). When stressful events occur, a couple must cope and adapt, but, depending on their vulnerabilities, some people are better able to do that than are others (Danner-Vlaardingerbroek et al., 2016). Failure to cope successfully can make the stresses worse, and if poor coping causes marital quality to decline, a couple's coping may be further impaired

(Karney & Neff, 2013). And ultimately, extended periods of dissatisfaction are presumed to lead to marital instability and divorce.

Take a look at Figure 13.2, and start tracing the paths from the bottom. Our inborn traits and past experiences equip all of us with strengths and weaknesses as relationship partners, and some of the weaknesses are "vulnerabilities" that undermine our abilities to cope effectively with stress and change (Solomon & Jackson, 2014). Some vulnerabilities also make life more stressful, increasing the difficulties with which we have to deal. But no matter who we are, stress happens. In addition to the intermittent conflicts that occur at home, any frustrations and difficulties we experience individually at work or school can cause **stress spill-over** in which we bring surly moods home and interact irascibly with our inno-cent partners (Sears et al., 2016). Then, our coping skills and other "adaptive processes" determine whether our stress grows or is managed and reduced. And ultimately, each partner's ability to adapt successfully influences the quality of their marriage at the same time that marital quality is influencing the partners' abilities to adapt.

There are feedback loops and overlapping influences in the vulnerability-stress-adaptation model, and when it comes to stress, what doesn't kill us may make us stronger. Couples with good communication skills who have already encountered moderate stress in their relationships are likely to be more resilient and to adjust better to new stressors—when they become parents, for instance, a change that's always stressful—than other couples who have similar skills but

FIGURE 13.2. **The Vulnerability-Stress-Adaptation Model of marriage.**
The model posits that partners bring vulnerabilities with them when they enter a mar-riage, and those vulnerabilities interact with both the stresses they encounter and their coping skills to determine how well their marriages function.

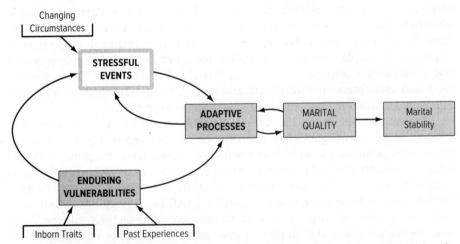

Source: Adapted from Karney, B. R., & Bradbury, T. N. "The longitudinal course of marital quality and stability: A review of theory, methods, and research," Psychological Bulletin, 118, 1995, 3–34.

who haven't yet been tested by having to deal with stress (Neff & Broady, 2011). Successfully coping with our difficulties can improve our abilities to adapt to new nuisances. But the bottom line is that the quality of our marriages emerges from the interplay of who we are, the circumstances we encounter, and the manner in which we respond to those circumstances, and, to some degree, these three important influences affect each other. It's possible for the roots of divorce to begin in childhood in an insecure attachment style or the lessons learned in a home filled with conflict. But if life treats us well, or we work hard and well with our spouses to overcome life's difficulties (or perhaps just take a good college course on close relationships!), divorce need not occur.

Results from the PAIR Project

For almost 30 years, Ted Huston (2009) and his colleagues (Wilson & Huston, 2013) kept track of 168 couples who married in 1981. The project focused on the manner in which spouses adapted to their lives together (or failed to do so) and was known as the Processes of Adaptation in Intimate Relationships (or PAIR) Project. There's enormous value in long-lasting studies like this, but their results can be a little sobering. Indeed, in the PAIR Project, after only 13 years, 35 percent of the couples had divorced and another 20 percent weren't happy; only 45 percent of the couples could be said to be happily married, and even they were less satisfied and less loving than they had been when they wed. And these, I should remind you, are typical results. Take a look back at Figure 6.7 on p. 189: Marital satisfaction routinely declines in most couples as time goes by.

Why? Huston and his colleagues examined three different explanations for why marriages go awry. One possibility is that spouses who are destined to be discontent begin their marriages being less in love and more at odds with each other than are those whose marriages ultimately succeed. This possibility, the *enduring dynamics* model, suggests that spouses bring to their marriages problems, incompatibilities, and enduring vulnerabilities that surface during their courtship; indeed, the partners may be well aware of these frustrations and shortcomings before they even wed (Lavner et al., 2014). According to this model, then, marriages that are headed for divorce are weaker than others from the very beginning (James, 2015).

In contrast, a second possibility known as the *emergent distress* model suggests that the problematic behavior that ultimately destroys a couple begins after they marry. As time goes by, some couples fall into a rut of increasing conflict and negativity that did not exist when the marriage began. Thus, unlike the enduring dynamics model, the emergent distress perspective suggests that, when they begin, there is no discernible difference between marriages that will succeed and those that will fail; the difficulties that ruin some marriages usually develop later (Williamson et al., 2016).

Finally, a third possibility is the *disillusionment* model. This approach suggests that couples typically begin their marriages with rosy, romanticized views of their relationship that are unrealistically positive. Then, as time goes by and the spouses stop working as hard to be adorable and charming to each other, reality slowly erodes these pleasant fictions. But there may be more disillusionment in some couples than in others (Niehuis et al., 2016); romance may fade and some disappointment may occur in any marriage as people realize that their partnership is less wonderful than it originally seemed, but in some couples, "the ink is barely dry on the marriage license when doubts and disillusionment about marriage and the partner can begin to set in" (Kayser & Rao, 2006, p. 206).

The particulars of the three models are meaningful because each suggests a different way to improve marriages and to reduce the risk of divorce. According to the enduring dynamics model, rocky courtships lead to bad marriages, and premarital interventions that keep ambivalent couples from ever marrying should prevent many subsequent divorces. By comparison, the emergent distress model argues that couples need to guard against slow slides into disagreeableness and negativity, and interventions that encourage spouses to remain cheerful, generous, attentive, and kind should keep divorce from their door. And finally, the disillusionment model suggests that dispassionate and accurate perceptions of one's lover and one's relationship that preclude subsequent disappointment and disenchantment should also prevent divorce.

All of these are reasonable possibilities, but Huston and his colleagues found that only two of the three seemed to be at work in the marriages they followed. (Let's pause a moment. Which two models do you think were the winners?) First, consistent with the enduring dynamics model, the PAIR Project determined that, compared to couples who were still happy after several years, spouses who were unhappy had been less loving and affectionate and more ambivalent and negative toward each other when their marriages began. Couples who were destined to be distressed were less generous and less tender and more uncertain and more temperamental from the very start. Thus, any doubts or difficulties that people faced when they were engaged did not disappear once they were married. To the contrary, any indecision or incompatibilities were simply imported into their marital relationship, so that they remained less content over the years that followed.

So, the enduring dynamics model predicted how happy marriages would be. However, the best predictor of which couples would actually divorce was the disillusionment model. The drop in marital satisfaction during the first years of marriage was sharper and more pronounced in some couples than in others, and they were the spouses who were most at risk for divorce. They did not necessarily grow cantankerous or spiteful as the emergent distress model would expect; instead, they simply experienced the greatest change in their romantic feelings for each other. Their love faded more, and more rapidly, than did the romances of other couples.

In addition, a striking feature of the disillusionment that Huston and his colleagues observed was that many of the couples who were destined to divorce were *more* affectionate than most when their marriages began, and it took some time for their disappointment to develop. Couples whose marriages were short-lived—who were divorced within 6 (or fewer) years—usually began their marriages with less love and more ambivalence than did couples whose marriages would succeed. (Thus, you can see why, when disillusionment set in, they were divorced relatively quickly.) However, couples who ultimately divorced after longer periods—after 7 or more years of marriage—were especially affectionate and romantic when their marriages began. They were more adoring than other couples, on average, and thus had further to fall (and, perhaps, were more surprised than most) when the usual drop in affectionate behavior following the honeymoon began. They ended up no less sentimental toward each other than other couples, but they experienced the biggest changes—that is, the steepest declines—in romantic behavior, and those changes predicted a delayed divorce.

Overall, then, the PAIR Project made two conclusions seem sound. First, the size and speed of changes in romance best predict which couples will divorce, and second, the problems couples bring to their marriage determine how quickly a divorce will occur. Similar results have been obtained from other studies (e.g., Lavner et al., 2014; Niehuis et al., 2015; Ogolsky et al., 2016), so we can safely conclude that both the *level* of satisfaction a couple experiences and the *change* in that satisfaction over time are key players in relational outcomes. Importantly, couples that are doomed to divorce do not always turn surly and spiteful, but they do tend to lose the joy they once experienced (Niehuis et al., 2016).[2]

Results from the Early Years of Marriage Project

Another impressive long-term study, the Early Years of Marriage (EYM) Project directed by Terri Orbuch, has been following 174 white couples and 199 black couples in and around Detroit, Michigan, since they married in 1986 (Fiori et al., 2017). The EYM researchers have been particularly interested in the manner in which the social conditions that couples encounter may affect marital outcomes. And some sociological variables are important. In 2002, 16 years after the project began, 46 percent of the couples had already divorced, but the couples' race seemed to make a big difference: Just over a third (36 percent) of the white couples had divorced, but more than half (55 percent) of the black couples had dissolved their marriages.

Why were black couples more prone to divorce? There could be several reasons. On average, the black couples had cohabited for a longer period and were more likely to have had children before getting married. They also had lower incomes and were more likely to come from broken homes, and all of these influences are positively correlated with one's risk of divorce (Wilcox & Marquardt, 2010). Overall, the EYM project is demonstrating, as other studies have (James, 2015), that the social context in which couples conduct their relationships may have substantial effects on the outcomes they encounter. Economic hardship can put any couple at risk for divorce no matter how much they respect and value marriage (Barton & Bryant, 2016).

---

[2] I encourage you to take a moment to consider how this pattern maps onto people's approach and avoidance motivations, which we encountered on p. 184 back in chapter 6. Evidently, some marriages fail not because they are aversive and unpleasant but because they are not pleasant and delightful enough.

People's Personal Perceptions of Their Problems

The various models and data we have encountered suggest that there are three general types of influences on our marital outcomes (Levinger & Levinger, 2003). At the broadest level are cultural norms and other variables that set the national stage for marriage. No-fault divorce laws and discrimination that constrains economic opportunity are examples of the ways in which the *cultural context* may either support or undermine marital success.

More idiosyncratic are our *personal contexts,* the social networks of family and friends and the physical neighborhoods we inhabit. For instance, as I noted earlier, women who work with a wide variety of interesting male colleagues are more prone to divorce than are women who do not work outside their homes (McKinnish, 2007). Finally, there is a *relational context* that describes the intimate environment couples create through their own perceptions of, and interactions with, each other. The individual characteristics that lead us to react to our partners with either chronic good humor or pessimistic caution are some of the building blocks of the particular atmosphere that pervades a partnership.

I mention these three levels of analysis because people tend to focus on only one of them when they generate explanations for their marital problems. Yet another impressive long-term study, the Marital Instability Over the Life Course project conducted by Alan Booth and his colleagues, conducted phone interviews with a random sample of 1,078 Americans every few years from 1980 to 2000. When those who divorced were asked what caused their divorces, the most frequently reported reasons all involved some characteristic of their marital relationships, as Table 13.1 shows. Women complained of infidelity,

TABLE 13.1.   "What Caused Your Divorce?"

Reason	Total Cases (%)	Described by: Men (%)	Women (%)
Infidelity	22	16	25
Incompatibility	19	19	19
Drinking or substance use	11	5	14
Grew apart	10	9	10
Personality problems	9	10	8
Communication difficulties	9	13	6
Physical or mental abuse	6	0	9
Love was lost	4	7	3
Don't know	3	9	0

Source: Adapted from Amato, P. R., & Previti, D. "People's reasons for divorcing: Gender, social class, the life course, and adjustment," Journal of Family Issues, 24, 2003, 602–626.

These values reflect the responses of 208 members of a random sample of spouses in the United States who were asked what had caused their divorces. Other causes such as financial problems or interference from family were mentioned on occasion, but the nine most frequent reasons are listed here.

substance use, or abuse more often than men, whereas men were more likely to complain of poor communication or to announce that they did not know what had gone wrong. Ex-wives also had more complaints than ex-husbands did, on average, but very few accounts from either sex acknowledged the possible influences of the cultural or personal contexts in which they conducted their relationships.

Nevertheless, those broader contexts may have been important. The higher a couple's income had been, the less often abuse was mentioned as a cause of divorce and the more often personality clashes were mentioned. The more education the respondents had, the more often they complained of incompatibility with their ex-spouses. Thus, a couple's socioeconomic status (which includes education and income) helped to predict the problems they would encounter. The age at which they married mattered, too; people who married at younger ages were more likely to report that they had grown apart or that alcohol and drug use had been a problem.

When they grow discontent, people always complain about the particulars of their partnerships (and think that their partners are more to blame than they are; Scott et al., 2013). But broader influences are often important, too. The various factors that shape a couple's likelihood of divorce include not only the day-to-day interactions that may cause them pleasure or pain; the surrounding circumstances and culture can either promote or undermine their marriage, as well (Williamson et al., 2013).

Specific Predictors of Divorce

We've encountered a variety of variables that may put people at risk for divorce, and I'm about to list them and several more in the big table that begins on the next page. However, let me offer this caveat: Statements of general trends sometimes gloss over important qualifications. No one generalization will apply to every marriage, predictors may hold for some groups or stages of marriage but not others, and the apparent influence of a particular variable may reflect the other factors to which it was compared in a given study. For instance, some classic correlates of divorce (such as low income) may be more influential in young marriages than in older marriages that have already stood the test of time (Booth et al., 1986). To some degree, marriages that survive the initial effects of certain stressors may be less susceptible to their influences many years later. It may also be important to recognize that when several risks are combined, each may have stronger effects than it would have had by itself; being poor *and* poorly educated, for instance, can be much worse than facing either difficulty by itself (Cutrona et al., 2011). Please keep these nuances in mind while inspecting Table 13.2, which presents a summary of key predictors of marital stability identified by modern research. These aren't passing influences; the effects of most of them haven't changed much for several decades (Amato, 2010). They have similar effects on the satisfaction and stability gays and lesbians experience in their relationships, as well (Khaddouma et al., 2015).

TABLE 13.2.　Predictors of Divorce: A Synthesis of the Literature

Predictor	Findings
Socioeconomic status	People with low-status occupations, less education, and lower incomes are more likely to divorce than are those with higher socioeconomic status. In particular, women with good educations are much less likely to divorce than women with poor educations are (Wilcox & Marquardt, 2010).
Race	Due to their greater exposure to other risk factors such as low income, premarital birth, parental divorce, and cohabitation—and despite their greater respect for marriage (Trail & Karney, 2012)—black Americans are more likely to divorce than white Americans are (Johnson, 2012).
Sex ratios	Around the world, divorce rates are higher when women outnumber men and the sex ratio is low (Barber, 2003).
Social mobility	People who move often from place to place are more prone to divorce than are those who stay in one place and put down roots (Magdol & Bessel, 2003).
No-fault legislation	Laws that make a divorce easier to obtain make divorce more likely (Wolfers, 2006).
Working women	Divorce rates increase when higher proportions of women enter the workforce (Fitch & Ruggles, 2000).
Age at marriage	People who marry as teenagers are more likely to divorce than are those who marry after age 25 (Glenn et al., 2010).
Prior marriage	Second marriages are more likely to end in divorce than first marriages are (Jensen et al., 2017).
Parental divorce	Parents who divorce increase the chances that their children will divorce. However, as divorce becomes commonplace, this effect is declining (Amato & Patterson, 2017).
Religion	Attendance at religious services is correlated with a lower risk of divorce, especially when both spouses attend regularly (Vaaler et al., 2009).
Teenage sex	First intercourse that is unwanted or that occurs before the age of 16 is associated with an increased risk of divorce (Paik, 2011).
Premarital cohabitation	Premarital cohabitation is associated with higher divorce rates, but the added risk isn't great if the couple is engaged to be married when cohabitation begins (Willoughby & Belt, 2016).
Premarital ambivalence	Mixed feelings and uncertainty during courtship about where the relationship is heading are associated with higher rates of divorce (Wilson & Huston, 2013).
Premarital birth	Having a baby before marriage is associated with a higher risk of divorce for both the mother and the father (Heaton, 2002).
Children	Spouses who have no children are more likely to divorce, but the risk-reducing effect of children is most noticeable when the children are very young (Lyngstad & Jalovaara, 2010).
Stepchildren	Women who bring children with them into a second marriage are more likely to divorce, but that's not true of men; evidently, women may find it easier to be a stepparent than men do (Teachman, 2008).
Similarity	Spouses with lots in common are less likely to divorce (Clarkwest, 2007).

Personality attributes	The higher one's neuroticism, the more likely one is to divorce (Solomon & Jackson, 2014).
Attachment styles	People who are high in avoidance of intimacy are more likely to divorce (Ceglian & Gardner, 1999).
Genetics	A person who has an identical twin who gets divorced is about 5 times more likely to divorce than he or she would have been if the twin had not divorced, even if the two twins were separated at birth and have never met (Lykken, 2002).
Stress hormones	During their first year of marriage, couples who are destined to divorce have chronically higher amounts of the stress hormones epinephrine and norepinephrine in their blood than do couples who will not be divorced 10 years later (Kiecolt-Glaser et al., 2003).
Stressful life events	The occurrence of stressful life events (other than parenthood) increases the likelihood of divorce (Randall & Bodenmann, 2009). As one example, post-traumatic stress disorder that results from exposure to combat increases one's risk of divorce (Foran et al., 2013).
Time together	Couples who share more time together are less likely to divorce (Poortman, 2005).
Alcohol and drug abuse	Drug dependency increases the likelihood of divorce (Amato & Previti, 2003).
Infidelity	Cheating by one's spouse makes divorce more likely, but one's own infidelity does not—as long as one doesn't get caught (Frisco et al., 2017).
Attitudes toward marriage	People who are pessimistic about marriage are more likely to divorce (Segrin et al., 2005). Favorable attitudes about divorce make divorce more likely, too (Hatemi et al., 2015).
Marital interactions	Positive interactions predict stability, and negative interaction predicts divorce (Lavner & Bradbury, 2012). Couples that fail to maintain a 5-to-1 ratio of positive to negative behaviors are more likely to divorce (Gottman, 1994a).
Sexual satisfaction	Greater satisfaction with one's sex life is associated with a lower likelihood of divorce (Karney & Bradbury, 1995).
Marital satisfaction	"Marital satisfaction has larger effects on marital stability than do most other variables" (Karney & Bradbury, 1995, p. 20). Individuals who are more satisfied with their marriages are less likely to divorce. Even so, satisfaction is far from being a perfect predictor of divorce.

BREAKING UP

I've spent some time describing who gets divorced, and now it's time to inspect *how* breakups happen. How do partners proceed when they want to dissolve their relationship? The first thing to note is that people do not lightly end relationships to which they were once committed. Most divorces, for instance, are characterized by multiple complaints that result in a long period of discontent, but there are also things that the partners like about each other. So, some ambivalence ordinarily occurs. Recall, too, from our discussion of interdependence theory in chapter 6, that people do not usually depart their partnerships just because they are dissatisfied. Although a long period of unhappiness and distress precedes most divorces,

---

The Rules of Relationships

Leslie Baxter (1986) once asked college students in Oregon to write essays describing why they had ended a premarital romantic relationship. In all cases, the respondents had initiated the breakup, and their narratives (a term we explore further in the box on page 409) provided intriguing insights into the standards with which they judged their relationships. Eight themes appeared in at least 10 percent of the essays, and they appear to be specific prescriptions that take the form of *relationship rules:* They describe standards that are expected of us and our relationships, and our partners may leave us if we consistently break them. Here they are, listed in order of the frequency with which they were mentioned:

- **Autonomy:** Allow your partner to have friends and interests outside your relationship; ***don't be too possessive.*** (Problems with possessiveness were mentioned 37 percent of the time.)
- **Similarity:** You and your partner should share similar attitudes, values, and interests; ***don't be too different.*** (Mentioned 30 percent of the time.)
- **Supportiveness:** Enhance your partner's self-worth and self-esteem; ***don't be thoughtless or inconsiderate.*** (27 percent)
- **Openness:** Self-disclose, genuinely and authentically; ***don't be close-lipped.*** (22 percent)
- **Fidelity:** Be loyal and faithful to your partner; ***don't cheat.*** (17 percent)
- **Togetherness:** Share plenty of time together; don't take a night shift or move out of town and ***don't spend too much time elsewhere.*** (16 percent)
- **Equity:** Be fair; ***don't exploit your partner.*** (12 percent)
- **Magic:** Be romantic; ***don't be ordinary.*** (10 percent)

Various other reasons were mentioned, but none as frequently as these. Men and women also differed somewhat in the frequency of their complaints; women were troubled by problems with autonomy, openness, and equity more often than men, whereas men complained about lost magic more often than women. As usual, women tended to be more pragmatic than men when they evaluated their relationships. But as we noted on page 400, both sexes typically focus on their relationship and ignore their personal and cultural contexts when they explain the failure of their partnerships.

---

people typically initiate divorce only when they finally come to believe that they will be better off without their spouses (that is, only when their CLalts promise better outcomes than they are experiencing now). The decision to divorce results from complex calculations of distress and delight involving alternative, sometimes uncertain, possibilities.

Then, when that global decision is made, more choices await. Let's inspect what people do when they want to pull the plug on a failing partnership.

Breaking Up with Premarital Partners

The next time you want to end a romantic relationship, what do you think you'll do? Will you break the news to your partner straightforwardly, or will you simply start ignoring your partner's texts, change your status on Facebook, and start avoiding him or her? When she analyzed college students' accounts of their break-ups, Leslie Baxter (1984) found that a major distinction between different trajec-tories of relationship dissolution involved the question of whether someone who wished to depart ever announced that intention to the partner who was to be left behind! In some instances, the effort to disengage was *direct,* or explicitly stated; however, in most cases, people used *indirect* strategies in which they tried to end the relationship without ever saying so.

A second key distinction, according to Baxter (1984), was whether one's effort to depart was *other-oriented,* trying to protect the partner's feelings, or *self-oriented,* being more selfish at the expense of the partner's feelings. On occasion, for instance, people announced their intention to end the relationship in a manner that allowed their partners a chance to respond and to save face; one direct, other-oriented strategy was to announce one's dissatisfaction but to talk things over and to negotiate, rather than demand, an end to the partnership. In contrast, when they were direct but more selfish, they sometimes simply announced that the relationship was over and ducked any further contact with their ex-partners.

A more indirect but rather selfish ploy was to behave badly, increasing the partner's costs so much that the partner decided to end the relationship. People were more considerate when they claimed that they wanted to be "just friends," but if they did so when they really wanted to end the relationship altogether, this, too, was an indirect approach, with them misrepresenting their desire to depart.

Obviously, people made various moves when they wanted to end their rela-tionships, and the differences between direct and indirect and other-oriented and self-oriented strategies were just two of the distinctions that Baxter (1984) observed. Other distinctions included:

- the *gradual* versus *sudden onset* of one's discontent. Only about a quarter of the time was there some critical incident that suddenly changed a partner's feelings about his or her relationship; more often, people gradually grew dissatisfied.
- an *individual* versus *shared desire* to end the partnership. Two-thirds of the time, only one partner wanted the relationship to end.
- the *rapid* versus *protracted* nature of one's *exit.* More often than not, people made several disguised efforts to end their relationships before they succeeded.
- the *presence* or *absence of repair attempts.* Most of the time, no formal effort to repair the relationship was made.

Add all this up, and the single most common manner in which premarital rela-tionships ended involved gradual dissatisfaction that led one of the two partners to make repeated efforts to dissolve the relationship without ever announcing that intention and without engaging in any attempts to improve or repair the partner-ship. But even this most frequent pattern, which Baxter (1984) labeled **persever-ing indirectness,** occurred only one-third of the time, so a variety of other specific trajectories were commonplace, too.

People differ in the strategies they prefer, as well. Attachment style is influ-ential: Those who are high in avoidance of intimacy dislike drama and are especially likely to employ indirect strategies that reduce the chances of an emotional confrontation with their (ex-)partners (Collins & Gillath, 2012). If they do straightforwardly announce their wish to break up, they're more likely than others are to do it from a distance, with a text, an e-mail, or a Facebook message (Weisskirch & Delevi, 2012).[3]

Nevertheless, despite such idiosyncrasies, people generally agree about the typical elements, if not the specific strategies, of partners' efforts to end their relationships (Battaglia et al., 1998). Surveys of young adults find that the end of a close relationship routinely involves several familiar elements that are listed in Table 13.3. The process usually begins when one partner grows bored with the

TABLE 13.3. A Typical Script for the End of a Close Relationship

The next time one of your relationships ends, you may find it following this general sequence of events. The mixed feelings that partners often experience when they contemplate a breakup are apparent in this generic script:

Step 1	One of the partners begins to lose interest in the relationship.
Step 2	The disinterested partner begins to notice other people.
Step 3	The disinterested partner withdraws and acts more distant.
Step 4	The partners try to work things out and resolve the problem.
Step 5	The partners spend less time together.
Step 6	Lack of interest resurfaces.
Step 7	Someone considers breaking up.
Step 8	They communicate their feelings in a "meeting of the minds."
Step 9	The partners again try to work things out.
Step 10	One or both partners again notice other people.
Step 11	They again spend less time together.
Step 12	They go out with other potential partners.
Step 13	They try to get back together.
Step 14	One or both again consider breaking up.
Step 15	They emotionally detach, with a sense of "moving on."
Step 16	They break up, and the relationship is dissolved.

Source: Data from Battaglia, D. M., Richard, F. D., Datteri, D. L., & Lord, C. G. "Breaking up is (relatively) easy to do: A script for the dissolution of close relationships," Journal of Social and Personal Relationships, 15, 1998, 829–845.

Actual breakups are often very idiosyncratic, of course, but it's clear from this shared script that people generally expect the end of a close relationship to be characterized by ambivalence and twists and turns before the partnership finally ends.

---

[3] Facebook didn't exist the last time I broke up with anybody, so I can't be certain, but this sounds rude and obnoxious to me. And indeed, American teens think that ending a relationship via social media or a text message is much less acceptable than breaking up in person. Nevertheless, 27 percent of young adults have broken up with someone through a text message, and almost a third (31 percent) have been the recipient of a breakup text (Anderson, 2015).

relationship and begins noticing other people. That partner grows distant and less involved emotionally, but this often leads to an initial effort to restore the relationship and put things back the way they were. The partners spend less time together, however, and when a lack of interest resurfaces, thoughts of breaking up begin. Discussion of the relationship ensues, and the couple agrees to try again to work things out, but they continue to notice other people, and they become more withdrawn. They see others, but that engenders a short-lived desire to reunite that is followed by more contemplation of calling it quits. They prepare themselves psychologically and then break up.

Thereafter, some online housekeeping known as *relational cleansing* often follows (LeFebvre et al., 2015). People may change or hide their relationship status on profile pages, defriend their ex-partners or block their texts, and edit the photos on their walls. There's often a lot of work to do these days if one is to end entirely a close relationship!

Steps to Divorce

Obtaining a divorce is usually more complicated than breaking up with a premarital partner, but the ambivalence and vacillation that is evident in the typical sequence of events in Table 13.3 characterizes divorces, too. And marriages don't end overnight. Whereas someone's efforts to end a premarital romantic relationship may last several weeks, the process of ending a marriage can take several years. In one study of couples who stayed married for about a dozen years, the dissatisfied spouses typically spent the last 5 years of their marriages thinking about separating (Stewart et al., 1997)!

Over such a span of time, many idiosyncratic events may occur, but Steve Duck (Rollie & Duck, 2006) suggested that five general stages occur during the dissolution of most relationships. In an initial *personal phase,* a partner grows dissatisfied, often feeling frustration and disgruntlement. Then, in a subsequent *dyadic phase,* the unhappy partner reveals his or her discontent. Long periods of negotiation, confrontation, or attempts at accommodation may follow, and common feelings include shock, anger, hurt, and, sometimes, relief. But if the end of the relationship nears, a *social phase* begins. The partners publicize their distress, explaining their side of the story to family and friends and seeking support and understanding. As the relationship ends, a *grave-dressing phase* begins. Mourning decreases, and the partners begin to get over their loss by doing whatever cognitive work and relational cleansing are required to put their past partnership behind them. Memories are revised and tidied up, and an acceptable story—a narrative—for the course of the relationship is created. Rationalization and reassessment are likely to occur. Finally, in a *resurrection phase*, the ex-partners reenter social life as singles, often telling others that their experiences have changed them and that they're smarter and wiser now.

Within this general framework, the manner in which people dissolve their partnerships is likely to affect their feelings about each other afterward. In general, couples who do not identify and discuss the sources of their dissatisfaction have less positive feelings toward each other and are less likely to stay in touch than are those who do discuss their difficulties. Furthermore, for some couples, a breakup is just a transition to another form of a continuing relationship (Dailey et al., 2013). Various outcomes are possible when intimate relationships end. Let's turn to those next.

THE AFTERMATH OF BREAKUPS

When people are asked how much stress and change various events would cause in their lives, the death of a spouse or a divorce consistently show up at the top of the list (Miller & Rahe, 1997). The ends of our romantic partnerships are often momentous events—and although divorces are usually more complicated, the end of nonmarital romances can be powerfully affecting, too (Morris et al., 2015). But when a couple breaks up, is that really the end of their relationship? Not necessarily.

Postdissolution Relationships

There's an impressive amount of **churning** in romantic relationships that occurs when partners break up but then reconcile and get back together (in some cases, doing so several times). Half of us experienced that unsettled pattern when we were dating as teenagers (Halpern-Meekin et al., 2012), and, more notably, over a third (37 percent) of those who are currently cohabiting and almost a quarter (23 percent) of those who are presently married in the United States have cycled through an on/off/on again experience of breakup and renewal during their relationship (Vennum et al., 2014).[4] Churning is usually disadvantageous, as it is associated with stress and uncertainty and chronically lower satisfaction even when a relationship continues (Vennum & Johnson, 2014)—but it does clearly indicate that the end of a relationship is sometimes temporary. Breakups are sometimes just a transitional phase in an enduring relationship (Dailey et al., 2013).

When a breakup is (finally) permanent, partners may remain friends, at least for a while (Mogilski & Welling, 2017), but in most cases their commitment to each other gradually fades away entirely. This occurs because most of the pivotal events they encounter after their breakup are setbacks that undermine their commitment to a friendly postdissolution relationship (Kellas et al., 2008). They may have awkward, uncomfortable interactions, become jealous of the other's new love, or have their sexual advances rebuffed. Their continued contact may interfere with their new romances (Rodriguez et al., 2016), and they may finally find it easier to avoid each other, screening their calls or moving away. Certainly, ex-lovers do sometimes hook up, provide needed support, and find forgiveness after a breakup occurs, and some maintain a worthy friendship. Gays and lesbians, in

---

[4]What's more, a quarter of us have had "sex with an ex" after a breakup, and in *most* of those cases—63 percent—either we or our ex-partners had already begun having sex with someone else when those booty calls occurred (Halpern-Meekin et al., 2012). With that in mind, I invite you to revisit our insightful discussion of "Safe, Sensible Sex" back on pages 288–292.

particular, are more likely than heterosexuals to remain connected to ex-lovers after a romance ends (Harkless & Fowers, 2005). But in most cases, the task we face when a breakup occurs is ultimately to get on with our lives without our ex-partners. What's that adjustment like?

Getting Over It

Some relationships are richer than others, of course, and it's especially difficult to lose a partnership that's been characterized by high degrees of mutuality and

---

Narratives: Our Stories of Our Pasts

Before you read this box, I encourage you to try a short exercise proposed by Ann Weber and John Harvey (1994, p. 294):

1. Think of a difficult or troublesome experience you have had in a close relationship.
2. What do you remember about this event? What happened? What did you do? How did you feel?
3. Why did this event occur in your relationship?
4. Have you ever told anyone about this experience and why it happened?

In answering these questions, you are creating a *narrative*, a story that explains your experience. Narratives are awash with descriptions, expectations, feelings, interpretations of people's actions, and accounts of how and why events occurred, and they tend to bring order and a plot sequence to life's complex, messy events (Slotter & Ward, 2015). When a relationship is ongoing, the positive or negative emotional tone of the narratives people construct about major events in their partnership provides an indication of how healthy and happy the relationship is (McCoy et al., 2017); when their stories have unhappy endings, partners are much less likely to still be together a year later (Frost, 2012).

Then, when a relationship is over, narratives about its end may provide a his-

tory of the relationship's beginning, understanding of the relationship's problems, reactions to the separation, and one's coping afterward. They are personal stories that spring from the narrator's perceptions, and they aren't necessarily "true." Indeed, depending on their past complaints, ex-partners routinely construct quite different accounts of a failed relationship (Harvey & Fine, 2006).

We do sometimes construct narratives that paint ourselves in a favorable light to justify our behaviors and to help maintain self-esteem. We may also use narratives to influence the way others think of us. But the best, most adaptive narratives help us find meaning in what has happened; they focus on redemption—the lessons we learned and the personal growth we earned—in the past relationship, and they're associated with less distress and depression as we adjust to being single (Frost et al., 2016). And the more complete our narratives are—the more coherence and detail we bring to the characters, feelings, sequence of events, and causes that constructed our relationships—the better our adjustment is likely to be (Kellas & Manusov, 2003). Thoughtful narratives facilitate personal well-being, empathy for others, and a sense of growth, so they are key elements in our recoveries from loss.

self-expansion.[5] Our self-concepts have to change when we lose a relationship that has been a rewarding, central part of our self-definition (Mason et al., 2012), and that can be a wrenching process. Strong emotions often occur (Morris et al., 2015). But they are usually not as intense as we think they will be, and they don't last forever. People do heal.

An intriguing experience-sampling study (Sbarra & Emery, 2005) obtained daily reports of the emotions experienced by young adults at the University of Virginia in the month after they ended a meaningful romantic relationship (that had been at least 4 months long). Participants carried beepers that prompted them to record their feelings at random times each day. Four emotional reactions were monitored (see Figure 13.3), and they demonstrated that, as you'd expect, break-ups were painful. Compared to another group of students whose relationships were continuing, the ex-lovers were angry and sad, and their feelings of courage and strength (that is, "relief") were eroding. Two weeks later, as their romantic love for their ex-partners continued to recede, their anger was reduced and their sadness was ebbing, but their relief was lower, too. Their adjustment continued, however, and after another 2 weeks, they were no sadder than their peers and their relief had rebounded. A month into the process, they were noticeably less in love and their courage and strength were returning.

And importantly, all of this was less awful than they thought it would be. Every 2 weeks, another study asked young adults what they expected to feel if their current romances ended—and it then started tracking the actual responses of those whose relationships *did* end (Eastwick et al., 2008). In advance of a breakup, the participants correctly predicted the rate with which their distress would fade with time—they knew that time would heal their wounds—but they overestimated the initial pain they would feel when the breakup occurred. This sort of mistake is common. Our forecasts of our emotional responses to breakups are often exaggerated (Tomlinson et al., 2010). In this case, though, the wrongful predictions offer some hopeful news: As awful as they often are, the average breakup doesn't hurt as much as we think it will.

Of course, some breakups are worse than others. It's generally harder to be rejected than to do the rejecting (Morris et al., 2015), and anyone who mopes and dwells on what they've lost and how lousy they feel during a breakup is likely to have a hard time; rumination prolongs our distress, whereas reflection—seeking meaning in our experiences and looking to learn from them—is associated with positive adjustment and recovery (Saffrey & Ehrenberg, 2007). But people with insecure styles of attachment who are anxious about abandonment are particu-larly likely to have trouble mentally letting go. They remain preoccupied with the ex-partner (and are especially upset at the thought of him or her with someone new), so they remain sadder longer than others do (Sbarra, 2006). (To get their minds off their ex-partners, they should start browsing dating sites to see who else is out there; anxious people detach more easily from a failed relationship when they set their sights on someone new [Spielmann et al., 2009]. But neither they nor anyone else should haunt an ex-partner's Facebook page; the more time

---

[5] These two concepts were introduced on pages 3 and 186, respectively.

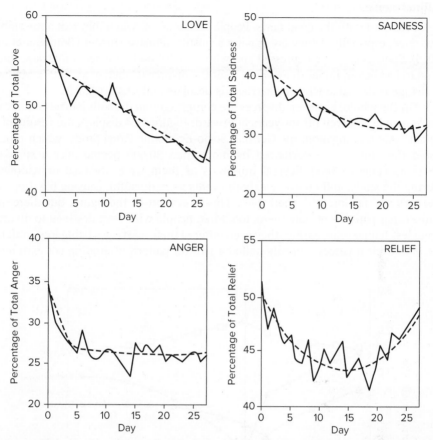

Source: Sbarra, D. A., & Emery, R. E. "The emotional sequelae of nonmarital relationship dissolution: Analysis of change and intraindividual variability over time," Personal Relationships, 12, 2005, 213–232.

FIGURE 13.3. **Adjusting to breakups.**
Young adults were sad and angry when they broke up with their romantic partners, but those negative emotions became less intense with time. A month after the breakup, they were more detached from their old relationships and bouncing back.

people spend examining an ex's page, the longer it takes them to heal and move on [Lukacs & Quan-Haase, 2015].) People with secure attachment styles fare better after breakups. They brood less, so they're less likely to stay angry. They're also more likely to accept the finality of the relationship's end, so they start healing and recover from sadness sooner (Sbarra, 2006).

Divorce Is Different

The end of a marriage is usually much more complex. Estates must be divided, children provided for, and laws followed, and the event changes one's life, sometimes for better but sometimes for worse.

Adjustment

Let's start with the good news. People are better off when they exit a miserable marriage, especially if they are leaving a hostile, abusive partner (Bourassa et al., 2015). Spouses who are depressed and who have hit bottom when a marriage ends tend to feel better, rather than worse, after the divorce (Cohen et al., 2007). Making a change is desirable when a marriage is desolate and unsalvageable.

On the whole, however, divorces are complex, often difficult journeys that can leave people less well off for years afterward. Figure 13.4 displays the results of a remarkable investigation, the German Socio-Economic Panel Study, which monitored the outcomes experienced by more than 30,000 people over a span of 18 years (Lucas, 2005). Several hundreds of them were divorced or widowed during the study, and on average, both events were dreadful, causing big drops in people's satisfaction with their lives. This is evident in the figure, but there are three other patterns of note there, too. First, people who were destined to divorce were less happy years earlier; they even entered their marriages being less content. Second, their divorces typically halted a painful pattern of eroding contentment,

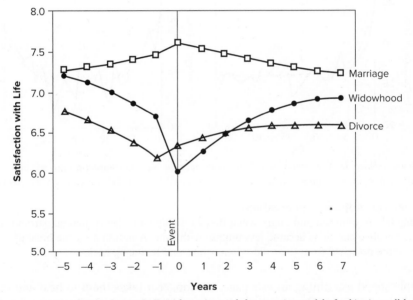

Source: Lucas, R. E. "Adaptation and the set-point model of subjective well-being," Current Directions in Psychological Science, 16, 2007, 75–79.

FIGURE 13.4. **Marriage, divorce, widowhood, and satisfaction with life.**
Here's what happened to thousands of people who got married, divorced, or were widowed in Germany. These are average trajectories, and individual outcomes were idiosyncratic. But on the whole, getting married did make people happier for a while, but a few years later they were no happier than they had been before they wed. Being widowed was dreadful, and despite substantial healing, it had lasting negative effects. And most divorces ended a long period of declining happiness—but years later, divorced people remained less happy than those whose marriages were intact.

and once they exited their distressed marriages, life started getting better. But third, years later, they still weren't as happy as they had been before the decline and fall of their marriages. There *was* a lot of idiosyncrasy in people's well-being after a divorce, and the average trajectory pictured here makes divorce look meaner than it turns out to be for most people, who carry on resiliently after their marriages end. And some people (9 percent) are much happier after a divorce than they had been before. For others, however, a decrease in well-being that accompanies divorce is long-lasting; years later, 19 percent of divorcees are less happy than they had been before their marriages failed (Mancini et al., 2011). Divorces are often monumental events in people's lives, and although time heals, it may not do so completely.

While Figure 13.4 is fresh in our minds, let's also acknowledge the devastating losses suffered by people who are widowed (Infurna & Luthar, 2017). The magnitude of the loss is hard for outsiders to comprehend. *Twenty years* later, widows and widowers still hold imaginary conversations with their lost loves about once a month (Carnelley et al., 2006), and as you can see in the figure, their satisfaction with life is diminished for a very long time, on average. Occasional bouts of grief may still occur a decade later, especially when the survivor is high in anxiety about abandonment (Meier et al., 2013) or the spouse's death was sudden and unexpected (Stroebe et al., 2012). So, like the loss of a child, this isn't a hurt that is ever forgotten, and generous, supportive friends will respect that. This is not a loss that people easily put behind them.

Back to divorce. Only two-thirds (68 percent) of those who get divorced after their mid-20s ever remarry, but those who do have usually taken the plunge for the second time within 4 years, on average (Elliott & Simmons, 2011). Remarrying is often a turning point for divorced singles that is associated with a boost in well-being (Blekesaune, 2008); indeed, if they stay unmarried, divorced people are 55 percent more likely than their remarried peers to *die* sometime during the next 40 years (Sbarra & Nietert, 2009). But whether or not they remarry, over three-fourths of those who divorce will report, 6 years later, that their divorce was a good thing (Hetherington, 2003).

> **A Point to Ponder**
>
> After all the difficulties divorce often entails, men are more likely to remarry than women are (Livingston & Caumont, 2017). Why?

So, outcomes vary. It can take years to adjust to the end of a marriage, but most people gradually bounce back. However, others end up defeated by their divorces, suffering distress and difficulty in their lives and their relationships for years thereafter (Sbarra et al., 2015). And almost everyone finds that the stresses don't end when the divorce is final; divorce changes one's social network and finances as well as one's intimate life.

Social Networks

People turn to their friends and family for support during a divorce, and the time they spend with friends increases, especially in the first year (Hanson et al., 1998). However, people usually lose about half of the members of their social networks (such as some friends and most of the in-laws) when their marriages end, and in many cases, ex-spouses never make enough new friends to replace

---

Want to Protect the Planet? Don't Get Divorced

Here's another reason to feel lousy when you get divorced: Because you and your ex are no longer sharing the same living space—and you're certainly not taking showers together—you're consuming a lot more energy and other resources per person than you would have had you stayed together. Couples consume fewer resources per capita—lights, air conditioning, water for cooking and cleaning; you name it—than singles do. Careful estimates suggest that if all the divorced people in the United States used the same resources per person as those who stayed married, the country would save 73 billion kilowatt-hours of electricity, 627 billion gallons of water, and 38 million rooms of living space each year (Yu & Liu, 2007). Yow. Feel free, when you break up and move out, to get a roommate.

---

the ones they've lost (Terhell et al., 2004). So, people typically have smaller social networks for years following a divorce.

Morever, not all of the remaining members of one's social network are likely to be supportive. About 50 percent of divorced people have interactions with their estranged spouses that are hostile or tense, and half of them also report that they have relatives who disapprove of their separation (Stewart et al., 1997). Not everyone who is close to a divorced person will offer desirable support.

Economic Resources

Women's finances usually deteriorate when they leave their marriages. National surveys in the United States find that their household incomes drop substantially, by about 27 percent, and this pattern has existed for decades (Emery et al., 2012). Men's household incomes tend to drop, too, but they're more likely than women to live by themselves after they divorce; the women are much more likely to have children in their households. So, if you count the number of mouths ex-spouses have to feed, men's per capita income goes *up* 34 percent in the year after they divorce whereas mothers' incomes drop 36 percent (Sayer, 2006). Men actually have more money to spend on their own needs and interests whereas women ordinarily have less. On average, then, a woman's standard of living decreases after she divorces, whereas a man's improves (Sharma, 2015).

Relationships Between Ex-Spouses

When a couple has children, a divorce doesn't mean they're done dealing with each other. Parents usually have continued contact, and antagonism, ambivalence, nostalgia, or regrets may all shape their ongoing interactions (Halford & Sweeper, 2013). Emerging from these conflicting feelings appear to be four broad types of postmarital relationships (Ahrons, 1994): Fiery Foes, Angry Associates, Cooperative Colleagues, and Perfect Pals. For both Fiery Foes and Angry Associates, the spouses' animosity toward each other still defines their relationship. Despite their open disrespect for each other, Angry Associates have some capacity to work together in co-parenting their children, but Fiery Foes have very little; their bitterness keeps them at constant odds. Cooperative Colleagues aren't good friends, but they are civil and pleasant to each other and they are able to cooperate successfully in parenting tasks. Finally, Perfect Pals maintain "a strong friendship with mutual respect that did not get eroded by their decision to live separate lives" (Ahrons, p. 116). In a sample of divorced parents in the midwestern United States, half the ex-spouses had amicable relationships (38% Cooperative Colleagues, 12% Perfect Pals) and half had distressed relationships (25% Angry Associates and 25% Fiery Foes) a year after their divorces. (Twenty years later, things had settled down a bit. Sixty percent of the ex-spouses had amicable connections, and only 22 percent were still Angry Associates or Fiery Foes. But 18 percent had become Dissolved Duos, having no contact with each other at all [Ahrons, 2007].)

The Children of Divorce

The verdict is in. Decades of research involving hundreds of thousands of people converge on the conclusion that, compared to those whose parents stay married, children whose parents divorce exhibit lower levels of well-being both as adolescents and as young adults. Their psychological adjustment is poorer; they experience more depression and anxiety and less satisfaction with life. Their behavior is more problematic; they use more drugs, break more laws, make more unwanted babies, and get poorer grades. And, as we've already seen, their adult relationships are more fragile; the children of divorce are more likely than others to get divorced themselves. These effects are usually not large, and many children experience their parents' divorce without much difficulty. Still, the global impact of a parental divorce, although modest, is routinely negative (Amato, 2010; Sbarra & Beck, 2013).

© *Photographee.eu/Shutterstock*

What do you think? Are these ex-spouses Fiery Foes, Angry Associates, or Cooperative Colleagues? (They don't appear to be Perfect Pals!)

Why are the children of divorce less well off? The outcomes I just noted are merely correlated with parental divorce, and there may be several reasons why these patterns exist. Spouses and families that experience a divorce may differ in several meaningful ways from those that don't, and a number of influences may be at work. For one thing, children of divorce *inherit* some of their greater risk for unstable marriages, so the stresses of their parents' divorce aren't entirely to blame (D'Onofrio et al., 2007). The same traits that make their parents poor partners—neuroticism or impulsivity, perhaps—may be passed on to the children when they're born, making the transmission of divorce from one generation to the next genetic instead of just experiential. Still, with due respect to the complexities involved, the divorce of one's parents often brings on several stresses that may also be very influential: the loss of a parent, parental stress, economic hardship, and family conflict (Lansford, 2009).

According to a **parental loss** view, children are presumed to benefit from having two parents who are devoted to their care, and children who lose a parent for any reason, including divorce, are likely to be less well off (Barber, 2000). Indeed, if a divorce does occur, children fare better when they spend time with both parents (Fabricius & Suh, 2017), and they do worse if one of their parents moves some distance away (Braver et al., 2003).

In contrast, a **parental stress** model holds that the quality, not the quantity, of the parenting a child receives is key, and any stressor (including divorce) that distracts or debilitates one's parents can have detrimental effects. According to this view, children's outcomes depend on how well a custodial parent adjusts to a divorce, and, consistent with this perspective, children of divorce usually start doing more poorly in school when their parents grow dissatisfied, long before they actually break up (Sun, 2001). Of course, one major stressor is **economic hardship,** and it may be the impoverished circumstances that sometimes follow divorce, not just the divorce per se, that adds to children's burdens (Neppl et al., 2016). Any difficulties faced by the children are reduced if the custodial parent has sufficient resources to support them well (Sun & Li, 2002). (Indeed, you may be personally familiar with one of the unfortunate outcomes routinely faced by children of divorce: Compared to parents who stay married, those who divorce contribute less money toward their children's college educations [Turley & Desmond, 2011].)

All of these factors are influential, but the most potent influence of them all is **parental conflict** (Lansford, 2009). Acrimonious interactions between parents appear to be hard on children, and whether or not a divorce occurs, conflict in the home is associated with more anxiety (Riggio, 2004), poorer health (Miller & Chen, 2010), and more problematic behavior (Clements et al., 2014) in children. Remarkably, even when babies are sleeping, the regions of their brains that regulate emotion and stress respond strongly to the sound of angry voices—if the babies live in high-conflict homes (Graham et al., 2013). So, take a look at Figure 13.5: As you might expect, children are happiest when they live in an intact family in which little conflict or discord occurs, and their well-being is much lower when divorce occurs in a low-conflict home. But if they live amidst constant conflict, children are worse off when the parents *don't* divorce; when a divorce breaks up

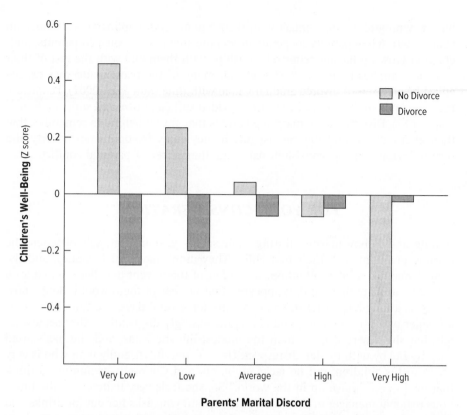

Source: Amato, P. R. "Reconciling divergent perspectives: Judith Wallerstein, quantitative family research, and children of divorce," Family Relations, 52, 2003, 332–339.

FIGURE 13.5. **Parents' marital discord, divorce, and children's psychological well-being.**
The figure takes note of family discord and conflict and compares the outcomes of children whose parents divorced to those of children who stayed in intact homes. When divorce occurred in low-conflict families, children fared poorly, but they were even worse off when there was a lot of discord at home and the parents did *not* divorce. Spouses who ponder "staying together for the sake of the children" should consider whether they can provide their children a peaceable home.

an angry, embattled household, there's almost no decrease in the children's well-being at all (Amato, 2003). Thus, the question of whether unhappy spouses should "stay together for the sake of the children" seems to depend on whether they can be civil toward each other; children suffer when a peaceable marriage is disrupted, but they are better off going through a divorce if their homes are full of conflict (Maleck & Papp, 2015).

There are two more points to make. First, there's no question that children are less affected by divorce if they are able to maintain high-quality relationships with their parents thereafter. Whatever their sources, the poorer outcomes often experienced by children of divorce are greatly reduced when the children continue to have meaningful, loving contact with their parents and grandparents (Henderson et al., 2009). When parents cooperate to become attentive, devoted co-parents, their children grow up having better relationships with them and with the rest of their extended families (Ahrons, 2007). Second, many of the poorer outcomes experienced by children of divorce gradually fade with time (Sun & Li, 2002). People are resilient, and children heal if they are provided sufficient love and support (Emery et al., 2012). Divorcing or remarrying parents may find it helpful to remember that their children will probably be just fine if they enjoy freedom from poverty and receive loving, reliable, consistent parenting that is free of parental conflict.

FOR YOUR CONSIDERATION

Connie and Bobby married during their senior year in high school when she became pregnant with their first child. They didn't have much money, and the baby demanded a lot of attention, so neither of them went to college, and after a few years and another child, it appeared that neither of them would. Bobby now works as a long-haul trucker, so he is gone for several days at a time. Connie is a cashier at a grocery store, and she is increasingly disgruntled. She has always felt that she deserved more than the modest life she leads, and she has started viewing Bobby with hidden disrespect. He is a cheerful, friendly man who is very warm to his children, but he lacks ambition, and Connie is beginning to think that he'll never "move up in the world." So, she feels very flattered by the flirtatious regional manager of the grocery store chain who asks her out for drinks and dinner when Bobby is on the road. She fantasizes about how much more exciting her life would be if she were married to the manager, and she has decided to sleep with him to see what that's like.

In your opinion, having read this chapter, what should Connie do? What does the future hold for Connie and Bobby? Why?

CHAPTER SUMMARY

The Changing Rate of Divorce

The Prevalence of Divorce. Divorce became much more common during the twentieth century, particularly in the United States.

Why Has the Divorce Rate Increased? High expectations for marriage, women working, changing gender roles, creeping individualism, no-fault divorce legislation, and premarital cohabitation may all have played a part. Children are also more likely to come from broken homes, and many of us have divorced friends.

The Predictors of Divorce

Levinger's Barrier Model. When attraction and barriers are low but alternative attractions are high, divorce is likely.

Karney and Bradbury's Vulnerability-Stress-Adaptation Model. Enduring *personal vulnerabilities, stressful events,* and the *adaptive processes* with which people cope with their difficulties combine to influence marital quality.

Results from the PAIR Project. *Enduring dynamics* predict how happy marriages will be, but *disillusionment* best predicts which couples will actually divorce.

Results from the Early Years of Marriage Project. The social context in which couples conduct their relationships is important.

People's Personal Perceptions of Their Problems. Divorced spouses identify infidelity, incompatibility, and drug use as the three most common reasons why they sought a divorce.

Specific Predictors of Divorce. A variety of societal, demographic, relational, and personal influences are related to an increased risk of divorce.

Breaking Up

Breaking Up with Premarital Partners. *Persevering indirectness* is the most common strategy for breaking up. Editing of social media known as *relational cleansing* often occurs.

Steps to Divorce. When spouses divorce, they often go through personal, dyadic, social, and grave-dressing phases that are followed by a resurrection phase.

The Aftermath of Breakups

Postdissolution Relationships. Some couples continue a friendship after a romantic breakup, but most partnerships fade away completely. Some *churning* may occur before a relationship finally ends.

Getting Over It. Strong emotions often occur, but they're usually not as intense as we expect, and they don't last forever.

Divorce Is Different. Divorces are often monumental events, and the consequences can last for years.

The Children of Divorce. Children of divorce exhibit reduced well-being, but they can prosper if their parents stay involved with them and are civil to each other. Children fare better if surly, hostile parents do divorce than if they do not because parental conflict is deleterious to children.

CHAPTER 14

Maintaining and Repairing Relationships

MAINTAINING AND ENHANCING RELATIONSHIPS
◆ REPAIRING RELATIONSHIPS ◆ IN CONCLUSION
◆ FOR YOUR CONSIDERATION ◆ CHAPTER SUMMARY

This is our last chapter, and we're nearing the end of the book. So, it's time to take stock. What do you know now that you didn't know before we started? Only you know for sure, but here are some possibilities:

- The styles of behavior that are often expected of men—the styles that encourage them to be assertive and self-reliant but that do not encourage them to be warm and tender—do not train them to be very desirable partners in long-term intimate relationships.
- People with low self-esteem sometimes sabotage their own relationships by making mountains out of molehills and perceiving rejection where none exists.
- Proximity, familiarity, and convenience are influential in determining whether or not rewarding relationships ever begin. There may be lots of people with whom we could have wonderful relationships that we'll simply never meet.
- Looks matter, and if you're not physically attractive, a lot of people will pass you by instead of wanting to get to know you.
- We don't know or understand our romantic partners as well as we think we do; a lot of misperception persists even in successful relationships.
- People try hard to make good impressions on us when we're getting to know them, but they put less effort into being polite, decorous, and delightful once we like or love them.
- Men generally do not do as well at nonverbal communication as women do, and deficiencies in nonverbal communication are correlated with dissatisfaction in close relationships.
- More often than we realize, our partners do not receive the messages we intend to send when we talk with them.
- Bad is stronger than good, and the occasional sour or critical interactions we have with our partners are more influential than the nice things we do for them.

- Over the long haul, intimate relationships are much more costly than we usually expect them to be. If you think that your relationship will provide you unending bliss and delight, you're certain to be disappointed.
- Romantic, passionate love is one of the primary reasons we choose to marry, but it tends to decline over time.
- About one-third of us are not comfortable and relaxed with interdependent intimacy; we either worry that our partners don't love us enough, or we are ill at ease when they get too close.
- Men tend to want more sex than women do, and frustration often results.
- Sooner or later, it's likely that our partners will betray us in some manner that causes us hurt and pain.
- Conflict is unavoidable.
- Marriages are less happy, on average, than they used to be, and divorce is more common.

Yikes. That's quite a list. And it's just a sampling of the unfortunate facts we've encountered; several other influences, such as the personality traits of neuroticism and narcissism or the states of jealousy or loneliness create difficulties in close relationships, too.

Altogether, these patterns may paint a gloomy picture, and, indeed, the surprisingly low success rates of modern marriages suggest that many partnerships are not as wonderful as we hope they will be. On the other hand, there are also a lot of optimistic facts among the topics we've encountered. Here are a few:

- A lot of men, about one-third of them, are just as warm and tender and sensitive and kind as women routinely are. And those that aren't can probably learn to be warmer and more expressive than they are now.
- Happy lovers perceive their partners and explain their behavior in generous ways that give the partners the benefit of any doubt and portray them as kind and caring even when they occasionally misbehave.

Relationships are complex, and they are usually more costly than we expect them to be. But now that you've read this book, you shouldn't be as pessimistic as this comic strip character is.

Jeff Macnelly's Shoe

Shoe © 2003 MacNelly, Inc. Distributed by King Features, Inc.

- Lots of people seek and are comfortable in an interdependent and intimate relationship with a romantic partner.
- In happy relationships, when passion decreases, it is replaced by a deep, affectionate friendship that is rich, warm, and satisfying to those who experience it.
- Authentic forgiveness benefits both the recipient and the giver, and it is easiest to attain in those close, satisfying relationships that are most worth saving.
- Perhaps most importantly, almost all of us can be more thoughtful, more charming, and more rewarding romantic partners if we try to be. Men do better at nonverbal communication when they are motivated to get it right. We can reduce or eliminate verbal misunderstandings when we take the time to check the accuracy of our interpretations. And with attentive effort, we can be more polite, less selfish, more considerate, and less critical toward our partners than we would otherwise be.

There are lots of reasons to hope that, with wisdom and work, we can live happily ever after. Indeed, I don't think there's any question that "knowledge is power": With better understanding of close relationships, we are better equipped to prevent some problems and to readily overcome others. And the best news of all may be that when we're committed to our partnerships, we engage in a variety of actions that help to protect and maintain the satisfaction we enjoy. Furthermore, if they occur, many problems can be fixed, and many wounds can be healed. When we encounter disappointments in our relationships, we are often able to fully surmount those difficulties if we wish.

In this concluding chapter, then, we'll survey both the mechanisms with which partners protect and perpetuate their satisfaction and the interventions with which faltering contentment can be restored. Despite the hurdles that must be overcome, many relationships not only survive, they thrive.

MAINTAINING AND ENHANCING RELATIONSHIPS

I introduced back in chapter 6 (on pages 203–204) the idea that people often behave in various ways that protect and maintain desirable relationships. **Relationship maintenance mechanisms**, the strategic actions people take to sustain their partnerships, have been studied by researchers from two different scholarly camps. Social psychologists schooled in Caryl Rusbult's *investment model*[1] have identified several behaviors that follow from commitment to a relationship, and communication scholars have noted other actions that distinguish happy partners from those who are less content. Let's examine both sets of findings.

Staying Committed

People who are committed to a partnership, who want and expect it to continue, *think* and *behave* differently than less committed partners do (Ogolsky &

[1] I suspect a look back at page 201 will come in handy.

Bowers, 2013). When they foresee future happiness with their partners (Lemay, 2016), they perceive themselves, their partners, and their relationship in ways that help to sustain the partnership, and they act in ways that avoid or defuse conflict and that enrich the relationship.

Cognitive Maintenance Mechanisms

People's perspectives change in several important ways when they are committed to their relationships. First, they think of themselves not as separate individuals but as part of a greater whole that includes them *and* their partners. They perceive greater overlap between their partners' lives and their own, and they use more plural pronouns, with *we, us,* and *ours* replacing *I, me,* and *mine* (Agnew et al., 1998). This change in self-definition is referred to as **cognitive interdependence,** and it makes some of the other maintenance mechanisms I mention below more likely to occur (Soulsby & Bennett, 2017). I'm likely, for instance, to be even more motivated to take care of "us" than I would be to take care of just "you."

Second, committed partners think of each other with **positive illusions,** idealizing each other and perceiving their relationship in the best possible light (Fletcher et al., 2013). A partner's faults are judged to be relatively trivial, the relationship's deficiencies are considered to be relatively unimportant, and a partner's misbehavior is dismissed as an unintentional or temporary aberration (Neff & Karney, 2003). A characteristic that makes these positive illusions interesting is that people are often well aware of the specific obnoxious and thoughtless things their partners sometimes do, but by misremembering them and explaining them away, they are able to maintain global evaluations of their partners that are more positive than the sum of their parts (Karney, 2015). And as long as they are not too unrealistic, these rose-colored perceptions help protect people's happiness by taking the sting out of a partner's occasional missteps.

A specific type of positive illusion can be said to be a third cognitive maintenance mechanism. Committed partners tend to think that their relationships are better than most, and the happier they are, the more exceptional they consider their relationships to be (Reis et al., 2011a). This **perceived superiority** makes one's partnership seem even more special and really does make a relationship more likely to last (Rusbult et al., 2000).

Satisfied partners are also less likely to be on the prowl, looking for other lovers. Attractive rivals can distract our partners and lure them away from us only when our partners know they exist, but contented lovers display an **inattention to alternatives** that leaves them relatively uninterested and unaware of how well they could be doing in alternative relationships (Miller, 2008). People who are not very committed to their current partnerships monitor their other options with more inquisitiveness and eagerness than do those who are more content with what they've already got; given the chance in a lab procedure, for instance, they linger longer and more carefully inspect photos of attractive members of the other sex (Miller, 1997a). Uncommitted lovers continue to shop around for better partners, and that puts their current relationships at risk: Young adults who are alert to their other options at the beginning of a college semester are less likely to still be with the same romantic partner when the semester is done (Miller, 1997a). In contrast, committed lovers are relatively heedless of how well they could be doing in other relationships—they're not paying much attention to such possibilities—and that helps to protect and maintain their current partnerships.

In addition, when committed partners do notice attractive rivals to their relationships, they judge them to be less desirable than others think them to be (Petit & Ford, 2015). Commitment leads people to disparage those who could lure them away from their existing relationships (Cole et al., 2016), and this **derogation of tempting alternatives** allows people to feel that other potential partners are less attractive than the ones they already have. One of the things that makes this perceptual bias interesting is that it is strongest when the alternatives are most tempting and thereby pose the greatest threat to one's relationship. For instance, committed partners do not derogate images of attractive members of the other sex when they are said to be in another city far away, but they do find them less attractive when they are said to be fellow students on one's own campus (Simpson et al., 1990). To protect their relationships, happy lovers tend to underestimate the desirability of other potential partners.

Behavioral Maintenance Mechanisms

As you can see, the cognitive things people do to maintain their relationships generally involve subtle changes in perception or judgment of others, their relationships, and themselves. Other maintenance mechanisms involve changes in the things people do.

For one thing, committed people are often willing to make various personal sacrifices, such as doing things they would prefer not to do, or not doing things that they would like to do, in order to promote the well-being of their partners or their relationships (Totenhagen et al., 2013). This **willingness to sacrifice** often involves trivial costs (such as seeing a movie that doesn't interest you because your partner wants to go), and contented partners frequently make such small sacrifices (Ruppel & Curran, 2012). But sacrifice can also involve substantial costs in which people endure rather long periods of deprivation in order to preserve or enrich their partnerships (Day & Impett, 2016). If you're already married, for instance, your spouse may be having to go to a lot of trouble to help you go to school; but, if he or she is committed to your future together, that's a price that your spouse may be willing to pay.

Prayer is helpful in this regard. Careful studies have found that those who begin praying for the success and well-being of their partners become more satisfied with the sacrifices they make (Lambert et al., 2012), and more forgiving, too (Lambert et al., 2013). And in general, those who pray for their partners tend to be more satisfied with, and more committed to, their relationships. Notably, however, prayer that is focused on one's own needs and desires doesn't have such effects (Fincham & Beach, 2014).

Relationships are also likely to prosper when our partners behave toward us in ways that encourage us to gradually become the people that we want to be.

A Point to Ponder

What is it about prayer for the well-being of our partners that makes us more forgiving and more generous toward them?

When our partners encourage us to be all that we can be—supporting the development of skills we want to learn, endorsing our acceptance of promising new roles and responsibilities, and promoting the self-growth we seek—both our relationships and our personal well-being are enhanced (Overall et al., 2010a). This is the **Michelangelo phenomenon,** named for the famous sculptor who created uplifting works of art from ordinary blocks of stone (Rusbult et al., 2009). People have rarely finished growing and changing when their partnerships begin, and committed partners help each other become who they wish to be when the partners' goals promote the health of their relationship (Hui et al., 2014).

Committed lovers also tend to swallow minor mistreatment from their partners without biting back. This is **accommodation,** the willingness to control the impulse to respond in kind to a partner's provocation and to instead respond constructively (Häfner & IJzerman, 2011). Accommodation occurs when people tolerate a partner's bad mood, pointless criticism, thoughtlessness, and other small nuisances with placidity and poise. It does not involve martyrdom; to the contrary, as long as a partner's offenses are only occasional or temporary, accommodation provides an effective means of avoiding useless conflict that might merely perpetuate an aversive interaction. And when both partners are inclined to "stay cool" instead of "fighting fire with fire," they tend to have a happy relationship (Rusbult et al.,2001).

I should note, however, that accommodation takes work. It requires us to bite our tongues and hold our tempers, so it involves active self-restraint—and in fact, **self-control** (the ability to manage one's impulses, control one's thoughts, persevere in pursuit of desired goals, and curb unwanted behavior) is generally good for our relationships. In general, self-control helps us do the right things and not to do the wrong things (Karremans et al., 2015)—and in particular, it enables us to refrain from lashing out in response to provocation, so people high in self-control rarely, if ever, engage in intimate partner violence (Finkel et al., 2009). To the contrary, people who are high in self-control make more sacrifices that benefit their partners (Pronk & Karremans, 2014). And forgiveness requires us to stop nursing a grudge, so self-control makes forgiveness more likely, too (Karremans et al., 2015). Finally, we use self-control to withstand temptation, so it aids our efforts to resist the lure of attractive alternatives; when they're already in relationships, people say it's easier for them to remain faithful—and they actually are less flirtatious toward new acquaintances—the more self-control they have (Pronk et al., 2011).

In fact, people differ in their dispositional levels of self-control (that is, their usual abilities to regulate their impulses) and, if you have any sense, you'll seek a partner with ample ability to persevere and refrain, as needed. That's because the more self-control two partners possess—that is, the greater the sum of their combined abilities to make good decisions and to do the right thing—the smoother and more satisfying their relationship will routinely be (Vohs et al., 2011). No matter who we are, though, self-control is reduced when we are stressed, distracted, or fatigued, so people are less accommodating, less forgiving, and more tempted by alternatives when they are temporarily spent (Luchies et al., 2011). We tend to be at our worst when we are tired and taxed. It's good news, then, that feeling connected to family and friends bolsters self-control; acceptance by a

---

The Most Obvious Box in the Book: Don't Cheat

Obviously, if you want to protect and maintain a valued relationship, you shouldn't subject it to potentially lethal stress and strain. So, don't cheat on your partner. Nearly all of us (91 percent) think that adultery is "morally wrong" (Dugan, 2015), and most of us (62 percent) think that if we found out that our spouses were having affairs, we'd leave and get a divorce (Jones, 2008). And sure enough, a partner's infidelity greatly increases the chances that a marriage (Frisco et al., 2017) or any other romantic relationship (Negash et al., 2014) will fail. It's the leading reason marriages end (Baucom et al., 2014). For most of us, faithlessness is an awful betrayal that ruins trust and damages a relationship more than other problems do; if they seek therapy, for instance, spouses who are grappling with infidelity are noticeably more distressed and depressed than other therapy couples typically are (Atkins et al., 2010). Nevertheless, therapy usually helps. On average, infidelity couples are much improved—being much less unhappy—after they complete

a program of marital therapy like those coming up in a few pages (Hargrave & Hammer, 2016).

Thus, here are two bits of good advice. First, if you discover that your partner in (what had been) a worthy relationship has been unfaithful, try not to act in haste. Calm counsel can assist you in understanding what happened and in reaching an informed, profitable decision about how best to put your pain behind you (Doherty & Harris, 2017). You may find that the relationship is reparable, so "couples should never throw away a marriage in the midst of a crisis of infidelity; you never know when you're going to need it later" (Pittman & Wagers, 2005, p. 1419). Second, do your part to protect your partnership by steering clear of temptation. Seek a social network that will support your faithfulness instead of undermining your monogamy, and handle attractive alternatives (including co-workers, Facebook confidants, and, especially, former lovers) with care (Glass & Staeheli, 2003).

---

loving partner enhances our abilities to behave in ways that protect our relationships (Blackhart et al., 2011).[2]

Self-control can be difficult, but there's another behavioral maintenance mechanism that is easier to enact: **play.** Couples are usually content when they find ways to engage in novel, challenging, exciting, and pleasant activities together (Sheldon et al., 2013). In short, those who play together tend to stay together. In formal studies of this simple truth, couples have been tied together on one side at the wrists and ankles and invited to crawl through an obstacle course while pushing

---

[2] Here's another benefit of self-control in close relationships: It shows that we care. We rarely improve our relationships by trying to change our partners—that usually just annoys them—but our efforts do pay off when we try to change *ourselves.* Our partners are typically pleased when they realize that we are striving to behave better—for instance, trying to communicate more clearly and to manage conflict more reasonably—and they're more satisfied when we successfully exert some self-control (Simpson et al., 2016). Think of the benefits to be gained when *both* partners do this.

a foam cylinder with their heads (Aron et al., 2000). Prizes could be won if they completed the course quickly enough, so the task was exciting, goofy fun. Compared to couples who engaged in a more mundane activity, those that played like this felt that their relationships were of higher quality when the day was done. And sure enough, out in the real world, spouses who get up and go out to hike, bike, dance, or to attend concerts, lectures, and shows feel that their marriages are of higher quality than do those who just stay home and watch television (Strong & Aron, 2006). Finding time to play in inventive and creative ways is beneficial in close relationships, so you may want to make a point of it. Consider this approach, pioneered by Kimberley Coulter and John Malouff (2013): Collaborate with your partner in creating a list of engaging and interesting things to do together. Then develop definite plans to *do* them, making time each week for one of the items on your list. What sorts of activities should you choose? The specifics are up to you, but try to pursue entertainments that are novel, exciting, playful, and passionate. Go somewhere you've never been. Be adventurous.[3] Meet your partner at a bar and pretend that you've just met. Be sensual. Take turns massaging each other without having sex. Have fun, and try to be spontaneous; these activities lose some of their value if they're rigidly scheduled (Tonietto & Malkoc, 2016), and they have beneficial effects only when both you and your partner want to participate (Girme et al., 2014). But if you're both game, spending 90 minutes doing something fun and exciting each week is likely to leave you happier and more satisfied with your relationship a few months from now (Malouff et al., 2015).

Contented couples also develop **rituals**, recurring patterns of behavior that become familiar routines that "if gone, would be missed" (Bruess & Kudak, 2008, p. 6). Pleasing rituals are often small actions—such as a quick kiss goodnight just before a couple turns out the lights each night—or comfortable habits, such as sitting for a bit before fixing dinner to chat about the day. But such events carry special meaning because they become traditions that symbolize the two partners' devotion to their relationship and their identity as a couple. Indeed, rituals can be quite idiosyncratic, involving pet names and private customs that may seem peculiar to others—but the more rituals a couple shares, the more intimate and satisfied they tend to be (Pearson et al., 2011).

Finally, those who are committed to a partnership are more likely to offer **forgiveness** after a partner's betrayal (Karremans et al., 2011). Forgiveness quickens the healing of both the relationship and the partner who was wronged—it is less stressful to forgive an intimate partner than to nurse a grudge—so forgiveness promotes good health both in relationships and in those who give it (Weir, 2017).

Staying Content

A second collection of maintenance activities has been identified by communication scholars Dan Canary and Laura Stafford (2001), who gathered hundreds of

---

[3]Try skydiving, for instance. On our honeymoon, my wife and I fell out of a perfectly good airplane, each of us strapped to someone who claimed to know what he was doing. Happily, we survived—and it's a shared experience that we'll never forget.

reports from people (including 500 term papers from college students) describing what they did to maintain their relationships. Canary and Stafford then distilled the strategies into the manageable number of categories that appear in Table 14.1. As you can see, contented partners try to foster *positivity,* being polite, staying cheerful, and remaining upbeat; they encourage *openness* and *relationship talk,* sharing their own thoughts and feelings and inviting their partners to do the same; they provide *assurances* that announce their love, commitment, and regard for each other; they share a *social network,* having friends in common and spending time with their partner's family; they *share tasks* around the home in an equitable fashion, handling their fair share of household responsibilities; and they spend time together, sharing *joint activities* (Girme et al., 2014; Ogolsky & Monk, 2018).

Similar activities are used to maintain close friendships (Oswald et al., 2004), and that should be no surprise. If you take a look (way back on p. 2) at the components of intimacy in chapter 1, you'll see that most of the maintenance mechanisms identified by Canary and Stafford promote and encourage intimacy between friends and lovers. Knowledge, caring, interdependence, mutuality, trust, responsiveness, and commitment are all likely to be enhanced by maintenance strategies that involve openness, assurances of one's love and commitment, and plenty of shared friends and activities. The actions people take to stay happy in close relationships seem to involve the creation and preservation of rewarding intimacy with their partners.

Furthermore, these various actions seem to work. Partners who routinely do the things listed in Table 14.1 enjoy greater fondness for each other and greater commitment to their relationships than do those who work less hard to maintain their partnerships (Stafford, 2003)—and this is especially true when *both* partners

TABLE 14.1. Canary and Stafford's Relational Maintenance Strategies

Strategy	Examples: "I . . ."
Positivity	Strive to make our interactions enjoyable
	Try to be cheerful and upbeat when we're together
Openness	Encourage my partner to disclose his/her thoughts and feelings to me
Relationship Talk	Encourage my partner to tell me what he/she wants from our relationship
Assurances	Try to show my partner how much he/she means to me
	Talk about our plans for the future
Understanding	Apologize when I'm wrong
	Strive to be patient and forgiving
Sharing Tasks	Help equally with tasks that need to be done
	Help my partner complete his/her projects
Social Networks	Do things with his/her friends and family
	Include our friends in our activities
Joint Activities	Share time together
	Do things together

Source: Adapted from Stafford (2011) and Marmo & Canary (2013).

A Prescription for Contentment:
1. Appreciate your partner. 2. Express your gratitude.
3. Repeat.

People adapt to pleasant circumstances, and if you're lucky (and wise and diligent) enough to have a great relationship, there's a danger that you'll come to take it for granted. (In the language of interdependence theory, your comparison level will creep upward.) But if you grow lazily accustomed to your good fortune, you won't be as delighted with it as you should be. That would be wasteful, so I have a specific prescription for how you can savor your satisfaction, maintain your relationship, and be happier and healthier all at the same time.

Tune in. Feel obligated to take notice of the thoughtful acts of affection, benevolence, and generosity your partner provides you (Dew & Wilcox, 2013). Then, each week, make a point of telling your partner which three kindnesses, large or small, you enjoyed the most.

Happy people are naturally adept at noticing their blessings (Fagley, 2012), but any of us can learn to pay better attention to them, and it's likely that our moods—and even our physical health (Mills et al., 2015)—will improve when we do. Indeed, people who start "gratitude journals" in which they keep track of their joys and good fortune become genuinely happier (Lyubomirsky & Layous, 2013).

Then, when we express our gratitude to our partners, we provide them powerfully rewarding acknowledgment and affection (Algoe et al., 2016). Our evident appreciation reduces the costs of the favors they do us so that their small sacrifices are easier for them to bear—and the result is that they take more pleasure in continuing their efforts on our behalf (Kubacka et al., 2011).

In our journey through this book, we've found that bad is stronger than good, and that couples are less affectionate toward each other as time goes by. But we know that now, so we're equipped to avoid the creeping disillusionment that erodes too many partnerships. Your assignment is clear: Take conscious note of the good things in your relationship, celebrate them, and communicate your recognition and appreciation of them to your partner. Both of you will be happier if you appreciate your partner, express your gratitude, and repeat (Algoe et al., 2013).

---

behave this way (Oswald & Clark, 2006). Don't fret if you find the long list of activities in Table 14.1 a little daunting; three of them are more important than the others, and they're easy to remember. Of the bunch, the best predictors of how happy a marriage will be are positivity, assurances, and sharing tasks (Canary et al., 2002). Spouses who do their fair share of housework, who are typically in good spirits, and who regularly express their love and regard for their partners are especially likely to be happily wed.

I do have a cautionary note, however: Kindnesses done for a partner on Valentine's Day are unlikely to still be keeping him or her satisfied on the Fourth of July. Canary and his colleagues (2002) found that the beneficial effects of these maintenance mechanisms were short lived: If these desirable activities stopped, contentment soon began to decline. The clear implication is that in order to maintain happy relationships, we have to *keep at it*. And here's where *self-control* is pertinent again (Kammrath & Peetz, 2011); over the long haul, we need to continue to strive to be routinely cheerful, loving, and fair. The effort we put into it is likely to matter (Shafer et al., 2014); those of us who take occasional breaks from being generous, jovial, and affectionate toward our partners do so at our peril.

REPAIRING RELATIONSHIPS

The maintenance mechanisms that protect and preserve relationships have something in common with taking good care of your car. If you shopped wisely and made a good buy, you're likely to be a happy driver if you conscientiously engage in a consistent program of thoughtful maintenance, regularly changing the oil, adding antifreeze, and generally taking care of business. Still, sooner or later, despite your efforts, things may break, and a repair rather than a tune-up will be in order. If the repair is simple, you may want to do it yourself, but there may also be occasions in which you'll need professional help. Happily, when relationships break, as with cars, help is available.

Do It Yourself

One way to solve the problems we encounter in our relationships is to fix them ourselves. Our perceptions of our own behavior tend to be contaminated by self-serving biases, and it's often hard for us to recognize how we are contributing to the relational difficulties we face. Third-party observers can usually be more dispassionate and fair in their perceptions of our relationships than we can. Nevertheless, if you want to do it yourself, there's plenty of advice available. Television shows, self-help books, websites, and podcasts are full of suggestions that may help you improve your relationships. And consumers of this material often feel that the advice has been helpful; people who read self-help books, for instance, usually feel that the books were beneficial to them (Ellis, 1993).

There are often problems, however, with the popular advice the media provide. For one thing, the backgrounds of people who sell their advice are sometimes as bogus as the advice itself; there are well-known authors who boast of their "Ph.D." degrees who either did not graduate from an accredited university or did not study a helping profession or behavioral science in graduate school. According to Wikipedia, John Gray, the best-selling author of *Men Are from Mars, Women Are from Venus* (1992), received his Ph.D. from Columbia Pacific University, an unaccredited distance-learning place you have never heard of (because it was shut down by the state of California). Dr. Laura Schlessinger, best-selling author of *The Proper Care and Feeding of Marriage* (2007), has a Ph.D. in physiology, not psychology. In addition, some advisers do not base their counsel on sound research; instead, they give voice to their personal opinions, which are sometimes at odds with the facts.

Indeed, too often, lay advice is simply wrong—with its popularity having nothing to do with its accuracy. Back in chapter 1, I asserted that relationship scientists disagree strongly with the simpleminded notion that men come from Mars and women come from Venus; now that you've read this book, what do you think?

Here's another example. A book entitled *The Rules: Time-Tested Secrets for Capturing the Heart of Mr. Right* was a number one "nonfiction" bestseller a while back. According to its authors (Fein & Schneider, 1995), *The Rules* described "a simple way of acting around men that can help any woman win the heart of the man of her dreams" (p. 5). If readers followed the advice provided, "he will not just marry you, but feel crazy about you forever! What we're promising you is 'happily ever after'" (p. 6). Sounds great, doesn't it? Unfortunately, the rules were wrong. In order to enhance their desirability, readers were advised to stay aloof and mysterious and to avoid seeming too eager to develop a new relationship. As the authors admitted, "in plain language, we're talking about playing hard to get" (p. 6). But playing hard-to-get doesn't work, and relationship science has known that for 40 years. Men are not particularly attracted to women who artificially delay the progress of a developing relationship; what's attractive to a man is a desirable woman who plays hard-to-get for everyone *but him* (Walster et al., 1973). Specifically, *The Rules* instructed women to avoid seeing a man more than twice a week, to avoid much self-disclosure early on, and to avoid telling him what they did when they were apart, and these and other rules are *negatively* correlated with men's interest in (Jonason & Li, 2013), and commitment to (Agnew & Gephart, 2000) a new partner. On the whole, women who followed *The Rules* probably had more trouble attracting and keeping men than did other women. That's not very useful advice. (Indeed, one of the authors filed for divorce a few years after the book came out.)

Of course, not all popular advice is flawed, and some of it is very credible. Some self-help books and websites, for instance, are written or run by reputable, well-respected scientists (e.g., Christensen et al., 2014; Gottman, 2011; Orbuch, 2009). And on the positive side, such help is inexpensive. Readers or visitors can refer to them repeatedly, absorbing material at their own pace. Credible books and self-help sites may also be particularly valuable to people who are too embarrassed to seek formal therapy. On average, doing it yourself isn't nearly as effective as face-to-face education and therapy are, but people can still learn skills and perspectives that facilitate their efforts to address their problems (McAllister et al., 2012). Along those lines, if you're seeking good (and free!) advice, I recommend the *Utah Marriage Handbook*, which is available for download at http://strongermarriage.org/engaged/free-utah-marriage-handbook. It's well done. (And did I mention it's free?)

Let me also acknowledge that I'm glad you read *this* book. It's not designed as a self-help book, but I hope that the information I gathered here has been useful to you. I believe that there is enormous value in the scientific study of close relationships, and I hope that I've provided you material that will help you understand your own relationships with more sophistication. I bet that there's a lot here that you can apply to your own circumstances to enjoy even richer, more rewarding partnerships.

Preventive Maintenance

There are also occasions, when you're taking care of your car, when the smart thing to do is to invest in major maintenance *before* anything goes wrong. After a few years, for instance, you should replace your timing belt (if you have one);

it's a part inside a gasoline engine that, at best, will leave you stranded, or, at worse, will destroy your engine if it breaks. It's an expensive change to make, and when your engine is running fine, it's easy to put off. But there's no question that it's a wise choice.

Similarly, couples who are engaged to be married usually feel that they're sailing along just fine, and there's no need to prepare for the new phase of their relationship that wedlock will bring. However, some preventive maintenance may be valuable then, too. Before problems begin, fine-tuning a couple's expectations and communication skills may pay big dividends.

Premarital counseling is available in various forms ranging from informal visits with a pastor, priest, or rabbi to structured training under the guidance of psychologists or marriage and family therapists. (Rolffs & Rogge, 2016, provide a review of these programs.) Web-based instruction that people access at home is also available (Doss et al., 2016). To keep things simple here, I'll touch on the PREP program, which is one of the best-known relationship skills courses.

The Prevention and Relationship Enhancement Program, or PREP, typically involves about 12 hours of training spread across five sessions (Markman et al., 1994). Meetings focus on several topics that may be familiar by now to readers of this book:

- *The power of commitment to change partners' outlooks and behavior.* Couples are encouraged to take a long-range view of the future they are striving to create together.
- *The importance of having fun together.* Couples are urged to make a point of playing together on a regular basis.
- *The value of open communication about sex.* Couples are advised to express their desires clearly and openly and to try something new every now and then.
- *The consequences of inappropriate expectations.* Couples are encouraged to be aware of their expectations, to be reasonable in what they expect, and to communicate their expectations clearly.

Participants are also taught the *speaker-listener technique*, which I described back on pages 356–357.

Does PREP work? In general, the answer seems to be yes: PREP and other programs like it are usually beneficial, at least for a while, particularly for high-risk couples who need them the most (Williamson et al., 2015). Engaged and newlywed couples who participate in a premarital prevention program are less than half as likely to separate over the next 3 years as are couples who do not receive such education (Rogge et al., 2013). The long-term effects of such training are still uncertain, and over time the effects of any one program may not be much different from those of another (Markman et al., 2013). Nevertheless, some premarital preventive maintenance appears to facilitate a few years of smooth sailing when marriages begin, and couples who participate in such programs are more likely than others to seek couples counseling if they need it later on (Williamson et al., 2014). It's likely that fewer marriages would fail if such education were more widespread (Halford et al., 2018).

Marital Therapy

Once real problems emerge, more intensive interventions may be needed. Professional helpers may use a variety of therapeutic approaches, and three different broad types of therapies appear to be helpful for most people most of the time. As we'll see, they differ with regard to (a) their focus on problematic behavior, thoughts, or feelings; (b) their focus on individual vulnerabilities or the couple's interaction as the source of dysfunction; and (c) their emphasis on past events or present difficulties as the source of distress (Baucom et al., 2006). Therapy that involves both members of a couple is most common, but people in troubled relationships often profit from individual therapy even when their partners refuse to seek help with them.

Behavioral Approaches

Most of the time, unhappy spouses aren't very nice to each other, and a classic intervention, **traditional behavioral couple therapy** (or TBCT), encourages them to be more pleasant and rewarding partners. TBCT focuses on the couple's present interactions and seeks to replace any negative and punishing behavior with more gracious and generous actions. Couples are taught communication skills that help them express affection and manage conflict coolly, and they are specifically encouraged to do things that benefit and please their partners in order to increase the rewards and decrease the costs of their interactions.

Desirable behavior is elicited in several ways. Therapists may schedule "love days" (Weiss et al., 1973) in which one partner deliberately sets out to do favors and kindnesses that are requested by the other. Alternatively, the couple may enter into agreements to reward positive behavior from their partners with desirable behavior of their own. In one such agreement, a *quid pro quo contract*,[4] behavior change from one partner is directly linked to behavior change by the other (Jacobson & Margolin, 1979). For instance, she may agree to do the laundry every Sunday if he cleans the bathroom on Saturday, and he'll clean the bathroom if she did the laundry on the previous Sunday. This sort of contract fails to increase positive exchanges if either partner falters, so *good faith contracts,* parallel agreements in which behavior change is rewarded with special privileges, are also used (Weiss et al., 1974). In a good faith contract, he may agree to clean the bathroom every Saturday, and when he does, he gets to choose the activity for that evening; she may agree to do the laundry every Sunday, and when she does, he assumes all the responsibility for bathing the children and putting them to bed that night.

Getting partners to behave more generously is important, but it doesn't always change the grudging disregard that distressed couples often feel for each other by the time they seek therapy. For that reason, a descendant of TBCT focuses on partners' cognitions and judgments of their relationship as well as their conduct (Epstein & Baucom, 2002). In addition to encouraging desirable behavior, **cognitive-behavioral couple therapy** (or CBCT) seeks to change various aspects of the ways partners think about and appraise their partnership. The therapy

---

[4] *Quid pro quo* is Latin that means "something for something" or "this for that."

addresses spouses' *selective attention,* their tendency to notice some things and to ignore others, and tries to instill more reasonable *expectations,* more forgiving *attributions,* and more adaptive *relationship beliefs* in each partner. Participants are taught to track and test their thoughts, actively considering various attributions for any negative behavior, recognizing and challenging unrealistic beliefs, and generating lists of the pros and cons of the expectations they hold. CBCT acknowledges that people often import into their marriages problematic habits of thinking that they have learned in past relationships, but it still focuses mainly on current patterns in a couple's interaction; the idea is that, no matter where maladaptive cognition came from, a couple will be more content when they are able to perceive and judge each other fairly, kindly, and reasonably (Fischer et al., 2016).

An even more recent descendant of TBCT is **integrative behavioral couple therapy** (IBCT), an approach that seeks both to encourage more desirable behavior and to teach the partners to tolerantly accept the incompatibilities that they cannot change (Gurman, 2013). IBCT teaches the communication skills and employs the behavior modification techniques of TBCT, but it also assumes that even when two partners behave desirably and well, some frustrating incompatibilities will always remain; for that reason, an important goal of therapy is to teach spouses adaptive emotional reactions to the nuisances they will inevitably face. Acceptance of one's own and one's partner's imperfections is promoted through three techniques (Wheeler & Christensen, 2002). With *empathic joining,* spouses are taught to express their pain and vulnerabilities without any blame or resentment that will make their partners defensive; the point is to engender empathy by helping each spouse understand the other's feelings. Spouses are also taught to view their problems with *unified detachment,* an intellectual perspective that defuses emotion and helps the couple understand with cool dispassion their problematic patterns of interaction. The couple is invited to describe the events that cause frustration and to identify the triggers that set them in motion while avoiding the negative emotion that usually results from such events. Finally, in *tolerance building,* spouses are taught to become less sensitive and to react less intensely when problematic behavior occurs; negative patterns of interaction are rehearsed and analyzed in therapy sessions, and the partners are actually encouraged to give up their efforts to change everything they dislike in each other. The focus of IBCT is on the couple's present patterns of interaction, whatever their origins, and it seeks collaborative change in both their interactive behavior and their individual emotional reactions to it.

Thus, the three behavioral approaches share a focus on the partners' actions toward each other, but they differ in their additional elements. TBCT seeks to change spouses' behavior, whereas CBCT seeks to change their behavior and their cognitions, and IBCT seeks to change their behavior and their emotions (see Table 14.2). Each approach may appeal to some couples more than others, but, importantly, they all work. Between 60 and 70 percent of the couples who seriously undertake any of these therapies achieve notable reductions in their dissatisfaction and distress that lasts for years (Baucom et al., 2018). And thanks to Brian Doss and his colleagues (Roddy et al., 2016), you can try a version of IBCT online at www.OurRelationship.com.

TABLE 14.2. Core Features of Marital Therapies

	Primary Focus on		
Therapeutic Approach	Behavior, Cognitions, or Emotions	Individual or Couple	Present or Past
Behavioral Couple Therapy	Behavior	Couple	Present
Cognitive-Behavioral Couple Therapy	Cognitions	Both	Present
Integrative Behavioral Couple Therapy	Emotions	Both	Present
Emotionally Focused Couple Therapy	Emotions	Both	Present
Insight-Oriented Couple Therapy	Emotions & Cognitions	Individual	Past

Source: Adapted from Baucom, D. H., Epstein, N., & Stanton, S. (2006). "The treatment of relationship distress: Theoretical perspectives and empirical findings." In A. Vangelisti & D. Perlman (Eds.), The Cambridge handbook of personal relationships (pp. 745–769). New York: Cambridge University Press, 2006.

Emotionally Focused Couple Therapy

Another relatively recent innovation, emotionally focused couple therapy (or EFCT), is derived from attachment theory (Wiebe & Johnson, 2016). Throughout this book, we've seen that people who are securely attached to their partners are content and comfortable in intimate relationships, and EFCT strives to improve relationships by increasing the partners' attachment security. Like the behavioral approaches, EFCT seeks to reestablish desirable patterns of interaction between spouses, but its primary focus is on the emotions the partners experience as they seek to fulfill their attachment needs. People are thought to need emotional security, and they seek it from their spouses, but frustration and distress can result when one spouse seeks reassurance and acceptance ineffectively and the other spouse responds in a negative manner. In one common pattern, a partner who wants more attention and affection will pursue it in a way that seems critical and blaming to the other, who then responds by retreating to an even greater distance. No one is soothed and no one is happy, and the cycle of obnoxious pursuit and withdrawal may intensify.

EFCT tries to identify such maladaptive cycles of emotional communication and to replace them with restructured interactions that allow the partners to feel safe, loved, and securely connected to one another. Three stages are involved (Johnson, 2004). In the first, problematic patterns of communication or conflict are identified, and the couple is encouraged to think of themselves as collaborators united in a fight against a common foe; the therapist also helps the spouses explore the unmet needs for acceptance and security that fuel their conflict. In the second stage, the partners begin to establish constructive new patterns of interaction that acknowledge the other's needs and that provide more reassurance and comfort. Finally, in the third stage, the partners rehearse and reinforce their responsiveness to each other, and they rely on their newfound security to fearlessly seek new solutions to old problems. The entire process covers nine steps, which are listed in Table 14.3, during 10–20 sessions of treatment.

The focus of therapy is a couple's present interaction, but the partners are encouraged to consider how their individual needs contribute to their joint outcomes, so both individual and interactive sources of dysfunction are examined. And EFCT is quite effective with couples who are moderately distressed; about 70 percent of them overcome their dissatisfaction by the time treatment is complete (Baucom et al., 2018).

Insight-Oriented Therapy

A final family of therapies has descended from the psychodynamic traditions of Sigmund Freud, who assumed that people often carried unconscious injuries and scars from their past relationships that could, without their knowledge, complicate and contaminate their present partnerships. (See the box on the next page.) Various interventions seek to promote partners' insights into such problematic "baggage," but a prototypical example of this approach is Douglas Snyder's (2002)

TABLE 14.3. Specific Steps in Emotionally Focused Couple Therapy

With the help of a therapist, couples who complete EFCT will encounter each of the following phases of treatment:

Stage One: Assessment of the Problem

Step 1: Partners describe their problems, often describing a recent fight in detail.

Step 2: Partners identify the emotional fears and needs that underlie their arguments.

Step 3: Partners put their emotions into words so that the other understands.

Step 4: Partners realize that they're both hurting and that neither of them is individually to blame.

Stage Two: Promoting New Styles of Interaction That Foster Bonding

Step 5: Partners identify and admit their deepest feelings, including their needs for reassurance, acceptance, and comfort.

Step 6: Partners acknowledge and begin to accept the other's feelings; they also explore their own new responses to what they have learned.

Step 7: Partners begin new patterns of interaction based on openness and understanding; they once again become allies rather than adversaries.

Stage Three: Rehearsal and Maintenance of Desirable New Styles of Interaction

Step 8: Partners collaboratively invent new solutions to old problems.

Step 9: Partners thoughtfully rehearse and consolidate their new, more accepting behavior toward each other.

Souce: Adapted from Johnson, S. M. Creating connection: The practice of emotionally focused couple therapy, *2e. New York: Brunner-Routledge, 2004.*

Central Tenets of Insight-Oriented Therapy

Most marital therapists who use a psychodynamic orientation stress three fundamental propositions:

1. In the ways they choose a mate and behave toward their partners, people are frequently influenced by hidden tensions and unresolved needs of which they are unaware.

2. Many of these unconscious conflicts stem from events that took place either in one's family of origin or in prior romantic relationships.

3. The major therapeutic goal is for the clients to gain insight into their unconscious conflicts—to understand why they feel and act the way they do—so that they have the freedom to choose to feel and act differently.

insight-oriented couple therapy (IOCT). IOCT emphasizes individual vulnerabilities to a greater extent than the other therapies I've mentioned (see Table 14.2); it strives to help people comprehend how the personal habits and assumptions they developed in other relationships may be creating difficulty with their present partners. Thus, it also examines past events to a fuller extent than other therapies do; IOCT assumes that the origins of marital dissatisfaction often lie in difficulties the spouses encountered in prior relationships.

A primary tool of IOCT is *affective reconstruction,* the process through which a spouse re-imagines and revisits past relationships in an effort to identify the themes and coping styles that characterized conflicts with past partners (Snyder & Schneider, 2002). A person is guided through close inspection of his or her relational history, and careful attention is given to the patterns of any interpersonal injuries. The therapist then helps the client understand the connections that may exist between the themes of the person's past relationships and his or her present problems.

The insight that emerges from affective reconstruction helps the partners adopt more benign judgments of the other's behavior. Each spouse becomes more aware of his or her vulnerabilities, and the joint expression of fears and needs builds empathy between the partners. The therapist is also likely to portray both spouses as doing the best that they can, given their personal histories, so that blaming and acrimony are reduced. Then, because (as we've seen before) knowledge is power, the spouses slowly construct new, more rewarding patterns of interaction that avoid the pitfalls of the past.

All of this typically takes 15–20 sessions with a therapist. Like the emotionally focused and behavioral approaches to therapy, IOCT appears to help most couples, and in at least one study (Snyder et al., 1991), it had substantial staying power, leaving spouses better adjusted 4 years later than TBCT did.

Common Features of Marital Therapy

There are several other varieties of marital therapy available in the marketplace, but I focused on just the behavioral approaches, EFCT, and IOCT because careful studies suggest that they work for most couples (Baucom et al., 2018). Most people who seriously participate in any of these therapies are likely to be better off afterward, and (as a rough average) about two-thirds of them will no longer be dissatisfied with their marriages (Lebow et al., 2012). There are no guarantees, and success in therapy is likely to depend on the sincerity of one's investment in, and the amount of effort one devotes to, the process. But *marital therapy helps* most couples. If you ever wish to repair a faltering intimate relationship, help is available.

So, which of these therapies is for you? Over the years, this question has aroused a lot of competition and occasional argument among professional helpers, but I have a very simple answer: Pick the therapy—and the therapist—that appeal to you the most. This is not an idle suggestion. The best therapy for you is very likely to be the one that sounded most interesting as you read these last few pages (Lindhiem et al., 2014), and there are three reasons why.

First, despite their different labels and different emphases, the therapies I have introduced all share some common features, and that may be why they all work (Baucom et al., 2018). Each provides a reasonable explanation of why a couple has been experiencing difficulty, and each provides a hopeful new perspective on how such difficulties can be overcome. Toward that end, each provides a means of changing patterns of interaction that have been causing distress, and each increases a couple's repertoire of more effective, more desirable behavior. They pursue these ends with different rationales, but all of these therapies equip couples with more constructive and more satisfying ways of relating to each other. So, these various approaches all share some core elements that make them more similar than they may superficially seem.

Second, given this, the *therapist* you select may be just as important as the therapy you choose. Marital therapy is much more likely to be successful when both members of the couple respect and trust their therapist (Summers & Barber, 2003), so you should seek an accomplished therapist who seems credible and persuasive to you. A professional helper who espouses a therapeutic approach you find plausible is likely to seem more skilled and knowledgeable than is one who uses an approach you find less compelling.

Finally, a therapeutic approach that interests you may be more likely to offer hope that real change is possible, and such optimism can be very influential (Snyder et al., 2006). Positive expectations make therapy more effective. Compared to those who are pessimistic about the outcome of therapy, spouses who believe that benefits will result from their efforts are likely to work harder and to maintain higher spirits, and both increase the chances that the therapy will succeed.

Along those lines, let me remind you of the dangers in believing, as some people do, that "great relationships just happen" and "partners cannot change." We encountered these and other dysfunctional relationship beliefs back in chapter 4, and I hope that the disadvantages of such beliefs now seem even clearer. People can and *do* change during therapy (Roberts et al., 2017). But if we think they can't, we'll be less likely to seek therapy when problems arise in our marriages, and if we do enter therapy, we'll probably do so halfheartedly. As a result, our situations will be less likely to improve.

You can lead a horse to water, but you can't make him drink. Indeed, that old cliché suggests one last thing that all these marital therapies have in common: They are all underutilized. Most people who divorce do so without ever consulting a marital therapist, and the minority who do usually wait to seek help until their problems are severe (Cordova, 2014). This is particularly true of men; they're slower to recognize that problems exist, less likely to believe that therapy will help, and slower to seek therapy when it's warranted than women are (Doss et al., 2003). Given the effectiveness of marital therapy, this is regrettable. I hope that, now that you know that you'll probably get your money's worth—and whether you're gay or straight (Whitton et al., 2016)—you'll not delay in contacting a therapist if the need arises.

> ### A Point to Ponder
>
> What would keep you from seeking help for your relationship if you ever need it? Why?

Indeed, time usually counts. The sooner marital problems are addressed, the easier they are to solve. The greater a couple's distress, the harder it is to reverse (Snyder et al., 2006). Why wait? Consider the possibilities: Therapy doesn't always work, and there is always the chance, once a couple's problems are understood, that a therapist will recommend dissolving the marriage. But if that's the case, a great deal of distressing uncertainty and pain may be avoided (Doherty & Harris, 2017). Alternatively, if a relationship is salvageable and therapy can be helpful, a couple can reduce their discomfort and return to profitable partnership sooner when therapy is sought promptly. Either way, there's little point in waiting to address the inevitable difficulties intimate partners will face.

IN CONCLUSION

Overall, then, just like cars, relationships can get preventive maintenance that can keep them from breaking down, and they can often be fixed when they do falter. I think that this is a clever analogy (which is why I used it), but I need to point out that there's one way in which it is quite misleading: Sooner or later, no matter how you take care of them, cars wear out and must be replaced, and that's not necessarily true of intimate relationships at all. Sure, there are some people who regularly trade in their lovers, like their cars, for newer, flashier models (Campbell & Foster, 2002), but most of you out there hope that you will ultimately construct an intimate relationship with a particular partner that you will find fulfilling for the rest of your life.

And you may. I hope that, having studied the modern science of close relationships, you are now better equipped to create, understand, and manage successful, happy, rewarding relationships that last. Hold sensible expectations, so that you're not disappointed when frustrations arise (Neff & Geers, 2013). But know, too, that our relationships are more resilient, being better able to withstand the inevitable difficulties of interdependency, when they are nurtured and nourished with plenty of shared affection (Horan, 2012), shared activities and pleasures (Feeney & Lemay, 2012), and shared expressions of devotion and commitment (Weigel & Ballard-Reisch, 2014). So, by shopping wisely and then making attentive and thoughtful investments in the care and feeding of your partnerships, you may very well be able to develop and maintain relationships that remain gratifying to you forever. After all, some people do. When 100 couples who had been contentedly married for 45 years were asked to explain their success (Lauer et al., 1990), they replied that:

- They valued marriage and considered it a long-term commitment.
- A sense of humor was a big help.
- They were similar enough that they agreed about most things.
- They genuinely liked their spouses and enjoyed spending time with them.

I hope that you're able to do the same.

FOR YOUR CONSIDERATION

When she reached the end of this book, Leslie decided to talk with her husband about her increasing discontent with him and their marriage. He had been considerate and charming when they were engaged, but she had come to feel that he had stopped trying to please her, and she felt lonely and hurt. She felt that she was constantly changing to accommodate his wishes but that he was doing little to satisfy her in return. He never asked her how her day had been. It was a little thing, but it nettled her, and it was just one example of his self-absorption and apparent lack of care. However, when she suggested that they seek therapy, he resolutely refused. So, she decided to go by herself; she went to the website of the American Association for Marriage and Family Therapy at www.aamft.org, found a therapist, and made an individual appointment.

Having read this chapter, what do you think the future holds for Leslie and her husband? Why?

CHAPTER SUMMARY

With better understanding of close relationships, people are better equipped to prevent some problems and to overcome others.

Maintaining and Enhancing Relationships

Relationship maintenance mechanisms are strategic actions people take to sustain their partnerships.

Staying Committed. People who want a relationship to continue think and behave differently than less committed partners do. Cognitive maintenance mechanisms include *cognitive interdependence, positive illusions, perceived superiority, inattention to alternatives,* and *derogation of alternatives.*

Behavioral maintenance mechanisms include *willingness to sacrifice, prayer,* the *Michelangelo phenomenon, accommodation, self-control, play, rituals,* and *forgiveness.*

Staying Content. Communication scholars have identified several more activities that seem to help partners stay content. The most important of these are *positivity, assurances,* and the *sharing* of *tasks.*

Partners who routinely engage in these activities are happier than are those who work less hard to maintain their relationships. However, people need to *keep doing them* in order for them to be beneficial.

Repairing Relationships

Regular maintenance helps keep relationships in good condition, but they may still break down and need repair.

Do It Yourself. There's plenty of advice available but some of it is faulty. However, some self-help information is provided by reputable scientists, and it may be very beneficial to its consumers.

Preventive Maintenance. Premarital counseling comes in various forms. One example, the Prevention and Relationship Enhancement Program, results in increased satisfaction during the first years of marriage.

Marital Therapy. Professional helpers may use several different therapies. *Traditional behavioral couple therapy* seeks to establish less punishing and more pleasant patterns of interaction between partners. *Cognitive-behavioral couple therapy* focuses on maladaptive cognitions. *Integrative behavioral couple therapy* tries to teach troubled spouses to accept the incompatibilities that they cannot change. *Emotionally focused couple therapy* seeks to make partners more secure. *Insight-oriented couple therapy* seeks to free spouses from the emotional baggage they carry from prior relationships.

All of these therapeutic approaches share certain core features. Couples who trust their therapists and enter therapy with positive expectations are likely to derive real benefit from any of them.

In Conclusion

My hope is that, having studied the modern science of close relationships, you are better equipped to create, understand, and manage successful, happy, rewarding relationships that last. I wish you the very best in the interpersonal journey that awaits you.

References

Aassve, A., Fuochi, G., & Mencarini, L. (2014). Desperate housework: Relative resources, time availability, economic dependency, and gender ideology across Europe. *Journal of Family Issues, 35,* 1000–1022.

AAUW. (2017). *The simple truth about the gender pay gap.* American Association of University Women. Retrieved from http://www.aauw.org/research/the-simple-truth-about-the-gender-pay-gap/

Abbey, A. (1982). Sex differences in attributions for friendly behavior: Do males misperceive females' friendliness? *Journal of Personality and Social Psychology, 42,* 830–838.

Abel, E. L., & Kruger, M. L. (2010). Smile intensity in photographs predicts longevity. *Psychological Science, 21,* 542–544.

Acevedo, B. P. (2015). Neural correlates of human attachment: Evidence from fMRI studies of adult pair-bonding. In V. Zayas & C. Hazan (Eds.), *Bases of adult attachment: Linking brain, mind and behavior* (pp. 185–194). New York: Springer.

Acevedo, B. P., & Aron, A. (2009). Does a long-term relationship kill romantic love? *Review of General Psychology, 13,* 59–65.

Acevedo, B. P., & Aron, A. P. (2014). Romantic love, pair-bonding, and the dopaminergic reward system. In M. Mikulincer & P. R. Shaver (Eds.), *Mechanisms of social connection: From brain to group* (pp. 55–69). Washington, DC: American Psychological Association.

Acevedo, B. P., Aron, A., Fisher, H. E., & Brown, L. L. (2012). Neural correlates of long-term intense romantic love. *Social Cognitive and Affective Neuroscience, 7,* 145–159.

Ackerman, D. (1994). *A natural history of love.* New York: Random House.

Ackerman, J. M., Griskevicius, V., & Li, N. P. (2011). Let's get serious: Communicating commitment in romantic relationships. *Journal of Personality and Social Psychology, 100,* 1079–1094.

Ackerman, J. M., & Kenrick, D. T. (2009). Cooperative courtship: Helping friends raise and raze relationship barriers. *Personality and Social Psychology Bulletin, 35,* 1285–1300.

Ackerman, R. A., Kashy, D. A., & Corretti, C. A. (2015). A tutorial on analyzing data from speed-dating studies with heterosexual dyads. *Personal Relationships, 22,* 92–110.

Adams, G. S., & Inesi, M. E. (2016). Impediments to forgiveness: Victim and transgressor attributions of intent and guilt. *Journal of Personality and Social Psychology, 111,* 866–881.

Adams, R. B., Jr., & Nelson, A. J. (2016). Eye behavior and gaze. In D. Matsumoto, H. C. Hwang, & M. G. Frank (Eds.), *APA handbook of nonverbal communication* (pp. 335–362). Washington, DC: American Psychological Association.

Afifi, T., Caughlin, J., & Afifi, W. (2007). The dark side (and light side) of avoidance and secrets. In B. H. Spitzberg & W. R. Cupach (Eds.), *The dark side of interpersonal communication* (2nd ed., pp. 61–92). Mahwah, NJ: Erlbaum.

Afifi, T. D., Joseph, A., & Aldeis, D. (2012). The "standards for openness hypothesis": Why women find (conflict) avoidance more dissatisfying than men. *Journal of Social and Personal Relationships, 29,* 102–125.

Afifi, T. D., Merrill, A. F., & Davis, S. (2016). The theory of resilience and relational load. *Personal Relationships, 23,* 663–683.

Afifi, T. O., MacMillan, H., Cox, B. J., Asmundson, G. J. G., Stein, M. B., & Sareen, J. (2009). Mental health correlates of intimate partner violence in marital relationships in a nationally representative sample of males and females. *Journal of Interpersonal Violence, 24,* 1398–1417.

Afifi, W. A., Falato, W. L., & Weiner, J. L. (2001). Identity concerns following a severe relational transgression: The role of discovery method for the relational outcomes of infidelity. *Journal of Social and Personal Relationships, 18,* 291–308.

Agnew, C. R., & Gephart, J. M. (2000). Testing *The Rules* of commitment enhancement: Separating fact from fiction. *Representative Research in Social Psychology, 24,* 41–47.

Agnew, C. R., Van Lange, P. A. M., Rusbult, C. E., & Langston, C. A. (1998). Cognitive interdependence: Commitment and the mental representation of close relationships. *Journal of Personality and Social Psychology, 74,* 939–954.

Agthe, M., Strobel, M., Spörrle, M., Pfundmair, M., & Maner, J. K. (2016). On the borders of harmful and helpful beauty biases: The biasing effects of physical attractiveness depend on sex and ethnicity. *Evolutionary Psychology, 14,* 1–14.

Ahmetoglu, G., Swami, V., & Chamorro-Premuzic, T. (2010). The relationship between dimensions of love, personality, and relationship length. *Archives of Sexual Behavior, 39,* 1181–1190.

Ahrons, C. (1994). *The good divorce.* New York: HarperCollins.

Ahrons, C. R. (2007). Family ties after divorce: Long-term implications for children. *Family Process, 46,* 53–65.

Aicken, C. R. H., Gray, M., Clifton, S., & . . . Mercer, C. H. (2013). Improving questions on sexual partnerships: Lessons learned from cognitive interviews for Britain's third National Survey of Sexual Attitudes and Lifestyles ("Natsal-3"). *Archives of Sexual Behavior, 42,* 173–185.

Ainsworth, M. D. S., Blehar, M. C., Waters, E., & Wall, S. (1978). *Patterns of attachment: A psychological study of the strange situation.* Hillsdale, NJ: Erlbaum.

Aitken, S. J., Lyons, M., & Jonason, P. K. (2013). Dads or cads? Women's strategic decisions in the mating game. *Personality and Individual Differences, 55,* 118–122.

Aizer, A. A., Chen, M. H., McCarthy, E. P., & . . . Nguyen, P. L. (2013). Marital status and survival in patients with cancer. *Journal of Clinical Oncology, 31,* 3869–3876.

Albrecht, S. L., & Kunz, P. R. (1980). The decision to divorce: A social exchange perspective. *Journal of Divorce, 3,* 319–337.

Albright, L., Cohen, A. I., Malloy, T. E., Christ, T., & Bromgard, G. (2004). Judgments of communicative intent in conversation. *Journal of Experimental Social Psychology, 40,* 290–302.

Aldeis, D., & Afifi, T. D. (2015). Putative secrets and conflict in romantic relationships over time. *Communication Monographs, 82,* 224–251.

Algoe, S. B., Fredrickson, B. L., & Gable, S. L. (2013). The social functions of the emotion of gratitude via expression. *Emotion, 13,* 605–609.

Algoe, S. B., Kurtz, L. E., & Hilaire, N. M. (2016). Putting the "You" in "Thank You": Examining other-praising behavior as the active relational ingredient in expressed gratitude. *Social Psychological and Personality Science, 7,* 658–666.

Allen, A. B., & Leary, M. R. (2010). Reactions to others' selfish actions in the absence of tangible consequences. *Basic and Applied Social Psychology, 32,* 26–34.

Allen, J. P., Uchino, B. N., & Hafen, C. A. (2015). Running with the pack: Teen peer-relationship qualities as predictors of adult physical health. *Psychological Science, 26,* 1574–1583.

Allen, K., Blascovich, J., & Mendes, W. B. (2002). Cardiovascular reactivity in the presence of pets, friends, and spouses: The truth about cats and dogs. *Psychosomatic Medicine, 64,* 727–739.

Allen, K., Shykoff, B. E., & Izzo, J. L., Jr. (2001). Pet ownership, but not ACE inhibitor therapy, blunts home blood pressure responses to mental stress. *Hypertension, 38,* 815–820.

Allik, J., Realo, A., Mõttus, R., Borkenau, P., Kuppens, P., & Hrebíčková, M. (2010). How people see others is different from how people see themselves: A replicable pattern across cultures. *Journal of Personality and Social Psychology, 99,* 870–882.

Allison, R., & Risman, B. J. (2013). A double standard for "hooking up": How far have we come toward gender equality? *Social Science Research, 42,* 1191–1206.

Alterovitz, S. S., & Mendelsohn, G. A. (2011). Partner preferences across the life span: Online dating by older adults. *Psychology of Popular Media Culture, 1,* 89–95.

Altman, I., & Taylor, D. A. (1973). *Social penetration: The development of interpersonal relationships.* New York: Holt, Rinehart & Winston.

Alvergne, A., & Lummaa, V. (2010). Does the contraceptive pill alter mate choice in humans? *Trends in Ecology & Evolution, 25,* 171–179.

Amato, P. R. (2003). Reconciling divergent perspectives: Judith Wallerstein, quantitative family research, and children of divorce. *Family Relations, 52,* 332–339.

Amato, P. R. (2009). Institutional, companionate, and individualistic marriage: A social psychological perspective on marital change. In H. Peters & C. Kamp Dush (Eds.), *Marriage and family: Perspectives and complexities* (pp. 75–90). New York: Columbia University Press.

Amato, P. R. (2010). Research on divorce: Continuing trends and new developments. *Journal of Marriage and Family, 72,* 650–666.

Amato, P. R., Booth, A., Johnson, D. R., & Rogers, S. J. (2007). *Alone together: How marriage in America is changing.* Cambridge, MA: Harvard University Press.

Amato, P. R., & Patterson, S. E. (2017). The intergenerational transmission of union instability in early adulthood. *Journal of Marriage and Family, 79,* 723–728.

Amato, P. R., & Previti, D. (2003). People's reasons for divorcing: Gender, social class, the life course, and adjustment. *Journal of Family Issues, 24,* 602–626.

Amato, P. R., & Rogers, S. J. (1999). Do attitudes toward divorce affect marital quality? *Journal of Family Issues, 20,* 69–86.

Ambadar, Z., Cohn, J. F., & Reed, L. I. (2009). All smiles are not created equal: Morphology and timing of smiles perceived as amused, polite, and embarrassed/nervous. *Journal of Nonverbal Behavior, 33,* 17–34.

Ambady, N., Hallahan, M., & Conner, B. (1999). Accuracy of judgments of sexual orientation from thin slices of behavior. *Journal of Personality and Social Psychology, 77,* 538–547.

Ambrose, C. E., & Gross, A. M. (2016). Interpreting sexual dating encounters: Social information processing differences in men and women. *Journal of Family Violence, 31,* 361–370.

American Society of Plastic Surgeons. (2016). *2015 plastic surgery statistics report.* Retrieved from https://www.plasticsurgery.org/news/plastic-surgery-statistics.

Ames, D. R., Kammrath, L. K., Suppes, A., & Bolger, N. (2010). Not so fast: The (not-quite-complete) dissociation between accuracy and confidence in thin-slice impressions. *Personality and Social Psychology Bulletin, 36,* 264–277.

Andersen, P. A., Guerrero, L. K., & Jones, S. M. (2006). Nonverbal behavior in intimate interactions and intimate relationships. In V. Manusov & M. L. Patterson (Eds.), *The Sage handbook of nonverbal communication* (pp. 259–277). Thousand Oaks, CA: Sage.

Anderson, J. R., Van Ryzin, M. J., & Doherty, W. J. (2010). Developmental trajectories of marital happiness in continuously married individuals: A group-based modeling approach. *Journal of Family Psychology, 24,* 587–596.

Anderson, K. G. (2006). How well does paternity confidence match actual paternity? Evidence from worldwide nonpaternity rates. *Current Anthropology, 47,* 513–520.

Anderson, K. J., Kanner, M., & Elsayegh, N. (2009). Are feminists man haters? Feminists' and non-feminists' attitudes toward men. *Psychology of Women Quarterly, 33,* 216–224.

Anderson, L. R. (2016a). Divorce rate in the U.S.: Geographic Variation, 2015. *Family Profiles,* FP-16-21. Bowling Green, OH: National Center for Family & Marriage Research.

Anderson, L. R. (2016b). High school seniors' attitudes on cohabitation as a testing ground for marriage. *Family Profiles,* FP-16-13. Bowling Green, OH: National Center for Family & Marriage Research.

Anderson, M. (2015, October 1). *6 facts about teen romance in the digital age.* Pew Research Center. Retrieved from http://www.pewresearch.org/fact-tank/2015/10/01/6-facts-about-teen-romance-in-the-digital-age/.

Anderson, M., Kunkel, A., & Dennis, M. R. (2011). "Let's (not) talk about that": Bridging the past sexual experiences taboo to build healthy romantic relationships. *Journal of Sex Research, 48,* 381–391.

Andrews, P. W., Gangestad, S. W., Miller, G. F., Haselton, M. G., Thornhill, R., & Neale, M. C. (2008). Sex differences in detecting sexual infidelity: Results of a maximum likelihood method for analyzing the sensitivity of sex differences to underreporting. *Human Nature, 19,* 347–373.

Angulo, S., Brooks, M. L., & Swann, W. B., Jr. (2011). Swimming serenely in a sea of words: Sexism, communication, and precarious couples. *Personal Relationships, 18,* 604–616.

Ansari, A. (2015). *Love* in the age of *like. Time, 185*(22), 40–45.

Antfolk, J., Salo, B., Alanko, K., & . . . Santilla, P. (2015). Women's and men's sexual preferences and activities with respect to the partner's age: Evidence for female choice. *Evolution and Human Behavior, 36,* 73–79.

Apostolou, M. (2009). Parent-offspring conflict over mating: The case of short-term mating strategies. *Personality and Individual Differences, 47,* 895–899.

Apostolou, M. (2015). Parent-offspring conflict over mating: Domains of agreement and disagreement. *Evolutionary Psychology, 13,* 1–12.

Archer, J. (2006). Cross-cultural differences in physical aggression between partners: A social-role analysis. *Personality and Social Psychology Review, 10,* 133–153.

Argyle, M., & Henderson, M. (1984). The rules of friendship. *Journal of Social and Personal Relationships, 1,* 211–237.

Ariely, D., & Loewenstein, G. (2006). The heat of the moment: The effect of sexual arousal on sexual decision making. *Journal of Behavioral Decision Making, 19,* 87–98.

Aron, A. (2010). Behavior, the brain, and the social psychology of close relationships. In C. Agnew, D. Carlston, W. Graziano, & J. Kelly (Eds.), *Then a miracle occurs: Focusing on behavior in social psychological theory and research* (pp. 283–298). New York: Oxford University Press.

Aron, A., Aron, E. N., & Allen, J. (1998). Motivations for unreciprocated love. *Personality and Social Psychology Bulletin, 24,* 787–796.

Aron, A., Aron, E. N., & Smollan, D. (1992). Inclusion of Other in the Self Scale and the structure of interpersonal closeness. *Journal of Personality and Social Psychology, 63,* 596–612.

Aron, A., Fisher, H. E., Strong, G., Acevedo, B., Riela, S., & Tsapelas, I. (2008). Falling in love. In S. Sprecher, A. Wenzel, & J. Harvey, (Eds.), *Handbook of relationship initiation* (pp. 315–336). New York: Psychology Press.

Aron, A., Lewandowski, G. W., Jr., Mashek, D., & Aron, E. N. (2013). The self-expansion model of motivation and cognition in close relationships. In J. A. Simpson & L. Campbell (Eds.), *The Oxford handbook of close relationships* (pp. 90–115). New York: Oxford University Press.

Aron, A., Mashek, D. J., & Aron, E. N. (2004). Closeness as including the other in the self. In D. J. Mashek & A. Aron (Eds.), *Handbook of closeness and intimacy* (pp. 27–41). Mahwah, NJ: Erlbaum.

Aron, A., Melinat, E., Aron, E. N., Vallone, R. D., & Bator, R. J. (1997). The experimental generation of interpersonal closeness: A procedure and some preliminary findings. *Personality and Social Psychology Bulletin, 23,* 363–377.

Aron, A., Norman, C. C., Aron, E. N., McKenna, C., & Heyman, R. E. (2000). Couples' shared participation in novel and arousing activities and experienced relationship quality. *Journal of Personality and Social Psychology, 78,* 273–284.

Aron, A., Paris, M., & Aron, E. N. (1995). Falling in love: Prospective studies of self-concept change. *Journal of Personality and Social Psychology, 69,* 1102–1112.

Aron, A., Steele, J. L., Kashdan, T. B., & Perez, M. (2006). When similars do not attract: Tests of a prediction from the self-expansion model. *Personal Relationships, 13,* 387–396.

Aronson, E., & Cope, V. (1968). My enemy's enemy is my friend. *Journal of Personality and Social Psychology, 8,* 8–12.

Arriaga, X. B., & Agnew, C. R. (2001). Being committed: Affective, cognitive, and conative components of relationship commitment. *Personality and Social Psychology Bulletin, 27,* 1190–1203.

Arriaga, X. B., Capezza, N. M., & Daly, C. A. (2016). Personal standards for judging aggression by a relationship partner: How much aggression is too much? *Journal of Personality and Social Psychology, 110,* 36–54.

Arriaga, X. B., Capezza, N. M., Goodfriend, W., Rayl, E. S., & Sands, K. J. (2013). Individual well-being and relationship maintenance at odds: The unexpected perils of maintaining a relationship with an aggressive partner. *Social Psychological and Personality Science, 4,* 676–684.

Arriaga, X. B., Capezza, N. M., Reed, J. T., Wesselmann, E. D., & Williams, K. D. (2014b). With partners like you, who needs strangers? Ostracism involving a romantic partner. *Personal Relationships, 21,* 557–569.

Arriaga, X. B., Cobb, R. J., & Daly, C. A. (2018). Aggression and violence in romantic relationships. In A. Vangelisti & D. Perlman (Eds.), *Cambridge handbook of personal relationships* (2nd ed.) New York: Cambridge University Press.

Arriaga, X. B., Kumashiro, M., Finkel, E. J., VanderDrift, L. E., & Luchies, L. B. (2014). Filling the void: Bolstering attachment security in committed relationships. *Social Psychological and Personality Science, 5,* 398–406.

Arriaga, X. B., & Rusbult, C. E. (1998). Standing in my partner's shoes: Partner perspective taking and reactions to accommodative dilemmas. *Personality and Social Psychology Bulletin, 24,* 927–948.

Arriaga, X. B., & Schkeryantz, E. L. (2015). Intimate relationships and personal distress: The invisible harm of psychological aggression. *Personality and Social Psychology Bulletin, 41,* 1332–1344.

Arriaga, X. B., Slaughterbeck, E. S., Capezza, N. M., & Hmurovic, J. L. (2007). From bad to worse: Relationship commitment and vulnerability to partner imperfections. *Personal Relationships, 14,* 389–409.

Arroyo, A., & Harwood, J. (2011). Communication competence mediates the link between shyness and relationship quality. *Personality and Individual Differences, 50,* 264–267.

Asch, S. E. (1946). Forming impressions of personality. *Journal of Abnormal and Social Psychology, 41,* 258–290.

Asendorpf, J. B., & Wilpers, S. (1998). Personality effects on social relationships. *Journal of Personality and Social Psychology, 74,* 1531–1544.

Ash, J., & Gallup, G. G., Jr. (2008). Brain size, intelligence, and paleoclimatic variation. In G. Geher & G. Miller (Eds.), *Mating intelligence: Sex, relationships, and the mind's reproductive system* (pp. 313–335). New York: Erlbaum.

Ashenhurst, J. R., Wilhite, E. R., Harden, K. P., & Fromme, K. (2017). Number of sexual partners and relationship status are associated with unprotected sex across emerging adulthood. *Archives of Sexual Behavior, 46,* 419–432.

Assad, K. K., Donnellan, M. B., & Conger, R. D. (2007). Optimism: An enduring resource for romantic relationships. *Journal of Personality and Social Psychology, 93,* 285–297.

Atkins, D. C., Marín, R. A., Lo, T. T. Y., Klann, N., & Hahlweg, K. (2010). Outcomes of couples with infidelity in a community-based sample of couple therapy. *Journal of Family Psychology, 24,* 212–216.

Attard-Johnson, J., Bindemann, M., & Ciardha, C. O. (2016). Pupillary response as an age-specific measure of sexual interest. *Archives of Sex Behavior, 45,* 855–870.

Aubé, J., Norcliffe, H., Craig, J., & Koestner, R. (1995). Gender characteristics and adjustment-related outcomes: Questioning the masculinity model. *Personality and Social Psychology Bulletin, 21,* 284–295.

Aubrey, J. S., & Rill, L. (2013). Investigating relations between Facebook use and social capital among college undergraduates. *Communication Quarterly, 61,* 479–496.

Averill, J. R. (1982). *Anger and aggression: An essay on emotion.* New York: Springer.

Aydin, N., Krueger, J. I., Fischer, J., & . . . Fischer, P. (2012). "Man's best friend": How the presence of a dog reduces mental distress after social exclusion. *Journal of Experimental Social Psychology, 48,* 446–449.

Aylor, B., & Dainton, M. (2001). Antecedents in romantic jealousy experience, expression, and goals. *Western Journal of Communication, 65,* 370–391.

Azizli, N., Atkinson, B. E., Baughman, H. M., & . . . Veselka, L. (2016). Lies and crimes: Dark Triad, misconduct, and high-stakes deception. *Personality and Individual Differences, 89,* 34–39.

Babcock, M. J., Ta, V. P., & Ickes, W. (2014). Latent semantic similarity and language style matching in initial dyadic interactions. *Journal of Language and Social Psychology, 33,* 78–88.

Bach, G. R., & Wyden, P. (1983). *The intimate enemy: How to fight fair in love and marriage.* New York: Avon Books.

Back, M. D., Schmukle, S. C., & Egloff, B. (2008a). Becoming friends by chance. *Psychological Science, 19,* 439–440.

Back, M. D., Schmukle, S. C., & Egloff, B. (2008b). How extraverted is honey.bunny77@hotmail.de? Inferring personality from e-mail addresses. *Journal of Research in Personality, 42,* 1116–1122.

Baddeley, J. L., Pennebaker, J. W., & Beevers, C. G. (2013). Everyday social behavior during a major depressive episode. *Social Psychological and Personality Science, 4,* 445–452.

Bahns, A. J., Crandall, C. S., Gillath, O., & Preacher, K. J. (2017). Similarity in relationships as niche construction: Choice, stability, and influence within dyads in a free choice environment. *Journal of Personality and Social Psychology, 112,* 329–355.

Bailenson, J. N., & Yee, N. (2005). Digital chameleons: Automatic assimilation of nonverbal gestures in immersive virtual environments. *Psychological Science, 16,* 814–819.

Bailey, J. M., Vasey, P. L., Diamond, L. M., Breedlove, S. M., Vilain, E., & Epprecht, M. (2016). Sexual orientation, controversy, and science. *Psychological Science in the Public Interest, 17,* 45–101.

Baker, L. R., McNulty, J. K., & Overall, N. C. (2014). When negative emotions benefit close relationships. In W. Parrott (Ed.), *The positive side of negative emotions* (pp. 101–125). New York: Guilford Press.

Bale, C., & Archer, J. (2013). Self-perceived attractiveness, romantic desirability and self-esteem: A mating sociometer perspective. *Evolutionary Psychology, 11,* 68–84.

Balsam, K. F., Beauchaine, T. P., Rothblum, E. D., & Solomon, S. E. (2008). Three-year follow-up of same-sex couples who had civil unions in Vermont, same-sex couples not in civil unions, and heterosexual married couples. *Developmental Psychology, 44,* 102–116.

Banai, I. P., Banai, B., & Bovan, K. (2017). Vocal characteristics of presidential candidates can predict the outcome of actual elections. *Evolution and Human Behavior,* doi:10.1016/j.evolhumbehav.2016.10.012

Bank, B. J., & Hansford, S. L. (2000). Gender and friendship: Why are men's best same-sex friendships less intimate and supportive? *Personal Relationships, 7,* 63–78.

Bar, M., Neta, M., & Linz, H. (2006). Very first impressions. *Emotion, 6,* 269–278.

Baranowski, A. M., & Hecht, H. (2015). Gender differences and similarities in receptivity to sexual invitations: Effects of location and risk perception. *Archives of Sex Behavior, 44,* 2257–2265.

Barber, N. (2000). *Why parents matter: Parental investment and child outcomes.* Westport, CT: Bergin and Garvey.

Barber, N. (2003). Divorce and reduced economic and emotional interdependence: A cross-national study. *Journal of Divorce and Remarriage, 39,* 113–124.

Bar-Kalifa, E., & Rafaeli, E. (2013). Disappointment's sting is greater than help's balm: Quasi-signal detection of daily support matching. *Journal of Family Psychology, 27,* 956–967.

Barnett, M. D., Fleck, L. K., Marsden, A. D., & Martin, K. J. (2017). Sexual semantics: The meanings of sex, virginity, and abstinence for university students. *Personality and Individual Differences, 106,* 203–208

Barnett, M. D., Melugin, P. R., & Cruze, R. M. (2016). Was it (or will it be) good for you? Expectations and experiences of first coitus among emerging adults. *Personality and Individual Differences, 97,* 25–29.

Barriger, M., & Vélez-Blasini, C. J. (2013). Descriptive and injunctive social norm overestimation in hooking up and their role as predictors of hook-up activity in a college student sample. *Journal of Sex Research, 50,* 84–94.

Barry, R. A., Bunde, M., Brock, R. L., & Lawrence, E. (2009). Validity and utility of a multidimensional model of received support in intimate relationships. *Journal of Family Psychology, 23,* 48–57.

Barry, R. A., & Lawrence, E. (2013). "Don't stand so close to me": An attachment perspective of disengagement and avoidance in marriage. *Journal of Family Psychology, 27,* 484–494.

Barthes, J., Godelle, B., & Raymond, M. (2013). Human social stratification and hypergyny: Toward an understanding of male homosexual preference. *Evolution and Human Behavior, 34,* 155–163.

Bartholomew, K. (1990). Avoidance of intimacy: An attachment perspective. *Journal of Social and Personal Relationships, 7,* 147–178.

Barton, A. W., & Bryant, C. M. (2016). Financial strain, trajectories of marital processes, and African American newlyweds' marital instability. *Journal of Family Psychology, 30,* 657–664.

Barton, A. W., Futris, T. G., & Nielsen, R. B. (2014). With a little help from *our* friends: Couple social integration in marriage. *Journal of Family Psychology, 28,* 986–991.

Barton, J., Braxton, J., Davis, D., & . . . Weston, E. (2016). *Sexually transmitted disease surveillance 2015.* Atlanta: Centers for Disease Control and Prevention.

Bartz, J. A. (2016). Oxytocin and the pharmacological dissection of affiliation. *Current Directions in Psychological Science, 25,* 104–110.

Bartz, J. A., & Lydon, J. E. (2008). Relationship-specific attachment, risk regulation, and communal norm adherence in close relationships. *Journal of Experimental Social Psychology, 44,* 655–663.

Bartz, J. A., Lydon, J. E., Kolevzon, A., & . . . Bolger, N. (2015). Differential effects of oxytocin on agency and communion for anxiously and avoidantly attached individuals. *Psychological Science, 26,* 1177–1186.

Basow, S. A., & Minieri, A. (2011). "You owe me": Effects of date cost, who pays, participant gender, and rape myth beliefs on perceptions of rape. *Journal of Interpersonal Violence, 26,* 479–497.

Bastian, B., & Haslam, N. (2010). Excluded from humanity: The dehumanizing effects of social ostracism. *Journal of Experimental Social Psychology, 46,* 107–113.

Bates, E. A., & Graham-Kevan, N. (2016). Is the presence of control related to help-seeking behavior? A test of Johnson's assumptions regarding sex differences and the role of control in intimate partner violence. *Partner Abuse, 7,* 3–25.

Battaglia, D. M., Richard, F. D., Datteri, D. L., & Lord, C. G. (1998). Breaking up is (relatively) easy to do: A script for the dissolution of close relationships. *Journal of Social and Personal Relationships, 15,* 829–845.

Baucom, B. R., McFarland, P. T., & Christensen, A. (2010). Gender, topic, and time in observed demand-withdraw interaction in cross- and same-sex couples. *Journal of Family Psychology, 24,* 233–242.

Baucom, D. H., Belus, J. M., Stanton, S., & Epstein, N. B. (2018). Treating relationship distress. In A. Vangelisti & D. Perlman (Eds.), *Cambridge handbook of personal relationships* (2nd ed.) New York: Cambridge University Press.

Baucom, D. H., Epstein, N., & Stanton, S. (2006). The treatment of relationship distress: Theoretical perspectives and empirical findings. In A. Vangelisti & D. Perlman (Eds.), *The Cambridge handbook of personal relationships* (pp. 745–769). New York: Cambridge University Press.

Baucom, D. H., Snyder, D. K., & Abbott, B. V. (2014). Infidelity. In L. Grossman & S. Walfish (Eds.), *Translating psychological research into practice* (pp. 419–426). New York: Springer.

Baumeister, R. F., & Bratslavsky, E. (1999). Passion, intimacy, and time: Passionate love as a function of change in intimacy. *Personality and Social Psychology Review, 3,* 49–67.

Baumeister, R. F., Bratslavsky, E., Finkenauer, C., & Vohs, K. D. (2001). Bad is stronger than good. *Review of General Psychology, 5,* 323–370.

Baumeister, R. F., & Leary, M. R. (1995). The need to belong: Desire for interpersonal attachments as a fundamental human motivation. *Psychological Bulletin, 117,* 497–529.

Baumeister, R. F., & Vohs, K. D. (2004). Sexual economics: Sex as a female resource for social exchange in heterosexual interactions. *Personality and Social Psychology Review, 8,* 339–363.

Baumeister, R. F., & Wotman, S. R. (1992). *Breaking hearts: The two sides of unrequited love.* New York: Guilford Press.

Baumeister, R. F., Wotman, S. R., & Stillwell, A. M. (1993). Unrequited love: On heartbreak, anger, guilt, scriptlessness, and humiliation. *Journal of Personality and Social Psychology, 64,* 377–394.

Baxter, L. A. (1984). Trajectories of relationship disengagement. *Journal of Social and Personal Relationships, 1,* 29–48.

Baxter, L. A. (1986). Gender differences in the heterosexual relationship rules embedded in break-up accounts. *Journal of Social and Personal Relationships, 3,* 289–306.

Baxter, L. A. (2004). Relationships as dialogues. *Personal Relationships, 11,* 1–22.

Baxter, L. A., Mazanec, M., Nicholson, J., Pittman, G., Smith, K., & West, L. (1997). Everyday loyalties and betrayals in personal relationships. *Journal of Social and Personal Relationships, 14,* 655–678.

Baxter, L. A., & West, L. (2003). Couple perceptions of their similarities and differences: A dialectical perspective. *Journal of Social and Personal Relationships, 20,* 491–514.

Baxter, L. A., & Wilmot, W. W. (1984). "Secret tests": Social strategies for acquiring information about the state of the relationship. *Human Communication Research, 11,* 171–201.

Baxter, L. A., & Wilmot, W. W. (1985). Taboo topics in close relationships. *Journal of Social and Personal Relationships, 2,* 253–269.

Beach, S. R. H., Whitaker, D. J., Jones, D. J., & Tesser, A. (2001). When does performance feedback prompt complementarity in romantic relationships? *Personal Relationships, 8,* 231–248.

Beall, A. T., & Tracy, J. L. (2013). Women are more likely to wear red or pink at peak fertility. *Psychological Science, 24,* 1837–1841.

Beck, C. J. A., Anderson, E. R., O'Hara, K. L., & Benjamin, G. A. H. (2013). Patterns of intimate partner violence in a large, epidemiological sample of divorcing couples. *Journal of Family Psychology, 27,* 743–753.

Beck, L. A., & Clark, M. S. (2009). Offering more support than we seek. *Journal of Experimental Social Psychology, 45,* 267–270.

Beck, L. A., & Clark, M. S. (2010a). Looking a gift horse in the mouth as a defense against increasing intimacy. *Journal of Experimental Social Psychology, 46,* 676–679.

Beck, L. A., & Clark, M. S. (2010b). What constitutes a healthy communal marriage and why relationship stage matters. *Journal of Family Theory & Review, 2,* 299–315.

Beck, L. A., Pietromonaco, P. R., DeBuse, C. J., Powers, S. I., & Sayer, A. G. (2013). Spouses' attachment pairings predict neuroendocrine, behavioral, and psychological responses to marital conflict. *Journal of Personality and Social Psychology, 105,* 388–424.

Becker, O. A. (2013). Effects of similarity of life goals, values, and personality on relationship satisfaction and stability: Findings from a two-wave panel study. *Personal Relationships, 20,* 443–461.

Becker, O. A., & Lois, D. (2010). Selection, alignment, and their interplay: Origins of lifestyle homogamy in couple relationships. *Journal of Marriage and Family, 72,* 1234–1248.

Beckes, L., & Coan, J. A. (2015). Relationship neuroscience. In M. Mikulincer, P. Shaver, J. Simpson, & J. Dovidio (Eds.), *APA handbook of personality and social psychology, Volume 3: Interpersonal relations* (pp. 119–149). Washington, DC: American Psychological Association.

Beetz, A., & Bales, K. (2016). Affiliation in human-animal interaction. In L. Freund, S. McCune, L. Esposito, N. Gee, & P. McCardle (Eds.), *The social neuroscience of human-animal interaction* (pp. 107–125). Washington, DC: American Psychological Association.

Belkin, A., Ender, M. G., Frank, N., & . . . Segal, D. R. (2013). Readiness and DADT repeal: Has the new policy of open service undermined the military? *Armed Forces & Society, 39,* 587–601.

Ben-Ari, A., & Lavee, Y. (2007). Dyadic closeness in marriage: From the inside story to a conceptual model. *Journal of Social and Personal Relationships, 24,* 627–644.

Bensman, L. (2012). Two people just make it better: The psychological differences between partnered orgasms and solitary orgasms. *Dissertation Abstracts International, 72*(11-B), 7107.

Bente, G., Leuschner, H., Al Issa, A., & Blascovich, J. J. (2010). The others: Universals and cultural specificities in the perception of status and dominance from nonverbal behavior. *Consciousness and Cognition, 19,* 762–777.

Berenson, K. R., & Andersen, S. M. (2006). Childhood physical and emotional abuse by a parent: Transference effects in adult interpersonal relations. *Personality and Social Psychology Bulletin, 32,* 1509–1522.

Berkman, L. F., & Glass, T. A. (2000). Social integration, social networks, social support and health. In L. F. Berkman & I. Kawachi (Eds.), *Social epidemiology* (pp. 137–174). New York: Oxford University Press.

Bernier, A., Matte-Gagné, C. & Bouvette-Turcot, A. (2014). Examining the interface of children's sleep, executive functioning, and caregiving relationships: A plea against silos in the study of biology, cognition, and relationships. *Current Directions in Psychological Science, 23,* 284–289.

Bernstein, W. M., Stephenson, B. O., Snyder, M. L., & Wicklund, R. A. (1983). Causal ambiguity and heterosexual affiliation. *Journal of Experimental Social Psychology, 19,* 78–92.

Berscheid, E. (2010). Love in the fourth dimension. *Annual Review of Psychology, 61,* 1–25.

Berscheid, E., Snyder, M., & Omoto, A. M. (1989). Issues in studying close relationships: Conceptualizing and measuring closeness. In C. Hendrick (Ed.), *Review of personality and social psychology: Vol. 10. Close relationships* (pp. 63–91). Newbury Park, CA: Sage.

Berscheid, E., Snyder, M., & Omoto, A. M. (2004). Measuring closeness: The Relationship Closeness Inventory (RCI) revisited. In D. J. Mashek & A. Aron (Eds.), *Handbook of closeness and intimacy* (pp. 81–101). Mahwah, NJ: Erlbaum.

Berscheid, E., & Walster, E. (1974). A little bit about love. In T. Huston (Ed.), *Foundations of interpersonal attraction* (pp. 355–381). New York: Academic Press.

Bialik, K. (2017, June 12). *Key facts about race and marriage, 50 years after Loving v. Virginia.* Pew Research Center. Retrieved from www.pewresearch.org/fact-tank/2017/06/12/key-facts-about-race-and-marriage-50-years-after-loving-v-virginia.

Biesen, J. N., Schooler, D. E., & Smith, D. A. (2016). What a difference a pronoun makes: *I/we* versus *you/me* and worried couples' perceptions of their interaction quality. *Journal of Language and Social Psychology, 35,* 180–205.

Birditt, K. S., Brown, E., Orbuch, T. L., & McIlvane, J. M. (2010). Marital conflict behaviors and implications for divorce over 16 years. *Journal of Marriage and Family, 72,* 1188–1204.

Birditt, K. S., Hope, S., Brown, E., & Orbuch, T. (2012). Developmental trajectories of marital happiness over 16 years. *Research in Human Development, 9,* 126–144.

Birnbaum, G. E., Reis, H. T., Mizrahi, M., & . . . Granovski-Milner, C. (2016). Intimately connected: The importance of partner responsiveness for experiencing sexual desire. *Journal of Personality and Social Psychology, 111,* 530–546.

Birnie, C., McClure, M. J., Lydon, J. E., & Holmberg, D. (2009). Attachment avoidance and commitment aversion: A script for relationship failure. *Personal Relationships, 16,* 79–97.

Black, M. C., Basile, K. C., Breiding, M. J., & . . . Stevens, M. R. (2011). *The National Intimate Partner and Sexual Violence Survey: 2010 summary report.* Atlanta: Centers for Disease Control and Prevention.

Blackhart, G. C., Nelson, B. C., Winter, A., & Rockney, A. (2011). Self-control in relation to feelings of belonging and acceptance. *Self and Identity, 10,* 152–165.

Blanch-Hartigan, D., Andrzejewski, S. A., & Hill, K. M. (2012). The effectiveness of training to improve person perception accuracy: A meta-analysis. *Basic and Applied Social Psychology, 34,* 483–498.

Bleakley, A., Hennessy, M., & Fishbein, M. (2010). Predicting preferences for types of sex education in U.S. Schools. *Sexuality Research and Social Policy, 7,* 50–57.

Blekesaune, M. (2008). Partnership transitions and mental distress: Investigating temporal order. *Journal of Marriage and Family, 70,* 879–890.

Bleske, A. L., & Shackelford, T. K. (2001). Poaching, promiscuity, and deceit: Combating mating rivalry in same-sex friendships. *Personal Relationships, 8,* 407–424.

Bleske-Rechek, A., Somers, E., Micke, E., & . . . Ritchie, L. (2012). Benefit or burden: Attraction in cross-sex friendship. *Journal of Social and Personal Relationships, 29,* 569–596.

Blickstein, I. (2005). Superfecundation and superfetation. In I. Blickstein & L. G. Keith (Eds.), *Multiple pregnancy: Epidemiology, gestation, and perinatal outcome* (2nd ed., pp. 102–107). London: Taylor and Francis.

Bloch, L., Haase, C. M., & Levenson, R. W. (2014). Emotion regulation predicts marital satisfaction: More than a wives' tale. *Emotion, 14,* 130–144.

Blumstein, P., & Schwartz, P. (1983). *American couples: Money, work, sex.* New York: William Morrow.

Bobst, C., & Lobmaier, J. S. (2014). Is preference for ovulatory female's faces associated with men's testosterone levels? *Hormones and Behavior, 66,* 487–492.

Bodenmann, G., Atkins, D. C., Schär, M., & Poffet, V. (2010). The association between daily stress and sexual activity. *Journal of Family Psychology, 24,* 271–279.

Bodie, G. D., Vickery, A. J., Cannava, K., & Jones, S. M. (2015). The role of "Active Listening" in informal helping conversations: Impact on perceptions of listener helpfulness, sensitivity, and supportiveness and discloser emotional improvement. *Western Journal of Communication, 79,* 151–173.

Bohns, V. K., & Flynn, F. J. (2010). "Why didn't you just ask?": Underestimating the discomfort of help-seeking. *Journal of Experimental Social Psychology, 46,* 402–409.

Bohns, V. K., Lucas, G. M., Molden, D. C., & . . . Higgins, E. T. (2013). Opposites fit: Regulatory focus complementarity and relationship well-being. *Social Cognition, 31,* 1–14.

Bohns, V. K., Scholer, A. A., & Rehman, U. (2015). Implicit theories of attraction. *Social Cognition, 33,* 284–307.

Bolger, N., Zuckerman, A., & Kessler, R. C. (2000). Invisible support and adjustment to stress. *Journal of Personality and Social Psychology, 79,* 953–961.

Bollich, K. L., Doris, J. M., Vazire, S., Raison, C. L., Jackson, J. J., & Mehl, M. R. (2016). Eavesdropping on character: Assessing everyday moral behaviors. *Journal of Research in Personality, 61,* 15–21.

Bond, C. F., Jr., & DePaulo, B. M. (2006). Accuracy of deception judgments. *Personality and Social Psychology Review, 10,* 214–234.

Booth, A., Johnson, D. R., White, L. K., & Edwards, J. N. (1986). Divorce and marital instability over the life course. *Journal of Family Issues, 7,* 421–442.

Boothroyd, L. G., Cross, C. P., Gray, A. W., Coombes, C., & Gregson-Curtis, K. (2011). Perceiving the facial correlates of sociosexuality: Further evidence. *Personality and Individual Differences, 50,* 422–425.

Boothroyd, L. G., Jones, B. C., Burt, D. M., DeBruine, L. M., & Perrett, D. I. (2008). Facial correlates of sociosexuality. *Evolution and Human Behavior, 29,* 211–218.

Boothroyd, L. G., Jones, B. C., Burt, D. M., & Perrett, D. I. (2007). Partner characteristics associated with masculinity, health, and maturity in male faces. *Personality and Individual Differences, 43,* 1161–1173.

Bosson, J. K., Johnson, A. B., Niederhoffer, K., & Swann, W. B., Jr. (2006). Interpersonal chemistry through negativity: Bonding by sharing negative attitudes about others. *Personal Relationships, 13,* 135–150.

Bosson, J. K., & Vandello, J. A. (2011). Precarious manhood and its links to action and aggression. *Current Directions in Psychological Science, 20,* 82–86.

Bouffard, J. A., Bouffard, L. A., & Miller, H. A. (2016). Examining the correlates of women's use of sexual coercion: Proposing an explanatory model. *Journal of Interpersonal Violence, 31,* 2360–2382.

Bouffard, J. A., & Miller, H. A. (2014). The role of sexual arousal and overperception of sexual intent within the decision to engage in sexual coercion. *Journal of Interpersonal Violence, 29,* 1967–1986.

Bourassa, K. J., Sbarra, D. A., & Whisman, M. A. (2015). Women in very low quality marriages gain life satisfaction following divorce. *Journal of Family Psychology, 29,* 490–499.

Boutwell, B. B., & Boisvert, D. (2014). Sexual promiscuity & self-control: A behavior genetic explanation to an evolutionary question. *Personality and Individual Differences, 63,* 112–116.

Bowlby, J. (1969). *Attachment and loss: Vol. 1. Attachment.* New York: Basic Books.

Boyce, C. J., Wood, A. M., Banks, J., Clark, A. E., & Brown, G. D. A. (2013). Money, well-being, and loss aversion: Does an income loss have a greater effect on well-being than an equivalent income gain? *Psychological Science, 24,* 2557–2562.

Boyce, C. J., Wood, A. M., & Ferguson, E. (2016). Individual differences in loss aversion: Conscientiousness predicts how life satisfaction responds to losses versus gains in income. *Personality and Social Psychology Bulletin, 42,* 471–484.

Boyes, A. D., & Fletcher, G. J. O. (2007). Metaperceptions of bias in intimate relationships. *Journal of Personality and Social Psychology, 92,* 286–306.

Boyle, A. M., & O'Sullivan, L. F. (2016). Staying connected: Computer-mediated and face-to-face communication in college students' dating relationships. *Cyberpsychology, Behavior, and Social Networking, 19,* 299–307.

Boynton, M. (2008, February). *What Rapunzel and Lady Godiva have in common: Using hair length as a cue for sexual availability.* Poster presented at the meeting of the Society for Personality and Social Psychology, Albuquerque, NM.

Brackett, M. A., Warner, R. M., & Bosco, J. S. (2005). Emotional intelligence and relationship quality among couples. *Personal Relationships, 12,* 197–212.

Bradford, S. A., Feeney, J. A., & Campbell, L. (2002). Links between attachment orientations and dispositional and diary-based measures of disclosure in dating couples: A study of actor and partner effects. *Personal Relationships, 9,* 491–506.

Bradshaw, C., Kahn, A. S., & Saville, B. K. (2010). To hook up or date: Which gender benefits? *Sex Roles, 62,* 661–669.

Bradshaw, S. D. (2006). Shyness and difficult relationships: Formation is just the beginning. In D. C. Kirkpatrick, S. Duck, & M. K. Foley (Eds.), *Relating difficulty: The processes of constructing and managing difficult interaction* (pp. 15–41). Mahwah, NJ: Erlbaum.

Braithwaite, S. R., Coulson, G., Keddington, K., & Fincham, F. D. (2015). The influence of pornography on sexual scripts and hooking up among emerging adults in college. *Archives of Sexual Behavior, 44,* 111–123.

Braithwaite, S. R., Mitchell, C. M., Selby, E. A., & Fincham, F. D. (2016). Trait forgiveness and enduring vulnerabilities: Neuroticism and catastrophizing influence relationship satisfaction via less forgiveness. *Personality and Individual Differences, 94,* 237–246.

Braithwaite, S. R., Selby, E. A., & Fincham, F. D. (2011). Forgiveness and relationship satisfaction: Mediating mechanisms. *Journal of Family Psychology, 25,* 551–559.

Brakefield, T. A., Mednick, S. C., Wilson, H. W., De Neve, J., Christakis, N. A., & Fowler, J. H. (2014). Same-sex sexual attraction does not spread in adolescent social networks. *Archives of Sexual Behavior, 43,* 335–344.

Brand, R. J., Markey, C. M., Mills, A., & Hodges, S. D. (2007). Sex differences in self-reported infidelity and its correlates. *Sex Roles, 57,* 101–109.

Brannon, S. M., & Gawronski, B. (2017). A second chance for first impression? Exploring the context-(In)Dependent updating of implicit evaluations. *Social Psychological and Personality Science, 8,* 275–283.

Braver, S. L., Ellman, I. M., & Fabricius, W. V. (2003). Relocation of children after divorce and children's best interests: New evidence and legal considerations. *Journal of Family Psychology, 17,* 206–219.

Braver, S. L., Shapiro, J. R., & Goodman, M. R. (2006). Consequences of divorce for parents. In M. A. Fine & J. H. Harvey (Eds.), *Handbook of divorce and relationship dissolution* (pp. 313–337). Mahwah, NJ: Erlbaum.

Bredow, C. A. (2015). Chasing Prince Charming: Partnering consequences of holding unrealistic standards for a spouse. *Personal Relationships, 22,* 476–501.

Brennan, K. A., Clark, C. L., & Shaver, P. R. (1998). Self-report measurement of adult attachment: An integrative overview. In J. A. Simpson & W. S. Rholes (Eds.), *Attachment theory and close relationships* (pp. 46–76). New York: Guilford Press.

Brewer, D. D., Potterat, J. J., Garrett, S. B., & . . . Darrow, W. W. (2000). Prostitution and the sex discrepancy in reported number of sexual partners. *Proceedings of the National Academy of Science, 97,* 12385–12388.

Brewer, G., & Archer, J. (2007). What do people infer from facial attractiveness? *Journal of Evolutionary Psychology, 5,* 39–49.

Brewer, G., & Hendrie, C. A. (2011). Evidence to suggest that copulatory vocalizations in women are not a reflexive consequence of orgasm. *Archives of Sexual Behavior, 40,* 559–564.

Brewer, G., Hunt, D., James, G., & Abell, L. (2015). Dark Triad traits, infidelity and romantic revenge. *Personality and Individual Differences, 83,* 122–127.

Bridges, A. J., Senn, C. Y., & Andrews, A. R., III. (2013). Women, erotica, and pornography. In D. Castañeda (Ed.), *The essential handbook of women's sexuality* (Vol. 1, pp. 253–271). Santa Barbara, CA: Praeger.

Bringle, R. G., Winnick, T., & Rydell, R. J. (2013). The prevalence and nature of unrequited love. *SAGE Open, 3,* 1–15.

Britt, S. L., & Huston, S. J. (2012). The role of money arguments in marriage. *Journal of Family and Economic Issues, 33,* 464–476.

Britt, S. L., & Roy, R. R. N. (2014). Relationship quality among young couples from an economic and gender perspective. *Journal of Family and Economic Issues, 35,* 241–250.

Brock, R. L., & Lawrence, E. (2014). Intrapersonal, interpersonal, and contextual risk factors for overprovision of partner support in marriage. *Journal of Family Psychology, 28,* 54–64.

Brody, L. R., & Hall, J. A. (2010). Gender, emotion, and socialization. In J. Chrisler & D. McCreary (Eds.), *Handbook of gender research in psychology* (Vol. 1, pp. 429–454). New York: Springer.

Brody, S., & Weiss, P. (2013). Slimmer women's waist is associated with better erectile function in men independent of age. *Archives of Sexual Behavior, 42,* 1191–1198.

Brooks, J. E., & Neville, H. A. (2017). Interracial attraction among college men: The influence of ideologies, familiarity, and similarity. *Journal of Social and Personal Relationships, 34,* 166–183.

Brown, G., Manago, A. M., & Trimble, J. E. (2016). Tempted to text: College students' mobile phone use during a face-to-face interaction with a close friend. *Emerging Adulthood, 4,* 440–443.

Brown, J. L., Sheffield, D., Leary, M. R., & Robinson, M. E. (2003). Social support and experimental pain. *Psychosomatic Medicine, 65,* 276–283.

Brown, S. L., Manning, W. D., & Payne, K. K. (2017). Relationship quality among cohabiting versus married couples. *Journal of Family Issues, 38,* 1730–1753.

Brownridge, D. A. (2010). Does the situational couple violence-intimate terrorism typology explain cohabitors' high risk of intimate partner violence? *Journal of Interpersonal Violence, 25,* 1264–1283.

Bruess, C. & Kudak, A. (2008). *Belly button fuzz and bare-chested hugs: What happy couples do—The loving little rituals of romance.* Minneapolis: Fairview Press.

Brumbaugh, C. C., & Wood, D. (2013). Mate preferences across life and across the world. *Social Psychological and Personality Science, 4,* 100–107.

Brummelman, E., Thomaes, S., & Sedikides, C. (2016). Separating narcissism from self-esteem. *Current Directions in Psychological Science, 25,* 8–13.

Brummett, E. A. (2017). "Race doesn't matter": A dialogic analysis of interracial romantic partners' stories about racial differences. *Journal of Social and Personal Relationships, 34,* 771–789.

Brunell, A. B., & Webster, G. D. (2013). Self-determination and sexual experience in dating relationships. *Personality and Social Psychology Bulletin, 39,* 970–987.

Brunet, P. M., & Schmidt, L. A. (2007). Is shyness context specific? Relation between shyness and online self-disclosure with and without a live webcam in young adults. *Journal of Research in Personality, 41,* 938–945.

Bryant, G., Fessler, D., Fusaroli, R., & . . . Zhou, Y. (2016). Detecting affiliation in colaughter across 24 societies. *PNAS, 113,* 4682–4687.

Buck, A. A., & Neff, L. A. (2012). Stress spillover in early marriage: The role of self-regulatory depletion. *Journal of Family Psychology, 26,* 698–708.

Buck, D. M., & Plant, E. A. (2011). Interorientation interactions and impressions: Does the timing of disclosure of sexual orientation matter? *Journal of Experimental Social Psychology, 47,* 333–342.

Buckley, K. E., Winkel, R. E., & Leary, M. R. (2004). Reactions to acceptance and rejection: Effects of level and sequence of relational evaluation. *Journal of Experimental Social Psychology, 40,* 14–28.

Buhrmester, D., & Furman, W. (1986). The changing functions of friends in childhood: A neo-Sullivanian perspective. In V. J. Derlega & B. A. Winstead (Eds.), *Friendship and social interaction* (pp. 41–62). New York: Springer-Verlag.

Buller, D. B., & Burgoon, J. K. (1994). Deception: Strategic and nonstrategic communication. In J. A. Daly & J. M. Wiemann (Eds.), *Strategic interpersonal communication* (pp. 191–223). Hillsdale, NJ: Erlbaum.

Burger, J. M., & Burns, L. (1988). The illusion of unique invulnerability and use of effective contraception. *Personality and Social Psychology Bulletin, 14,* 264–270.

Burgoon, J. K., Schuetzler, R., & Wilson, D. W. (2015). Kinesic patterning in deceptive and truthful interactions. *Journal of Nonverbal Behavior, 39,* 1–24.

Burke, M., & Kraut, R. E. (2016). The relationship between Facebook use and well-being depends on communication type and tie strength. *Computer-Mediated Communication, 21,* 265–281.

Burleson, B. R., Kunkel, A. W., Samter, W., & Werking, K. J. (1996). Men's and women's evaluations of communication skills in personal relationships: When sex differences make a difference—and when they don't. *Journal of Social and Personal Relationships, 13,* 201–224.

Burleson, M. H., Roberts, N. A., Vincelette, T. M., & Guan, X. (2013). Marriage, affectionate touch, and health. In M. Newman & N. Roberts (Eds.), *Health and social relationships: The good, the bad, and the complicated* (pp. 67–93). Washington, DC: American Psychological Association.

Burleson, M. H., Trevathan, W. R., & Todd, M. (2007). In the mood for love or vice versa? Exploring the relations among sexual activity, physical affection, affect, and stress in the daily lives of mid-aged women. *Archives of Sexual Behavior, 36,* 357–368.

Burnette, J. L., Davisson, E. K., Finkel, E. J., Van Tongeren, D. R., Hui, C. M., & Hoyle, R. H. (2014). Self-control and forgiveness: A meta-analytic review. *Social Psychological and Personality Science, 5,* 443–450.

Burnette, J. L., Taylor, K. W., Worthington, E. L., & Forsyth, D. R. (2007). Attachment and trait forgivingness: The mediating role of angry rumination. *Personality and Individual Differences, 42,* 1585–1596.

Burns, G. L., & Farina, A. (1992). The role of physical attractiveness in adjustment. *Genetic, Social, and General Psychology Monographs, 118,* 157–194.

Burton-Chellew, M. N., & Dunbar, R. I. M. (2015). Romance and reproduction are socially costly. *Evolutionary Behavioral Sciences, 9,* 229–241.

Busby, D. M., & Holman, T. B. (2009). Perceived match or mismatch on the Gottman conflict styles: Associations with relationship outcome variables. *Family Process, 48,* 531–545.

Buss, D. M. (1989). Sex differences in human mate preferences: Evolutionary hypotheses tested in 37 cultures. *Behavioral and Brain Sciences, 12,* 1–14.

Buss, D. M. (2000). *The dangerous passion: Why jealousy is as necessary as love and sex.* New York: Free Press.

Buss, D. M. (2003). *The evolution of desire: Strategies of human mating* (rev. ed.). New York: Basic Books.

Buss, D. M. (2013). Seven tools for teaching evolutionary psychology. In D. Dunn, R. Gurung, K. Naufel, & J. Wilson (Eds.), *Controversy in the psychology classroom: Using hot topics to foster critical thinking* (pp. 49–64). Washington, DC: American Psychological Association.

Buss, D. M. (2015). *Evolutionary psychology: The new science of the mind* (5th ed.). New York: Routledge.

Buss, D. M., & Duntley, J. D. (2006). The evolution of aggression. In M. Schaller, J. A. Simpson, & D. T. Kenrick (Eds.), *Evolution and social psychology* (pp. 263–285). New York: Psychology Press.

Buss, D. M., Goetz, C., Duntley, J. D., Asao, K., & Conroy-Beam, D. (2017). The mate switching hypothesis. *Personality and Individual Differences, 104,* 143–149.

Buss, D. M., Larsen, R. J., Westen, D., & Semmelroth, J. (1992). Sex differences in jealousy: Evolution, physiology, and psychology. *Psychological Science, 3,* 251–255.

Buss, D. M., & Schmitt, D. P. (1993). Sexual strategies theory: An evolutionary perspective on human mating. *Psychological Review, 100,* 204–232.

Buss, D. M., & Shackelford, T. K. (2008). Attractive women want it all: Good genes, economic investment, parenting proclivities, and emotional commitment. *Evolutionary Psychology, 6,* 134–146.

Buss, D. M., Shackelford, T. K., Kirkpatrick, L. A., & . . . Bennett, K. (1999). Jealousy and the nature of beliefs about infidelity: Tests of competing hypotheses about sex differences in the United States, Korea, and Japan. *Personal Relationships, 6,* 125–150.

Buss, D. M., Shackelford, T. K., Kirkpatrick, L. A., & Larsen, R. J. (2001). A half century of mate preferences: The cultural evolution of values. *Journal of Marriage and the Family, 63,* 491–503.

Butzer, B., & Campbell, L. (2008). Adult attachment, sexual satisfaction, and relationship satisfaction: A study of married couples. *Personal Relationships, 15,* 141–154.

Buunk, A. P., Dijkstra, P., & Massar, K. (2018). The universal threat and temptation of extradyadic affairs. In A. Vangelisti & D. Perlman (Eds.), *Cambridge handbook of personal relationships* (2nd ed.) New York: Cambridge University Press.

Buunk, A. P., Park, J. H., & Duncan, L. A. (2010). Cultural variation in parental influence on mate choice. *Cross-Cultural Research, 44,* 23–40.

Buunk, A. P., & Solano, A. C. (2010). Conflicting preferences of parents and offspring over criteria for a mate: A study in Argentina. *Journal of Family Psychology, 24,* 391–399.

Buunk, A. P., Solano, A. C., Zurriaga, R., & González, P. (2011). Gender differences in the jealousy-evoking effect of rival characteristics: A study in Spain and Argentina. *Journal of Cross-Cultural Psychology, 42,* 323–339.

Buunk, B. (1987). Conditions that promote breakups as a consequence of extra-dyadic involvements. *Journal of Social and Clinical Psychology, 5,* 271–284.

Buunk, B. P. (1995). Sex, self-esteem, dependency and extradyadic sexual experience as related to jealousy responses. *Journal of Social and Personal Relationships, 12,* 147–153.

Buunk, B. P., & Dijkstra, P. (2006). Temptation and threat: Extradyadic relations and jealousy. In A. L. Vangelisti & D. Perlman (Eds.), *The Cambridge handbook of personal relationships* (pp. 533–555). New York: Cambridge University Press.

Buunk, B. P., Dijkstra, P., Fetchenhauer, D., & Kenrick, D. T. (2002). Age and gender differences in mate selection criteria for various involvement levels. *Personal Relationships, 9,* 271–278.

Byers, E. S., & Cohen, J. N. (2017). Validation of the interpersonal exchange model of sexual satisfaction with women in a same-sex relationship. *Psychology of Women Quarterly, 41,* 32–45.

Byrne, D., Ervin, C. E., & Lamberth, J. (1970). Continuity between the experimental study of attraction and real-life computer dating. *Journal of Personality and Social Psychology, 16,* 157–165.

Byrne, D., & Nelson, D. (1965). Attraction as a linear function of proportion of positive reinforcements. *Journal of Personality and Social Psychology, 1,* 659–663.

Cacioppo, J. T., Berntson, G. G., Norris, C. J., & Gollan, J. K. (2012). The evaluative space model. In P. Van Lange, A. Kruglanski, & E. T. Higgins (Eds.), *Handbook of theories of social psychology* (Vol. 1, pp. 50–72). Thousand Oaks, CA: Sage.

Cacioppo, J. T., Cacioppo, S., Gonzaga, G. C., Ogburn, E. L., & VanderWeele, T. J. (2013). Marital satisfaction and break-ups differ across on-line and off-line meeting venues. *PNAS, 110,* 10135–10140.

Cacioppo, J. T., Fowler, J. H., & Christakis, N. A. (2009). Alone in the crowd: The structure and spread of loneliness in a large social network. *Journal of Personality and Social Psychology, 97,* 977–991.

Cacioppo, J. T., & Hawkley, L. C. (2009). Loneliness. In M. R. Leary & R. H. Hoyle (Eds.), *Handbook of individual differences in social behavior* (pp. 227–240). New York: Guilford Press.

Cacioppo, J. T., Hawkley, L. C., Ernst, J. M., & . . . Spiegel, D. (2006). Loneliness within a nomological net: An evolutionary perspective. *Journal of Research in Personality, 40,* 1054–1085.

Cacioppo, S., & Cacioppo, J. T. (2016). Comment: Demystifying the neuroscience of love. *Emotion Review, 8,* 108–114.

Cacioppo, S., Grippo, A. J., London, S., Goossens, L., & Cacioppo, J. T. (2015). Loneliness: Clinical import and interventions. *Perspectives on Psychological Science, 10,* 238–249.

Cafferky, B. M., Mendez, M., Anderson, J. R., & Stith, S. M. (2017). Substance use and intimate partner violence: A meta-analytic review. *Psychology of Violence.* doi:10.1037/vio0000074.

Call, V., Sprecher, S., & Schwartz, P. (1995). The incidence and frequency of marital sex in a national sample. *Journal of Marriage and the Family, 57,* 639–652.

Cameron, J. J., & Vorauer, J. D. (2008). Feeling transparent: On metaperceptions and miscommunications. *Social and Personality Psychology Compass, 2,* 1093–1108.

Campbell, J., Miller, P., Cardwell, M., & Belknap, R. A. (1994). Relationship status of battered women over time. *Journal of Family Violence, 9,* 99–111.

Campbell, K., & Kaufman, J. (2017). Do you pursue your heart or your art: Creativity, personality, and love. *Journal of Family Issues, 38,* 287–311.

Campbell, K., Wright, D. W., & Flores, C. G. (2012). Newlywed women's marital expectations: Lifelong monogamy? *Journal of Divorce & Remarriage, 53,* 108–125.

Campbell, L., Cronk, L., Simpson, J. A., Milroy, A., Wilson, C. L., & Dunham, B. (2009). The association between men's ratings of women as desirable long-term mates and individual differences in women's sexual attitudes and behaviors. *Personality and Individual Differences, 46,* 509–513.

Campbell, L., Simpson, J. A., Kashy, D. A., & Rholes, W. S. (2001). Attachment orientations, dependence, and behavior in a stressful situation: An application of the actor-partner interdependence model. *Journal of Social and Personal Relationships, 18,* 821–843.

Campbell, W. K., & Foster, C. A. (2002). Narcissism and commitment in romantic relationships: An investment model analysis. *Personality and Social Psychology Bulletin, 28,* 484–495.

Canary, D. J., & Emmers-Sommer, T. M. (1997). *Sex and gender differences in personal relationships.* New York: Guilford Press.

Canary, D. J., & Lakey, S. (2013). *Strategic conflict.* New York: Routledge.

Canary, D. J., & Stafford, L. (2001). Equity in the preservation of personal relationships. In J. Harvey & A. Wenzel (Eds.), *Close romantic relationships: Maintenance and enhancement* (pp. 133–151). Mahwah, NJ: Erlbaum.

Canary, D. J., Stafford, L., & Semic, B. A. (2002). A panel study of the associations between maintenance strategies and relational characteristics. *Journal of Marriage and the Family, 64,* 395–406.

Cann, A., & Baucom, T. R. (2004). Former partners and new rivals as threats to a relationship: Infidelity type, gender, and commitment as factors related to distress and forgiveness. *Personal Relationships, 11,* 305–318.

Cantú, S. M., Simpson, J. A., Griskevicius, V., Weisberg, Y. J., Durante, K. M., & Beal, D. J. (2014). Fertile and selectively flirty: Women's behavior toward men changes across the ovulatory cycle. *Psychological Science, 25,* 431–438.

Carli, L. L. (1999). Gender, interpersonal power, and social influence. *Journal of Social Issues, 55,* 81–98.

Carli, L. L. (2001). Gender and social influence. *Journal of Social Issues, 57,* 725–741.

Carlsmith, K. M., Wilson, T. D., & Gilbert, D. T. (2008). The paradoxical consequences of revenge. *Journal of Personality and Social Psychology, 95,* 1316–1324.

Carlson, D. L., & Lynch, J. L. (2017). Purchases, penalties, and power: The relationship between earnings and housework. *Journal of Marriage and Family, 79,* 199–224.

Carlson, D. L., Miller, A. J., Sassler, S., & Hanson, S. (2016). The gendered division of housework and couples' sexual relationships: A reexamination. *Journal of Marriage and Family, 78,* 975–995.

Carlson, E. N. (2016). Meta-accuracy and relationship quality: Weighing the costs and benefits of knowing what people really think about you. *Journal of Personality and Social Psychology, 111,* 250–264.

Carnegie, D. (1936). *How to win friends and influence people.* New York: Pocket Books.

Carnelley, K. B., Wortman, C. B., Bolger, N., & Burke, C. T. (2006). The time course of grief reactions to spousal loss: Evidence from a national probability sample. *Journal of Personality and Social Psychology, 91,* 476–492.

Carney, D. R., Colvin, C. R., & Hall, J. A. (2007). A thin slice perspective on the accuracy of first impressions. *Journal of Research in Personality, 41,* 1054–1072.

Carney, D. R., Cuddy, A. C., & Yap, A. J. (2015). Review and summary of research on the embodied effects of expansive (vs. contractive) nonverbal displays. *Psychological Science, 26,* 657–663.

Carpenter, C. J. (2012). Meta-analyses of sex differences in responses to sexual versus emotional infidelity: Men and women are more similar than different. *Psychology of Women Quarterly, 36,* 25–37.

Carrère, S., & Gottman, J. M. (1999). Predicting divorce among newlyweds from the first three minutes of a marital conflict discussion. *Family Process, 38,* 293–301.

Carstensen, L. L., Isaacowitz, D. M., & Charles, S. T. (1999). Taking time seriously: A theory of socioemotional selectivity. *American Psychologist, 54,* 165–181.

Cartmill, E. A., & Goldin-Meadow, S. (2016). Gesture. In D. Matsumoto, H. C. Hwang, & M. G. Frank (Eds.), *APA handbook of nonverbal communication* (pp. 307–333). Washington, DC: American Psychological Association.

Carton, H., & Egan, V. (2017). The dark triad and intimate partner violence. *Personality and Individual Differences, 105,* 84–88.

Carver, C. S., & Scheier, M. F. (2009). Optimism. In M. R. Leary & R. H. Hoyle (Eds.), *Handbook of individual differences in social behavior* (pp. 330–342). New York: Guilford Press.

Casey, E. A., Masters, N. T., Beadnell, B., & . . . Wells, E. A. (2017). Predicting sexual assault perpetration among heterosexually active young men. *Violence Against Women, 23,* 3–27.

Castro, F. N., & de Araújo Lopes, F. (2010). Romantic preferences in Brazilian undergraduate students: From the short term to the long term. *Journal of Sex Research, 47,* 1–7.

Catalyst. (2017). Women CEOs of the S&P 500. Catalyst, Inc. Retrieved from http://www.catalyst.org/knowledge/women-ceos-sp-500

Cate, R. M., Levin, L. A., & Richmond, L. S. (2002). Premarital relationship stability: A review of recent research. *Journal of Social and Personal Relationships, 19,* 261–284.

Cate, R. M., Lloyd, S. A., & Long, E. (1988). The role of rewards and fairness in developing premarital relationships. *Journal of Marriage and the Family, 50,* 443–452.

Caughlin, J. P., Afifi, W. A., Carpenter-Theune, K. E., & Miller, L. E. (2005). Reasons for, and consequences of, revealing personal secrets in close relationships: A longitudinal study. *Personal Relationships, 12,* 43–59.

Caughlin, J. P., & Basinger, E. D. (2015). Completely open and honest communication: Is that really what we want? *NCFR Report: Family Focus, FF64,* F1–F3.

Caughlin, J. P., Huston, T. L., & Houts, R. M. (2000). How does personality matter in marriage? An examination of trait anxiety, interpersonal negativity, and marital satisfaction. *Journal of Personality and Social Psychology, 78,* 326–336.

Caughlin J. P., & Vangelisti, A. L. (2009). Why people conceal or reveal secrets: A multiple goals theory perspective. In T. D. Afifi & W. A. Afifi (Eds.), *Uncertainty, information management, and disclosure decisions: Theories and applications* (pp. 279–299). New York: Routledge.

Cavallo, J. V., Murray, S. L., & Holmes, J. G. (2014). Risk regulation in close relationships. In M. Mikulincer & P. R. Shaver (Eds.), *Mechanisms of social connection: From brain to group* (pp. 237–254). Washington, DC: American Psychological Association.

CAWP. (2017). *Current numbers.* Center for American Women and Politics. Retrieved from http://www.cawp.rutgers.edu/current-numbers

Ceglian, C. P., & Gardner, S. (1999). Attachment style: A risk for multiple marriages? *Journal of Divorce & Remarriage, 31,* 125–139.

Çelik, P., Lammers, J., van Beest, I., Bekker, M. H. J., & Vonk, R. (2013). Not all rejections are alike: Competence and warmth as a fundamental distinction in social rejection. *Journal of Experimental Social Psychology, 49,* 635–642.

Centers for Disease Control and Prevention (2014). *Understanding intimate partner violence: Fact sheet.* Washington, DC: U.S. Department of Health & Human Services. Retrieved from https://www.cdc.gov/violenceprevention/pub/index.html.

Chaladze, G. (2016). Heterosexual male carriers could explain persistence of homosexuality in men: Individual-based simulations of an X-linked inheritance model. *Archives of Sexual Behavior, 45,* 1705–1711.

Chaplin, W. F., Phillips, J. B., Brown, J. D., Clanton, N. R., & Stein, J. L. (2000). Handshaking, gender, personality, and first impressions. *Journal of Personality and Social Psychology, 79,* 110–117.

Chartrand, T. L., Dalton, A. N., & Fitzsimons, G. J. (2007). Nonconscious relationship reactance: When significant others prime opposing goals. *Journal of Experimental Social Psychology, 43,* 719–726.

Chartrand, T. L., & Lakin, J. L. (2013). The antecedents and consequences of human behavioral mimicry. *Annual Review of Psychology, 64,* 285–308.

Cheek, J. M., & Buss, A. H. (1981). Shyness and sociability. *Journal of Personality and Social Psychology, 41,* 330–339.

Chen, H., Cohen, P., Kasen, S., Johnson, J. G., Ehrensaft, M., & Gordon, K. (2006). Predicting conflict within romantic relationships during the transition to adulthood. *Personal Relationships, 13,* 411–427.

Chen, H., Luo, S., Yue, G., Xu, D., & Zhaoyang, R. (2009). Do birds of a feather flock together in China? *Personal Relationships, 16,* 167–186.

Chen, R., Austin, J. P., Miller, J. K., & Piercy, F. P. (2015). Chinese and American individuals' mate selection criteria: Updates, modifications, and extensions. *Journal of Cross-Cultural Psychology, 46,* 101–118.

Chen, S., Boucher, H. C., Andersen, S. M., & Saribay, S. A. (2013). Transference and the relational self. In J. A. Simpson & L. Campbell (Eds.), *The Oxford handbook of close relationships* (pp. 281–305). New York: Oxford University Press.

Chen, S., Fitzsimons, G. M., & Andersen, S. M. (2007). Automaticity in close relationships. In J. A. Bargh (Ed.), *Social psychology and the unconscious: The automaticity of higher mental processes* (pp. 133–172). New York: Psychology Press.

Chen, S., Lee-Chai, A. Y., & Bargh, J. A. (2001). Relationship orientation as a moderator of the effects of social power. *Journal of Personality and Social Psychology, 80,* 173–187.

Cheng, Z., & Smyth, R. (2015). Sex and happiness. *Journal of Economic Behavior and Organization, 112,* 26–32.

Cherlin, A. J. (2009). *The marriage-go-round: The state of marriage and the family in America today.* New York: Knopf.

Chester, D. S., & DeWall, C. N. (2017). Combating the sting of rejection with the pleasure of revenge: A new look at how emotion shapes aggression. *Journal of Personality and Social Psychology, 112,* 413–430.

Child Trends. (2017, February). *Teen pregnancy prevention.* Retrieved from https://www.childtrends.org/publications/teen-pregnancy-prevention-research-based-policy-recommendations-executive-legislative-officials-2017/

Choi, K. H., & Tienda, M. (2017). Marriage-market constraints and mate-selection behavior: Racial, ethnic, and gender differences in intermarriage. *Journal of Marriage and Family, 79,* 301–317.

Choi, N., Fuqua, D. R., & Newman, J. L. (2007). Hierarchical confirmatory factor analysis of the Bem Sex Role Inventory. *Educational and Psychological Measurement, 67,* 818–832.

Chopik, W. J., & Edelstein, R. S. (2014). Age differences in romantic attachment around the world. *Social Psychological and Personality Science, 5,* 892–900.

Chopik, W. J., Edelstein, R. S., & Fraley, R. C. (2013). From the cradle to the grave: Age differences in attachment from early adulthood to old age. *Journal of Personality, 81,* 171–183.

Chopik, W. J., Edelstein, R. S., van Anders, S. M., & . . . Samples-Steele, C. R. (2014). Too close for comfort? Adult attachment and cuddling in romantic and parent-child relationships. *Personality and Individual Differences, 69,* 212–216.

Christakis, N. A., & Fowler, J. H. (2009). *Connected: The surprising power of our social networks and how they shape our lives.* New York: Little, Brown.

Christensen, A., Doss, B. D., & Jacobson, N. S. (2014). *Reconcilable differences: Rebuild your relationship by rediscovering the partner you love—without losing yourself.* New York: Guilford Press.

Christensen, A., Eldridge, K., Catta-Preta, A. B., Lim, V. R., & Santagata, R. (2006). Cross-cultural consistency of the demand/withdraw interaction pattern in couples. *Journal of Marriage and Family, 68,* 1029–1044.

Chun, J. S., Ames, D. R., Uribe, J. N., & Higgins, E. T. (2017). Who do we think of as good judges? Those who agree with us *about* us. *Journal of Experimental Social Psychology, 69,* 121–129.

Ciarrochi, J., Parker, P. D., Sahdra, B. K., Kashdan, T. B., Kiuru, N., & Conigrave, J. (2017). When empathy matters: The role of sex and empathy in close friendships. *Journal of Personality, 85,* 494–504.

Clark, M. S., & Aragón, O. R. (2013). Communal (and other) relationships: History, theory development, recent findings, and future directions. In J. A. Simpson & L. Campbell (Eds.), *The Oxford handbook of close relationships* (pp. 255–280). New York: Oxford University Press.

Clark, M. S., & Grote, N. K. (1998). Why aren't indices of relationship costs always negatively related to indices of relationship quality? *Personality and Social Psychology Review, 2,* 2–17.

Clark, M. S., Lemay, E. P., Jr., Graham, S. M., Pataki, S. P., & Finkel, E. J. (2010). Ways of giving benefits in marriage: Norm use, relationship satisfaction, and attachment-related variability. *Psychological Science, 21,* 944–951.

Clark, M. S., & Mills, J. R. (2012). A theory of communal (and exchange) relationships. In P. Van Lange, A. Kruglanski, & E. T. Higgins (Eds.), *Handbook of theories of social psychology* (Vol. 2, pp. 232–250). Thousand Oaks, CA: Sage.

Clark, M. S., Pataki, S. P., & Carver, V. H. (1996). Some thoughts and findings on self-presentation of emotions in relationships. In G. J. O. Fletcher & J. Fitness (Eds.), *Knowledge structures in close relationships: A social psychological approach* (pp. 247–274). Mahwah, NJ: Erlbaum.

Clark, R. D., III, & Hatfield, E. (1989). Gender differences in receptivity to sexual offers. *Journal of Psychology and Human Sexuality, 2,* 39–55.

Clark, R. D., III, & Hatfield, E. (2003). Love in the afternoon. *Psychological Inquiry, 14,* 227–231.

Clarkwest, A. (2007). Spousal dissimilarity, race, and marital dissolution. *Journal of Marriage and Family, 69,* 639–653.

Claxton, A., O'Rourke, N., Smith, J. Z., & DeLongis, A. (2012). Personality traits and marital satisfaction within enduring relationships: An intra-couple discrepancy approach. *Journal of Social and Personal Relationships, 29,* 375–396.

Clayton, R. B., Nagurney, A., & Smith, J. R. (2013). Cheating, breakup, and divorce: Is Facebook use to blame? *Cyberpsychology, Behavior, and Social Networking, 16,* 717–720.

Cleere, C., & Lynn, S. J. (2013). Acknowledged versus unacknowledged sexual assault among college women. *Journal of Interpersonal Violence 28,* 2593–2611.

Clements, M. L., Martin, S. E., Randall, D. W., & Kane, K. L. (2014). Child and parent perceptions of interparental relationship conflict predict preschool children's adjustment. *Couple and Family Psychology: Research and Practice, 3,* 110–125.

Clore, G. L., & Byrne, D. (1974). A reinforcement-affect model of attraction. In T. L. Huston (Ed.), *Foundations of interpersonal attraction* (pp. 143–170). New York: Academic Press.

Coan, J. A., Schaefer, H. S., & Davidson, R. J. (2006). Lending a hand: Social regulation of the neural response to threat. *Psychological Science, 17,* 1032–1039.

Cobb, R. A., DeWall, C. N., Lambert, N. M., & Fincham, F. D. (2013). Implicit theories of relationship and close relationship violence: Does believing your relationship can grow relate to lower perpetration of violence? *Personality and Social Psychology Bulletin, 39,* 279–290.

Coffelt, T. A., & Hess, J. A. (2014). Sexual disclosures: Connections to relational satisfaction and closeness. *Journal of Sex and Marital Therapy, 40,* 577–591.

Cohen, S., Doyle, W. J., Turner, R., Alper, C. M., & Skoner, D. P. (2003). Sociability and susceptibility to the common cold. *Psychological Science, 14,* 389–395.

Cohen, S., Janicki-Deverts, D., Turner, R. B., & Doyle, W. J. (2015). Does hugging provide stress-buffering social support? A study of susceptibility to upper respiratory infection and illness. *Psychological Science, 26,* 135–147.

Cohen, S., Klein, D. N., & O'Leary, D. (2007). The role of separation/divorce in relapse into and recovery from major depression. *Journal of Social and Personal Relationships, 24,* 855–873.

Cohn, D. (2010, June 4). At long last, divorce. *Pew Research Center.* Retrieved from http://pewresearch.org/pubs/1617/long-duration-marriage-end-divorce-gore

Cohn, D., & Caumont, A. (2016, March 31). *10 demographic trends that are shaping the U.S. and the world.* Pew Research Center. Retrieved from http://www.pewresearch.org/fact-tank/2016/03/31/10-demographic-trends-that-are-shaping-the-u-s-and-the-world/

Cohn, E. S., Dupuis, E. C., & Brown, T. M. (2009). In the eye of the beholder: Do behavior and character affect victim and perpetrator responsibility for acquaintance rape? *Journal of Applied Social Psychology, 39,* 1513–1535.

Cole, S., Trope, Y., & Balcetis, E. (2016). In the eye of the betrothed: Perceptual downgrading of attractive alternative romantic partners. *Personality and Social Psychology Bulletin, 42,* 879–892.

Collibee, C., & Furman, W. (2016). The relationship context for sexual activity and its associations with romantic cognitions among emerging adults. *Emerging Adulthood, 4,* 71–81.

Collins, N. L., & Allard, L. M. (2001). Cognitive representations of attachment: The content and function of working models. In G. J. O. Fletcher & M. S. Clark (Eds.), *Blackwell handbook of social psychology: Interpersonal processes* (pp. 60–85). Malden, MA: Blackwell.

Collins, N. L., & Feeney, B. C. (2004). Working models of attachment shape perceptions of social support: Evidence from experimental and observational studies. *Journal of Personality and Social Psychology, 87,* 363–383.

Collins, N. L., & Feeney, B. C. (2010). An attachment theoretical perspective on social support dynamics in couples: Normative processes and individual differences. In K. Sullivan & J. Davila (Eds.), *Support processes in intimate relationships* (pp. 89–120). New York: Oxford University Press.

Collins, N. L., Ford, M. B., Guichard, A. C., Kane, H. S., & Feeney, B. C. (2010). Responding to need in intimate relationships: Social support and caregiving processes in couples. In M. Mikulincer & P. R. Shaver (Eds.), *Prosocial motives, emotions, and behavior: The better angels of our nature* (pp. 367–389). Washington, DC: American Psychological Association.

Collins, N. L., Kane, H. S., Metz, M. A., & . . . Prok, T. (2014). Psychological, physiological, and behavioral responses to a partner in need: The role of compassionate love. *Journal of Social and Personal Relationships, 31,* 601–629.

Collins, N. L., & Miller, L. C. (1994). Self-disclosure and liking: A meta-analytic review. *Psychological Bulletin, 116,* 457–475.

Collins, T. J., & Gillath, O. (2012). Attachment, breakup strategies, and associated outcomes: The effects of security enhancement on the selection of breakup strategies. *Journal of Research in Personality, 46,* 210–222.

Coltrane, S., & Shih, K. Y. (2010). Gender and the division of labor. In J. Chrisler & D. McCreary (Eds.), *Handbook of gender research in psychology* (Vol. 2, pp. 401–422). New York: Springer.

Confer, J. C., Easton, J. A., Fleischman, D. S., Goetz, C. D., Lewis, D. M. G., Perilloux, C., & Buss, D. M. (2010). Evolutionary psychology: Controversies, questions, prospects, and limitations. *American Psychologist, 65,* 110–126.

Conley, T. D. (2011). Perceived proposer personality characteristics and gender differences in acceptance of casual sex offers. *Journal of Personality and Social Psychology, 100,* 309–329.

Connelly, B. S., & Ones, D. S. (2010). An other perspective on personality: Meta-analytic integration of observers' accuracy and predictive validity. *Psychological Bulletin, 136,* 1092–1122.

Conroy-Beam, D., & Buss, D. M. (2016). Do mate preferences influence actual mating decisions? Evidence from computer simulations and three studies of mated couples. *Journal of Personality and Social Psychology, 111,* 53–66.

Conroy-Beam, D., Buss, D. M., Pham, M. N., & Shackelford, T. K. (2015). How sexually dimorphic are human mate preferences? *Personality and Social Psychology Bulletin, 41,* 1082–1093.

Conway, J. R., Noë, N., Stulp, G., & Pollet, T. V. (2015). Finding your soulmate: Homosexual and heterosexual age preferences in online dating. *Personal Relationships, 22,* 666–678.

Coontz, S. (2005). *Marriage, a history: From obedience to intimacy or how love conquered marriage.* New York: Viking.

Coontz, S. (2015). Revolution in intimate life and relationships. *Journal of Family Theory & Review, 7,* 5–12.

Cooper, E. B., Fenigstein, A., & Fauber, R. L. (2014). The Faking Orgasm Scale for Women: Psychometric properties. *Archives of Sexual Behavior, 43,* 423–435.

Cooper, M., O'Donnell, D., Caryl, P. G., Morrison, R., & Bale, C. (2007). Chat-up lines as male displays: Effects of content, sex, and personality. *Personality and Individual Differences, 43,* 1075–1085.

Cooper, M. L., Barber, L. L., Zhaoyang, R., & Talley, A. E. (2011). Motivational pursuits in the context of human sexual relationships. *Journal of Personality, 79,* 1031–1066.

Copen, C. E., Chandra, A., & Febo-Vazquez, I. (2016). *Sexual behavior, sexual attraction, and sexual orientation among adults aged 18–44 in the United States: Data from the 2011–2013 National Survey of Family Growth.* National Health Statistics Reports, 88. Hyattsville, MD: National Center for Health Statistics.

Cordaro, D. T., Keltner, D., Tshering, S., Wangchuk, D., & Flynn, L. M. (2016). The voice conveys emotion in ten globalized cultures and one remote village in Bhutan. *Emotion, 16,* 117–128.

Cordova, J. V. (2014). *The Marriage Checkup practitioner's guide: Promoting lifelong relationship health.* Washington, DC: American Psychological Association.

Côté, S., Kraus, M. W., Cheng, B. H., & . . . Keltner, D. (2011). Social power facilitates the effect of prosocial orientation on empathic accuracy. *Journal of Personality and Social Psychology, 101,* 217–232.

Couch, L. L., & Jones, W. H. (1997). Conceptualizing levels of trust. *Journal of Research in Personality, 31,* 319–336.

Coughlin, P., & Wade, J. C. (2012). Masculinity ideology, income disparity, and romantic relationship quality among men with higher earning female partners. *Sex Roles, 67,* 311–322.

Coulter, K., & Malouff, J. M. (2013). Effects of an intervention designed to enhance romantic relationship excitement: A randomized-control trial. *Couple and Family Psychology: Research and Practice, 2,* 24–44.

Cowan, G., & Mills, R. D. (2004). Personal inadequacy and intimacy predictors of men's hostility toward women. *Sex Roles, 51,* 67–78.

Cowley, A. D. (2014). "Let's get drunk and have sex": The complex relationship of alcohol, gender, and sexual victimization. *Journal of Interpersonal Violence, 29,* 1258–1278.

Coyne, J. C., Rohrbaugh, M. J., Shoham, V., Sonnega, J. S., Nicklas, J. M., & Cranford, J. A. (2001). Prognostic importance of marital quality for survival of congestive heart failure. *American Journal of Cardiology, 88,* 526–529.

Coyne, S. M., Nelson, D. A., Graham-Kevan, N., Keister, E., & Grant, D. M. (2010). Mean on the screen: Psychopathy, relationship aggression, and aggression in the media. *Personality and Individual Differences, 48,* 288–293.

Crane, R. D., Dollahite, D. C., Griffin, W., & Taylor, V. L. (1987). Diagnosing relationships with spatial distance: An empirical test of a clinical principle. *Journal of Marital and Family Therapy, 13,* 307–310.

Croom, C., Gross, B., Rosen. L. D., & Rosen, B. (2016). What's her Face(book)? How many of their Facebook "friends" can college students actually identify? *Computers in Human Behavior, 56,* 135–141.

Cross, E. J., Overall, N. C., Hammond, M. D., & Fletcher, G. J. O. (2017). When does men's hostile sexism predict relationship aggression? The moderating role of partner commitment. *Social Psychological and Personality Science, 8,* 331–340.

Cross, S. E., Hardin, E. E., & Gercek-Swing, B. (2011). The what, how, why, and where of self-construal. *Personality and Social Psychology Review, 15,* 142–179.

Cross, S. E., & Morris, M. L. (2003). Getting to know you: The relational self-construal, relational cognition, and well-being. *Personality and Social Psychology Bulletin, 29,* 512–523.

Croy, I., Bojanowski, V., & Hummel, T. (2013). Men without a sense of smell exhibit a strongly reduced number of sexual relationships, women exhibit reduced partnership security: A reanalysis of previously published data. *Biological Psychology, 92,* 292–294.

Cruz, J. (2013). *Divorce rate in the U.S., 2011.* National Center for Family & Marriage Research. Retrieved from http://ncfmr.bgsu.edu/pdf/family_profiles/file131530.pdf

Cuddy, A. (2015). *Presence: Bringing your boldest self to your biggest challenges.* New York: Little, Brown.

Cundiff, J. M., Smith, T. W., Butner, J., Critchfield, K. L., & Nealey-Moore, J. (2015). Affiliation and control in marital interaction: Interpersonal complementarity is present but is not associated with affect or relationship quality. *Personality and Social Psychology Bulletin, 41,* 35–51.

Cunningham, G. B., & Melton, E. N. (2013). The moderating effects of contact with lesbian and gay friends on the relationships among religious fundamentalism, sexism, and sexual prejudice. *Journal of Sex Research, 50,* 401–408.

Cunningham, M. R. (1989). Reactions to heterosexual opening gambits: Female selectivity and male responsiveness. *Personality and Social Psychology Bulletin, 15,* 27–41.

Cunningham, M. R., Barbee, A. P., & Philhower, C. L. (2002). Dimensions of facial physical attractiveness: The intersection of biology and culture. In G. Rhodes & L. A. Zebrowitz (Eds.), *Facial attractiveness: Evolutionary, cognitive and social perspectives* (pp. 193–238). Westport, CT: Ablex.

Cunningham, M. R., Roberts, A. R., Barbee, A. P., Druen, P. B., & Wu, C. (1995). "Their ideas of beauty are, on the whole, the same as ours": Consistency and variability in the cross-cultural perception of female physical attractiveness. *Journal of Personality and Social Psychology, 68,* 261–279.

Cunningham, M. R., Shamblen, S. R., Barbee, A. P., & Ault, L. K. (2005). Social allergies in romantic relationships: Behavioral repetition, emotional sensitization, and dissatisfaction in dating couples. *Personal Relationships, 12,* 273–295.

Cupach, W. R. (2007). "You're bugging me!": Complaints and criticism from a partner. In B. Spitzberg & W. Cupach (Eds.), *The dark side of interpersonal communication* (2nd ed., pp. 143–168). Mahwah, NJ: Erlbaum.

Cupach, W. R., & Spitzberg, B. H. (Eds.). (2011). *The dark side of close relationships II.* New York: Routledge.

Cuperman, R., & Ickes, W. (2009). Big five predictors of behavior and perceptions in initial dyadic interactions: Personality similarity helps extraverts and introverts, but hurts "disagreeables." *Journal of Personality and Social Psychology, 97,* 667–684.

Curtis, R. C., & Miller, K. (1986). Believing another likes or dislikes you: Behaviors making the beliefs come true. *Journal of Personality and Social Psychology, 51,* 284–290.

Cutrona, C. E. (1982). Transition to college: Loneliness and the process of social adjustment. In L. A. Peplau & D. Perlman (Eds.), *Loneliness: A sourcebook of current theory, research, and therapy* (pp. 291–309). New York: Wiley Interscience.

Cutrona, C. E., Russell, D. W., Burzett, R. G., Wesner, K. A., & Bryant, C. M. (2011). Predicting relationship stability among midlife African American couples. *Journal of Consulting and Clinical Psychology, 79,* 814–825.

Czarna, A. Z., Leifeld, P., Śmieja, M., Dufner, M., & Salovey, P. (2016). Do narcissism and emotional intelligence win us friends? Modeling dynamics of peer popularity using inferential network analysis. *Personality and Social Psychology Bulletin, 42,* 1588–1599.

Daigen, V., & Holmes, J. G. (2000). Don't interrupt! A good rule for marriage? *Personal Relationships, 7,* 185–201.

Dailey, R. M., McCracken, A. A., Jin, B., Rossetto, K. R., & Green, E. W. (2013). Negotiating breakups and renewals: Types of on-again/off-again dating relationships. *Western Journal of Communication, 77,* 382–410.

Dainton, M. (2017). Equity, equality, and self-interest in marital maintenance. *Communication Quarterly, 65,* 247–267.

Daly, J. A., Hogg, E., Sacks, D., Smith, M., & Zimring, L. (1983). Sex and relationship affect social self-grooming. *Journal of Nonverbal Behavior, 7,* 183–189.

Daneback, K., Cooper, A., & Månsson, S. (2005). An Internet study of cybersex participants. *Archives of Sexual Behavior, 34,* 321–328.

Daniels, K., Jones, J., & Abma, J. (2013). Use of emergency contraception among women aged 15–44. *NCHS Data Brief,* no. 112. Hyattsville, MD: National Center for Health Statistics.

Danner-Vlaardingerbroek, G., Kluwer, E. S., Van Steenbergen, E. F., & Van Der Lippe, T. (2016). How work spills over into the relationship: Self-control matters. *Personal Relationships, 23,* 441–455.

Darbyshire, D., Kirk, C, Wall, H. J., & Kaye, L. K. (2016). Don't judge a (face)book by its cover: Exploring judgment accuracy of others' personality of Facebook. *Computers in Human Behavior, 58,* 380–387.

Dardis, C. M., & Gidycz, C. A. (2017). The frequency and perceived impact of engaging in in-person and cyber unwanted pursuit after relationship break-up among college men and women. *Sex Roles, 75,* 56–72.

Darley, J. M., & Gross, P. H. (1983). A hypothesis-confirming bias in labeling effects. *Journal of Personality and Social Psychology, 44,* 20–33.

Das, A., Waite, L. J., & Laumann, E. O. (2011). Sexual expression over the life course: Results from three landmark surveys. In J. DeLamater and L. Carpenter (Eds.), *Sex for life: From virginity to Viagra, how sexuality changes throughout our lives* (pp. 236–259). New York: NYU Press.

Daugherty, J., & Copen, C. (2016). *Trends in attitudes about marriage, childbearing, and sexual behavior: United States, 2002, 2006–2010, and 2011–2013.* National Health Statistics Reports, 92. Hyattsville, MD: National Center for Health Statistics.

Davies, A. P. C., Shackelford, T. K., & Hass, R. G. (2007). When a "poach" is not a poach: Redefining human mate poaching and re-estimating its frequency. *Archives of Sexual Behavior, 36,* 702–716.

Davies, A. P. C., Shackelford, T. K., & Hass, R. G. (2010). Sex differences in perceptions of benefits and costs of mate poaching. *Personality and Individual Differences, 49,* 441–445.

Davila, J., & Cobb, R. J. (2004). Predictors of change in attachment security during adulthood. In W. S. Rholes & J. A. Simpson (Eds.), *Adult attachment: Theory, research, and clinical implications* (pp. 133–156). New York: Guilford Press.

Davila, J., & Kashy, D. A. (2009). Secure base processes in couples: Daily associations between support experiences and attachment security. *Journal of Family Psychology, 23,* 76–88.

Davis, D., Shaver, P. R., & Vernon, M. L. (2004). Attachment style and subjective motivations for sex. *Personality and Social Psychology Bulletin, 30,* 1076–1090.

Davis, D., Shaver, P. R., Widaman, K. F., Vernon, M. L., Follette, W. C., & Beitz, K. (2006). "I can't get no satisfaction": Insecure attachment, inhibited sexual communication, and sexual dissatisfaction. *Personal Relationships, 13,* 465–483.

Davis, K. C., Jacques-Tiura, A. J., Stappenbeck, C. A., & . . . George, W. H. (2016). Men's condom use resistance: Alcohol effects on theory of planned behavior constructs. *Health Psychology, 35,* 178–186.

Davis, K. C., Stappenbeck, C. A., Norris, J., & . . . Kajumulo, K. F. (2014). Young men's condom use resistance tactics: A latent profile analysis. *Journal of Sex Research, 51,* 454–465.

Davis, K. E., Swan, S. C., & Gambone, L. J. (2012). Why doesn't he just leave me alone? Persistent pursuit: A critical review of theories and evidence. *Sex Roles, 66,* 328–339.

Day, L. C., & Impett, E. A. (2016). For it is in giving that receive: the benefits of sacrifice in relationships. In C. Knee & H. Reis (Eds.), *Positive approaches to optimal relationship development* (pp. 211–231). Cambridge, UK: Cambridge University Press.

Day, L. C., Muise, A., Joel, S., & Impett, E. A. (2015). To do it or not to do it? How communally motivated people navigate sexual interdependence dilemmas. *Personality and Social Psychology Bulletin, 41,* 791–804.

De Bro, S. C., Campbell, S. M., & Peplau, L. A. (1994). Influencing a partner to use a condom: A college student perspective. *Psychology of Women Quarterly, 18,* 165–182.

Debrot, A., Schoebi, D., Perrez, M., & Horn, A. B. (2013). Touch as an interpersonal emotion regulation process in couples' daily lives: The mediating role of psychological intimacy. *Personality and Social Psychology Bulletin, 39,* 1373–1385.

Deci, E. L., & Ryan, R. M. (2012). Self-determination theory. In P. Van Lange, A. Kruglanski, & E. T. Higgins (Eds.), *Handbook of theories of social psychology* (Vol. 1, pp. 416–436). Thousand Oaks, CA: Sage.

Deckman, T., DeWall, C. N., Way, B., Gilman, R., & Richman, S. (2014). Can marijuana reduce social pain? *Social Psychological and Personality Science, 5,* 131–139.

de Graaf, H., Vanwesenbeeck, I., Meijer, S., Woertman, L., & Meeus, W. (2009). Sexual trajectories during adolescence: Relation to demographic characteristics and sexual risk. *Archives of Sexual Behavior, 38,* 276–282.

de Groot, J. H. B., Smeets, M. A. M., Rowson, M. J, & . . . Semin, G. R. (2015). A sniff of happiness. *Psychological Science, 26,* 684–700.

DeGue, S., & DiLillo, D. (2005). "You would if you loved me": Toward an improved conceptual and etiological understanding of nonphysical male sexual coercion. *Aggression and Violent Behavior, 10,* 513–532.

de Jong, D. C., & Reis, H. T. (2014). Sexual kindred spirits: Actual and overperceived similarity, complementarity, and partner accuracy in heterosexual couples. *Personality and Social Psychology Bulletin, 40,* 1316–1329.

De Jong, D. C., & Reis, H. T. (2015). Sexual similarity, complementarity, accuracy, and overperception in same-sex couples. *Personal Relationships, 22,* 647–665.

DeLamater, J. (2012). Sexual expression in later life: A review and synthesis. *Journal of Sex Research, 49,* 125–141.

De La Ronde, C., & Swann, W. B., Jr. (1998). Partner verification: Restoring shattered images of our intimates. *Journal of Personality and Social Psychology, 75,* 374–382.

Della Sala, S. (Ed.). (2010). *Forgetting.* New York: Psychology Press.

DelPriore, D. J., Hill, S. E., & Buss, D. M. (2012). Envy: Functional specificity and sex-differentiated design features. *Personality and Individual Differences, 53,* 317–322.

DeMaris, A. (2013). Burning the candle at both ends: Extramarital sex as a precursor of marital disruption. *Journal of Family Issues, 34,* 1474–1499.

Denes, A., Lannutti, P. J., & Bevan, J. L. (2015). Same-sex infidelity in heterosexual romantic relationships: Investigating emotional, relational, and communicative responses. *Personal Relationships, 22,* 414–430.

Denissen, J. J. A., Penke, L., Schmitt, D. P., & van Aken, M. A. G. (2008). Self-esteem reactions to social interactions: Evidence for sociometer mechanisms across days, people, and nations. *Journal of Personality and Social Psychology, 95,* 181–196.

Dennison, R. P., Koerner, S. S., & Segrin, C. (2014). A dyadic examination of family-of-origin influence on newlyweds' marital satisfaction. *Journal of Family Psychology, 28,* 429–435.

Denrell, J. (2005). Why most people disapprove of me: Experience sampling in impression formation. *Psychological Review, 112,* 951–978.

Denton, W. H., & Burleson, B. R. (2007). The Initiator Style Questionnaire: A scale to assess initiator tendency in couples. *Personal Relationships, 14,* 245–268.

DePaulo, B. (2014). A singles studies perspective on Mount Marriage. *Psychological Inquiry, 25,* 64–68.

DePaulo, B. (2015). *How we live now.* New York: Atria Books.

DePaulo, B. M., Ansfield, M. E., Kirkendol, S. E., & Boden, J. M. (2004). Serious lies. *Basic and Applied Social Psychology, 26,* 147–167.

DePaulo, B. M., & Bell, K. L. (1996). Truth and investment: Lies are told to those who care. *Journal of Personality and Social Psychology, 71,* 703–716.

DePaulo, B. M., Charlton, K., Cooper, H., Lindsay, J. J., & Muhlenbruck, L. (1997). The accuracy–confidence correlation in the detection of deception. *Personality and Social Psychology Review, 1,* 346–357.

DePaulo, B. M., & Kashy, D. A. (1998). Everyday lies in close and casual relationships. *Journal of Personality and Social Psychology, 74,* 63–79.

DePaulo, B. M., Kashy, D. A., Kirkendol, S. E., Wyer, M. M., & Epstein, J. A. (1996). Lying in everyday life. *Journal of Personality and Social Psychology, 70,* 979–995.

DePaulo, B. M., Lanier, K., & Davis, T. (1983). Detecting the deceit of the motivated liar. *Journal of Personality and Social Psychology, 45,* 1096–1103.

DePaulo, B. M., Morris, W. L., & Sternglanz, R. W. (2009). When the truth hurts: Deception in the name of kindness. In A. L. Vangelisti (Ed.), *Feeling hurt in close relationships* (pp. 167–190). New York: Cambridge University Press.

Derlega, V. J., Winstead, B. A., & Greene, K. (2008). Self-disclosure and starting a close relationship. In S. Sprecher, A. Wenzel, & J. Harvey (Eds.), *Handbook of relationship initiation* (pp. 153–174). New York: Psychology Press.

Dermer, M., & Pyszczynski, T. A. (1978). Effects of erotica upon men's loving and liking responses for women they love. *Journal of Personality and Social Psychology, 36,* 1302–1309.

Derrick, J. L., Houston, R. J., Quigley, B. M., & . . . Leonard, K. E. (2016). (Dis)similarity in impulsivity and marital satisfaction: A comparison of volatility, compatibility, and incompatibility hypotheses. *Journal of Research in Personality, 61,* 35–49.

DeShong, H. L., Helle, A. C., Lengel, G. J., Meyer, N., & Mullins-Sweatt, S. N. (2017). Facets of the Dark Triad: Utilizing the Five-Factor Model to describe Machiavellianism. *Personality and Individual Differences, 105,* 218–223.

De Smet, O., Uzieblo, K., Loeys, T., Buysse, A., & Onraedt, T. (2015). Unwanted pursuit behavior after breakup: Occurrence, risk factors, and gender differences. *Journal of Family Violence, 30,* 753–767.

DeSteno, D. (2010). Mismeasuring jealousy: A cautionary comment on Levy and Kelly (2010). *Psychological Science, 21,* 1355–1356.

DeSteno, D. A., & Salovey, P. (1994). Jealousy in close relationships: Multiple perspectives on the green-eyed monster. In A. L. Weber & J. H. Harvey (Eds.), *Perspectives on close relationships* (pp. 217–242). Boston: Allyn & Bacon.

DeSteno, D. A., & Salovey, P. (1996). Evolutionary origins of sex differences in jealousy? Questioning the "fitness" of the model. *Psychological Science, 7,* 367–372.

DeSteno, D., Valdesolo, P., & Bartlett, M. Y. (2006). Jealousy and the threatened self: Getting to the heart of the green-eyed monster. *Journal of Personality and Social Psychology, 91,* 626–641.

Deters, F. G., & Mehl, M. R. (2013). Does posting Facebook status updates increase or decrease loneliness? An online social networking experiment. *Social Psychological and Personality Science, 4,* 570–586.

De Vogli, R., Chandola, T., & Marmot, M. G. (2007). Negative aspects of close relationships and heart disease. *Archives of Internal Medicine, 167,* 1951–1957.

Dew, J., & Wilcox, W. B. (2011). If Momma ain't happy: Explaining declines in marital satisfaction among new mothers. *Journal of Marriage and Family, 73,* 1–12.

Dew, J., & Wilcox, W. B. (2013). Generosity and the maintenance of marital quality. *Journal of Marriage and Family, 75,* 1218–1228.

DeWall, C. N. (2015). Teaching students why a good marriage is hard to find. *Observer, 28*(8), 31–32.

DeWall, C. N., Finkel, E. J., Lambert, N. M., & . . . Fincham, F. D. (2013). The Voodoo Doll Task: Introducing and validating a novel method for studying aggressive inclinations. *Aggressive Behavior, 39,* 419–439.

DeWall, C. N., MacDonald, G., Webster, G. D., & . . . Eisenberger, N. I. (2010). Acetaminophen reduces social pain: Behavioral and neural evidence. *Psychological Science, 21,* 931–937.

DeWall, C. N., Twenge, J. M., Gitter, S. A., & Baumeister, R. F. (2009). It's the thought that counts: The role of hostile cognition in shaping aggressive responses to social exclusion. *Journal of Personality and Social Psychology, 96,* 45–59.

Dewsbury, D. A. (1981). Effects of novelty on copulatory behavior: The Coolidge effect and related phenomena. *Psychological Bulletin, 89,* 464–482.

Diamond, L. M. (2013). Sexuality in relationships. In J. A. Simpson & L. Campbell (Eds.), *The Oxford handbook of close relationships* (pp. 589–614). New York: Oxford University Press.

Diamond, L. M. (2014). Romantic love. In M. M. Tugade, M. N. Shiota, & L. D. Kirby (Eds.), *Handbook of positive emotions* (pp. 311–328). New York: Guilford Press.

Diamond, L. M. (2015). Sexuality and same-sex sexuality in relationships. In M. Mikulincer, P. Shaver, J. Simpson, & J. Dovidio (Eds.), *APA handbook of personality and social psychology: Vol. 3. Interpersonal relations* (pp. 523–553). Washington, DC: American Psychological Association.

Dickerson, S. S., & Zoccola, P. M. (2013). Cortisol responses to social exclusion. In C. N. DeWall (Ed.), *The Oxford handbook of social exclusion* (pp. 143–151). New York: Oxford University Press.

Dillon, L. M., Nowak, N., Weisfeld, G. E., & . . . Shen, J. (2015). Sources of marital conflict in five cultures. *Evolutionary Psychology, 13,* 1–15.

Dillow, M. R., Dunleavy, K. N., & Weber, K. D. (2009). The impact of relational characteristics and reasons for topic avoidance on relational closeness. *Communication Quarterly, 57,* 205–223.

Dindia, K. (2002). Self-disclosure research: Knowledge through meta-analysis. In M. Allen, R. W. Preiss, B. M. Gayle, & N. A. Burrell (Eds.), *Interpersonal communication research: Advances through meta-analysis* (pp. 169–185). Mahwah, NJ: Erlbaum.

Dindia, K. (2006). Men are from North Dakota, women are from South Dakota. In K. Dindia & D. J. Canary (Eds.), *Sex differences and similarities in communication* (pp. 3–20). Mahwah, NJ: Erlbaum.

Dindia, K., & Timmerman, L. (2003). Accomplishing romantic relationships. In J. O. Greene & B. R. Burleson (Eds.), *Handbook of communication and social interaction skills* (pp. 685–721). Mahwah, NJ: Erlbaum.

Dion, K. K., Berscheid, E., & Walster, E. (1972). What is beautiful is good. *Journal of Personality and Social Psychology, 24,* 285–290.

DiPaola, B. M., Roloff, M. E., & Peters, K. M. (2010). College students' expectations of conflict intensity: A self-fulfilling prophecy. *Communication Quarterly, 58,* 59–76.

Dixson, B. J., Dixson, A. F., Bishop, P. J., & Parish, A. (2010). Human physique and sexual attractiveness in men and women: A New Zealand–U.S. comparative study. *Archives of Sexual Behavior, 39,* 798–806.

Dixson, B. J., Grimshaw, G. M., Linklater, W. L., & Dixson, A. F. (2011). Eye-tracking of men's preferences for waist-to-hip ratio and breast size of women. *Archives of Sexual Behavior, 40,* 43–50.

Doherty, W. J., & Harris, S. M. (2017). *Helping couples on the brink of divorce: Discernment counseling for troubled relationships.* Washington, DC: American Psychological Association.

Don, B. P., & Mickelson, K. D. (2014). Relationship satisfaction trajectories across the transition to parenthood among low-risk parents. *Journal of Marriage and Family, 76,* 677–692.

Donnellan, M. B., Conger, R. D., & Bryant, C. M. (2004). The Big Five and enduring marriages. *Journal of Research in Personality, 38,* 481–504.

Donnelly, K., & Twenge, J. M. (2017). Masculine and feminine traits on the Bem Sex-Role Inventory, 1993–2012: A cross-temporal meta-analysis. *Sex Roles, 76,* 556–565.

Donnelly, K., Twenge, J. M., Clark, M. A., Shaikh, S. K., Beiler-May, A., & Carter, N. T. (2016). Attitudes toward women's work and family roles in the United States, 1976–2013. *Psychology of Women Quarterly, 40,* 41–54.

D'Onofrio, B. M., Turkheimer, E., Harden, K. P., Slutske, W. S., Heath, A. C., Madden, P. A. F., & Martin, N. G. (2007). A genetically informed study of the intergenerational transmission of marital instability. *Journal of Marriage and Family, 69,* 793–809.

Dooley, T. (2010, March 1). This is not your parents' marriage. *Houston Chronicle,* pp. D1–D2.

Dosmukhambetova, D., & Manstead, A. S. R. (2012). Fear attenuated and affection augmented: Male self-presentation in a romantic context. *Journal of Nonverbal Behavior, 36,* 135–147.

Doss, B. D., Atkins, D. C., & Christensen, A. (2003). Who's dragging their feet? Husbands and wives seeking marital therapy. *Journal of Marital & Family Therapy, 29,* 165–177.

Doss, B. D., Cicila, L. N., Georgia, E. J., & . . . Christensen, A. (2016). A randomized controlled trial of the web-based OurRelationship program: Effects on relationship and individual functioning. *Journal of Consulting and Clinical Psychology, 84,* 285–296.

Doss, B. D., Rhoades, G. K., Stanley, S. M., & Markman, H. J. (2009). The effect of the transition to parenthood on relationship quality: An 8-year prospective study. *Journal of Personality and Social Psychology, 96,* 601–619.

Doumas, D. M., Pearson, C. L., Elgin, J. E., & McKinley, L. L. (2008). Adult attachment as a risk factor for intimate partner violence: The "mispairing" of partners' attachment styles. *Journal of Interpersonal Violence, 23,* 616–634.

Downs, A. C., & Lyons, P. M. (1991). Natural observations of the links between attractiveness and initial legal judgments. *Personality and Social Psychology Bulletin, 17,* 541–547.

Doyle, D. M., & Molix, L. (2015). Social stigma and sexual minorities'' romantic relationship functioning: A meta-analytic review. *Personality and Social Psychology Bulletin, 4,* 1363–1381.

Drigotas, S. M., Rusbult, C. E., Wieselquist, J., & Whitton, S. W. (1999). Close partner as sculptor of the ideal self: Behavioral affirmation and the Michelangelo phenomenon. *Journal of Personality and Social Psychology, 77,* 293–323.

Drouin, M., Miller, D., Wehle, S. M. J. & Hernandez, E. (2016). Why do people lie online? "Because everyone lies on the internet." *Computers in Human Behavior, 64,* 134–142.

Dugan, A. (2015, June 19). *Men, women differ on morals of sex, relationships.* Gallup Social Issues. Retrieved from http://www.gallup.com/poll/183719/men-women-differ-morals-sex-relationships.aspx.

Dunbar, N. E., & Burgoon, J. K. (2005). Perceptions of power and interactional dominance in interpersonal relationships. *Journal of Social and Personal Relationships, 22,* 207–233.

Dunbar, N. E., Gangi, K., Coveleski, S., & Giles, G. (2016). When is it acceptable to lie: Interpersonal and intergroup perspectives on deception. *Communication Studies, 67,* 129–146.

Dunn, M. J., Brinton, S., & Clark, L. (2010). Universal sex differences in online advertisers' age preferences: Comparing data from 14 cultures and 2 religious groups. *Evolution and Human Behavior, 31,* 383–393.

Dunn, M. J., & McLean, H. (2015). Jealousy-induced sex differences in eye gaze directed at either emotional- or sexual infidelity-related mobile phone messages. *Cyberpsychology, Behavior, and Social Networking, 18,* 38–41.

Duntley, J. D., & Buss, D. M. (2012). The evolution of stalking. *Sex Roles, 66,* 311–327.

Durante, K. M., Griskevicius, V., Simpson, J. A., Cantú, S. M., & Tybur, J. M. (2012). Sex ratio and women's career choice: Does a scarcity of men lead women to choose briefcase over baby? *Journal of Personality and Social Psychology, 103,* 121–134.

Durante, K. M., Li, N. P., & Haselton, M. G. (2008). Changes in women's choice of dress across the ovulatory cycle: Naturalistic and laboratory task-based evidence. *Personality and Social Psychology Bulletin, 34,* 1451–1460.

Durtschi, J. A., Fincham, F. D., Cui, M., Lorenz, F. O., & Conger, R. D. (2011). Dyadic processes in early marriage: Attributions, behavior, and marital quality. *Family Relations, 60,* 421–434.

Dutton, D. G., & Aron, A. P. (1974). Some evidence for heightened sexual attraction under conditions of high anxiety. *Journal of Personality and Social Psychology, 30,* 510–517.

Dworkin, S. L., & O'Sullivan, L. (2005). Actual versus desired initiation patterns among a sample of college men: Tapping disjunctures within traditional male sexual scripts. *Journal of Sex Research, 42,* 150–158.

Eagly, A. H., & Wood, W. (2012). Social role theory. In P. Van Lange, A. Kruglanski, & E. Higgins (Eds.), *Handbook of theories of social psychology* (Vol. 2, pp. 458–476). Thousand Oaks, CA: Sage.

Eagly, A. H., & Wood, W. (2013a). Feminism and evolutionary psychology: Moving forward. *Sex Roles, 69,* 549–556.

Eagly, A. H., & Wood, W. (2013b). The nature-nurture debates: 25 years of challenges in understanding the psychology of gender. *Perspectives on Psychological Science, 8,* 340–357.

Eaker, E. D., Sullivan, L. M., Kelly-Hayes, M., D'Agostino, R. B., Sr., & Benjamin, E. J. (2007). Marital status, marital strain, and risk of coronary heart disease or total mortality: The Framingham Offspring Study. *Psychosomatic Medicine, 69,* 509–513.

Eastwick, P. W. (2013). Cultural influences on attraction. In J. A. Simpson & L. Campbell (Eds.), *The Oxford handbook of close relationships* (pp. 161–182). New York: Oxford University Press.

Eastwick, P. W. (2016). The emerging integration of close relationships research and evolutionary psychology. *Current Directions in Psychological Science, 25,* 183–190.

Eastwick, P. W., & Hunt, L. L. (2014). Relational mate value: Consensus and uniqueness in romantic evaluations. *Journal of Personality and Social Psychology, 106,* 728–751.

Eastwick, P. W., & Finkel, E. J. (2008). Sex differences in mate preferences revisited: Do people know what they initially desire in a romantic partner? *Journal of Personality and Social Psychology, 94,* 245–264.

Eastwick, P. W., Finkel, E. J., & Eagly, A. H. (2011). When and why do ideal partner preferences affect the process of initiating and maintaining romantic relationships? *Journal of Personality and Social Psychology, 101,* 1012–1032.

Eastwick, P. W., Finkel, E. J., Krishnamurti, T., & Loewenstein, G. (2008). Mispredicting distress following romantic breakup: Revealing the time course of the affective forecasting error. *Journal of Experimental Social Psychology, 44,* 800–807.

Eastwick, P. W., Finkel, E. J., Mochon, D., & Ariely, D. (2007). Selective versus unselective romantic desire. *Psychological Science, 18,* 317–319.

Eastwick, P. W., Luchies, L. B., Finkel, E. J., & Hunt, L. L. (2014). The predictive validity of ideal partner preferences: A review and meta-analysis. *Psychological Bulletin, 140,* 623–665.

Eastwick, P. W., Saigal, S. D., & Finkel, E. J. (2010). Smooth operating: A structural analysis of social behavior (SASB) perspective on initial romantic encounters. *Social Psychological and Personality Science, 1,* 344–352.

Eastwick, P. W., & Tidwell, N. D. (2013). To pair bond or not: The evolutionary psychological approach to human mating. In C. Hazan & M. I. Campa (Eds.), *Human bonding: The science of affectional ties* (pp. 132–160). New York: Guilford Press.

Ebbesen, E. B., Kjos, G. L., & Konecni, V. J. (1976). Spatial ecology: Its effects on the choice of friends and enemies. *Journal of Experimental Social Psychology, 12,* 505–518.

Ebel-Lam, A. P., MacDonald, T. K., Zanna, M. P., & Fong, G. T. (2009). An experimental investigation of the interactive effects of alcohol and sexual arousal on intentions to have unprotected sex. *Basic and Applied Social Psychology, 31,* 226–233.

Eberhart, N. K., & Hammen, C. L. (2006). Interpersonal predictors of onset of depression during the transition to adulthood. *Personal Relationships, 13,* 195–206.

Ebesu Hubbard, A. S., Hendrickson, B., Fehrenbach, K. S., & Sur, J. (2013). Effects of timing and sincerity of an apology on satisfaction and changes in negative feelings during conflicts. *Western Journal of Communication, 77,* 305–322.

Edwards, G. L., & Barber, B. L. (2010). Women may underestimate their partners' desires to use condoms: Possible implications for behaviour. *Journal of Sex Research, 47,* 59–65.

Edwards, K. M., Gidycz, C. A., & Murphy, M. J. (2011). College women's stay/leave decisions in abusive dating relationships: A prospective analysis of an expanded investment model. *Journal of Interpersonal Violence, 26,* 1446–1462.

Eidelson, R. J. (1980). Interpersonal satisfaction and level of involvement: A curvilinear relationship. *Journal of Personality and Social Psychology, 39,* 460–470.

Eidelson, R. J., & Epstein, N. (1982). Cognition and relationship maladjustment: Development of a measure of dysfunctional relationship beliefs. *Journal of Consulting and Clinical Psychology, 50,* 715–720.

Eisenberg, A. R. (1992). Conflicts between mothers and their young children. *Merrill-Palmer Quarterly, 38,* 21–43.

Eisenberger, N. I. (2013). Why rejection hurts: The neuroscience of social pain. In C. N. DeWall (Ed.), *The Oxford handbook of social exclusion* (pp. 152–162). New York: Oxford University Press.

Eisenbruch, A. B., Simmons, Z. L., & Roney, J. R. (2015). Lady in red: Hormonal predictors of women's clothing choices. *Psychological Science, 26,* 1332–1338.

Ekman, P., & Cardaro, D. (2011). What is meant by calling emotions basic. *Emotion Review, 3,* 364–370.

Elaad, E., Lavy, S., Cohenca, D., Berholz, E., Thee, P., & Ben-Gigi, Y. (2012). Lies, truths, and attachment orientations in late adolescence. *Personality and Individual Differences, 52,* 670–673.

Eldridge, K. A., & Baucom, B. (2012). Demand-withdraw communication in couples: Recent developments and future directions. In P. Noller & G. C. Karantzas (Eds.), *The Wiley-Blackwell handbook of couple and family relationships* (pp. 144–158). Hoboken, NJ: Wiley.

Elfenbein, H. A. (2013). Nonverbal dialects and accents in facial expressions of emotion. *Emotion Review, 5,* 90–96.

Elliot, A. J., & Niesta, D. (2008). Romantic red: Red enhances men's attraction to women. *Journal of Personality and Social Psychology, 95,* 1150–1164.

Elliot, A. J., Greitemeyer, T., & Pazda, A. D. (2013a). Women's use of red clothing as a sexual signal in intersexual interaction. *Journal of Experimental Social Psychology, 49,* 599–602.

Elliot, A. J., Kayser, D. N., Greitemeyer, T., Lichtenfeld, S., Gramzow, R. H., Maier, M. A., & Liu, H. (2010). Red, rank, and romance in women viewing men. *Journal of Experimental Psychology: General, 139,* 399–417.

Elliot, A. J., Tracy, J. L., Pazda, A. D., & Beall, A. T. (2013b). Red enhances women's attractiveness to men: First evidence suggesting universality. *Journal of Experimental Social Psychology, 49,* 165–168.

Elliott, D. B., & Simmons, T. (2011). Marital events of Americans: 2009. *American Community Survey Reports* (ACS-13). Washington, DC: U. S. Census Bureau.

Elliott, S., & Umberson, D. (2008). The performance of desire: Gender and sexual negotiation in long-term marriages. *Journal of Marriage and Family, 70,* 391–406.

Ellis, A. (1993). The advantages and disadvantages of self-help therapy materials. *Professional Psychology: Research & Practice, 24,* 335–339.

Ellyson, S. L., Dovidio, J. F., & Brown, C. E. (1992). The look of power: Gender differences and similarities in visual dominance behavior. In C. Ridgeway (Ed.), *Gender and interaction: The role of microstructures in inequality* (pp. 50–80). New York: Springer-Verlag.

Elmquist, J., Shorey, R. C., Labrecque, L., & . . . Stuart, G. L. (2016). The relationship between family-of-origin violence, hostility, and intimate partner violence in men arrested for domestic violence: Testing a mediational model. *Violence Against Women, 22,* 1243–1258.

Elphinston, R. A., Feeney, J. A., Noller, P., Connor, J. P., & Fitzgerald, J. (2013). Romantic jealousy and relationship satisfaction: The cost of rumination. *Western Journal of Communication, 77,* 293–304.

El-Sheikh, M., Kelly, R., & Rauer, A. (2013). Quick to berate, slow to sleep: Interpartner psychological conflict, mental health, and sleep. *Health Psychology, 32,* 1057–1066.

Elshout, M., Nelissen, R. M. A., & Van Beest, I. (2015). A prototype analysis of vengeance. *Personal Relationships, 22,* 502–523.

Elwert, F., & Christakis, N. A. (2008). The effect of widowhood on mortality by the causes of death of both spouses. *American Journal of Public Health, 98,* 2092–2098.

Emery, L. F., & Le, B. (2014). Imagining the white picket fence: Social class, future plans, and romantic relationship quality. *Social Psychological and Personality Science, 5,* 653–661.

Emery, R. E., Shim, J. J., & Horn, E. (2012). Examining divorce consequences and policies and the question is: Is marriage more than a piece of paper? In L. Campbell & T. J. Loving (Eds.), *Interdisciplinary research on close relationships: The case for integration* (pp. 227–250). Washington, DC: American Psychological Association.

Epley, N. (2014). *Mindwise: How we understand what others think, believe, feel, and want.* New York: Knopf.

Epley, N., Akalis, S., Waytz, A., & Cacioppo, J. T. (2008). Creating social connection through inferential reproduction: Loneliness and perceived agency in gadgets, gods, and greyhounds. *Psychological Science, 19,* 114–120.

Epley, N., & Whitchurch, E. (2008). Mirror, mirror on the wall: Enhancement in self-recognition. *Personality and Social Psychology Bulletin, 34,* 1159–1170.

Epstein, N., & Baucom, D. H. (2002). *Enhanced cognitive-behavioral therapy for couples: A contextual approach.* Washington, DC: American Psychological Association.

Erbert, L. A. (2000). Conflict and dialectics: Perceptions of dialectical contradictions in marital conflict. *Journal of Social and Personal Relationships, 17,* 638–659.

Erchull, M. J., Liss, M., Axelson, S. J., Staebell, S. E., & Askari, S. F. (2010). Well . . . she wants it more: Perceptions of social norms about desires for marriage and children and anticipated chore participation. *Psychology of Women Quarterly, 34,* 253–260.

Erikson, E. (1950). *Childhood and society.* New York: Norton.

Erol, R. Y., & Orth, U. (2013). Actor and partner effects of self-esteem on relationship satisfaction and the mediating role of secure attachment between the partners. *Journal of Research in Personality, 47,* 26–35.

Etcheverry, P. E., & Agnew, C. R. (2004). Subjective norms and the prediction of romantic relationship state and fate. *Personal Relationships, 11,* 409–428.

Etcheverry, P. E., Le, B., & Hoffman, N. G. (2013a). Predictors of friend approval for romantic relationships. *Personal Relationships, 20,* 69–83.

Etcheverry, P. E., Le, B., Wu, T., & Wei, M. (2013b). Attachment and the investment model: Predictors of relationship commitment, maintenance, and persistence. *Personal Relationships, 20,* 546–567.

Exline, J. J., Baumeister, R. F., Zell, A. L., Kraft, A. J., & Witvliet, C. V. O. (2008). Not so innocent: Does seeing one's own capability for wrongdoing predict forgiveness? *Journal of Personality and Social Psychology, 94,* 495–515.

Fabricius, W. V., & Suh, G. W. (2017). Should infants and toddlers have frequent overnight parenting time with fathers? The policy debate and new data. *Psychology, Public Policy, and Law, 23,* 68–84.

Fagley, N. S. (2012). Appreciation uniquely predicts life satisfaction above demographics, the Big 5 personality factors, and gratitude. *Personality and Individual Differences, 53,* 59–63.

Falbo, T., & Peplau, L. A. (1980). Power strategies in intimate relationships. *Journal of Personality and Social Psychology, 38,* 618–628.

Faries, M. D., & Bartholomew, J. B. (2012). The role of body fat in female attractiveness. *Evolution and Human Behavior, 33,* 672–681.

Farley, S. D. (2008). Attaining status at the expense of likeability: Pilfering power through conversational interruption. *Journal of Nonverbal Behavior, 32,* 241–260.

Farley, S. D., Hughes, S. M., & LaFayette, J. N. (2013). People will know we are in love: Evidence of differences between vocal samples directed toward lovers and friends. *Journal of Nonverbal Behavior, 37,* 123–138.

Farrell, A. K., Simpson, J. A., Overall, N. C., & Shallcross, S. L. (2016). Buffering the responses of avoidantly attached romantic partners in strain test situations. *Journal of Family Psychology, 30,* 580–591.

Farris, C., Treat, T. A., Viken, R. J., & McFall, R. M. (2008). Sexual coercion and the misperception of sexual intent. *Clinical Psychology Review, 28,* 48–66.

Farvid, P., & Braun, V. (2006). 'Most of us guys are raring to go anytime, anyplace, anywhere': Male and female sexuality in *Cleo* and *Cosmo. Sex Roles, 55,* 295–310.

Fast, N. J., Gruenfeld, D. H., Sivanathan, N., & Galinsky, A. D. (2009). Illusory control: A generative force behind power's far-reaching effects. *Psychological Science, 20,* 502–508.

Favez, N., & Tissot, H. (2017). Attachment tendencies and sexual activities: The mediating role of representations of sex. *Journal of Social and Personal Relationships.* doi: 10.1177/0265407516658361

Feeney, B. C., & Cassidy, J. (2003). Reconstructive memory related to adolescent-parent conflict interactions: The influence of attachment-related representations on immediate perceptions and changes in perceptions over time. *Journal of Personality and Social Psychology, 85,* 945–955.

Feeney, B. C., & Collins, N. L. (2015). A new look at social support: A theoretical perspective on thriving through relationships. *Personality and Social Psychology Review, 19,* 113–147.

Feeney, B. C., & Lemay, E. P., Jr. (2012). Surviving relationship threats: The role of emotional capital. *Personality and Social Psychology Bulletin, 38,* 1004–1017.

Feeney, J. A. (1999). Adult attachment, emotional control, and marital satisfaction. *Personal Relationships, 6,* 169–185.

Feeney, J. A. (2002). Attachment, marital interaction, and relationship satisfaction: A diary study. *Personal Relationships, 9,* 39–55.

Feeney, J. A. (2005). Hurt feelings in couple relationships: Exploring the role of attachment and perceptions of personal injury. *Personal Relationships, 12,* 253–271.

Feeney, J. A., & Hill, A. (2006). Victim-perpetrator differences in reports of hurtful events. *Journal of Social and Personal Relationships, 23,* 587–608.

Feeney, J. A., Noller, P., & Roberts, N. (2000). Attachment and close relationships. In C. Hendrick & S. S. Hendrick (Eds.), *Close relationships: A sourcebook* (pp. 185–201). Thousand Oaks, CA: Sage.

Fehr, B. (1996). *Friendship processes.* Thousand Oaks, CA: Sage.

Fehr, B. (2015). Love: Conceptualization and experience. In M. Mikulincer, P. Shaver, J. Simpson, & J. Dovidio (Eds.), *APA handbook of personality and social psychology: Vol. 3. Interpersonal relations* (pp. 495–522). Washington, DC: American Psychological Association.

Fehr, B., & Broughton, R. (2001). Gender and personality differences in conceptions of love: An interpersonal theory analysis. *Personal Relationships, 8,* 115–136.

Fehr, B., Harasymchuk, C., & Sprecher S. (2014). Compassionate love in romantic relationships: A review and some new findings. *Journal of Social and Personal Relationships, 31,* 575–600.

Fein, E., & Schneider, S. (1995). *The rules: Time-tested secrets for capturing the heart of Mr. Right.* New York: Warner Books.

Feingold, A. (1992). Good-looking people are not what we think. *Psychological Bulletin, 111,* 304–341.

Feldman, R., Weller, A., Zagoory-Sharon, O., & Levine, A. (2007). Evidence for a neuroendocrinological foundation of human affiliation: Plasma oxytocin levels across pregnancy and postpartum period predict mother-infant bonding. *Psychological Science, 18,* 965–970.

Felmlee, D. H. (2001). From appealing to appalling: Disenchantment with a romantic partner. *Sociological Perspectives, 44,* 263–280.

Felmlee, D. H., Sweet, E., & Sinclair, H. C. (2012). Gender rules: Same- and cross-gender friendships norms. *Sex Roles, 66,* 518–529.

Fenigstein, A., & Preston, M. (2007). The desired number of sexual partners as a function of gender, sexual risks, and the meaning of "ideal." *Journal of Sex Research, 44,* 89–95.

Fergusson, D. M., Horwood, L. J., & Ridder, E. M. (2005). Partner violence and mental health outcomes in a New Zealand birth cohort. *Journal of Marriage and Family, 67,* 1103–1119.

Festinger, L., Schachter, S., & Back, K. W. (1950). *Social pressures in informal groups: A study of human factors in housing.* New York: Harper & Brothers.

Fetterolf, J. C., & Rudman, L. A. (2017). Exposure to sexual economics theory promotes a hostile view of heterosexual relationships. *Psychology of Women Quarterly, 41,* 77–88.

Figueredo, A. J., Sefcek, J. A., & Jones, D. N. (2006). The ideal romantic partner personality. *Personality and Individual Differences, 41,* 431–441.

Finch, E. (2001). *The criminalization of stalking: Constructing the problem and evaluating the solution.* London: Cavendish.

Fincham, F. D. (2001). Attributions in close relationships: From Balkanization to integration. In G. J. O. Fletcher & M. S. Clark (Eds.), *Blackwell handbook of social psychology: Interpersonal processes* (pp. 3–31). Malden, MA: Blackwell.

Fincham, F. D., & Beach, S. R. H. (2002). Forgiveness in marriage: Implications for psychological aggression and constructive communication. *Personal Relationships, 9,* 239–251.

Fincham, F. D., & Beach, S. R. H. (2010). Of memes and marriage: Toward a positive relationship science. *Journal of Family Theory & Review, 2,* 4–24.

Fincham, F. D., & Beach, S. R. H. (2013). Gratitude and forgiveness in relationships. In J. A. Simpson & L. Campbell (Eds.), *The Oxford handbook of close relationships* (pp. 638–663). New York: Oxford University Press.

Fincham, F. D., & Beach, S. R. H. (2014). I say a little prayer for you: Praying for partner increases commitment in romantic relationships. *Journal of Family Psychology, 28,* 587–593.

Fingerhut, H. (2016, May 12). *Support steady for same-sex marriage and acceptance of homosexuality.* Pew Research Center. Retrieved from http://www.pewresearch.org/fact-tank/2016/05/12/support-steady-for-same-sex-marriage-and-acceptance-of-homosexuality/

Fingerman, K. L., & Charles, S. T. (2010). It takes two to tango: Why older people have the best relationships. *Current Directions in Psychological Science, 19,* 172–176.

Fink, B., Hugill, N., & Lange, B. P. (2012a). Women's body movements are a potential cue to ovulation. *Personality and Individual Differences, 53,* 759–763.

Fink, B., Neave, N., Manning, J. T., & Grammer, K. (2006). Facial symmetry and judgments of attractiveness, health and personality. *Personality and Individual Differences, 41,* 491–499.

Fink, B., Weege, B. Flügge, J., Röder, S., Neave, N., & McCarty, K. (2012b). Men's personality and women's perception of their dance quality. *Personality and Individual Differences, 52,* 232–235.

Finkel, E. J. (2008). Intimate partner violence perpetration: Insights from the science of self-regulation. In J. P. Forgas & J. Fitness (Eds.), *Social relationships: Cognitive, affective and motivational processes* (pp. 271–288). New York: Psychology Press.

Finkel, E. J. (2014). The I^3 model: Metatheory, theory, and evidence. *Advances in Experimental Social Psychology, 49,* 1–104.

Finkel, E. J., Cheung, E. O., Emery, L. F., Carswell, K. L., & Larson, G. M. (2015a). The suffocation model: Why marriage in America is becoming an all-or-nothing institution. *Current Directions in Psychological Science, 24,* 238–244.

Finkel, E. J., DeWall, C. N., Slotter, E. B., Oaten, M., & Foshee, V. A. (2009). Self-regulatory failure and intimate partner violence perpetration. *Journal of Personality and Social Psychology, 97,* 483–499.

Finkel, E. J., & Eastwick, P. W. (2015). Interpersonal attraction: In search of a theoretical Rosetta stone. In M. Mikulincer, P. Shaver, J. Simpson, & J. Dovidio (Eds.), *APA handbook of personality and social psychology, Volume 3: Interpersonal relations* (pp. 179–210). Washington, DC: American Psychological Association.

Finkel, E. J., Eastwick, P. W., Karney, B. R., Reis, H. T., & Sprecher, S. (2012). Online dating: A critical analysis from the perspective of psychological science. *Psychological Science in the Public Interest, 13,* 3–66.

Finkel, E. J., Norton, M. I., Reis, H. T., & . . . Maniaci, M. R. (2015b). When does familiarity promote versus undermine interpersonal attraction? A proposed integrative model from erstwhile adversaries. *Perspectives on Psychological Science, 10,* 3–19.

Finkel, E. J., Slotter, E. B., Luchies, L. B., Walton, G. M., & Gross, J. J. (2013). A brief intervention to promote conflict reappraisal preserves marital quality over time. *Psychological Science, 24,* 1595–1601.

Finkenauer, C., Buyukcan-Tetik, A., Baumeister, R. F., & . . . Vohs, K. D. (2015). Out of control: Identifying the role of self-control strength in family violence. *Current Directions in Psychological Science, 24,* 261–266.

Finkenauer, C., Kubacka, K. E., Engels, R. C. M. E., & Kerkhof, P. (2009). Secrecy in close relationships: Investigating its intrapersonal and interpersonal effects. In T. D. Afifi & W. A. Afifi (Eds.), *Uncertainty, information management, and disclosure decisions: Theories and applications* (pp. 300–319). New York: Routledge.

Guéguen, N. (2009). Menstrual cycle phases and female receptivity to a courtship solicitation: An evaluation in a nightclub. *Evolution and Human Behavior, 30,* 351–355.

Guéguen, N. (2011). Effects of solicitor sex and attractiveness on receptivity to sexual offers: A field study. *Archives of Sexual Behavior, 40,* 915–919.

Guéguen, N. (2012). Makeup and menstrual cycle: Near ovulation, women use more cosmetics. *Psychological Record, 62,* 541–548.

Guéguen, N. (2013). Effects of a tattoo on men's behavior and attitudes towards women: An experimental field study. *Archives of Sexual Behavior, 42,* 1517–1524.

Guéguen, N., & Lamy, L. (2012). Men's social status and attractiveness: Women's receptivity to men's date requests. *Swiss Journal of Psychology, 71,* 157–160.

Guerrero, L. K. (1998). Attachment-style differences in the experience and expression of romantic jealousy. *Personal Relationships, 5,* 273–291.

Guerrero, L. K., & Andersen, P. A. (1998). Jealousy experience and expression in romantic relationships. In P. A. Andersen & L. K. Guerrero (Eds.), *Handbook of communication and emotion* (pp. 155–188). San Diego: Academic Press.

Guerrero, L. K., La Valley, A. G., & Farinelli, L. (2008). The experience and expression of anger, guilt, and sadness in marriage: An equity theory explanation. *Journal of Social and Personal Relationships, 25,* 699–724.

Guerrero, L. K., Trost, M. R., & Yoshimura, S. M. (2005). Romantic jealousy: Emotions and communicative responses. *Personal Relationships, 12,* 233–252.

Guinote, A., Weick, M., & Cai, A. (2012). Does power magnify the expression of dispositions? *Psychological Science, 23,* 475–482.

Gunaydin, G., Selcuk, E., & Zayas, V. (2017). Impressions based on a portrait predict, 1-month later, impression following a live interaction. *Social Psychological and Personality Science, 8,* 36–44.

Gunnery, S. D., Hall, J. A., & Ruben, M. A. (2013). The deliberate Duchenne smile: Individual differences in expressive control. *Journal of Nonverbal Behavior, 37,* 29–141.

Gurman, A. S. (2013). Behavioral couple therapy: Building a secure base for therapeutic integration. *Family Process, 52,* 115–138.

Gute, G., Eshbaugh, E. M., & Wiersma, J. (2008). Sex for you, but not for me: Discontinuity in undergraduate emerging adults' definitions of "having sex." *Journal of Sex Research, 45,* 329–337.

Guthrie, J., & Kunkel, A. (2013). Tell me sweet (and not-so-sweet) little lies: Deception in romantic relationships. *Communication Studies, 64,* 141–157.

Guttentag, M., & Secord, P. F. (1983). *Too many women? The sex ratio question.* Beverly Hills, CA: Sage.

Guttmacher Institute. (2012, February). *Facts on American teens' sources if information about sex.* Retrieved from http://www.guttmacher.org/pubs/FB-Teen-Sex-Ed.html

Guttmacher Institute. (2013, June). *Facts on American teens' sexual and reproductive health.* Retrieved from http://www.guttmacher.org/pubs/FB-ATSRH.pdf

Guttmacher Institute. (2016, September). *American teens' sexual and reproductive health.* Retrieved from https://www.guttmacher.org/fact-sheet/american-teens-sexual-and-reproductive-health

Guzzo, K. B. (2014). Trends in cohabitation outcomes: Compositional changes and engagement among never-married young adults. *Journal of Marriage and Family, 76,* 826–842.

Ha, T., van den Ber, J. E. M., Engels, R. C. M. E., & Lichtwarck-Aschoff, A. (2012). Effects of attractiveness and status in dating desire in homosexual and heterosexual men and women. *Archives of Sexual Behavior, 41,* 673–682.

Haak, E. A., Keller, P. S., & DeWall, C. N. (2017). Daily variations in attachment anxiety and avoidance: A density distributions approach. *Journal of Research in Personality, 69,* 218–224.

Haas, S. M., & Whitton, S. W. (2015). The significance of living together and importance of marriage in same-sex couples. *Journal of Homosexuality, 62,* 1241–1263.

Haase, C. M., Holley, S., Bloch, L., Verstaen, A., & Levenson, R. W. (2016). Interpersonal emotional behaviors and physical health: A 20-year longitudinal study of long-term married couples. *Emotion, 16,* 965–977.

Hadden, B. W., Smith, C. V., & Webster, G. D. (2014). Relationship duration moderates associations between attachment and relationship quality: Meta-analytic support for the temporal adult romantic attachment model. *Personality and Social Psychology Review, 18,* 42–58.

Haden, S. C., & Hojjat, M. (2006). Aggressive responses to betrayal: Type of relationship, victim's sex, and nature of aggression. *Journal of Social and Personal Relationships, 23,* 101–116.

Haeffel, G. J., Voelz, Z. R., & Joiner, T. E., Jr. (2007). Vulnerability to depressive symptoms: Clarifying the role of excessive reassurance seeking and perceived social support in an interpersonal model of depression. *Cognition & Emotion, 21,* 681–688.

Hafen, C. A., Laursen, B., Burk, W. J., Kerr, M., & Stattin, H. (2011). Homophily in stable and unstable adolescent friendships: Similarity breeds constancy. *Personality and Individual Differences, 51,* 607–612.

Häfner, M., & IJzerman, H. (2011). The face of love: Spontaneous accommodation as social emotion regulation. *Personality and Social Psychology Bulletin, 37,* 1551–1563.

Hagen, E. H. (2016). Evolutionary psychology and its critics. In D. Buss (Ed.), *The handbook of evolutionary psychology* (2nd ed., Vol. 1, pp. 136–160). New York: Wiley.

Haines, E. L., Deaux, K., & Lofaro, N. (2016). The times they are a-changing . . . or are they not? A comparison of gender stereotypes, 1983–2014. *Psychology of Women Quarterly, 40,* 353–363.

Halatsis, P., & Christakis, N. (2009). The challenge of sexual attraction within heterosexuals' cross-sex friendship. *Journal of Social and Personal Relationships, 26,* 919–937.

Hald, G. M., & Høgh-Olesen, H. (2010). Receptivity to sexual invitations from strangers of the opposite gender. *Evolution and Human Behavior, 31,* 453–458.

Hales, A. H., Kassner, M. P., Williams, K. D., & Graziano, W. G. (2016). Disagreeableness as a cause and consequence of ostracism. *Personality and Social Psychology Bulletin, 42,* 782–797.

Halford, W. K., Pepping, C., & Petch, J. (2018). Promoting healthy relationships. In A. Vangelisti & D. Perlman (Eds.), *Cambridge handbook of personal relationships* (2nd ed.) New York: Cambridge University Press.

Halford, W. K., Sanders, M. R., & Behrens, B. C. (2000). Repeating the errors of our parents? Family-of-origin spouse violence and observed conflict management in engaged couples. *Family Process, 39,* 219–235.

Halford, W. K., & Sweeper, S. (2013). Trajectories of adjustment to couple relationship separation. *Family Process, 52,* 228–243.

Hall, E. T. (1966). *The hidden dimension.* Garden City, NY: Doubleday.

Hall, J. A. (2012). Friendship standards: The dimensions of ideal expectations. *Journal of Social and Personal Relationships, 29,* 884–907.

Hall, J. A. (2016). Interpreting social-sexual communication: Relational framing theory and social-sexual communication, attraction, and intent. *Human Communication Research, 42,* 138–164.

Hall, J. A., Andrzejewski, S. A., & Yopchick, J. E. (2009). Psychosocial correlates of interpersonal sensitivity: A meta-analysis. *Journal of Nonverbal Behavior, 33,* 149–180.

Hall, J. A., Coats, E. J., & LeBeau, L. S. (2005). Nonverbal behavior and the vertical dimension of social relations: A meta-analysis. *Psychological Bulletin, 131,* 898–924.

Hall, J. A., & Mast, M. S. (2008). Are women always more interpersonally sensitive than men? Impact of goals and content domain. *Personality and Social Psychology Bulletin, 34,* 144–155.

Hall, J. A., Park, N., Song, H., & Cody, M. J. (2010). Strategic misrepresentation in online dating: The effects of gender, self-monitoring, and personality traits. *Journal of Social and Personal Relationships, 27,* 117–135.

Hall, J. K., Hutton, S. B., & Morgan, M. J. (2010). Sex differences in scanning faces: Does attention to the eyes explain female superiority in facial expression recognition? *Cognition & Emotion, 24,* 629–637.

Hall, K. S., Sales, J. M., Komro, K. A., & Santelli, J. (2016). The state of sex education in the United States. *Journal of Adolescent Health, 58,* 595–597.

Halpern-Meekin, S., Manning, W. D., Giordano, P. C. & Longmore, M. A. (2012). Relationship churning in emerging adulthood: On/off relationships and sex with an ex. *Journal of Adolescent Research, 28,* 166–188.

Hamberger, L. K., & Larsen, S. E. (2015). Men's and women's experience of intimate partner violence: A review of ten years of comparative studies in clinical samples; Part 1. *Journal of Family Violence, 30,* 699–717.

Hamermesh, D. (2013). *Beauty pays: Why attractive people are more successful.* Princeton, NJ: Princeton University Press.

Hamilton, B. E., Martin, J. A., & Osterman, M. J. K. (2016, June 2). Births: Preliminary data for 2015. *National Vital Statistics Reports, 65*(3), 1–15.

Hamilton, B. E., & Mathews, T. J. (2016). *Continued declines in teen births in the United States, 2015.* NCHS Data Brief, 259. Hyattsville, MD: National Center for Health Statistics.

Hamilton, N. F. (2016). Romantic relationships and online dating. In A. Attrill & C. Fullwood (Eds.), *Applied cyberpsychology: Practical applications of cyberpsychological theory and research* (pp. 144–160). New York: Palgrave Macmillan.

Hampel, A. D., & Vangelisti, A. L. (2008). Commitment expectations in romantic relationships: Application of a prototype interaction-pattern model. *Personal Relationships, 15,* 81–102.

Han, J. J., Beltran, T. H., Song, J. W., Klaric, J., & Choi, S. (2017). Prevalence of genital human papillomavirus infection and human papillomavirus vaccination rates among US adult men. *JAMA Oncology, 3,* 810–816.

Hannon, P. A., Finkel, E. J., Kumashiro, M., & Rusbult, C. E. (2012). The soothing effects of forgiveness on victims' and perpetrators' blood pressure. *Personal Relationships, 19,* 279–289.

Hansen, T. (2012). Parenthood and happiness: a review of folk theories versus empirical evidence. *Social Indicators Research, 108,* 29–64.

Hanson, T. L., McLanahan, S. S., & Thomson, E. (1998). Windows on divorce: Before and after. *Social Science Research, 27,* 329–349.

Harasymchuk, C., & Fehr, B. (2013). A prototype analysis of relational boredom. *Journal of Social and Personal Relationships, 30,* 627–646.

Harden, K. P. (2014a). A sex-positive framework for research on adolescent sexuality. *Perspectives on Psychological Science, 9,* 455–469.

Harden, K. P. (2014b). Genetic influences on adolescent sexual behavior: Why genes matter for environmentally oriented researchers. *Psychological Bulletin, 140,* 434–465.

Hardesty, J. L., Crossman, K. A., Haselschwerdt, M. L., & . . . Johnson, M. P. (2015). Toward a standard approach to operationalizing coercive control and classifying violence types. *Journal of Marriage and Family, 77,* 833–843.

Hargrave, T. D., & Hammer, M. Y. (2016). Restoration of relationships after affairs. In G. Weeks, S. Fife, & C. Peterson (Eds.), *Techniques for the couple therapist: Essential interventions from the experts* (pp. 190–193). New York: Routledge.

Harinck, F., & De Dreu, C. K. W. (2011). When does taking a break help in negotiations? The influence of breaks and social motivation on negotiation processes and outcomes. *Negotiation and Conflict Management Research, 4,* 33–46.

Harkless, L. E., & Fowers, B. J. (2005). Similarities and differences in relational boundaries among heterosexuals, gay men, and lesbians. *Psychology of Women Quarterly, 29,* 167–176.

Harlow, H. F. (1958). The nature of love. *American Psychologist, 13,* 673–685.

Harris, C. R. (2013). Shifts in masculinity preferences across the menstrual cycle: Still not there. *Sex Roles, 69,* 507–515.

Harris, C. R., Chabot, A., & Mickes, L. (2013). Shifts in methodology and theory in menstrual cycle research on attraction. *Sex Roles, 69,* 525–535.

Harris, C. R., & Darby, R. S. (2010). Jealousy in adulthood. In S. L. Hart & M. Legerstee (Eds.), *Handbook of jealousy: Theory, research, and multidisciplinary approaches* (pp. 547–571). Malden, MA: Blackwell.

Harris, M. J., & Garris, C. P. (2008). You never get a second chance to make a first impression: Behavioral consequences of first impressions. In N. Ambady & J. Skowronski (Eds.), *First impressions* (pp. 147–168). New York: Guilford.

Hartgerink, C. H., van Beest, I., Wicherts, J. M., & Williams, K. D. (2015). The ordinal effects of ostracism: A meta-analysis of 120 Cyberball studies. *PLoS ONE, 10,* e0127002.

Hartl, A. C., Laursen, B., & Cillessen, A. H. N. (2015). A survival analysis of adolescent friendships: The downside of dissimilarity. *Psychological Science, 26,* 1304–1315.

Harvey, J. H., & Fine, M. A. (2006). Social construction of accounts in the process of relationship termination. In M. A. Fine & J. H. Harvey (Eds.), *Handbook of divorce and relationship dissolution* (pp. 189–199). Mahwah, NJ: Erlbaum.

Haselton, M. G., & Buss, D. M. (2000). Error Management Theory: A new perspective on biases in cross-sex mind reading. *Journal of Personality and Social Psychology, 78,* 81–91.

Haselton, M. G., Buss, D. M., Oubiad, V., & Angleitner, A. (2005). Sex, lies, and strategic interference: The psychology of deception between the sexes. *Personality and Social Psychology Bulletin, 31,* 3–23.

Haselton, M. G., & Galperin, A. (2013). Error management in relationships. In J. A. Simpson & L. Campbell (Eds.), *The Oxford handbook of close relationships* (pp. 234–254). New York: Oxford University Press.

Haselton, M. G., & Gildersleeve, K. (2011). Can men detect ovulation? *Current Directions in Psychological Science, 20,* 87–92.

Hatemi, P. K., McDermott, R., & Eaves, L. (2015). Genetic and environmental contributions to relationships and divorce attitudes. *Personality and Individual Differences, 72,* 135–140.

Hatfield, E., & Rapson, R. L. (2008). Passionate love and sexual desire: Multidisciplinary perspectives. In J. P. Forgas & J. Fitness (Eds.), *Social relationships: Cognitive, affective and motivational processes* (pp. 21–37). New York: Psychology Press.

Hatfield, E., & Rapson, R. L. (2012). Equity theory in close relationships, In P. Van Lange, A. Kruglanski, & E. T. Higgins (Eds.), *Handbook of theories of social psychology* (Vol. 2, pp. 200–217). Thousand Oaks, CA: Sage.

Hatfield, E., & Sprecher, S. (1986). Measuring passionate love in intimate relationships. *Journal of Adolescence, 9,* 383–410.

Hauch, V., Blandón-Gitlin, I., Masip, J., & Sporer, S. L. (2015). Are computers effective lie detectors? A meta-analysis of linguistic cues to deception. *Personality and Social Psychology Review, 19,* 307–342.

Havlíček, J., Třebický, V., Valentova, J. V., & . . . Roberts, S. C. (2017). Men's preferences for women's breast size and shape in four cultures. *Evolution and Human Behavior, 38,* 217–226.

Hawkins, A. J. (2014). Continuing the important debate on government-supported healthy marriages and relationships initiatives: A brief response to Johnson's (2014) comment. *Family Relations, 63,* 305–308.

Hawkins, A. J., Amato, P. R., & Kinghorn, A. (2013). Are government-supported healthy marriage initiatives affecting family demographics? A state-level analysis. *Family Relations, 62,* 501–513.

Hawkley, L. C., Browne, M. W., & Cacioppo, J. T. (2005). How can I connect with thee? Let me count the ways. *Psychological Science, 16,* 798–803.

Haydon, A. A., Cheng, M. M., Herring, A. H., McRee, A., & Halpern, C. T. (2014). Prevalence and predictors of sexual inexperience in adulthood. *Archives of Sexual Behavior, 43,* 221–230.

Haydon, K. C., & Roisman, G. I. (2013). What's past is prologue: Social developmental antecedents of close relationships. In J. A. Simpson & L. Campbell (Eds.), *The Oxford handbook of close relationships* (pp. 750–770). New York: Oxford University Press.

Hayford, S. R., Guzzo, K. B., & Smock, P. J. (2014). The decoupling of marriage and parenthood? Trends in the timing of marital first births, 1945–2002. *Journal of Marriage and Family, 76,* 520–538.

Hazan, C., & Shaver, P. (1987). Romantic love conceptualized as an attachment process. *Journal of Personality and Social Psychology, 52,* 511–524.

Hazan, C., & Zeifman, D. (1994). Sex and the psychological tether. In K. Bartholomew & D. Perlman (Eds.), *Attachment processes in adulthood* (pp. 151–178). London: Jessica Kingsley.

Heaton, T. B. (2002). Factors contributing to increasing marital stability in the U.S. *Journal of Family Issues, 23,* 392–409.

Heaven, P. C. L., Smith, L., Prabhakar, S. M., Abraham, J., & Mete, M. E. (2006). Personality and conflict communication patterns in cohabiting couples. *Journal of Research in Personality, 40,* 829–840.

Hebl, M. R., Foster, J. B., Mannix, L. M., & Dovidio, J. F. (2002). Formal and interpersonal discrimination: A field study of bias toward homosexual applicants. *Personality and Social Psychology Bulletin, 28,* 815–825.

Hecht, M. L., Marston, P. J., & Larkey, L. K. (1994). Love ways and relationship quality in heterosexual relationships. *Journal of Social and Personal Relationships, 11,* 25–43.

Heerey, E. A. (2015). Decoding the dyad: Challenges in the study of individual differences in social behavior. *Current Directions in Psychological Science, 24,* 285–291.

Hefner, V., & Wilson, B. J. (2013). From love at first sight to soul mate: The influence of romantic ideals in popular films on young people's beliefs about relationships. *Communication Monographs, 80,* 150–175.

Hehman, E., Leitner, J. B., Deegan, M. P., & Gaertner, S. L. (2013). Facial structure is indicative of explicit support for prejudicial beliefs. *Psychological Science, 24,* 289–296.

Heider, F. (1958). *The psychology of interpersonal relations.* New York: Wiley.

Heiman, J. R., Long, J. S., Smith, S. N., Fisher, W. A., Sand, M. S., & Rosen, R. C. (2011). Sexual satisfaction and relationship happiness in midlife and older couples in five countries. *Archives of Sexual Behavior, 40,* 741–753.

Hellmuth, J. C., & McNulty, J. K. (2008). Neuroticism, marital violence, and the moderating role of stress and behavioral skills. *Journal of Personality and Social Psychology, 95,* 166–180.

Helms, H. M., Proulx, C. M., Klute, M. M., McHale, S. M., & Crouter, A. C. (2006). Spouses' gender-typed attributes and their links with marital quality: A pattern analytic approach. *Journal of Social and Personal Relationships, 23,* 843–864.

Henderson, C. E., Hayslip, B., Jr., Sanders, L. M., & Louden, L. (2009). Grandmother-grandchild relationship quality predicts psychological adjustment among youth from divorced families. *Journal of Family Issues, 30,* 1245–1264.

Henderson, L., Gilbert, P., & Zimbardo, P. (2014). Shyness, social anxiety, and social phobia. In S. Hofmann & P. DiBartolo (Eds.), *Social anxiety: Clinical, developmental, and social perspectives* (3rd ed., pp. 95–115). San Diego: Academic Press.

Hendrick, C., & Hendrick, S. S. (2006). Styles of romantic love. In R. J. Sternberg & K. Weis (Eds.), *The new psychology of love* (pp. 149–170). New Haven, CT: Yale University Press.

Hendrick, S. S., & Hendrick, C. (1993). Lovers as friends. *Journal of Social and Personal Relationships, 10,* 459–466.

Hendrick, S. S., Hendrick, C., & Logue, E. M. (2010). Respect and the family. *Journal of Family Theory & Review, 2,* 126–136.

Henline, B. H., Lamke, L. K., & Howard, M. D. (2007). Exploring perceptions of online infidelity. *Personal Relationships, 14,* 113–128.

Henrich, J., Heine, S. J., & Norenzayan, A. (2010). The weirdest people in the world? *Behavioral and Brain Sciences, 33,* 61–135.

Hepper, E. G., & Carnelley, K. B. (2012). Attachment and romantic relationships: The roles of working models of self and other. In M. A. Paludi (Ed.), *The psychology of love* (Vol. 1, pp. 133–154). Santa Barbara, CA: Praeger.

Herbenick, D., Reece, M., Schick, V., Sanders, S. A., Dodge, B., & Fortenberry, J. D. (2010a). An event-level analysis of the sexual characteristics and composition among adults ages 18 to 59: Results from a national probability sample in the United States. *Journal of Sexual Medicine, 7* (Suppl. 5), 346–361.

Herbenick, D., Reece, M., Schick, V., Sanders, S. A., Dodge, B., & Fortenberry, J. D. (2010b). Sexual behavior in the United States: Results from a national probability sample of men and women ages 14–94. *Journal of Sexual Medicine, 7* (Suppl. 5), 255–265.

Herbst, K. C., Gaertner, L., & Insko, C. A. (2003). My head says yes but my heart says no: Cognitive and affective attraction as a function of similarity to the ideal self. *Journal of Personality and Social Psychology, 84,* 1206–1219.

Herek, G. M., Norton, A. T., Allen, T. J., & Sims, C. L. (2010). Demographic, psychological, and social characteristics of self-identified lesbian, gay, and bisexual adults in a U.S. probability sample. *Sexuality Research and Social Policy, 7,* 176–200.

Herrero, J., Rodriguez, F. J., & Torres, A. (2017). Acceptability of partner violence in 51 societies: The role of sexism and attitudes toward violence in social relationships. *Violence Against Women, 23,* 351–367.

Herrero, J., Torres, A., Rodríguez, F. J., & Juarros-Basterretxea, J. (2018). Intimate partner violence against women in the European Union: The influence of male partners' traditional gender roles and general violence. *Psychology of Violence.* doi:10.1037/vio0000099

Hertenstein, M. J. (2011). The communicative functions of touch in adulthood. In M. Hertenstein & S. Weiss (Eds.), *The handbook of touch: Neuroscience, behavioral, and health perspectives* (pp. 299–327). New York: Springer.

Hertenstein, M. J., Hansel, C. A., Butts, A. M., & Hile, S. N. (2009). Smile intensity in photographs predicts divorce later in life. *Motivation and Emotion, 33,* 99–105.

Herz, R. S., & Inzlicht, M. (2002). Sex differences in response to physical and social factors involved in human mate selection. *Evolution and Human Behavior, 23,* 359–364.

Hesse, C., & Mikkelson, A. C. (2017). Affection deprivation in romantic relationships. *Communication Quarterly, 65,* 20–38.

Hesse, C., & Trask, S. L. (2014). Trait affection and adult attachment styles: Analyzing relationships and group differences. *Communication Research Reports, 31,* 53–61.

Hetherington, E. M. (2003). Intimate pathways: Changing patterns in close personal relationships across time. *Family Relations, 52,* 318–331.

Hettinger, V. E., Hutchinson, D. M., & Bosson, J. K. (2014). Influence of professional status on perceptions of romantic relationship dynamics. *Psychology of Men & Masculinity, 15,* 470–480.

Heyman, R. E., Hunt-Martorano, A. N., Malik, J., & Smith-Slep, A. M. (2009). Desired change in couples: Gender differences and effects on communication. *Journal of Family Psychology, 23,* 474–484.

Hicks, T. V., & Leitenberg, H. (2001). Sexual fantasies about one's partner versus someone else: Gender differences in incidence and frequency. *Journal of Sex Research, 38,* 43–50.

Hill, P. L., Nickel, L. B., & Roberts, B. W. (2014). Are you in a healthy relationship? Linking conscientiousness to health via implementing and immunizing behaviors. *Journal of Personality, 82,* 485–492.

Hill, S. E. (2007). Overestimation bias in mate competition. *Evolution and Human Behavior, 28,* 118–123.

Hinchliff, S., & Gott, M. (2004). Intimacy, commitment, and adaptation: Sexual relationships within long-term marriages. *Journal of Social and Personal Relationships, 21,* 595–609.

Hitsch, G. J., Hortaçsu, A., & Ariely, D. (2010). What makes you click? Mate preferences in online dating. *Quantitative Marketing and Economics, 8,* 393–427.

Hogerbrugge, M. J. A., Komter, A. E., & Scheepers, P. (2012). Dissolving long-term romantic relationships: Assessing the role of the social context. *Journal of Social and Personal Relationships, 30,* 320–342.

Hohmann-Marriott, B. E. (2006). Shared beliefs and the union stability of married and cohabiting couples. *Journal of Marriage and Family, 68,* 1015–1028.

Hojjat, M., & Ayotte, B. J. (2013). Forgiveness and positive psychology. In M. Hojjat & D. Cramer (Eds.), *Positive psychology of love* (pp. 121–133). New York: Oxford University Press.

Holland, R. W., Roeder, U. R., van Baaren, R. B., Brandt, A. C., & Hannover, B. (2004). Don't stand so close to me: The effects of self-construal on interpersonal closeness. *Psychological Science, 15,* 237–242.

Holleran, S. E., Mehl, M. R., & Levitt, S. (2009). Eavesdropping on social life: The accuracy of stranger ratings of daily behavior from thin slices of natural conversations. *Journal of Research in Personality, 43,* 660–672.

Holley, S. R., Haase, C. M., & Levenson, R. W. (2013). Age-related changes in demand-withdraw communication behaviors. *Journal of Marriage and Family, 75,* 822–836.

Holley, S. R., Sturm, V. E., & Levenson, R. W. (2010). Exploring the basis for gender differences in the demand-withdraw pattern. *Journal of Homosexuality, 57,* 666–684.

Holloway, R. A., Waldrip, A. M., & Ickes, W. (2009). Evidence that a *simpático* self-schema accounts for differences in the self-concepts and social behavior of Latinos versus whites (and blacks). *Journal of Personality and Social Psychology, 96,*1012–1028.

Holman, T. B., & Jarvis, M. O. (2003). Hostile, volatile, avoiding, and validating couple-conflict types: An investigation of Gottman's couple-conflict types. *Personal Relationships, 10,* 267–282.

Holmes, J. G., & Levinger, G. (1994). Paradoxical effects of closeness in relationships on perceptions of justice: An interdependence-theory perspective. In M. J. Lerner & G. Mikula (Eds.), *Entitlement and the affectional bond: Justice in close relationships* (pp. 149–173). New York: Plenum.

Holmes, J. G., & Wood, J. V. (2009). Interpersonal situations as affordances: The example of self-esteem. *Journal of Research in Personality, 43,* 250.

Holtgraves, T. (2011). Text messaging, personality, and the social context. *Journal of Research in Personality, 45,* 92–99.

Holt-Lunstad, J., Birmingham, W. C., & Light, K. C. (2015a). Relationship quality and oxytocin: Influence of stable and modifiable aspects of relationships. *Journal of Social and Personal Relationships, 32,* 472–490.

Holt-Lunstad, J., Smith, T. B., Baker, M., Harris, T., & Stephenson, D. (2015b). Loneliness and social isolation as risk factors for mortality: A meta-analytic review. *Perspectives on Psychological Science, 10,* 227–237.

Holtzman, N. S., & Strube, M. J. (2013). People with dark personalities tend to create a physically attractive veneer. *Social Psychological and Personality Science, 4,* 461–467.

Iemmola, F., & Ciani, A. C. (2009). New evidence of genetic factors influencing sexual orientation in men: Female fecundity increase in the maternal line. *Archives of Sexual Behavior, 38,* 393–399.

Imhoff, R., & Schmidt, A. F. (2014). Sexual disinhibition under sexual arousal: Evidence for domain specificity in men and women. *Archives of Sexual Behavior, 43,* 1123–1136.

Impett, E. A., Breines, J. G., & Strachman, A. (2010). Keeping it real: Young adult women's authenticity in relationships and daily condom use. *Personal Relationships, 17,* 573–584.

Impett, E. A., Gere, J., Kogan, A., Gordon, A. M., & Keltner, D. (2014a). How sacrifice impacts the giver and the recipient: Insights from approach-avoidance motivational theory. *Journal of Personality, 82,* 390–401.

Impett, E. A., Javam, L., Le, B. M., Asyabi-Eshghi, B., & Kogan, A. (2013). The joys of genuine giving: Approach and avoidance sacrifice motivation and authenticity. *Personal Relationships, 20,* 740–754.

Impett, E. A., Muise, A., & Peragine, D. (2014b). Sexuality in the context of relationships. In D. L. Tolman, L. Diamond, J. Bauermeister et al. (Eds.), *APA handbook of sexuality and psychology* (Vol. 1, pp. 269–315). Washington, DC: American Psychological Association.

Impett, E. A., & Peplau, L. A. (2006). "His" and "her" relationships? A review of the empirical evidence. In A. L. Vangelisti & D. Perlman (Eds.), *The Cambridge handbook of personal relationships* (pp. 273–291). New York: Cambridge University Press.

Impett, E. A., Peplau, L. A., & Gable, S. L. (2005). Approach and avoidance sexual motives: Implications for personal and interpersonal well-being. *Personal Relationships, 12,* 465–482.

Impett, E. A., Strachman, A., Finkel, E. J., & Gable, S. L. (2008). Maintaining sexual desire in intimate relationships: The importance of approach goals. *Journal of Personality and Social Psychology, 94,* 808–823.

Infurna, F. J., & Luthar, S. S. (2017). The multidimensional nature of resilience to spousal loss. *Journal of Personality and Social Psychology, 112,* 926–947.

Ireland, M. E., Slatcher, R. B., Eastwick, P. W., Scissors, L. E., Finkel, E. J., & Pennebaker, J. W. (2011). Language style matching predicts relationship initiation and stability. *Psychological Science, 22,* 39–44.

Italie, L. (2011, January 26). Pups or paramours? 14 percent prefer pets. *Houston Chronicle,* p. A6.

Ivcevic, Z., & Ambady, N. (2013). Face to (Face)book: The two faces of social behavior? *Journal of Personality, 81,* 290–301.

Izhaki-Costi, O., & Schul, Y. (2011). I do not know you and I am keeping it that way: Attachment avoidance and empathic accuracy in the perception of strangers. *Personal Relationships, 18,* 321–340.

Jackson, G. L., Trail, T. E., Kennedy, D. P., Williamson, H. C., Bradbury, T. N., & Karney, B. R. (2016). The salience and severity of relationship problems among low-income couples. *Journal of Family Psychology P, 30,* 2–11.

Jackson, J. J., Wood, D., Bogg, T., Walton, K. E., Harms, P. D., & Roberts, B. W. (2010). What do conscientious people do? Development and validation of the Behavioral Indicators of Conscientiousness (BIC). *Journal of Research in Personality, 44,* 501–511.

Jackson, T., Chen, H., Guo, C., & Gao, X. (2006). Stories we love by: Conceptions of love among couples from the People's Republic of China and the United States. *Journal of Cross-Cultural Psychology, 37,* 446–464.

Jacobson, N. S., Follette, W. C., & McDonald, D. W. (1982). Reactivity to positive and negative behavior in distressed and nondistressed married couples. *Journal of Consulting and Clinical Psychology, 50,* 706–714.

Jacobson, N. S., & Margolin, G. (1979). *Marital therapy: Strategies based on social learning and behavior exchange principles.* New York: Brunner/Mazel.

Jacques-Tiura, A. J., Abbey, A., Parkhill, M. R., & Zawacki, T. (2007). Why do some men misperceive women's sexual intentions more frequently than others do? An application of the Confluence Model. *Personality and Social Psychology Bulletin, 33,* 1467–1480.

Jakubiak, B. K., & Feeney, B. C. (2016). A sense of security: Touch promotes state attachment security. *Social Psychological and Personality Science, 7,* 745–753.

James, S. L. (2015). Variation in trajectories of women's marital quality. *Social Science Research, 49,* 16–30.

Jasieńska, G., Lipson, S. F., Ellison, P. T., Thune, I., & Ziomkiewicz, A. (2006). Symmetrical women have higher potential fertility. *Evolution and Human Behavior, 27,* 390–400.

Jasieńska, G., Ziomkiewicz, A., Ellison, P. T., Lipson, S. F., & Thune, I. (2004). Large breasts and narrow waists indicate high reproductive potential in women. *Proceedings of the Royal Society of London B, 271,* 1213–1217.

Jauk, E., Neubauer, A. C., Mairunteregger, T., & . . . Rauthmann, J. F. (2016). How alluring are dark personalities? The Dark Triad and attractiveness in speed dating. *European Journal of Personality, 30, 125–138.*

Jayamaha, S. D., Girme, Y. U., & Overall, N. C. (2017). When attachment anxiety impedes support provision: The role of feeling unvalued and unappreciated. *Journal of Family Psychology, 31,* 191–191.

Jemmott, J. B. (2010). Efficacy of a theory-based abstinence-only intervention over 24 months: A randomized controlled trial with young adolescents. *Archives of Pediatrics & Adolescent Medicine, 164,* 152–159.

Jena, A. B., Goldman, D. P., & Seabury, S. A. (2015). Incidence of sexually transmitted infections after human papillomavirus vaccination among adolescent females. *JAMA Internal Medicine, 175,* 617–623.

Jensen, J. F., & Rauer, A. J. (2014). Turning inward versus outward: Relationship work in young adults and romantic functioning. *Personal Relationships, 21,* 451–467.

Jensen, T. M., Shafer, K., Guo, S., Larson, J. H. (2017). Differences in relationship stability between individuals in first and second marriages: A propensity score analysis. *Journal of Family Issues, 38,* 406–432.

Jensen-Campbell, L. A., & Graziano, W. G. (2001). Agreeableness as a moderator of interpersonal conflict. *Journal of Personality, 69,* 323–362.

Jensen-Campbell, L. A., Graziano, W. G., & West, S. G. (1995). Dominance, prosocial orientation, and female preferences: Do nice guys really finish last? *Journal of Personality and Social Psychology, 68,* 427–440.

Jensen-Campbell, L. A., Knack, J. M., Waldrip, A. M., & Campbell, S. D. (2007). Do Big Five personality traits associated with self-control influence the regulation of anger and aggression? *Journal of Research in Personality, 41,* 403–424.

Jeronimus, B. F., Riese, H., Sanderman, R., & Ormel, J. (2014). Mutual reinforcement between neuroticism and life experiences: A five-wave, 16-year study to test reciprocal causation. *Journal of Personality and Social Psychology, 107,* 751–764.

Jiang, L. C., & Hancock, J. T. (2013). Absence makes the communication grow fonder: Geographic separation, interpersonal media, and intimacy in dating relationships. *Journal of Communication, 63,* 556–577.

Jöchle, W. (1973). Coitus-induced ovulation. *Contraception, 7,* 523–564.

Joel, S., Teper, R., & MacDonald, G. (2014). People overestimate their willingness to reject potential romantic partners by overlooking their concern for other people. *Psychological Science, 25,* 2233–2340.

Johnson, K. L., Gill, S., Reichman, V., & Tassinary, L. G. (2007). Swagger, sway, and sexuality: Judging sexual orientation from body motion and morphology. *Journal of Personality and Social Psychology, 93,* 321–334.

Johnson, M. D. (2012). Healthy marriage initiatives: On the need for empiricism in policy implementation. *American Psychologist, 67,* 296–308.

Johnson, M. D. (2014). Government-supported healthy marriage initiatives are not associated with changes in family demographics: A comment on Hawkins, Amato, and Kinghorn (2013). *Family Relations, 63,* 300–304.

Johnson, M. D., Galambos, N. L., & Anderson, J. R. (2016). Skip the dishes? Not so fast! Sex and housework revisited. *Journal of Family Psychology, 30,* 203–213.

Johnson, M. P. (1999). Personal, moral, and structural commitment to relationships: Experiences of choice and constraint. In J. M. Adams & W. H. Jones (Eds.), *Handbook of interpersonal commitment and relationship stability* (pp. 73–87). New York: Kluwer Academic/Plenum.

Johnson, M. P. (2008). *A typology of domestic violence: Intimate terrorism, violent resistance, and situational couple violence.* Boston: Northeastern University Press.

LaBrie, J. W., Hummer, J. F., Ghaidarov, T. M., Lac, A., & Kenney, S. R. (2014). Hooking up in the college context: The event-level effects of alcohol use and partner familiarity on hookup behaviors and contentment. *Journal of Sex Research, 51,* 62–73.

Lachance-Grzela, M., & Bouchard, G. (2010). Why do women do the lion's share of housework? A decade of research. *Sex Roles, 63,* 767–780.

Lachance-Grzela, M., & Bouchard, G. (2016). The effects of parental divorce in single and romantically involved emerging adults. *Journal of Divorce & Remarriage, 57,* 504–516.

Lackenbauer, S. D., Campbell, L., Rubin, H., Fletcher, G. J. O., & Troister, T. (2010). The unique and combined benefits of accuracy and positive bias in relationships. *Personal Relationships, 17,* 475–493.

Lakey, B. (2013). Perceived social support and happiness: The role of personality and relational processes. In S. A. David, I. Boniwell, & A. C. Ayers (Eds.), *The Oxford handbook of happiness* (pp. 847–859). New York: Oxford University Press.

Lakey, B., Vander Molen, R. J., Fles, E., & Andrews, J. (2016). Ordinary social interaction and the main effect between perceived support and affect. *Journal of Personality, 84,* 671–684.

Lam, A. G., Mak, A., & Lindsay, P. D. (2004). What really works? An exploratory study of condom negotiation strategies. *AIDS Education & Prevention, 16,* 160–171.

Lam, B. C. P., Cross, S. E., Wu, T., Yeh, K., Wang, Y., & Su, J. C. (2016). What do you want in a marriage? Examining marriage ideals in Taiwan and the United States. *Personality and Social Psychology Bulletin, 42,* 703–732.

Lambert, N. M., Fincham, F. D., DeWall, N. C., Pond, R., & Beach, S. R. (2013). Shifting toward cooperative tendencies and forgiveness: How partner-focused prayer transforms motivation. *Personal Relationships, 20,* 184–197.

Lambert, N. M., Fincham, F. D., & Stanley, S. (2012). Prayer and satisfaction with sacrifice in close relationships. *Journal of Social and Personal Relationships, 29,* 1058–1070.

Lamidi, E. & Manning, W. D. (2016). Marriage and cohabitation experiences among young adults. *Family Profiles,* FP-16-17. Bowling Green, OH: National Center for Family & Marriage Research.

Lammers, J., & Maner, J. (2016). Power and attraction to the counternormative aspects of infidelity. *Journal of Sex Research, 53,* 54–63.

Lammers, J., Stapel, D. A., & Galinsky, A. D. (2010). Power increases hypocrisy: Moralizing in reasoning, immorality in behavior. *Psychological Science, 21,* 737–744.

Lamy, L. (2016). Beyond emotion: Love as an encounter of myth and drive. *Emotion Review, 8,* 97–107.

Landers, A. (1982). *Love or sex . . . and how to tell the difference.* Chicago: Field Enterprises.

Lane, B. L., Piercy, C. W., & Carr, C. T. (2016). Making it Facebook official: The warranting value of online relationship status disclosures on relational characteristics. *Computers in Human Behavior, 56,* 1–8.

Lang, F. R., Wagner, J., Wrzus, C., & Neyer, F. J. (2013). Personal effort in social relationships across adulthood. *Psychology and Aging, 28,* 529–539.

Langeslag, S. J. E., Muris, P., & Franken, I. H. A. (2013). Measuring romantic love: Psychometric properties of the infatuation and attachment scales. *Journal of Sex Research, 50,* 739–747.

Langeslag, S. J. E., Olivier, J. R., Köhlen, M. E., Nijs, I. M., & Van Strien, J. W. (2015). Increased attention and memory for beloved-related information during infatuation: behavioral and electrophysiological data. *Social Cognitive and Affective Neuroscience, 10,* 136–144.

Långström, N., Rahman, Q., Carlström, E., & Lichtenstein, P. (2010). Genetic and environmental effects on same-sex sexual behavior: A population study of twins in Sweden. *Archives of Sexual Behavior, 39,* 75–80.

Lannin, D. G., Bittner, K. E., & Lorenz, F. O. (2013). Longitudinal effect of defensive denial on relationship instability. *Journal of Family Psychology, 27,* 968–977.

Lansford, J. E. (2009). Parental divorce and children's adjustment. *Perspectives on Psychological Science, 4,* 140–152.

Lapierre, M. A., & Lewis, M. N. (2017). Should it stay or should it go now? Smartphones and relational health. *Psychology of Popular Media Culture.* doi: 10.1037/ppm0000119.

Larmuseau, M. H. D., Matthijs K., & Wenseleers, T. (2016). Cuckolded fathers rare in human populations. *Trends in Ecology & Evolution, 31,* 327–329.

Larose, S., Guay, F., & Boivin M. (2002). Attachment, social support, and loneliness in young adulthood: A test of two models. *Personality and Social Psychology Bulletin, 28,* 684–693.

Larrick, R. P., Timmerman, T. A., Carton, A. M., & Abrevaya, J. (2011). Temper, temperature, and temptation: Heat-related retaliation in baseball. *Psychological Science, 22,* 423–428.

Larsen, S. E., & Hamberger, L. K. (2015). Men's and women's experience of IPV Part II: A review of new developments in comparative studies in clinical populations. *Journal of Family Violence, 30,* 1007–1030.

Larson, C. M., Haselton, M. G., Gildersleeve, K. A., & Pillsworth, E. G. (2013). Changes in women's feelings about their romantic relationships across the ovulatory cycle. *Hormones and Behavior, 63,* 128–135.

Larson, D. G., Chastain, R. L., Hoyt, W. T., & Ayzenberg, R. (2015). Self-concealment: Integrative review and working model. *Journal of Social and Clinical Psychology, 34,* 705–774.

Larson, G. M., & Sbarra, D. A. (2015). Participating in research on romantic breakups promotes emotional recovery via changes in self-concept clarity. *Social Psychological and Personality Science, 6,* 399–406.

Larson, R., Richards, M. H., Moneta, G., Holmbeck, G., & Duckett, E. (1996). Changes in adolescents' daily interactions with their families from ages 10 to 18: Disengagement and transformation. *Developmental Psychology, 32,* 744–754.

Larson, R. W., & Bradney, N. (1988). Precious moments with family members and friends. In R. M. Milardo (Ed.), *Families and social networks* (pp. 107–126). Thousand Oaks, CA: Sage.

Lassek, W. D., & Gaulin, S. J. C. (2009). Costs and benefits of fat-free muscle mass in men: Relationship to mating success, dietary requirements, and native immunity. *Evolution and Human Behavior, 30,* 322–328.

Lassek, W. D., & Gaulin, S. J. C. (2016). What makes Jessica Rabbit sexy? Contrasting roles of waist and hip size. *Evolutionary Psychology, 14,* 1–16.

Lauer, J., & Lauer, R. (1985, June). Marriages made to last. *Psychology Today,* pp. 22–26.

Lauer, R. H., Lauer, J. C., & Kerr, S. T. (1990). The long-term marriage: Perceptions of stability and satisfaction. *International Journal of Aging and Human Development, 31,* 189–195.

Laumann, E. O., Gagnon, J. H., Michael, R. T., & Michaels, S. (1994). *The social organization of sexuality: Sexual practices in the United States.* Chicago: University of Chicago Press.

Laurenceau, J., Barrett, L. F., & Rovine, M. J. (2005). The interpersonal process model of intimacy in marriage: A daily-diary and multilevel modeling approach. *Journal of Family Psychology, 19,* 314–323.

Laurenceau, J., Rivera, L. M., Schaffer, A. R., & Pietromonaco, P. R. (2004). Intimacy as an interpersonal process: Current status and future directions. In D. J. Mashek & A. Aron (Eds.), *Handbook of closeness and intimacy* (pp. 81–101). Mahwah, NJ: Erlbaum.

Laurin, K., Fitzsimmons, G. M., Finkel, E. J., & . . . Brown, P. C. (2016). Power and the pursuit of a partner's goals. *Journal of Personality and Social Psychology, 110,* 840–868.

Lavner, J. A., & Bradbury, T. N. (2012). Why do even satisfied newlyweds eventually go on to divorce? *Journal of Family Psychology, 26,* 1–10.

Lavner, J. A., Karney, B. R., & Bradbury, T. N. (2012). Do cold feet warn of trouble ahead? Premarital uncertainty and four-year marital outcomes. *Journal of Family Psychology, 26,* 1012–1017.

Lavner, J. A., Karney, B. R., & Bradbury, T. N. (2013). Newlyweds' optimistic forecasts of their marriage: For better or for worse? *Journal of Family Psychology, 27,* 531–540.

Lavner, J. A., Karney, B. R., & Bradbury, T. N. (2014). Relationship problems over the early years of marriage: Stability or change? *Journal of Family Psychology, 28,* 979–985.

Lavner, J. A., Karney, B. R., & Bradbury, T. N. (2016). Does couples' communication predict marital satisfaction, or does marital satisfaction predict communication? *Journal of Marriage and Family, 78,* 680–694.

Lavner, J. A., Lamkin, J., Miller, J. D., Campbell, W. K., & Karney, B. R. (2015). Narcissism and newlywed marriage: Partner characteristics and marital trajectories. *Personality Disorders: Theory, Research, and Treatment, 7,* 169–179.

Lawrence, E., & Bradbury, T. N. (2007). Trajectories of change in physical aggression and marital satisfaction. *Journal of Family Psychology, 21,* 236–247.

Lawrence, E., Orengo-Aguayo, R., Langer, A., & Brock, R. L. (2012). The impact and consequences of partner abuse on partners. *Partner Abuse, 3,* 406–428.

Lawson, J. F., James, C., Jannson, A. C., Koyama, N. F., & Hill, R. A. (2014). A comparison of heterosexual and homosexual mating preferences in personal advertisements. *Evolution and Human Behavior, 35,* 408–414.

Le, B., Dove, N. L., Agnew, C. R., Korn, M. S., & Mutso, A. A. (2010). Predicting nonmarital romantic relationship dissolution: A meta-analytic synthesis. *Personal Relationships, 17,* 377–390.

Le, B. M., Impett, E. A., Kogan, A., Webster, G. D., & Cheng, C. (2012). The personal and interpersonal rewards of communal orientation. *Journal of Social and Personal Relationships, 30,* 694–710.

Le, B. M., Korn, M. S., Crockett, E. E., & Loving, T. J. (2011). Missing you maintains us: Missing a romantic partner, commitment, relationships maintenance, and physical infidelity. *Journal of Social and Personal Relationships, 28,* 653–667.

Leaper, C., & Ayres, M. M. (2007). A meta-analytic review of gender variations in adults' language use: Talkativeness, affiliative speech, and assertive speech. *Personality and Social Psychology Review, 11,* 328–363.

Leaper, C., & Robnett, R. D. (2011). Women are more likely than men to use tentative language, aren't they? A meta-analysis testing for gender differences and moderators. *Psychology of Women Quarterly, 35,* 129–142.

Leary, M. R. (1986). The impact of interactional impediments on social anxiety and self-presentation. *Journal of Experimental Social Psychology, 22,* 122–135.

Leary, M. R. (2001). Toward a conceptualization of interpersonal rejection. In M. R. Leary (Ed.), *Interpersonal rejection* (pp. 3–20). New York: Oxford University Press.

Leary, M. R. (2005). Varieties of interpersonal rejection. In K. D. Williams, J. P. Forgas, & W. von Hippel (Eds.), *The social outcast: Ostracism, social exclusion, rejection, and bullying* (pp. 35–51). New York: Psychology Press.

Leary, M. R. (2012). Sociometer theory. In P. Van Lange, A. Kruglanski, & E. T. Higgins (Eds.), *Handbook of theories of social psychology* (Vol. 2, pp. 151–159). Thousand Oaks, CA: Sage.

Leary, M. R. (2017). *Introduction to behavioral research methods* (7th ed.). New York: Pearson.

Leary, M. R., & Acosta, J. (2018). Acceptance, rejection, and the quest for relational value. In A. Vangelisti & D. Perlman (Eds.), *Cambridge handbook of personal relationships* (2nd ed.) New York: Cambridge University Press.

Leary, M. R., & Cottrell, C. A. (2013). Evolutionary perspectives on interpersonal acceptance and rejection. In C. N. DeWall (Ed.), *The Oxford handbook of social exclusion* (pp. 9–19). New York: Oxford University Press.

Leary, M. R., Haupt, A. L., Strausser, K. S., & Chokel, J. T. (1998). Calibrating the sociometer: The relationship between interpersonal appraisals and state self-esteem. *Journal of Personality and Social Psychology, 74,* 1290–1299.

Leary, M. R., Herbst, K. C., & McCrary, F. (2003). Finding pleasure in solitary activities: Desire for aloneness or disinterest in social contact? *Personality and Individual Differences, 35,* 59–68.

Leary, M. R., & Jongman-Sereno, K. P. (2014). Social anxiety as an early warning system: A refinement and extension of the self-presentation theory of social anxiety. In S. Hofmann & P. DiBartolo (Eds.), *Social anxiety: Clinical, developmental, and social perspectives* (3rd ed., pp. 579–597). San Diego: Academic Press.

Leary, M. R., & Kowalski, R. M. (1995). *Social anxiety.* New York: Guilford Press.

Leary, M. R., & Leder, S. (2009). The nature of hurt feelings: Emotional experience and cognitive appraisals. In A. Vangelisti (Ed.), *Feeling hurt in close relationships* (pp. 15–33). New York: Cambridge University Press.

Leary, M. R., & Miller, R. S. (2000). Self-presentational perspectives on personal relationships. In W. Ickes & S. Duck (Eds.), *The social psychology of personal relationships* (pp. 129–155). Chichester, England: Wiley.

Leary, M. R., & Miller, R. S. (2012). The pursuit of relational value as a foundation of intimate relationships. In M. A. Paludi (Ed.), *The psychology of love* (Vol. 2, pp. 107–123). Santa Barbara, CA: Praeger.

Leary, M. R., Nezlek, J. B., Downs, D. L., Radford-Davenport, J., Martin, J., & McMullen, A. (1994). Self-presentation in everyday interactions. *Journal of Personality and Social Psychology, 67,* 664–673.

Leary, M. R., Twenge, J. M., & Quinlivan, E. (2006). Interpersonal rejection as a determinant of anger and aggression. *Personality and Social Psychology Review, 10,* 111–132.

Lease, S. H., Montes, S. H., Baggett, L. R., & . . . Boyraz, G. (2013). A cross-cultural exploration of masculinity and relationships in men from Turkey, Norway, and the United States. *Journal of Cross-Cultural Psychology, 44,* 84–105.

Lebow, J. L., Chamber, A. L., Christensen, A., & Johnson, S. M. (2012). Research on the treatment of couple distress. *Journal of Marital & Family Therapy, 38,* 145–168.

Lee, A. J., Mitchem, D. G., Wright, M. J., Martin, N. G., Keller, M. C., & Ziestsch, B. P. (2016). Facial averageness and genetic quality: Testing heritability, genetic correlation with attractiveness, and the paternal age effect. *Evolution and Human Behavior, 37,* 61–66.

Lee, D. M., Nazroo, J., O'Connor, D. B., Blake, M., & Pendleton, N. (2016). Sexual health and well-being among older men and women in England: Findings from the English Longitudinal Study of Ageing. *Archives of Sexual Behavior, 45,* 133–144.

Lee, J. A. (1988). Love-styles. In R. J. Sternberg & M. L. Barnes (Eds.), *The psychology of love* (pp. 38–67). New Haven, CT: Yale University Press.

Lee, L., Loewenstein, G., Ariely, D., Hong, J., & Young, J. (2008). If I'm not hot, are you hot or not? *Psychological Science, 19,* 669–677.

Lee, S. W. S., & Schwarz, N. (2014). Framing love: When it hurts to think we were made for each other. *Journal of Experimental Social Psychology, 54,* 61–67.

LeFebvre, L., Blackburn, K., & Brody, N. (2015). Navigating romantic relationship dissolution model to social networking environments. *Journal of Social and Personal Relationships, 32,* 78–98.

Legate, N., Ryan, R. M., & Weinstein, N. (2012). Is coming out always a "good thing"? Exploring the relations of autonomy support, outness, and wellness for lesbian, gay, and bisexual individuals. *Social Psychological and Personality Science, 3,* 145–152.

Lehmiller, J. J., & Agnew, C. R. (2007). Perceived marginalization and the prediction of romantic relationship stability. *Journal of Marriage and Family, 69,* 1036–1049.

Lehmiller, J. J., VanderDrift, L. E., & Kelly, J. R. (2011). Sex differences in approaching friends with benefits relationships. *Journal of Sex Research, 48,* 275–284.

Lehmiller, J. J., VanderDrift, L. E., & Kelly, J. R. (2014). Sexual communication, satisfaction, and condom use behavior in friends with benefits and romantic partners. *Journal of Sex Research, 51,* 74–85.

Leising, D., Gallrein, A. B., & Dufner, M. (2014). Judging the behavior of people we know: Objective assessment, confirmation of preexisting views, or both? *Personality and Social Psychology Bulletin, 40,* 153–163.

Lemay, E. P. Jr. (2014). Accuracy and Bias in self-perceptions of responsive behavior: Implications for security in romantic relationships. *Journal of Personality and Social Psychology, 107,* 638–656.

Lemay, E. P., Jr. (2016). The forecast model of relationship commitment. *Journal of Personality and Social Psychology, 111,* 34–52.

Lemay, E. P., Jr., Bechis, M. A., Martin, J., Neal, A. M., & Coyne, C. (2013). Concealing negative evaluations of a romantic partner's physical attractiveness. *Personal Relationships, 20,* 669–689.

Lemay, E. P., Jr., & Cannon, K. T. (2012). Dysphoric reassurance seeking breeds contempt: Experimental evidence. *Journal of Social and Clinical Psychology, 31,* 1023–1050.

Lemay, E. P., Jr., Clark, M. S., & Greenberg, A. (2010). What is beautiful is good because what is beautiful is desired: Physical attractiveness stereotyping as projection of interpersonal goals. *Personality and Social Psychology Bulletin, 36,* 339–353.

Lemay, E. P., Jr., & Dobush, S. (2015). When do personality and emotion predict destructive behavior during relationship conflict? The role of perceived commitment asymmetry. *Journal of Personality, 83,* 523–534.

Lemay, E. P., Jr., Lin, J. L., & Muir, H. J. (2015). Daily affective and behavioral forecasts in romantic relationships: Seeing tomorrow through the lens of today. *Personality and Social Psychology Bulletin, 4,* 1005–1019.

Lemay, E. P., Jr., & Neal, A. M. (2013). The wishful memory of interpersonal responsiveness. *Journal of Personality and Social Psychology, 104,* 653–672.

Lemay, E. P., Jr., & Neal, A. M. (2014). Accurate and biased perceptions of responsive support predict well-being. *Motivation and Emotion, 38,* 270–286.

Lemay, E. P., Jr., & Spongberg, K. (2015). Perceiving and wanting to be valued by others: Implications for cognition, motivation, and behavior in romantic relationships. *Journal of Personality, 83,* 464–478.

Lemay, E. P., Jr., & Wolf, N. R. (2016a). Human mate poaching tactics are effective: Evidence from a dyadic prospective study on opposite-sex "Friendships." *Social Psychological and Personality Science, 7,* 374–380.

Lemay, E. P. Jr., & Wolf, N. R. (2016b). Projection of romantic and sexual desire in opposite-sex friendships: How wishful thinking creates a self-fulfilling prophecy. *Personality and Social Psychology Bulletin, 42,* 864–878.

Lennon, C. A., Stewart, A. L., & Ledermann, T. (2013). The role of power in intimate relationships. *Journal of Social and Personal Relationships, 30,* 95–114.

Lenton, A. P., & Francesconi, M. (2010). How humans cognitively manage an abundance of mate options. *Psychological Science, 21,* 528–533.

Lenton, A. P., & Webber, L. (2006). Cross-sex friendships: Who has more? *Sex Roles, 54,* 809–820.

Leone, C., & Hawkins, L. B. (2006). Self-monitoring and close relationships. *Journal of Personality, 74,* 739–778.

Leone, J. M., Lape, M. E., & Xu, Y. (2014). Women's decisions to not seek formal help for partner violence: A comparison of intimate terrorism and situational couple violence. *Journal of Interpersonal Violence, 29,* 1850–1876.

Letzring, T. D., & Noftle, E. E. (2010). Predicting relationship quality from self-verification of broad personality traits among romantic couples. *Journal of Research in Personality, 44,* 353–362.

Letzring, T. D., Wells, S. M., & Funder, D. C. (2006). Information quantity and quality affect the realistic accuracy of personality judgment. *Journal of Personality and Social Psychology, 91,* 111–123.

Levant, R. F., & Rankin, T. J. (2014). The gender role socialization of boys to men. In R. J. Burke & D. A. Major (Eds.), *Gender in organizations: Are men allies or adversaries to women's career advancement?* (pp. 55–72). Northampton, MA: Elgar Publishing.

Levenson, R. W., Carstensen, L. L., & Gottman, J. M. (1994). Influence of age and gender on affect, physiology, and their interrelations: A study of long-term marriages. *Journal of Personality and Social Psychology, 67,* 56–68.

Lever, J., Frederick, D. A., & Peplau, L. A. (2006). Does size matter? Men's and women's views on penis size across the lifespan. *Psychology of Men and Masculinity, 7,* 129–143.

Levine, E. E., & Schweitzer, M. E. (2014). Are liars ethical? On the tension between benevolence and honesty. *Journal of Experimental Social Psychology, 53,* 107–112.

Levine, T. R. (2016). Examining sender and judge variability in honesty assessments and deception detection accuracy: Evidence for a transparent liar but no evidence of deception-general ability. *Communication Research Reports, 33,* 188–194.

Levine, T. R., Clare D. D., Blair, J. P., & . . . Park, H. S. (2014). Expertise in deception detection involves actively prompting diagnostic information rather than passive behavioral observation. *Human Communication Research, 40,* 442–462.

Levine, T. R., Serota, K. B., Shulman, H., & . . . Lee, J. H. (2011). Sender demeanor: Individual differences in sender believability have a powerful impact on deception detection judgments. *Human Communication Research, 37,* 377–403.

Levinger, G. (1976). A social psychological perspective on marital dissolution. *Journal of Social Issues, 32,* 21–47.

Levinger, G., & Levinger, A. C. (2003). Winds of time and place: How context has affected a 50-year marriage. *Personal Relationships, 10,* 285–306.

Levitt, M. J., Silver, M. E., & Franco, N. (1996). Troublesome relationships: A part of human experience. *Journal of Social and Personal Relationships, 13,* 523–536.

Lewicki, R., Polin, B., & Lount, R. (2016). An exploration of the structure of effective apologies. *Negotiation and Conflict Management Research, 9,* 177–196.

Lewis, M. A., Granato, H., Blayney, J. A., Lostutter, T. W., & Kilmer, J. R. (2012). Predictors of hooking up sexual behaviors and emotional reactions among U.S. college students. *Archives of Sexual Behavior, 41,* 1219–1229.

Lewis, M. A., Litt, D. M., Cronce, J. M., Blayney, J. A., & Gilmore, A. K. (2014). Underestimating protection and overestimating risk: Examining descriptive normative perceptions and their association with drinking and sexual behaviors. *Journal of Sex Research, 51,* 86–96.

Lewis, R. J., Mason, T. B., Winstead, B. A., & Kelley, M. L. (2017). Empirical investigation of a model of sexual minority specific and general risk factors for intimate partner violence among lesbian women. *Psychology of Violence, 7,* 110–119.

Lewis, T., & Manusov, V. (2009). Listening to another's distress in everyday relationships. *Communication Quarterly, 57,* 282–301.

Li, H., Zeigler-Hill, V., Yang, J. J., & . . . Zhang, Q. (2012). Low self-esteem and the neural basis of attentional bias for social rejection cues: Evidence from the N2pc ERP component. *Personality and Individual Differences, 53,* 947–951.

Li, N. P. (2008). Intelligent priorities: Adaptive long- and short-term mate preferences. In G. Geher & G. Miller (Eds.), *Mating intelligence: Sex, relationships, and the mind's reproductive system* (pp. 105–119). New York: Erlbaum.

Li, N. P., Bailey, J. M., Kenrick, D. T., & Linsenmeier, J. A. W. (2002). The necessities and luxuries of mate preferences: Testing the tradeoffs. *Journal of Personality and Social Psychology, 82,* 947–955.

Li, N. P., Sng, O., & Jonason, P. K. (2012). Sexual conflict in mating strategies. In T. K. Shackleford & A. T. Goetz (Eds.), *The Oxford handbook of sexual conflict in humans* (pp. 49–71). New York: Oxford University Press.

Li, N. P., Valentine, K. A., & Patel, L. (2011). Mate preferences in the US and Singapore: A cross-cultural test of the mate preference priority model. *Personality and Individual Differences, 50,* 291–294.

Li, N. P., Yong, J. C., Tov, W. S., & . . . Balliet, D. (2013). Mate preferences do predict attraction and choices in the early stages of mate selection. *Journal of Personality and Social Psychology, 105,* 757–776.

Li, X., Chen, W., & Popiel, P. (2015). What happens on Facebook stays on Facebook? The implications of Facebook interaction for perceived, receiving and giving social support. *Computers in Human Behavior, 51,* 106–113.

Liberman, V., Anderson, N. R., & Ross, L. (2010). Achieving difficult agreements: Effects of positive expectations on negotiation processes and outcomes. *Journal of Experimental Social Psychology, 46,* 494–504.

Lick, D. J., Cortland, C. I., & Johnson, K. L. (2016). The pupils are the windows to sexuality: Pupil dilation as a visual cue to others' sexual interest. *Evolution and Human Behavior, 37,* 117–124.

Liebold, J. M., & McConnell, A. R. (2004). Women, sex, hostility, power, and suspicion: Sexually aggressive men's cognitive associations. *Journal of Experimental Social Psychology, 40,* 256–263.

Lim, B. H., Valdez, C. E., & Lilly, M. M. (2015). Making meaning out of interpersonal victimization: The narratives of IPV survivors. *Violence Against Women, 21,* 1065–1086.

Lin, A. J., & Santelli, J. S. (2008). The accuracy of condom information in three selected abstinence-only education curricula. *Sexuality Research & Social Policy, 5,* 56–70.

Lin, Y. W., & Rusbult, C. E. (1995). Commitment to dating relationships and cross-sex friendships in America and China. *Journal of Social and Personal Relationships, 12,* 7–26.

Lindberg, L., Santelli, J., & Desai, S. (2106). Understanding the decline in adolescent fertility in the United States, 2007–2012. *Journal of Adolescent Health, 59,* 577–583.

Lindgren, K. P., Jacques-Tiura, A. J., & Westgate, E. C. (2012). Sexual-intent perceptions: A primer on methods, theories, and applications. In M. A. Paludi (Ed.), *The psychology of love* (Vol. 2, pp. 141–155). Santa Barbara, CA: Praeger.

Lindhiem, O., Bennett, C. B., Trentacosta, C. J., & McLear, C. (2014). Client preferences affect treatment satisfaction, completion, and clinical outcome: A meta-analysis. *Clinical Psychology Review, 34,* 506–517.

Linville, P., Fischhoff, B., & Fischer, G. (1993). AIDS risk perceptions and decision bias. In J. B Pryor & G. D. Reeder (Eds.), *The social psychology of HIV infection* (pp. 1–38). Hillsdale, NJ: Erlbaum.

Lipinski-Harten, M., & Tafarodi, R. W. (2012). A comparison of conversational quality in online and face-to-face first encounters. *Journal of Language and Social Psychology, 31,* 331–341.

Lippa, R. A. (2005). Sexual orientation and personality. *Annual Review of Sex Research, 16,* 119–153.

Lippa, R. A. (2007). The preferred traits of mates in a cross-national study of heterosexual and homosexual men and women: An examination of biological and cultural influences. *Archives of Sexual Behavior, 36,* 193–208.

Lippa, R. A. (2009). Sex differences in sex drive, sociosexuality, and height across 53 nations: Testing evolutionary and social structural theories. *Archives of Sexual Behavior, 38,* 631–651.

Lippa, R. A., & Hershberger, S. (1999). Genetic and environmental influences on individual differences in masculinity, femininity, and gender diagnosticity: Analyzing data from a classic twin study. *Journal of Personality, 67,* 127–155.

Lishner, D. A., Nguyen, S., Stocks, E. L., & Zillmer, E. J. (2008). Are sexual and emotional infidelity equally upsetting to men and women? Making sense of forced-choice responses. *Evolutionary Psychology, 6,* 667–675.

Little, A. C. (2015). Attraction and human mating. In V. Zeigler-Hill, L. Welling, & T. Shackelford (Eds.), *Evolutionary perspectives on social psychology* (pp. 319–329). Cham, Switzerland: Springer.

Little, A. C., Burt, D. M., & Perrett, D. I. (2006). Assortative mating for perceived facial personality traits. *Personality and Individual Differences, 40,* 973–984.

Little, A. C., Penton-Voak, I. S., Burt, D. M., & Perrett, D. I. (2002). Evolution and individual differences in the perception of attractiveness: How cyclic hormonal changes and self-perceived attractiveness influence female preferences for male faces. In G. Rhodes & L. A. Zebrowitz (Eds.), *Facial attractiveness: Evolutionary, cognitive, and social perspectives* (pp. 59–90). Westport, CT: Ablex.

Liu, E., & Roloff, M. E. (2016). Regret for complaint withholding. *Communication Quarterly, 64,* 72–92.

Liu, H., & Waite, L. (2014). Bad marriage, broken heart? Age and gender differences in the link between marital quality and cardiovascular risks among older adults. *Journal of Health and Social Behavior, 55,* 403–423.

Liu, M., & Wang, Y. (2016). Comparison of face-to-face and web surveys on the topic of homosexual rights. *Journal of Homosexuality, 63,* 838–854.

Livingston, G. (2016, October 26). *Births outside of marriage decline for immigrant women.* Pew Research Center. Retrieved from http://www.pewsocialtrends.org/2016/10/26/births-outside-of-marriage-decline-for-immigrant-women/

Livingston, G., & Caumont, A. (2017, February 13). *5 facts on love and marriage in America.* Pew Research Center. Retrieved from http://www.pewresearch.org/fact-tank/2017/02/13/5-facts-about-love-and-marriage/.

Lloyd, S. A. (1987). Conflict in premarital relationships: Differential perceptions of males and females. *Family Relations, 36,* 290–294.

Lloyd, S. A., & Emery, B. C. (2000). The context and dynamics of intimate aggression against women. *Journal of Social and Personal Relationships, 17,* 503–521.

Löckenhoff, C. E., & Carstensen, L. F. (2004). Socioemotional Selectivity Theory, aging, and health: The increasingly delicate balance between regulating emotions and making tough choices. *Journal of Personality, 72,* 1395–1424.

Löckenhoff, C. E., Chan, W., McCrae, R. R., & . . . Terracciano, A. (2014). Gender stereotypes of personality: Universal and accurate? *Journal of Cross-Cultural Psychology, 45,* 675–694.

Loewenstein, G., Krishnamurti, T., Kopsic, J., & McDonald, D. (2015). Does increased sexual frequency enhance happiness? *Journal of Economic Behavior and Organization, 116,* 206–218.

Logan, J. M., & Cobb, R. J. (2016). Benefits of capitalization in newlyweds: Predicting marital satisfaction and depression symptoms. *Journal of Social and Clinical Psychology, 35,* 87–106.

Lohr, J. M., Olatunji, B. O., Baumeister, R. F., & Bushman, B. J. (2007). The psychology of anger venting and empirically supported alternatives that do not harm. *Scientific Review of Mental Health Practice, 5,* 53–64.

Long, E. C. J., Angera, J. J., Carter, S. J., Nakamoto, M., & Kalso, M. (1999). Understanding the one you love: A longitudinal assessment of an empathy training program for couples in romantic relationships. *Family Relations, 48,* 235–242.

Longmore, M. A., Manning, W. D., Giordano, P. C., & Copp, J. E. (2014). Intimate partner victimization, poor relationship quality, and depressive symptoms during young adulthood. *Social Science Research, 48,* 77–89.

Lorber, M. F., Erlanger, A. C. E., Heyman, R. E., & O'Leary, K. D. (2015). The honeymoon effect: Does it exist and can it be predicted? *Prevention Science, 16,* 550–559.

Lorber, M. F., & O'Leary, K. D. (2004). Predictors of the persistence of male aggression in early marriage. *Journal of Family Violence, 19,* 329–338.

Lorenzo, G. L., Biesanz, J. C., & Human, L. J. (2010). What is beautiful is good and more accurately understood: Physical attractiveness and accuracy in first impressions of personality. *Psychological Science, 21,* 1777–1782.

Loving, T. J. (2006). Predicting dating relationship fate with insiders' and outsiders' perspectives: Who and what is asked matters. *Personal Relationships, 13,* 349–362.

Loving, T. J., & Sbarra, D. A. (2015). In M. Mikulincer, P. Shaver, J. Simpson, & J. Dovidio (Eds.), *APA handbook of personality and social psychology, Volume 3: Interpersonal relations* (pp. 151–176). Washington, DC: American Psychological Association.

Lucas, R. E. (2005). Time does not heal all wounds: A longitudinal study of reaction and adaptation to divorce. *Psychological Science, 16,* 945–950.

Lucas, R. E. (2007). Adaptation and the set-point model of subjective well-being. *Current Directions in Psychological Science, 16,* 75–79.

Luchies, L. B, Finkel, E. J., & Fitzsimons, G. M. (2011). The effects of self-regulatory strength, content, and strategies on close relationships. *Journal of Personality, 79,* 1251–1279.

Luchies, L. B., Finkel, E. J., McNulty, J. K., & Kumashiro, M. (2010). The doormat effect: When forgiving erodes self-respect and self-concept clarity. *Journal of Personality and Social Psychology, 98,* 734–749.

Luciano, E. C., & Orth, U. (2017). Transitions in romantic relationships and development of self-esteem. *Journal of Personality and Social Psychology, 112,* 307–328.

Luhmann, M., Hofmann, W., Eid, M., & Lucas, R. E. (2012). Subjective well-being and adaptation to life events: A meta-analysis. *Journal of Personality and Social Psychology, 102,* 592–615.

Lukacs, V., & Quan-Haase, A. (2015). Romantic breakups on Facebook: New scales for studying post-breakup behaviors, digital distress, and surveillance. *Information, Communication & Society, 18,* 492–508.

Luke, M. A., Maio, G. R., & Carnelley, K. B. (2004). Attachment models of the self and others: Relations with self-esteem, humanity-esteem, and parental treatment. *Personal Relationships, 11,* 281–303.

Luo, S. (2009). Partner selection and relationship satisfaction in early dating couples: The role of couple similarity. *Personality and Individual Differences, 47,* 133–138.

Luo, S., & Snider, A. G. (2009). Accuracy and biases in newlyweds' perceptions of each other: Not mutually exclusive but mutually beneficial. *Psychological Science, 20,* 1332–1339.

Luo, S., & Zhang, G. (2009). What leads to romantic attraction: Similarity, reciprocity, security, or beauty? Evidence from a speed-dating study. *Journal of Personality, 77,* 933–964.

Luo, S., Zhang, G., Watson, D., & Snider, A. G. (2010). Using cross-sectional couple data to disentangle the causality between positive partner perceptions and marital satisfaction. *Journal of Research in Personality, 44,* 665–668.

Luong, G., Charles, S. T., & Fingerman, K. L. (2011). Better with age: Social relationships across adulthood. *Journal of Social and Personal Relationships, 28,* 9–23.

Lutfey, K. E., Link, C. L., Rosen, R. C., Wiegel, M., & McKinlay, J. B. (2009). Prevalence and correlates of sexual activity and function in women: Results from the Boston Area Community Health (BACH) survey. *Archives of Sexual Behavior, 38,* 514–527.

Lutz-Zois, C. J., Bradley, A. C., Mihalik, J. L., & Moorman-Eavers, E. R. (2006). Perceived similarity and relationship success among dating couples: An idiographic approach. *Journal of Social and Personal Relationships, 23,* 865–880.

Luxen, M. F., & Buunk, B. P. (2006). Human intelligence, fluctuating asymmetry and the peacock's tail: General intelligence (g) as an honest signal of fitness. *Personality and Individual Differences, 41,* 897–902.

Lydon, J., Pierce, T., & O'Regan, S. (1997). Coping with moral commitment to long-distance dating relationships. *Journal of Personality and Social Psychology, 73,* 104–113.

Lykken, D. T. (2002). How relationships begin and end: A genetic perspective. In A. L. Vangelisti, H. T. Reis, & M. A. Fitzpatrick (Eds.), *Stability and change in relationships* (pp. 83–102). Cambridge, England: Cambridge University Press.

Lyngstad, T. H., & Jalovaara, M. (2010). A review of the antecedents of union dissolution. *Demographic Research, 23,* 257–292.

Lytle, A., & Levy, S. R. (2015). Reducing heterosexuals' prejudice toward gay men and lesbian women via an induced cross-orientation friendship. *Psychology of Sexual Orientation and Gender Diversity, 2,* 447–455.

Lyubomirsky, S., & Layous, K. (2013). How do simple positive activities increase well-being? *Current Directions in Psychological Science, 22,* 57–62.

Määttä, K., & Uusiautti, S. (2013). Silence is not golden: Review of studies of couple interaction. *Communication Studies, 64,* 33–48.

MacDonald, G., Zanna, M. P., & Holmes, J. G. (2000). An experimental test of the role of alcohol in relationship conflict. *Journal of Experimental Social Psychology, 36,* 182–193.

MacDonald, T. K., MacDonald, G., Zanna, M. P., & Fong, G. (2000). Alcohol, sexual arousal, and intentions to use condoms in young men: Applying alcohol myopia theory to risky sexual behavior. *Health Psychology, 19,* 290–298.

MacDonald, T. K., & Ross, M. (1999). Assessing the accuracy of predictions about dating relationships: How and why do lovers' predictions differ from those made by observers? *Personality and Social Psychology Bulletin, 25,* 1417–1429.

Macdowall, W., Gibson, L. J., Tanton, C., & . . . Wellings, K. (2013). Lifetime prevalence, associated factors, and circumstances of non-volitional sex in women and men in Britain: Findings from the third National Survey of Sexual Attitudes and Lifestyles (Natsal-3). *Lancet, 382,* 1845–1855.

MacGeorge, E. L., & Hall, E. D. (2014). Relationship advice. In C. R. Agnew (Ed.), *Social influences on romantic relationships: Beyond the dyad* (pp. 188–208). Cambridge, UK: Cambridge University Press.

Magdol, L., & Bessel, D. R. (2003). Social capital, social currency, and portable assets: The impact of residential mobility on exchanges of social support. *Personal Relationships, 10,* 149–169.

Mahoney, A. R., & Knudson-Martin, C. (2009). Gender equality in intimate relationships. In C. Knudson-Martin & A. Mahoney (Eds.), *Couples, gender, and power: Creating change in intimate relationships* (pp. 3–16). New York: Springer.

Maisel, N. C., & Gable, S. L. (2009). The paradox of received social support: The importance of responsiveness. *Psychological Science, 20,* 928–932.

Maisel, N. C., & Karney, B. R. (2012). Socioeconomic status moderates associations among stressful events, mental health, and relationship satisfaction. *Journal of Family Psychology, 26,* 654–660.

Major, B., Carrington, P. I., & Carnevale, P. J. D. (1984). Physical attractiveness and self-esteem: Attributions for praise from an other-sex evaluator. *Personality and Social Psychology Bulletin, 10,* 43–50.

Malachowski, C. C., & Frisby, B. N. (2015). The aftermath of hurtful events: Cognitive, communicative, and relational outcomes. *Communication Quarterly, 63,* 187–203.

Maldonado, R. C., Watkins, L. E., DiLillo, D. (2015). The interplay of trait anger, childhood physical abuse, and alcohol consumption in predicting intimate partner aggression. *Journal of Interpersonal Violence, 30,* 1112–1127.

Maleck, S., & Papp, L. M. (2015). Childhood risky family environments and romantic relationship functioning among young adult dating couples. *Journal of Family Issues, 36,* 567–588.

Malle, B. F. (2006). The actor-observer asymmetry in attribution: A (surprising) meta-analysis. *Psychological Bulletin, 132,* 895–919.

Malouff, J. M., Mundy, S. A., Galea, T. R., & Bothma, V. N. (2015). Preliminary findings supporting a new model of how couples maintain excitement in romantic relationships. *American Journal of Family Therapy, 43,* 227–237.

Malouff, J. M., Thorsteinsson, E. B., Schutte, N. S., Bhullar, N., & Rooke, S. E. (2010). The five-factor model of personality and relationship satisfaction of intimate partners: A meta-analysis. *Journal of Research in Personality, 44,* 124–127.

Maltby, J., Wood, A. M., Day, L., Kon, T. W. H., Colley, A., & Linley, P. A. (2008). Personality predictors of levels of forgiveness two and a half years after the transgression. *Journal of Research in Personality, 42,* 1088–1094.

Mancini, A. D., Bonanno, G. A., & Clark, A. E. (2011). Stepping off the hedonic treadmill: Individual differences in response to major life events. *Journal of Individual Differences, 32,* 144–152.

Maner, J. K., DeWall, N., Baumeister, R. F., & Schaller, M. (2007). Does social exclusion motivate interpersonal reconnection? Resolving the "porcupine problem." *Journal of Personality and Social Psychology, 92,* 42–55.

Maner, J. K., Rouby, D. A., & Gonzaga, G. C. (2008). Automatic inattention to attractive alternatives: The evolved psychology of relationship maintenance. *Evolution and Human Behavior, 29,* 343–349.

Manglos-Weber, N. D., & Weinreb, A. A. (2017). Own-choice marriage and fertility in Turkey. *Journal of Marriage and Family, 79,* 372–389.

Mannes, A. E. (2013). Shorn scalps and perceptions of male dominance. *Social Psychological and Personality Science, 4,* 198–205.

Manning, W. D., Brown, S. L., & Stykes, J. B. (2016). Same-sex and different-sex cohabiting couple relationship stability. *Demography, 53,* 937–953.

Manning, W. D., Giordano, P. C., Longmore, M. A., & Flanigan, C. M. (2012). Young adult dating relationships and the management of sexual risk. *Populations Research and Policy Review, 31,* 165–185.

Marcus, D. K., & Miller, R. S. (2003). Sex differences in judgments of physical attractiveness: A social relations analysis. *Personality and Social Psychology Bulletin, 29,* 325–335.

Markey, P. M., Lowmaster, S., & Eichler, W. (2010). A real-time assessment of interpersonal complementarity. *Personal Relationships, 17,* 13–25.

Markey, P. M., & Markey, C. N. (2007). Romantic ideals, romantic obtainment, and relationship experiences: The complementarity of interpersonal traits among romantic partners. *Journal of Social and Personal Relationships, 24,* 517–533.

Markman, H. J. (1981). Prediction of marital distress: A 5-year follow-up. *Journal of Consulting and Clinical Psychology, 49,* 760–762.

Markman, H. J., Rhoades, G. K., Stanley, S. M., & Peterson, K. M. (2013). A randomized clinical trial of the effectiveness of premarital intervention: Moderators of divorce outcomes. *Journal of Family Psychology, 27,* 165–172.

Markman, H. J., Rhoades, G. K., Stanley, S. M., Ragan, E. P., & Whitton, S. W. (2010). The premarital communication roots of marital distress and divorce: The first five years of marriage. *Journal of Family Psychology, 24,* 289–298.

Markman, H. J., Stanley, S., & Blumberg, S. L. (1994). *Fighting for your marriage: Positive steps for preventing divorce and preserving a lasting love.* San Francisco: Jossey-Bass.

Marmo, J. & Canary, D. J. (2013). Connecting happiness to relational maintenance: Understanding the importance of fairness. In M. Hojjat & D. Cramer (Eds.), *Positive psychology of love* (pp. 203–217). New York: Oxford University Press.

Marshall, A. D., & Holtzworth-Munroe, A. (2010). Recognition of wives' emotional expressions: A mechanism in the relationship between psychopathology and intimate partner violence perpetration. *Journal of Family Psychology, 24,* 21–30.

Marshall, L. L., Weston, R., & Honeycutt, T. C. (2000). Does men's positivity moderate or mediate the effect of their abuse on women's relationship quality? *Journal of Social and Personal Relationships, 17,* 660–675.

Marshall, T. C. (2010). Gender, peer relations, and intimate romantic relationships. In J. Chrisler & D. McCreary (Eds.), *Handbook of gender research in psychology* (Vol. 2, pp. 281–310). New York: Springer.

Martin, C. L., Cook, R. E., & Andrews, N. Z. (2017). Reviving androgyny: A modern day perspective on flexibility of gender identity and behavior. *Sex Roles, 76,* 592–603.

Martins, Y., Preti, G., Crabtree, C. R., Runyan, T., Vainius, A. A., & Wysocki, C. J. (2005). Preference for human body odors is influenced by gender and sexual orientation. *Psychological Science, 16,* 694–701.

Martos, A. J., Nezhad, S., & Meyer, I. H. (2015). Variations in sexual identity milestones among lesbians, gay men, and bisexuals. *Sexuality Research and Social Policy, 12,* 24–33.

Masarik, A. S., Conger, R. D., Donnellan, M. B., & . . . Widaman, K. F. (2014). For better and for worse: Genes and parenting interact to predict future behavior in romantic relationships. *Journal of Family Psychology, 28,* 357–367.

Mason, A. E., Law, R. W., Bryan, A. E., Portley, R. M., & Sbarra, D. A. (2012). Facing a breakup: Electromyographic responses moderate self-concept recovery following a romantic separation. *Personal Relationships, 19,* 551–568.

Mason, M. F., Tatkow, E. P., & Macrae, C. N. (2005). The look of love: Gaze shifts and person perception. *Psychological Science, 16,* 236–239.

Massar, K., & Buunk, A. P. (2009). Rivals in the mind's eye: Jealous responses after subliminal exposure to body shapes. *Personality and Individual Differences, 46,* 129–134.

Massar, K., Winters, C. L., Lenz, S., & Jonason, P. K. (2017). Green-eyed snakes: The associations between psychopathy, jealousy, and jealousy induction. *Personality and Individual Differences, 115,* 164–168.

Master, S. L., Eisenberger, N. I., Taylor, S. E., Naliboff, B. D., Shirinyan, D., & Lieberman, M. D. (2009). A picture's worth: Partner photographs reduce experimentally induced pain. *Psychological Science, 20,* 1316–1318.

Masters, W. H., & Johnson, V. F. (1970). *Human sexual inadequacy.* Boston: Little, Brown.

Matsumoto, D., & Hwang, H. C. (2016). The cultural bases of nonverbal communication. In D. Matsumoto, H. C. Hwang, & M. G. Frank (Eds.), *APA handbook of nonverbal communication* (pp. 77–101). Washington, DC: American Psychological Association.

Matsumoto, D., Hwang, H. C., & Frank, M. G. (2016). The body: Postures, gait, proxemics, and haptics. In D. Matsumoto, H. C. Hwang, & M. G. Frank (Eds.), *APA handbook of nonverbal communication* (pp. 387–400). Washington, DC: American Psychological Association.

Maxwell, J. A., Muise, A., MacDonald, G., & . . . Impett, E. A. (2017). How implicit theories of sexuality shape sexual and relationship well-being. *Journal of Personality and Social Psychology, 112,* 238–279.

Mayer, J. D., Caruso, D. R., & Salovey, P. (2016). The ability model of emotional intelligence: Principles and updates. *Emotion Review, 8,* 290–300.

McAllister, S., Duncan, S. F., & Hawkins, A. J. (2012). Examining the early evidence for self-directed marriage and relationship education: A meta-analytic study. *Family Relations, 61,* 742–755.

McAndrew, F. T., & De Jonge, C. R. (2011). Electronic person perception: What do we infer about people from the style of their e-mail messages? *Social Psychological and Personality Science, 2,* 403–407.

McCabe, M. P., & Goldhammer, D. L. (2012). Demographic and psychological factors related to sexual desire among heterosexual women in a relationship. *Journal of Sex Research, 49,* 78–87.

McClure, M. J., & Lydon, J. E. (2014). Anxiety doesn't become you: How attachment anxiety compromises relational opportunities. *Journal of Personality and Social Psychology, 106,* 89–111.

McClure, M. J., Xu, J. H., Craw, J. P., Lane, S. P., Bolger, N., & Shrout, P. E. (2014). Understanding the costs of support transactions in daily life. *Journal of Personality, 82,* 563–574.

McCormack, M. (2014). Innovative sampling and participant recruitment in sexuality research. *Journal of Social and Personal Relationships, 31,* 475–481.

McCoy, A., Rauer, A., & Sabey, A. (2017). The meta marriage: Links between older couples' relationship narratives and marital satisfaction. *Family Process.* doi: 10.1111/famp.12217.

McCrae, R. R., & Costa, P. T., Jr. (2010). The Five-Factor Theory of personality. In O. P. John, R. W. Robins, & L. A. Pervin (Eds.), *Handbook of personality: Theory and research* (3rd ed., pp. 159–181). New York: Guilford.

McCullough, M. E. (2008). *Beyond revenge: The evolution of the forgiveness instinct.* New York: Jossey-Bass.

McCullough, M. E., Bono, G., & Root, L. M. (2007). Rumination, emotion, and forgiveness: Three longitudinal studies. *Journal of Personality and Social Psychology, 92,* 490–505.

McCullough, M. E., Emmons, R. A., Kilpatrick, S. D., & Mooney, C. N. (2003). Narcissists as "victims": The role of narcissism in the perception of transgressions. *Personality and Social Psychology Bulletin, 29,* 885–893.

McDaniel, B. T., & Coyne, S. M. (2016). "Technoference": The interference of technology in couple relationships and implications for women's personal and relational well-being. *Psychology of Popular Media Culture, 5,* 85–98.

McDermott, R., Fowler, J. H., & Christakis, N. A. (2013). Breaking up is hard to do, unless everyone else is doing it too: Social network effects on divorce in a longitudinal sample. *Social Forces, 92,* 491–519.

McEwan, B., & Horn, D. (2016). ILY & Can U Pick Up Some Milk: Effects of relational maintenance via text messaging on relational satisfaction and closeness in dating partners. *Southern Communication Journal, 81,* 168–181.

McEwan, T. E., Mullen, P. E., & MacKenzie, R. (2009). A study of the predictors of persistence in stalking situations. *Law and Human Behavior, 33,* 149–158.

McGonagle, K. A., Kessler, R. C., & Schilling, E. A. (1992). The frequency and determinants of marital disagreements in a community sample. *Journal of Social and Personal Relationships, 9,* 507–524.

McGuire, J. E., & Leaper, C. (2016). Competition, coping, and closeness in young heterosexual adults' same-gender friendships. *Sex Roles, 74,* 422–435.

McHugh, M. C., & Hambaugh, J. (2010). She said, he said: Gender, language, and power. In J. Chrisler & D. McCreary (Eds.), *Handbook of gender research in psychology* (Vol. 1, pp. 379–410). New York: Springer.

McKibbin, W. F., Goetz, A. T., Shackelford, T. K., Schipper, L. D., Starratt, V. G., & Stewart-Williams, S. (2007). Why do men insult their intimate partners? *Personality and Individual Differences, 43,* 231–241.

McKinnish, T. G. (2007). Sexually integrated workplaces and divorce: Another form of on-the-job search. *Journal of Human Resources, 42,* 331–352.

McNulty, J. K. (2010). When positive processes hurt relationships. *Current Directions in Psychological Science, 19,* 167–171.

McNulty, J. K. (2011). The dark side of forgiveness: The tendency to forgive predicts continued psychological and physical aggression in marriage. *Personality and Social Psychology Bulletin, 37,* 770–783.

McNulty, J. K. (2016). Should spouses be demanding less from marriage? A contextual perspective on the implications of interpersonal standards. *Personality and Social Psychology Bulletin, 42,* 444–457.

McNulty, J. K., & Fincham, F. D. (2012). Beyond positive psychology? *American Psychologist, 67,* 101–110.

McNulty, J. K., & Karney, B. R. (2002). Expectancy confirmation in appraisals of marital interactions. *Personality and Social Psychology Bulletin, 28,* 764–775.

McNulty, J. K., & Russell, V. M. (2010). When "negative" behaviors are positive: A contextual analysis of the long-term effects of problem-solving behaviors on changes in relationship satisfaction. *Journal of Personality and Social Psychology, 98,* 587–604.

McNulty, J. K., Wenner, C. A., & Fisher, T. D. (2016). Longitudinal associations among relationship satisfaction, sexual satisfaction, and frequency of sex in early marriage. *Archives of Sexual Behavior, 45,* 85–97.

McPherson, M., Smith-Lovin, L., & Brashears, M. E. (2006). Social isolation in America: Changes in core discussion networks over two decades. *American Sociological Review, 71,* 353–375.

Mehl, M. R., & Conner, T. S. (Eds.). (2012). *Handbook of research methods for studying daily life.* New York: Guilford Press.

Mehl, M. R., & Robbins, M. L. (2012). Naturalistic observation sampling: The electronically activated recorder (EAR). In M. R. Mehl & T. S. Conner (Eds.), *Handbook of research methods for studying daily life* (pp. 176–192). New York: Guilford.

Mehl, M. R., Vazire, S., Holleran, S. E., & Clark, C. S. (2010). Eavesdropping on happiness: Well-being is related to having less small talk and more substantive conversations. *Psychological Science, 21,* 539–541.

Mehl, M. R., Vazire, S., Ramirez-Esparza, N., Slatcher, R. B., & Pennebaker, J. W. (2007). Are women really more talkative than men? *Science, 317,* 82.

Meier, A. M., Carr, D. R., & Currier, J. M. (2013). Attachment anxiety and avoidance in coping with bereavement: Two studies. *Journal of Social and Clinical Psychology, 32,* 315–334.

Mellor, D., Stokes, M., Firth, L., Hayashi, Y., & Cummins, R. (2008). Need for belonging, relationship satisfaction, loneliness, and life satisfaction. *Personality and Individual Differences, 45,* 213–218.

Meltzer, A. L. (2017). Wives with masculine husbands report increased marital satisfaction near peak fertility. *Evolutionary Behavioral Sciences, 11,* 161–172.

Meltzer, A. L., McNulty, J. K., Jackson, G. L., & Karney, B. R. (2014). Sex differences in the implications of partner physical attractiveness for the trajectory of marital satisfaction. *Journal of Personality and Social Psychology, 106,* 418–428.

Meltzer, A. L., McNulty, J. K., Novak, S. A., Butler, E. A., & Karney, B. R. (2011). Marriages are more satisfying when wives are thinner than their husbands. *Social Psychological and Personality Science, 2,* 416–424.

Meltzer, A. L., Novak, S. A., McNulty, J. K., Butler, E. A., & Karney, B. R. (2013). Marital satisfaction predicts weight gain in early marriage. *Health Psychology, 32,* 824–827.

Merali, N. (2012). Arranged and forced marriage. In M. A. Paludi (Ed.), *The psychology of love* (Vol. 3, pp. 143–168). Santa Barbara, CA: Praeger.

Merolla, A. J. (2014). The role of hope in conflict management and relational maintenance. *Personal Relationships, 21,* 365–386.

Merrill, A. F., & Afifi, T. D. (2015). Attachment-related differences in secrecy and rumination in romantic relationships. *Personal Relationships, 22,* 259–274.

Meston, C. M., & Buss, D. M. (2007). Why humans have sex. *Archives of Sexual Behavior, 36,* 477–507.

Metts, S. (1994). Relational transgressions. In W. R. Cupach & B. H. Spitzberg (Eds.), *The dark side of interpersonal communication* (pp. 217–239). Hillsdale, NJ: Erlbaum.

Metts, S., & Cupach, W. R. (1990). The influence of romantic beliefs and problem-solving responses on satisfaction in romantic relationships. *Human Communication Research, 17,* 170–185.

Meuwly, N., Bodenmann, G., Germann, J., Bradbury, T. N., Ditzen, B., & Heinrichs, M. (2012). Dyadic coping, insecure attachment, and cortisol stress recovery following experimentally induced stress. *Journal of Family Psychology, 26,* 937–947.

Michalski, R. L., Shackelford, T. K., & Salmon, C. A. (2007). Upset in response to a sibling's partner's infidelities. *Human Nature, 18,* 74–84.

Mickelson, K. D., Kessler, R. C., & Shaver, P. R. (1997). Adult attachment in a nationally representative sample. *Journal of Personality and Social Psychology, 73,* 1092–1106.

Mikulincer, M. (1998). Attachment working models and the sense of trust: An exploration of interaction goals and affect regulation. *Journal of Personality and Social Psychology, 74,* 1209–1224.

Mikulincer, M., & Shaver, P. R. (2013). The role of attachment security in adolescent and adult close relationships. In J. A. Simpson & L. Campbell (Eds.), *The Oxford handbook of close relationships* (pp. 66–89). New York: Oxford University Press.

Mikulincer M., & Shaver, P. R. (2016). *Attachment in adulthood: Structure, dynamics, and change* (2nd ed.). New York: Guilford Press.

Mikulincer, M., Shaver, P. R., & Avihou-Kanza, N. (2011). Individual differences in adult attachment are systematically related to dream narratives. *Attachment & Human Development, 13,* 105–123.

Milardo, R. M., Johnson, M. P., & Huston, T. L. (1983). Developing close relationships: Changing patterns of interaction between pair members and social networks. *Journal of Personality and Social Psychology, 44,* 964–976.

Miles, L. K. (2009). Who is approachable? *Journal of Experimental Social Psychology, 45,* 262–266.

Miller, G. E., & Chen, E. (2010). Harsh family climate in early life presages the emergence of a pro-inflammatory phenotype in adolescence. *Psychological Science, 21,* 848–856.

Miller, J. B., & Noirot, M. (1999). Attachment memories, models and information processing. *Journal of Social and Personal Relationships, 16,* 147–173.

Miller, L. C., Berg, J. H., & Archer, R. L. (1983). Openers: Individuals who elicit intimate self-disclosure. *Journal of Personality and Social Psychology, 44,* 1234–1244.

Miller, M. A., & Rahe, R. H. (1997). Life changes scaling for the 1990s. *Journal of Psychomatic Research, 43,* 279–292.

Miller, M. J., Denes, A., Diaz, B., & Buck, R. (2014). Attachment style predicts jealous reactions to viewing touch between a romantic partner and close friend: Implications for internet social communication. *Journal of Nonverbal Behavior, 38,* 451–476.

Miller, P. J. E., Caughlin, J. P., & Huston, T. L. (2003). Trait expressiveness and marital satisfaction: The role of idealization processes. *Journal of Marriage and the Family, 65,* 978–995.

Miller, P. J. E., Niehuis, S., & Huston, T. L. (2006). Positive illusions in marital relationships: A 13-year longitudinal study. *Personality and Social Psychology Bulletin, 32,* 1579–1594.

Miller, P. J. E., & Rempel, J. K. (2004). Trust and partner-enhancing attributions in close relationships. *Personality and Social Psychology Bulletin, 30,* 695–705.

Miller, R. S. (1996). *Embarrassment: Poise and peril in everyday life.* New York: Guilford Press.

Miller, R. S. (1997a). Inattentive and contented: Relationship commitment and attention to alternatives. *Journal of Personality and Social Psychology, 73,* 758–766.

Miller, R. S. (1997b). We always hurt the ones we love: Aversive interactions in close relationships. In R. Kowalski (Ed.), *Aversive interpersonal interactions* (pp. 11–29). New York: Plenum.

Miller, R. S. (2001). Breaches of propriety. In R. M. Kowalski (Ed.), *Behaving badly: Aversive behaviors in interpersonal relationships* (pp. 29–58). Washington, DC: American Psychological Association.

Miller, R. S. (2008). Attending to temptation: The operation (and perils) of attention to alternatives in close relationships. In J. P. Forgas & J. Fitness (Eds.), *Social relationships: Cognitive, affective and motivational processes* (pp. 321–337). New York: Psychology Press.

Miller, R. S. (2009). Social anxiousness, shyness, and embarrassability. In M. R. Leary & R. H. Hoyle (Eds.), *Handbook of individual differences in social behavior* (pp. 176–191). New York: Guilford Press.

Miller, R. S., Bernhard, P., & Bowen, T. (2014, July). *Who are some of these people? An analysis of Facebook "friends."* Paper presented at the meeting of the International Association for Relationship Research, Melbourne, Australia.

Miller, R. S., & Schlenker, B. R. (1985). Egotism in group members: Public and private attributions of responsibility for group performance. *Social Psychology Quarterly, 48,* 85–89.

Miller, S. L., & Maner, J. K. (2008). Coping with romantic betrayal: Sex differences in responses to partner infidelity. *Evolutionary Psychology, 6,* 413–426.

Miller, S. L., & Maner, J. K. (2010). Scent of a woman: Men's testosterone responses to olfactory ovulation cues. *Psychological Science, 21,* 276–283.

Miller, S. L., & Maner, J. K. (2011). Ovulation as a male mating prime: Subtle signs of women's fertility influence men's mating cognition and behavior. *Journal of Personality and Social Psychology, 100,* 295–308.

Miller, W. B., Sable, M. R., & Beckmeyer, J. J. (2009). Preconception motivation and pregnancy wantedness: Pathways to toddler attachment security. *Journal of Marriage and Family, 71,* 1174–1192.

Miller-Ott, A. E., & Kelly, L. (2016). Competing discourses and meaning making in talk about romantic partners' cell-phone contact with non-present others. *Communication Studies, 67,* 58–76.

Miller-Ott, A. E., Kelly, L., & Duran, R. L. (2012). The effects of cell phone usage rules on satisfaction in romantic relationships. *Communication Quarterly, 60,* 17–34.

Mills, J., Clark, M. S., Ford, T. E., & Johnson, M. (2004). Measurement of communal strength. *Personal Relationships, 11,* 213–230.

Mills, P. J., Redwine, L., Wilson, K., & . . . Chopra, D. (2015). The role of gratitude in spiritual well-being in asymptomatic heart failure patients. *Spirituality in Clinical Practice, 2,* 5–17

Milojev, P., & Sibley, C. G. (2017). Normative personality trait development in adulthood: A 6-year cohort-sequential growth model. *Journal of Personality and Social Psychology, 112,* 510–526.

Mischkowski, D., Kross, E., & Bushman, B. J. (2012). Flies on the wall are less aggressive: Self-distancing "in the heat of the moment" reduces aggressive thoughts, angry feelings, and aggressive behavior. *Journal of Experimental Social Psychology, 48,* 1187–1191.

Mitchell, A. E., Castellani, A. M., Herrington, R. L., Joseph, J. I., Doss, B. D., & Snyder, D. K. (2008). Predictors of intimacy in couples' discussions of relationship injuries: An observational study. *Journal of Family Psychology, 22,* 21–29.

Mitchell, C. (2010). Are divorce studies trustworthy? The effects of survey nonresponse and response errors. *Journal of Marriage and Family, 72,* 893–905.

Mitchell, J. W., Lee, J., Woodyatt, C., & . . . Stephenson, R. (2016). Perceived challenges and rewards of forming a sexual agreement among HIV-negative male couples. *Archives of Sexual Behavior, 45,* 1525–1534.

Mitchell, K., & Sugar, M. (2007, November 8). Annie's mailbox. *The Bryan-College Station Eagle,* A6.

Mitchell, K., & Sugar, M. (2008, January 24). Annie's mailbox. *The Bryan-College Station Eagle,* B2.

Mitchell, S. A. (2002). *Can love last? The fate of romance over time.* New York: Norton.

Mogilski, J. K., & Welling, L. L. M. (2017). Staying friends with an ex: Sex and dark personality traits predict motivations for post-relationship friendship. *Personality and Individual Differences, 115,* 114–119.

Moilanen, K. L. (2015). Short- and long-term self-regulation and sexual risk-taking behaviors in unmarried heterosexual young adults. *Journal of Sex Research, 52,* 758–769.

Monfort, S. S., Kaczmarek, L. D., Kashdan, T. B., & . . . Gracanin, A. (2014). Capitalizing on the success of romantic partners: A laboratory investigation on subjective, facial, and physiological emotional processing. *Personality and Individual Differences, 68,* 149–153.

Mongeau, P. A., Knight, K., Williams, J., Eden, J., & Shaw, C. (2013). Identifying and explicating variation among friends with benefits relationships. *Journal of Sex Research, 50,* 37–47.

Montoya, R. M. (2008). I'm hot, so I'd say you're not: The influence of objective physical attractiveness on mate selection. *Personality and Social Psychology Bulletin, 34,* 1315–1331.

Montoya, R. M., & Horton, R. S. (2004). On the importance of cognitive evaluation as a determinant of interpersonal attraction. *Journal of Personality & Social Psychology, 86,* 696–712.

Montoya, R. M., & Horton, R. S. (2013). A meta-analytic investigation of the processes underlying the similarity-attraction effect. *Journal of Social and Personal Relationships, 30,* 64–94.

Montoya, R. M., & Horton, R. S. (2014). A two-dimensional model for the study of interpersonal attraction. *Personality and Social Psychology Review, 18,* 59–86.

Mooney, L., Strelan, P., & McKee, I. (2016). How forgiveness promotes offender pro-relational intentions: The mediating role of offender gratitude. *British Journal of Social Psychology, 55,* 44–64.

Moore, T. M., Stuart, G. L., McNulty, J. K., Addis, M. E., Cordova, J. V., & Temple, J. R. (2008). Domains of masculine gender role stress and intimate partner violence in a clinical sample of violent men. *Psychology of Men & Masculinity, 9,* 82–89.

Moreland, R. L., & Beach, S. R. (1992). Exposure effects in the classroom: The development of affinity among students. *Journal of Experimental Social Psychology, 28,* 255–276.

Moreno, J. L. (1934). *Who shall survive? A new approach to the problem of human interrelationships.* Washington, DC: Nervous and Mental Disease Publishing.

Morgentaler, A. (2003). *The Viagra myth: The surprising impact on love and relationships.* San Francisco: Jossey-Bass.

Morin, R., & Cohn, D. (2008, September 25). Women call the shots at home; public mixed on gender roles in jobs. *Pew Research Center.* Retrieved from http://pewresearch.org/pubs/967/gender-power

Morris, C. E., Reiber, C., & Roman, E. (2015). Quantitative sex differences in response to the dissolution of a romantic relationship. *Evolutionary Behavioral Sciences, 9,* 270–282.

Morrow, G. D., Clark, E. M., & Brock, K. F. (1995). Individual and partner love styles: Implications for the quality of romantic involvements. *Journal of Social and Personal Relationships, 12,* 363–387.

Morry, M. M., Kito, M., Mann, S., & Hill, L. (2013). Relational-interdependent self-construal: Perceptions of friends and friendship quality. *Journal of Social and Personal Relationships, 30,* 44–63.

Morry, M. M., Kito, M., & Ortiz, L. (2011). The attraction–similarity model and dating couples: Projection, perceived similarity, and psychological benefits. *Personal Relationships, 18,* 125–143.

Moss-Racusin, C. A., & Rudman, L. A. (2010). Disruptions in women's self-promotion: The backlash avoidance model. *Psychology of Women Quarterly, 34,* 186–202.

Muehlenhard, C. L., & Peterson, Z. D. (2011). Distinguishing between *sex* and *gender:* History, current conceptualizations, and implications. *Sex Roles, 64,* 791–803.

Muise, A., Boudreau, G. K., & Rosen, N. O. (2017). Seeking connection versus avoiding disappointment: An experimental manipulation of approach and avoidance sexual goals and the implications for desire and satisfaction. *Journal of Sex Research, 54,* 296–307.

Muise, A., Christofides, E., & Desmarais, S. (2009). More information than you ever wanted: Does Facebook bring out the green-eyed monster of jealousy? *Cyberpsychology & Behavior, 12,* 441–444.

Muise, A., Christofides, E., & Desmarais, S. (2014). "Creeping" or just information seeking? Gender differences in partner monitoring in response to jealousy on Facebook. *Personal Relationships, 21,* 35–50.

Muise, A., & Impett, E. A. (2016). Applying theories of communal motivation to sexuality. *Social and Personality Psychology Compass, 10,* 455–467.

Muise, A., Impett, E. A., & Desmarais, S. (2013). Getting it on versus getting it over with: Sexual motivation, desire, and satisfaction in intimate bonds. *Personality and Social Psychology Bulletin, 39,* 1320–1332.

Muise, A., Schimmack, U., & Impett, E. A. (2016a). Sexual frequency predicts greater well-being, but more is not always better. *Social Psychological and Personality Science, 7,* 295–302.

Muise, A., Stanton, S. C. E., Kim, J. J., & Impett, E. A. (2016b). Not in the mood? Men under- (not over-) perceive their partner's sexual desire in established intimate relationships. *Journal of Personality and Social Psychology, 110,* 725–742.

Mund, M., Finn, C., Hagemeyer, B., & Neyer, F. J. (2016). Understanding dynamic transactions between personality traits and partner relationships. *Current Directions in Psychological Science, 25,* 411–416.

Mund, M., Finn, C., Hagemeyer, B., Zimmermann, J., & Neyer, F. J. (2015). The dynamics of self-esteem in partner relationships. *European Journal of Personality, 29,* 235–249.

Mundy, L. (2012). *The richer sex: How the new majority of female breadwinners is transforming sex, love, and family.* New York: Simon & Schuster.

Murray, S. L., Aloni, M., Holmes, J. G., Derrick, J. L., Stinson, D. A., & Leder, S. (2009). Fostering partner dependence as trust insurance: The implicit contingencies of the exchange script in close relationships. *Journal of Personality and Social Psychology, 96,* 324–348.

Murray, S. L., Bellavia, G. M., Rose, P., & Griffin, D. W. (2003). Once hurt, twice hurtful: How perceived regard regulates daily marital interactions. *Journal of Personality and Social Psychology, 84,* 126–147.

Murray, S. L., Griffin, D. W., Derrick, J. L, Harris, B., Aloni, M., & Leder, S. (2011). Tempting fate or inviting happiness? Unrealistic idealization prevents the decline of marital satisfaction. *Psychological Science, 22,* 619–626.

Murray, S. L., Griffin, D. W., Rose, P., & Bellavia, G. M. (2003). Calibrating the sociometer: The relational contingencies of self-esteem. *Journal of Personality and Social Psychology, 85,* 63–84.

Murray, S. L., Holmes, J. G., Derrick, J. L., Harris, B., Griffin, D. W., & Pinkus, R. T. (2013). Cautious to a fault: Self-protection and the trajectory of marital satisfaction. *Journal of Experimental Social Psychology, 49,* 522–533.

Murray, S. L., Holmes, J. G., & Griffin, D. W. (1996). The self-fulfilling nature of positive illusions in romantic relationships: Love is not blind, but prescient. *Journal of Personality and Social Psychology, 71,* 1155–1180.

Murray, S. L., Holmes, J. G., & Griffin, D. W. (2000). Self-esteem and the quest for felt security: How perceived regard regulates attachment processes. *Journal of Personality and Social Psychology, 78,* 478–498.

Murray, S. L., Holmes, J. G., Griffin, D. W., Bellavia, G., & Rose, P. (2001). The mismeasure of love: How self-doubt contaminates relationship beliefs. *Personality and Social Psychology Bulletin, 27,* 423–436.

Murray, S. L., Rose, P., Bellavia, G. M., Holmes, J. G., & Kusche, A. G. (2002). When rejection stings: How self-esteem constrains relationship-enhancement processes. *Journal of Personality and Social Psychology, 83,* 556–573.

Murstein, B. I. (1987). A clarification and extension of the SVR theory of dyadic pairing. *Journal of Marriage and the Family, 49,* 929–933.

Muscanell, N. L., Guadagno, R. E., Rice, L., & Murphy, S. (2013). Don't it make my brown eyes green? An analysis of Facebook use and romantic jealousy. *Cyberpsychology, Behavior, and Social Networking, 16,* 237–242.

Myers, D. (2013). Sexual orientation, marriage, and students of faith. In D. Dunn, R. Gurung, K. Naufel, & J. Wilson (Eds.), *Controversy in the psychology classroom: Using hot topics to foster critical thinking* (pp. 81–104). Washington, DC: American Psychological Association.

Myers, D. G. (2008). *Social psychology* (9th ed.). Boston: McGraw-Hill.

Myers, D. G. (2016). Is narcissism extreme self-esteem? *Observer, 29*(3), 35–36.

Myers, S. A., & Berscheid, E. (1997). The language of love: The difference a preposition makes. *Personality and Social Psychology Bulletin, 23,* 347–362.

Nater, C., & Zell, E. (2015). Accuracy of social perception: An integration and review of meta-analyses. *Social and Personality Psychology Compass, 9,* 481–494.

National Center for Health Statistics (2013). *Number of sexual partners in lifetime.* Retrieved from https://www.cdc.gov/nchs/nsfg/key_statistics/n.htm#numberlifetime

Nedelec, J. L., & Beaver, K. M. (2014). Physical attractiveness as a phenotypic marker of health: An assessment using a nationally representative sample of American adults. *Evolution and Human Behavior, 35,* 456–463.

Ne'eman, R., Perach-Barzialy, N., Fischer-Shofty, M., Atias, A., & Shamaty-Tsoory, S. G. (2016). Intranasal administration of oxytocin increases human aggressive behavior. *Hormones and Behavior, 80,* 125–131.

Neff, L. A., & Broady, E. F. (2011). Stress resilience in early marriage: Can practice make perfect? *Journal of Personality and Social Psychology, 101,* 1050–1067.

Neff, L. A., & Geers, A. L. (2013). Optimistic expectations in early marriage: A resource or vulnerability for adaptive relationship functioning? *Journal of Personality and Social Psychology, 105,* 38–60.

Neff, L. A., & Karney, B. R. (2002). Judgments of a relationship partner: Specific accuracy but global enhancement. *Journal of Personality, 70,* 1079–1112.

Neff, L. A., & Karney, B. R. (2003). The dynamic structure of relationship perceptions: Differential importance as a strategy of relationship maintenance. *Personality and Social Psychology Bulletin, 29,* 1433–1446.

Neff, L. A., & Karney, B. R. (2005). To know you is to love you: The implications of global adoration and specific accuracy for marital relationships. *Journal of Personality and Social Psychology, 88,* 480–497.

Neff, L. A., & Karney, B. R. (2009). Compassionate love in early marriage. In B. Fehr, S. Sprecher, & L. Underwood (Eds.), *The science of compassionate love: Theory: research, and applications* (pp. 201–221). Chichester, England: Wiley-Blackwell.

Negash, S., Cui, M., Fincham, F. D., & Pasley, K. (2014). Extradyadic involvement and relationship dissolution in heterosexual women university students. *Archives of Sexual Behavior, 43,* 531–539.

Neighbors, C., Walker, D. D., Mbilinyi, L. F., O'Rourke, A., Edleson, J. L., Zegree, J., & Roffman, R. A. (2010). Normative misperceptions of abuse among perpetrators of intimate partner violence. *Violence Against Women, 16,* 370–386.

Nelson, L. D., & Morrison, E. L. (2005). The symptoms of resource scarcity: Judgments of food and finances influence preferences for potential partners. *Psychological Science, 16,* 167–173.

Nelson, S. K., Kushlev, K., English, T., Dunn, E. W., & Lyubomirsky, S. (2013). In defense of parenthood: Children are associated with more joy than misery. *Psychological Science, 24,* 3–10.

Neppl, T. K., Senia, J. M., & Donnellan, M. B. (2016). Effects of economic hardship: Testing the family stress model over time. *Journal of Family Psychology, 30,* 12–21.

Nestler, S., & Back, M. D. (2013). Applications and extensions of the lens model to understand interpersonal judgments at zero acquaintance. *Current Directions in Psychological Science, 22,* 374–379.

Newall, N. E., Chipperfield, J. G., Clifton, R. A., Perry, R. P., Swift, A. U., & Ruthig, J. C. (2009). Causal beliefs, social participation, and loneliness among older adults: A longitudinal study. *Journal of Social and Personal Relationships, 26,* 273–290.

Newcomb, T. M. (1961). *The acquaintance process.* New York: Holt, Rinehart & Winston.

Nezlek, J. B., & Leary, M. R. (2002). Individual differences in self-presentational motives in daily social interaction. *Personality and Social Psychology Bulletin, 28,* 211–223.

Nezlek, J. B., Schütz, A., & Sellin, I. (2007). Self-presentational success in daily interaction. *Self and Identity, 6,* 361–379.

Nicholls, T. L., & Hamel, J. (2015). Intimate partner violence. In B. Cutler & P. Zapf (Eds.), *APA handbook of forensic psychology, Vol. 1: Individual and situational influences in criminal and civil contexts* (pp. 381–422). Washington, DC: American Psychological Association.

Niehuis, S., Lee, K., Reifman, A., Swenson, A., & Hunsaker, S. (2011). Idealization and disillusionment in intimate relationships: A review of theory, method, and research. *Journal of Family Therapy, 3,* 273–302.

Niehuis, S., Reifman, A., Feng, D., & Huston, T. L. (2016). Courtship progression rate and declines in expressed affection early in marriage: A test of the disillusionment model. *Journal of Family Issues, 37,* 1074–1100.

Niehuis, S., Reifman, A., & Lee, K. (2015). Disillusionment in cohabiting and married couples: A national study. *Journal of Family Issues, 36,* 951–973.

Nissan, T., Shapira, O., & Liberman, N. (2015). Effects of power on mental rotation and emotion recognition in women. *Personality and Social Psychology Bulletin, 41,* 1425–1437.

Noller, P. (1980). Misunderstandings in marital communication: A study of couples' nonverbal communications. *Journal of Personality and Social Psychology, 39,* 1135–1148.

Noller, P. (1981). Gender and marital adjustment level differences in decoding messages from spouses and strangers. *Journal of Personality and Social Psychology, 41,* 272–278.

Noller, P. (2006). Nonverbal communication in close relationships. In V. Manusov & M. L. Patterson (Eds.), *The Sage handbook of nonverbal communication* (pp. 403–420). Thousand Oaks, CA: Sage.

Noller, P. (2012). Conflict in family relationships. In P. Noller & G. C. Karantzas (Eds.), *The Wiley-Blackwell handbook of couple and family relationships* (pp. 129–143). Hoboken, NJ: Wiley.

Noller, P., & Venardos, C. (1986). Communication awareness in married couples. *Journal of Social and Personal Relationships, 3,* 31–42.

North, R. J., Holahan, C. J., Moos, R. H., & Cronkite, R. C. (2008). Family support, family income, and happiness: A 10-year perspective. *Journal of Family Psychology, 22,* 475–483.

Norton, M. I., Frost, J. H., & Ariely, D. (2007). Less is more: The lure of ambiguity, or why familiarity breeds contempt. *Journal of Personality and Social Psychology, 92,* 97–105.

Norton, M. I., Frost, J. H., & Ariely, D. (2013). Less is often more, but not always: Additional evidence that familiarity breeds contempt and a call for future research. *Journal of Personality and Social Psychology, 105,* 921–923.

Notarius, C. I., Lashley, S. L., & Sullivan, D. J. (1997). Angry at your partner? Think again. In R. J. Sternberg & M. Hojjat (Eds.), *Satisfaction in close relationships* (pp. 219–248). New York: Guilford Press.

Oakman, J., Gifford, S., & Chlebowsky, N. (2003). A multilevel analysis of the interpersonal behavior of socially anxious people. *Journal of Personality, 71,* 397–434.

O'Boyle, E. H., Forsyth, D. R., Banks, G. C., Story, P. A., & White, C. D. (2015). A meta-analytic test of redundancy and relative importance of the Dark Triad and Five-Factor Model of personality. *Journal of Personality, 83,* 644–664.

Ochs, E., & Kremer-Sadlik, T. (2013). *Fast-forward family: Home, work, and relationships in middle-class America.* Berkeley: University of California Press.

O'Connell, D., & Marcus, D. K. (2016). Psychopathic personality traits predict positive attitudes toward sexually predatory behaviors in college men and women. *Personality and Individual Differences, 94,* 372–376.

O'Connor, J. J. M., Fraccaro, P. J., Pisanski, K., & . . . Feinberg, D. R. (2014). Social dialect and men's voice pitch influence women's mate preferences. *Evolution and Human Behavior, 35,* 368–375.

OECD. (2016). *SF3.1: Marriage and divorce rates.* Organisation for Economic Co-operation and Development. Retrieved from https://www.oecd.org/els/family/database.htm.

Ogolsky, B. G., & Bowers, J. R. (2013). A meta-analytic review of relationship maintenance and its correlates. *Journal of Social and Personal Relationships, 30,* 343–367.

Ogolsky, B. G., Dennison, R. P., & Monk, J. K. (2014). The role of couple discrepancies in cognitive and behavioral egalitarianism in marital quality. *Sex Roles, 70,* 320–342.

Ogolsky, B. G., & Monk, J. K. (2018). Maintaining relationships. In A. Vangelisti & D. Perlman (Eds.), *Cambridge handbook of personal relationships* (2nd ed.) New York: Cambridge University Press.

Ogolsky, B. G., & Surra, C. A. (2014). A comparison of concurrent and retrospective trajectories of commitment to wed. *Personal Relationships, 21,* 620–639.

Ogolsky, B. G., Surra, C. A., & Monk, J. K. (2016). Pathways of commitment to wed: The development and dissolution of romantic relationships. *Journal of Marriage and Family, 78,* 293–310.

Oh, S. Y., Bailenson, J., Krämer, N., & Li, B. (2016). Let the avatar brighten your smile: Effects of enhancing facial expressions in virtual environments. *PloS One, 11,* e0161794.

Ohtsubo, Y., Matsumura, A., Noda, C., & . . . Yamaguchi, M. (2014). It's the attention that counts: interpersonal attention fosters intimacy and social exchange. *Evolution and Human Behavior, 35,* 237–244.

Ohtsubo, Y., & Yagi, A. (2015). Relationship value promotes costly apology-making: testing the valuable relationships hypothesis from the perpetrator's perspective. *Evolution and Human Behavior, 36,* 232–239.

Oishi, S. (2010). The psychology of residential mobility: Implications for the self, social relationships, and well-being. *Perspectives on Psychological Science, 5,* 5–21.

Okimoto, T. G., & Brescoll, V. L. (2010). The price of power: Power seeking and backlash against female politicians. *Personality and Social Psychology Bulletin, 36,* 923–936.

Olatunji, B. O., Lohr, J. M., & Bushman, B. J. (2007). The pseudopsychology of venting in the treatment of anger: Implications and alternatives for mental health practice. In T. A. Cavell & K. T. Malcolm (Eds.), *Anger, aggression, and interventions for interpersonal violence* (pp. 119–141). Mahwah, NJ: Erlbaum.

O'Leary, K. D., Acevedo, B. P., Aron, A., Huddy, L., & Mashek, D. (2012). Is long-term love more than a rare phenomenon? If so, what are its correlates? *Social Psychological and Personality Science, 3,* 241–249.

Olivola, C. Y., & Todorov, A. (2010a). Elected in 100 milliseconds: Appearance-based trait inferences and voting. *Journal of Nonverbal Behavior, 34,* 83–110.

Olivola, C. Y., & Todorov, A. (2010b). Fooled by first impressions? Reexamining the diagnostic value of appearance-based inferences. *Journal of Experimental Social Psychology, 46,* 315–324.

Olmstead, S. B., Negash, S., Pasley, K., & Fincham, F. D. (2013). Emerging adults' expectations for pornography use in the context of future committed romantic relationships: A qualitative study. *Archives of Sexual Behavior, 42,* 625–635.

Olson, I. R., & Marshuetz, C. (2005). Facial attractiveness is appraised in a glance. *Emotion, 5,* 498–502.

Online dating statistics. (2017, July). Retrieved from http://www.statisticbrain.com/online-dating-statistics/

Orbuch, T. L. (2009). *5 simple steps to take your marriage from good to great.* New York: Delacorte Press.

Oriña, M. M., Collins, W. A., Simpson, J. A., Salvatore, J. E., Haydon, K. C., & Kim, J. S. (2011). Developmental and dyadic perspectives on commitment in adult romantic relationships. *Psychological Science, 22,* 908–915.

Oriña, M. M., Wood, W., & Simpson, J. A. (2002). Strategies of influence in close relationships. *Journal of Experimental Social Psychology, 38,* 459–472.

Ormiston, M. E., Wong, E. M., & Haselhuhn, M. P. (2017). Facial-width-to-height ratio predicts perceptions of integrity in males. *Personality and Individual Differences, 105,* 40–42.

Orth, U., & Robins, R. W. (2014). The development of self-esteem. *Current Directions in Psychological Science, 23,* 381–387.

Osman, M., Pupic, D., & Baigent, N. (2017). How many slaps is equivalent to one punch? New approaches to assessing the relative severity of violent acts. *Psychology of Violence, 7,* 69–81.

Osterhout, R. E., Frame, L. E., & Johnson, M. D. (2011). Maladaptive attributions and dyadic behavior are associated in engaged couples. *Journal of Social and Clinical Psychology, 30,* 787–818.

Ostovich, J. M., & Sabini, J. (2004). How are sociosexuality, sex drive, and lifetime number of sexual partners related? *Personality and Social Psychology Bulletin, 30,* 1255–1266.

Oswald, D. L., & Clark, E. M. (2006). How do friendship maintenance behaviors and problem-solving styles function at the individual and dyadic levels? *Personal Relationships, 13,* 333–348.

Oswald, D. L., Clark, E. M., & Kelly, C. M. (2004). Friendship maintenance: An analysis of individual and dyad behaviors. *Journal of Social and Clinical Psychology, 23,* 413–441.

Overall, N. C. (2012). The costs and benefits of trying to change intimate partners. In P. Noller & G. C. Karantzas (Eds.), *The Wiley-Blackwell handbook of couple and family relationships* (pp. 234–247). Hoboken, NJ: Wiley.

Overall, N. C., Girme, Y. U., Lemay, E. P., Jr., & Hammond, M. D. (2014). Attachment anxiety and reactions to relationship threat: The benefits and costs of inducing guilt in romantic partners. *Journal of Personality and Social Psychology, 106,* 235–256.

Overall, N. C., Fletcher, G. J. O., & Simpson, J. A. (2010a). Helping each other grow: Romantic partner support, self-improvement, and relationship quality. *Personality and Social Psychology Bulletin, 36,* 1496–1513.

Overall, N. C., Fletcher, G. J. O., Simpson, J. A., & Fillo, J. (2015). Attachment insecurity, biased perceptions of romantic partners' negative emotions, and hostile relationship behavior. *Journal of Personality and Social Psychology, 108,* 730–749.

Overall, N. C., Fletcher, G. O., Simpson, J. A., & Sibley, C. G. (2009). Regulating partners in intimate relationships: The costs and benefits of different communication strategies. *Journal of Personality and Social Psychology, 96,* 620–639.

Overall, N. C., & Sibley, C. G. (2008). Attachment and attraction toward romantic partners versus relevant alternatives within daily interactions. *Personality and Individual Differences, 44,* 1126–1137.

Overall, N. C., Sibley, C. G., & Travaglia, L. K. (2010b). Loyal but ignored: The benefits and costs of constructive communication behavior. *Personal Relationships, 17,* 127–148.

Overall, N. C., & Simpson, J. A. (2013). Regulation processes in close relationships. In J. A. Simpson & L. Campbell (Eds.), *The Oxford handbook of close relationships* (pp. 427–451). New York: Oxford University Press.

Overall, N. C., Simpson, J. A., & Struthers, H. (2013). Buffering attachment-related avoidance: Softening emotional and behavioral defenses during conflict discussions. *Journal of Personality and Social Psychology, 104,* 854–871.

Owen, J., Fincham, F. D., & Manthos, M. (2013). Friendship after a friends with benefits relationship: Deception, psychological functioning, and social connectedness. *Archives of Sexual Behavior, 42,* 1443–1449.

Owen, P. R., & Laurel-Seller, E. (2000). Weight and shape ideals: Thin is dangerously in. *Journal of Applied Social Psychology, 30,* 979–990.

Pachankis, J. E., Cochran, S. D., & Mays, V. M. (2015). The mental health of sexual minority adults in and out of the closet: A population-based study. *Journal of Consulting and Clinical Psychology, 83,* 890–901.

Padgett, P. M. (2007). Personal safety and sexual safety for women using online personal ads. *Sexuality Research & Social Policy, 4,* 27–37.

Paik, A. (2011). Adolescent sexuality and the risk of marital dissolution. *Journal of Marriage and Family, 73,* 472–485.

Paik, A., Sanchagrin, K. J., & Heimer, K. (2016). Broken promises: Abstinence pledging and sexual and reproductive health. *Journal of Marriage and Family, 78,* 546–561.

Palomares, N. A. (2009). Women are sort of more tentative than men, aren't they? How men and women use tentative language differently, similarly, and counterstereotypically as a function of gender salience. *Communication Research, 36,* 538–560.

Papp, L. M., Cummings, E. M., & Goeke-Morey, M. C. (2009). For richer, for poorer: Money as a topic of marital conflict in the home. *Family Relations, 58,* 91–103.

Papp, L. M., Danielewicz, J., & Cayemberg, C. (2012). "Are we Facebook official?" Implications of dating partners' Facebook use and profiles for intimate relationship satisfaction. *Cyberpsychology, Behavior, and Social Networking, 15,* 85–90.

Park, G., Schwartz, H. A., Eichstaedt, J. C., Kern, M. L., Kosinski, M., & Stillwell, D. J. (2014). Automatic personality assessment through social media language. *Journal of Personality and Social Psychology, 108,* 934–952.

Park, H. S., & Levine, T. R. (2015). Base rates, deception detection, and deception theory: A reply to Burgoon (2015). *Human Communication Research, 41,* 350–366.

Parks-Leduc, L., Pattie, M. W., Pargas, F., & Eliason, R. G. (2014). Self-monitoring as an aggregate construct: Relationships with personality and values. *Personality and Individual Differences, 58,* 3–8.

Pascoal, P. M., de Santa Bárbara Narciso, I., & Pereira, N. M. (2014). What is sexual satisfaction? Thematic analysis of lay people's definitions. *Journal of Sex Research, 51,* 22–30.

Patterson, M. L. (2011). *More than words: The power of nonverbal communication.* Barcelona, Spain: Aresta.

Paul, A. (2014). Is online better than offline for meeting partners? Depends: Are you looking to marry or to date? *Cyberpsychology, Behavior, and Social Networking, 17,* 664–667.

Payne, J. W. (2006, January 8). Health risk indicator may be all in the belly. *Houston Chronicle,* p. G7.

Pazda, A. D., Prokop, P., & Elliot, A. J. (2014). Red and romantic rivalry: Viewing another woman in red increases perceptions of sexual receptivity, derogation, and intentions to mate-guard. *Personality and Social Psychology Bulletin, 40,* 1260–1269.

Pazzaglia, M. (2015). Body and odors: Not just molecules, after all. *Current Directions in Psychological Science, 24,* 329–333.

Pearce, A. R., Chuikova, T., Ramsey, A., & Galyautdinova, S. (2010). A positive psychology perspective on mate preferences in the United States and Russia. *Journal of Cross-Cultural Psychology, 41,* 742–757.

Pearson, J. C., Child, J. T., & Carmon, A. F. (2011). Rituals in dating relationships: The development and validation of a measure. *Communication Quarterly, 59,* 359–379.

Pedersen, W. C., Miller, L. C., Putcha-Bhagavatula, A. D., & Yang, Y. (2002). Evolved sex differences in the number of partners desired? The long and the short of it. *Psychological Science, 13,* 157–161.

Peer, E., Acquisti, A., & Shalvi, S. (2014). "I cheated, but only a little": Partial confessions to unethical behavior. *Journal of Personality and Social Psychology, 106,* 202–217.

Peetz, J., & Kammrath, L. (2011). Only because I love you: Why people make and why they break promises in romantic relationships. *Journal of Personality and Social Psychology, 100,* 887–904.

Peipert, J. F., Madden, T., Allsworth, J. E., & Secura, G. M. (2012). Preventing unintended pregnancies by providing no-cost contraception. *Obstetrics and Gynecology, 120,* 1291–1297.

Pelham, B. W., Carvallo, M., & Jones, J. T. (2005). Implicit egotism. *Current Directions in Psychological Science, 14,* 106–110.

Peplau, L. A., & Fingerhut, A. W. (2007). The close relationships of lesbians and gay men. *Annual Review of Psychology, 58,* 405–424.

Peplau, L. A., Fingerhut, A., & Beals, K. P. (2004). Sexuality in the relationships of lesbians and gay men. In J. H. Harvey, A. Wenzel, & S. Sprecher (Eds.), *The handbook of sexuality in close relationships* (pp. 349–369). Mahwah, NJ: Erlbaum.

Perelli-Harris, B., & Lyons-Amos, M. (2015). Changes in partnership patterns across the life course: An examination of 14 countries in Europe and the United States. *Demographic Research, 33,* 145–178.

Perilloux, C., Duntley, J. D., & Buss, D. M. (2012). The costs of rape. *Archives of Sexual Behavior, 41,* 1099–1106.

Perilloux, H. K., Webster, G. D., & Gaulin, S. J. C. (2010). Signals of genetic quality and maternal investment capacity: The dynamic effects of fluctuating asymmetry and waist-to-hip ratio on men's ratings of women's attractiveness. *Social Psychology and Personality Science, 1,* 34–42.

Perlman, D., Stevens, N. L., & Carcedo, R. J. (2015). Friendship. In M. Mikulincer, P. Shaver, J. Simpson, & J. Dovidio (Eds.), *APA handbook of personality and social psychology: Vol. 3. Interpersonal relations* (pp. 463–493). Washington, DC: American Psychological Association.

Perrett, D. (2010). *In your face: The new science of human attraction.* New York: Palgrave Macmillan.

Petersen, J. L., & Hyde, J. S. (2010). A meta-analytic review of research on gender differences in sexuality, 1993-2007. *Psychological Bulletin, 136,* 21–38.

Peterson, D. R. (2002). Conflict. In H. H. Kelley, E. Berscheid, A. Christensen, et al. (Eds.), *Close relationships* (pp. 265–314). Clinton Corners, NY: Percheron Press.

Petit, W. E., & Ford, T. E. (2015). Effect of relationship status on perceptions of physical attractiveness for alternative partners. *Personal Relationships, 22,* 348–355.

Petronio, S. (2010). Communication privacy management theory: What do we know about family privacy regulation? *Journal of Family Theory & Review, 2,* 175–196.

Pew Research. (2015, June 26). *Gay marriage around the world.* Retrieved from http://www.pewforum.org/2015/06/26/gay-marriage-around-the-world-2013/

Pew Research. (2017, June 26). *Support for same-sex marriage grows, even among groups that had been skeptical.* Retrieved from http://www.people-press.org/2017/06/26/support-for-same-sex-marriage-grows-even-among-groups-that-had-been-skeptical/

Pew Research Center. (2013, June). *A survey of LGBT Americans: Attitudes, experiences and values in changing times.* Washington, DC: Pew Research Center. Retrieved from pewresearch.org/lgbt.

Pew Research Center. (2013, June). *In gay marriage debate, both supporters and opponents see legal recognition as "inevitable."* Retrieved from http://www.people-press.org/2013/06/06/in-gay-marriage-debate-both-supporters-and-opponents-see-legal-recognition-as-inevitable/

Pew Research Center. (2015a, November 4). *Raising kids and running a household: How working parents share the load.* Retrieved from www.pewsocialtrends.org/2015/11/04/raising-kids-and-running-a-household-how-working-parents-share-the-load/

Pew Research Center. (2015b, January 14). *Women and leadership.* Washington, DC: Pew Research Center. Retrieved from http://www.pewsocialtrends.org/2015/01/14/chapter-1-women-in-leadership/

Pham, M. N., DeLecce, T., & Shackelford, T. K. (2017). Sperm competition in marriage: Semen displacement, male rivals, and spousal discrepancy in sexual interest. *Personality and Individual Differences, 105,* 229–232.

Pham, M. N., & Shackelford, T. K, (2015). Sperm competition and the evolution of human sexuality. In T. Shackelford & R. Hansen (Eds.), *The evolution of sexuality* (pp. 257–275). New York: Springer.

Pierce, L., Dahl, M. S., & Nielsen, J. (2013). In sickness and in wealth: Psychological and sexual costs of income comparison in marriage. *Personality and Social Psychology Bulletin, 39,* 359–374.

Pillsworth, E. G., & Haselton, M. G. (2006). Women's sexual strategies: The evolution of long-term bonds and extrapair sex. *Annual Review of Sex Research, 17,* 59–100.

Pines, A. M. (1998). *Romantic jealousy: Causes, symptoms, cures.* New York: Routledge.

Pinquart, M. (2003). Loneliness in married, widowed, divorced, and never-married older adults. *Journal of Social and Personal Relationships, 20,* 31–53.

Pipitone, R. N., & Gallup, G. G., Jr. (2008). Women's voice attractiveness varies across the menstrual cycle. *Evolution and Human Behavior, 29,* 268–274.

Pipitone, R. N., Gallup, G. G. Jr., & Bartels, A. (2016). Variation in men's masculinity affects preferences for women's voices at different points in the menstrual cycle. *Evolutionary Behavioral Sciences, 10,* 188–201.

Pittman, F. S., & Wagers, T. P. (2005). Teaching fidelity. *Journal of Clinical Psychology, 61,* 1407–1419.

Pitts, M. K., Smith, A. M. A., Grierson, J., O'Brien, M., & Misson, S. (2004). Who pays for sex and why? An analysis of social and motivational factors associated with male clients of sex workers. *Archives of Sexual Behavior, 33,* 353–358.

Place, S. S., Todd, P. M., Penke, L., & Asendorpf, J. B. (2009). The ability to judge the romantic interest of others. *Psychological Science, 20,* 22–26.

Pollet, T. V., Roberts, S. G. B., & Dunbar, R. I. M. (2011). Use of social network sites and instant messaging does not lead to increased offline social network size, or to emotionally closer relationships with offline network members. *Cyberpsychology, Behavior, and Social Networking, 14,* 253–258.

Pollmann, M. M. H., & Finkenauer, C. (2009). Investigating the role of two types of understanding in relationship well-being: Understanding is more important than knowledge. *Personality and Social Psychology Bulletin, 35,* 1512–1527.

Ponzi, D., Klimczuk, A. C. E., Traficonte, D. M., & Maestripieri, D. (2015). Perceived dominance in young heterosexual couples in relation to sex, context, and frequency of arguing. *Evolutionary Behavioral Sciences, 9,* 43–54.

Poortman, A. (2005). The mediating role of financial and time pressures. *Journal of Family Issues, 26,* 168–195.

Poortman, A., & Liefbroer, A. C. (2010). Singles' relational attitudes in a time of individualization. *Social Science Research, 39,* 938–949.

Poortman, A., & Seltzer, J. A. (2007). Parents' expectations about childrearing after divorce: Does anticipating difficulty deter divorce? *Journal of Marriage and Family, 69,* 254–269.

Porter, S., & ten Brinke, L. (2010). The truth about lies: What works in detecting high-stakes deception? *Legal and Criminological Psychology, 15,* 57–75.

Porter, S., ten Brinke, L., & Wallace, B. (2012). Secrets and lies: Involuntary leakage in deceptive facial expressions as a function of emotional intensity. *Journal of Nonverbal Behavior, 36,* 23–37.

Potarca, G. (2017). Does the internet affect assortative mating? Evidence from the U.S. and Germany. *Social Science Research, 61,* 278–292.

Powers, S. I., Pietromonaco, P. R., Gunlicks, M., & Sayer, A. (2006). Dating couples' attachment styles and patterns of cortisol reactivity and recovery in response to a relationship conflict. *Journal of Personality and Social Psychology, 90,* 613–628.

Prager, K. J., Shirvani, F. K., Garcia, J. J., & Coles, M. (2013). Intimacy and positive psychology. In M. Hojjat & D. Cramer (Eds.), *Positive psychology of love* (pp. 16–29). New York: Oxford University Press.

Pratto, F., & Walker, A. (2004). The bases of gendered power. In A. H. Eagly, A. E. Beall, & R. J. Sternberg (Eds.), *The psychology of gender* (2nd ed., pp. 242–268). New York: Guilford Press.

Pressman, S. D., Cohen, S., Miller, G. E., Barkin, A., Rabin, B. S., & Treanor, J. J. (2005). Loneliness, social network size, and immune response to influenza vaccination in college freshmen. *Health Psychology, 24,* 297–306.

Previti, D., & Amato, P. R. (2003). Why stay married? Rewards, barriers, and marital stability. *Journal of Marriage and Family, 65,* 561–573.

Price, M. (2011). Alone in the crowd. *Monitor on Psychology, 26*(4), 26–28.

Priem, J. S., & Solomon, D. (2015). Emotional support and physiological stress recovery: The role of support matching, adequacy, and invisibility. *Communication Monographs, 82,* 88–112.

Priem, J. S., Solomon, D. H., & Steuber, K. R. (2009). Accuracy and bias in perceptions of emotionally supportive communication in marriage. *Personal Relationships, 16,* 531–552.

Prokop, P., & Pazda, A. D. (2016). Women's red clothing can increase mate-guarding from their male partner. *Personality and Individual Differences, 98,* 114–117.

Prokosch, M. D., Coss, R. G., Scheib, J. E., & Blozis, S. A. (2009). Intelligence and mate choice: Intelligent men are always appealing. *Evolution and Human Behavior, 30,* 11–20.

Pronin, E., Lin, D. Y., & Ross, L. (2002). The bias blind spot: Perceptions of bias in self versus others. *Personality and Social Psychology Bulletin, 28,* 369–381.

Pronk, T. M., & Karremans, J. C. (2014). Does executive control relate to sacrificial behavior during conflicts of interests? *Personal Relationships, 21,* 168–175.

Pronk, T. M., Karremans, J. C., & Wigboldus, D. H. J. (2011). How can you resist? Executive control helps romantically involved individuals to stay faithful. *Journal of Personality and Social Psychology, 100,* 827–837.

Proost, K., Schreurs, B., de Witte, K., & Derous, E. (2010). Ingratiation and self-promotion in the selection interview: The effects of using single tactics or a combination of tactics on interviewer judgments. *Journal of Applied Social Psychology, 40,* 2155–2169.

Przybylinski, E., & Andersen, S. M. (2015). Systems of meaning and transference: Implicit significant-other activation evokes shared reality. *Journal of Personality and Social Psychology, 109,* 636–661.

Przybylski, A. K., & Weinstein, N. (2013). Can you connect with me now? How the presence of mobile communication technology influences face-to-face conversation quality. *Journal of Social and Personal Relationships, 30,* 237–246.

Puccinelli, N. M. (2010). Nonverbal communication competence. In D. Matsumoto (Ed.), *APA handbook of interpersonal communication* (pp. 273–288). Washington, DC: American Psychological Association.

Pulerwitz, J., Gortmaker, S. L., & DeJong, W. (2000). Measuring sexual relationship power in HIV/STD research. *Sex Roles, 42,* 637–660.

Purvis, J. A., Dabbs, J. M., Jr., & Hopper, C. H. (1984). The "opener": Skilled user of facial expression and speech pattern. *Personality and Social Psychology Bulletin, 10,* 61–66.

Qureshi, C., Harris, E., Atkinson, B. E. (2016). Relationships between age of females and attraction to the Dark Triad personality. *Personality and Individual Differences, 95,* 200–203.

Raby, K. L., Roisman, G. I., Simpson, J. A., Collins, W. A., & Steele, R. D. (2015). Greater maternal insensitivity in childhood predicts greater electrodermal reactivity during conflict discussions with romantic partners in adulthood. *Psychological Science, 26,* 348–353.

Rains, S. A., Brunner, S R., & Oman, K. (2016). Self-disclosure and new communication technologies: The implications of receiving superficial self-disclosures from friends. *Journal of Social and Personal Relationships, 33,* 42–61.

Ramirez, A., Jr. (2008). An examination of the tripartite approach to commitment: An actor-partner interdependence model analysis of the effect of relational maintenance behavior. *Journal of Social and Personal Relationships, 25,* 943–965.

Ramirez, A., Jr., Sumner, E. M., Fleuriet, C., & Cole, M. (2015). When online dating partners meet offline: The effect of modality switching on relational communication between online daters. *Computer-Mediated Communication, 20,* 99–114.

Rammstedt, B., Spinath, F. M., Richter, D., & Schupp, J. (2013). Partnership longevity and personality congruence in couples. *Personality and Individual Differences, 54,* 832–835.

Randall, A. K., & Bodenmann, G. (2009). The role of stress on close relationships and marital satisfaction. *Clinical Psychology Review, 29,* 105–115.

Randolph, M. E., Pinkerton, S. D., Bogart, L. M., Cecil, H., & Abramson, P. R. (2007). Sexual pleasure and condom use. *Archives of Sexual Behavior, 36,* 844–848.

Rasmussen, K. (2016). A historical and empirical review of pornography and romantic relationships: Implication for family researchers. *Journal of Family Theory & Review, 8,* 173–191.

Rasmussen, K., & Boon, S. D. (2016, July). *Sex, power, and punishment: Perceptions of sexual desire and gender differences in relationship power.* Paper presented at the meeting of the International Association for Relationship Research, Toronto.

Ratliff, K. A., & Oishi, S. (2013). Gender differences in implicit self-esteem following a romantic partner's success or failure. *Journal of Personality and Social Psychology, 105,* 688–702.

Rauer, A., Williams, L., & Jensen, J. (2017). Finer distinctions: Variability in satisfied older couples' problem-solving behaviors. *Family Process, 56,* 501–517.

Raven, B. H. (2001). Power/interaction and interpersonal influence: Experimental investigations and case studies. In A. Y. Lee-Chai & J. A. Bargh (Eds.), *The use and abuse of power: Multiple perspectives on the causes of corruption* (pp. 217–240). Philadelphia: Psychology Press.

Re, D. E., & Rule, N. O. (2016). The big man has a big mouth: Mouth width correlates with perceived leadership ability and actual leadership performance. *Journal of Experimental Social Psychology, 63,* 86–93.

Redlick, M. (2016). The green-eyed monster: Mate value, relational uncertainty, and jealousy in romantic relationships. *Personal Relationships, 23,* 505–516.

Reed, L. A., Tolman, R, M., Ward, L. M., & Safyer, P. (2016). Keeping tabs: Attachment anxiety and electronic intrusion in high school dating relationships. *Computers in Human Behavior, 58,* 259–268.

Regan, P. C. (2013). Sexual desire in women. In D. Castañeda (Ed.), *The essential handbook of women's sexuality* (Vol. 1, pp. 3–24). Santa Barbara, CA: Praeger.

Regan, P. C. (2015). Sexual desire: Conceptualization, correlates, and causes. In W. Hofmann & L. Nordgren (Eds.), *The psychology of desire* (pp. 347–368). New York: Guilford Press.

Reiber, C., & Garcia, J. R. (2010). Hooking up: Gender differences, evolution, and pluralistic ignorance. *Evolutionary Psychology, 8,* 390–404.

Reinhard, M., Sporer, S. L., Scharmach, M., & Marksteiner, T. (2011). Listening, not watching: Situational familiarity and the ability to detect deception. *Journal of Personality and Social Psychology, 101,* 467–484.

Reinhardt, J. P., Boerner, K., & Horowitz, A. (2006). Good to have but not to use: Differential impact of perceived and received support on well-being. *Journal of Social and Personal Relationships, 23,* 117–129.

Reis, H. T. (1986). Gender effects in social participation: Intimacy, loneliness, and the conduct of social interaction. In R. Gilmour & S. Duck (Eds.), *The emerging field of personal relationships* (pp. 91–105). London: Academic Press.

Reis, H. T. (1998). Gender differences in intimacy and related behaviors: Context and process. In D. J. Canary & K. Dindia (Eds.), *Sex differences and similarities in communication: Critical essays and empirical investigations of sex and gender in interaction* (pp. 203–234). Mahwah, NJ: Erlbaum.

Reis, H. T. (2012). A history of relationship research in social psychology. In A. W. Kruglanski & W. Stroebe (Eds.), *Handbook of the history of social psychology* (pp. 363–382). New York: Psychology Press.

Reis, H. T. (2013). Relationship well-being: The central role of perceived partner responsiveness. In C. Hazan & M. I. Campa (Eds.), *Human bonding: The science of affectional ties* (pp. 283–307). New York: Guilford Press.

Reis, H. T., Aron, A., Clark, M. S., & Finkel, E. J. (2013). Ellen Berscheid, Elaine Hatfield, and the emergence of relationship science. *Perspectives on Psychological Science, 8,* 558–572.

Reis, H. T., Caprariello, P. A., & Velickovic, M. (2011a). The relationship superiority effect is moderated by the relationship context. *Journal of Experimental Social Psychology, 47,* 481–484.

Reis, H. T., & Carothers, B. J. (2014). Black and white or shades of gray: Are gender differences categorical or dimensional? *Current Directions in Psychological Science, 23,* 19–26

Reis, H. T., Clark, M. S., & Holmes, J. G. (2004). Perceived partner responsiveness as an organizing construct in the study of intimacy and closeness. In D. Mashek & A. Aron (Eds.), *Handbook of closeness and intimacy* (pp. 201–225). Mahwah, NJ: Erlbaum.

Reis, H. T., & Gable, S. L. (2003). Toward a positive psychology of relationships. In C. L. M. Keyes & J. Haidt (Eds.), *Flourishing: positive psychology and the life well-lived* (pp. 129–159). Washington, DC: American Psychological Association.

Reis, H. T., Lin, Y., Bennett, M. E., & Nezlek, J. B. (1993). Change and consistency in social participation during early adulthood. *Developmental Psychology, 29,* 633–645.

Reis, H. T., Maniaci, M. R., Caprariello, P. A., Eastwick, P. W., & Finkel, E. J. (2011). Familiarity does indeed promote attraction in live interaction. *Journal of Personality and Social Psychology, 101,* 557–570.

Reis, H. T., Maniaci, M. R., & Rogge, R. D. (2014). The expression of compassionate love in everyday compassionate acts. *Journal of Social and Personal Relationships, 31,* 651–676.

Reis, H. T., Maniaci, M. R., & Rogge, R. D. (2017). Compassionate acts and everyday emotional well-being among newlyweds. *Emotion, 17,* 751–763.

Reis, H. T., & Patrick, B. C. (1996). Attachment and intimacy: Component processes. In E. T. Higgins & A. W. Kruglanski (Eds.), *Social psychology: Handbook of basic principles* (pp. 523–563). New York: Guilford Press.

Reis, H. T., & Shaver, P. (1988). Intimacy as an interpersonal process. In S. Duck (Ed.), *Handbook of personal relationships: Theory, research, and interventions* (pp. 367–389). Chichester, England: Wiley.

Reis, H. T., Sheldon, R. M., Gable, S. L., Roscoe, J., & Ryan, R. M. (2000). Daily well-being: The role of autonomy, competence, and relatedness. *Personality and Social Psychology Bulletin, 26,* 419–435.

Reis, H. T., Smith, S. M., Carmichael, C. L., Caprariello, P. A., Tsai, F., Rodrigues, A., & Maniaci, M. R. (2010). Are you happy for me? How sharing positive events with others provides personal and interpersonal benefits. *Journal of Personality and Social Psychology, 99,* 311–329.

Reis, H. T., Wheeler, L., Spiegel, N., Kernis, M. H., Nezlek, J., & Perri, M. (1982). Physical attractiveness in social interaction: II. Why does appearance affect social experience? *Journal of Personality and Social Psychology, 43,* 979–996.

Reissing, E. D., Andruff, H. L., & Wentland, J. J. (2012). Looking back: The experience of first sexual intercourse and current sexual adjustment in young heterosexual adults. *Journal of Sex Research, 49,* 27–35.

Reitz, A. K., Motti-Stefanidi, F., & Asendorpf, J. B. (2016). Me, us, and them: Testing sociometer theory in a socially diverse real-life context. *Journal of Personality and Social Psychology, 110,* 908–920.

Rempel, J. K., Ross, M., & Holmes, J. G. (2001). Trust and communicated attributions in close relationships. *Journal of Personality and Social Psychology, 81,* 57–64.

Ren, D., Arriaga, X. B., & Mahan, E. R. (2017). Attachment insecurity and perceived importance of relational features. *Journal of Social and Personal Relationships, 34,* 446–466.

Ren, P. (2011, November). *Lifetime mobility in the United States: 2010.* U. S. Census Bureau. Retrieved from http://www.census.gov/prod/2011pubs/acsbr10-07.pdf

Renshaw, K. D., Blais, R. K., & Smith, T. W. (2010). Components of negative affectivity and marital satisfaction: The importance of actor and partner anger. *Journal of Research in Personality, 44,* 328–334.

Renshaw, K. D., McKnight, P., Caska, C. M., & Blais, R. K. (2011). The utility of the relationship assessment scale in multiple types of relationships. *Journal of Social and Personal Relationships, 28,* 435–447.

Repetti, R. L., Reynolds, B. M., & Sears, M. S. (2015). Families under the microscope: Repeated sampling of perceptions, experiences, biology, and behavior. *Journal of Marriage and Family, 77,* 126–146.

Rey, L., & Extremera, N. (2014). Positive psychological characteristics and interpersonal forgiveness: Identifying the unique contribution of emotional intelligence abilities, Big Five traits, gratitude and optimism. *Personality and Individual Differences, 68,* 199–204.

Rhoades, G. K., Stanley, S. M., & Markman, H. J. (2009). The pre-engagement cohabitation effect: A replication and extension of previous findings. *Journal of Family Psychology, 23,* 107–111.

Rhoades, G. K., Stanley, S. M., & Markman, H. J. (2012). A longitudinal investigation of commitment dynamics in cohabiting relationships. *Journal of Family Issues, 33,* 369–390.

Rhodes, G. (2006). The evolutionary psychology of facial beauty. *Annual Review of Psychology, 57,* 199–226.

Rhodes, G., Harwood, K., Yoshikawa, S., Nishitani, M., & MacLean, I. (2002). The attractiveness of average faces: Cross-cultural evidence and possible biological basis. In G. Rhodes & L. A. Zebrowitz (Eds.), *Facial attractiveness: Evolutionary, cognitive and social perspectives* (pp. 35–58). Westport, CT: Ablex.

Richman, L. S., & Leary, M. R. (2009). Reactions to discrimination, stigmatization, ostracism, and other forms of interpersonal rejection: A multimotive model. *Psychological Review, 116,* 365–383.

Rick, S. I., Small, D. A., & Finkel, E. J. (2011). Fatal (fiscal) attraction: Spendthrifts and tightwads in marriage. *Journal of Marketing Research, 48,* 228–237.

Riek, B. M., & Mania, E. W. (2012). The antecedents and consequences of interpersonal forgiveness: A meta-analytic review. *Personal Relationships, 19,* 304–325.

Riela, S., Rodriguez, G., Aron, A., Xu, X., & Acevedo, B. P. (2010). Experiences of falling in love: Investigating culture, ethnicity, gender, and speed. *Journal of Social and Personal Relationships, 27,* 473–493.

Riggio, H. R. (2004). Parental marital conflict and divorce, parent–child relationships, social support, and relationship anxiety in young adulthood. *Personal Relationships, 11,* 99–114.

Riggle, E. D. B., Rostosky, S. S., Black, W. W., & Rosenkrantz, D. E. (2017). Outness, concealment, and authenticity: Associations with LGB individuals' psychological distress and well-being. *Psychology of Sexual Orientation and Gender Diversity, 4,* 54–62.

Righetti, F., Luchies, L. B., van Gils, S., & . . . Kumashiro, M. (2015). The prosocial versus proself power holder: How power influences sacrifice in romantic relationships. *Personality and Social Psychology Bulletin, 41,* 779–790.

Rizkalla, L., Wertheim, E. H., & Hodgson, L. K. (2008). The roles of emotion management and perspective taking in individuals' conflict management styles and disposition to forgive. *Journal of Research in Personality, 42,* 1594–1601.

Roberts, B. W., Luo, J., Briley, D. A., Chow, P. I., Su, R., & Hill, P. L. (2017). A systematic review of personality trait change through intervention. *Psychological Bulletin, 143,* 117–141.

Roberts, J. A., & David, M. E. (2016). My life has become a major distraction from my cell phone: Partner phubbing and relationship satisfaction among romantic partners. *Computers in Human Behavior, 54,* 134–141.

Roberts, S. G. B., & Dunbar, R. I. M. (2011). The costs of family and friends: An 18-month longitudinal study of relationship maintenance and decay. *Evolution and Human Behavior, 32,* 186–197.

Robillard, S. L. (2008). The effect of intra-sexual competition and restraint status on the eating behaviour of single females: An experimental investigation. *Dissertation Abstracts International, 68,* 83–86.

Robillard, S. L., & Jarry, J. L. (2007, May). *Intrasexual competition for evolutionarily desirable men: The effect on women's eating behavior.* Poster presented at the meeting of the Association for Psychological Science, Washington, DC.

Robins, R. W., Mendelsohn, G. A., Connell, J. B., & Kwan, V. S. Y. (2004). Do people agree about the causes of behavior? A social relations analysis of behavior ratings and causal attributions. *Journal of Personality and Social Psychology, 86,* 334–344.

Robinson, K. J., & Cameron, J. J. (2012). Self-esteem is a shared relationship resource: Additive effects of dating partners' self-esteem levels predict relationship quality. *Journal of Research in Personality, 46,* 227–230.

Robles, T. F., Slatcher, R. B., Trombello, J. M., & McGinn, M. M. (2014). Marital quality and health: A meta-analytic review. *Psychological Bulletin, 140,* 140–187.

Roddy, M. K., Nowlan, K. M., Doss, B. D., & Christensen, A. (2016). Integrative behavioral couple therapy: Theoretical background, empirical research, and dissemination. *Family Process, 55,* 408–422.

Rodrigues, D., Lopes, D., & Pereira, M. (2017). Sociosexuality, commitment, sexual infidelity, and perceptions of infidelity: Data from the second love web site. *Journal of Sex Research, 54,* 241–253.

Rodriguez, L. M., Øverup, C. A., Wickham, R. E., Knee, C. R., & Amspoker, A. B. (2016). Communication with former romantic partners and current relationship outcomes among college students. *Personal Relationships, 23,* 409–424.

Rogers, S. J. (1999). Wives' income and marital quality: Are there reciprocal effects? *Journal of Marriage and the Family, 61,* 123–132.

Rogge, R. D., Cobb, R. J., Lawrence, E., Johnson, M. D., & Bradbury, T. N. (2013). Is skills training necessary for the primary prevention of marital distress and dissolution? A 3-year experimental study of three interventions. *Journal of Consulting and Clinical Psychology, 81,* 949–961.

Roisman, G. I., Clausell, E., Holland, A., Fortuna, K., & Elieff, C. (2008). Adult romantic relationships as contexts of human development: A multimethod comparison of same-sex couples with opposite-sex dating, engaged, and married dyads. *Developmental Psychology, 44,* 91–101.

Rolffs, J. L., & Rogge, R. D. (2016). Brief interventions to strengthen relationships and prevent dissolution. In C. Knee & H. Reis (Eds.), *Positive approaches to optimal relationship development* (pp. 326–349). Cambridge, UK: Cambridge University Press.

Rollie, S. S., & Duck, S. (2006). Divorce and dissolution of romantic relationships: Stage models and their limitations. In M. Fine & J. Harvey (Eds.), *Handbook of divorce and relationship dissolution* (pp. 223–240). Mahwah, NJ: Erlbaum.

Roloff, M. E., & Cloven, D. H. (1990). The chilling effect in interpersonal relationships: The reluctance to speak one's mind. In D. Cahn (Ed.), *Intimates in conflict: A communication perspective* (pp. 49–76). Hillsdale, NJ: Erlbaum.

Romero-Canyas, R., Anderson, V. T., Reddy, K. S., & Downey, G. (2009). Rejection sensitivity. In M. R. Leary & R. H. Hoyle (Eds.), *Handbook of individual differences in social behavior* (pp. 466–479). New York: Guilford Press.

Romero-Canyas, R., Downey, G., Berenson, K., Ayduk, O., & Kang, N. J. (2010). Rejection sensitivity and the rejection-hostility link in romantic relationships. *Journal of Personality, 78,* 119–148.

Ronay, R., & von Hippel, W. (2010). The presence of an attractive woman elevates testosterone and physical risk taking in young men. *Social Psychological and Personality Science, 1,* 57–64.

Roney, J. R., & Simmons, Z. L. (2016). Within-cycle fluctuations in progesterone negatively predict changes in both in-pair and extra-pair desire among partnered women. *Hormones and Behavior, 81,* 45–52.

Rosenbaum, J. E. (2009). Patient teenagers? A comparison of the sexual behavior of virginity pledgers and matched nonpledgers. *Pediatrics, 123,* 110–120.

Rosenberg, J., & Tunney, R. J. (2008). Human vocabulary use as display. *Evolutionary Psychology, 6,* 538–549.

Rosenfeld, J. J., & Thomas, R. J. (2012). Searching for a mate: The rise of the internet as a social intermediary. *American Sociological Review, 77,* 523–547.

Rosenthal, L., & Starks, T. J. (2015). Relationship stigma and relationship outcomes in interracial and same-sex relationships: Examination of sources and buffers. *Journal of Family Psychology, 29,* 818–830.

Rosenthal, N. L., & Kobak, R. (2010). Assessing adolescents' attachment hierarchies: Differences across developmental periods and associations with individual adaptation. *Journal of Research on Adolescence, 20,* 678–706.

Rosenthal, R. (2006). Applying psychological research on interpersonal expectations and covert communication in classrooms, clinics, corporations, and courtrooms. In S. I. Donaldson, D. E. Berger, & K. Pedzek (Eds.), *Applied psychology: New frontiers and rewarding careers* (pp. 107–118). Mahwah, NJ: Erlbaum.

Ross, M. W. (2005). Typing, doing, and being: Sexuality and the Internet. *Journal of Sex Research, 42,* 342–352.

Rossetto, K. R. (2013). Relational coping during deployment: Managing communication and connection in relationships. *Personal Relationships, 20,* 568–586.

Rostosky, S. S., & Riggle, E. D. B. (2017). Same-sex couple relationship strengths: A review and synthesis of the empirical literature (2000–2016). *Psychology of Sexual Orientation and Gender Diversity, 4,* 1–13.

Rowatt, W. C., Cunningham, M. R., & Druen, P. B. (1999). Lying to get a date: The effect of facial physical attractiveness on the willingness to deceive prospective dating partners. *Journal of Social and Personal Relationships, 16,* 209–223.

Rubenstein, A. J., Langlois, J. H., & Roggman, L. A. (2002). What makes a face attractive and why: The role of averageness in defining facial beauty. In G. Rhodes & L. A. Zebrowitz (Eds.), *Facial attractiveness: Evolutionary, cognitive and social perspectives* (pp. 1–33). Westport, CT: Ablex.

Rubin, H., & Campbell, L. (2012). Day-to-day changes in intimacy predict heightened relationship passion, sexual occurrence, and sexual satisfaction: A dyadic diary analysis. *Social Psychological and Personality Science, 3,* 224–231.

Rubin, L. B. (1986). On men and friendship. *Psychoanalytic Review, 73,* 165–181.

Rubin, Z. (1973). *Liking and loving.* New York: Holt, Rinehart & Winston.

Rudman, L. A., Fetterolf, J. C., & Sanchez, D. T. (2013). What motivates the sexual double standard? More support for male versus female control theory. *Personality and Social Psychology Bulletin, 39,* 250–263.

Rudman, L. A., & Mescher, K. (2012a). Feminism and romance. In M. A. Paludi (Ed.), *The psychology of love* (Vol. 3, pp. 109–129). Santa Barbara, CA: Praeger.

Rudman, L. A., & Mescher, K. (2012b). Of animals and objects: Men's implicit dehumanization of women and likelihood of sexual aggression. *Personality and Social Psychology Bulletin, 38,* 734–746.

Rudman, L. A., Moss-Racusin, C. A., Phelan, J. E., & Nauts, S. (2012). Status incongruity and backlash effects: Defending the gender hierarchy motivates prejudice against female leaders. *Journal of Experimental Social Psychology, 48,* 165–179.

Rule, N. O. (2014). Snap-judgment science: Intuitive decisions about other people. *Observer, 27*(5), 18–19, 50.

Rule, N. O. (2017). Perceptions of sexual orientation from minimal cues. *Archives of Sexual Behavior, 46,* 129–139.

Rule, N. O., Ishii, K., Ambady, N., Rosen, K. S., & Hallett, K. C. (2011a). Found in translation: Cross-cultural consensus in the accurate categorization of male sexual orientation. *Personality and Social Psychology Bulletin, 37,* 1499–1507.

Rule, N. O., Rosen, K. S., Slepian, M. L., & Ambady, N. (2011b). Mating interest improves women's accuracy in judging male sexual orientation. *Psychological Science, 22,* 881–886.

Ruppel, E. K., & Curran, M. A. (2012). Relational sacrifices in romantic relationships: Satisfaction and the moderating role of attachment. *Journal of Social and Personal Relationships, 29,* 508–529.

Rusbult, C. E., Agnew, C. R., & Arriaga, X. B. (2012). The investment model of commitment processes. In P. Van Lange, A. Kruglanski, & E. T. Higgins (Eds.), *Handbook of theories of social psychology* (Vol. 2, pp. 218–231). Thousand Oaks, CA: Sage.

Rusbult, C. E., Bissonnette, V. L., Arriaga, X. B., & Cox, C. L. (1998). Accommodation processes during the early years of marriage. In T. Bradbury (Ed.), *The developmental course of marital dysfunction* (pp. 74–113). New York: Cambridge University Press.

Rusbult, C. E., Finkel, E. J., & Kumashiro, M. (2009). The Michelangelo phenomenon. *Current Directions in Psychological Science, 18,* 305–309.

Rusbult, C. E., & Martz, J. M. (1995). Remaining in abusive relationships: An investment model analysis of nonvoluntary dependence. *Personality and Social Psychology Bulletin, 21,* 558–571.

Rusbult, C. E., Olsen, N., Davis, J. L., & Hannon, P. A. (2001). Commitment and relationship maintenance mechanisms. In J. Harvey & A. Wenzel (Eds.), *Close romantic relationships: Maintenance and enhancement* (pp. 87–113). Mahwah, NJ: Erlbaum.

Rusbult, C. E., Van Lange, P. A. M., Wildschut, T., Yovetich, N. A., & Verette, J. (2000). Perceived superiority in close relationships: Why it exists and persists. *Journal of Personality and Social Psychology, 79,* 521–545.

Rusbult, C. E., Zembrodt, I. M., & Gunn, L. K. (1982). Exit, voice, loyalty, and neglect: Responses to dissatisfaction in romantic involvements. *Journal of Personality and Social Psychology, 43,* 1230–1242.

Rusbult, C. E., Zembrodt, I. M., & Iwaniszek, J. (1986). The impact of gender and sex-role orientation on responses to dissatisfaction in close relationships. *Sex Roles, 15,* 1–20.

Russell, D. W. (1996). The UCLA Loneliness Scale (Version 3): Reliability, validity and factorial structure. *Journal of Personality Assessment, 66,* 20–40.

Russell, V. M., Baker, L. R., & McNulty, J. K. (2013). Attachment insecurity and infidelity in marriage: Do studies of dating relationships really inform us about marriage? *Journal of Family Psychology, 27,* 242–251.

Rycyna, C. C., Champion, C. D., & Kelly, A. E. (2009). First impressions after various types of deception: Less favorable following expectancy violation. *Basic and Applied Social Psychology, 31,* 40–48.

Rydell, R. J., McConnell, A. R., & Bringle, R. G. (2004). Jealousy and commitment: Perceived threat and the effect of relationship alternatives. *Personal Relationships, 11,* 451–468.

Sabey, A. K., Rauer, A. J., & Haselschwerdt, M. L. (2016). "It's not just words coming from the mouth": The nature of compassionate love among older couples. *Journal of Social and Personal Relationships, 33,* 640–665.

Saffrey, C., & Ehrenberg, M. (2007). When thinking hurts: Attachment, rumination, and postrelationship adjustment. *Personal Relationships, 14,* 351–368.

Sagarin, B. J., Becker, D. V., Guadagno, R. E., Nicastle, L. D., & Millevoi, A. (2003). Sex differences (and similarities) in jealousy. The moderating influence of infidelity experience and sexual orientation of the infidelity. *Evolution and Human Behavior, 24,* 17–23.

Sagarin, B. J., Martin, A. L., Coutinho, S. A., & . . . Zengel, B. (2012). Sex differences in jealousy: A meta-analytic examination. *Evolution and Human Behavior, 33,* 595–614.

Sagarin, B. J., Rhoads, K. V. L., & Cialdini, R. B. (1998). Deceiver's distrust: Denigration as a consequence of undiscovered deception. *Personality and Social Psychology Bulletin, 24,* 1167–1176.

Sahlstein, E. M. (2006). The trouble with distance. In D. C. Kirkpatrick, S. Duck, & M. K. Foley (Eds.), *Relating difficulty: The processes of constructing and managing difficult interaction* (pp. 119–140). Mahwah, NJ: Erlbaum.

Salkicevic, S., Stanic, A. L., & Grabovac, M. T. (2014). Good mates retain us right: Investigating the relationship between mate retention strategies, mate value, and relationship satisfaction. *Evolutionary Psychology, 12,* 1038–1052.

Salovey, P., & Rodin, J. (1988). Coping with envy and jealousy. *Journal of Social and Clinical Psychology, 7,* 15–33.

Salvatore, J. E., Kuo, S. I., Steele, R. D., Simpson, J. A., & Collins, W. A. (2011). Recovering from conflict in romantic relationships: A developmental perspective. *Psychological Science, 22,* 376–383.

Sanchez, D. T., Fetterolf, J. C., & Rudman, L. A. (2012a). Eroticizing inequality in the United States: The consequences and determinants of traditional gender role adherence in intimate relationships. *Journal of Sex Research, 49,* 168–183.

Sanchez, D. T., Phelan, J. E., Moss-Racusin, C. A., & Good, J. J. (2012b). The gender role motivation model of women's sexually submissive behavior and satisfaction in heterosexual couples. *Personality and Social Psychology Bulletin, 38,* 528–539.

Sandstrom, G. M., & Dunn, E. W. (2014). Social interactions and well-being: The surprising power of weak ties. *Personality and Social Psychology Bulletin, 40,* 910–922.

Sanford, K. (2014). A latent change score model of conflict resolution in couples: Are negative behaviors bad, benign, or beneficial? *Journal of Social and Personal Relationships, 31,* 1068–1088.

Sanford, K., & Grace, A. J. (2011). Emotion and underlying concerns during couples' conflict: An investigation of within-person change. *Personal Relationships, 18,* 96–109.

Sarkisian, N., & Gerstel, N. (2016). Does singlehood isolate or integrate? Examining the link between marital status and ties to kin, friends, and neighbors. *Journal of Social and Personal Relationships, 33,* 361–384.

Saslow, L. R., Muise, A., Impett, E. A., & Dubin. M. (2013). Can you see how happy we are? Facebook images and relationship satisfaction. *Social Psychological and Personality Science, 4,* 411–418.

Sassler, S., & Miller, A. J. (2011). Waiting to be asked: Gender, power, and relationship progression among cohabiting couples. *Journal of Family Issues, 32,* 482–506.

Savage, D. (2016, July 14). Straight up. *Eugene Weekly,* p. 31.

Savin-Williams, R. C. (2005). *The new gay teenager.* Cambridge, MA: Harvard University Press.

Savin-Williams, R. C. (2006). Who's gay? Does it matter? *Current Directions in Psychological Science, 15,* 40–44.

Savin-Williams, R. C. (2014). An exploratory study of the categorical versus spectrum nature of sexual orientation. *Journal of Sex Research, 51,* 446–453.

Savitsky, K., Keysar, B., Epley, N., Carter, T., & Swanson, A. (2011). The closeness-communication bias: Increased egocentrism among friends versus strangers. *Journal of Experimental Social Psychology, 47,* 269–273.

Sayer, L. C. (2006). Economic aspects of divorce and relationship dissolution. In M. A. Fine & J. H. Harvey (Eds.), *Handbook of divorce and relationship dissolution* (pp. 385–406). Mahwah, NJ: Erlbaum.

Sbarra, D. A. (2006). Predicting the onset of emotional recovery following nonmarital relationship dissolution: Survival analyses of sadness and anger. *Personality and Social Psychology Bulletin, 32,* 298–312.

Sbarra, D. A., & Beck, C. J. A. (2013). Divorce and close relationships: Findings, themes, and future directions. In J. A. Simpson & L. Campbell (Eds.), *The Oxford handbook of close relationships* (pp. 795–822). New York: Oxford University Press.

Sbarra, D. A., & Emery, R. E. (2005). The emotional sequelae of nonmarital relationship dissolution: Analysis of change and intraindividual variability over time. *Personal Relationships, 12,* 213–232.

Sbarra, D. A., Hasselmo, K., & Bourassa, K. J. (2015). Divorce and health: Beyond individual differences. *Current Directions in Psychological Science, 24,* 109–113.

Sbarra, D. A., & Nietert, P. J. (2009). Divorce and death: Forty years of the Charleston Heart Study. *Psychological Science, 20,* 107–113.

Schachter, S. (1959). *The psychology of affiliation: Experimental studies of the sources of gregariousness.* Stanford, CA: Stanford University Press.

Schaffhuser, K., Allemand, M., & Martin, M. (2014). Personality traits and relationship satisfaction in intimate couples: Three perspectives on personality. *European Journal of Personality, 28,* 120–133.

Schick, V., Calabrese, S. K., & Herbenick, D. (2014). Survey methods in sexuality research. In D. L. Tolman, Diamond, L. M., Bauermeister, J. A., et al. (Eds.), *APA handbook of sexuality and psychology* (Vol. 1, pp. 81–98). Washington, DC: American Psychological Association.

Schlenker, B. R. (2003). Self-presentation. In M. R. Leary & J. P. Tangney (Eds.), *Handbook of self and identity* (pp. 492–518). New York: Guilford Press.

Schlenker, B. R. (2012). Self-presentation. In M. R. Leary & J. P. Tangney (Eds.), *Handbook of self and identity* (2nd ed., pp. 542–570). New York: Guilford Press.

Schmitt, D. P. (2005). Sociosexuality from Argentina to Zimbabwe: A 48-nation study of sex, culture, and strategies of human mating. *Behavioral and Brain Sciences, 28,* 247–275.

Schmitt, D. P. (2008). Attachment matters: Patterns of romantic attachment across gender, geography, and cultural forms. In J. P. Forgas & J. Fitness (Eds.), *Social relationships: Cognitive, affective and motivational processes* (pp. 75–97). New York: Psychology Press.

Schmitt, D. P. (2016). Fundamentals of human mating strategies. In D. Buss (Ed.), *The handbook of evolutionary psychology* (2nd ed., Vol. 1, pp. 294–316). New York: Wiley.

Schmitt, D. P., & Buss, D. M. (2001). Human mate poaching: Tactics and temptations for infiltrating existing mateships. *Journal of Personality and Social Psychology, 80,* 894–917.

Schmitt, D. P., Couden, A., & Baker, M. (2001). The effects of sex and temporal context on feelings of romantic desire: An experimental evaluation of sexual strategies theory. *Personality and Social Psychology Bulletin, 27,* 833–847.

Schmitt, D. P., & Jonason, P. K. (2015). Attachment and sexual permissiveness: Exploring differential associations across sexes, cultures, and facets of short-term mating. *Journal of Consulting and Clinical Psychology, 46,* 119–133.

Schmitt, D. P., Jonason, P. K., Byerley, G. J., & . . . Qudrat, A. (2012). A reexamination of sex differences in sexuality: New studies reveal old truths. *Current Directions in Psychological Science, 21,* 135–139.

Schmitt, D. P., & Shackelford, T. K. (2003). Nifty ways to leave your lover: The tactics people use to entice and disguise the process of human mate poaching. *Personality and Social Psychology Bulletin, 29,* 1018–1035.

Schmitt, D. P., & Shackelford, T. K. (2008). Big five traits related to short-term mating: From personality to promiscuity across 46 nations. *Evolutionary Psychology, 6,* 246–282.

Schmitt, D. P., & the International Sexuality Description Project. (2003). Universal sex differences in the desire for sexual variety: Tests from 52 nations, 6 continents, and 13 islands. *Journal of Personality and Social Psychology, 85,* 85–104.

Schmitt, D. P., & the International Sexuality Description Project. (2004). Patterns and universals of mate poaching across 53 nations: The effects of sex, culture, and personality on romantically attracting another person's partner. *Journal of Personality and Social Psychology, 86,* 560–584.

Schneider, D., Harknett, K., & McLanahan, S. (2016). Intimate partner violence in the great recession. *Demography, 53,* 471–505.

Schoenfeld, E. A., Loving, T. J., Pope, M. T., Huston, T. L., & Štulhofer, A. (2017). Does sex really matter? Examining the connections between spouses' nonsexual behaviors, sexual frequency, sexual satisfaction, and marital satisfaction. *Archives of Sexual Behavior, 46,* 489–501.

Schröder, J., & Schmiedeberg, C. (2015). Effects of relationship duration, cohabitation, and marriage on the frequency of intercourse in couples: Findings from German panel data. *Social Science Research, 52,* 72–82.

Schrodt, P., Witt, P. L., & Shimkowski, J. R. (2014). A meta-analytical review of the demand/withdraw pattern of interaction and its associations with individual, relational, and communicative outcomes. *Communication Monographs, 81,* 28–58.

Schütz, A. (1999). It was your fault! Self-serving biases in autobiographical accounts of conflicts in married couples. *Journal of Social and Personal Relationships, 16,* 193–208.

Schützwohl, A. (2005). Sex differences in jealousy: The processing of cues to infidelity. *Evolution and Human Behavior, 26,* 288–299.

Schützwohl, A. (2006). Sex differences in jealousy: Information search and cognitive preoccupation. *Personality and Individual Differences, 40,* 285–292.

Schützwohl, A. (2008a). Relief over the disconfirmation of the prospect of sexual and emotional infidelity. *Personality and Individual Differences, 44,* 666–676.

Schützwohl, A. (2008b). The intentional object of romantic jealousy. *Evolution and Human Behavior, 29,* 92–99.

Schwartz, P., Diefendorf, S., & McGlynn-Wright, A. (2014). Sexuality in aging. In D. L. Tolman, L. Diamond, J. Bauermeister, et al. (Eds.), *APA handbook of sexuality and psychology* (Vol. 1, pp. 523–551). Washington, DC: American Psychological Association.

Schwarz, S., & Hassebrauck, M. (2008). Self-perceived and observed variations in women's attractiveness throughout the menstrual cycle—A diary study. *Evolution and Human Behavior, 29,* 282–288.

Schweinle, W. E., Ickes, W., & Bernstein, I. H. (2002). Empathic accuracy in husband to wife aggression: The overattribution bias. *Personal Relationships, 9,* 141–158.

Scott, S. B., Parsons, A., Post, K. M., & . . . Rhoades, G. K. (2017). Changes in the sexual relationship and relationship adjustment precede extradyadic sexual involvement. *Archives of Sexual Behavior, 46,* 395–406.

Scott, S. B., Rhoades, G. K., Stanley, S. M., Allen, E. S., & Markman, H. J. (2013). Reasons for divorce and recollections of premarital intervention: Implications for improving relationship education. *Couple and Family Psychology: Research and Practice, 2,* 131–145.

Scott-Sheldon, L. A. J., & Johnson, B. T. (2006). Eroticizing creates safer sex: A research synthesis. *Journal of Primary Prevention, 27,* 619–640.

Sczesny, S., Moser, F., & Wood. W. (2015). Beyond sexist beliefs: How do people decide to use gender-inclusive language? *Personality and Social Psychology Bulletin, 4,* 943–954.

Seabrook, R. C., Ward, L. M., Reed, L., Manago, A., Giaccardi, S., & Lippman, J. R. (2016). Our scripted sexuality: The development and validation of a measure of the heterosexual script and its relation to television consumption. *Emerging Adulthood, 4,* 338–355.

Seal, D. W., Agostinelli, G., & Hannett, C. A. (1994). Extradyadic romantic involvement: Moderating effects of sociosexuality and gender. *Sex Roles, 31,* 1–22.

Sears, M. S., Repetti, R. L., Robles, T. F., & Reynolds, B. M. (2016). I just want to be left alone: Daily overload and marital behavior. *Journal of Family Psychology, 30,* 569–579.

Secord, P. F. (1983). Imbalanced sex ratios: The social consequences. *Personality and Social Psychology Bulletin, 9,* 525–543.

Seder, J. P., & Oishi, S. (2012). Intensity of smiling in Facebook photos predicts future life satisfaction. *Social Psychological and Personality Science, 3,* 407–413.

Sedikides, C., Campbell, W. K., Reeder, G. D., & Elliot, A. J. (1998). The self-serving bias in relational context. *Journal of Personality and Social Psychology, 74,* 378–386.

Sedikides, C., Oliver, M. B., & Campbell, W. K. (1994). Perceived benefits and costs of romantic relationships for women and men: Implications for exchange theory. *Personal Relationships, 1,* 5–21.

Seeman, T. E., Singer, B. H., Ryff, C. D., Love, G. D., & Levy-Storms, L. (2002). Social relationships, gender, and allostatic load across two age cohorts. *Psychosomatic Medicine, 64,* 395–406.

Segal, M. W. (1974). Alphabet and attraction: An unobtrusive measure of the effect of propinquity in a field setting. *Journal of Personality and Social Psychology, 30,* 654–657.

Segal, N., & Fraley, R. C. (2016). Broadening the investment model: An intensive longitudinal study on attachment and perceived partner responsiveness in commitment dynamics. *Journal of Social and Personal Relationships, 33,* 581–599.

Segal-Caspi, L., Roccas, S., & Sagiv, L. (2012). Don't judge a book by its cover, revisited: Perceived and reported traits and values of attractive women. *Psychological Science, 23,* 1112–1116.

Segrin, C., Taylor, M. E., & Altman, J. (2005). Social cognitive mediators and relational outcomes associated with parental divorce. *Journal of Social and Personal Relationships, 22,* 361–377.

Seidman, G. (2012). Positive and negative: Partner derogation and enhancement differentially related to relationship satisfaction. *Personal Relationships, 19,* 51–71.

Seidman, G., & Burke, C. T. (2015). Partner enhancement versus verification and emotional responses to daily conflict. *Journal of Social and Personal Relationships, 32,* 304–329.

Seidman, G., & Miller, O. S. (2013). Effects of gender and physical attractiveness on visual attention to Facebook profiles. *Cyberpsychology, Behavior, and Social Networking, 16,* 20–24.

Seih, Y., Buhrmester, M. D., Lin, Y., Huang, C., & Swann, W. B. Jr. (2013). Do people want to be flattered or understood: The cross-cultural universality of self-verification. *Journal of Experimental Social Psychology, 49,* 169–172.

Sela, Y., Shackelford, T. K., Pham, M. N., & Euler, H. A. (2015). Do women perform fellatio as a mate retention behavior? *Personality and Individual Differences, 73,* 61–66.

Selcuk, E., Gunaydin, G., Ong, A. D., & Almeida, D. M. (2016). Does partner responsiveness predict hedonic and eudaimonic well-being? A 10-year longitudinal study. *Journal of Marriage and Family, 78,* 311–325.

Selcuk, E., Stanton, S. C. E., Slatcher, R. B., & Ong, A. D. (2017). Perceived partner responsiveness predicts better sleep quality through lower anxiety. *Social Psychological and Personality Science, 8,* 83–92.

Sells, T. G. C., & Ganong, L. (2017). Emerging adults' expectations and preferences for gender role arrangements in long-term heterosexual relationship. *Sex Roles, 76,* 125–137.

Seltzer, L. J., Prososki, A. R., Ziegler, T. E., & Pollak, S. D. (2012). Instant messages vs. speech: Hormones and why we still need to hear each other. *Evolution and Human Behavior, 33,* 42–45.

Serota, K. B., & Levine, T. R. (2015). A few prolific liars: Variation in the prevalence of lying. *Journal of Language and Social Psychology, 34,* 138–157.

Sewell, K. K., & Strassberg, D. S. (2015). How do heterosexual undergraduate students define having sex? A new approach to an old question. *Journal of Sex Research, 52,* 507–516.

Shackelford, T. K., Goetz, A. T., Buss, D. M., Euler, H. A., & Hoier, S. (2005). When we hurt the ones we love: Predicting violence against women from men's mate retention. *Personal Relationships, 12,* 447–463.

Shackelford, T. K., Michalski, R. L., & Schmitt, D. P. (2004). Upset in response to a child's partner's infidelities. *European Journal of Social Psychology, 34,* 489–497.

Shafer, K., Jensen, T. M., & Larson, J. H. (2014). Relationship effort, satisfaction, and stability: Differences across union type. *Journal of Marital & Family Therapy, 40,* 212–232.

Shaffer, D. R., Pegalis, L. J., & Bazzini, D. G. (1996). When boy meets girl (revisited): Gender, gender-role orientation, and prospect of future interaction as determinants of self-disclosure among same- and opposite-sex acquaintances. *Personality and Social Psychology Bulletin, 22,* 495–506.

Shaffer, D. R., Ruammake, C., & Pegalis, L. J. (1990). The "opener": Highly skilled as interviewer or interviewee. *Personality and Social Psychology Bulletin, 16,* 511–520.

Shallcross, A. J., Ford, B. Q., Floerke, V. A., & Mauss, I. B. (2013). Getting better with age: The relationship between age, acceptance, and negative affect. *Journal of Personality and Social Psychology, 104,* 734–749.

Shanteau, J., & Nagy, G. F. (1979). Probability of acceptance in dating choice. *Journal of Personality and Social Psychology, 37,* 522–533.

Sharma, A. (2015). Divorce/separation in later-life: A fixed effects analysis of economic well-being by gender. *Journal of Family and Economic Issues, 36,* 299–306.

Sharp, E. A., & Ganong, L. H. (2000). Raising awareness about marital expectations: Are unrealistic beliefs changed by integrative teaching? *Family Relations, 49,* 71–76.

Shaver, P., Furman, W., & Buhrmester, D. (1985). Transition to college: Network changes, social skills, and loneliness. In S. Duck & D. Perlman (Eds.), *Understanding personal relationships: An interdisciplinary approach* (pp. 193–219). London: Sage.

Shaver, P. R., & Mikulincer, M. (2013). Attachment orientations and reactions to ostracism in close relationships and groups. In C. N. DeWall (Ed.), *The Oxford handbook of social exclusion* (pp. 238–247). New York: Oxford University Press.

Sheets, V.L. (2014). Passion for life: Self-expansion and passionate love across the life span. *Journal of Social and Personal Relationships, 31,* 958–974.

Sheldon, K. M., Boehm, J., & Lyubomirsky, S. (2013). Variety is the spice of life: The hedonic adaptation prevention model. In S. David, I. Boniwell, & A. Ayers (Eds.), *The Oxford handbook of happiness* (pp. 901–914). New York: Oxford University Press.

Shettel-Neuber, J., Bryson, J. B., & Young, L. E. (1978). Physical attractiveness of the "other person" and jealousy. *Personality and Social Psychology Bulletin, 4,* 612–615.

Shimizu, M., Seery, M. D., Weisbuch, M., & Lupien, S. P. (2011). Trait social anxiety and physiological activation: Cardiovascular threat during social interaction. *Personality and Social Psychology Bulletin, 37,* 94–106.

Shorey, R. C., Cornelius, T. L., & Bell, K. M. (2011). Reactions to participating in dating violence research: Are our questions distressing participants? *Journal of Interpersonal Violence, 26,* 2890–2907.

Shrout, P. E., Herman, C. M., & Bolger, N. (2006). The costs and benefits of practical and emotional support on adjustment: A daily diary study of couples experiencing acute stress. *Personal Relationships, 13,* 115–134.

Shu, X., Zhu, Y., & Zhang, Z. (2012). Patriarchy, resources, and specialization: Marital decision-making power in urban china. *Journal of Family Issues, 34,* 885–917.

Siegler, I. C., Brummett, B. H., Martin, P., & Helms, M. J. (2013). Consistency and timing of marital transitions and survival during midlife: The role of personality and health risk behaviors. *Annals of Behavioral Medicine, 45,* 338–347.

Simmons, C. A., & Lehmann, P. (2007). Exploring the link between pet abuse and controlling behaviors in violent relationships. *Journal of Interpersonal Violence, 22,* 1211–1222.

Simpson, J. A. (2007). Psychological foundations of trust. *Current Directions in Psychological Science, 16,* 264–268.

Simpson, J. A., Collins, W. A., Salvatore, J. E., & Sung, S. (2014). The impact of early interpersonal experience on adult romantic relationship functioning. In M. Mikulincer & P. R. Shaver (Eds.), *Mechanisms of social connection: From brain to group* (pp. 221–234). Washington, DC: American Psychological Association.

Simpson, J. A., Collins, W. A., Tran, S., & Haydon, K. C. (2007). Attachment and the experience and expression of emotions in romantic relationships: A developmental perspective. *Journal of Personality and Social Psychology, 92,* 355–367.

Simpson, J. A., Farrell, A. K., Oriña, M. M., & Rothman, A. J. (2015). Power and social influence in relationships. In M. Mikulincer, P. Shaver, J. Simpson, & J. Dovidio (Eds.), *APA handbook of personality and social psychology: Vol. 3. Interpersonal relations* (pp. 393–420). Washington, DC: American Psychological Association.

Simpson, J. A., Fillo, J., & Myers, J. (2012). Partner knowledge and relationship outcomes. In S. Vazire & T. W. Wilson (Eds.), *Handbook of self-knowledge* (pp. 225–241). New York: Guilford Press.

Simpson, J. A., & Gangestad, S. W. (1991). Individual differences in sociosexuality: Evidence for convergent and discriminant validity. *Journal of Personality and Social Psychology, 60,* 870–883.

Simpson, J. A., Gangestad, S. W., & Lerma, M. (1990). Perception of physical attractiveness: Mechanisms involved in the maintenance of romantic relationships. *Journal of Personality and Social Psychology, 59,* 1192–1201.

Simpson, J. A., & Howland, M. (2012). Bringing the partner into attachment theory and research. *Journal of Family Theory & Review, 4,* 282–289.

Simpson, J. A., Ickes, W., & Blackstone, T. (1995). When the head protects the heart: Empathic accuracy in dating relationships. *Journal of Personality and Social Psychology, 69,* 629–641.

Simpson, J. A., Ickes, W., & Grich, J. (1999). When accuracy hurts: Reactions of anxious-ambivalent dating partners to a relationship-threatening situation. *Journal of Personality and Social Psychology, 76,* 754–769.

Simpson, J. A., Kim, J. S., Fillo, J., & . . . Winterheld, H. A. (2011). Attachment and the management of empathic accuracy in relationship-threatening situations. *Personality and Social Psychology Bulletin, 37,* 242–254.

Simpson, J. A., Overall, N. C., Farrell, A. K., & Girme, Y. U. (2016). Regulation processes in romantic relationships. In K. Vohs & R. Baumeister (Eds.), *Handbook of self-regulation: Research, theory, and applications* (3rd ed., pp. 283–304). New York: Guilford Press.

Simpson, J. A., Wilson, C. L., & Winterheld, H. A. (2004). Sociosexuality and romantic relationships. In J. H. Harvey, A. Wenzel, & S. Sprecher (Eds.), *The handbook of sexuality in close relationships* (pp. 87–112). Mahwah, NJ: Erlbaum.

Sinclair, H. C., Felmlee, D., Sprecher, S., & Wright, B. L. (2015). Don't tell me who I can't love: A multimethod investigation of social network and reactance effects on romantic relationships. *Social Psychology Quarterly, 78,* 77–99.

Sinclair, H. C., & Frieze, I. H. (2005). When courtship persistence becomes intrusive pursuit: Comparing rejecter and pursuer perspectives of unrequited attraction. *Sex Roles, 52,* 839–852.

Singh, D. (1993). Adaptive significance of female physical attractiveness: Role of waist-to-hip ratio. *Journal of Personality and Social Psychology, 65,* 293–307.

Singh, D. (1995). Female judgment of male attractiveness and desirability for relationships: Role of waist-to-hip ratio and financial status. *Journal of Personality and Social Psychology, 69,* 1089–1101.

Singh, D., & Luis, S. (1995). Ethnic and gender consensus for the effect of waist-to-hip ratio on judgment of women's attractiveness. *Human Nature, 6,* 51–65.

Singh, D., & Singh, D. (2011). Shape and significance of feminine beauty: An evolutionary perspective. *Sex Roles, 64,* 723–731.

Skakoon-Sparling, S., Cramer, K. M., & Shuper, P, A. (2016). The impact of sexual arousal on sexual risk-taking and decision-making in men and women. *Archives of Sexual Behavior, 45,* 33–42.

Slatcher, R. B. (2010). When Harry and Sally met Dick and Jane: Creating closeness between couples. *Personal Relationships, 17,* 279–297.

Slatcher, R. B., Selcuk, E., & Ong, A. D. (2015). Perceived partner responsiveness predicts diurnal cortisol profiles 10 years later. *Psychological Science, 26,* 972–982.

Slater, A., Bremner, G., Johnson, S. P., Sherwood, P., Hayes, R., & Brown, E. (2000). Newborn infants' preference for attractive faces: The role of internal and external facial features. *Infancy, 1,* 265–274.

Slater, D. (2013). *Love in the time of algorithms: What technology does to meeting and mating.* New York: Current.

Slater, P. E. (1968). Some social consequences of temporary systems. In W. G. Bennes & P. E. Slater (Eds.), *The temporary society* (pp. 77–96). New York: Harper & Row.

Sloan, D. M. (2010). Self-disclosure and psychological well-being. In J. Maddux & J. P. Tangney (Eds.), *Social psychological foundations of clinical psychology* (pp. 212–225). New York: Guilford.

Slotter, E. B., Duffy, C.W., & Gardner, W. L. (2014). Balancing the need to be "me" with the need to be "we": Applying optimal distinctiveness theory to the understanding of multiple motives within romantic relationships. *Journal of Experimental Social Psychology, 52,* 71–81.

Slotter, E. B., Finkel, E. J., DeWall, C. N., Pond, R. S., Jr., Lambert, N. M., Bodenhausen, G. V., & Fincham, F. D. (2012). Putting the brakes on aggression toward a romantic partner: The inhibitory influence of relationship commitment. *Journal of Personality and Social Psychology, 102,* 291–305.

Slotter, E. B., & Ward, D. E. (2015). Finding the silver lining: The relative roles of redemptive narratives and cognitive reappraisal in individuals' emotional distress after the end of a romantic relationship. *Journal of Social and Personal Relationships, 32,* 737–756.

Smith, A. (2016, February 11). *15% of American adults have used online dating sites or mobile dating apps.* Pew Research Center. Retrieved from http://www.pewinternet.org/2016/02/11/15-percent-of-american-adults-have-used-online-dating-sites-or-mobile-dating-apps/

Smith, G., Mysak, K., & Michael, S. (2008). Sexual double standards and sexually transmitted illnesses: Social rejection and stigmatization of women. *Sex Roles, 58,* 391–401.

Smith, H. M. J., Dunn, A. K., Baguley, T., & Stacey, P. C. (2016). Concordant cues in faces and voices: Testing the backup signal hypothesis. *Evolutionary Psychology, 14,* 1–10.

Smith, J. L., Ickes, W., Hall, J. A., & Hodges, S. D. (Eds.). (2011). *Managing interpersonal sensitivity: Knowing when and when not to understand others.* Hauppauge, NY: Nova Science.

Smith, T. W. (2006). Sexual behavior in the United States. In R. D. McAnulty & M. M. Burnette (Eds.), *Sex and sexuality, Vol. 1: Sexuality today: Trends and controversies* (pp. 103–131). Westport, CT: Praeger.

Smith, T. W., & Baron, C. E. (2016). Marital discord in the later years. In J. Bookwala (Ed.), *Couple relationships in the middle and later years* (pp. 37–56). Washington, DC: American Psychological Association.

Smith, T. W., Ruiz, J. M., & Uchino, B. N. (2004). Mental activation of supportive ties, hostility, and cardiovascular reactivity to laboratory stress in young men and women. *Health Psychology, 23,* 476–785.

Smith-Marek, E. N., Cafferky, B., Dharnidharka, P., & . . . Mendez, M. (2015). Effects of childhood experiences of family violence on adult partner violence: A meta-analytic review. *Journal of Family Theory & Review, 7,* 498–519.

Snyder, D. K. (2002). Integrating insight-oriented techniques into couple therapy. In J. H. Harvey & A. Wenzel (Eds.), *A clinician's guide to maintaining and enhancing close relationships* (pp. 259–275). Mahwah, NJ: Erlbaum.

Snyder, D. K., Castellani, A. M., & Whisman, M. A. (2006). Current status and future directions in couple therapy. *Annual Review of Psychology, 57,* 317–344.

Snyder, D. K., & Schneider, W. J. (2002). Affective reconstruction: A pluralistic, developmental approach. In A. S. Gurman & N. S. Jacobson (Eds.), *Clinical handbook of couple therapy* (3rd ed., pp. 151–179). New York: Guilford Press.

Snyder, D. K., Wills, R. M., & Grady-Fletcher, A. (1991). Long-term effectiveness of behavioral versus insight-oriented therapy: A four-year follow-up study. *Journal of Consulting and Clinical Psychology, 59,* 138–141.

Snyder, M. (1981). Seek, and ye shall find: Testing hypotheses about other people. In E. T. Higgins, C. P. Herman, & M. P. Zanna (Eds.), *Social cognition: The Ontario symposium* (Vol. 1, pp. 277–303). Hillsdale, NJ: Erlbaum.

Snyder, M. (1987). *Public appearances, private realities: The psychology of self-monitoring.* New York: W. H. Freeman.

Snyder, M., & Gangestad, S. (1986). On the nature of self-monitoring: Matters of assessment, matters of validity. *Journal of Personality and Social Psychology,* 51, 125–139.

Snyder, M., & Swann, W. B., Jr. (1978a). Behavioral confirmation in social interaction: From social perception to social reality. *Journal of Experimental Social Psychology, 14,* 148–163.

Snyder, M., & Swann, W. B., Jr. (1978b). Hypothesis-testing processes in social interaction. *Journal of Personality and Social Psychology, 36,* 1202–1212.

Snyder, M., Tanke, E. D., & Berscheid, E. (1977). Social perception and interpersonal behavior: On the self-fulfilling nature of social stereotypes. *Journal of Personality and Social Psychology, 35,* 656–666.

Sohn, K. (2016). Men's revealed preferences regarding women's ages: Evidence from prostitution. *Evolution and Human Behavior, 37,* 272–280.

Sohn, K. (2017). Men's revealed preference for the mates' ages. *Evolution and Human Behavior, 38,* 58–62.

Solomon, B. C., & Jackson, J. J. (2014). Why do personality traits predict divorce? Multiple pathways through satisfaction. *Journal of Personality and Social Psychology, 106,* 978–996.

Solomon, B. C., & Vazire, S. (2014). You are so beautiful . . . to me: Seeing beyond biases and achieving accuracy in romantic relationships. *Journal of Personality and Social Psychology,* 107, 516–528.

Solomon, D., & Theiss, J. (2013). *Interpersonal communication: Putting theory into practice.* New York: Routledge.

Solomon, D. H., Knobloch, L. K., Theiss, J. A., & McLaren, R. M. (2016). Relational turbulence theory: Explaining variation in subjective experiences and communication within romantic relationships. *Human Communication Research, 42,* 507–532.

Solomon, S. E., Rothblum, E. D., & Balsam, K. F. (2005). Money, housework, sex, and conflict: Same-sex couples in civil unions, those not in civil unions, and heterosexual married siblings. *Sex Roles, 52,* 561–575.

Sommer, K. L., & Rubin, Y. S. (2005). Role of social expectancies in cognitive and behavioral responses to social rejection. In K. D. Williams, J. P. Forgas, & W. von Hippel (Eds.), *The social outcast: Ostracism, social exclusion, rejection, and bullying* (pp. 171–183). New York: Psychology Press.

Sommer, K. L., Williams, K. D., Ciarocco, N. J., & Baumeister, R. F. (2001). When silence speaks louder than words: Explorations into the intrapsychic and interpersonal consequences of social ostracism. *Basic and Applied Social Psychology, 23,* 225–243.

Soons, J. P. M., Liefbroer, A. C., & Kalmijn, M. (2009). The long-term consequences of relationship formation for subjective well-being. *Journal of Marriage and Family, 71,* 1254–1270.

Soto, C. J. (2015). Is happiness good for your personality? Concurrent and prospective relations of the Big Five with subjective well-being. *Journal of Personality, 83,* 45–55.

Soulsby, L. K., & Bennett, K. M. (2017). When two become one: Exploring identity in marriage and cohabitation. *Journal of Family Issues, 38,* 358–380.

South, S. J., Trent, K., & Shen, Y. (2001). Changing partners: Toward a macrostructural-opportunity theory of marital dissolution. *Journal of Marriage and the Family, 63,* 743–754.

Southard, A. C., Noser, A. E., Pollock, N. C., Mercer, S. H., & Zeigler-Hill, V. (2015). The interpersonal nature of dark personality features. *Journal of Social and Clinical Psychology, 34,* 555–586.

Southworth, C., Finn, J., Dawson, S., Fraser, C., & Tucker, S. (2007). Intimate partner violence, technology, and stalking. *Violence Against Women, 13,* 842–856.

Spielmann, S. S., MacDonald, G., Joel, S., & Impett, E. A. (2016). Longing for ex-partners out of fear of being single. *Journal of Personality, 84,* 799–808.

Spielmann, S. S., MacDonald, G., Maxwell, J. A., & . . . Impett, E. A. (2013b). Settling for less out of fear of being single. *Journal of Personality and Social Psychology, 105,* 1049–1073.

Spielmann, S. S., MacDonald, G., & Wilson, A. E. (2009). On the rebound: Focusing on someone new helps anxiously attached individuals let go of ex-partners. *Personality and Social Psychology Bulletin, 35,* 1382–1394.

Spielmann, S. S., MacDonald, G., & Tackett, J. L. (2012). Social threat, social reward, and regulation of investment in romantic relationships. *Personal Relationships, 19,* 601–622.

Spielmann, S. S., Maxwell, J. A., MacDonald, G., & Baratta, P. L. (2013a). Don't get your hopes up: Avoidantly attached individuals perceive lower social reward when there is potential for intimacy. *Personality and Social Psychology Bulletin, 39,* 219–236.

Spitzberg, B. H. (1999). An analysis of empirical estimates of sexual aggression, victimization, and perpetration. *Violence and Victims, 14,* 241–260.

Spitzberg, B. H. (2017). Acknowledgment of unwanted pursuit, threats, assault, and stalking in a college population. *Psychology of Violence, 7,* 265–275.

Spitzberg, B. H., & Cupach, W. R. (2014). *The dark side of relationship pursuit: From attraction to obsession and stalking* (2nd ed.). New York: Routledge.

Spitzberg, B. H., Cupach, W. R., & Ciceraro, L. D. L. (2010). Sex differences in stalking and obsessive relational intrusion: Two meta-analyses. *Partner Abuse, 1,* 259–285.

Sprecher, S. (1986). The relation between inequity and emotions in close relationships. *Social Psychology Quarterly, 49,* 309–321.

Sprecher, S. (2002). Sexual satisfaction in premarital relationships: Associations with satisfaction, love, commitment, and stability. *Journal of Sex Research, 39,* 190–196.

Sprecher, S. (2014). Effects of actual (manipulated) and perceived similarity on liking in get-acquainted interactions: The role of communication. *Communication Monographs, 81,* 4–27.

Sprecher, S. (2017). Inequity leads to distress and a reduction in satisfaction: Evidence from a priming experiment. *Journal of Family Issues.* doi: 10.1177/0192513X16637098.

Sprecher, S., Barbee, A., & Schwartz, P. (1995). "Was it good for you, too?" Gender differences in first sexual intercourse experiences. *Journal of Sex Research, 32,* 3–15.

Sprecher, S., & Fehr, B. (2005). Compassionate love for close others and humanity. *Journal of Social and Personal Relationships, 22,* 629–651.

Sprecher, S., & Fehr, B. (2011). Dispositional attachment and relationship-specific attachment as predictors of compassionate love for a partner. *Journal of Social and Personal Relationships, 28,* 558–574

Sprecher, S., Fehr, B., & Zimmerman, C. (2007). Expectation for mood enhancement as a result of helping: The effects of gender and compassionate love. *Sex Roles, 56,* 543–549.

Sprecher, S., & Hatfield, E. (2017). The importance of love as a basis of marriage: Revisiting Kephart (1967). *Journal of Family Issues, 38,* 312–335.

Sprecher, S., & Metts, S. (1999). Romantic beliefs: Their influence on relationships and patterns of change over time. *Journal of Social and Personal Relationships, 16,* 834–851.

Sprecher, S., & Metts, S. (2013). Logging on, hooking up: The changing nature of romantic relationship initiation and romantic relating. In C. Hazan & M. I. Campa (Eds.), *Human bonding: The science of affectional ties* (pp. 197–225). New York: Guilford Press.

Sprecher, S., & Regan, P. C. (1998). Passionate and companionate love in courting and young married couples. *Sociological Inquiry, 68,* 163–185.

Sprecher, S., Regan, P. C., & McKinney, K. (1998). Beliefs about the outcomes of extramarital sexual relationships as a function of the gender of the "cheating spouse." *Sex Roles, 38,* 301–311.

Sprecher, S., Schmeeckle, M., & Felmlee, D. (2006). Inequality in emotional involvement in romantic relationships. *Journal of Family Issues, 27,* 1255–1280.

Sprecher, S., & Treger, S. (2015). The benefits of turn-taking reciprocal self-disclosure in get-acquainted interactions. *Personal Relationships, 22,* 460–475.

Sprecher, S., Treger, S., & Sakaluk, J. K. (2013a). Premarital sexual standards and sociosexuality: Gender, ethnicity, and cohort differences. *Archives of Sexual Behavior, 42,* 1395–1405.

Sprecher, S., Treger, S., & Wondra, J. D. (2013b). Effects of self-disclosure role on liking, closeness, and other impressions in get-acquainted interactions. *Journal of Social and Personal Relationships, 30,* 497–514.

Srivastava, S., McGonigal, K. M., Richards, J. M., Butler, E. A., & Gross, J. J. (2006). Optimism in close relationships: How seeing things in a positive light makes them so. *Journal of Personality and Social Psychology, 91,* 143–153.

Stackert, R. A., & Bursik, K. (2003). Why am I unsatisfied? Adult attachment style, gendered irrational relationship beliefs, and young adult romantic relationship satisfaction. *Personality and Individual Differences, 34,* 1419–1429.

Stafford, L. (2003). Maintaining romantic relationships: A summary and analysis of one research program. In D. J. Canary & M. Dainton (Eds.), *Maintaining relationships through communication: Relational, contextual, and cultural variations* (pp. 51–77). Mahwah, NJ: Erlbaum.

Stafford, L. (2011). Measuring relationship maintenance behaviors: Critique and development of the revised relationship maintenance behavior scale. *Journal of Social and Personal Relationships, 28,* 278–303.

Stafford, L., & Dainton, M. (1994). The dark side of "normal" family interaction. In W. R. Cupach & B. H. Spitzberg (Eds.), *The dark side of interpersonal communication* (pp. 259–280). Hillsdale, NJ: Erlbaum.

Stafford, L., David, P., & McPherson, S. (2014). Sanctity of marriage and marital quality. *Journal of Social and Personal Relationships, 31,* 54–70.

Stafford, L., Merolla, A. J., & Castle, J. D. (2006). When long-distance dating partners become geographically close. *Journal of Social and Personal Relationships, 23,* 901–919.

Stake, J. E., & Eisele, H. (2010). Gender and personality. In J. Chrisler & D. McCreary (Eds.), *Handbook of gender research in psychology* (Vol. 2, pp. 19–40). New York: Springer.

Stanik, C. E., & Bryant, C. M. (2012). Marital quality of newlywed African American couples: Implications of egalitarian gender role dynamics. *Sex Roles, 66,* 256–267.

Stanik, C. E., & Ellsworth, P. C. (2010). Who cares about marrying a rich man? Intelligence and variation in women's mate preferences. *Human Nature, 21,* 203–217.

Stanik, C. E., McHale, S. M., & Crouter, A. C. (2013). Gender dynamics predict changes in marital love among African American couples. *Journal of Marriage and Family, 75,* 795–807.

Stanley, S. M., Bradbury, T. N., & Markman, H. J. (2000). Structural flaws in the bridge from basic research on marriage to interventions. *Journal of Marriage and the Family, 62,* 256–264.

Stanley, S. M., Rhoades, G. K., Amato, P. R., Markman, H. J., & Johnson, C. A. (2010). The timing of cohabitation and engagement: Impact on first and second marriages. *Journal of Marriage and Family, 72,* 906–918.

Starks, T. J., & Parsons, J. T. (2014). Adult Attachment among partnered gay men: Patterns and associations with sexual relationship quality. *Archives of Sexual Behavior, 43,* 107–117.

Steinberg, M., & Diekman, A. B. (2016). The double-edged sword of stereotypes of men. In Y. J. Wong & S. R. Wester (Eds.), *APA handbook of men and masculinities* (pp. 433–456). Washington, DC: American Psychological Association.

Stepler, R. (2017, March 9). *Led by Baby Boomers, divorce rates climb for America's 50+ population.* Pew Research Center. Retrieved from http://www.pewresearch.org/fact-tank/2017/03/09/led-by-baby-boomers-divorce-rates-climb-for-americas-50-population/.

Sternberg, R. J. (1987). *The triangle of love: Intimacy, passion, commitment.* New York: Basic Books.

Sternberg, R. J. (2006). A duplex theory of love. In R. J. Sternberg & K. Weis (Eds.), *The new psychology of love* (pp. 184–199). New Haven, CT: Yale University Press.

Stewart, A. J., Copeland, A. P., Chester, N. L., Malley, J. E., & Barenbaum, N. B. (1997). *Separating together: How divorce transforms families.* New York: Guilford Press.

Stewart-Williams, S., Butler, C. A., & Thomas, A. G. (2017). Sexual history and present attractiveness: People want a mate with a bit of a past, but not too much. *Journal of Sex Research.* doi:10.1080/00224499.2016.1232690

Stickney, L. T., & Konrad, A. M. (2007). Gender-role attitudes and earnings: A multinational study of married women and men. *Sex Roles, 57,* 801–811.

Stillwell, A. M., Baumeister, R. F., & Del Priore, R. E. (2008). We're all victims here: Toward a psychology of revenge. *Basic and Applied Social Psychology, 30,* 253–263.

Stinson, D. A., Cameron, J. J., Wood, J. V., Gaucher, D., & Holmes, J. G. (2009). Deconstructing the "reign of error": Interpersonal warmth explains the self-fulfilling prophecy of anticipated acceptance. *Personality and Social Psychology Bulletin, 35,* 1165–1178.

Stinson, D. A., Logel, C., Holmes, J. G., & . . . Kath, J. (2010). The regulatory function of self-esteem: Testing the epistemic and acceptance signaling systems. *Journal of Personality and Social Psychology, 99,* 993–1013.

Stoeber, J. (2012). Dyadic perfectionism in romantic relationships: Predicting relationship satisfaction and longterm commitment. *Personality and Individual Differences, 53,* 300–305.

Stokes, J. E. (2017). Marital quality and loneliness in later life: A dyadic analysis of older married couples in Ireland. *Journal of Social and Personal Relationships, 34,* 114–135.

Strachman, A., & Gable, S. L. (2006). What you want (and do not want) affects what you see (and do not see): Avoidance social goals and social events. *Personality and Social Psychology Bulletin, 32,* 1446–1458.

Strachman, A., & Impett, E. A. (2009). Attachment orientations and daily condom use in dating relationships. *Journal of Sex Research, 46,* 319–329.

Strassberg, D. S., & English, B. L. (2015). An experimental study of men's and women's personal ads. *Archives of Sex Behavior, 44,* 2249–2255.

Strauss, C., Morry, M. M., & Kito, M. (2012). Attachment styles and relationship quality: Actual perceived, and ideal partner matching. *Personal Relationships, 19,* 14–36.

Strelan, P., McKee, I., & Feather, N. T. (2016). When and how forgiving benefits victims: Post-transgression offender effort and the mediating role of deservingness judgements. *European Journal of Social Psychology, 46,* 308–322.

Stroebe, M. S., Abakoumkin, G., Stroebe, W., & Schut, H. (2012). Continuing bonds in adjustment to bereavement: Impact of abrupt versus gradual separation. *Personal Relationships, 19,* 255–266.

Strokoff, J., Owen, J., & Fincham, F. D. (2015). Diverse reactions to hooking up among U.S. university students. *Archives of Sexual Behavior, 44,* 935–943.

Strong, G., & Aron, A. (2006). The effect of shared participation in novel and challenging activities on experienced relationship quality: Is it mediated by high positive affect? In K. D. Vohs & E. J. Finkel (Eds.), *Self and relationships: Connecting intrapersonal and interpersonal processes* (pp. 342–359). New York: Guilford Press.

Strübel, J., & Petrie, T. (2016, August). *Love me Tinder: Objectification and psychosocial well-being.* Poster presented at the meeting of the American Psychological Association, Denver.

Stuart, G. L., Moore, T. M., Elkins, S. R., & . . . Shorey, R. C. (2013). The temporal association between substance use and intimate partner violence among women arrested for domestic violence. *Journal of Consulting and Clinical Psychology, 81,* 681–690.

Stucke, T. S. (2003). Who's to blame? Narcissism and self-serving attributions following feedback. *European Journal of Personality, 17,* 465–478.

Stukas, A. A., Jr., & Snyder, M. (2002). Targets' awareness of expectations and behavioral confirmation in ongoing interactions. *Journal of Experimental Social Psychology, 38,* 31–40.

Stulp, G., Buunk, A. P., & Pollet, T. V. (2013). Women want taller men more than men want shorter women. *Personality and Individual Differences, 54,* 877–883.

Subotnik, R. (2007). Cyber-infidelity. In P. Peluso (Ed.), *Infidelity: A practitioner's guide to working with couples in crisis* (pp. 169–190). New York: Routledge.

Sullivan, K. T., Pasch, L. A., Johnson, M. D., & Bradbury, T. N. (2010). Social support, problem solving, and the longitudinal course of newlywed marriage. *Journal of Personality and Social Psychology, 98,* 631–644.

Summers, R. F., & Barber, J. P. (2003). Therapeutic alliance as a measurable psychotherapy skill. *Academic Psychiatry, 27,* 160–165.

Sun, Y. (2001). Family environment and adolescents' well-being before and after parents' marital disruption: A longitudinal analysis. *Journal of Marriage and the Family, 63,* 697–713.

Sun, Y., & Li, Y. (2002). Children's well-being during parents' marital disruption process: A pooled time-series analysis. *Journal of Marriage and the Family, 64,* 472–488.

Sunderani, S., Arnocky, S., & Vaillancourt, T. (2013). Individual differences in mate poaching: An examination of hormonal, dispositional, and behavioral mate-value traits. *Archives of Sexual Behavior, 42,* 533–542.

Sundie, J. M., Kenrick, D. T., Griskevicius, V., Tybur, J. M., Vohs, K. D., & Beal, D. J. (2011). Peacocks, Porsches, and Thorstein Veblen: Conspicuous consumption as a sexual signaling system. *Journal of Personality and Social Psychology, 100,* 664–680.

Surra, C. A., & Longstreth, M. (1990). Similarity of outcomes, interdependence, and conflict in dating relationships. *Journal of Personality and Social Psychology, 59,* 501–516.

Swami, V., Greven, C., & Furnham, A. (2007). More than just skin deep? A pilot study integrating physical and non-physical factors in the perception of physical attractiveness. *Personality and Individual Differences, 42,* 563–572.

Swami, V., & IBP Project Members. (2010). The attractive female body weight and female body dissatisfaction in 26 countries across 10 world regions: Results of the International Body Project 1. *Personality and Social Psychology Bulletin, 36,* 309–325.

Swann, W. B., Jr. (1996). *Self-traps: The elusive quest for higher self-esteem.* New York: W. H. Freeman.

Swann, W. B., Jr., & Bosson. J. K. (2010). Self and identity. In S. Fiske, D. Gilbert, & G. Lindzey (Eds.), *Handbook of social psychology* (5th ed., Vol. 1, pp. 589–628). Hoboken, NJ: Wiley.

Swann, W. B., Jr., & Buhrmester, M. D. (2012). Self-verification: The search for coherence. In M. R. Leary & J. P. Tangney (Eds.), *Handbook of self and identity* (2nd ed., pp. 405–424). New York: Guilford Press.

Swann, W. B., Jr., De La Ronde, C., & Hixon, J. G. (1994). Authenticity and positivity strivings in marriage and courtship. *Journal of Personality and Social Psychology, 66,* 857–869.

Swann, W. B., Jr., & Gill, M. J. (1997). Confidence and accuracy in person perception: Do we know what we think we know about our relationship partners? *Journal of Personality and Social Psychology, 73,* 747–757.

Swann, W. B., Jr., Hixon, J. G., Stein-Seroussi, A., & Gilbert, D. T. (1990). The fleeting gleam of praise: Cognitive processes underlying behavioral reactions to self-relevant feedback. *Journal of Personality and Social Psychology, 59,* 17–26.

Swann, W. B., Jr., & Pelham, B. (2002). Who wants out when the going gets good? Psychological investment and preference for self-verifying roommates. *Self and Identity, 1,* 219–233.

Swann, W. B., Jr., & Rentfrow, P. J. (2001). Blirtatiousness: Cognitive, behavioral, and physiological consequences of rapid responding. *Journal of Personality and Social Psychology, 81,* 1160–1175.

Swann, W. B., Jr., Rentfrow, P. J., & Gosling, S. D. (2003). The precarious couple effect: Verbally inhibited men + critical, disinhibited women = bad chemistry. *Journal of Personality and Social Psychology, 85,* 1095–1106.

Swann, W. B., Jr., Sellers, J. G., & McClarty, K. L. (2006). Tempting today, troubling tomorrow: The roots of the precarious couple effect. *Personality and Social Psychology Bulletin, 32,* 93–103.

Swann, W. B., Jr., Silvera, D. H., & Proske, C. U. (1995). On "knowing your partner": Dangerous illusions in the age of AIDS? *Personal Relationships, 2,* 173–186.

Syme, M. L., Cohn, T. J., & Barnack-Tavlaris, J. (2017). A comparison of actual and perceived sexual risk among older adults. *Journal of Sexual Research, 54,* 149–160.

Tabak, J. A., & Zayas, V. (2012). The roles of featural and configural face processing in snap judgments of sexual orientation. *PLoS ONE, 7,* 1–7.

Tach, L. M., & Halpern-Meekin, S. (2012). Marital quality and divorce decisions: How do premarital cohabitation and nonmarital childbearing matter? *Family Relations, 61,* 571–585.

Tackett, S. L., Nelson, L. J., & Busby, D. M. (2013). Shyness and relationship satisfaction: Evaluating the associations between shyness, self-esteem, and relationship satisfaction in couples. *American Journal of Family Therapy, 41,* 34–45.

Tafoya, M. A., & Spitzberg, B. H. (2007). The dark side of infidelity: Its nature, prevalence, and communicative functions. In B. H. Spitzberg & W. R. Cupach (Eds.), *The dark side of interpersonal communication* (2nd ed., pp. 201–242). Mahwah, NJ: Erlbaum.

Takahashi, H., Matsuura, M., Yahata, N., Koeda, M., Suhara, T., & Okubo, Y. (2006). Men and women show distinct brain activations during imagery of sexual and emotional infidelity. *NeuroImage, 32,* 1299–1307.

Talhelm, T., & Oishi, S. (2014). Residential mobility affects self-concept, group support, and happiness of individuals and communities. In P. Rentfrow (Ed.), *Geographical psychology: Exploring the interaction of environment and behavior* (pp. 219–239). Washington, DC: American Psychological Association.

Tan, R., Overall, N. C., & Taylor, J. K. (2012). Let's talk about us: Attachment, relationship-focused disclosure, and relationship quality. *Personal Relationships, 19,* 521–534.

Tanha, M., Beck, C. J. A., Figueredo, A. J., & Raghavan, C. (2010). Sex differences in intimate partner violence and the use of coercive control as a motivational factor for intimate partner violence. *Journal of Interpersonal Violence, 25,* 1836–1854.

Tatum, A. K. (2017). The interaction of same-sex marriage access with sexual minority identity on mental health and subjective wellbeing. *Journal of Homosexuality, 64,* 638–653.

Tausczik, Y. R., & Pennebaker, J. W. (2010). The psychological meaning of words: LIWC and computerized text analysis methods. *Journal of Language and Social Psychology, 29,* 24–54.

Tavris, C. (1989). *Anger: The misunderstood emotion.* New York: Simon and Schuster.

Taylor, L. S., Fiore, A. T., Mendelsohn, G. A., & Cheshire, C. (2011). "Out of my league": A real-world test of the matching hypothesis. *Personality and Social Psychology Bulletin, 37,* 942–954.

Teachman, J. (2008). Complex life course patterns and the risk of divorce in second marriages. *Journal of Marriage and Family, 70,* 294–305.

Teding van Berkhout, E., & Malouff, J. (2016). The efficacy of empathy training: A meta-analysis of randomized controlled trials. *Journal of Counseling Psychology, 63,* 32–41.

Tellegen, A., Lykken, D. T., Bouchard, T. J., Wilcox, K. J., Segal, N. L., & Rich, S. (1988). Personality similarity in twins reared apart and together. *Journal of Personality and Social Psychology, 54,* 1031–1039.

ten Brinke, L., & Porter, S. (2012). Cry me a river: Identifying the behavioral consequences of extremely high-stakes interpersonal deception. *Law and Human Behavior, 36,* 469–477.

Tenney, E. R., & Spellman, B. A. (2011). Complex social consequences of self-knowledge. *Social Psychological and Personality Science, 2,* 343–350.

Terhell, E. L., van Groenou, M. I. B., & van Tilburg, T. (2004). Network dynamics in the long-term period after divorce. *Journal of Social and Personal Relationships, 21,* 719–738.

Theiss, J. A., & Estlein, R. (2014). Antecedents and consequences of the perceived threat of sexual communication: A test of the relational turbulence model. *Western Journal of Communication, 78,* 404–425.

Theiss, J. A., Estlein, R., & Weber, K. M. (2013). A longitudinal assessment of relationship characteristics that predict new parents' relationship satisfaction. *Personal Relationships, 20,* 216–235.

Theiss, J. A., & Knobloch, L. K. (2014). Relational turbulence and the post-deployment transition: Self, partner, and relationship focused turbulence. *Communication Research, 41,* 27–51.

Thibaut, J. W., & Kelley, H. H. (1959). *The social psychology of groups.* New York: Wiley.

Thielmann, I., & Hilbig, B. E. (2015). The traits one can trust: Dissecting reciprocity and kindness as determinants of trustworthy behavior. *Personality and Social Psychology Bulletin, 41,* 1523–1536.

Thomae, M., & Houston, D. M. (2016). The impact of gender ideologies on men's and women's desire for a traditional or non-traditional partner. *Personality and Individual Differences, 95,* 152–158.

Thomas, V., & Azmitia, M. (2016). Tapping into the app: Updating the experience sampling method for the 21st century. *Emerging Adulthood, 4,* 60–67.

Thompson, A. E., & Voyer, D. (2014). Sex differences in the ability to recognise non-verbal display of emotion: A meta-analysis. *Cognition and Emotion, 28,* 1164–1195.

Thompson, S. C., & Kelley, H. H. (1981). Judgments of responsibility for activities in close relationships. *Journal of Personality and Social Psychology, 41,* 469–477.

Thornhill, R., Chapmen, J. F., & Gangestad, S. W. (2013). Women's preferences for men's scents associated with testosterone and cortisol levels: Patterns across the ovulatory cycle. *Evolution and Human Behavior, 34,* 216–221.

Thornhill, R., Gangestad, S. W., Miller, R., Scheyd, G., McCollough, J. K., & Franklin, M. (2003). Major histocompatibility complex genes, symmetry, and body scent attractiveness in men and women. *Behavioral Ecology, 14,* 668–678.

Thornton, A., Axinn, W. G., & Xie, Y. (2007). *Marriage and cohabitation.* Chicago: University of Chicago Press.

Thornton, A., & Young-DeMarco, L. (2001). Four decades of trends in attitudes toward family issues in the United States: The 1960s through the 1990s. *Journal of Marriage and the Family, 63,* 1009–1037.

Tice, D. M., & Baumeister, R. F. (1993). Controlling anger: Self-induced emotion change. In D. M. Wegner & J. W. Pennebaker (Eds.), *Handbook of mental control* (pp. 393–409). Englewood Cliffs, NJ: Prentice Hall.

Tidwell, N. D., & Eastwick, P. W. (2013). Sex differences in succumbing to sexual temptations: A function of impulse or control? *Personality and Social Psychology Bulletin, 39,* 1620–1633.

Tidwell, N. D., Eastwick, P. W., & Finkel, E. J. (2013). Perceived, not actual, similarity predicts initial attraction in a live romantic context: Evidence from the speed-dating paradigm. *Personal Relationships, 20,* 199–215.

Timmons, A. C., Arbel, R., & Margolin, G. (2017). Daily patterns of stress and conflict in couples: Associations with marital aggression and family-of-origin aggression. *Journal of Family Psychology, 31,* 93–104.

Todorov, A., Olivola, C. Y., Dotsch, R., Mende-Siedlecki (2015). Social attributions from faces: Determinants, consequences, accuracy, and functional significance. *Annual Review of Psychology, 66,* 519–545.

Tokunaga, R. S. (2011). Friend me or you'll strain us: Understanding negative events that occur over social networking sites. *Cyberpsychology, Behavior, and Social Networking, 14,* 425–432.

Toller, P. (2011). Bereaved parents' experiences of supportive and unsupportive communication. *Southern Communication Journal, 76,* 17–34.

Tomlinson, J. M., & Aron, A. (2012). Relationship neuroscience: Where we are and where we might be going. In O. Gillath, G. Adams, & A. Kunkel (Eds.), *Relationship science: Integrating evolutionary, neuroscience, and sociocultural approaches* (pp. 13–26). Washington, DC: American Psychological Association.

Tomlinson, J. M., Aron, A., Carmichael, C. L., Reis, H. T., & Holmes, J. G. (2014). The costs of being put on a pedestal: Effects of feeling over-idealized. *Journal of Social and Personal Relationships, 31,* 384–409.

Tomlinson, J. M., Carmichael, C. L., Reis, H. T., & Aron, A. (2010). Affective forecasting and individual differences: Accuracy for relational events and anxious attachment. *Emotion, 10,* 447–453.

Tonietto, G. N., & Malkoc, S. A. (2016). The calendar mindset: Scheduling takes the fun out and puts the work in. *Journal of Marketing Research, 53,* 922–936.

Totenhagen, C. J., Butler, E. A., Curran, M. A., & Serido, J. (2016). The calm after the storm: Relationship length as associated with couples' daily variability. *Journal of Social and Personal Relationships, 33,* 768–791.

Totenhagen, C. J., Curran, M. A., Serido, J., & Butler, E. A. (2013). Good days, bad days: Do sacrifices improve relationship quality? *Journal of Social and Personal Relationships, 30,* 881–900.

Totenhagen, C. J., Serido, J., Curran, M. A., & Butler, E. A. (2012). Daily hassles and uplifts: A diary study on understanding relationship quality. *Journal of Family Psychology, 26,* 719–728.

Tracy, J. L., & Robins, R. W. (2008). The automaticity of emotion recognition. *Emotion, 8,* 81–95.

Trail, T. E., & Karney, B. R. (2012). What's (not) wrong with low-income marriages. *Journal of Marriage and Family, 74,* 413–427.

Tran, S., Simpson, J. A., & Fletcher, G. J. O. (2008). The role of ideal standards in relationship initiation processes. In S. Sprecher, A. Wenzel, & J. Harvey (Eds.), *Handbook of relationship initiation* (pp. 487–498). New York: Psychology Press.

Treat, T. A., Viken, R. J., Farris, C. A., & Smith, J. R. (2016). Enhancing the accuracy of men's perceptions of women's sexual interest in the laboratory. *Psychology of Violence, 6,* 562–572.

Troy, A. B., Lewis-Smith, J., & Laurenceau, J. (2006). Interracial and intraracial romantic relationships: The search for differences in satisfaction, conflict, and attachment style. *Journal of Social and Personal Relationships, 23,* 65–80.

Tsai, F., & Reis, H. T. (2009). Perceptions by and of lonely people in social networks. *Personal Relationships, 16,* 221–238.

Tsapelas, I., Aron, A., & Orbuch, T. (2009). Marital boredom now predicts less satisfaction 9 years later. *Psychological Science, 20,* 543–545.

Tsapelas, I., Fisher, H. E., & Aron, A. (2011). Infidelity: When, where, why. In W. Cupach & B. Spitzberg (Eds.), *The dark side of close relationships II* (pp. 175–195). New York: Routledge.

Tucker, J. S., & Anders, S. L. (1998). Adult attachment style and nonverbal closeness in dating couples. *Journal of Nonverbal Behavior, 22,* 109–124.

Tucker, P., & Aron, A. (1993). Passionate love and marital satisfaction at key transition points in the family life cycle. *Journal of Social and Clinical Psychology, 12,* 135–147.

Turchik, J. A., & Hassija, C. M. (2014). Female sexual victimization among college students: Assault severity, health risk behaviors, and sexual functioning. *Journal of Interpersonal Violence, 29,* 2439–2457.

Turley, R. N. L., & Desmond, M. (2011). Contributions to college costs by married, divorced, and remarried parents. *Journal of Family Issues, 32,* 767–790.

Tuscherer, T., Sacco, D. F., Wirth, J. H., & . . . Wesselmann, E. D. (2015). Responses to exclusion are moderated by its perceived fairness. *European Journal of Social Psychology, 46,* 280–293.

Twenge, J. M. (2013). Overwhelming evidence for generation me: A reply to Arnett. *Emerging Adulthood, 1,* 21–26.

Twenge, J. M., Campbell, W. K., & Carter, N. T. (2014). Declines in trust in others and confidence in institutions among American adults and late adolescents, 1972–2012. *Psychological Science, 25,* 1914–1923.

Twenge, J. M., Catanese, K. R., & Baumeister, R. F. (2003). Social exclusion and the deconstructed state: Time perception, meaninglessness, lethargy, lack of emotion, and self-awareness. *Journal of Personality and Social Psychology, 85,* 409–423.

Twenge, J. M., & Kasser, T. (2013). Generational changes in materialism and work centrality, 1976–2007: Associations with temporal changes in societal insecurity and materialistic role modeling. *Personality and Social Psychology Bulletin, 39,* 883–897.

Twenge, J. M., Sherman, R. A., & Wells, B. E. (2015). Changes in American adults' sexual behavior and attitudes, 1972–2012. *Archives of Sexual Behavior, 44,* 2273–2285.

Twenge, J. M., Sherman, R. A., & Wells, B. E. (2016). Changes in American adults' reported same-sex sexual experiences and attitudes, 1973–2014. *Archives of Sexual Behavior, 45,* 1713–1730.

Ueno, K., Gayman, M. D., Wright, E. R., & Quantz, S. D. (2009). Friends' sexual orientation, relational quality, and mental health among gay, lesbian, and bisexual youth. *Personal Relationships, 16,* 659–670.

U. S. Census Bureau. (2013). *America's families and living arrangements: 2013.* Retrieved from http://www.census.gov/hhes/families/data/cps2013.html

Uleman, J. S., & Saribay, S. A. (2012). Initial impressions of others. In K. Deaux & M. Snyder (Eds.), *The Oxford handbook of personality and social psychology* (pp. 337–366). New York: Oxford University Press.

Urquia, M. L., O'Campo, P. J., & Ray, J. G. (2013). Marital status, duration of cohabitation, and psychosocial well-being among childbearing women: A Canadian nationwide survey. *American Journal of Public Health, 103,* e8–e15.

Uskul, A. K., Paulmann, S., & Weick, M. (2016). Social power and recognition of emotional prosody: High power is associated with lower recognition accuracy than low power. *Emotion, 16,* 11–15.

Utz, S., Muscanell, N., & Khalid, C. (2015). Snapchat elicits more jealousy than Facebook: A comparison of Snapchat and Facebook Use. *Cyberpsychology, Behavior, and Social Networking, 18,* 141–146.

Uysal, A., Lin, H. L., & Knee, C. R. (2010). The role of need satisfaction in self-concealment and well-being. *Personality and Social Psychology Bulletin, 36,* 187–199.

Vaaler, M. L., Ellison, C. G., & Powers, D. A. (2009). Religious influences on the risk of marital dissolution. *Journal of Marriage and Family, 71,* 917–934.

Vacharkulksemsuk, T., Reit, E., Khambatta, P., Eastwick, P. W., Finkel, E. J., & Carney, D. R. (2016). Dominant, open nonverbal displays are attractive at zero-acquaintance. *PNAS, 113,* 4009–4014.

Valentine, K. A., Li, N. P., Penke, L., & Perrett, D. I. (2014). Judging a man by the width of his face: The role of facial ratios and dominance in mate choice at speed-dating events. *Psychological Science, 25,* 806–811.

Valentova, J. V., Bártova, K., Štěrbova, Z., & Varella, M. A. C. (2017). Influence of sexual orientation, population, monogamy, and imprinting-like effect on preferences and choices for female buttock size, breast size and shape, and WHR. *Personality and Individual Differences, 104,* 313319.

Valtorta, N. K., Kanaan, M., Gilbody, S., Ronzi, S., & Hanratty, B. (2016). Loneliness and social isolation as risk factors for coronary heart disease and stroke: Systematic review and meta-analysis of longitudinal observational studies. *Heart, 102,* 1009–1016.

Van Buren, A. (2013, January 30). Man wants wife along for ride. *The Eagle,* E4.

Vanden Abeele, M., Schouten, A. P., & Antheunis, M. L. (2017). Personal editable, and always accessible: An affordance approach to the relationship between adolescents' mobile messaging behavior and their friendship quality. *Journal of Social and Personal Relationships, 34,* 1–19.

van den Boom, D. C. (1994). The influence of temperament and mothering on attachment and exploration: An experimental manipulation of sensitive responsiveness among lower-class mothers with irritable infants. *Child Development, 65,* 1457–1477.

VanderDrift, L. E., & Agnew, C. R. (2016, July). *The multidimensionality of stay-leave behavior in nonmarital romantic relationships.* Paper presented at the meeting of the International Association for Relationship Research, Toronto.

VanderDrift, L. E., Agnew, C. R., Harvey, S. M., & Warren, J. T. (2013a). Whose intentions predict? Power over condom use within heterosexual dyads. *Health Psychology, 32,* 1038–1046.

VanderDrift, L. E., Lehmiller, J. J., & Kelly, J. R. (2012). Commitment in friends with benefits relationships: Implications for relational and safe-sex outcomes. *Personal Relationships, 19,* 1–13.

VanderDrift, L. E., Wilson, J. E., & Agnew, C. R. (2013b). On the benefits of valuing being friends for non-marital romantic partners. *Journal of Social and Personal Relationships, 30,* 115–131.

van der Land, S. F., Schouten, A. P., Feldberg, F., Huysman, M., & van den Hooff, B. (2015). Does avatar appearance matter? How team visual similarity and member-avatar similarity influence virtual team performance. *Human Communication Research, 41,* 128–153.

van der Linden, D., Scholte, R. H. J., Cillessen, A. H. N., te Nijenhuis, J., & Segers, E. (2010). Classroom ratings of likeability and popularity are related to the Big Five and the general factor of personality. *Journal of Research in Personality, 44,* 669–672.

Van Dongen, S., & Gangestad, S. W. (2011). Human fluctuating asymmetry in relation to health and quality: A meta-analysis. *Evolution and Human Behavior, 32,* 380–398.

Vangelisti, A. L. (2015). Communication in personal relationships. In M. Mikulincer, P. Shaver, J. Simpson, & J. Dovidio (Eds.), *APA handbook of personality and social psychology: Vol. 3. Interpersonal relations* (pp. 371–392). Washington, DC: American Psychological Association.

Vangelisti, A. L., & Hampel, A. D. (2010). Hurtful communication: Current research and future directions. In S. Smith & S. Wilson (Eds.), *New directions in interpersonal communication research* (pp. 221–241). Thousand Oaks, CA: Sage.

Vanhalst, J., & Leary, M. R. (2014). Sociotropic differentiation: Differential anticipatory reactions to rejection by close versus distal others predict well-being. *Personality and Individual Differences, 68,* 176–182.

Vanhalst, J., Luyckx, K., Teppers, E., & Goossens, L. (2012). Disentangling the longitudinal relation between loneliness and depressive symptoms: Prospective effects and the intervening role of coping. *Journal of Social and Clinical Psychology, 31,* 810–834.

Vanhalst, J., Soenens, B., Luyckx, & . . . Asher, S. R. (2015). Why do the lonely stay lonely? Chronically lonely adolescents' attributions and emotions in situations of social inclusion and exclusion. *Journal of Personality and Social Psychology, 109,* 932–948.

Vannier, S. A., & O'Sullivan, L. F. (2011). Communicating interest in sex: Verbal and nonverbal initiation of sexual activity in young adults' romantic dating relationships. *Archives of Sexual Behavior, 40,* 961–969.

Vannier, S. A., & O'Sullivan, L. F. (2017). Passion, connection, and destiny: How romantic expectations help predict satisfaction and commitment in young adults' dating relationships. *Journal of Social and Personal Relationships, 34,* 235–257.

van Steenbergen, H., Langeslag, S. J. E., Band, G. P. H., & Hommel, B. (2014). Reduced cognitive control in passionate lovers. *Motivation and Emotion, 38,* 444–450.

Van Zalk, M. H. W., Branje, S. J. T., Denissen, J., Van Aken, M. A. G., & Meeus, W. H. J. (2011). Who benefits from chatting, and why? The roles of extraversion and supportiveness in online chatting and emotional adjustment. *Personality and Social Psychology Bulletin, 37,* 1202–1215.

Vasey, P. L., & VanderLaan, D. P. (2010). Avuncular tendencies and the evolution of male androphilia in Samoan fa'afafine. *Archives of Sexual Behavior, 39,* 821–830.

Vazire, S. (2010). Who knows what about a person? The self-other knowledge asymmetry (SOKA) model. *Journal of Personality and Social Psychology, 98,* 281–300.

Vazire, S., & Carlson, E. N. (2011). Others sometimes know us better than we know ourselves. *Current Directions in Psychological Science, 20,* 104–108.

Vedes, A., Hilpert, P., Nussbeck, F. W. & . . . Lind, W. R. (2016). Love styles, coping, and relationship satisfaction: A dyadic approach. *Personal Relationships, 23,* 84–97.

Vennum, A., & Johnson, M. D. (2014). The impact of premarital cycling on early marriage. *Family Relations, 63,* 439–452.

Vennum, A., Lindstrom, R., Monk, J. K., & Adams, R. (2014). "It's complicated": The continuity and correlates of cycling in cohabiting and marital relationships. *Journal of Social and Personal Relationships, 31,* 410–430.

Verhage, M. L., Schuengel, C., Madigan, S., & . . . van IJzendoorn, M. H. (2016). Narrowing the transmission gap: A synthesis of three decades of research on intergenerational transmission of attachment. *Psychological Bulletin, 142,* 337–366.

Verhofstadt, L. L. L., Buysse, A., Ickes, W., de Clercq, A., & Peene, O. J. (2005). Conflict and support interactions in marriage: An analysis of couples' interactive behavior and on-line cognition. *Personal Relationships, 12,* 23–42.

Verhofstadt, L. L. L., Lemmens, G. M. D., & Buysse, A. (2013). Support-seeking, support-provision and support-perception in distressed married couples: A multi-method analysis. *Journal of Family Therapy, 35,* 320–339.

Vescio, T. K., Schlenker, K. A., & Lenes, J. G. (2010). Power and sexism. In A. Guinote & T. Vescio (Eds.), *The social psychology of power* (pp. 363–380). New York: Guilford Press.

Vincent, J. P., Weiss, R. L., & Birchler, G. R. (1975). Dyadic problem solving behavior as a function of marital distress and spousal vs. stranger interactions. *Behavior Therapy, 6,* 475–487.

Vohs, K. D., & Baumeister, R. F. (2015). Correcting some misrepresentations about gender and sexual economics theory: Comment on Rudman and Fetterolf (2014). *Psychological Science, 26,* 1522–1523.

Vohs, K. D., Finkenauer, C., & Baumeister, R. F. (2011). The sum of friends' and lovers' self-control scores predicts relationship quality. *Social Psychological and Personality Science, 2,* 138–145.

Volk, A. A., & Atkinson, J. A. (2013). Infant and child death in the human environment of evolutionary adaptation. *Evolution and Human Behavior, 34,* 182–192.

von Hippel, W., Baker, E., Wilson, R., Brin, L., & Page, L. (2016). Detecting deceptive behaviour after the fact. *British Journal of Social Psychology, 55,* 195–205.

Voracek, M., & Fisher, M. L. (2006). Success is all in the measures: Androgenousness, curvaceousness, and starring frequencies in adult media actresses. *Archives of Sexual Behavior, 35,* 297–304.

Vorauer, J. D., Cameron, J. J., Holmes, J. G., & Pearce, D. G. (2003). Invisible overtures: Fears of rejection and the signal amplification bias. *Journal of Personality and Social Psychology, 84,* 793–812.

Vorderer, P., Krömer, N., & Schneider, F. M. (2016). Permanently online—Permanently connected: Explorations into university students' use of social media and mobile smart devices. *Computers in Human Behavior, 63,* 694–703.

Vrangalova, Z. (2015). Does casual sex harm college students' well-being? A longitudinal investigation of the role of motivation. *Archives of Sexual Behavior, 44,* 945–959.

Vrij, A. (2006). Nonverbal communication and deception. In V. Manusov & M. L. Patterson (Eds.), *The Sage handbook of nonverbal communication* (pp. 341–359). Thousand Oaks, CA: Sage.

Vrij, A. (2007). Deception: A social lubricant and a selfish act. In K. Fiedler (Ed.), *Social communication* (pp. 309–342). New York: Psychology Press.

Vrij, A., Granhag, P. A., & Porter, S. (2010). Pitfalls and opportunities in nonverbal and verbal lie detection. *Psychological Science in the Public Interest, 11,* 89–121.

Vukasović, T., & Bratko, D. (2015). Heritability of personality: A meta-analysis of behavior genetic studies. *Psychological Bulletin, 141,* 769–785.

Waas, G. A., & Graczyk, P. A. (1998). Group interventions for the peer-rejected child. In K. C. Stoiber & T. R. Kratochwill (Eds.), *Handbook of group intervention for children and families* (pp. 141–158). Needham Heights, MA: Allyn & Bacon.

Wade, J. C., & Donis, E. (2007). Masculinity ideology, male identity, and romantic relationship quality among heterosexual and gay men. *Sex Roles, 57,* 775–786.

Wagner, M. F., Milner, J. S., McCarthy, R. J., & . . . Skowronski, J. J. (2015). Facial emotion recognition accuracy and child physical abuse: An experiment and a meta-analysis. *Psychology of Violence, 5,* 154–162.

Waite, L. J., & Joyner, L. (2001). Emotional and physical satisfaction with sex in married, cohabiting, and dating sexual unions: Do men and women differ? In E. O. Laumann & R. T. Michael (Eds.),

Sex, love, and health in America: Private choices and public policies (pp. 239–269). Chicago: University of Chicago Press.

Waldinger, R. J., Cohen, S., Schulz, M. S., & Crowell, J. A. (2015). Security of attachment to spouses in late life: Concurrent and prospective links with cognitive and emotional well-being. *Clinical Psychological Science, 3,* 516–529.

Waldinger, R. J., & Schulz, M. S. (2016). The long reach of nurturing family environments: Links with midlife emotion-regulatory styles and late-life security in intimate relationships. *Psychological Science, 27,* 1443–1450.

Waldron, V. R., & Kelley, D. K. (2008). *Communicating forgiveness.* Thousand Oaks, CA: Sage.

Waller, W. (1937). The rating and dating complex. *American Sociological Review, 2,* 727–734.

Waller, W. W., & Hill, R. (1951). *The family, a dynamic interpretation.* New York: Dryden Press.

Walsh, J. L., Ward, L. M., Caruthers, A., & Merriwether, A. (2011). Awkward or amazing: Gender and age trends in first intercourse experiences. *Psychology of Women Quarterly, 35,* 59–71.

Walster, E., & Walster, G. W. (1978). *A new look at love.* Reading, MA: Addison-Wesley.

Walster, E., Walster, G. W., Piliavin, J., & Schmidt, L. (1973). "Playing hard to get": Understanding an elusive phenomenon. *Journal of Personality & Social Psychology, 26,* 113–121.

Wänke, M., Samochowiec, J., & Landwehr, J. (2012). Facial politics: Political judgment based on looks. In J. P. Forgas, K. Fiedler, & C. Sedikides (Eds.), *Social thinking and interpersonal behavior* (pp. 143–160). New York: Psychology Press.

Watkins, L. E., Jaffe, A. E., Hoffman, L., & . . . DiLillo, D. (2014). The longitudinal impact of intimate partner aggression and relationship status on women's physical health and depression symptoms. *Journal of Family Psychology, 28,* 655–665.

Watkins, S. J., & Boon, S. D. (2016). Expectations regarding partner fidelity in dating relationships. *Journal of Social and Personal Relationships, 33,* 237–256.

Watson, D., Beer, A., & McDade-Montez, E. (2014). The role of active assortment in spousal similarity. *Journal of Personality, 82,* 116–129.

Watson, D., Klohnen, E. C., Casillas, A., Simms, E. N., Haig, J., & Berry, D. S. (2004). Match makers and deal breakers: Analyses of assortative mating in newlywed couples. *Journal of Personality, 72,* 1029–1068.

Watts, T. M., Holmes, L., Savin-Williams, R. C., & Rieger, G. (2017). Pupil dilation to explicit and non-explicit sexual stimuli. *Archives of Sex Behavior, 46,* 155–165.

Weaver, S. E., & Ganong, L. H. (2004). The factor structure of the Romantic Beliefs Scale for African Americans and European Americans. *Journal of Social and Personal Relationships, 21,* 171–185.

Weber, A. L., & Harvey, J. H. (1994). Accounts in coping with relationship loss. In A. L. Weber & J. H. Harvey (Eds.), *Perspectives on close relationships* (pp. 285–306). Boston: Allyn & Bacon.

Weber, K., Goodboy, A. K., & Cayanus, J. L. (2010). Flirting competence: An experimental study on appropriate and effective opening lines. *Communication Research Reports, 27,* 184–191.

Weeden, J., & Sabini, J. (2007). Subjective and objective measures of attractiveness and their relation to sexual behavior and sexual attitudes in university students. *Archives of Sexual Behavior, 36,* 79–88.

Weeks, D. G., Michela, J. L., Peplau, L.A., & Bragg, M. E. (1980). The relation between loneliness and depression: A structural equation analysis. *Journal of Personality and Social Psychology, 39,* 1238–1244.

Wegner, R., & Abbey, A. (2016). Individual differences in men's misperception of women's sexual intent: Application and extension of the confluence model. *Personality and Individual Differences, 94,* 16–20.

Wegner, R., Davis, K. C., Stappenbeck, C. A., Kajumulo, K. F., Norris, J., & George, W. H. (2017). The effects of men's hostility toward women, acute alcohol intoxication, and women's condom request style on men's condom use resistance tactics. *Psychology of Violence.* doi:10.1037/vio0000069

Wei, M., Russell, D. W., Mallinckrodt, B., & Vogel, D. L. (2007). The Experiences in Close Relationship Scale (ECR)-Short Form: Reliability, validity, and factor structure. *Journal of Personality Assessment, 88,* 187–204.

Weidman, A. C., Fernandez, K. C., Levinson, C. A., Augustine, A. A., Larsen, R. J., & Rodebaugh, T. L. (2012). Compensatory Internet use among individuals higher in social anxiety and its implications for well-being. *Personality and Individual Differences, 53,* 191–195.

Weigel, D. J., & Ballard-Reisch, D. S. (2014). Constructing commitment in intimate relationships: Mapping interdependence in the everyday expressions of commitment. *Communication Research, 41,* 311–332.

Weigel, D. J., Davis, B. A., & Woodard, K. C. (2015). A two-sided coin: Mapping perceptions of the pros and cons of relationship commitment. *Journal of Social and Personal Relationships, 32,* 344–367.

Weigel, D. J., Lalasz, C. B., & Weiser, D. A. (2016). Maintaining relationships: The role of implicit relationship theories and partner fit. *Communication Research, 29,* 23–34.

Weir, K. (2017, January). Forgiveness can improve mental and physical health. *Monitor on Psychology,* 31–33.

Weisbuch, M., Ambady, N., Clarke, A. L., Achor, S., & Weele, J. V. (2010). On being consistent: The role of verbal-nonverbal consistency in first impressions. *Basic and Applied Social Psychology, 32,* 261–268.

Weiser, D. A., & Weigel, D. J. (2014). Testing a model of communication responses to relationship infidelity. *Communication Quarterly, 62,* 416–435.

Weiss, R. L., Birchler, G. R., & Vincent, J. P. (1974). Contractual models for negotiating training in marital dyads. *Journal of Marriage and the Family, 36,* 321–330.

Weiss, R. L., Hops, H., & Patterson, G. R. (1973). A framework for conceptualizing marital conflict, a technology for altering it, some data for evaluating it. In L. A. Hamerlynck, L. C. Handy, & E. J. Mash (Eds.), *Behavior change: Methodology, concepts and practice* (pp. 309–342). Champaign, IL: Research Press.

Weiss, R. S. (1973). *Loneliness.* Cambridge, MA: MIT Press.

Weisskirch, R. S., & Delevi, R. (2012). Its ovr b/n u n me: Technology use, attachment styles, and gender roles in relationship dissolution. *Cyberpsychology, Behavior, and Social Networking, 15,* 486–490.

Wendorf, C. A., Lucas, T., Imamoğlu, E. O., Weisfeld, C. C., & Weisfeld, G. E. (2011). Marital satisfaction across three cultures: Does the number of children have an impact after accounting for other marital demographics? *Journal of Cross-Cultural Psychology, 42,* 340–354.

Wenzel, A., & Emerson, T. (2009). Mate selection in socially anxious and nonanxious individuals. *Journal of Social and Clinical Psychology, 28,* 341–363.

Werking, K. (1997). *We're just good friends: Women and men in nonromantic relationships.* New York: Guilford Press.

Wesselmann, E. D., & Williams, K. D. (2013). Ostracism and stages of coping. In C. N. DeWall (Ed.), *The Oxford handbook of social exclusion* (pp. 20–30). New York: Oxford University Press.

Wesselmann, E. D., Wirth, J. H., Mroczek, D. K., & Williams, K. D. (2012). Dial a feeling: Detecting moderation of affect decline during ostracism. *Personality and Individual Differences, 53,* 580–586.

Whalen, J. M., Pexman, P. M., & Gill, A. J. (2009). "Should be fun—not!" Incidence and marking of nonliteral language in e-mail. *Journal of Language and Social Psychology, 28,* 263–280.

Wheeler, J., & Christensen, A. (2002). Creating a context for change: Integrative Couple Therapy. In A. L. Vangelisti, H. T. Reis, & M. A. Fitzpatrick (Eds.), *Stability and change in relationships* (pp. 285–305). Cambridge, England: Cambridge University Press.

Wheeler, L., & Kim, Y. (1997). What is beautiful is culturally good: The physical attractiveness stereotype has different content in collectivistic cultures. *Personality and Social Psychology Bulletin, 23,* 795–800.

Wheeler, L., Reis, H., & Nezlek, J. (1983). Loneliness, social interaction, and sex roles. *Journal of Personality and Social Psychology, 45,* 943–953.

Whisman, M. A. (2013). Relationship discord and the prevalence, incidence, and treatment of psychopathology. *Journal of Social and Personal Relationships, 30,* 163–170.

Whisman, M. A., Snyder, D. K., & Beach, S. R. H. (2009). Screening for marital and relationship discord. *Journal of Family Psychology, 23,* 247–254.

Whitaker, D. J., Le, B., & Niolon, P. H. (2010). Persistence and desistance of the perpetration of physical aggression across relationships: Findings from a national study of adolescents. *Journal of Interpersonal Violence, 25,* 591–609.

White, G. L. (1980). Inducing jealousy: A power perspective. *Personality and Social Psychology Bullein, 6,* 222–227.

White, G. L. (1981). Some correlates of romantic jealousy. *Journal of Personality,* 49, 129–147.

White, G. L., Fishbein, S., & Rutstein, J. (1981). Passionate love: The misattribution of arousal. *Journal of Personality and Social Psychology, 41,* 56–62.

Whitley, B. E., Jr. (1993). Reliability and aspects of the construct validity of Sternberg's Triangular Love Scale. *Journal of Social and Personal Relationships, 10,* 475–480.

Whitton, S. W., James-Kangal, N., Rhoades, G. K., & Markman, H. J. (2018). Understanding couple conflict. In A. Vangelisti & D. Perlman (Eds.), *Cambridge handbook of personal relationships* (2nd ed.) New York: Cambridge University Press.

Whitton, S. W., Stanley, S. M., Markman, H. J., & Johnson, C. A. (2013). Attitudes toward divorce, commitment, and divorce proneness in first marriages and remarriages. *Journal of Marriage and Family, 75,* 276–287.

Whitton, S. W., Weitbrecht, E. M., Kuryluk, A. D., & Hutsell, D. W. (2016). A randomized waitlist-controlled trial of culturally sensitive relationship education for male same-sex couples. *Journal of Family Psychology, 30,* 763–768.

Whitty, M. T., & Quigley, L. (2008). Emotional and sexual infidelity offline and in cyberspace. *Journal of Marital & Family Therapy, 34,* 461–468.

Whyte, W. F. (1955). *Street corner society: The social structure of an Italian slum.* Chicago: University of Chicago Press.

Wickham, R. E., Reed, D. E., & Williamson, R. E. (2015). Establishing the psychometric properties of the self and perceived-partner Authenticity in Relationships Scale-Short Form (AIRS-SF): Measurement invariance, reliability, and incremental validity. *Personality and Individual Differences, 77,* 62–67.

Widmer, E. D., Treas, J., & Newcomb, R. (1998). Attitudes toward nonmarital sex in 24 countries. *Journal of Sex Research, 35,* 349–358.

Wiebe, S. A., & Johnson, S. M. (2016). A review of the research in emotionally focused therapy for couples. *Family Process, 55,* 390–407.

Wight, R. G., LeBlanc, A. J., & Lee Badgett, M. V. (2013). Same-sex legal marriage and psychological well-being: Findings from the California health interview survey. *American Journal of Public Health, 103,* 339–346.

Wiik, K. A., Keizer, R., & Lappegård, T. (2012). Relationship quality in marital and cohabiting unions across Europe. *Journal of Family Issues, 74,* 389–398.

Wilcox, W. B., & Marquardt, E. (Eds.). (2010). *When marriage disappears: The new middle America.* The National Marriage Project. Retrieved from http://www.stateofourunions.org

Wildsmith, E., Schelar, E., Kristen-Peterson, K., & Manlove, J. (2010, May). Sexually transmitted diseases among young adults: Prevalence, perceived risk, and risk-taking behaviors. *Child Trends Research Brief.* Retrieved from http://www.childtrends.org/Files//Child_Trends-2010_05_01_RB_STD.pdf

Wile, D. B. (1995). *After the fight: Using your disagreements to build a stronger relationship.* New York: Guilford Press.

Willetts, M. C., Sprecher, S., & Beck, F. D. (2004). Overview of sexual practices and attitudes within relational contexts. In J. H. Harvey, A. Wenzel, & S. Sprecher (Eds.), *The handbook of sexuality in close relationships* (pp. 57–85). Mahwah, NJ: Erlbaum.

Williams, J., Stönner, C., Wicker, J., & . . . Kramer, S. (2016). Cinema audiences reproducibly vary the chemical composition of air during films, by broadcasting scene specific emissions on breath. *Scientific Reports, 6*(25464), 1–10.

Williams, K. D. (2001). *Ostracism: The power of silence.* New York: Guilford Press.

Williams, K. D. (2007). Ostracism. *Annual Review of Psychology, 58,* 425–452.

Williams, L. E., & Bargh, J. A. (2008). Experiencing physical warmth promotes interpersonal warmth. *Science, 322,* 606–607.

Williams, M. J., & Mendelsohn, G. A. (2008). Gender clues and cues: Online interactions as windows into lay theories about men and women. *Basic and Applied Social Psychology, 30,* 278–294.

Williams, M. J., & Tiedens, L. Z. (2016). The subtle suspension of backlash: A meta-analysis of penalties for women's implicit and explicit dominance behavior. *Psychological Bulletin, 142,* 165–197.

Williams, S. L., & Frieze, I. H. (2005). Courtship behaviors, relationship violence, and breakup persistence in college men and women. *Psychology of Women Quarterly, 29,* 248–257.

Williamson, H. C., Karney, B. R., & Bradbury, T. N. (2013). Financial strain and stressful events predict newlyweds' negative communication independent of relationship satisfaction. *Journal of Family Psychology, 27,* 65–75.

Williamson, H. C., Nguyen, T. P., Bradbury, T. N., & Karney, B. R. (2016). Are problems that contribute to divorce present at the start of marriage, or do they emerge over time? *Journal of Social and Personal Relationships, 33,* 1120–1134.

Williamson, H. C., Rogge, R. D., Cobb, R. J., & . . . Bradbury, T. N. (2015). Risk moderates the outcome of relationship education: A randomized controlled trial. *Journal of Consulting and Clinical Psychology, 83,* 617–629.

Williamson, H. C., Trail, T. E., Bradbury, T. N., & Karney, B. R. (2014). Does premarital education decrease or increase couples' later help-seeking? *Journal of Family Psychology, 28,* 112–117.

Willis, J., & Todorov, A. (2006). First impressions: Making up your mind after a 100-ms exposure to a face. *Psychological Science, 17,* 592–598.

Willoughby, B. J., & Belt, D. (2016). Marital orientation and relationship well-being among cohabiting couples. *Journal of Family Psychology, 30,* 181–192.

Willoughby, B. J., Carroll, J. S., & Busby, D. M. (2014a). Differing relationship outcomes when sex happens before, on, or after first dates. *Journal of Sex Research, 51,* 52–61.

Willoughby, B. J., Carroll, J. S., Busby, D. M., & Brown, C. C. (2016). Differences in pornography use among couples: Associations with satisfaction, stability, and relationship processes. *Archives of Sexual Behavior, 45,* 145–158.

Willoughby, B. J., Farero, A M., & Busby, D. M. (2014b). Exploring the effects of sexual desire discrepancy among married couples. *Archives of Sexual Behavior, 43,* 551–562.

Willoughby, B. J., & Hall, S. S. (2015). Enthusiasts, delayers, and the ambiguous middle: Marital paradigms among emerging adults. *Emerging Adulthood, 3,* 123–135.

Willoughby, B. J., Hall, S. S., & Luczak, H. P. (2015a). Marital paradigms: A conceptual framework for marital attitudes, values, and beliefs. *Journal of Family Issues, 36,* 188–211.

Willoughby, B. J., Medaris, M., James, S., & Bartholomew, K. (2015b). Changes in marital beliefs among emerging adults: Examining martial paradigms over time. *Emerging Adulthood, 3,* 219–228.

Wilson, A. C., & Huston, T. L. (2013). Shared reality and grounded feelings during courtship: Do they matter for marital success? *Journal of Marriage and Family, 75,* 681–696.

Wilson, B., & Lamidi, E. (2013). *Living alone in the U.S., 2011.* National Center for Family and Marriage Research. Retrieved from http://ncfmr.bgsu.edu/pdf/family_profiles/file138254.pdf

Wimmer, A., & Lewis, K. (2010). Beyond and below racial homophily: ERG models of a friendship network documented on Facebook. *American Journal of Sociology, 116,* 583–642.

Wincentak, K., Connolly, J., & Card, N. (2017). Teen dating violence: A meta-analytic review of prevalence rates. *Psychology of Violence, 7,* 224–241.

Winczewski, L. A., Bowen, J. D., & Collins, N. L. (2016). Is empathic accuracy enough to facilitate responsive behavior in dyadic interaction? Distinguishing ability from motivation. *Psychological Science, 27,* 394–404.

Winslett, A. H., & Gross, A. M. (2008). Sexual boundaries: An examination of the importance of talking before touching. *Violence Against Women, 14,* 542–562.

Winston, R. (2002). *Human instinct.* London: Bantam Press.

Winterheld, H. A., Simpson, J. A., & Oriña, M. M. (2013). It's in the way that you use it: Attachment and the dyadic nature of humor during conflict negotiation in romantic couples. *Personality and Social Psychology Bulletin, 39,* 496–508.

Witt, E. A., Donnellan, M. B., & Orlando, M. J. (2011). Timing and selection effects within a psychology subject pool: Personality and sex matter. *Personality and Individual Differences, 50,* 355–359.

Wolbring, T., & Riordan, P. (2016). How beauty works. Theoretical mechanisms and two empirical applications on students' evaluation of teaching. *Social Science Research, 57,* 253–272.

Wolfers, J. (2006). Did unilateral divorce raise divorce rates? A reconciliation and new results. *American Economic Review, 96,* 1802–1820.

Wolfinger, N. H. (2005). *Understanding the divorce cycle: The children of divorce in their own marriages.* New York: Cambridge University Press.

Wong, J. S., & Schonlau, M. (2013). Does bully victimization predict future delinquency? A propensity score matching approach. *Criminal Justice and Behavior, 40,* 1184–1208.

Wood, D., & Furr, R. M. (2016). The correlates of similarity estimates are often misleadingly positive: The nature and scope of the problem, and some solutions. *Personality and Social Psychology Review, 20,* 79–99.

Wood, J. T. (2004). Monsters and victims: Male felons' accounts of intimate partner violence. *Journal of Social and Personal Relationships, 21,* 555–576.

Wood, W. (2016). Reply to Gangestad's (2016) comment on Wood, Kressel, Joshi, and Louie (2014). *Emotion Review, 8,* 90–94.

Wood, W., & Carden, L. (2014). Elusiveness of menstrual cycle effects on mate preferences: Comment on Gildersleeve, Haselton, and Fales (2014). *Psychological Bulletin, 140,* 1265–1271.

Wood, W., & Eagly, A. H. (2007). Social structural origins of sex differences in human mating. In S. W. Gangestad & J. A. Simpson (Eds.), *The evolution of mind: Fundamental questions and controversies* (pp. 383–390). New York: Guilford Press.

Woodley, H. J. R., & Allen, N. J. (2014). The dark side of equity sensitivity. *Personality and Individual Differences, 67,* 103–108.

Woolf, S. E., & Maisto, S. A. (2008). Gender differences in condom use behavior? The role of power and partner-type. *Sex Roles, 58,* 689–701.

World Health Organization. (2013). *Global and regional estimates of violence against women.* Retrieved from http://www.who.int/reproductivehealth/publications/violence/9789241564625/en/#

Worley, T. R., & Samp, J. (2016a). Complaint avoidance and complaint-related appraisals in close relationships: A dyadic power theory perspective. *Communication Research, 43,* 391–413.

Worley, T. R., & Samp, J. A. (2016b). Gendered associations of decision-making power, topic avoidance, and relational satisfaction: A differential influence model. *Communication Reports, 29,* 1–12.

Wortman, C. B., & Boerner, K. (2007). Beyond the myths of coping with loss: Prevailing assumptions versus scientific evidence. In H. S. Friedman & R. C. Silver (Eds.), *Foundations of health psychology* (pp. 285–324). New York: Oxford University Press.

Wotipka, C. D., & High, A. C. (2016). An idealized self or the real me? Predicting attraction to online dating profiles using selective self-presentation and warranting. *Communication Monographs, 83,* 281–302.

Wright, B. L., & Loving, T. J. (2011). Health implications of conflict in close relationships. *Social and Personality Psychology Compass, 5,* 552–562.

Wright, C. N., Holloway, A., & Roloff, M. E. (2007). The dark side of self-monitoring: How high self-monitors view their romantic relationships. *Communication Reports, 20,* 101–114.

Wright, C. N., & Roloff, M. E. (2015). You should *just know* why I'm upset: Expectancy violation theory and the influence of mind reading expectations (MRE) on responses to relational problems. *Communication Research Reports, 32,* 10–19.

Wright, P. H. (1982). Men's friendships, women's friendships and the alleged inferiority of the latter. *Sex Roles, 8,* 1–20.

Wright, P. J. (2013). U.S. males and pornography, 1973–2010: Consumption, predictors, correlates. *Journal of Sex Research, 50,* 60–71.

Wright, P. J., & Bae, S. (2016). Pornography and male socialization. In Y. Wong & S. Wester (Eds.), *APA handbook of men and masculinities* (pp. 551–568), Washington, DC: American Psychological Association.

Wrzus, C., Hänel, M., Wagner, J., & Neyer, F. J. (2013). Social network changes and life events across the life span: A meta-analysis. *Psychological Bulletin, 139,* 53–80.

Wu, K., Chen, C., & Greenberger, E. (2015). The sweetness of forbidden fruit: Interracial daters are more attractive than interracial daters. *Journal of Social and Personal Relationships, 32,* 650–666.

Wu, T., Cross, S. E., Wu, C., Cho, W., & Tey, S. (2016). Choosing your mother or your spouse: Close relationship dilemmas in Taiwan the United States. *Journal of Cross-Cultural Psychology, 47,* 558–580.

Wurst, S. N., Gerlach, T. M., Dufner, M., & . . . Back, M. D. (2017). Narcissism and romantic relationships: The differential impact of narcissistic admiration and rivalry. *Journal of Personality and Social Psychology, 112,* 280–306.

Xu, X., Aron, A., Brown, L., Cao, G., Feng, T., & Weng, X. (2011). Reward and motivation systems: A brain mapping study of early-stage intense romantic love in Chinese participants. *Human Brain Mapping, 32,* 249–257.

Xue, M., & Silk, J. B. (2012). The role of tracking and tolerance in relationship among friends. *Evolution and Human Behavior, 33,* 17–25.

Yager, J. (1997). *Friendshifts: The power of friendship and how it shapes our lives.* Stamford, CT: Hannacroix Creek Books.

Yagil, D., Karnieli-Miller, O., Eisikovits, Z., & Enosh, G. (2006). Is that a "No"? The interpretation of responses to unwanted sexual attention. *Sex Roles, 54,* 251–260.

Yan, W., Wu, Q., Liang, J., Chen, Y., & Fu, X. (2013). How fast are the leaked facial expressions: The duration of micro-expressions. *Journal of Nonverbal Behavior, 37,* 217–230.

Yancey, G., & Emerson, M. O. (2016). Does height matter? An examination of height preferences in romantic coupling. *Journal of Family Issues, 37,* 53–73.

Yarkoni, T. (2010). Personality in 100,000 words: A large-scale analysis of personality and word use among bloggers. *Journal of Research in Personality, 44,* 363–373.

Yavorsky, J. E., Kamp Dush, C. M., & Schoppe-Sullivan, S. J. (2015). The production of inequality: The gender division of labor across the transition to parenthood. *Journal of Marriage and Family, 77,* 662–679.

York, C., & Turcotte, J. (2015). Vacationing from Facebook: Adoption, temporary discontinuance, and readoption of an innovation. *Communication Research Reports, 32,* 54–62.

Yoshimura, S. M., & Boon, S. D. (2014). Exploring revenge as a feature of family life. *Journal of Family Theory & Review, 6,* 222–240.

Young, B. J., & Furman, W. (2013). Predicting commitment in young adults' physically aggressive and sexually coercive dating relationships. *Journal of Interpersonal Violence, 28,* 3245–3264.

Young, S. D., & Jordan, A. H. (2013). The influence of social networking photos on social norms and sexual health behaviors. *Cyberpsychology, Behavior, and Social Networking, 16,* 243–247.

Younger, J., Aron, A., Parke, S., Chatterjee, N., & Mackey, S. (2010). Viewing pictures of a romantic partner reduces experimental pain: Involvement of neural reward systems. *PLoS ONE, 5*(10), e13309.

Ysseldyk, R., Matheson, K., & Anisman, H. (2007). Rumination: Bridging a gap between forgivingness, vengefulness, and psychological health. *Personality and Individual Differences, 42,* 1573–1584.

Yu, E., & Liu, J. (2007). Environmental impacts of divorce. *Proceedings of the National Academy of Sciences, 104,* 20629–20634.

Yucel, D., & Gassanov, M. A. (2010). Exploring actor and partner correlates of sexual satisfaction among married couples. *Social Science Research, 39,* 725–738.

Zacchilli, T. L., Hendrick, C., & Hendrick, S. S. (2009). The Romantic Partner Conflict Scale: A new Scale to measure relationship conflict. *Journal of Social and Personal Relationships, 26,* 1073–1096.

Zadro, L., Williams, K. D., & Richardson, R. (2004). How low can you go? Ostracism by a computer is sufficient to lower self-reported levels of belonging, control, self-esteem, and meaningful existence. *Journal of Experimental Social Psychology, 40,* 560–567.

Zajonc, R. B. (2001). Mere exposure: A gateway to the subliminal. *Current Directions in Psychological Science, 10,* 224–228.

Zandbergen, D. L., & Brown, S. G. (2015). Culture and gender differences in romantic jealousy. *Personality and Individual Differences, 72,* 122–127.

Zawacki, T. (2011). Effects of alcohol on women's risky sexual decision making during social interactions in the laboratory. *Psychology of Women Quarterly, 35,* 107–118.

Zayas, V., & Shoda, Y. (2007). Predicting preferences for dating partners from past experiences of psychological abuse: Identifying the psychological ingredients of situations. *Personality and Social Psychology Bulletin, 33,* 123–138.

Zayas, V., & Shoda, Y. (2015). Love you? Hate you? Maybe it's both: Evidence that significant others trigger bivalent-priming. *Social Psychological and Personality Science, 6,* 56–64.

Zeidner, M., & Kloda, I. (2013). Emotional intelligence (EI), conflict resolution patterns, and relationship satisfaction: Actor and partner effects revisited. *Personality and Individual Differences, 54,* 278–283.

Zell, E., Krizan, Z., & Teeter, S. R. (2015). Evaluating gender similarities and differences using meta-synthesis. *American Psychologist, 70,* 10–20.

Zell, E., Strickhouser, J. E., Lane, T. N., & Teeter, S. R. (2016). Mars, Venus, or Earth? Sexism and the exaggeration of psychological gender differences. *Sex Roles, 75,* 287–300.

Zengel, B., Edlund, J. E., & Sagarin, B. J. (2013). Sex differences in jealousy in response to infidelity: Evaluation of demographic moderators in a national random sample. *Personality and Individual Differences, 54,* 47–51.

Zentner, M., & Mitura, K. (2012). Stepping out of the caveman's shadow: Nations' gender gap predicts degree of sex differentiation in mate preferences. *Psychological Science, 23,* 1176–1185.

Zhang, F., & Parmley, M. (2011). What your best friend sees that I don't see: Comparing female close friends and casual acquaintances on the perception of emotional facial expressions of varying intensities. *Personality and Social Psychology Bulletin, 37,* 28–39.

Zhang, S., & Kline, S. L. (2009). Can I make my own decision? A cross-cultural study of perceived social network influence in mate selection. *Journal of Cross-Cultural Psychology, 40,* 3–23.

Zhang, Y., & Epley, N. (2009). Self-centered social exchange: Differential use of costs versus benefits in prosocial reciprocity. *Journal of Personality and Social Psychology, 97,* 796–810.

Zhang, Y., & Van Hook, J. (2009). Marital dissolution among interracial couples. *Journal of Marriage and Family, 71,* 95–107.

Zhang, Z., Lui, H., & Yu, Y. (2016). Marital biography and health in middle and late life. In J. Bookwala (Ed.), *Couple relationships in the middle and later years* (pp. 199–218). Washington, DC: American Psychological Association.

Zhong, C., & Leonardelli, G. J. (2008). Cold and lonely: Does social exclusion literally feel cold? *Psychological Science, 19,* 838–842.

Zilcha-Mano, S., Mikulincer, M., & Shaver, P. R. (2011). An attachment perspective on human-pet relationships: Conceptualization and assessment of pet attachment orientations. *Journal of Research in Personality, 45,* 345–357.

Zimmerman, D. H., & West, C. (1975). Sex roles, interruptions and silences in conversations. In B. Thorne & N. Henley (Eds.), *Language and sex: Difference and dominance* (pp. 105–129). Rowley, MA: Newbury House.

Zinzow, H. M., & Thompson, M. (2015). A longitudinal study of risk factors for repeated sexual coercion and assault in U.S. college men. *Archives of Sexual Behavior, 44,* 213–222.

Zipp, J. F., Prohaska, A., & Bemiller, M. (2004). Wives, husbands, and hidden power in marriage. *Journal of Family Issues, 25,* 933–958.

Zuckerman, M., Koestner, R., & Alton, A. O. (1984). Learning to detect deception. *Journal of Personality and Social Psychology, 46,* 519–528.

Zuniga, A., Stevenson, R. J., Mahmut, M. K., & Stephen, I. D. (2017). Diet quality and the attractiveness of male body odor. *Evolution and Human Behavior, 38,* 136–143.

Zurbriggen, E. L., & Morgan, E. M. (2006). Who wants to marry a millionaire? Reality dating television programs, attitudes toward sex, and sexual behaviors. *Sex Roles, 54,* 1–17.

Name Index

Aassve, A., 366
Abbey, A., 296, 297
Abel, E. L., 140
Acevedo, B. P., 45, 245, 246, 255, 267
Ackerman, D., 240, 241, 246
Ackerman, J. M., 211, 263
Ackerman, R. A., 61, 62
Acosta, J., 29, 303
Adams, G. S., 331
Adams, R. B., Jr., 141
Afifi, T. D., 154, 157, 348, 395
Afifi, T. O., 381
Afifi, W. A., 329
Agnew, C. R., 3, 106, 174, 175, 199., 200, 201, 203, 211, 423, 431
Agthe, M., 72
Ahmetoglu, G., 245, 256, 266, 267
Ahrons, C. R., 414, 415, 418
Aicken, C. R. H., 55
Ainsworth, M. D. S., 15
Aitken, S. J., 79
Aizer, A. A., 5
Albrecht, S. L., 175
Albright, L., 136
Aldeis, D., 154
Algoe, S. B., 429
Allard, L. M., 261
Allen, A. B., 199
Allen, J. P., 5
Allen, K., 223
Allen, N. J., 197
Allik, J., 131
Allison, R., 271
Alterovitz, S. S., 94

Altman, I., 152
Alvergne, A., 79, 81
Amato, P. R., 92, 197, 220, 328, 372, 373, 389, 390, 391, 392, 393, 395, 400, 401, 402, 403, 415, 417
Ambadar, Z., 141
Ambady, N., 144, 235
Ambrose, C. E., 296
Ames, D. R., 105
Anders, S. L., 157
Andersen, P. A., 149, 320
Andersen, S. M., 120
Anderson, J. R., 189
Anderson, K. G., 198
Anderson, L. R., 8, 9, 389
Anderson, M., 155, 406
Andrews, P. W., 314
Angulo, S., 161
Ansari, A., 70
Antfolk, J., 94
Apostolou, M., 261
Aragón, O. R., 193, 194
Archer, J., 29, 72, 73, 85, 153
Argyle, M., 215
Ariely, D., 290
Aron, A., 3, 45, 58, 96, 151, 186, 245, 246, 247, 248, 253–254, 255, 259, 264, 265, 267, 268, 427
Aron, E. N., 253–254
Arriaga, X. B., 19, 109, 163, 199, 200, 203, 308, 374, 375, 377, 378, 384
Arroyo, J., 227, 231
Asch, S. E., 103
Asendorpf, J. B., 230
Ash, J., 33

Ashenhurst, J. R., 291
Assad, K. K., 119
Atkins, D. C., 426
Atkinson, J. A., 36
Attard-Johnson, J., 141
Aubé, J., 160
Aubrey, J. S., 235
Aung, T., 85
Averett, S. L., 5
Averill, J. R., 180
Aydin, N., 223
Aylor, B., 321
Ayotte, B. J., 331
Ayres, M. M., 159
Azizli, N., 226
Azmitia, M., 57

Babcock, M. J., 44
Bach, G. R., 356, 358
Back K. W., 42
Back, M. D., 66, 67, 102, 123, 158
Baddeley, J. L., 236
Bae, S., 287
Bahns, A. J., 87, 89
Bailenson, J. N., 44, 148
Bailey, J. M., 30
Baker, L. R., 343
Bale, C., 29, 85
Bales, K., 223
Ballard-Reisch, D. S., 199, 439
Balsam, K. F., 31
Banai, I. P., 147
Bank, B. J., 224
Bar-Kalifa, E., 212
Bar, M., 101
Baranowski, A. M., 48

Barber, B. L., 290
Barber, J. P., 438
Barber, N., 390, 402, 416
Bargh, J. A., 107, 363
Barnes, M. L., 258
Barnes, R. D., 25
Barnett, M. D., 54, 276, 281
Baron, C. E., 338
Barriger, M., 290
Barry, R. A., 210, 338
Barthes, J., 274
Bartholomew, J. B., 76
Bartholomew, K., 16
Barton, A. W., 220, 390, 399
Barton, J., 276, 289
Bartz, J. A., 58, 202, 255–256
Basinger, E. D., 154
Basow, S. A., 288
Bastian, B., 308
Bates, E. A., 376
Battaglia, D. M., 406
Baucom, B. R., 163, 347, 348
Baucom, D. H., 426, 433,
    434, 435, 436, 438
Baucom, T. R., 313
Baumeister, R. F., 4, 5, 181,
    259, 265, 288, 343
Baxter, L. A., 38, 96, 154,
    155, 303, 326, 336, 337,
    404, 405
Beach, S. R. H., 68, 95, 184,
    330, 424
Beall, A. T., 80
Beaver, K. M., 78
Beck, C. J. A., 193, 195, 202,
    375, 415
Beck, L. A., 338
Becker, O. A., 89, 92
Beckes, L., 58
Beetz, A., 223
Belkin, A., 144
Bell, K. L., 323
Bellavia, G. M., 31
Belt, D., 11, 392, 402
Bem, S. L., 234
Ben-Ari, A., 2
Bennett, K. M., 3, 423
Bensman, L., 270
Bente, G., 143
Berenson, K. R., 120

Berg, J., 153
Běrkman, L. F., 5
Bernier, A., 19
Bernstein, W. M., 85
Berscheid, E., 2, 42, 72, 208,
    246, 247, 258, 264, 345
Bessel, D. R., 391, 402
Bialik, K., 90
Biesanz, J. C., 130
Biesen, J. N., 349
Birditt, K. S., 45, 189, 346
Birnbaum, G. E., 297
Birnie, C., 116
Black, M. C., 375, 383
Blackhart, G. C., 426
Blanch-Hartigan, D., 151
Bleakley, A., 277
Blekesaune, M., 413
Bleske, A. L., 313
Bleske-Rechek, A., 225
Blickstein, I., 285
Bloch, L., 166, 344
Blumberg, S. L., 357
Blumstein, P., 279, 280,
    282, 292
Bobst, C., 80
Bodenmann, G., 403
Bodie, G. D., 166
Boerner, K., 164
Bohns, V. K., 95, 212, 295
Boisvert, D., 36
Bolger, N., 212
Bollich, K. L., 45
Bond, C. F., Jr., 325
Boon, S. D., 280, 288, 330
Booth, A., 220, 373, 392,
    395, 400, 401
Booth-Butterfield, M., 323
Boothroyd, L. G., 96, 284
Bosson. J. K., 29, 381
Bouchard, G., 366, 393
Bouffard, J. A., 297, 300
Bourassa, K. J., 412
Boutwell, B. B., 36
Bowers, J. R., 203, 423
Bowlby, J., 14
Boyce, C. J., 181, 185
Boyes, A. D., 108
Boyle, A. M., 158
Boynton, M., 77

Brackett, M. A., 130
Bradbury, T. N., 111, 189,
    190, 384, 395, 396, 403
Bradford, S. A., 157
Bradney, N., 208
Bradshaw, C., 271
Bradshaw, S. D., 229, 230
Braithwaite, S. R., 287,
    330, 331
Brakefield, T. A., 273
Brand, R. J., 311
Brannon, S. M., 105
Bratko, D., 27, 29
Bratslavsky, E., 265
Braun, V., 293
Braver, S. L., 416
Bredow, C. A., 85
Brehm, S. S. ix, 111
Brennan, K. A., 56
Brescoll, V. L., 365
Brewer, D. D., 281
Brewer, G., 72, 73, 123,
    322, 330
Bridges, A. J., 287
Bringle, R. G., 259
Britt, S. L., 197, 340
Broady, E. F., 397
Brock, R. L., 212
Brody, L. R., 149, 263
Brody, S., 76
Brooks, J. E., 90
Broughton, R., 264
Brown, G., 13
Brown, J. L., 210
Brown, S. G., 312
Brown, S. L., 11
Brownridge, D. A., 380
Bruess, C., 427
Brumbaugh, C. C., 23, 97
Brummelman, E., 124
Brummett, E. A., 90
Brunell, A. B., 294
Brunet, P. M., 231
Bryant, C. M., 26, 390, 399
Bryant, G., 147
Buck, A. A., 180
Buck, D. M., 153
Buckley, K. E., 305,
    306, 307
Buhrmester, D., 217

Buhrmester, M. D., 119, 121, 174
Buller, D. B., 322
Burch, R. L., 285
Burdette, M. P., 326, 327, 328
Burger, J. M., 289
Burgoon, J. K., 322, 324, 368
Burke, C. T., 121
Burke, M., 235
Burleson, B. R., 161, 337
Burleson, M. H., 144, 156, 298
Burnette, J. L., 330
Burns, G. L., 83
Burns, L., 289
Bursik, K., 116
Burton-Chellew, M. N., 219, 337
Busby, D. M., 353
Buss, A. H., 224–225, 228
Buss, D. M., 35, 36, 37, 78, 83, 85, 93, 263, 278, 284, 285, 311, 314, 315, 316, 317, 318, 321, 340, 341, 376, 377, 383
Butzer, B., 298
Buunk, A. P., 242, 261, 280, 314
Buunk, B. P., 96, 110, 310, 311, 313, 328
Byers, E. S., 297
Byrne, D., 42, 52, 65, 87, 88

Cacioppo, J. T., 71, 183, 211, 231, 232, 234, 236, 237, 245
Cacioppo, S., 245
Cafferky, B. M., 380
Call, V., 265
Cameron, J. J., 33, 137
Campbell, J., 384
Campbell, K., 265, 391
Campbell, L., 262, 279, 284, 298
Campbell, W. K., 124, 439
Canary, D. J., 22, 335, 344, 346, 349, 355–356, 427, 428, 429
Cann, A., 313

Cannon, K. T., 236
Cantú, S. M., 80
Caprariello, P. A., 214
Cardaro, D., 248
Carden, L., 81
Carli, L. L., 365
Carlsmith, K. M., 328
Carlson, D. L., 198, 366
Carlson, E. N., 131
Carnegie, D., 215
Carnelley, K. B., 164, 262, 413
Carney, D. R., 101, 369
Carothers, B. J., 21, 22
Carpenter, C. J., 316
Carrère, S., 163, 198
Carstensen, L. L., 220, 221
Cartmill, E. A., 142
Carton, H., 379
Carver, C. S., 119
Casey, E. A., 297, 379
Cassidy, J., 116
Castro, F. N., 97
Cate, R. M., 197
Caughlin, J. P., 154, 190
Caumont, A., 11, 95, 240, 365, 389, 413
Cavallo, J. V., 31
Ceglian, C. P., 403
Çelik, P., 305
Chaladze, G., 274
Chaplin, W. F., 144
Charles, S. T., 221
Chartrand, T. L., 120, 148
Cheek, J. M., 228
Chen, E., 416
Chen, H., 89, 338
Chen, R., 97
Chen, S., 120, 338, 349, 356, 374
Cheng, Z., 292
Cherlin, A. J., 9, 12, 60, 179
Chester, D. S., 328
Choi, K. H., 90
Choi, N., 25
Chokel, J. T., 306
Chopik, W. J., 18, 145, 216
Chorost, A. F., 264
Christakis, N. A., 5, 211, 225
Christensen, A., 345, 347, 431, 434

Chun, J. S., 123
Ciani, A. C., 274
Ciarrochi, J., 224
Clark, E. M., 429
Clark, M. S., 126, 193, 194, 195, 198, 202
Clark, R. D., III, 47, 48, 50
Clarkwest, A., 402
Claxton, A., 28
Clayton, R. B., 13
Cleere, C., 301
Clements, M. L., 416
Clore, G. L., 65
Cloven, D. H., 337
Coan, J. A., 5, 58
Cobb, R. A., 115
Cobb, R. J., 19, 210
Coffelt, T. A., 296
Cohen, J. N., 297
Cohen, L. M., 54
Cohen, P., 339
Cohen, S., 145, 346, 412
Cohn, D., 11, 365, 389
Cohn, E. S., 300
Cole, S., 424
Collibee, C., 225
Collins, N. L., 116, 156, 210, 213, 256, 261, 308
Collins, T. J., 406
Coltrane, S., 197
Confer, J. C., 33, 34
Conley, J. J., 28
Connelly, B. S., 129
Conner, T. S., 42
Conroy-Beam, D., 35, 82, 85, 94
Conway, J. R., 35
Coons, J. V., 96
Coontz, S., 240, 241, 390
Cooper, E. B., 322
Cooper, M., 86
Cooper, M. L., 183
Copen, C. E., 271, 281
Cordaro, D. T., 147
Cordova, J. V., 439
Costa, P. T., Jr., 27, 28
Côté, S., 374
Cottrell, C. A., 305
Couch, L. L., 327

Coughlin, P., 11
Coulter, K., 427
Cowan, G., 381
Cowley, A. D., 397
Coyne, J. C., 6
Coyne, S. M., 379
Crane, R. D., 146
Cranford, J. A., 6
Croom, C., 235
Cross, E. J., 23
Cross, S. E., 23, 226, 349
Croy, I., 146
Cuddy, A., 143
Cummings, E. M., 340
Cummings, E. M., 340
Cundiff, J. M., 95
Cunningham, G. B., 272
Cunningham, M. R., 74, 78,
    86, 190, 341
Cupach, W. R., 23, 38, 341
Cuperman, R., 89
Curran, M. A., 424
Curtis, R. C., 87, 118
Cutrona, C. E., 236, 237, 401
Czarna, A. Z., 124, 130

Daigen, V., 162
Dailey, R. M., 408
Dainton, M., 191, 199, 321
Daly, J. A., 127
Daneback, K., 287
Daniels, K., 12
Danner-Vlaardingerbroek,
    G., 395
Darbyshire, D., 125
Dardis, C. M., 383
Darley, J. M., 103, 104
Das, A., 286
Datteri, D. L., 406
Daugherty, J., 271
David, M, E, 13, 159
Davies, A. P. C., 317
Davila, J., 19, 211, 262
Davis, D., 179, 262, 298
Davis, K. C., 292
Davis, K. E., 217, 383
Davis, S., 290
Dawes, R. M., 181
Day, L. C., 194, 424
Dean, G. O., 86

de Araújo Lopes, F., 97
De Bro, S. C., 371
Debrot, A., 144
Deckman, T., 307
de Graaf, H., 276
de Groot, J. H. B., 146
DeGue, S., 299
de Jong, D. C., 89, 95, 297
De Jonge, C. R., 158
DeLamater, J., 279
De La Ronde, C., 122, 132
Delevi, R., 406
Della Sala, S., 112
DelPriore, D. J., 315
Denes, A., 319
Denissen, J. J. A., 31
Dennison, R. P., 393
Denrell, J., 101
Denton, W. H., 347
DePaulo (09), B. M., 303
DePaulo, B. M., 9, 323,
    324, 325
Derlega, V. J., 152
Dermer, M., 246
Derrick, J. L., 96
DeShong, H. L., 226
De Smet, O., 383
Desmond, M., 416
DeSteno, D. A., 311,
    312, 316
Deters, F. G., 235
De Vogli, R., 346
Dew, J., 191, 429
DeWall, C. N., 179, 307, 309,
    328, 329
Dewsbury, D. A., 265
Diamond, L. M., 30, 38,
    245, 248, 255, 273,
    279, 281
Dickerson, S. S., 308
Diekman, A. B., 27
Dijkstra, P., 311, 313
DiLillo, D., 299
Dillon. L. M., 340
Dillow, M. R., 156
Dindia, K., 22, 152, 160, 320
Dion, K. K., 72
DiPaola, B. M., 349
Dixson, B. J., 76, 77
Doherty, W. J., 426, 439

Don, B. P., 191
Donis, E., 26, 30
Donnelly, K., 24, 25, 27,
    372, 391
D'Onofrio, B. M., 416
Donovan-Kicken, E., 188
Dooley, T., 11
Dosmukhambetova, D., 123
Doss, B. D., 191, 432, 439
Doumas, D. M., 380
Downey, G., 119
Downs, A. C., 73
Doyle, D. M., 274
Drigotas, S. M., 201
Drouin, M., 322
Duck, S., 407
Dugan, A., 426
Dunbar, N. E., 219, 323,
    337, 368
Dunbar, R. I. M., 218
Dunn, E. W., 4
Dunn, M. J., 94, 318
Duntley, J. D., 376, 377, 383
Durante, K. M., 1
Durtschi, J. A., 111
Dutton, D. G., 247
Dweck, C., 344
Dworkin, S. L., 294

Eagly, A. H., 24, 37, 94, 263
Eaker, E. D., 355
Eastwick, P. W., 36, 55, 66,
    81, 82, 83, 87, 96, 214,
    215, 242, 286, 314, 410
Ebbesen, E. B., 69
Ebel-Lam, A. P., 290
Eberhart, N. K., 5
Ebesu Hubbard, A. S., 331
Edelstein, R. S., 18
Edwards, G. L., 290
Edwards, K. M., 173, 384
Egan, V., 379
Ehrenberg, M., 410
Ehrensaft, M., 339
Eidelson, R. J., 113, 187, 354
Eisele, H., 26–27
Eisenberg, A. R., 337
Eisenberger, N. I., 307
Eisenbruch, A. B., 78
Ekman, P., 248

Elaad, E., 325
Eldridge, K. A., 163, 347. 348
Elfenbein, H. A., 140
Elliot, A. J., 78
Elliott, D. B., 189, 389, 413
Elliott, S., 341
Ellis, A., 430
Ellsworth, P. C., 94
Ellyson, S. L., 142
Elmquist, J., 379
Elphinston, R. A., 321
El-Sheikh, M., 338
Elshout, M., 328
Elwert, F., 5
Emerson, M. O., 77
Emerson, T., 85
Emery, B., 382, 383–384
Emery, L. F., 60
Emery, R. E., 410, 411, 414, 417
Emmers-Sommer, T. M., 22
English, B. L., 94
Epley, N., 131, 183, 223, 356
Epstein, N., 113, 354, 433, 435
Erbert, L. A., 336, 337
Erikson, E., 218
Erol, R. Y., 33
Estlein, R., 295
Etcheverry, P. E., 106, 202, 211
Exline, J. J., 331
Extremera, N., 330

Fabricius, W. V., 416
Fagley, N. S., 429
Falbo, T., 370, 371
Fales, M. R., 74, 79, 320
Faries, M. D., 76
Farina, A., 83
Farley, S. D., 147, 368
Farrell, A. K., 211
Farris, C., 297
Farvid, P., 293
Fast, N. J., 366
Favez, N., 298
Feeney, B. C., 116, 145, 210, 213, 439
Feeney, J. A., 261, 307, 323, 328

Fehr, B., 185, 208, 219, 222, 224, 246, 247, 251, 256, 257, 258, 260, 262, 263, 264, 267, 337
Fein, E., 431
Feingold, A., 83
Feldman, R., 255
Feldman, R. S., 324
Felmlee, D. H., 91, 215
Fenigstein, A., 281
Fergusson, D. M., 375
Festinger, L., 42, 67
Fetterolf, J. C., 288
Figueredo, A. J., 92
Finch, E., 383
Fincham, F. D., 111, 184, 330, 332, 344, 424
Fine, M. A., 409
Fingerhut, A. W., 31
Fingerhut, H., 31, 272
Fingerman, K. L., 221
Fink, B., 75, 80, 142
Finkel, E. J., 11, 43, 55, 66, 71, 72, 120, 166, 179, 214, 314, 343, 350, 378, 379, 380, 381, 389, 425
Finkenauer, C., 129, 154, 380
Fiori, K. L., 45
Fischer, M. S., 434
Fish, J. N., 298
Fishbein, S., 249
Fisher, H., 245, 264
Fisher, M. L., 76
Fisher, T. D., 55, 281, 286
Fisher, W. A., 298, 301
Fiske, S. T., 46, 100, 253
Fitch, C. A., 362, 391, 402
Fitness, J., 149, 151, 326, 369, 379
Fitzgerald, C. J., 97
Fitzsimons, G. M., 2, 95, 120
Fivecoat, H. C., 186
Flannery, K. M., 223
Fleischmann, A. A., 321
Fletcher, G. J. O., 4, 96, 97, 108, 129, 245, 246, 248, 260, 423
Floyd, K., 144, 156, 161, 255, 256

Flynn, F. J., 212
Foa, U. G., 365
Follingstad, D. R., 55
Fong, K., 123
Foran, H. M., 403
Forbes, M. K., 294
Ford, M. B., 308
Ford, T. E., 204, 424
Forest, A. L., 33, 235
Forrest, J. A., 324
Forsyth, D. R., 109
Foster, C. A., 439
Foster, J. D., 124, 317, 327
Fournier, B., 380
Fowers, B. J., 53, 54, 409
Fowler, J. H., 211
Fowler, K. A., 381
Fox, A. B., 157
Fox, J., 13, 315
Fraley, R. C., 18, 19, 213, 217, 262
Francesconi, M., 82
Frank, M. G., 146, 324
Frederick, D. A., 76, 96, 268, 295, 320
Frei, J. R., 209
French, B. H., 300
French, J. R. P., Jr., 363
Friesen, M. D., 331
Frieze, I. H., 55, 254, 255, 369, 381, 383
Frisby, B. N., 190, 303, 307
Frisco, M. L., 280, 403, 426
Frost, D. M., 30, 409
Frye, N. E., 112
Fugère, M. A., 275
Fuglestad, P. T., 127
Fuhrman, R. W., 208, 209, 224
Fung, H. H., 220, 221
Funk, F., 330
Furman, W., 217, 225, 384
Furr, R. M., 89

Gable, S. L., 182, 183, 184, 185, 209, 210, 213
Gagné, F. M., 107
Gaines, S. O., Jr., 113
Galínha, I. C., 5
Galinsky, A. D., 367

Galinsky, A. M., 276
Gallrein, A. B., 131
Gallup, G. G., Jr., 33, 76, 147, 285
Galperin, A., 263, 271, 296, 314
Galupo, M. P., 225
Gangestad, S. W., 35, 78, 81, 93, 128, 282, 283
Ganong, L. H., 116, 366, 372
Garcia, J. R., 12, 271, 290
Garcia, L. T., 297
Gardner, S., 403
Gardner, W. L., 373–374
Garris, C. P., 101
Garver-Apgar, C. E., 285
Garza, R., 57, 76
Gassanov, M. A., 297
Gatzeva, M., 10
Gaulin, S. J. C., 75, 76
Gaunt, R., 92
Gawronski, B., 105
Gayle, B. M., 347
Geary, D. C., 34
Gebauer, J. E., 89
Geers, A. L., 190, 191, 439
Gephart, J. M., 431
Gere, J., 185, 202
Gerressu, M., 286
Gerstel, N., 9
Gerstorf, D., 5, 221
Gesselman, A. N., 271
Giancola, P. R., 290
Gidycz, C. A., 301, 383
Gigerenzer, G., 149
Gilbert, S. E., 384
Gildersleeve, K. A., 74, 79, 80, 81, 284
Gill, M. J., 105, 106
Gillath, O., 16, 57, 102, 116, 263, 324, 391, 406
Gillespie, B. J., 220, 222
Gilovich, T., 110
Giordano, P. C., 378
Girme, Y. U., 212, 427, 428
Givertz, M., 232
Glass, S. P., 426
Glass, T. A., 5
Glasser, C. L., 82
Gleason, M. E. J., 212

Glenn, N. D., 179, 402
Godbout, N., 380
Goel, S., 9
Gohar, D., 125
Goldberg, A. E., 273
Goldhammer, D. L., 288
Goldin-Meadow, S., 142
Gonsalkorale, K., 310
Gonso, J., 137
Gonzaga, G. C., 92, 248, 253
Goodfriend, W., 174
Goodman-Deane, J., 158
Goodwin, R., 113
Goodwin, S. A., 252, 253
Goossens, L., 232
Gordon, A. K., 323
Gordon, A. M., 338, 349, 356
Gordon, K. C., 384
Gore, J. S., 349
Gosling, S. D., 47
Gosnell, C. L., 183
Gott, M., 298
Gottman, J., 59
Gottman, J. M., 45, 59, 136, 137, 161, 162, 163, 166, 180, 181, 182, 198, 347, 349, 351, 352, 353, 355, 356, 403, 431
Gouin, J., 5, 256, 346
Graber, E. C., 180
Grace, A. J., 349
Graczyk, P. A., 217
Graham, A. M., 416
Graham, J. M., 256, 259, 260
Graham, S. M., 280
Graham-Kevan, N., 376
Gray, J., 20, 430
Gray, J. S., 96
Graziano, W. G., 338
Grebe, N. M., 81
Green, M. C., 320
Greenstein, T. N., 179
Greenwood, S., 12
Greiling, H., 35
Grello, C. M., 288
Grieve, R., 325
Griffin, D. W., 31
Griffitt, W., 87
Grijalva, E., 124

Grillot, R. L., 80
Griskevicius, V., 14
Grollman, E. A., 30
Gross, A. M., 296, 301
Gross, P. H., 103, 104
Grossman, I., 11
Grote, N. K., 55, 194, 198, 254, 255
Grov, C., 287
Guéguen, N., 48, 80, 94, 123
Guerrero, L. K., 196, 310, 312, 313, 320
Guinote, A., 366
Gunaydin, G., 118
Gunn, L. K., 350
Gunnery, S. D., 141
Gurman, A. S., 434
Gute, G., 281
Guthrie, J., 323
Guttentag, M., 14
Guttmacher Institute, 275, 293
Guzzo, K. B., 11

Ha, T., 82
Haak, E. A., 19
Haas, S. M., 274
Haase, C. M., 343
Hadden, B. W., 19, 202
Haeffel, G. J., 236
Hafen, C. A., 92
Häfner, M., 203, 425
Hagen, E. H., 37
Haines, E. L., 27
Halatsis, P., 225
Hald, G. M., 48
Hales, A. H., 309
Halford, W. K., 355, 414, 432
Hall, E. D., 41
Hall, E. T., 145
Hall, J. A., 69, 130, 149, 151, 215, 263, 277, 291, 296, 369
Hall, J. K., 151
Hall, K. S., 277
Hall, S. S., 113
Halpern-Meekin, S., 393, 408
Hambaugh, J., 157, 159

Hamberger, L. K., 376, 377
Hamel, J., 375, 376, 377, 378
Hamermesh, D., 73
Hamilton, B. E., 8, 276
Hamilton, N. F., 70
Hammen, C. L., 5
Hammer, M. Y., 426
Hampel, A. D., 199, 326
Han, J. J., 289
Hancock, J. T., 69
Hannon, P. A., 331
Hansen, T., 191
Hansford, S. L., 224
Hanson, T. L., 413
Harasymchuk, C., 185, 267, 337
Harden, K. P., 276, 277
Hardesty, J. L., 375
Hargrave, T. D., 426
Harinck, F., 350
Harkless, L. E., 409
Harlow, H. F., 42
Harris, C. R., 81
Harris, M. J., 101
Harris, S. M., 426, 439
Hartgerink, C. H., 310
Hartl, A. C., 88
Harvey, J. H., 327, 409
Harwood, J., 227, 231
Haselton, M. G., 74, 79, 81, 96, 263, 284, 296, 314, 315, 322
Haslam, N., 308
Hassebrauck, M., 80
Hassija, C. M., 300
Hatemi, P. K., 403
Hatfield, E., 42, 48, 50, 195, 196, 240, 242, 247, 249–250, 251
Hauch, V., 324
Haupt, A. L., 306
Havlíček, J., 76
Hawkins, A. J., 41, 60
Hawkins, L. B., 127
Hawkley, L. C., 232, 234, 236
Haydon, A. A., 275
Haydon, K. C., 262
Hayes, J., 325
Hayford, S. R., 9

Hazan, C., 15, 218
Heaton, T. B., 402
Heaven, P. C. L., 338
Hebl, M. R., 138
Hecht, H., 48
Hecht, M. L., 267
Heerey, E. A., 38
Hefner, V., 9, 114
Hehman, E., 102
Heiman, J. R., 292
Hellmuth, J. C., 380
Helms, H. M., 26, 92
Henderson, C. E., 418
Henderson, L., 230
Henderson, M., 215
Hendrick, C., 254, 260
Hendrick, S. S., 209, 254, 260
Hendrie, C. A., 123, 322
Henline, B. H., 287
Henrich, J., 47
Hepper, E. G., 262
Herbenick, D., 292
Herbst, K. C., 92
Herold, A. L., 369
Herrero, J., 379, 380
Hershberger, S., 24
Hertenstein, M. J., 59, 140, 144
Herz, R. S., 77
Hess, J. A., 296
Hesse, C., 156, 157
Hetherington, E. M., 413
Hettinger, V. E., 365
Heyman, R. E., 183
Hicks, T. V., 311
High, A. C., 126
Hilbig, B. E., 2
Hill, A., 323, 328
Hill, P. L., 27
Hill, R., 361
Hill, S. E., 314
Hinchliff, S., 298
Hitsch, G. J., 77, 84, 88, 93, 124
Hixon, J. G., 122
Hodges, S. D., 131
Hogerbrugge, M. J. A., 393
Høgh-Olesen, H., 48
Hohmann-Marriott, B. E., 92
Hojjat, M., 331

Holland, R. W., 146
Holleran, S. E., 159
Holley, S. R., 338, 347, 348
Holloway, R. A., 215
Holman, T. B., 352, 353
Holmes, J. G., 31, 162, 198
Holt-Lunstad, J., 5, 58, 232, 256
Holtgraves, T., 158
Holtzman, N. S., 124
Holtzworth-Munroe, A., 150, 381
Hook, J. N., 111, 331
Hopwood, C. J., 95
Horan, S. M., 226, 322, 323, 439
Horn, D., 158
Horner, E. M., 179
Horstman, J., 272
Horton, R. S., 85, 87, 92
Hostetler, A. J., 390
Houston, D. M., 27
Houts, R. M., 338, 355
Howard, E. S., 181, 374
Howes, C., 216
Howland, M., 212, 349
Hoyt, T., 300
Hrapczynski, K. M., 112
Hsueh, A. C., 10
Huang, K., 14
Hudson, N. W., 28
Huebner. D. M., 191
Hughes, S. M., 76, 85
Hui, C. M., 425
Huibregtse, B. M., 276
Human, L. J., 58, 101, 130, 255
Humbad, M. N., 57
Hunt, L. L., 84, 87
Hunt, M. M., 241
Hunter, S., 155
Huston, S. J., 340
Huston, T. L., 264, 338, 397, 402
Huynh, A. C., 349
Hwang, H. S., 139, 140, 142
Hyde, J. S., 22, 23, 271

Iacovelli, A. M., 158
Ickes, W., 25, 44, 62, 89, 129, 131, 227, 228

Iemmola, F., 274
Iida, M., 212
IJzerman, H., 203, 425
Imhof, M., 144
Imhoff, R., 290
Impett, E. A., 185, 194, 276, 277, 280, 285, 291, 295, 298, 300, 364, 424
Inesi, M.E., 331
Infurna, F. J., 413
Inzlicht, M., 77
Ireland, M. E., 159
Italie, L., 223
Ivcevic, Z., 235
Izhaki-Costi, O., 130

Jackson, G. L., 60
Jackson, J. J., 28, 396, 403
Jackson, T., 260
Jacobson, N. S., 195, 433
Jacques-Tiura, A. J., 296
Jakubiak, B. K., 145
Jalovaara, M., 402
James, S. L., 189, 397, 399
Jarvis, M. O., 352
Jasieńska, G., 78
Jauk, E., 226
Jayamaha, S. D., 211
Jena, A. B., 277
Jensen, J. F., 355
Jensen, T. M., 402
Jensen-Campbell, L. A., 98, 338, 380
Jeronimus, B. F., 28
Jiang, L. C., 69
Jöchle, W., 79
Joel, S., 259
Johnson, B. T., 291
Johnson, C., 158
Johnson, D. R., 220, 373, 392
Johnson, J. G., 339
Johnson, K. L., 144
Johnson, M. D., 60, 198, 402, 408, 435
Johnson, M. P., 202, 375, 376, 377, 382
Johnson, P. B., 369
Johnson, S. M., 435, 436

Johnson, V. F., 296
Jokela, M., 79
Jonason, P. K., 97, 225, 271, 298, 431
Jones, D., 74, 78
Jones, D. N., 226, 286, 313
Jones, E. E., 125
Jones, J. D., 19
Jones, J. M., 272, 426
Jones, J. T., 66, 88
Jones, W. H., 2, 326, 327, 328
Jong, E., 264–265
Jongman-Sereno, K. P., 230
Jordan, A. H., 291
Jose, A., 10, 392
Joyner, L., 292

Kachadourian, L. K., 330
Kafetsios, K., 157, 262
Kahneman, D., 1
Kaighobadi, F., 377
Kail, B. L., 274
Kalbfleisch, P. J., 369
Kammrath, L. K., 194, 327, 344, 430
Kamp Dush, C. M., 355
Kandrik, M., 13
Kane, H. S., 212
Kaplar, M. E., 323
Karbowski, A., 77
Kardum, I., 317
Karney, B. R., 49, 60, 108, 111, 112, 118, 121, 190, 258, 395–396, 402, 403, 419, 423
Karraker, A., 279
Karremans, J. C., 76, 331, 425, 427
Kasen, S., 339
Kashdan, T. B., 231
Kashy, D. A., 211, 262, 323
Kasser, T., 11
Kassin, S. M., 111
Kato, T., 331
Katz, J., 300
Kaufman, J., 265
Kaukinen, C. E., 382
Kavanagh, P. S., 29, 85
Kawamoto, T., 38

Kayser, K., 398
Keefer, L. A., 391
Kellas, J. K., 167, 408, 409
Kellerman, J., 142
Kelley, D. K., 330
Kelley, H. H., 109, 171, 174, 192, 345, 360
Kelly, E. L., 28
Kelly, L., 337
Kelmer, G., 69, 71
Keltner, D., 248, 366, 368
Keneski, E., 211
Kennedy, K. A., 342
Kenrick, D. T., 6, 211
Kephart, W., 240
Kerr, P. G., 108, 129
Khaddouma, A., 401
Kiecolt-Glaser, J. K., 347, 403
Kiefer, A. K., 294
Kifer, Y., 366
Kille, D. R., 107
Kim, J. L., 293
Kim, Y., 73, 347
Kimmes, J. G., 111, 112, 116
King, K. B., 6
King, M. E., 188
Kleinke, C. L., 86, 142
Kline, S. L., 216, 261
Kloda, I., 355
Klohnen, E. C., 92
Klusmann, D., 286, 288
Kluwer, E. S., 344
Knäuper, B., 289
Knee, C. R., 114, 115, 294
Knobloch, L. K., 69, 155, 186, 187, 188
Knoester, C., 395
Knöfler, T., 144
Knopp, K. C., 202, 203
Knowles, M. L., 13
Knudson-Martin, C., 367
Kobak, R., 218
Koch, S. C., 142
Kogan, A., 194
Kohn, J. L., 5
Kohut, T., 287
Konrad, A. M., 27
Konrath, S. H., 18

Kosinksi, M., 58, 125
Kossinets, G., 6
Kouzakova, M., 149
Kowalski, R. M., 227
Krahé, B., 300
Krasnova, H., 235, 315
Kraut, R. E., 235
Kreager, D. A., 70
Kremer-Sadlik, T., 58
Kross, E., 235
Kruger, D. J., 97, 280, 288, 310, 361
Kruger, J., 110, 158
Kruger, M. L., 140
Kubacka, K. E., 429
Kudak, A., 427
Kuhle, B. X., 319
Kuijer, R. G., 199
Kunkel, A., 323
Kunstman, J. W., 367
Kunz, P. R., 175
Kuperberg, A., 10, 271, 290
Kurdek, L. A., 30, 189, 201, 223
Kurzban, R., 82
Kuster, F., 33
Kuyper, L., 60

LaBrie, J. W., 288
Lachance-Grzela, M., 366, 393
Lackenbauer, S. D., 121
Lakey, B., 212, 213
Lakey, S., 335, 344, 346, 349, 355–356
Lakin, J. L., 148
Lam, A. G., 371
Lam, B. C. P., 96
Lambert, N. M., 424
Lamidi, E., 7, 227
Lammers, J., 367
Lamy, L., 94, 248
Landers, A., 242
Lane, B. L., 13, 315
Lang, F. R., 221
Lang, S. F., 54
Langeslag, S. J. E., 252, 256
Långström, N., 273, 274
Lannin, D. G., 163
Lansford, J. E., 416

Lapierre, M. A., 13
Larmuseau, M. H. D., 285, 314
Larose, S., 236
Larrick, R. P., 380
Larsen, S. E., 376, 377
Larson, C. M., 285
Larson, D. G., 154
Larson, G. M., 60
Larson, R. W., 208, 217
Lassek, W. D., 75, 76
Lauer, J. C., 254, 267
Lauer, R. H., 254, 267, 440
Laumann, E. O., 286
Laurel-Seller, E., 81
Laurenceau, J., 54, 151, 154
Laurin, K., 368
Lavee, Y., 2
Lavner, J. A., 124, 163, 188, 189, 190, 341, 397, 399, 403
Lawrence, E., 212, 338, 384
Lawson, J. F., 97
Layous, K., 429
Le, B. M., 60, 69, 180, 192, 194, 201
Leaper, C., 159, 221
Leary, M. R., 4, 5, 29, 42, 126, 127, 199, 227, 230, 231, 303, 304, 305, 306, 307, 309, 326
Lease, S. H., 26
Lebow, J. L., 438
Leder, S., 307, 326
Lee, A. J., 75
Lee, D. M., 265
Lee, J. A., 258, 260
Lee, L., 84
Lee, S. W. S, 115
Lee-Chai, A. Y., 363
LeFebvre, L., 407
Legate, N., 155
Lehmann, P., 381
Lehmiller, J. J., 211, 224–225
Leising, D., 106, 113
Leitenberg, H., 311
Lemay, E. P., Jr., 31, 73, 110, 112, 117, 119, 201, 212, 224, 236, 317, 323, 423, 439

Lennon, C. A., 361, 362
Lenton, A. P., 82, 224
Leonardelli, G. J., 308
Leone, C., 127
Leone, J. M., 376
Letzring, T. D., 129
Levant, R. F., 24, 27
Levenson, R. W., 162, 166, 181, 182, 263
Lever, J., 293
Levine, E. E., 323
Levine, T. R., 322, 324, 325
Levinger, A. C., 400
Levinger, G., 198, 394–395, 400
Levitt, M. J., 38, 303
Levy, S. R., 272
Lewicki, R., 331
Lewis, K., 58
Lewis, M. A., 289, 290, 291
Lewis, M. N., 13
Lewis, R. J., 380
Lewis, T., 164
Li, B., 44
Li, H., 33
Li, N. P., 34, 35, 82, 96, 97, 263, 431
Li, X., 235
Li, Y., 416, 418
Liberman, V., 349
Lick, D. J., 141
Liebold, J. M., 381
Liefbroer, A. C., 9
Lim, B. H., 384
Lin, A. J., 277, 291
Lin, Y. W., 201
Lindberg, L., 277
Lindgren, K. P., 296
Lindheim, O., 438
Linville, P., 289
Lipinski-Harten, M., 158
Lippa, R. A., 24, 30, 97, 286
Lishner, D. A., 316
Little, A. C., 74, 75, 80, 84
Liu, E., 355
Liu, H., 38
Liu, J., 414
Livingston, G., 12, 95, 240, 413
Lloyd, S. A., 337, 382, 384
Lobmaier, J. S., 80

Löckenhoff, C. E., 24, 220
Loewenstein, G., 290, 294
Logan, J. M., 210
Lohr, J. M., 343
Lois, D., 92
Long, E. C. J., 131
Longmore, M. A., 380
Longstreth, M., 338
Lorber, M. F., 375, 381
Lord. C. G., 406
Lorenzo, G. L., 130
Loving, T. J., 5, 106, 211, 346
Lucas, R. E., 175, 179, 412
Luchies, L. B., 332, 425
Luciano, E. C., 33, 45
Luhmann, M., 191
Luis, S., 82
Lukacs, V., 411
Luke, M. A., 261
Lummaa, V., 79, 81
Luo, S., 55, 82, 90, 92, 108, 129
Luong, G., 216
Lutfey, K. E., 292
Luthar, S. S., 413
Lutz-Zois, C. J., 92
Luxen, M. F., 78
Lydon, J. E., 82, 107,
  202, 203
Lykken, D. T., 403
Lynch, J. L., 366
Lyngstad, T. H., 402
Lynn, S. J., 301
Lyons, P. M., 73
Lyons-Amos, M., 7, 389
Lytle, A., 272
Lyubomirsky, S., 429

Määttä, K., 150
MacDonald, G., 338
MacDonald, T. K., 106, 290
Macdowall, W., 300
MacGeorge, E. L., 41
Magdol, L., 391, 402
Mahoney, A. R., 367
Maisel, N. C., 213, 395
Maisto, S. A., 291, 371
Major, B., 84
Malachowski, C. C., 190,
  303, 307
Maldonado, R. C., 379

Maleck, S., 417
Malkoc, S. A., 427
Malle, B. F., 109
Malouff, J. M., 28, 50, 131,
  186, 427
Maltby, J., 330
Mancini, A. D., 413
Maner, J. K., 80, 253, 309,
  321, 367
Manglos-Weber, N. D., 242
Mania, E. W., 330
Maniaci, M. R., 214, 257
Mannes, A. E., 77
Manning, W. D., 7, 30, 289
Manusov, V., 164, 409
Mar, R. A., 123
Marcus, D. K., 73, 300
Margolin, G., 433
Markey, C. N., 95, 297
Markey, P. M., 95
Markman, H. J., 136, 137, 163,
  166, 167, 330, 356, 357, 432
Marks, M. J., 271
Marmo, J., 428
Marquardt, E., 390, 391,
  399, 402
Marshall, A. D., 150
Marshall, L. L., 384
Marshall, T. C., 26, 27, 221,
  222, 224–225
Marshuetz, C., 72
Martin, C. L., 25
Martins, Y., 77
Martos, A. J., 155
Martz, J. M., 174, 201
Masarik, A. S., 19
Mason, A. E., 410
Mason, M. F., 141
Mason, W., 47
Massar, K., 313, 314
Mast, M. S., 130, 151
Master, S. L., 5
Masters, W. H., 296
Mathews, T. J., 276
Matsumoto, D., 139, 140,
  142, 146
Maxwell, J. A., 295
Mayer, J. D., 130
McAllister, S., 431
McAndrew, F. T., 158

McCabe, M. P., 288
McClure, M. J., 82, 212
McConnell, A. R., 381
McCormack, M., 47
McCoy, A., 409
McCrae, R. R., 27, 28
McCullough, M. E., 124,
  330, 331
McDaniel, B. T., 13
McDermott, R., 393
McEwan, B., 158
McEwan, T. E., 383
McGonagle, K. A., 180, 337
McGuire, J. E., 221
McHugh, M. C., 157, 159
McKibbin, W. F., 377
McKinnish, T. G., 390, 400
McLean, H., 318
McNulty, J. K., 111, 118,
  179, 297, 332, 355, 380
McPherson, M., 227
Meehan, J. C., 381
Mehl, M. R., 42, 45, 57, 156,
  159, 235
Meier, A. M., 413
Mellor, D., 231
Melton, E. N., 272
Meltzer, A. L., 76, 82, 127, 284
Mendelsohn, G. A., 94, 159
Merali, N., 241, 261
Merino, S. M., 225
Merolla, A. J., 349
Merrill, A. F., 157
Mescher, K., 198, 300
Meston, C. M., 278
Metts, S., 23, 113, 263
Meuwly, N., 210
Michalski, R. L., 318
Mickelson, K. D., 18, 191
Mikkelson, A. C., 156
Mikulincer, M., 17, 38, 116,
  157, 261, 262, 298,
  308, 338
Milardo, R. M., 219
Miles, L. K., 215
Miller, A. J., 366
Miller, G. E., 416
Miller, H. A., 297
Miller, J. B., 116
Miller, K., 87, 118

Miller, L. C., 153, 156
Miller, M. A., 408
Miller, M. J., 313
Miller, O. S., 82
Miller, P. J. E., 26, 209
Miller, R. S., 4, 12, 38, 46, 73, 109, 124, 127, 143, 174, 180, 190, 191, 202, 227, 230, 235, 303, 305, 315, 326, 335, 423–424
Miller, S. L., 80, 321
Miller, W. B., 19
Miller-Ott, A. E., 12, 337
Mills, J. R., 193, 194
Mills, P. J., 429
Mills, R. D., 381
Milojev, P., 27
Minieri, A., 288
Mischkowski, D., 343
Misra, T. A., 327
Mitchell, A. E., 154
Mitchell, C., 55
Mitchell, J. W., 280
Mitchell, K., 192, 288
Mitchell, S. A., 264, 266
Mitura, K., 37, 94
Mogilski, J. K., 408
Moilanen, K. L., 291
Molix, L., 274
Monfort, S. S., 209
Mongeau, P. A., 225
Monk, J. K., 428
Montoya, R. M., 84, 85, 87, 92
Mooney, L., 331
Moore, T. M., 381
Moreland, J. J., 13
Moreland, R. L., 68
Moreno, J. L., 42
Morgentaler, A., 270
Morin, R., 365
Morris, C. E., 408, 410
Morris, M. L., 226
Morrison, E. L., 81
Morrow, G. D., 260
Morry, M. M., 90, 226
Moss-Racusin, C. A., 126
Muehlenhard, C. L., 24, 123
Muise, A., 194, 293, 295, 297, 315

Mund, M., 33, 37
Mundy, L., 11, 390
Murray, S. L., 31, 32, 33, 108, 192
Murstein, B. I., 90, 91
Muscanell, N. L., 13, 315
Myers, D. G., 124, 273
Myers, S. A., 246
Myhr, L., 300

Nagy, G. F., 85
Nater, C., 129
Neal, A. M., 112, 212
Nedelec, J. L., 78
Ne'eman, R., 255
Neff, L. A., 108, 121, 180, 190, 191, 258, 396, 397, 423, 439
Negash, S., 426
Neighbors, C., 379
Nelson, A. J., 141
Nelson, D., 42, 52, 88
Nelson, L. D., 81
Nelson, S. K., 191
Neppl, T. K., 416
Nestler, S., 102
Neville, H.A., 90
Newall, N. E., 236
Newcomb, T. M., 87, 90
Newton, I, 42
Nezlek, J. B., 125, 126, 234, 262
Nicholls, T. L., 375, 376, 377, 378
Niehuis, S., 108, 191, 398, 399
Nietert, P. J., 413
Nissan, T., 370
Noirot, M., 116
Noller, P., 149–150, 355
North, R. J., 210
Norton, M. I., 69, 71
Notarius, C. I., 137, 344

Oakman, J., 228
O'Boyle, E. H., 226
Ochs, E., 58
O'Connell, D., 300
O'Connor, J. J. M., 147
Ogolsky, B. G., 112, 188, 203, 373, 399, 422, 428

Oh, S. Y., 44
Ohtsubo, Y., 213, 331
Oishi, S., 11, 139, 391
Okimoto, T. G., 365
Olatunji, B. O., 343
O'Leary, K. D., 267
Olivola, C. Y., 73, 101
Olmstead, S. B., 287
Olson, I. R., 72
O'Neil, J. M., 27
Ones, D. S., 129
Orbuch, T. L., 45, 399, 431
Oriña, M. M., 217, 366
Ormiston, M. E., 102
Orth, U., 29, 33, 45
Osman, M., 374
Osterhout, R. E., 110
O'Sullivan, L. F., 158, 173, 294, 295
Oswald, D. L., 428, 429
Overall, N. C., 18, 157, 202, 338, 347, 349, 351, 372, 425
Owen, J., 225
Owen, P. R., 81
Owenz, M. B., 54

Pachankis, J. E., 155
Padgett, J. E., 271, 290
Padgett, P. M., 29
Paik, A., 10, 276, 277, 402
Palomares, N. A., 159
Papp, L. M., 315, 337, 340, 417
Park, G., 125
Park, H. S., 325
Parks-Leduc, L., 126
Parmley, M., 151
Parsons, J. E., 369
Parsons, J. T., 298
Pascoal, P. M., 295
Pasipandoya, E., 54
Patterson, M. L., 139, 149
Patterson, S. E., 393, 402
Paul, A., 71
Paymar, M., 376
Payne, J. W., 78
Pazda, A. D., 78
Pazzaglia, M., 146
Pearce, A. R., 7

Pearson, J. C., 427
Pedersen, W. C., 317
Peer, E., 329
Peetz, J., 327, 430
Peipert, J. F., 277
Pelham, B. W., 66, 121
Pence, E., 376
Pennebaker, J. W., 57
Peplau, L. A., 31, 280, 364, 370, 371
Perelli-Harris, B., 7, 389
Perilloux, C., 300
Perilloux, H. K., 78
Perlman, D. viii, 208, 209, 216
Perrett, D., 79
Petersen, J. L., 22
Peterson, D. R., 339, 340, 341, 344, 353, 354
Peterson, Z. D., 22, 24
Petit, W. E., 204, 424
Petrie, T., 70
Petronio, S., 154, 190, 336
Petty, K. N., 114, 115
Pew Research Center, 7, 155, 197, 198, 272, 273, 274–275, 365, 366
Pham, M. N., 285
Pierce, L., 11
Pillsworth, E. G., 284
Pines, A. M., 321
Pinquart, M., 234
Pipitone, R. N., 80, 147
Pittman, F. S., 426
Pittman, T., 125
Pitts, M. K., 286
Place, S. S., 130
Plant, E. A., 153
Pollet, T. V., 235
Pollmann, M. M. H., 129
Ponzi, D., 366
Poore, J., 185
Poortman, A., 9, 395, 403
Porter, S., 324
Potarca, G., 71
Powers, R. A., 382
Powers, S. I., 347
Prager, K. J., 2
Pratto, F., 364
Pressman, S. D., 5
Preston, M., 281

Previti, D., 328, 395, 400, 403
Price, M., 13
Priem, J. S., 212, 213
Prokop, P., 78
Prokosch, M. D., 77
Pronin, E., 109, 342
Pronk, T. M., 425
Proost, K., 125, 126
Przbylinski, E., 120
Przybylski, A. K., 13
Puccinelli, N. M., 137, 149
Pulerwitz, J., 291
Pupic, D., 374
Purvis, J. A., 153
Pyszczynski, T. A., 246

Quan-Haase, A., 411
Quigley, L., 318
Qureshi, C., 226

Raby, K. L., 19
Rafaeli, E., 212
Rahe, R. H., 408
Rains, S. A., 158
Ramirez, A., Jr., 69, 204
Rammstedt, B., 92
Randall, A. K., 403
Randolph, M. E., 291
Rankin, T. J., 24, 27
Rao, S. S., 398
Rapson, R. L., 195, 196, 240, 242
Rasmussen, K., 287, 288
Ratliff, K. A., 11
Rauer, A. J., 353, 355
Raven, B. H., 363, 364
Re, D. E., 102
Redlick, M., 312
Reed, L. A., 377
Regan, P. C., 30, 264, 267, 286
Reiber, C., 271
Reinhard, M., 324
Reinhardt, J. P., 212
Reis, H. S., 223, 297
Reis, H. T., 3, 6, 21, 22, 26, 42, 43, 71, 83, 84, 90, 95, 153, 157, 160, 184, 209, 210, 213, 214, 218, 223, 224, 234, 236, 257, 297, 423

Reissing, E. D., 276
Reitz, A. K., 29
Rempel, J. K., 209
Ren, D., 17, 18
Ren, P., 179, 391
Renshaw, K. D., 180
Rentfrow, P. J., 161
Repetti, R. L., 53
Rey, L., 330
Rhoades, G. K., 11, 203, 393
Rhodes, G., 74, 75
Richard, F. D., 406
Richman, L. S., 309
Rick, S. I., 91
Riek, B. M., 330
Riela, S., 260
Riggio, H. R., 416
Riggle, E. D. B., 155, 273
Righetti, F., 373
Rill, L., 235
Riordan, P., 73
Risman, B. J., 271
Rizkalla, L., 349
Robbins, M. L., 57
Roberts, B. W., 438
Roberts, J. A., 13, 159
Roberts, S. G. B., 218
Robillard, S. L., 123
Robins, R. W., 29, 109, 140
Robinson, M. D., 33
Robles, T. F., 5, 62
Robnett, R. D., 159
Roddy, M. K., 434
Rodin, J., 321
Rodrigues, D., 283
Rodriguez, L. M., 408
Rogers, M. J., 55
Rogers, S. J., 220, 373, 391, 392
Rogge, R. D., 257, 432
Rohrbaugh, M. J., 6
Roisman, G. I., 30, 262
Rolffs, J. L., 432
Rollie, S. S., 407
Roloff, M. E., 113, 337, 355
Romero-Canyas, R., 119
Ronay, R., 123
Roney, J. R., 80
Rosen, L. D., 253
Rosenbaum, J. E., 277

Rosenberg, J., 77
Rosenthal, A. M., 253
Rosenthal, L., 211
Rosenthal, N. L., 218
Rosenthal, R., 116, 117
Ross, M., 106
Ross, M. W., 287
Rossetto, K. R., 69
Rostosky, S. S., 273
Rowatt, W. C., 83
Roy, R. R. N., 197, 340
Rubin, H., 279
Rubin, L. B., 222, 223
Rubin, Y. S., 310
Rubin, Z., 251, 263
Ruble, D. N., 369
Rudman, L. A., 126, 198,
    271, 288, 300, 365
Ruggles, S., 362, 391, 402
Rule, N. O., 79, 101,
    102, 144
Ruppel, E. K., 424
Rusbult, C. E., 109, 132, 174,
    200, 201, 203, 350, 351,
    423, 425
Russell, D. W., 233
Russell, V. M., 286, 355
Rutstein, J., 249
Rycyna, C. C., 329
Rydell, R. J., 312

Sabey, A. K., 258
Sabini, J., 83, 320
Saffrey, C., 410
Sagarin, B. J., 316, 318,
    319, 323
Sahlstein, E. M., 69, 71
Salkicevic, S., 377
Salovey, P., 310, 316, 321
Salvatore, J. E., 347
Samp, J. A., 372, 373, 391
Sanchez, D. T., 294
Sandstrom, G. M., 4
Sanford, K., 349, 353
Santelli, J. S., 277, 291
Saribay, S. A., 101
Sarkisian, N., 9
Saslow, L. R., 125
Sassler, S., 366
Savage, D., 266

Savin-Williams, R. C., 30,
    155, 273
Savitsky, K., 137
Sayer, L. C., 414
Sbarra, D. A., 5, 60, 410, 411,
    413, 415
Schachter, S., 1, 4, 42, 67
Schaffhuser, K., 27
Scheier, M. F., 119
Schick, V., 55, 281
Schkeryantz, E. L., 375
Schlenker, B. R., 109, 123, 124
Schlessinger, L., 430
Schmidt, A. F., 290
Schmidt, L. A., 231
Schmiedeberg, C., 265
Schmitt, D. P., 18, 35, 37, 48,
    83, 93, 262, 282, 286,
    298, 317
Schneider, D., 380
Schneider, S., 431
Schneider, W. J., 437
Schoenfeld, E. A., 293
Schonlau, M., 217
Schröder, J., 265
Schrodt, P., 347
Schul, Y., 130
Schulz, M.S., 19
Schütz, A., 110
Schützwohl, A., 35, 311,
    318, 319
Schwartz, P., 266, 279, 280,
    282, 292
Schwarz, S., 80, 115
Schweinle, W. E., 130, 131
Schweitzer, M. E., 323
Scott, S. B., 285, 401
Scott-Sheldon, L. A. J., 291
Scrutton, H. E., 29
Sczesny, S., 23
Seabrook, R. C., 293
Seal, D. W., 283
Sears, M. S., 396
Secord, P. F., 14
Seder, J. P., 139
Sedikides, C., 110, 172
Seeley, E. A., 374
Seeman, T. E., 210
Segal, M. W., 68
Segal, N., 213

Segal-Caspi, L., 72
Segrin, C., 403
Seidman, G., 82, 121, 181
Seih, Y., 121
Sela, Y., 377
Selcuk, E., 214
Sells, T. G. C., 366, 372
Seltzer, J. A., 395
Seltzer, L. J., 159
Serota, K. B., 322
Sewell, K.K., 54, 281
Shackelford, T. K., 85, 285,
    286, 313, 317, 318, 377
Shafer, K., 190, 430
Shaffer, D. R., 153, 160
Shallcross, A. J., 263
Shanteau, J., 85
Sharma, A., 414
Sharp, E. A., 116
Shaver, P. R., 15, 17, 38, 153,
    157, 209, 218, 261, 262,
    298, 308, 338
Sheets, V. L., 186, 254
Sheldon, K. M., 178, 186,
    337, 426
Shettel-Neuber, J., 320
Shih, K. Y., 197
Shimizu, M., 230
Shippee, S. K., 123
Shoda, Y., 120, 385
Shoham, V., 6
Shorey, R. C., 60
Shrout, P. E., 212
Shu, X., 365
Sibley, C. G., 27, 202
Siegler, I. C., 9
Silk, J. B., 194
Simmons, C. A., 381
Simmons, T., 189, 389, 413
Simmons, Z. L., 80
Simpson, J. A., 18, 19, 35, 37,
    132, 209, 282, 283, 344,
    349, 360, 362, 424, 426
Sinclair, H. C., 211, 383
Singh, D., 76, 78, 82
Skakoon-Sparling, S., 290
Slatcher, R. B., 151, 156, 214
Slater, A., 74, 78
Slater, D., 70, 179
Slater, P. E., 390

Sloan, D. M., 156
Slotter, E. B., 336, 380, 409
Smith, A., 70
Smith, G., 271, 291
Smith, H. M. J., 147
Smith, J. L., 129
Smith, J. Z., 273
Smith, R. L., 223
Smith, T. W., 210, 278, 338
Smith-Marek, E. N., 378, 382
Smollan, D., 3
Smyth, R., 292
Snider, A. G., 129
Snyder, D. K., 436, 437, 438, 439
Snyder, M., 104, 117, 118, 127, 128
Sohn, K., 94
Solano, A. C., 261
Solomon, B. C., 108, 396, 403
Solomon, D. H., 151, 186, 188, 212
Solomon, S. E., 342
Sommer, K. L., 308, 310
Sonenstein, F. L., 276
Sonnega, J. S., 6
Soons, J. P. M., 179
Soto, C. J., 29
Soulsby, L. K., 3, 423
South, S. J., 11
Southard, A. C., 226
Southworth, C., 383
Spellman, B. A., 125
Spielmann, S. S., 4, 9, 183, 410
Spitzberg, B. H., 38, 280, 300, 314, 383
Spongberg, K., 31
Sprecher, S., 90, 113, 153, 156, 178, 196, 240, 249–250, 251, 257, 262, 263, 264, 265, 266, 267, 286, 318
Srivastava, S., 119
Stackert, R. A., 116
Staeheli, J. C., 426
Stafford, L., 69, 191, 202, 216, 427, 428
Stake, J. E., 26, 27

Stanik, C. E., 26, 94, 198
Stanley, S. M., 10, 168, 357
Stanton, S., 435
Starks, T. J., 211, 298
Steinberg, M., 27
Stepler, R., 389
Sternberg, R. J., 242, 243, 244, 245, 258, 264
Stewart-Williams, S., 272
Stewart, A. J., 407, 414
Stickney, L. T., 27
Stillwell, A. M., 328
Stinson, D. A., 119, 123
Stoeber, J., 191
Stokes, J. E., 232
Strachman, A., 185, 298
Strassberg, D. S., 54, 94, 281
Strauss, C., 92
Strausser, K. S., 306
Strelan, P., 332
Stroebe, M. S., 413
Strokoff, J., 271
Strong, G., 186, 265, 267, 427
Strube, M. J., 124
Strübel, J., 70
Stucke, T. S., 124
Stukas, A. A., Jr., 117
Stulp, G., 77
Subotnik, R., 287
Sugar, M., 192, 288
Suh, G. W., 416
Sullivan, K. T., 210
Summers, R. F., 438
Sun, Y., 416, 418
Sunderani, S., 317
Sundie, J. M., 94, 123
Surra, C. A., 112, 338
Svetieva, E., 324
Swami, V., 76, 81
Swann, W. B., 29, 104, 105, 106, 117, 119, 121, 122, 132, 161, 174
Sweeper, S., 414
Syme, M. L., 290

Tabak, J. A., 144
Tach, L. M., 393
Tackett, S. L., 227, 230
Tafarodi, R. W., 158

Tafoya, M. A., 280, 314
Takahashi, H., 318
Talhelm, T., 391
Tan, R., 157
Tanha, M., 385
Tatum, A. K., 274
Tausczik, Y. R., 57
Tavris, C., 167, 343
Taylor, D. A., 152
Taylor, L. S., 84
Taylor, M. G., 355
Taylor, S. E., 100
Teachman, J., 402
Teding van Berkhout, E., 131
Tellegen, A., 34
Ten Brinke, L., 324
Tenney, E. R., 125
Terhell, E. L., 414
Theiss, J. A., 151, 187, 188, 295
Thibaut, J. W., 171, 360
Thielman, I., 2
Thomas, R. J., 70
Thomas, V., 57
Thompson, A. E., 151, 369
Thompson, M., 300
Thompson, S. C., 109
Thornhill, R., 77, 79
Thornton, A., 10, 360
Tice, D. M., 343
Tidwell, N. D., 50, 81, 89, 286
Tiedens, L. Z., 27
Tienda, M., 90
Timmerman, L., 320
Timmons, A. C., 338, 378, 380
Tissot, H., 298
Todorov, A., 65, 73, 82, 101, 105
Tokunaga, R. S., 315
Toller, P., 164
Tomlinson, J. M., 58, 108, 410
Tonietto, G. N., 427
Totenhagen, C. J., 37, 203, 424
Tracy, J. L., 80, 140
Trail, T. E., 60, 402
Tran, S., 107

Trask, S. L., 157
Treat, T. A., 297
Treger, S., 153
Troy, A. B., 90
Tsai, F., 234, 236
Tsapelas, I., 35, 185,
    268, 285
Tucker, J. S., 157
Tucker, P., 264
Tunney, R. J., 77
Turchik, J. A., 300
Turcotte, J., 235
Turley, R. N. L., 416
Tuscherer, T., 309
Twenge, J. M., 11, 24, 25,
    27, 30, 271, 275, 308,
    372, 391

Ueno, K., 225
Uleman, J. S., 101
Umberson, D., 341
Urquia, M. L., 10
U. S. Census Bureau, 7
Uskul, A. K., 370
Utz, S., 13
Uusiautti, S., 150

Vaaler, M. L., 402
Vacharkulksemsuk, T.,
    43, 143
Valentine, K. A., 102
Valentova, J. V., 75
Valtorta, N. K., 5
Van Buren, A., 294
van den Boom, D. C., 19
van der Land, S. F., 89
van der Linden, D., 27
Van Dongen, S., 78, 93
Van Hook, J., 90
van Steenbergen, H., 253
van Straaten, I., 84
Van Zalk, M. H. W., 158
Vandello, J. A., 381
Vanden Abeele, M., 158
VanderDrift, L. E., 175, 216,
    225, 371
VanderLaan, D. P., 274
Vangelisti, A. L., 136, 137,
    154, 199, 326, 435
Vanhalst, J., 236, 305

Vannier, S. A., 173, 295
Varnum, M. E. W., 11
Vasey, P. L., 274
Vazire, S., 108, 130, 131
Vedes, A., 260
Veitch, R., 87
Vélez-Blasini, C. J., 290
Venardos, C., 150
Vennum, A., 408
Verhage, M. L., 19
Verhofstadt, L. L. L.,
    168, 210
Vescio, T. K., 374
Vincent, J. P., 180
Vohs, K. D., 288, 425
Volk, A. A., 36
von Hippel, W., 123, 325
Voracek, M., 76
Vorauer, J. D., 137
Vorderer, P., 13
Voyer, D., 151, 369
Vrangalova, Z., 271
Vrij, A., 147, 322, 324, 325
Vukasović, T., 27, 29

Waas, G. A., 217
Wade, J. C., 11, 26, 30
Wagers, T. P., 426
Wagner, M.F., 150
Waite, L. J., 38, 292
Waldinger, R. J., 19, 202
Waldron, V. R., 330
Walker, A., 364
Waller, W. W., 42, 361
Walsh, J. L., 276
Walster, E., 72, 87, 247, 264,
    265, 266, 431
Walster, G. W., 264,
    265, 266
Wänke, M., 102
Warber, K. M., 13, 315
Ward, D. E., 409
Watkins, L. E., 384
Watkins, S. J., 280
Watson, D., 88, 89
Watts, D. J., 68
Watts, T. M., 141
Weaver, S. E., 113
Webber, L., 224
Weber, A. L., 327, 409

Weber, K., 86
Webster, G. D., 294
Weeden, J., 82, 83
Weeks, D. G., 236, 237
Wegner, R., 297, 371
Wehrman, E. C., 69
Wei, M., 56
Weidman, A. C., 231
Weigel, D. J., 114, 199, 336,
    351, 439
Weinreb, A. A., 242
Weinstein, N., 13
Weir, K., 331, 427
Weisbuch, M., 147
Weiser, D. A., 286, 313, 351
Weiss, P., 76
Weiss, R. L., 433
Weiss, R. S., 232
Weisskirch, R. S., 406
Welling, L. L. M., 408
Wells, B. E., 275, 293
Wendorf, C. A., 191, 340
Wenzel, A., 85
Werking, K., 219
Wesselmann, E. D.,
    308, 309
West, C., 368
West, L., 96
Westen, D., 381
Whalen, J. M., 158
Wheeler, J., 434
Wheeler, L., 73, 160, 234
Whisman, M. A., 5
Whitaker, D. J., 381
Whitchurch, E., 131
White, G. L., 248, 249,
    312, 321
Whitley, B. E., Jr., 246, 267
Whitton, S. W., 274, 355,
    392, 439
Whitty, M. T., 318
Whyte, W. F., 42
Wickham, R. E., 154
Widmer, E. D., 275
Wiebe, S. A., 435
Wiederman, M. W., 49
Wight, R. G., 5
Wiik, K. A., 10
Wilcox, W. B., 191, 390, 391,
    399, 402, 429

Wildsmith, E., 290
Wile, D. B., 166
Willetts, M. C., 278
Williams, J., 146
Williams, K. D., 308, 309, 310
Williams, L. E., 107
Williams, M. J., 27, 146, 159
Williams, S. L., 381
Williamson, H. C., 397, 401, 432
Willis, J., 65, 82, 101
Willoughby, B. J., 11, 112, 113, 115, 276, 287, 288, 392, 402
Wilmot, W. W., 154, 155
Wilpers, S., 230
Wilson, A. C., 397, 402
Wilson, B., 227
Wilson, B. J., 9, 114
Wimmer, A., 58
Wincentak, K., 377
Winczewski, L. A., 3
Winkel, R. E., 307
Winslett, A. H., 301
Winston, R., 36
Winterheld, H. A., 344, 349
Witt, E. A., 49
Wolbring, T., 73
Wolf, N. R., 117, 224, 317
Wolfers, J., 392, 402
Wolfinger, N. H., 10, 11
Wong, J. S., 217
Wood, D., 97

Wood, J. T., 382
Wood, J. V., 31, 33, 235
Wood, W., 23, 24, 37, 81, 89, 94, 263
Woodley, H. J. R., 197
Woolf, S. E., 291, 371
World Health Organization, 375, 376
Worley, T. R., 372, 373, 391
Wortman, C. B., 164
Wotipka, C. D., 126
Wotman, S. R., 259
Wright, B. L., 346
Wright, C. N., 113, 127
Wright, P. H., 222
Wright, P. J., 287
Wrzus, C., 219
Wu, K., 90
Wu, T., 12
Wurst, S. N., 124
Wyden, P., 356, 358

Xu, X., 245, 248, 260
Xue, M., 194

Yager, J., 219
Yagi, A., 331
Yagil, D., 297
Yan, W., 141
Yancey, G., 77
Yarkoni, T., 159
Yavorsky, J. E., 197
Yeater, E. A., 300
Yee, N., 148
York, C., 235
Yoshimura, S., 329, 330

Young, B. J., 384
Young, S. D., 291
Young-DeMarco, L., 360
Younger, J., 246
Ysseldyk, R., 331
Yu, E., 414
Yucel, D., 297

Zacchilli, T. L., 344, 354
Zadro, L., 310
Zajonc, R. B., 68, 71
Zandbergen, D. L., 312
Zayas, V., 120, 144, 385
Zeidner, M., 355
Zeifman, D., 218
Zell, E., 22, 23, 129
Zellman, G. L., 369
Zembrodt, I. M., 350
Zengel, B., 318
Zentner, M., 37, 94
Zhang, F., 151
Zhang, G., 55, 82
Zhang, L., 124
Zhang, S., 261
Zhang, Y., 90, 183
Zhang, Z., 5
Zhong, C., 308
Zilcha-Mano, S., 223
Zimbardo, P., 230
Zimmerman, D. H., 368
Zinzow, H. M., 300
Zipp, J. F., 372
Zoccola, P. M., 308
Zuckerman, M., 325
Zuniga, A., 77

Subject Index

Abstinence-only sex
  education, 277–278,
  291, 302
Acceptance
  degrees of, in relationships,
    18–19, 304
  emotional support
    and, 210
  expectations of, 85–87
  relational value,
    303–305
  self-esteem and, 33,
    122–123
Accommodation, 203, 351,
  359, 367, 425, 440
Acetaminophen, 307
Active exclusion, 304
Active inclusion, 304
Active listening, 165–166
Actor/observer effects, 109,
  118, 134, 342, 359
Adolescence
  divorce and, 415
  first sexual experience
    during, 276
  friendship during,
    217–218, 238
  parenting of, and
    attachment style, 19
Advice support, 210
Affection
  communication and,
    149, 156
  as component of
    intimacy, 2
  emotional support
    and, 210
  fMRI and, 58, 245

in friendship, 208, 237
love and, 245, 263–264,
  422
need to belong and, 4–5
nonverbal behavior
  and, 144
permissiveness-with
  affection standard, 271
relationship success and,
  198, 199, 398
rewarding nature of,
  181–182
Affective reconstruction, 437
African Americans
  divorce and, 399
  Early Years of Marriage
    Project and, 45, 399
  Facebook and, 125
  interaction with, 215
  physical attractiveness
    and, 81
  sexual attitudes in, 275
Agape, 258, 259
Age. See also Adolescence;
  Elderly
  conflict and, 338
  first marriage, 7, 8
  first sexual experience, 402
  love affected by, 263
  at marriage, divorce and,
    76, 402
  sexual frequency and,
    266, 279, 298
Agreeableness
  body movement and, 142
  conflict and, 338, 359
  the Dark Triad and, 226
  forgiveness and, 330

infidelity and, 286, 317
IPV and, 379
jealousy and, 313
loneliness and, 232
mates, preferences for,
  97–98, 99
mate poaching and, 317
nature of, 27–28
relationship functioning
  and, 27, 29, 88
stalking and, 383
vengefulness and, 330
word use and, 125, 159
AIDS/HIV, 7, 36, 105, 289
Alcohol
  condom use and, 290
  conflict and, 338–339
  as predictor of divorce,
    403
  sexual coercion, 299, 301
Alcohol myopia, 290
Ambivalence, 304
American Psychological
  Association, 273
American Sociological
  Association, 274
Androgyny
  instrumental and
    expressive traits in,
    24–25
  interaction and, 25, 160
  nature of, 24, 40
  in relationships, 26, 40
Anger
  attributions and,
    342–344
  breakups, reacting to,
    408–411

communication and, 139,
140, 166–167
conflict and, 342
controlling, 343–344
forgiveness and, 330
jealousy and, 333
low self-esteem and, 33
neuroticism and, 28
Annie Hall (film), 288
Annoyances,
cumulative, 341
Anxiety about
abandonment,
17–18, 39
assessment of, 56–57
communication and, 157
conflict and, 347
controlling men and, 385
forgiveness and, 330
grief and, 413
hurt feelings and, 308
infidelity and, 286, 298
judgments of, 82, 102
loneliness and, 232
love and, 261–262
pets and, 223
relationship satisfaction
and, 202
sex and, 298
Anxious-ambivalent
attachment, 15, 18
Approach motivation,
183–186, 202, 205, 294,
295, 302
Archives, 59, 64
Argentina, 274
Arousal, 185, 223, 243,
247–251, 253–254, 266,
269, 290
Attachment
four components of,
217–218
friendship and, 217–218
love and, 246
Attachment styles, 14–20.
See also Anxiety about
abandonment;
Avoidance of intimacy;
Insecure attachment;
Secure attachment

assessment of, 56–57
attributions and, 111
breakups and, 405–406,
410–411
communication
and, 157
conflict and, 338, 347
forgiveness and, 330
hurt feelings and, 308
interdependency and,
182, 202
IPV and, 379, 380
jealousy and, 313,
320, 330
loneliness and, 232, 239
love and, 261–262
lying and, 324
perception of partners
and, 116, 132
sexual orientation
and, 30
sexuality and, 298
social support and,
211–212, 213
Attention to alternative
partners, 252–253,
423, 440
Attitudes
about casual sex,
270–272, 301
about same-sex sexuality,
272–274, 301
cultural differences in,
275, 301
similarities in, 42–43, 88
Attraction
arousal and, 247–251
physical appearance and,
72–84
proximity and,
66–72, 98
qualities desired in mates,
96–98
reciprocity and, 85–87
rewards and, 65–66
sex differences, 96–98
similarity and, 87–96
in Triangular Theory of
Love, 246
Attributional conflict, 342

Attributional processes
defined, 108
made by happy and
unhappy couples, 111
patterns, 108–112
Australia, 93, 275, 286
Autonomy and connection
dialectic, 336
Avoidance motivation,
183–18691, 205
Avoidance of conflict, 344
Avoidance of intimacy
assessment of, 56–57
caregiving and, 262
communication and,
157, 262
divorce and, 403
forgiveness and, 330
interdependency
and, 202
loneliness and, 232
love and, 262
nature of, 17, 39
pets and, 223
sex and, 298
Avoidant style of
attachment, 15
Avoiders, 352, 359

Bachelor, The (TV show),
60, 293
Bachelorette, The (TV show),
60, 293
Bad stronger than good,
181, 356, 420
Barrier model of breakups,
394–395
Beauty. *See* Physical
attractiveness
Behavior control, 362
Behavior description,
163, 164
Behavioral approaches to
marital therapy,
433–435
Behavioral couple therapy,
433–435, 441
Behavioral relationship
maintenance
mechanisms, 424–427

Beliefs about relationships, 112–116, 134. *See also* Relationships
  behavioral, 424–427, 441
  cognitive, 423–424, 441
  destiny and growth, 114–115
  difficulties in relationships and, 113–114
  dysfunctional, 113
  mechanisms, 422–430, 440
  preventive, 431–432, 441
  romanticism, 113
  sexual destiny, 295
  sexual growth, 295
Belligerence, 163
Belong, need to, 4–6
Best friends, 219
Betrayal, 326–330, 334
  defined, 326
  getting away with, 329
  individual differences in, 327, 334
  two sides to every, 327–328
Bias
  for beauty, 72–73
  confirmation, 104–105
  self-serving, 55, 109–110
  social desirability, 55, 281
  truth, 325
  volunteer, 49
Big Five personality traits, 27–28. *See also* Agreeableness; Conscientiousness; Extraversion; Neuroticism; Openness to experience
Bilateral style of power, 370–371
Births out of wedlock, 7–8
Blirtatiousness, 161, 169
Body, attractiveness in, 75–76
Body movement, 142–143, 169
Booty calls, 70, 225, 408
Boredom, 184–185, 186, 231, 267
Brazil, 97, 272, 292

Breakups, trajectories of, 403–408
Breast size, 76
Bulgaria, 83

Canada, 257, 274, 275, 389
Capitalization, in friendships, 209–210, 238
Caring
  attachment style and, 262
  compassionate love and, 256–258
  in friendship, on the Love Scale
  as part of intimacy, 2
Casual sex, attitudes about, 47–50
Census Bureau, U.S., 7
Centers for Disease Control and Prevention, 375
Cheaters (TV show), 319
Cheating. *See* Infidelity
Chemosignals, 146
Children
  care of, 197
  of divorce, 415–418, 419
  friendship among, 216–217, 238
  having without marriage, 7–8
  mother's influence on attachment styles of, 18–19
  predictor of divorce, 403
  in single-parent homes, 8, 389
China, 14, 75, 89, 97, 245, 260–261, 292
Churning, 408
Cisnormativity, 30
Civil unions, 274
Closedness and openness dialectic, 336
Coding procedures (scientific observations), 57
Coercion, sexual, 299–301, 302
Coercive power, 363, 366
Cognitive interdependence, 423, 440

Cognitive relationship maintenance mechanisms, 423–424
Cognitive-behavioral couple therapy (CBCT), 433–434, 435, 441
Cohabitation, 392–393
  changes in, 7
  divorce and, 9–11, 39, 402
Columbia Pacific University, 430
Coming out, 155
Commitment, 199–204
  attachment style and, 262
  between best friends, 219
  cognitive relationship maintenance mechanisms for, 423–424
  as component of love, 243, 246, 259–260, 262, 267, 268
  consequences of, 203–204
  definition of, 199–200, 206
  investment model of, 200–203
  as part of intimacy, 3
  sex and, 276–280
  three types of, 202–203
Commitment Scale, 200
Communal relationships, 193–195, 205, 373
  vs. exchange relationships, 193–195
Communal Strength scale, 194
Communication, 136–170. *See also* Dysfunctional; Nonverbal communication; Verbal communication
  about sex, 295–297, 302
  active listening in, 165–166
  attachment styles and, 157
  behavior descriptions in, 163
  computer-mediated, 158–159

dysfunctional, 161–168
error and
    misunderstanding in,
    136–138
gender differences in
    verbal, 156–161
I-statements in, 163–164
miscommunication in,
    161–163
model of, 137
respect and validation in,
    167–168
saying what we mean in,
    163–165
secrets, 154–156
self-disclosure in, 151–156
sympathy and
    concern, 164
taboo topics, 154–156
talk table, 136
verbal, 151–156
Communion, in friendship,
    208, 237
Companionate love, 244,
    245, 246, 254–256, 258,
    260, 262, 267, 268
Companionship, 208
Comparison level (CL),
    172–173, 175–179, 205
Comparison level for
    alternatives (CLalt),
    173–177, 205, 362
Compassionate love,
    256–258, 259, 262, 269
Compassionate Love Acts
    Diary, 257
Compassionate Love Scale,
    256–257
Competence, 294
Complementarity, 95–96
Compromise, 354
Computer-mediated
    communication,
    158–159
Concern,
    communicating, 164
Condoms, 277, 289–291,
    302, 371
Confirmation bias,
    104–105, 133

Conflict. *See* Interpersonal
    conflict
Connection with others, 3,
    4, 5, 33, 158–159, 219,
    232, 294, 336
Conscientiousness
    dancing and, 142
    infidelity and, 286
    IPV and, 379, 380
    judgments of, 101, 131
    loneliness and, 232
    mate poaching and, 317
    nature of, 28
    in relationships, 27, 28,
    40, 88
    research participation
    and, 49
Constraint commitment,
    202–203
Consummate love, 244
Contempt, 162
Contrition, forgiveness and,
    330–331
Convenience, proximity
    and, 71, 98
Convenience samples,
    47–50, 64
Conversation, 159
    dysfunctional, 161–163
    styles of, 159
    topics of, 157, 159
Coolidge effect, 265
Correlational designs,
    50–51, 64
Correlations, 50–51
Cosmetic surgery, 82
Cosmopolitan
    (magazine), 293
Costs
    avoidance motivation
    and, 183–186
    in interdependency
    theory, 172, 204
    relationship satisfaction
    and, 180–192
    to rewards ratio, 181
    as time goes by, 186–192
    unanticipated, 191
Counterpower, 362–363
Courtly love, 241

Criticism
    in communication, 162
    conflict and, 341, 359
Cross-complaining, 18, 162
Cultural influences, 7–14, 39
    changes in, 7–14, 39
    cohabitation and, 7, 9–11
    divorce and, 389–394
    gestures and, 142
    importance of, 9
    individualism, 11
    love and, 260–261, 269
    physical attractiveness
    and, 78, 81–82
    sex ratio, 13–14
    sexual attitudes and,
    274–275
    socioeconomic
    development and, 11–13
    sources of change in,
    11–14, 39
    technology and, 12–13
Cumulative annoyances,
    conflict and, 341, 359
Cyberball, 310
Cybersex, 287

"Dark side" of relationships,
    38, 40
Dark Triad, 226, 238, 313,
    317, 330
Data, research
    analysis of, 61–62
    archival materials, 59, 64
    observational, 55, 58
    paired, interdependent,
    61–6264
    self-report, 53–55
Dating, apps, 70
    online, 69, 70–71
Dealbreakers, 97
Deceiver's distrust, 323
Deception
    in close *vs.* casual
    relationships, 322–323
    deceiver's distrust and,
    323, 333
    defined, 322
    detecting a partner's,
    324–325

Deception—*Cont.*
   getting away with, 329
   impression management
      and, 123–124
Defensiveness, 162
Demand/withdrawal
   pattern of conflict,
      347–348, 359
Denmark, 48, 274
Department of Health
   and Human Services,
   U.S., 60
Derogation of tempting
   alternatives, 204,
   424, 440
Designs, research
   correlational, 50–51, 52
   experimental, 51–53, 64
Destiny beliefs, 114, 134
Devaluation, relational, 307
Dialectics, 336–337
Direct rewards, 65
Direct strategies of breaking
   up, 403–408
Direct style of power, 370
Direct tactics in conflict,
   346, 349
Disillusionment model of
   breakups, 397–399
Dismissing style of
   attachment, 16–17, 39,
   132, 182
Display rules, 140–141
Dissolution of relationships.
   See also Divorce
   adjustments after, 408–411
   aftermath of, 408–418
   barrier model of,
      394–395, 418
   postdissolution
      relationships, 408–409,
      414–415
   process of breaking up,
      403–408
   relationship rules and, 404
   types of relationship and,
      388–394
   Vulnerability-Stress-
      Adaptation Model of,
      395–397, 419

Distressed relationships, 184
Distress-maintaining
   attributions, 111
Divorce
   children of, 415–418
   cohabitation and,
      9–11, 39
   comparison level for
      alternatives and, 175
   cultural changes in, 8,
      389–394, 418
   Early Years of Marriage
      Project on, 399, 419
   economic resources
      and, 414
   effects on social network,
      413–414
   environmental impact
      of, 414
   high-risk *vs.* low-risk
      couples for, 181, 182
   PAIR Project on,
      397–399, 419
   perceived cause of,
      400–401, 419
   predictors of, 394–403
   rates of, 8, 11,
      388–394
   reasons for increase in,
      389–394
   relationship with
      ex-spouses following,
      414–415
   sex ratios, 407–408
   specific predictors of, 59,
      401–403, 419
   steps to, 407–408, 419
   Vulnerability-Stress-
      Adaptation Model of,
      395–397, 419
Domestic violence. *See*
   Violence in
   relationships
Domination in conflict, 354
Dopamine, 246, 255–256,
   266–267
Double standard, sexual,
   271, 301
Dyadic phase of dissolution
   of relationships, 407

Dyadic withdrawal, 238,
   21926
Dysfunctional
   active listening and,
      165–166
   communication, 161–168
   miscommunication,
      161–163
   polite interaction and,
      166–167
   respect and validation,
      167–168
   saying what we mean
      and, 163–165
Dysfunctional beliefs, 113

Early Years of Marriage
   (EYM) Project, 45, 185,
   399, 419
Economic hardship model
   of children of divorce,
   416–418
Economics
   and relationships, 11
   of relationships, 171,
      180–192
Effort, in impression
   management, 127–128
Elderly, the
   frequency of sex in, 266,
      278–279
   friendships of, 220–221
   love in, 263
Electronically activated
   recorders (EARs), 45, 57
Emergent distress model of
   breakups, 397–398
Emotional constraint, 224
Emotional infidelity,
   315–316, 318–320
Emotional intelligence,
   130–131
Emotional sharing, 221, 238
Emotional support, 210
Emotionally focused therapy
   (EFCT), 435–436, 441
Emotions
   facial expressions
      revealing, 139–140
   feigned expressions of, 141

nature of, 248
romantic love as an, 248
Empathic joining, 434
Empathy, 131, 154, 217, 229, 256, 331, 352, 353, 409, 434, 437 *see also* Nonverbal Sensitivity
Empty love, 243, 245
Encoding, 137, 149–150
Enduring dynamics model of, breakups, 397–399
England, 14, 286, 346
Equality, in close relationships, 364–367, 372
Equitable relationships, 195–199
Equity, 195–199, 205–206, 363, 364, 404, 428
Eros, 258
Escalation, of conflict, 344–347, 359
Ethical issues in research, 59–61, 64
Ethnicity
    divorce and, 402
    interethnic relationships, 90
    judgments of attractiveness and, 74, 81–82
Evolutionary perspectives
    on attraction, 93–95, 993
    on conflict, 341
    on cultural change, 36
    disagreement regarding, 36, 81–82, 94, 263–264
    explaining patterns in relationships, 33–37
    on infidelity, 284–285
    on mate-guarding, 377
    on need to belong, 5–6, 33
    on parental investment, 33–34
    on physical attractiveness, 76, 78–81
    on same-sex sexuality, 274

sex differences in love and, 263–264
    on sexual selection, 33–35
Excessive reassurance seeking, 236
Exchange relationships, 193–195, 205
    vs. communal relationships, 193–195
Exclusion, degrees of, 305–308
Exit as response to conflict, 351
Expectations
    interaction, and 121–124, 134
    of marriage, 190, 389–390, 397–399
    of rewards in relationships, 172–173, 190
Experience, influence of, 39
Experience-sampling, 55, 208, 217, 410
Experimental research designs, 51–53, 64
Expert power, 363, 364
Expressive traits, 24–27
Expressivity, 24–27, 40, 421
    friendships and, 224
    in gays and lesbians, 30
    loneliness and, 234, 239
    marital satisfaction and, 26, 27, 198
    self-disclosure and, 160–161, 224
Extradyadic sex
    attitudes toward, 280–281
    divorce and, 403
    emotional infidelity *vs.*, 315–316, 318–320
    evolutionary perspective on, 284–285
    gender and sexual orientation differences in, 280–281
    jealousy and, 318–320
    sociosexual orientation and, 282–284

Extraversion, 27, 28, 40, 125, 159, 317
Eye contact, 141 *see also* Gazing; Pupil dilation; Visual dominance ratio
Eye-tracking methodology, 57

Facebook, 12–13, 33, 58, 70, 139, 158–159, 235, 383
    impression management and, 125
Facebook friends, 12–13, 235
    individual differences in, 225–226
    jealousy and, 315
    networks of, and marital adjustment, 220
    proximity and, 66–72
    self-monitoring and, 126–128
    in young adulthood, 218
"Face-to-face" friendships, 222
Facial expressions, 139–170
    display rules regarding, 140–141
    microexpressions, 141
    smiles, 139–140
    universality of, 140
Facial features, attractive, 74–75
Facial symmetry, 75, 78
Facial width-to-height ratio (fWHR), 102
Familiarity, attraction and, 67–71, 98
Fantasy, 264, 269
Fatal attraction, 91, 124, 191
Fate control, 362
Fatuous love, 244, 245
Fearful style of attachment, 16–17, 39, 182
Femininity, 24–27
Feminism, 198
Fertility, 74, 78, 80, 93, 274, 284
Fight Effects Profile, 356–358
    speaker-listener technique, 356–357

Fighting, 354–358
  benefits of, 354–358
Financial status, attraction
  and, 76, 94
Finland, 274
First impressions, 101–107
  accuracy of perceptions
    and, 105
  confirmation bias in,
    104–105, 133
  influencing use of
    subsequent
    information, 104–105
  overconfidence in,
    105–107, 133
  physical attractiveness
    and, 72–73
  primacy effect,
    103–104, 133
  rapidity of, 101
  stereotypes in, 101–102
Florida State University,
  47–48
"Flourishing"
  relationships, 184
Forgiveness, 330–332, 334,
  427, 440
Framingham Heart Study,
  393
France, 48, 142, 274
"Friends with benefits,"
  209, 225
Friendship-Based Love
  Scale, 254–255
Friendships, 207–237
  during adolescence,
    217–218
  after marriage, 219–220
  attributes of, 208–214
  best, 219
  during childhood,
    216–217, 238
  compared to love, 208–209
  defined, 208
  difficulties in, 226–237
  enjoyment of, 208
  between men and
    women, 224–225
  during midlife,
    219–220, 238

during old age,
  220–221, 238
Functional magnetic
  resonance imaging
  (fMRI), 45, 58, 245, 260

Gay men. *See also* same-sex
  relationships
  attitudes about, 272–273
  coming out, 155
  friendships of, 225, 238
  evolutionary origins, 274
  expressivity in, 30
  online dating by, 70
  pupil dilation in, 141
  recognizing, 79, 114
  sexual communication
    by, 296
  mate preferences of, 82, 97
  smell and, 77
Gay relationships. *See*
  Same-sex relationships
"Gaydar," 144
Gazing, 74, 141–142, 144,
  153, 157, 169
Gender differences
  in casual sex, 47–50
  conflict and, 347–348
  in control of power
    resources, 364–366
  in desired rewards, 183
  expressive *vs.* instrumental
    traits, 24–25
  in friendships, 221–225, 238
  in intimate violence,
    376–377
  in loneliness, 234
  in love, 263–264, 269
  nature of, 24, 40
  in nonverbal
    communication,
    149–151
  in number of sexual
    partners, 281
  in pressures to adhering
    to "proper" gender
    roles, 27
  responses to jealousy, 320
  in same-sex friendships,
    221–224

sex differences *vs.*, 22–24
  in targets of betrayal, 327
  in use of power, 368–372
  in verbal
    communication, 159
Gender roles
  divorce and, 391
  pressure on adhering to
    "proper," 27
Genetics
  loneliness and, 232
  as predictor of divorce, 403
  same-sex sexual
    orientation and,
    272–274
German Socio-Economic
  Panel Study, 412–413
Germany, 45, 48, 75, 83, 94,
  179, 275, 288, 292, 412
Gestures, 142, 169
Glee (TV show), 272
Good faith contracts, 433
Good genes hypothesis,
  284–285, 302
Gratitude, 429
Grave-dressing phase of
  dissolution of
  relationships, 407
Great Britain, 214, 275, 300
Grindr (app), 70
Growth beliefs, 114–115, 134

Hair length, attractiveness
  and, 77
Half-truths, 322
Handshaking, 144
Hard-to-get, playing, 87
Health
  connections with others
    and, 4–6
  emotional support
    and, 210
  pets and, 223
Height, attractiveness and, 77
HER (app), 70
High self-monitors, 126–127
HIV/AIDS, 36
Homosexual relationships.
  See Same-sex
  relationships

Hookups, 271, 288–289, 289–290, 302
Hostile conflict style, 353, 359
Household tasks, 92, 197, 366
How to Win Friends and Influence People (book), 215
Human nature
  in intimate relationships, 33–37, 40
  need to belong, 4–6
Humor, 86, 97, 400
Hurt feelings, 305–308, 310, 326, 332

I-cubed (I³) model, 378
Ideal selves, and attraction, 92
Idealizing, of partners, 107–108, 134, 252–253, 264
Illegitimate demands, 341, 359
Illusion of unique invulnerability, 289–290
Illusions regarding partners, 107–108, 134–135
Impelling influences, 378–379
Impression management, 123–128, 134
  deception in, 123–124
  effort in, 127–128, 420
  on Facebook, 125
  individual differences in, 126–128
  strategies of, 124–126
Impressions of others. *See* First impressions
Inadequacy as partner, 312
Inattention to alternatives, 174, 423–424
Inclusion, degrees of, 304, 305–308
Inclusion of Other in the Self Scale, 3
Income, divorce and, 390–391, 401, 402
Indirect power, 370
Indirect rewards, 65, 66

Indirect strategies of breaking up, 403–408
Indirect style of power, 370
Indirect tactics in conflict, 346, 349
Individual differences, 20–23. *See also* Attachment styles; Dark Triad; Gender differences; Nonverbal sensitivity Personality; Sex differences; Sexual orientation
  approach and avoidance motivations, 185
  betrayal, 327
  communal strength, 194
  emotional intelligence, 130
  friendships, 225–226
  jealousy, susceptibility to, 312–313
  optimism, 119
  relational self-construal, 225–226
  rejection sensitivity, 119
  self-esteem, 29–33
  self-monitoring, 126–128
  sociosexuality, 281–284
Individualism, 11, 39
Indonesia, 83
Inequity, 196
Infatuation, 243, 245
Infidelity. *See also* Extradyadic sex
  avoiding, 426, 4042
  sexual *vs.* emotional, 315–316, 318–320
Informational power, 363, 364, 386
Ingratiation, 125, 134
Inhibiting influences, 380
Insecure style of attachment, 18–19
  breakups and, 408–411
  coming out, 155
  conflict and, 338
  distress-maintaining attributions and, 111
  loneliness and, 232
  love and, 261–262

  parenting and, 18–19
  perceptions of partners and, 116
  social support provision and, 211–212
Insight-oriented couple therapy (IOCT), 436–437, 441
Instigating triggers, 378
Instrumental traits, 24–27, 160–161, 372
Instrumentality, in attraction, 66
Integrative agreements, 354
Integrative behavioral couple therapy (IBCT), 434–435, 441
Intelligence, attractiveness and, 77
Interaction, influence of, 37–38, 40
Intercourse, for the first time, 275–276, 302, 402
Interdependence theory, 171–172
  businesslike emphasis of, 180
  comparison level, 172–173, 175–179
  comparison level for alternatives, 173–177
  four types of relationships, 175–177, 205
  outcomes, 172
  power, 178, 360–361
  principle of lesser interest, 178, 361, 386
  rewards and costs in, 172, 181, 186–192
Interdependency
  approach and avoidance motivations, 183–186
  attachment and, 202
  commitment and, 199–204
  in communal relationships, 193–195
  in exchange relationships, 193–195
  nature of, 192, 205

Interdependency—*Cont.*
  as part of intimacy, 2
  power and, 178, 360–361
  relational turbulence
    model, 186–188
  rewards and costs,
    197–198, 421
  social exchange, 171–179
Interdependent self-
    construal, 238
Interethnic relationships, 90
International Association
    for Relationship
    Research, 46
Internet
  cybersex, 287
  dating, 70–71, 289
  impression management
    on, 69
  ostracism on, 310
  research involving, 47, 58
Interpersonal Betrayal
    Scale, 37, 327
Interpersonal conflict anger
    and, 341, 343–344,
    attributions and
  defined, 335–336
  demand/withdraw
    pattern in, 347–348
  dialectics causing, 336–337
  ending, 353–354, 359
  engagement and
    escalation of, 344–347
  events instigating,
    339–342, 359
  evolutionary perspective,
    341
  fighting in, 354–358
  four different responses
    to, 350–351
  frequency of, 337–339, 359
  inevitability of, 336
  issues producing, 340
  negotiation and
    accommodation,
    348–351
  possible courses of, 345
  tactics of, 349
  types of couples in,
    351–353

Interpersonal distance,
    145–146, 169
Interpersonal gap, 137
Interpersonal process model
    of intimacy, 153–154
Interrupting, 162, 368
Intimacy
  attachment styles and, 261
  in childhood
    friendships, 217
  as component of love,
    242–243, 246, 256,
    259–260, 267, 268
  costs of, 190
  on the Love Scale, 251
  nature and importance of,
    2–6, 39, 221
Intimacy *vs.* isolation, 218
Intimate partner violence
    (IPV), 375–385; *see
    also* Violence in
    relationships
  gender differences in,
    376–377, 387
  impelling influences on,
    378–380
  instigating triggers of, 378
  rationales for, 382–384
  types of, 375–376, 387
Intimate terrorism (IT),
    375–376, 378, 381–382
  leaving a relationship
    with, 384–385
  rationales for, 382–384
Intimate zone, 145
Intimidation, 126, 134
Intoxication, safe sex
    and, 290
Investment model of
    commitment,
    200–20309, 206
Investments, in
    relationships, 174,
    200–203, Invisible
    support
Invisible support, 212
Isolation, 232
Israel, 275
I-statements, 163–164, 166,
    349, 356, 357

Japan, 12, 75, 142, 215, 292,
    318, 389
Jealousy
  coping constructively
    with, 321, 333
  defining feelings, 310, 333
  evolutionary perspective
    on, 314, 316, 318
  people prone to, 312–3138
  reactive, 311, 333
  responses to, 320–321
  rivals and, 313–314
  sex differences in, 318–320
  for sexual *vs.* emotional
    infidelity, 315–316,
    318–320, 333
  suspicious, 311, 333
  therapy for, 321
  types of, 311–312
*Journal of Marriage and the
    Family,* 46
*Journal of Social and Personal
    Relationships,* 46

Kansas State University, 87
Kitchen-sinking, 161–162
Knowledge, 129, 134
  between best friends, 219
  in friendship, 207
  as part of intimacy, 2
Korea, 93, 94, 318

Language, influence of, 23
  and intimacy, 423
  and personality, 125, 129
Laughter, 147, 157, 186, 249,
    254, 255
Legitimate power, 363, 364
Lesbians 30. *See* Same-sex
    relationships
  coming out, 155
  attitudes about, 272–273
  coming out, 155
  friendships of, 225, 238
  evolutionary origins, 274
  online dating by, 70
  sexual communication
    by, 296
  mate preferences of, 82, 97
Liars, 324

Liking, 243
loving *vs.*, 208–209
romantic love *vs.*, 243, 245
Liking Scale, 251–254
Listening, active, 165–166
Loneliness
attributions and, 239
defined, 231, 239
emotional loneliness, 239
Facebook and, 235
gender differences in, 234
genetics and, 232
interactive effects of, 239
personality and, 232
self-esteem and, 234
social loneliness, 239
UCLA Loneliness
Scale, 233
with *vs.* without a
romantic partner, 234
Long-distance
relationships, 69
Long-term mating
strategies, 35, 96
Love. *See also*
Companionate love;
Compassionate love;
Romantic love
age and, 263
arousal in, 247–251, 266
attachment style and,
261–262
changing nature of,
264–266
in choice of a spouse,
240–242
commitment and, 243
companionate, 244, 245,
254–256
compared to friendship,
208–209
compassionate, 256–258
consummate, 244, 245
courtly, 241
cultural influences
on, 269
empty, 243, 245
fatuous, 244, 245
fMRI and, 58
history of, 241–242

idealization of partners
and, 252–253, 264
individual differences in,
260–264
intimacy and, 242–243
lust and, 58, 245–246
novelty and, 265–266
passion and, 243
romantic, passionate,
246–254
sex differences and,
263–264, 269
styles of loving,
258–260, 269
thought and, 251–254
through the passage of
time, 264–268, 269
Triangular Theory, 242–245
types of, 242–260
unrequited, 259
Love Attitudes Scale, 260
"Love is blind," 252–253
Love Scale, 251–254, 263
Low self-esteem, 26, 29–33,
40, 85, 235, 308, 420
Low self-monitors, 126–127
Loyalty, as response to
conflict, 350–351
Ludus, 258, 259
Lust, 58, 245–246
Lying, 322–325, 333
in close *vs.* casual
relationships, 322–323
detecting, 324–325
getting away with, 329
liar characteristics and, 324

Machiavellianism, 226, 313
Machismo, loneliness in
men and, 234
Maintaining relationships.
See Relationships
Male attractiveness, 75–77
Male dominance in power,
364–366
Mania, 258, 259
Marital Instability Over the
Life Course project,
400–401
Marital paradigms, 113, 134

Marital satisfaction
aggression and, 375
average trajectory of,
188–189, 205
dysfunctional
communication and,
161–163
health and, 7
nonverbal sensitivity and,
149–151
parenthood and, 191
power and, 373
reasons for waning, 187–
188
self-disclosure and, 156
sex and, 298
stress and, 396
traditional gender roles
and, 25
Marital therapy, 433–439
behavioral approaches,
433–435
common features of,
437–439
emotionally focused,
435–436, 441
insight-oriented,
436–437, 441
Marriage. *See also* Divorce
age at first, 7–8
attitudes, as predictor of
divorce, 403
balance of power in,
364–366, 373
boredom in, 185
changes in, 7–8
cohabitation before, 7, 9–11
doubts about, 188
friendships and, 220
high expectations of, 190,
389–390
history of romance and
passion in, 241–242
household tasks and, 92,
197, 198, 366
life satisfaction and, 412
parents' preferences, 261
prior, as predictor of
divorce, 402
rates of, 7

Marriage—*Cont.*
  romantic love decreasing
    after, 264–266
  satisfaction in, 188–192
Marriage shift, 121–122
Masculinity, 24–27
Massachusetts Institute of
  Technology, 66–67
Masturbation, 286
Matching, 84, 99, 313
  as broad process, 93–95
Mate poaching, 317
Mate value, 85, 86, 93, 94,
  97, 99, 147, 263, 312,
  313, 367, 377
Mate-guarding, 377
Material support, 210
Mating
  long-term *vs.* short-term,
    35, 96
  preferences for, 96–98, 99
Maximal exclusion, 304
Maximal inclusion, 304
Memories, 112
Men. *See also* Gender
  differences; Sex
  differences
  extradyadic sex by,
    280–281
  interest in physical
    attractiveness, 82–83
  jealousy in, 315–316,
    318–320
  language used by, 368
  love in, 263–264, 269
  misperceptions of sexual
    interest by, 296–297
  number of sex partners, 281
  opening lines used by, 86
  rationale for violence,
    382–384, 387
  sex drive in, 286–288, 302
  sexual double standard
    and, 271
  sexual satisfaction in,
    292, 296
  verbal communication
    styles, 159
  violence committed by,
    376–377, 382–384

*Men Are From Mars, Women
  Are From Venus* (book),
  20, 430
Menstrual cycle preferences
  during, 74, 79
  behavior during, 80
  men's reaction to, 80
  voice and, 147
Mere exposure effect, 68, 98
Meta-analyses, 62, 64, 285, 325
Michelangelo phenomenon,
  425, 440
Microexpressions, 141
Midlife, friendship during,
  219–220
Military service, "don't ask,
  don't tell," 144
  stresses of, 69, 187–188
Mimicry, 147–149, 169
Mindreading, 162
Miscommunication,
  149–151, 158–159. *See
  also* Dysfunctional
  communication
Misperceptions of sexual
  interest, 296–297
Modern Family
  (TV show), 272
Moral commitment, 202–203
Mothers
  influence on attachment
    styles of children, 18–19
  working, 8
Motivation, 129–130, 134
Mutuality, as part of
  intimacy, 3

Narcissism, 124, 226, 313, 421
Narratives, 404, 407, 409
National Center for Health
  Statistics, U.S., 7, 281
Natural selection, 33
Nature of commitment,
  199–204
Nature of
  interdependency, 192
Need to belong, 4–6, 39
  human nature and, 33
  loneliness and, 232
Negative affect, 162

Negative affect reciprocity,
  166, 346–347, 359
Negative self-concept,
  121–123
Neglect, as response to
  conflict and, 350–351
Negotiation, 346, 348–351
Neuroticism
  conflict and, 337–338, 359
  detection of, 130
  divorce and, 403
  forgiveness and, 330
  IPV and, 379
  jealousy and, 313
  loneliness and, 232
  nature of, 28
  in relationships, 28, 40,
    50, 189, 421
  word use and, 159
Nigeria, 75, 83
No-fault divorce laws, 392,
  402, 418
Nonconscious social
  cognition, 120
Nonlove, 243
Nonverbal communication,
  138–151
  body movement,
    142–143, 169
  combining components
    of, 147–149, 169
  components of, 138–149
  facial expressions,
    139–141, 169
  functions of, 138
  gazing, 141–142, 169
  gender differences in,
    149–151, 420
  gestures, 142
  interpersonal distance,
    145–146, 169
  lying and, 324
  mimicry, 147–149, 169
  misunderstanding in,
    149–151
  paralanguage,
    146–147, 169
  power expressed through,
    369–370
  touch, 143–145

Nonverbal sensitivity, 149–151; 369–370
Normal curves, 20–22
Northwestern University, 43, 337
Norway, 274
Novelty, 265–266, 269

Observational studies, 55–58, 64
Off-beam conversations, 162
Old age, friendship during, 220–221
Online dating, 69, 70–71
Opener Scale, 153
Opening lines, 86
Openness and closedness dialectic, 336, 404
Openness to experience, 28
Optimism
    beneficial, 116, 119
    unhelpful, 105
Orgasm, 54, 123, 270
Ostracism, 308–310, 333
Other-oriented strategies of breaking up, 403–408
Others' judgments
    of one's relationship, 106–107
    of oneself, 131
Outcomes, 172–179, 204
"Overbenefited," 196, 206
Overconfidence, 105–107, 133
Ovulatory shift, 74, 78–81
Oxytocin, 58, 255–256

PAIR Project, 397–399
Pairfam, 45
Paralanguage, 146–147, 169
Paraphrasing, 165–166, 170
Parental conflict model of divorce, 416–418
Parental investment, 34, 37, 94
Parental loss model of divorce, 416–418
Parental stress model of children of divorce, 416–418
Parenthood
    attachment and, 18–19

childcare, 197–198
    with or without marriage, 7–8
    reactions to "coming out," 155
    relationship satisfaction and, 191
    single-parent homes, 8
    working mothers and, 8
Participants in research, 47–50, 64
Particularistic resources of power, 365
Partner legibility, 130, 135
Passion
    attachment style and, 262
    as component of love, 243, 246, 256, 259–260, 262, 263–264, 268
    fantasy and, 264
    in marriage, history of, 241–242
    men and, 263–264
    over time, 265–266, 279
    romantic passionate love, 246–254
Passionate Love Scale, 249–250, 263
Passive exclusion, 304
Passive inclusion, 304
Paternity uncertainty, 34–35, 314
Penis shape, 285
Penis size, 293
Perceived partner responsiveness, 213–214, 238
Perceived relational value, 303–305, 326, 332
Perceived Responsiveness Scale, 214
Perceived similarity, 89–90, 99
Perceived superiority, 423, 440
Perceiver ability, 130–131, 135
Perceiver influence, 132, 135
Perception checking, 165–166, 170

Permissiveness-with-affection standard, 271
Persevering indirectness, 405, 419
Personal commitment, 202–203
Personal phrase of dissolution of relationships, 407
Personal Relationships, 46
Personal zone, 145–146
Personality, 27–29, 40. *See also* Agreeableness; Conscientiousness; Dark Triad; Extraversion; Neuroticism; Individual differences
    conflict and, 337–338
    jealousy and, 313
    loneliness and, 232
    as predictor of divorce, 403
    similarities in, 88
Pets, as friends, 223
"Phantom stranger" technique, 43
Phubbing, 13
Phones, *see* Smartphones
Physical attractiveness, 72–84, 420
    averageness and, 75
    bias for beauty, 72–73, 98
    of bodies, 75–76
    consensus regarding, 74–75
    culture and, 81–82
    evolutionary perspective on, 78–81, 93–95
    height and, 77
    impact on interactions with others, 83–84, 99
    judgments of others with, 72–73
    matching in, 84, 93–95
    in men, 74
    smell and, 77
    speed-dating and, 82–83
    symmetry and, 75
    weight and, 76
    in women, 74

Physical comfort, 210
Physical proximity, 66–72
Physiological measures, 45,
   58, 64, 245–246,
   308–309
Platonic love, 241
Play, relationship
   maintenance through,
   426–427, 440
Playboy Playmates, 81
Playing "hard to get," 87
Pluralistic ignorance,
   290–291
Points to ponder, 5, 13, 18,
   27, 60, 62, 80, 82, 89,
   110, 112, 123, 142, 166,
   173, 196, 216, 229, 258,
   265, 275, 276, 291, 297,
   311, 327, 336, 356, 366,
   381, 393, 413, 424, 439
Politeness, in
   communication,
   166–167
Pornography, 287
Positive illusions,
   107–108, 423
Post-dissolution
   relationships, 408–409,
   414–415
Posture, body, 39
Power, 360–385, 386
   behavior control, 362, 386
   in conversation, 368
   defined, 360
   and (in)dependence,
      360–361
   fate control, 362, 386
   gender differences in
      control of resources,
      364–366, 386
   indirect, 370
   interdependence theory
      and, 360–363, 386
   nonverbal behavior and,
      369–370
   outcome of, 372–373
   resources underlying,
      363–364, 386
   sex differences in use of,
      368–372

styles of, 370–372
two faces of, 373–374
Pragma, 258, 259
Prayer, 424
"Precarious" relationships,
   184–185
Prejudice against singles, 9
Premarital sex, attitudes
   toward, 270–271
Preoccupied style of
   attachment, 16, 39, 132
Prevention and Relationship
   Enhancement Program
   (PREP), 432
Preventive relationship
   maintenance,
   431–432
Primacy effect, 103–104, 133
Princeton University, 103
Principle of lesser interest,
   178, 361, 386
Prior marriage, as predictor
   of divorce, 402
Processes of Adaptation in
   Intimate Relationships
   (PAIR Project),
   397–399
*Proper Care and Feeding
   of Marriage, The*
   (book), 430
Proximity, attraction and,
   66–72, 98, 420
   convenience and, 71
   familiarity and, 67–71
   power of, 71–72
Proximity seeking, 218
Psychopathy, 226, 313
Public zone, 146
Pupil dilation, 141

Quid pro quid contract, 433

Race, divorce and, 402
Rape, 300
Ratings (scientific
   observations), 57
Reactive jealousy, 311
Reactivity, 58, 59
Rebuffs, conflict and,
   341, 359

Reciprocity, 99
   of benefits, 192
   liking and, 85–87
   in self-disclosure, 152
Reconstructive memory,
   112, 134
Red color, attractiveness
   and, 77–78
Referent power, 363, 364
Regulating interaction,
   nonverbal
   communication
   and, 138
Rejection
   degrees of, 304
   hurt feelings, 305–308
   ostracism, 308–310
   relational value, 305
Rejection sensitivity, 119
Relatedness, 294
Relational cleansing, 407, 419
Relational devaluation,
   307–308
Relational Maintenance
   Strategies, 428–430
Relational self-construals,
   225–226
Relational turbulence
   model, 186–188, 205
Relational value,
   303–305, 332
Relationship beliefs,
   112–116, 134. *See also*
   Relationships
   behavioral,
      424–427, 441
   cognitive, 423–424, 441
   destiny and growth,
      114–115
   difficulties in
      relationships and,
      113–114
   dysfunctional, 113
   mechanisms,
      422–430, 440
   preventive,
      431–432, 441
   romanticism, 113
Relationship Flourishing
   Scale, 54

Relationship satisfaction
  attributions and, 111
  compassionate acts and,
    256–258
  in interdependence
    theory, 172–173
  nonverbal communication
    and, 149–151
  over time, 177–179,
    188–192
  perceived support and,
    212–213
  relational turbulence
    model on, 186
  self-disclosure and, 16
  sexual satisfaction and,
    297–298, 302
  shared friendships
    and, 220
Relationship science.
    See Research,
    relationship
Relationships
  approach and avoidance
    processes in, 183–186
  continuing after
    breakups, 408–409
  ending (*see* Dissolution of
    relationships)
  exchange and communal
    differences, 193–195
  forecasts regarding, 106
  gay and lesbian (*see*
    Same-sex relationships)
  illusions in, 107–108
  importance of, 2–6
  pornography and, 287
  repairing, 430–439
  rewards-costs and,
    183–192
  romantic (*see*
    Romantic love)
  rules for, 214–216, 404
Religion, divorce and, 402
  importance of, 92
Remarriage, 402
Repairing relationships,
    430–439, 441
  advice from the media,
    430–431

marital therapy,
    433–439, 441
  preventive maintenance,
    431–432
Representative samples,
    47–50, 64
Research, relationship,
    41–64
  archival materials for,
    59, 64
  beginnings of, 42–43
  correlational designs,
    50–51
  current nature of, 43
  ethical issues in, 59–61, 64
  examples of, 42–45
  experimental designs,
    51–53, 64
  goals of, 46
  history of, 42–46, 63
  imposters and, 41
  interpreting and
    integrating results of,
    61–62, 64
  need for understanding,
    41–42
  observations of behavior,
    55, 58
  participants for, 47–50, 64
  physiological measures
    in, 58, 64
  question development,
    46, 63–64
  self-report data in, 53–55
Respect
  in communication,
    167–168
  in friendships, 209, 237
Responsiveness
  in communication,
    153–154
  in friendship,
    213–214, 238
  as part of intimacy, 2–3
  perceived partner,
    213–214
Resurrection phase of
    dissolution of
    relationships, 407
Reward power, 363

Rewards
  in attraction, 65–66
  in interdependence theory,
    172, 198, 204, 205
  over time, 186–192
  relationship satisfaction,
    183–192
Rituals, 427, 440
Romance
  enhanced by
    fantasy, 264
  feminism's compatibility
    with, 198
  in marriage, history of,
    241–242
Romantic love
  as an emotion, 248
  arousal in, 247–251
  companionate love, *vs.*,
    255–256
  decreasing after marriage,
    264–266, 421
  friendship *vs.*, 208–209
  infatuation, *vs.*, 242
  involving passion, 244–245
  nature of, 246–247
  as reason for marriage,
    241–242
  role of thoughts in,
    251–254
  through the passage of
    time, 264–268
  in Triangular Theory of
    Love, 244, 245
  unrequited, 259
Romanticism, 113
Rules of relationships,
    214–216, 238, 404
*Rules: Time-Tested Secrets
    for Capturing the Heart
    of Mr. Right, The*
    (book), 431
Russia, 97, 275

Sacrifice, willingness to,
    203, 424, 440
Safe haven, 218
Safe sex, 288–292
Sam Houston State
    University, 12

Same-sex relationships,
  30–31
  attitudes about, 272–274,
    275, 301
  conflict in, 342
  conversation in, 368
  demand/withdraw
    pattern in, 347
  equity in, 197
  expressivity in, 26
  extradyadic sex,
    280–281, 282
  friendships in,
    221–224, 238
  frequency of sex in,
    279–280
  IPV in, 375, 380
  investment model in, 201
  the need to belong in, 5
  marital therapy in, 439
  online dating and, 70
  predictors of divorce
    in, 401
  satisfaction in, 189
  sexual satisfaction in, 296
  use of power in, 374
Same-sex sexuality attitudes
    about, 272–274
  perceived origins, 272
Sarcasm, 147
Satisfaction. *see*
    Relationship
    satisfaction; Sexual
    satisfaction
Scales
  Attachment
    dimensions, 56
  Betrayal, 327
  Commitment, 200
  Compassionate Love, 257
  Destiny and Growth
    Beliefs, 115
  Friendship-Based Love,
    254–255
  Inclusion of Other in
    Self, 3
  Loneliness, 232–233
  Love and Liking, 251–252
  Communal Strength, 194
  Opener, 153
  Passionate Love, 249–250

Perceived
  Responsiveness, 214
Perceptions by Partner, 32
Relationship
  Flourishing, 54
Self-monitoring, 128
Shyness, 228
Secrets, 154–156, 169
Secure base, 218
Secure style of attachment,
    14–20, 39, 202, 320
  communication and,
    155, 157
  conflict and, 338
  forgiveness, and, 330
  jealousy and, 320
  love and, 261–262
  perception of partners, 116
  relationship-enhancing
    attributions and, 111
  sex and, 298
  social support and,
    211–212
Self-concepts, 119–123, 254
Self-control, 355, 378,
    425–426, 429–430, 440
Self-Determination
    Theory, 294
Self-disclosure, 151–156
  coming out, 155
  in cybersex, 287
  defined, 151, 169
  gender differences in,
    160, 224
  high openers, 153
  reciprocity in, 152
  relationship
    satisfaction, 156
  small talk, *vs.*, 156
  social penetration theory,
    152–153
  taboo topics, 154–156
Self-enhancement, 121–123
Self-esteem, 40, 254
  based on rejection and
    acceptance, 308
  effects on relationships,
    29–33, 40
  hurt feelings and, 305–308
  loneliness and, 234
  ostracism and, 308

Self-expansion, 186, 253,
    409–410
Self-fulfilling prophecies,
    116–119, 134
Self-monitoring, 126–128
Self-Monitoring Scale, 128
Self-oriented strategies of
    breaking up, 403–408
Self-perceptions,
    119–123, 134
Self-promotion, 125–126, 134
Self-reports, 53–55, 64
  potential problems with,
    53–55
Self-serving bias, 19–110,
    134, 342
Self-verification, 121–123, 134
Sensitivity, nonverbal,
    149–151
Separation from conflict,
    353–354
Separation protest, 218
Separation *versus* integration
    dialectic, 337
Separations,
  effects of, 69, 187
Sex
  attachment styles and, 298
  coercive, 299–301
  frequency of, 266
  initiation of, 276, 302, 402
  motives for, 294–295
  number of partners, 281
  online, 287
Sex differences, 40
  betrayal, 327
  demand/withdraw
    pattern, 347–348
  extradyadic sex, 280–281
  gender differences *vs.*,
    22–23
  housework, 366
  love and, 263–264
  mate preferences, 96–98
  nature of, 20–23
  nonverbal sensitivity,
    149–151, 421
  number of sex partners, 281
  parental investment, 34
  paternity uncertainty
    and, 34–35

relative resources, 365
reproductive potential,
    33–34
sex drives, 286–288, 302
sexual attitudes, 271
stereotypes about, 20–23
Sex drives. *see* Sexual desire
Sex education, 277–278, 291
Sex ratio, 13–14, 39, 402
Sexting, 12
Sexual behavior, unwanted,
    299–301, 402
Sexual coercion, 299–301
Sexual desire, 286–288, 302
Sexual destiny beliefs, 295
Sexual double standard,
    271, 301
Sexual growth beliefs, 295
Sexual orientation, 30–31
    beliefs regarding, 272–274
    disclosure of, 155
    evolution and, 274
    on Facebook, 125
    frequency of sex, 279–280
    friendships and, 225
    genetic basis, 272–273
    history of love and, 241
    nonverbal behavior
        and, 144
Sexual satisfaction,
    292–298
    attachment styles
        and, 298
    divorce and, 403
    in gays and lesbians, 296
    in men, 292, 296
    motives for sex and,
        294–295
    relationship satisfaction
        and, 297–298, 302
    sexual communication
        and, 295–297, 302
    unwanted sexual
        behavior and, 299–301
    in women, 296
Sexual selection, 33–36, 40,
    93, 274, 284, 315, 377
Sexuality, 270–301
    adolescent friendships
        and, 217
    age of first experience, 275

attachment and, 298
attitudes about, 270–275
causes of conflict and, 342
in committed
    relationships, 276–280
first experiences,
    275–276
frequency of sexual
    activity, 266
in homosexual vs
    heterosexual
    relationships, 30–31
numbers of sexual
    partners and, 281
online sex, 287
paternity uncertainty
    and, 34–35
power and, 360–361
problems with self-report
    research on, 55
responses to offers for,
    47–50
safe sex, 288–292
sex ratio and, 13–14
sexual coercion,
    299–301, 302
without love or
    commitment, 282–284
Sexually transmitted
    infections (STIs), 276,
    277, 289–290
Shared activities, 221, 238
Short-term mating
    strategies, 35, 96
Shyness, 227–231, 239
    alleviating, 230–231
    doing better with excuse
        for failure, 230–2317
    interpersonal effects of,
        229–230
Shyness Scale, 228
"Side-by-side"
    friendships, 222
Silent treatment, 308–310
Similarity, 87–96, 99, 404
    attitudes, 42–43, 88
    complementarity and,
        95–96
    conflict and, 338
    divorce and, 402
    examples of, 87

opposites and attraction,
    89–96
over time, 90–91
perceived *vs.* real, 52, 89–90
personalities, 88
types of, 92
Single, staying, 7, 9
Single-parent homes, 8, 389
Singlism, 9
Situational couple violence
    (SCV), 375, 378–380
Sleep, 338
Small talk, 156
Smartphones, 7, 12, 13, 57,
    70, 337
Smell, 146, 169
    attractiveness and, 77
Smiling, 139–140
Social allergies, 341
Social cognition, 100–135
    accuracy of perceptions,
        128–133
    attributions in, 108–112
    definition of, 100
    expectations, 116–119
    first impressions in,
        101–107
    illusions in, 107–108
    impression management,
        123–128
    memories and, 112
    nonconscious, 120
    relationship beliefs,
        112–116
    self-perception and,
        119–123
Social desirability bias, 55
Social exchange, 171–179
    comparison level and,
        172–173, 175–179
    comparison level for
        alternatives, 173–177
    defined, 171
    outcome, 172
    rewards and costs, 172
Social loneliness, 239
Social mobility, as predictor
    of divorce, 402
Social norms, 365
Social penetration theory,
    152–153

Social phase of dissolution of relationships, 407
Social responsibility norm, 364
Social skills, 23
Social support, 210–214, 238, 404
  perceptions of, 212–213
  physical effects, 210
  types of, 210, 211
Social zone, 146
Socioeconomic development, cultural changes and, 11–12
Socioeconomic status, divorce and, 401, 402
Socioemotional selectivity theory, 220–221, 238
Sociometer model of self-esteem, 29, 40
Sociosexual orientation, 281–284, 302
Sociosexual Orientation Inventory, 283
Solitary confinement, 1
South Africa, 274
Spain, 275, 292
Speaker-listener technique, 356–357, 359
Speed-dating, 43, 50, 82–83, 87
Sperm competition, 285, 302
Stability and change dialectic, 337
Stage of life, conflict and, 338
Stalking, 383
Star Wars (movie), 288
Statistical significance, 22, 61–62
Stepchildren, as predictor of divorce, 402
Stereotypes
  about communication, 159
  about sex differences in intimate relationships, 20–23
  first impressions and, 101–102

physical attractiveness, 72–73
power and gender, 365
Stimulus-value-role theory, 90–91
Stonewalling, 163
Stony Brook University, 45
Storge, 258, 259
Street Corner Society (book), 42
Stress hormones, as predictor of divorce, 403
Stress spillover, 396
Stresses and strains in divorce and, 395–397, 403
  pets and, 223
  relationships, 37–38, 303–332
  Vulnerability-Stress-Adaptation Model, 395–397
Structural improvement, 354
Styles of loving, 258–260, 269
Supplication, 126, 134
Survivor (TV show), 304–305
Suspicious jealousy, 311
Sweden, 275
Symmetry, facial, 75, 78
Sympathy, communicating, 164

Taboo topics, 157, 159, 169
Talk table, 136
Technoference, 13
Technology. *See also* Internet
  dating online and, 70–71
  influences on relationships, 12–13
  for observational studies, 57
Teen sex, as predictor of divorce, 402
Texting, 158–159
Therapy. *See also* Marital therapy
  coping with jealousy, 321
  for shyness, 230
Thought, romantic love and, 251–254

Threatening perceptions, 131–132, 135
Time, passage of, cohabitation outcomes, 10
  love and, 264–268, 269
  marital satisfaction, 189
Tinder (app), 70, 143
Togetherness, 336–337, 404
Tolerance building, 434
Touch, 143–145, 169
Traditional behavioral couple therapy, 441
Traditional behavioral couple therapy (TBCT), 433
Transgendered people, 30
Triangular Theory of Love, 242–245, 268
Trust
  between best friends, 219
  as component of intimacy, 2
  in friendships, 209, 237
Truth bias, 325
20 questions, 44
Twitter, 158

UCLA, 294–295
UCLA Loneliness Scale, 233
"Underbenefitted," 196, 206
Unified detachment, 434
Unilateral style of power, 370–371
United Kingdom, 70, 322, 374
Universalistic resources of power, 365
University of Arizona, 45
University of Denver, 218
University of Kansas, 102
University of Michigan, 87, 340
University of Minnesota, 118
University of Texas at Arlington, 44
University of Texas at Austin, 87, 105, 276–277
University of Virginia, 41

Unmarried birthrate, 7–8
Unrequited love, 259
Unwanted sexual behavior, 299–301
Utah Marriage Handbook, 431

Validation, in communication, 167–168, 170, 351–352
Validator conflict style, 359
Value, relational, 303–305
Values, similarities in, 88, 91
Vengefulness, 328–330, 334
Verbal communication, 151–156
  affection in, 156
  attachment styles, 157
  gender differences in, 156–161, 159, 169
  interpersonal model of intimacy, 153–154
  secrets, 154–156
  self-disclosure, 151–156, 160
  styles of, 159
  taboo topics, 154–156
Viagra, 270
Violence in relationships, 374–385, 386–387
  correlates of, 378–382, 387
  escaping from, 384–385, 387
  gender differences in, 376–377, 387
  impelling influences, 378–380

instigating triggers, 378
mate-guarding and, 377
prevalence of, 375
rationales of, 382–384, 387
situational couple violence, 378–380
stalking, 383
types of, 375–376, 386
Violent resistance, 375–376
Virtual Human Interaction Lab, 44
Virtual reality, 44, 148
Visual Dominance Ratio (VDR), 142
Voice
  nonverbal communication through, 146–147
  as response to conflict, 350–351
Volatile couples, 351, 359
Volunteer bias, 49
Vulnerability-Stress-Adaptation Model of marital instability, 395–397

Waist-to-hip ratios (WHR), 75–76, 81–82, 98
Weight, attractiveness and, 76
"Weird" research participants, 47
Widowhood, 412–413
Wild and Crazy Guy, A (recording), 249
Will and Grace (TV show), 272

Willingness to sacrifice, 203, 424, 440
Women. *See also* Gender differences; Sex differences
  language style of, 368
  love in, 263–264, 269
  number of sex partners, 281
  opening lines used by, 86
  response to emotional infidelity, 315–316, 318–320
  sex drives in, 286–288, 302
  sexual double standard and, 271
  sexual satisfaction in, 296
  verbal communication styles, 159
  violence committed by, 376–377
  violent relationships, leaving, 384–385
Women's intuition, 149
Work, effects of, 390–391, 402
Working mothers, 8
World Health Organization, 375

XYZ statements, 164, 170

Yes-butting, 162
Young adulthood, friendship in, 218

Zambia, 93